Séfer haḤinnuch סֵפֶר הַחִנּוּךְ
THE BOOK OF [MITZVAH] EDUCATION

סֵפֶר הַחִנּוּךְ

מיוחס לרבנו אהרן הלוי
איש ברצלונה

מהדורה מנוקדת, מבוססת על
ההוצאה הראשונה (וֶנֶצְיָה רפ״ג)
בהשוואה עם ארבעה כתבי־יד עתיקים,
עם תרגום והערות באנגלית, מאת
אלחנן וֶנגרוב

כרך ראשון: ספר בראשית ושמות
מצוות א-קיד

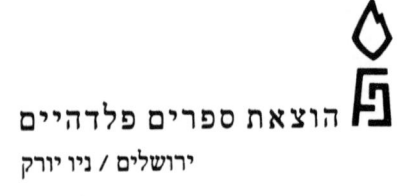

הוצאת ספרים פלדהיים
ירושלים / ניו יורק

Séfer haḤinnuch

༝༝༝༝༝ THE BOOK OF [MITZVAH] EDUCATION ༝༝༝

ascribed to Rabbi Aaron haLévi of Barcelona

the Hebrew text (with *n'kudoth*)
based on the first edition (Venice 1523)
compared with four old manuscripts,
with a translation and notes, by
Charles Wengrov

VOLUME I: GENESIS AND EXODUS
mitzvoth §1–114

FELDHEIM PUBLISHERS
Jerusalem/New York

כל הזכויות שמורות
למוציאים לאור
הוצאת ספרים פלדהיים בע״מ
ירושלים

First published 1984
Student Edition 1992
ISBN 0- 87306- 605- 7

Entire contents, with all special features,
copyright © 1984, 1992 by
Feldheim Publishers Ltd.

All rights reserved

No part of this publication may be translated,
reproduced, stored in a retrieval system or transmitted,
in any form or by any means, electronic, mechanical, photocopying, recording or otherwise,
without prior permission in writing from the publishers.

Feldheim Publishers
200 Airport Executive Park
Spring Valley, NY 10977

POB 35002 / Jerusalem, Israel

Printed in Israel

מכתב ברכה

ממרן הגאון ר' מרדכי גיפטר שליט"א

Dedicated to our dear parents

החבר ר׳ שרגא יהודה בן החבר ר׳ צבי מרדכי ז״ל פלדהיים
כ״ט באייר תש״ן

וזוגתו מרת גיטל בת החבר ר׳ יצחק קאליש ז״ל
כ״א בניסן תנש״א

Mr. and Mrs. Philipp Feldheim ז״ל
founders of Feldheim Publishers

ת.נ.צ.ב.ה.

contents   תוכן הענינים

Translator's preface | vii
A foreword by the author | 3   אגרת המחבר | 2
The order & reckoning
of the *mitzvoth* | 7   סדר ומנין המצוות | 6
Author's note | 53   הערת המחבר | 52
Preface | 57   הקדמה | 56
The *mitzvoth*:   ספר החינוך
   The Book of Genesis | 83   ספר בראשית | 82
   The Book of Exodus | 93   ספר שמות | 92

לעילוי נשמת
הר"ר אלחנן צבי ז"ל
ב"ר שמואל עוזר
ונגרוב

איש תם וישר, איש אמת, עניו וצנוע.
נקי כפיים, בר אוריין ויר"ש,
אהוב ואוהב את הבריות.

"בעל קורא" מנעוריו, ולא מחזיק טיבותא לנפשיה.
זכה וראה צאצאיו גדלים בתורה ויראה

נלב"ע בשיבה טובה
אור ליום כ"ה בתמוז תשס"ב
ת.נ.צ.ב.ה.

Translator's Preface

THE AUTHOR

Among the early writers of works on the *mitzvoth*, the author of *Séfer haḤinnuch* has achieved a fairly rare distinction: he has succeeded in remaining anonymous. Near the end of his Preface he describes himself as "a Jew of the house [tribe] of Lévi, of Barcelona"; near the beginning of *mitzvah* § 95 he refers, again, to "the Levites my brothers." But he remains otherwise unidentified.

In 5309 (1549) R. G'dalya ibn Yaḥya ascribed the work to R. Aaron haLévi of Barcelona, a well-known Talmudic scholar and early authority (*rishon*).[1] Evidently earlier, two Hebrew lines were written onto a manuscript of the *Ḥinnuch* dated 5093 (1333),[2] on the originally blank first page: "I have heard that the author of this work was R. Aaron of blessed memory." It can be assumed, however, that this was written at some time after the manuscript had come into existence. The first printed edition, Venice 5283 (1523), simply states on the title-page, "written by R. Aaron." In the second edition, Venice 5360 (1600) a marginal note finds support for this in the fact that in *mitzvah* § 95, after "the Levites my brothers," the author cites a passage from Scripture which mentions "Aaron."

Both a 19th-century scholar and the writer of a recent commentary on the *Ḥinnuch* have suggested that while our author was evidently not the renowned R. Aaron haLévi of Barcelona, whose works on Talmud and *halachah* are in print and are studied to this day, he did bear the same personal name; and because there were two scholars of the same name, both Levites, and both living in Barcelona at the same time, the relatively unknown one eventually became confused with the prominent one.[3]

---

1. R. G'dalya ibn Yaḥya, *Shalsheleth haKabbalah*, p. 44. For certain of the facts and references given here I am indebted to Gersion Appel, *A Philosophy of Mitzvot*, New York 1975, pp. 191 ff. As he states there on p. 256 (note 1), the question of the authorship is considered fairly fully in: David Rosin, *Ein Compendium der Jüdischen Gesetzeskunde* (Jahresbericht des Juedisch-theologischen Seminars, Breslau 1871; also offprint); Rabbi Charles B. Chavel, ed. *Séfer haḤinnuch*, Jerusalem 1956, pp. 5–7 and supplement; *Kuntres Hagahoth* in *Séfer haHashlamah l'Minḥath Ḥinnuch*, II p. 133.

2. About this manuscript see below, especially notes 8 and 9.

3. David Rosin, *op. cit.* p. 88; R. Mord'chai Yehuda haLévi From, *Torath haLévi*, Jerusalem 1952, p. 5.

This, however, remains conjecture. What is quite certain is that our author was not the well-known R. Aaron haLévi of Barcelona. As already noted by R. Hayyim Joseph David Azulai, in quite a few instances in the *Hinnuch* our author gives as *halachah* (law) rulings and views which differ from R. Aaron haLévi's decisions found in print.[4] Moreover, while (as noted) our author succeeded in concealing his identity, R. Aaron haLévi recorded not only his name but his illustrious genealogy as well, in the Introduction to his *Bedek haBa-yith*. On the other hand, there is enough evidence to indicate that R. Sh'lomo ibn Adreth (Rashba)—a colleague of R. Aaron haLévi in Barcelona, who differed with him on many points of law—was probably our author's *rav muvhak*, his master teacher or instructor in Talmud and *halachah*.

HUMILITY/HONESTY/ACKNOWLEDGMENTS

Our author goes further in his modesty, beyond remaining anonymous. He has added a preliminary *iggereth* (Foreword), which, he insists by the force of an oath, must always be included whenever a scribe copies his volume. And there he gives the lion's share of credit for his work to three great scholars who preceded him. All he did, he informs us, was only to make use of their writings (in the main), arranging them in a new form to catch the interest of his young son and the boy's friends. Needless to say, the work itself belies the author's modesty. He displays the full command of a *rishon* (early authority) over the field of Talmudic and post-Talmudic law.

Such humility, however, imposes a strong obligation on me to attempt something of the kind, in some small measure: to give an account of what I sought to do in this edition of the *Hinnuch*, and who provided what invaluable help.

The format, with its range of footnotes, will probably give an impression of immense scholarship on my part. That, alas, is a bit short of the truth. To start at the beginning, however, I initially sought to establish a Hebrew text of some degree of reliability. Details of this process are given below. Having a text, I rendered it into English to the best of my ability. It was my hope that the English would be used as a guide to the Hebrew rather than be read by itself; and I have therefore tended to "stretch" or "bend" the language somewhat to gain a greater fidelity to the wording and style of the original. Where the result is occasionally awkward or stiff, I ask the reader's indulgence.

4. See David Rosin, *op. cit.* in note 1, pp. 132–34.

TRANSLATOR'S PREFACE

In supplying the footnotes I became (if you will) a giant by standing on the shoulders of my predecessors. First and foremost I owe homage to R. Yitzḥak *ha-kohen* Aronovsky (of blessed memory), a 19th-century scholar of Eastern Europe, for his *Minḥath Yitzḥak*,[5] a learned commentary on the *Ḥinnuch*, in which he meticulously noted sources in Talmud, Midrash, and Rambam's *Mishneh Torah*, to just about every law and point of law in the text. Of the scholarship reflected in the notes of this edition, some ninety-odd percent is probably his. I have merely made the references available in English, in keeping with the apparent intention of the *Ḥinnuch* itself. Invariably, after giving laws and details of a particular *mitzvah*, our author notes where these and additional laws can be found in the Rabbinic literature—evidently with the hope of getting the interested reader (originally his son and the boy's friends) to go and study further. As a rule, though, he could give no more precise reference than a chapter of a Talmud tractate or the name of a Midrash. Printing being unknown, these works existed then in manuscripts only, with no standard pagination. Today, however, the pagination of the printed Talmud is standardized, and references can be given by exact page. Other sources can likewise be located fairly precisely. Hence the notes in this edition, in the similar hope that the reader will go on to learn more about the *mitzvoth*.

In addition to *Minḥath Yitzḥak*, I was aided by the ground-breaking monograph of David Rosin (see note 1), particularly in finding occasional sources or parallels to our author's reasons for the *mitzvoth*. Further guidance, especially in supplying explanatory notes or emending errors in the text,[6] came from the glosses, notes and comments of the great scholars who have written on this work, including the famed *Minḥath Ḥinnuch*, as well as the edition of Rabbi Chavel (*Mosad Rav Kook*). In a certain few instances I was able to add new (previously unnoted) sources in works of Midrash or *halachah* published from manuscript only in the last decades, and hence unavailable to the scholars previously. In this I was often guided by the monumental *Torah Shelemah* of my revered teacher, mentor and friend, R. Menaḥem M. Kasher, with whom I have been privileged to be associated for over a quarter of a century.

---

5. Issued in two volumes: I (part 1), Vilna 1908; II (parts 2–3), Piotrkov 1909–10; recently reissued in Jerusalem, in three volumes.

6. Where the text has been emended, standard scholarly practice has been followed: words or letters to be deleted are in parentheses; words or letters to be inserted are in brackets.

SCHOLARLY EMENDATION

This, in sum, has been my main work on the *Hinnuch*: translation and annotation. It fell, unfortunately, somewhat short of perfection. Encountering as I did many thousands of details of Talmudic teaching and law, inevitably my Talmudic-halachic knowledge was not always equal to the task, and many a mistranslation crept in, to say nothing of faulty nuances of understanding, which affected the notes as well.

The first to tackle this problem was Rabbi Aharon Feldman of the faculty of Yeshiva Ohr Somayach, in Jerusalem. He alerted me to many things that needed correction or improvement, battling, when necessary, the obstinacy which sometimes accompanied a misconception of mine. This work has been considerably improved as a result, and I acknowledge my gratitude.

More credit for such accuracy as the work may have is due Rabbi Yaakov Schatz, a modest but brilliant Talmudic scholar whose knowledge of the *Hinnuch* and *Minhath Hinnuch* is as intimate and thorough as mine is not. He has done his work with a surgeon's scalpel—ruthless but skilled. In addition, he has checked just about every reference and corrected occasional inaccuracies. Between his acumen and my English, there is hope that the result is satisfactory. (Shortcomings remain my own, of course. He could not be expected to fix everything. Readers who may find remaining errors or points for improvement are asked to kindly write us, and we shall try to correct matters in future editions.)

THE HEBREW TEXT

As noted above, I wanted to have a reasonably accurate text, fairly close to what the author wrote. My initial thought was to use the first edition, of Venice 5283 (1523), as Rabbi Chavel did in his edition. This, however, proved unsatisfactory. In many instances the first edition differs from later printings, in a word or a phrase, or even in a line or more. While at times the version of the first edition is superior, in a good number of cases the version of the later printings makes good sense, while the first edition does not. David Rosin, in fact, has a list of such instances which he simply calls errors in the first edition.[7]

Again, there are occasional passages in the first edition not found in the later printings. In Rabbi Chavel's work they are accepted as

---

7. David Rosin, *op. cit.* in note 1, p. 93 note 1. In ed. Chavel, except where these errors are blatant, they generally appear in the text, and the standard readings are noted below as variants.

⟨x⟩

authentic beyond question, giving a superior text. But were these passages really written by our author? Those who work in the field of old manuscripts know that one manuscript's marginal note is another's part of the text. In other words: A scholar in olden times studying a manuscript volume in his possession (before printed books existed) feels moved to write a note in the margin, for his own edification. Some time later another man wants to have the same work, and he pays a scribe to make him a copy of this scholar's manuscript. When the scribe comes to the marginal note, he thinks it a correction —something omitted originally, by mistake, in the text he is copying. So he adds it in the text.

Perhaps, then, this is how the first edition came to have added passages, not found in later printings? After all, this first edition was printed from one manuscript. The next edition, Venice 5360 (1600), was produced from a different manuscript. How could one simply assume the first edition to have the most accurate text?

I therefore decided to take the first edition and compare it with the four oldest existing manuscripts that bear dates. In order of age, these (which I consulted on microfilm at the *béth ha-s'farim ha-le'umi* in Jerusalem) are as follows:

MS Parma 928/1—bears an owner's date of 5087 (1327)
MS Vatican 163/1—dated 5093 (1333)[8]
MS Casanatense 134—dated 5103 (1343)
MS Parma 741—written in Fano, Italy, in 5111 (1351)

As best I could, I compared the first edition's text with the first (oldest) manuscript; where that was illegible I used the next manuscript; and noted all variants—where printed text and manuscript differed. Then I checked the other manuscripts to see if they confirmed the variant readings or not, or if perhaps they had some version of their own. (In many instances where the oldest MS was too faint and unclear to read, one could still go back and detect if it agreed with a variant reading in MS Vatican.) On the basis of majority or context (or the source that our author might have been quoting) I then decided which variant readings to accept and which to ignore.

As a rule, no record of such variants has been made in this edition. I have simply let the text stand on its merits. Only where a variant proved to be of unusual interest has notice been taken of it in the notes.

8. While this date in the manuscript's colophon is correctly given in Assemani's catalogue (Rome 1756, I p. 129), it was earlier recorded erroneously, as 5073 (1313), in Bartolocci, *Bibliotheca Magna Rabbinica*, Rome 1675, I p. 90a; and thence the error has been copied by Rosin, pp. 78, 92; Chavel, p. 19; and Appel, p. 192.

Where added passages in the first edition are not found in the manuscripts, I have nevertheless left them in, since they generally have their own interest and value (and there is the very slight chance, however small and unlikely, that they derive from our author). I have, however, put them in parentheses and noted them, as a rule, as probably later interpolations.

It will be obvious to anyone familiar with manuscript research that no claim can thus be made here for a scientifically accurate text. No attempt has been made to determine the relative value of the manuscripts or their relationship to one another, on the basis of internal evidence, etc. In general, I was left with the impression that none of the four manuscripts is wholly free of error, but the two older ones are more accurate than the later two (a scribe would necessarily copy into his work all the errors in a work he was transcribing, and being human, might add a few of his own). While the oldest has a few accurate readings not found elsewhere, the second manuscript proved superior in many instances; and it seems to show some kinship with the first edition.[9]

The factors of fatigue and human error being what they are, I will not even insist that my work has been entirely thorough or absolutely accurate. There are perhaps minor variants which have been overlooked. Yet I think the result is the most correct text to appear thus far.

Checking this text has been the task of Rabbi Moshe Goldstein, a young but veteran researcher who has published from manuscript new editions of such *rishonim* (early commentaries) as Ritba to certain tractates of the Talmud. He has managed to alert me to some manuscript readings which I originally missed, and to an occasional manuscript version that was untenable. To him both the publisher and I owe a good measure of thanks.

The painstaking, thankless task of adding vowel marks (*nikkud*) to the Hebrew was begun by Shulamith Ḥovav and done mainly by Rachel Klein, both of Jerusalem. Their work too has benefited by Rabbi Moshe Goldstein's careful scrutiny.

---

9. I.e. with the manuscript from which the first edition was printed. They often agree in peculiarities of spelling and other minor points; and in the short list of *mitzvoth* at the beginning of the work, both are identically erroneous in §§ 199–200. Very likely, both derive from one "parent" manuscript. This would also explain why the first edition has on its title-page "written by R. Aaron," while MS Vatican has on the first page (as noted above), "I have heard that the author of this work was R. Aaron of blessed memory."

TRANSLATOR'S PREFACE

Two more points should be noted: In writing the *Séfer haḤinnuch*, for each *sidrah* (weekly portion of the Torah) our author dealt with all the positive precepts first, and then all the negative precepts in the *sidrah*. Evidently he adopted this order under the influence of Rambam's *Séfer haMitzvoth* (our author's acknowledged source for the *mitzvoth* he describes): There the positive precepts form the first part of the work, and the negative precepts the second. Apparently, however, the printers of the *Ḥinnuch* in Frankfort 5543 (1783) found our author's arrangement confusing. Often Scripture gives a positive and a negative command about one thing in the very same verse (sentence) or in one verse after the other (to give a hypothetical example: to keep the Sabbath, and not to desecrate it). Necessarily the discussion of the two precepts must be interlinked. Yet in our author's arrangement the two *mitzvoth* may be as much as ten pages apart. Hence the Frankfort printers decided to rearrange the *mitzvoth* strictly in the order of their appearance in Scripture, be they positive or negative.

Purists may argue that this does violence to our author's work. Yet beyond any doubt the result is better for the reader (and thus perhaps it fulfills the better our author's purpose). This new order has been followed in all further printings (except ed. Chavel, which reprints the first edition), and it has been adopted here as well.

The second point to be noted is that in preparing the translation, I automatically broke it into paragraphs, to make it somewhat easier to read. Subsequently, the Hebrew was similarly divided into paragraphs, to correspond. In the original each *mitzvah* is divided into but four sections: (1) the nature or substance of the *mitzvah*; (2) its possible reason or purpose; (3) some of its laws and details; (4) when, where, and to whom it applies.

THE TIME OF WRITING

One interesting question remains: When did our author write his work? In the *mitzvah* of observing *sh'mittah* every seventh year (§330), in the last section (on when and where it is to be observed), he gives the next, approaching year of *sh'mittah* as either 5017 (1257) or 5018 (1258), depending on which of two authorities is followed. If this is correct, he wrote the work somewhere between 5012 (1252) and 5016 (1256). R. Ḥayyim Joseph David Azulai, however, suspects a scribal error here: for Ramban (R. Moshe b. Naḥman) was still living then, and yet, wherever his name appears in the *Ḥinnuch*, it is followed by the standard Hebrew abbreviation for "of blessed memory," indicating that Ramban was then no longer alive. Therefore, writes David

Rosin,[10] the dates our author gives must contain a scribal error in one letter, and should be corrected to 5067 (1307) and 5068 (1308). Manuscripts, he confidently suggests, will quite certainly have the correct dates.

The four manuscripts I consulted, however, confirm the original dates: 5017/18 (1257/58). Hence I believe they must be accepted. As to the objection that Ramban is invariably referred to as being deceased, and he was then among the living, to my mind that presents no difficulty. At the end of his *iggereth* (Foreword) our author invites all scribes copying his work to correct any patent or blatant error that they may discover. If he added a suitable title of honor for a living sage wherever he mentioned Ramban, it would be a simple matter for later scribes to change that title to the Hebrew for "of blessed memory" when Ramban was no longer among the living.[11] There are, in fact, instances enough in this work where after the Sages are mentioned, the editions add "of blessed memory"; or after a reference to the Almighty, they add "be He blessed"; and in the manuscripts these epithets are not to be found. Later copyists added their own touches of piety.

IN THANKS & IN MEMORIAM

First, my gratitude to Jerusalem's *béth ha-s'farim ha-le'umi* and the staff of its Manuscript-Microfilm Room for giving me the means to examine the four oldest dated manuscripts of the *Ḥinnuch*. I am equally grateful to the directors of the Biblioteca Palatina of Parma, the Vatican Library, and the Biblioteca Casanatense of Rome (all in Italy) for their kind permission to make use of these manuscripts, the originals of which are lodged with them.

It is a pleasant duty to express my warmest thanks to the publisher, Yaakov Feldheim, and his dear father, Philipp, both very good friends of many years standing, for a matchless opportunity to gain a thorough familiarity with an important 13th-century classic of Torah Judaism, which I might otherwise have known but indifferently. I am grateful, too, for the patience and grace with which they have accepted the *sturm und drang* through which this work has passed to make it truly fit for publication. Above all, I am in their debt for the opportunity to add

10. *Op. cit.* in note 1, p. 78. See R. Ḥayyim Joseph David Azulai, *Shém ha-G'dolim* (ed. Benjacob, Vilna 1853), *ma'arecheth ha-g'dolim*, I p. 132.

11. Having arrived at this solution independently, I then found that Appel (*op. cit.* in note 1) makes the same point on p. 257 note 8. On p. 192, however, he accepts the verdict of Rosin without demur.

(I hope) something of worth in English to our enduring classical literature.

In closing, whatever value my work on this *séfer* may have, I should like to leave it in memoriam to a very dear friend who was taken from us too soon and too painfully. Bernard Merling was a close friend since our days together at school. I guided his first steps on the road to the graphic arts, where he found such signal success by his talents and resources. Thereafter, neither time nor distance diminished the friendship or darkened its luster. Whenever or however I called on him for anything, if it was in his power to grant it I knew he would. And others could tell far more of him. In his own way he was a model figure in the observant Jewish community, always accessible, unspoiled by success. Perhaps that is why Heaven saw fit to make his stay so short on this troubled earth. Heaven's gain, however, was our tragic loss.

Two regrets marred his brief but memorable life: first, that his creative work was so ephemeral; he would leave no lasting body of work behind. And he longed to settle in Eretz Yisrael, but could not manage to do so. Perhaps by offering this work, my first major translation done in Jerusalem, as a memorial to him, both regrets may be, posthumously, somewhat mitigated. . . . Blessed be his memory.

Charles Wengrov

List of abbreviations, etc.

§	numbered section or *mitzvah*
ad loc.	*ad locum*, at the place
b.	*ben*, the son of
cf.	*confer*, compare
Deut.	the Book of Deuteronomy (*d'varim*)
ed.	edition of; edited by; editor
e.g.	*exempli gratia*, for example
et al.	*et alii*, and others
etc.	*et cetera*, and others
ff.	and pages following
ibid.	*ibidem*, at the place
idem	the same (person)
i.e.	*id est*, that is
l.	line
Lev.	the Book of Leviticus (*va-yikra*)
MdRSbY	*Midrash d'Rabbi Shimon ben Yohai* (ed. Epstein-Melamed)
MH	R. Joseph Babad, *Minhath Hinnuch* (commentary on the *Hinnuch*)
MhG	*Midrash haGadol*, compiled in Yemen, 14th century
MS (plural, MSS)	*manuscriptum*, manuscript (plural, *manuscripta*, manuscripts)
MT	Rambam (R. Moshe b. Maimon, Maimonides), *Mishneh Torah* (also titled *Yad haHazakah*)
MY	R. Yitzhak ha-kohén Aronovsky, *Minhath Yitzhak* (commentary on the *Hinnuch*)
op. cit.	*opera citato*, in the work cited
p. / pp.	page / pages
q.v.	*quod vide*, which see
R.	Rabbi, Rabbénu, Rav
ShM	Rambam (Maimonides), *Séfer haMitzvoth*
s.v.	*sub verbo*, *sub voce*, under the word (or words)
TB	*Talmud Bavli*, Babylonian Talmud
TJ	*Talmud Yerushalmi*, Jerusalem Talmud

Séfer haḤinnuch סֵפֶר הַחִנּוּךְ
THE BOOK OF [MITZVAH] EDUCATION

אִגֶּרֶת הַמְחַבֵּר

אוּלַי יַחְשֹׁב מְעַיֵּן בְּסֵפֶר זֶה שֶׁהַמְחַבְּרוֹ קִבֵּץ כָּל דִּינָיו בִּיגִיעוֹ וְטוּב עִיּוּנוֹ מִדִּבְרֵי הַתַּנָּאִים וְהָאֲמוֹרָאִים, וְאִלּוּ כֵן הָיָה יִתְחַיֵּב לִהְיוֹת הַמְחַבֵּר בָּקִי בְּכָל פִּנּוֹת הַתַּלְמוּד בַּבְלִי וּבִירוּשַׁלְמִי וְסִפְרָא וְסִפְרֵי וְתוֹסֶפְתָּא, לָכֵן הוּא הַיּוֹדֵעַ עַצְמוֹ וְחָכְמַת מָה לוֹ, רָאוּי לְפַרְסֵם הָאֱמֶת לְכָל הַשּׁוֹמֵעַ קוֹלוֹ, וְאַל יַעֲשֶׂה מְלֶאכֶת הַשֵּׁם תְּמִימָה כְּקֶשֶׁת רְמִיָּה בְּצִדְיָה וְעָרְמָה, כְּמִתְהַדֵּר בְּיַלְדֵי נָכְרִים, כְּחַלָּשׁ מִזְדַּיֵּן בְּשַׁלְטֵי הַגִּבּוֹרִים, וְכִשְׁפַל אֲנָשִׁים מִתְעַטֵּר בְּכִתְרֵי הַמְּלָכִים. וְהִנֵּה הוּא קוֹרֵא מִמְּקוֹמוֹ, מוֹדִיעַ וּמֵעִיד עֵדוּת נֶאֱמָנָה לְכָל קוֹרֵא בוֹ, שֶׁרֹב דִּבְרֵי הַסֵּפֶר נִלְקָטִים מִסִּפְרֵי עַמּוּדֵי הָאָרֶץ הַמְפֻרְסָמִים בְּמַעֲלָה וְחָכְמָה בְּכָל הַגּוֹיִם, הָרַב רַבִּי יִצְחָק אַלְפָסִי וְהָרַב רַבִּי מֹשֶׁה בַּר מַיְמוֹן לְטוֹבָה זְכוּרִים. לָהֶם מִשְׁפַּט הַבְּכוֹרָה הַהוֹד וְהַגְּדֻלָּה בְּחִבּוּר זֶה. וְאַל הַחוּט הַמְשֻׁלָּשׁ בְּחָכְמָה בִּתְבוּנָה וּבְדַעַת, הָרַב רַבִּי מֹשֶׁה בַּר נַחְמָן זִכְרוֹנוֹ לִבְרָכָה, הוּא חִבֵּר סֵפֶר נִכְבָּד מְאֹד בְּחֶשְׁבּוֹן הַמִּצְווֹת לְבַד כַּמָּה וְכַמָּה חִבּוּרִים יְקָרִים. אֵלֶּה הַגִּבּוֹרִים אֲשֶׁר מֵעוֹלָם, שֶׁהוֹצִיאוּ רֹב זְמַנָּם לְבָרֵר דִּבְרֵי חֲכָמִים לִבְרָכָה זִכְרָם, צְלוּלִים בְּמַיִם אַדִּירִים וְהֶעֱלוּ מִדִּבְרֵי הַגְּמָרָא פְּנִינִים בְּיָדָם. וְיוֹם בּוֹאֵנוּ אֶל בֵּית מִקְדָּשָׁם וְאֶל חֲדַר הוֹרָתָם, מָצָאנוּ שָׁם בְּאֵר מַיִם חַיִּים גַּנּוֹת וּפַרְדֵּסִים, גַּלְסְקָאוֹת וּכְלֵי מִלָּת לְפָנֵינוּ עֲרוּכִים. אָמַרְתִּי בַּמֶּה אֶתְרַצֶּה לָבוֹא וּלְשַׁמֵּשׁ לִפְנֵי הַגִּבּוֹרִים, וּכְבָר בֵּרְרוּ לָנוּ הֵם כָּל הַדְּבָרִים, הֲלֹא בְּסֵדֶר תרי"ג מִצְווֹת וְעַל דֶּרֶךְ הַסְּדָרִים,

1. Literally, a missive.
2. Respectively, the Sages of the Mishnah (the earlier part of the Talmud) and the Sages of the *g'mara* (the later part).
3. Sifra is on Leviticus; Sifre, on Numbers and Deuteronomy; both contain halachic teachings and rulings by the Talmudic Sages. The Tosefta is a collection of teachings by the Sages of the Mishnah which were not included in the Mishnah.
4. Expression from Jeremiah 8:9.
5. Expression from Hosea 7:16.
6. I.e. the work of others. Expression from Isaiah 2:6.
7. Expression from Song of Songs 4:4.
8. Expression from Job 9:6.
9. R. Isaac b. Jacob Alfasi (1013–1103) made a compendium of the Talmud, extracting and condensing its halachic material which is applicable to Jewish life in exile since the destruction of the Holy Temple. While at first glance it seems only a shortened version of the Talmud, his work is actually a code of law—the most important one produced before Rambam's *Mishneh Torah*. Known as *'Alfas* (from his name, which derives from his having lived many years in Fez, North Africa) the work is printed with the Talmud in the standard Vilna edition, each section behind its respective tractate.

⟨2⟩

A foreword[1] by the author

Perhaps a person who studies this work will think its author gathered all its laws by his toil and the fine quality of his study in the words of the Talmudic Sages, the *tanna'im* and *amora'im*.[2] Were that the case, the author would have had to be well versed in every corner of the Babylonian and Jerusalem Talmud, Midrash Sifra and Sifre, and the Tosefta.[3] Hence, as he knows himself and what wisdom there is in him,[4] it is seemly to let the truth be known to everyone who hears his voice, that he may not do the whole and perfect work of the Lord like a deceitful bow,[5] with trickery and guile, as one who takes pride in the brood of strangers,[6] as a weak man girding himself in the armor of the mighty[7] and as the lowliest of men adorning himself with the crowns of kings.

Here, then, the author proclaims from his place, informing and attesting faithfully to everyone who reads this, that most of the contents of the work are culled from the writings of the "pillars of the earth,"[8] renowned for virtue and wisdom among all the nations: R. Isaac Alfasi[9] and R. Moses b. Maimon,[10] be they remembered for good. To them goes the lion's share of the credit,[11] the glory and honor for this volume. And with the "threefold cord"[12] [braided] of wisdom, understanding and knowledge, [we have] R. Moses b. Naḥman of blessed memory:[13] he composed a most esteemed work on the reckoning of the *mitzvoth* (the Torah's precepts), in addition to many precious, valuable works.

These are the "mighty men" of old[14] who spent most of their time clarifying the words of the Talmudic Sages of blessed memory. They delved deep into the mighty waters[15] [of the Talmud] and out of the words of the Talmud[16] they brought up pearls in their hands, so that the day we entered their holy temple[17] and the chamber of their instruction, we found there "a well of living waters,"[18] gardens and orchards, "loaves and fine wool garments"[19] arrayed before us.

Said I: How can I be accepted cordially, to come and serve before these great men, when they have already clarified for us all the topics?—surely by arranging the 613 *mitzvoth* according to the *sidroth* (the weekly portions of the Written Torah read on the Sabbath in the

ספר החינוך A FOREWORD BY THE AUTHOR

אוּלַי יִתְעוֹרְרוּ יוֹתֵר בָּהֶן מִתּוֹךְ כַּף הַנְּעָרִים, יָשִׂימוּ לֵב בָּהֶם בַּשַּׁבָּתוֹת וּבַחַגִּים, וְיָשׁוּבוּ מֵהִשְׁתַּגֵּעַ בִּרְחוֹב הֶעָרִים, לְאוֹר הַחַיִּים, אִישׁ אֶת רֵעֵהוּ הַיְלָדִים רַבִּים, יִשְׁאֲלוּ מִצְוֹת שַׁבָּת זוֹ כַּמָּה, וּמָלְאָה הָאָרֶץ דֵּעַת וְזִמָּה. וְהִנֵּה פֵּרוּשׁ כָּל אַחַת נָכוֹן לִפְנֵיהֶם, וּמִבְּלִי יְגִיעָה יִמְצְאוּ דִּבְרֵי חֵפֶץ בְּסִימָנֵיהֶם, זֶרַע קֹדֶשׁ יִתְבָּרְכוּ מֵאֵל, הֵם וּבְנֵיהֶם וְכָל אֲשֶׁר לָהֶם, בְּכָל מְקוֹמוֹת מוֹשְׁבוֹתֵיהֶם, וַאֲנִי בִּכְלַל הַבְּרָכָה עִמָּהֶם.

וּמַשְׁבִּיעַ אֲנִי בַּשֵּׁם הַמְיֻחָד לְכָל מַעְתִּיקוֹ שֶׁיִּכְתֹּב אִגֶּרֶת זוֹ בְּרֹאשׁוֹ, וְהַחַיִּים וְהַשָּׁלוֹם יִהְיוּ אִתּוֹ, לְמַעַן יִתְּנוּ הַכֹּל הוֹדוֹ וְתִפְאַרְתּוֹ לְיוֹלְדוֹ וְהוֹרָתוֹ. וְהַמְתַקֵּן בּוֹ כָּל שְׁגִיאָה אַחַר הָעִיּוּן הַמְכֻוָּן מֵאֵל תְּהִי שְׁלֵמָה מַשְׂכֻּרְתּוֹ. וְשָׁלוֹם עַל יִשְׂרָאֵל.

10. Rambam (abbreviation from the Hebrew initials of his name), known also as Maimonides (1135–1204). A noted philosopher and physician, he is important to our author because of his *Séfer haMitzvoth*, a detailed listing of the 613 precepts of the Torah (with definitions, explanations, etc.) which, as our author freely acknowledges in his brief statement before his list of precepts and again before their exposition, he used in writing this work. Our author also drew greatly on Rambam's monumental code of Jewish law, *Mishneh Torah*.

11. Literally, the right of the firstborn—from Deuteronomy 21:17.

12. Expression from Ecclesiastes 4:12.

13. Ramban (1194–c. 1270), also known as Naḥmanides. Originally rabbi of Gerona, northern Spain, he was a physician, philosopher, Talmudic scholar, author of a Bible commentary, poet and kabbalist—with a range of knowledge unequalled in his time. His work on the *mitzvoth*, which our author goes on to mention, is his *hassagoth* (objections) to the *Sefer haMitzvoth* of Rambam (see note 10), in which he defends the listing of the precepts in *Halachoth G'doloth* (a work of geonic times) where Rambam differs.

14. Expression from Genesis 6:4.

15. Expression from Exodus 15:10.

16. Literally, the *g'mara*—the later part of the Talmud, which analyzes and discusses the Mishnah, the earlier part.

17. The "edifice of learning" which they built by their writings.

18. Expression from Song of Songs 4:15.

19. Expression from TB K'thuboth 111b.

20. Expression from Job 33:30.

21. Expression from Ecclesiastes 12:10.

22. Expression from Malachi 2:5.

23. I.e. R. Isaac Alfasi, Rambam and Ramban, on whose writings our author drew.

24. Expression from Ruth 2:12.

⟨4⟩

synagogue). Perhaps as a result, the young will become more interested in them, giving their attention to them on Sabbaths and Festival days, and will turn back from going wild in the street of the cities, to be enlightened by the light of [eternal] life.[20] The youngsters of tender age will ask one another, "How many are the *mitzvoth* [in the *sidrah*] of this Sabbath?"—*and the earth shall be full of knowledge* (Isaiah 11:9) *and wise thought* (Proverbs 1:4).

Here, then, is the explanation of every single [*mitzvah*] prepared before them. Without effort they will find words of delight[21] in the sections [of this work]. May the holy progeny be blessed of God, they and their children and all their dear ones, in all their places of habitation, and may I be included in the blessing with them.

By the unique name [of the Lord] I adjure every copyist [of this work] that he write this missive at its beginning; then may life and peace[22] be with him, for it is in order that all may give credit, honor and esteem for it to its proper "parents."[23] Whoever corrects any error in it after intent study, may his reward be complete[24] from God. And let peace be upon Israel (Psalms 128:6).

סֵדֶר וּמִנְיַן הַמִּצְווֹת

🕎🕎🕎🕎🕎

כָּל הַמִּצְווֹת שֶׁנָּתַן הָאֵל בָּרוּךְ הוּא לְעַמּוֹ יִשְׂרָאֵל הַכְּלוּלוֹת בְּסֵפֶר הַתּוֹרָה שֶׁהֵן קְבוּעוֹת לְדוֹרוֹת, בֵּין מִצְווֹת עֲשֵׂה וְלֹא־תַעֲשֶׂה, הֵן תרי״ג מִצְווֹת. וְאֵלּוּ הֵן הַסְּדָרִים שֶׁהֵן כְּתוּבוֹת בָּהֶן לְפִי הַחֶשְׁבּוֹן שֶׁחָשַׁב אוֹתָן הָרַב הַגָּדוֹל רַבִּי מֹשֶׁה בַּר מַיְמוֹן זִכְרוֹנוֹ לִבְרָכָה. וְכַסֵּדֶר הַזֶּה שֶׁאֲנִי כּוֹתְבָן זוֹ אַחַר זוֹ הֵן כְּתוּבוֹת בְּסֵפֶר הַתּוֹרָה.

מִצְוַת הַשְׁבָּתַת חָמֵץ	ט	בְּרֵאשִׁית	
מִצְוַת אֲכִילַת מַצָּה	י	מִצְוַת פְּרִיָּה וּרְבִיָּה	א
שֶׁלֹּא יִמָּצֵא חָמֵץ בִּרְשׁוּתֵנוּ בְּפֶסַח	יא	לֶךְ לְךָ	
שֶׁלֹּא לֶאֱכֹל מִכָּל דָּבָר שֶׁיֵּשׁ בּוֹ חָמֵץ	יב	מִצְוַת מִילָה	ב
שֶׁלֹּא נַאֲכִיל מִן הַפֶּסַח לְיִשְׂרָאֵל מְשֻׁמָּד	יג	וַיִּשְׁלַח	
		שֶׁלֹּא לֶאֱכֹל גִּיד הַנָּשֶׁה	ג
שֶׁלֹּא נַאֲכִיל מִן הַפֶּסַח לְגֵר וְתוֹשָׁב	יד	בֹּא אֶל פַּרְעֹה	
		מִצְוַת קִדּוּשׁ הַחֹדֶשׁ	ד
שֶׁלֹּא לְהוֹצִיא מִבְּשַׂר הַפֶּסַח חוּצָה	טו	מִצְוַת שְׁחִיטַת הַפֶּסַח	ה
		מִצְוַת אֲכִילַת בְּשַׂר הַפֶּסַח	ו
שֶׁלֹּא לִשְׁבֹּר עֶצֶם מִן הַפֶּסַח	טז	שֶׁלֹּא לֶאֱכֹל הַפֶּסַח נָא וּמְבֻשָּׁל	ז
		שֶׁלֹּא לְהוֹתִיר מִבְּשַׂר הַפֶּסַח	ח

1. This is taught in the Talmud and Midrash. TB Makkoth 23b: R. Simla'i expounded: 613 *mitzvoth* were given orally to Moses—365 negative precepts, as the number of days in the solar year; and 248 positive precepts, corresponding to the limbs and organs of a man. Said R. Hamnuna: Which verse bears this out? *Moses commanded us the Torah* (Deuteronomy 33:4). The numerical value of the Hebrew letters in the word *torah* is 611 [each Hebrew letter also denotes a number; tav = 400, vav = 6, resh = 200, hé = 5; and the first two of the Ten Commandments] *I am the Lord your God*, and *You shall have no other gods* (Exodus 20:2-3) we heard directly from the Almighty. (This last part, about the first two Commandments, is a teaching of the School of R. Ishmael in TB Horayoth 8a. The same way of reckoning 613 is found in Shir haShirim Rabbah 1:2—2 or 1, 13).

Similarly Bamidbar Rabbah 13, 15-16: For 613 *mitzvoth* were commingled with them [with the Ten Commandments]; and thus you will find there are 613 letters [in the Hebrew text of the Ten Commandments] from *I am the Lord your God* until [but excluding] the last two words, *'asher l'ré'echa*, "that is your neighbor's" (Exodus 20:14).

⟨6⟩

The order and reckoning of the *mitzvoth*

All the *mitzvoth* (precepts) that God, blessed is He, gave to His people Israel, which are incorporated in the Written Torah, being fixed permanently for all generations—whether positive precepts (acts to be done) or negative (acts not to be done)—are 613 precepts [in number].[1] The following are the *sidroth* in which they are written, according to the listing that the great master R. Moses b. Maimon of blessed memory made of them.[2] In the order that I now write them, so are they written in the Torah scroll.

sidrah b'réshith (Genesis 1–6:8)
1. the precept to "be fruitful and multiply"

sidrah lech l'cha (Genesis 12–17)
2. the precept of circumcision

sidrah va-yishlah (Genesis 32:3–36:43)
3. not to eat the sinew of the thigh-vein

sidrah bo (Exodus 10–13:16)
4. the precept of sanctifying the new month
5. the precept of ritually slaying the Passover offering
6. the precept of eating the flesh of the Passover offering
7. not to eat the Passover offering underroasted or cooked
8. not to leave over any flesh of the Passover offering
9. the precept of removing *hamétz* (leavened food) [from one's possession]
10. the precept of eating *matzah* (unleavened bread) [on the first night of Passover]
11. that no *hamétz* is to be found in our possession during Passover
12. not to eat anything [during Passover] that has *hamétz* in it
13. that we should not give a Jewish apostate any part of the Passover offering to eat
14. that we should not give anything of the Passover offering to a [partial] proselyte and resident [a heathen who has rejected idol-worship] to eat
15. not to carry any flesh of the Passover offering outside [the house]
16. not to break any bone of the Passover offering

ספר החינוך — THE LIST OF MITZVOTH

לא	מִצְוַת קִדּוּשׁ שַׁבָּת בִּדְבָרִים		שֶׁלֹּא יֹאכַל עָרֵל מִן הַפֶּסַח	יז
לב	שֶׁלֹּא לַעֲשׂוֹת מְלָאכָה בְּשַׁבָּת		מִצְוַת קִדּוּשׁ בְּכוֹרוֹת בְּאֶרֶץ יִשְׂרָאֵל	יח
לג	מִצְוַת כִּבּוּד אָב וָאֵם		שֶׁלֹּא לֶאֱכֹל חָמֵץ בְּפֶסַח	יט
לד	שֶׁלֹּא לַהֲרֹג נָקִי		שֶׁלֹּא יֵרָאֶה לָנוּ חָמֵץ בְּפֶסַח	כ
לה	שֶׁלֹּא לְגַלּוֹת עֶרְוַת אֵשֶׁת אִישׁ		מִצְוַת סִפּוּר יְצִיאַת מִצְרַיִם	כא
לו	שֶׁלֹּא לִגְנֹב נֶפֶשׁ מִיִּשְׂרָאֵל		מִצְוַת פִּדְיוֹן פֶּטֶר חֲמוֹר	כב
לז	שֶׁלֹּא לְהָעִיד בְּשֶׁקֶר		מִצְוַת עֲרִיפַת פֶּטֶר חֲמוֹר	כג
לח	שֶׁלֹּא לַחְמֹד			
לט	שֶׁלֹּא לַעֲשׂוֹת צוּרוֹת, אֲפִלּוּ לְנוֹי		וַיְהִי בְּשַׁלַּח	
מ	שֶׁלֹּא לִבְנוֹת אַבְנֵי מִזְבֵּחַ גָּזִית		שֶׁלֹּא נֵצֵא בְּשַׁבָּת חוּץ לַתְּחוּם	כד
מא	שֶׁלֹּא לִפְסֹעַ עַל הַמִּזְבֵּחַ			
			וַיִּשְׁמַע יִתְרוֹ	
	מִשְׁפָּטִים		מִצְוַת הָאֲמָנָה בִּמְצִיאוּת הַשֵּׁם יִתְבָּרַךְ	כה
מב	מִצְוַת דִּין עֶבֶד עִבְרִי		שֶׁלֹּא נַאֲמִין אֱלֹהוּת בִּלְתִּי הַשֵּׁם לְבַדּוֹ	כו
מג	מִצְוַת יִעוּד שֶׁל אָמָה הָעִבְרִיָּה		שֶׁלֹּא לַעֲשׂוֹת פֶּסֶל	כז
מד	מִצְוַת פִּדְיוֹן אָמָה הָעִבְרִיָּה		שֶׁלֹּא לְהִשְׁתַּחֲווֹת לַעֲבוֹדָה זָרָה	כח
מה	שֶׁלֹּא יִמְכֹּר אָמָה עִבְרִיָּה הַקּוֹנֶה אוֹתָהּ מִיַּד הָאָב		שֶׁלֹּא לַעֲבֹד עֲבוֹדָה זָרָה בְּמָה שֶׁדַּרְכָּהּ לְהֵעָבֵד	כט
מו	שֶׁלֹּא לִגְרֹעַ שְׁאֵר כְּסוּת וְעוֹנָה		שֶׁלֹּא לִשָּׁבַע לַשָּׁוְא	ל
מז	מִצְוַת בֵּית־דִּין לַהֲרֹג בְּחֶנֶק הַמְחֻיָּב			
מח	שֶׁלֹּא לְהַכּוֹת אָב וָאֵם			

    Ibid. 18, 21: In the stone tablets of the Ten Commandments were 613 *mitzvoth*, corresponding to the [number of] Hebrew letters [in the Commandments] from *'anochi* (I am the Lord your God) to *'asher l'ré'echa* [exclusive].

    So also, the "613 precepts" are mentioned in TB Shabbath 87a; Sifre, Deuteronomy §76; and Midrash haGadol, Genesis 15:1. The first attempt at a detailed listing is found in *Halachoth G'doloth*, from the eighth or ninth century. R. Héfetz b. Yatzliah, a blind scholar in the latter part of the tenth century, apparently established a different listing in his Arabic-language *Book of Commandments*, but only a small part is extant. Beginning with R. Sa'adyah Ga'on (10th century) or perhaps earlier, it became the fashion to cast the precepts into rhymed form, for inclusion in the liturgy. It remained for Rambam to establish a new detailed listing (by criteria that he carefully defined) in his *Séfer haMitzvoth* (the Book of the Precepts; hereafter abbreviated as ShM). As our author goes on to state, it is this listing which he utilizes in the present work.

    2. I.e. what follows are the 613 precepts as set down by Rambam (in ShM; listed also in brief form at the beginning of his *Mishneh Torah*—hereafter abbreviated as MT) listed and grouped according to the *sidroth* (plural of *sidrah*), the portions of the Pentateuch (Five Books of Moses) read in the synagogue on the Sabbaths of the year.

⟨8⟩

17. that no uncircumcised person should eat of the Passover offering
18. the precept of sanctifying firstborn [animals] in the land of Israel
19. not to eat any *hamétz* on Passover
20. that no *hamétz* should be seen with us during Passover
21. the precept of recounting the exodus from Egypt
22. the precept of redeeming a firstborn donkey
23. the precept of beheading a firstborn donkey [if it is not redeemed]

sidrah b'shallah (Exodus 13:17–17:16)
24. that we should not go out beyond permitted limits on the Sabbath

sidrah yithro (Exodus 18–20)
25. the *mitzvah* of belief in the existence of the Eternal Lord, be He blessed
26. that we should not believe in any divinity but the Eternal Lord alone
27. not to make a graven image
28. not to prostrate oneself in idol-worship
29. not to worship an idol [3] in the way it is customarily worshipped
30. not to swear in vain
31. the precept of hallowing the Sabbath in words
32. not to do any work on the Sabbath
33. the precept of honoring one's father and mother
34. not to murder an innocent man
35. not to uncover the nakedness of another's wife
36. not to kidnap any Jewish person
37. not to bear false witness
38. not to covet what belongs to another
39. not to make [carved human] images, even for ornamentation
40. not to build an altar of hewn stones
41. not to stride by steps to the altar

sidrah mishpatim (Exodus 21–24) [4]
42. the precept of the law of the Hebrew slave
43. the precept of marital designation of the Hebrew maidservant
44. the *mitzvah* of the redemption of the Hebrew maidservant
45. that one who buys a Hebrew maidservant from her father's hand may not sell her
46. not to diminish (withhold) [from one's wife] food, clothing or conjugal due
47. the precept that the court is to execute by strangulation anyone punishable by this death
48. not to strike a father or mother

THE LIST OF MITZVOTH

סד	שֶׁלֹּא לְהוֹנוֹת הַגֵּר בְּמָמוֹן	מט	מִצְוַת דִּינֵי קְנָסוֹת
סה	שֶׁלֹּא לְעַנּוֹת יָתוֹם וְאַלְמָנָה	נ	מִצְוַת בֵּית־דִּין לַהֲרֹג בְּסַיִף הַמְחֻיָּב
סו	מִצְוַת הַלְוָאָה לְעָנִי	נא	מִצְוַת בֵּית־דִּין לָדוּן בְּנִזְקֵי בְּהֵמָה
סז	שֶׁלֹּא נִתְבַּע חוֹב מֵעָנִי שֶׁאֵין לוֹ בַּמֶּה לְפָרְעוֹ	נב	שֶׁלֹּא לֶאֱכֹל שׁוֹר הַנִּסְקָל
		נג	מִצְוַת בֵּית־דִּין לָדוּן בְּנִזְקֵי הַבּוֹר
סח	שֶׁלֹּא נָשִׂית יָד בֵּין לֹוֶה לְמַלְוֶה בְּרִבִּית	נד	מִצְוַת בֵּית־דִּין לָדוּן גַּנָּב בְּתַשְׁלוּמִין אוֹ בְּמִיתָה
סט	שֶׁלֹּא לְקַלֵּל הַדַּיָּן	נה	מִצְוַת בֵּית־דִּין לָדוּן בְּנִזְקֵי הַבְּעֵר
ע	לָאו דְּבִרְכַּת הַשֵּׁם		
עא	שֶׁלֹּא לְקַלֵּל הַנָּשִׂיא	נו	מִצְוַת בֵּית־דִּין לָדוּן בְּנִזְקֵי הָאֵשׁ
עב	שֶׁלֹּא לְהַקְדִּים חֻקֵּי הַתְּבוּאוֹת	נז	מִצְוַת בֵּית־דִּין בְּדִין שׁוֹמֵר חִנָּם
עג	שֶׁלֹּא לֶאֱכֹל טְרֵפָה		
עד	שֶׁלֹּא לִשְׁמֹעַ טַעֲנַת בַּעַל דִּין שֶׁלֹּא בִּפְנֵי בַעַל דִּינוֹ	נח	מִצְוַת בֵּית־דִּין לָדוּן טוֹעֵן וְכוֹפֵר
עה	שֶׁלֹּא יָעִיד בַּעַל עֲבֵרָה	נט	מִצְוַת בֵּית־דִּין לָדוּן נוֹשֵׂא שָׂכָר וְשׂוֹכֵר
עו	שֶׁלֹּא לִנְטוֹת אַחֲרֵי רַבִּים בְּדִינֵי נְפָשׁוֹת בִּשְׁבִיל אֶחָד	ס	מִצְוַת בֵּית־דִּין בְּדִין הַשּׁוֹאֵל
		סא	מִצְוַת בֵּית־דִּין לָדוּן בְּדִין מְפַתֶּה
עז	שֶׁלֹּא יְלַמֵּד חוֹבָה מִי שֶׁלִּמֵּד זְכוּת תְּחִלָּה בְּדִינֵי נְפָשׁוֹת	סב	שֶׁלֹּא לְהַחֲיוֹת מְכַשֵּׁף
עח	מִצְוַת הַטָּיָה אַחֲרֵי רַבִּים	סג	שֶׁלֹּא לְהוֹנוֹת הַגֵּר בִּדְבָרִים

3. Literally, an alien worship.

4. In our author's original work, this comprises only Exodus 21–22:23, while Exodus 22:24–24:18 is listed as *sidrah 'im kessef* (i.e. a separate Scriptural portion). R. Bahya similarly treats it as a separate *sidrah* in his commentary on the Pentateuch (see note to Exodus 22:23 in ed. Chavel); and so R. Aaron haKohen of Lunel mentions it in his *Orḥoth Ḥayyim, hilchoth k'ri'ath ha-torah,* §63.

5. The Hebrew original has the euphemism, "blessing."

⟨10⟩

49. the precept of the laws of fines (penalties)
50. the precept that the court should execute by the sword [decapitation] one punishable by this death
51. the duty of the court to judge damages by domestic animals
52. not to eat an ox that was sentenced to death by stoning
53. the obligation of the court to judge damages done by a pit
54. the obligation of the court to judge a thief, [whether he has incurred a pecuniary penalty,] payment, or [deserved] death
55. the obligation of the court to judge damages of *hev'er* [done by a domestic animal's] eating or trampling
56. the obligation of the court to judge damage by fire
57. the obligation of the court to judge cases involving an unpaid custodian
58. the obligation of the court to judge the case of a plaintiff and a denier [defendant]
59. the obligation of the court to judge cases involving a paid custodian, or a hirer
60. the obligation of the court to judge cases concerning a borrower [of some object]
61. the obligation of the court to judge the case of a seducer
62. not to allow a sorcerer to live
63. not to verbally oppress a convert (proselyte)
64. not to wrong a convert in matters of property
65. not to afflict any orphan or widow
66. the *mitzvah* of lending to the poor
67. that we should not demand payment of a debt from a poor man who has not the means to pay it
68. that we should not lend a hand to either a borrower or a lender for interest [in effecting a loan between them]
69. not to curse a judge
70. the prohibition against cursing[5] the name [of the Eternal Lord]
71. not to curse a sovereign leader
72. not to separate the dues from produce in improper order
73. not to eat of an animal clawed by beasts
74. not to hear the claim of a litigant when his opponent is not present
75. that a sinner should not give testimony
76. not to follow a majority [of judges] in a capital case on the strength of a majority of one
77. that [a judge] who first argued for the innocence of the accused in a capital case should not then argue for his guilt
78. the precept of following the majority [in rendering legal decisions]

THE LIST OF MITZVOTH   ספר החינוך

עט	שֶׁלֹּא לְרַחֵם עַל עָנִי בַּדִּין		צד	שֶׁלֹּא לְהוֹשִׁיב עוֹבֵד עֲבוֹדָה זָרָה בְּאַרְצֵנוּ
פ	מִצְוַת פְּרוּק מַשָּׂא			
פא	שֶׁלֹּא לְהַטּוֹת מִשְׁפַּט חוֹטֵא מִפְּנֵי רִשְׁעוֹ			וְיִקְחוּ לִי [תְּרוּמָה]
פב	שֶׁלֹּא לַחְתּוֹךְ הַדִּין בְּאֹמֶד הַדַּעַת		צה	מִצְוַת בִּנְיַן בֵּית הַבְּחִירָה
פג	שֶׁלֹּא לִקַּח שֹׁחַד		צו	שֶׁלֹּא לְהוֹצִיא בַּדֵּי הָאָרוֹן מִמֶּנּוּ
פד	מִצְוַת שְׁמִטַּת קַרְקָעוֹת		צז	מִצְוַת סִדּוּר לֶחֶם הַפָּנִים וּלְבוֹנָה
פה	מִצְוַת שְׁבִיתָה בְּשַׁבָּת			
פו	שֶׁלֹּא לִשָּׁבַע בַּעֲבוֹדָה זָרָה			וְאַתָּה תְּצַוֶּה
פז	שֶׁלֹּא לְהַדִּיחַ בְּנֵי־יִשְׂרָאֵל אַחַר עֲבוֹדָה זָרָה		צח	מִצְוַת עֲרִיכַת נֵרוֹת בַּמִּקְדָּשׁ
פח	מִצְוַת חֲגִיגָה בָרְגָלִים		צט	מִצְוַת לְבִישַׁת בִּגְדֵי הַכֹּהֲנִים
פט	שֶׁלֹּא נִשְׁחַט שֵׂה הַפֶּסַח בְּאַרְבָּעָה עָשָׂר בְּנִיסָן בְּעוֹד שֶׁהֶחָמֵץ בִּרְשׁוּתֵנוּ		ק	שֶׁלֹּא יַזַּח הַחֹשֶׁן מֵעַל הָאֵפוֹד
			קא	שֶׁלֹּא לִקְרֹעַ הַמְּעִיל שֶׁל כֹּהֲנִים
			קב	מִצְוַת אֲכִילַת בְּשַׂר חַטָּאת וְאָשָׁם
צ	שֶׁלֹּא נַנִּיחַ אֵמוּרֵי הַפֶּסַח לִפָּסֵל בְּלִינָה		קג	מִצְוַת הַקְּטֹרֶת קְטֵרֶת
			קד	שֶׁלֹּא לְהַקְטִיר וּלְהַקְרִיב עַל מִזְבַּח הַזָּהָב
צא	מִצְוַת הֲבָאַת בִּכּוּרִים			
צב	שֶׁלֹּא לְבַשֵּׁל בָּשָׂר בְּחָלָב			כִּי תִשָּׂא
צג	שֶׁלֹּא לִכְרֹת בְּרִית לְשִׁבְעָה עֲמָמִים, וְכֵן לְכָל עוֹבֵד עֲבוֹדָה זָרָה		קה	מִצְוַת נְתִינַת מַחֲצִית הַשֶּׁקֶל בְּשָׁנָה
			קו	מִצְוַת קִדּוּשׁ יָדַיִם וְרַגְלַיִם בִּשְׁעַת עֲבוֹדָה

---

6. The descendants of Aaron (singular, *kohen*) who ministered at the Sanctuary; sometimes translated "priests."

7. Literally, the "great *kohen*"—chief of the *kohanim*; he had duties and privileges beyond the others.

⟨12⟩

79. not to take pity on a poor man in judgment
80. the *mitzvah* of unloading a burden [from another's beast]
81. not to pervert justice in a sinner's trial because he is wicked
82. not to decide a [capital] case on the basis of probability
83. not to take any bribe
84. the precept of *sh'mittah* (release) of the land [to leave its produce ownerless in the seventh, sabbatical year]
85. the *mitzvah* of resting on the Sabbath
86. not to swear by an idol
87. not to lead Israelites astray into idolatry
88. the precept of *ḥagigah*, the celebration offering, on the pilgrimage festivals
89. that we should not ritually slay the paschal lamb (Passover offering) on the fourteenth of Nissan while there is yet *ḥametz* in our possession
90. that we should not let the *émurim* (parts to be burned on the altar) of the Passover offering become impermissible by being left overnight
91. the precept of bringing *bikkurim* (first-fruits)
92. not to cook meat in milk
93. not to make a covenant (treaty) with the seven nations [that were to be extirpated], and so too not with any idol-worshipper
94. not to settle any idol-worshipper in our land

sidrah t'rumah (Exod. 25–27:19)
95. the precept of building the holy Temple
96. not to remove the staves of the ark from it
97. the precept of arranging the showbread and the frankincense

sidrah tetzavveh (Exodus 27:20–30:10)
98. the precept of preparing the lamps [in the *menorah*] in the Sanctuary
99. the precept that the *kohanim*[6] should wear their [special] garments
100. that the breastplate should not come loose from the *éphod* [worn by the *kohen gadol*][7]
101. not to tear the *me'il* (robe) of the *kohanim*
102. the precept to eat the flesh of the *ḥattath* (sin-offering) and the *'asham* (guilt-offering)
103. the precept of burning incense
104. not to burn [alien] incense or offer up sacrifices on the golden altar

sidrah ki thissa (Exodus 30:11–34:35)
105. the precept of giving half a shekel each year
106. the precept of hallowing [rinsing] hands and feet when ministering [at the Sanctuary]

ספר החינוך   THE LIST OF MITZVOTH

קז	מִצְוַת מְשִׁיחַת כֹּהֲנִים גְּדוֹלִים וּמְלָכִים בְּשֶׁמֶן הַמִּשְׁחָה	קכ	מִצְוַת קָרְבַּן בֵּית־דִּין אִם טָעוּ בְהוֹרָאָה
קח	שֶׁלֹּא יָסוּךְ זָר בְּשֶׁמֶן הַמִּשְׁחָה	קכא	מִצְוַת קָרְבַּן חַטָּאת לְיָחִיד שֶׁשָּׁגַג בְּמִצְוַת לֹא־תַעֲשֶׂה שֶׁחַיָּבִין עָלֶיהָ כָּרֵת
קט	שֶׁלֹּא לַעֲשׂוֹת בְּמַתְכֹּנֶת שֶׁמֶן הַמִּשְׁחָה	קכב	מִצְוַת עֵדוּת
קי	שֶׁלֹּא לַעֲשׂוֹת בְּמַתְכֹּנֶת הַקְּטֹרֶת	קכג	מִצְוַת קָרְבַּן עוֹלֶה וְיוֹרֵד
קיא	שֶׁלֹּא לֶאֱכֹל וְלִשְׁתּוֹת תִּקְרֹבֶת עֲבוֹדָה זָרָה	קכד	שֶׁלֹּא לְהַבְדִּיל [הָרֹאשׁ] בְּחַטַּאת הָעוֹף
קיב	מִצְוַת שְׁבִיתַת הָאָרֶץ בִּשְׁנַת הַשְּׁמִטָּה	קכה	שֶׁלֹּא לִתֵּן שֶׁמֶן זַיִת בְּמִנְחַת חוֹטֵא
קיג	שֶׁלֹּא לֶאֱכֹל בָּשָׂר בְּחָלָב	קכו	שֶׁלֹּא לִתֵּן לְבוֹנָה בְּמִנְחַת חוֹטֵא
	ויקהל	קכז	מִצְוַת תּוֹסֶפֶת חֹמֶשׁ לְאוֹכֵל מִן הַתְּרוּמָה אוֹ מוֹעֵל בָּהּ
קיד	שֶׁלֹּא יַעֲשׂוּ בֵית־דִּין מִשְׁפַּט מָוֶת בְּשַׁבָּת	קכח	מִצְוַת קָרְבַּן אָשָׁם תָּלוּי
	ויקרא	קכט	מִצְוַת קָרְבַּן אָשָׁם וַדַּאי
קטו	מִצְוַת מַעֲשֵׂה הָעוֹלָה	קל	מִצְוַת הֲשָׁבַת גֵּזֶל
קטז	מִצְוַת קָרְבַּן מִנְחָה		צו
קיז	שֶׁלֹּא לְהַקְרִיב שְׂאוֹר אוֹ דְּבַשׁ	קלא	מִצְוַת הֲרָמַת הַדֶּשֶׁן
קיח	שֶׁלֹּא לְהַקְרִיב קָרְבָּן בְּלֹא מֶלַח	קלב	מִצְוַת הַדְלָקַת אֵשׁ עַל הַמִּזְבֵּחַ בְּכָל יוֹם
קיט	מִצְוַת מְלִיחַת הַקָּרְבָּן	קלג	שֶׁלֹּא לְכַבּוֹת אֵשׁ מֵעַל הַמִּזְבֵּחַ
		קלד	מִצְוַת אֲכִילַת שְׁיָרֵי מְנָחוֹת

---

8. I.e. anyone but a *kohen gadol* or a king assuming his position.

9. These are two *sidroth*, which are generally read together in the synagogue, on one Sabbath.

⟨14⟩

107. the precept of anointing oil to apply to each *kohen gadol*[7] and king

108. that an outsider[8] should not rub anointing oil on himself

109. not to make anointing oil according to the [Scriptural] formula

110. not to make incense according to the [sacred] formula

111. not to eat or drink [from] an offering to an idol

112. the precept of letting the land rest, lie fallow in the year of *sh'mittah*

113. not to eat meat and milk [cooked together]

sidroth va-yakhél and *p'kudé*[9] (Exodus 35–40)

114. that the court should not carry out a death penalty on the Sabbath

sidrah va-yikra (Leviticus 1–5)

115. the precept of the sacrifice of the *'olah* (burnt-offering)

116. the precept of the *minḥah* (meal) offering

117. not to offer yeast or honey on the altar

118. not to offer up any sacrifice without salt

119. the precept of salting an offering

120. the precept of the offering by the high (supreme) court if it erred in a ruling

121. the precept of a *ḥattath* (sin-offering) for an individual who unintentionally violated a negative precept over which [when done intentionally] one incurs *karéth* [Divine severance of existence]

122. the precept of giving testimony

123. the precept of an *oleh v'yoréd* offering (of greater or lesser value)

124. not to separate the head of a fowl brought as a *ḥattath* (sin-offering)

125. not to put olive oil in the *minḥah* (meal-offering) of an unintentional sinner

126. not to put frankincense in an unintentional sinner's *minḥah*

127. the precept of adding a fifth [of the value in repayment] when one has eaten of sanctified food [the *kohen*'s hallowed portion, etc. or any sacred property] or enjoyed its use

128. the precept of *'asham talu-y*, an offering for doubtful guilt

129. the precept of *'asham vaddai*, an offering for certain guilt

130. the precept of returning property seized in robbery

sidrah tzav (Leviticus 6–8)

131. the precept of lifting off the ash [from the altar]

132. the precept of kindling the fire on the altar

133. not to extinguish fire on the altar

134. the precept of eating the

ספר החינוך   THE LIST OF MITZVOTH

קנ	שֶׁלֹּא יִכָּנְסוּ הַכֹּהֲנִים לַמִּקְדָּשׁ קְרוּעֵי בְגָדִים	קלה	שֶׁלֹּא לַעֲשׂוֹת שְׁיָרֵי מְנָחוֹת חָמֵץ
קנא	שֶׁלֹּא יֵצְאוּ הַכֹּהֲנִים מִן הַמִּקְדָּשׁ בִּשְׁעַת עֲבוֹדָה	קלו	מִצְוַת קָרְבַּן מִנְחָה שֶׁל כֹּהֵן גָּדוֹל בְּכָל יוֹם
קנב	שֶׁלֹּא לְהִכָּנֵס שְׁתוּיֵי יַיִן בַּמִּקְדָּשׁ, וְכֵן שֶׁלֹּא יוֹרֶה שָׁתוּי	קלז	שֶׁלֹּא תֵאָכֵל מִנְחַת כֹּהֵן
קנג	מִצְוַת בְּדִיקַת סִימָנֵי בְהֵמָה וְחַיָּה	קלח	מִצְוַת מַעֲשֵׂה הַחַטָּאת
		קלט	שֶׁלֹּא לֶאֱכֹל מִבְּשַׂר חַטָּאת הַנַּעֲשֵׂית בִּפְנִים
קנד	שֶׁלֹּא לֶאֱכֹל בְּהֵמָה וְחַיָּה טְמֵאָה	קמ	מִצְוַת מַעֲשֵׂה הָאָשָׁם
קנה	מִצְוַת בְּדִיקַת סִימָנֵי דָגִים	קמא	מִצְוַת מַעֲשֵׂה זֶבַח הַשְּׁלָמִים
קנו	שֶׁלֹּא לֶאֱכֹל דָּג טָמֵא	קמב	שֶׁלֹּא לְהוֹתִיר מִבְּשַׂר קָרְבַּן הַתּוֹדָה
קנז	שֶׁלֹּא לֶאֱכֹל עוֹף טָמֵא	קמג	מִצְוַת שְׂרֵפַת נוֹתַר הַקֳּדָשִׁים
קנח	מִצְוַת בְּדִיקַת סִימָנֵי חֲגָבִים	קמד	שֶׁלֹּא לֶאֱכֹל פִּגּוּל
קנט	מִצְוַת טֻמְאַת שְׁמוֹנָה שְׁרָצִים	קמה	שֶׁלֹּא לֶאֱכֹל בְּשַׂר קָדָשִׁים שֶׁנִּטְמָא
קס	מִצְוַת עִנְיַן טֻמְאַת אֳכָלִים	קמו	מִצְוַת שְׂרֵפַת בְּשַׂר קֹדֶשׁ שֶׁנִּטְמָא
קסא	מִצְוַת עִנְיַן טֻמְאַת נְבֵלָה	קמז	שֶׁלֹּא נֹאכַל חֵלֶב
קסב	שֶׁלֹּא לֶאֱכֹל שֶׁרֶץ הָאָרֶץ	קמח	שֶׁלֹּא נֹאכַל דָּם בְּהֵמָה חַיָּה וְעוֹף
קסג	שֶׁלֹּא לֶאֱכֹל מִינֵי שְׁרָצִים דַּקִּים		

וַיְהִי בַּיּוֹם הַשְּׁמִינִי

קמט	שֶׁלֹּא יִכָּנְסוּ הַכֹּהֲנִים לַמִּקְדָּשׁ מְגֻדְּלֵי שֵׂעָר

⟨16⟩

remainders of meal-offerings

135. not to make the remainders of meal-offerings (*minḥah*) become leavened

136. the precept of the daily meal-offering of the *kohen gadol*

137. that the meal-offering of a *kohen* should not be eaten

138. the precept of the procedure of the *ḥattath* (sin-offering)

139. not to eat of the flesh of any *ḥattath* whose blood is sprinkled within [the Sanctuary]

140. the precept of the procedure of the *'asham* (guilt-offering)

141. the precept of the procedure of *sh'lamim* (a peace-offering)

142. not to let any flesh of a *todah* (thank-offering) be left over [past the time for eating it]

143. the precept of burning the remnants of the sacred offerings

144. not to eat *piggúl* ["vile meat"—of an offering sacrificed with certain forbidden intentions]

145. not to eat the flesh of holy offerings that became defiled

146. the precept of burning holy flesh that became defiled

147. that we should not eat *ḥélev*, forbidden animal fat

148. that we should not eat the blood of any beast or fowl

sidrah sh'mini (Leviticus 9–11)

149. that the *kohanim* should not enter the Sanctuary with hair grown long

150. that the *kohanim* should not enter the Sanctuary with torn clothing

151. that the *kohanim* should not go out from the Sanctuary in the midst of [their holy] service

152. that [a *kohen*] should not enter the Sanctuary having drunk wine, nor [should any judge] give a ruling while inebriated

153. the precept of examining the signs of domestic and wild animals [which determine if they are kosher]

154. not to eat an unclean [non-kosher species of] domestic or wild animal

155. the precept of examining the signs of fish [which determine if they are kosher]

156. not to eat an unclean [non-kosher species of] fish

157. not to eat unclean [non-kosher species of] fowl

158. the precept of examining the signs of locusts, etc. [to see if they are kosher]

159. the precept of the ritual uncleanness of eight crawling creatures

160. the precept regarding ritual uncleanness of food

161. the precept regarding the ritual uncleanness of animal carcasses

162. not to eat creatures that swarm on the earth

163. not to eat the species of

THE LIST OF MITZVOTH ספר החינוך

קעד	מִצְוַת תִּגְלַחַת מְצֹרָע בַּיּוֹם הַשְּׁבִיעִי		הַנּוֹלָדִים בְּזוֹרְעִים וּבְפֵרוֹת
קעה	מִצְוַת טְבִילָה לַטְּמֵאִים	קסד	שֶׁלֹּא לֶאֱכֹל מִשֶּׁרֶץ הַמַּיִם
קעו	מִצְוַת קָרְבַּן מְצֹרָע כְּשֶׁיִּתְרַפֵּא מִצָּרַעְתּוֹ	קסה	שֶׁלֹּא לֶאֱכֹל מִן הַשְּׁרָצִים הַמִּתְהַוִּים מִן הָעִפּוּשׁ
קעז	מִצְוַת עִנְיַן טֻמְאַת בַּיִת שֶׁיִּהְיֶה בּוֹ נֶגַע		תזריע
קעח	מִצְוַת עִנְיַן טֻמְאַת זָב לִהְיוֹת טָמֵא וּמְטַמֵּא	קסו	מִצְוַת עִנְיַן טֻמְאַת יוֹלֶדֶת
		קסז	שֶׁלֹּא יֹאכַל טָמֵא מִן הַקֳּדָשִׁים
קעט	מִצְוַת קָרְבַּן זָב כְּשֶׁיִּתְרַפֵּא מִזּוֹבוֹ	קסח	מִצְוַת קָרְבַּן יוֹלֶדֶת
קפ	מִצְוַת עִנְיַן טֻמְאַת שִׁכְבַת זֶרַע שֶׁהוּא טָמֵא וּמְטַמֵּא	קסט	מִצְוַת עִנְיַן טֻמְאַת מְצֹרָע
		קע	שֶׁלֹּא לְגַלֵּחַ שְׂעַר הַנֶּתֶק
קפא	מִצְוַת עִנְיַן טֻמְאַת נִדָּה שֶׁטְּמֵאָה וּמְטַמְּאָה	קעא	מִצְוַת הַנְהָגַת הַמְצֹרָע וְכָל מְטַמְּאֵי אָדָם (בִּקְרִיעָה) [בִּפְרִיעָה] וּפְרִימָה
קפב	מִצְוַת עִנְיַן טֻמְאַת זָבָה שֶׁטְּמֵאָה וּמְטַמְּאָה	קעב	מִצְוַת עִנְיַן נִגְעֵי בְגָדִים
קפג	מִצְוַת קָרְבַּן זָבָה כְּשֶׁתִּתְרַפֵּא מִזּוֹבָהּ		מצרע
	אחרי מות	קעג	מִצְוַת הַטָּהֳרָה מִן הַצָּרַעַת שֶׁתִּהְיֶה בְּמִינִים יְדוּעִים
קפד	שֶׁלֹּא יִכָּנְסוּ הַכֹּהֲנִים בְּכָל עֵת		

⟨18⟩

minute insects that are engendered in grains and fruits
164. not to eat of creatures that swarm in the water
165. not to eat of swarming creatures that come into being from decay

sidrah thazriʿa (Leviticus 12–13)
166. the precept regarding the ritual uncleanness of a woman who gives birth
167. that a ritually unclean person should not eat of holy sacrifices
168. the precept of the offering brought by a woman who has given birth
169. the ritual uncleanness of a man with *tzaraʿath*
170. not to shave the hair of a *nethek* infection [of head or beard]
171. the precept of the practice by a man with *tzaraʿath* or anyone who can defile others, to leave his hair untrimmed and his his clothes torn
172. the precept regarding *tzaraʿath* in clothing

sidrah m'tzora (Leviticus 14–15)
173. the precept that ritual cleansing from a leprous ailment should be through certain specific ingredients
174. the precept of the shaving of a man with *tzaraʿath* on the seventh day [of his ritual purification]
175. the precept of ritual immersion in a *mikveh* for [cleansing] the defiled
176. the precept of the offering of a man with *tzaraʿath* when he is cured of his illness
177. the precept regarding the ritual uncleanness of a house contaminated with *tzaraʿath*
178. the precept regarding the ritual uncleanness of a person with a venereal discharge, that he is both the subject and cause of defilement
179. the precept of the offering by a person who has suffered a venereal discharge, when he is healed of his discharge
180. the precept concerning the ritual uncleanness of seminal fluid, that it is unclean and defiles
181. the precept concerning the ritual uncleanness of a menstruant, that she is herself defiled and is a cause of defilement
182. the precept concerning the ritual uncleanness of a woman with an irregular discharge, that she is defiled and causes defilement
183. the precept of the offering by a woman who has suffered an irregular discharge, when she recovers from her discharge

sidrah aḥaré moth (Leviticus 16–18)
184. that the *kohanim* should not enter the Sanctuary at all times

THE LIST OF MITZVOTH

ר	שֶׁלֹּא לָבוֹא עַל אֵשֶׁת אֲחִי הָאָב		קפה	בַּמִּקְדָּשׁ, וְכָל־שֶׁכֵּן זָרִים
רא	שֶׁלֹּא לָבוֹא עַל אֵשֶׁת הַבֵּן		קפו	מִצְוַת עֲבוֹדַת יוֹם הַכִּפּוּרִים
רב	שֶׁלֹּא לָבוֹא עַל אֵשֶׁת אָח		קפז	שֶׁלֹּא לִשְׁחֹט קָדָשִׁים חוּץ לָעֲזָרָה
רג	שֶׁלֹּא לָבוֹא עַל אִשָּׁה וּבִתָּהּ		קפח	מִצְוַת כִּסּוּי הַדָּם
רד	שֶׁלֹּא לְגַלּוֹת עֶרְוַת אִשָּׁה וּבַת בְּנָהּ			שֶׁלֹּא לְהִתְעַדֵּן בְּאַחַת מִכָּל הָעֲרָיוֹת
רה	שֶׁלֹּא לְגַלּוֹת עֶרְוַת אִשָּׁה וּבַת בִּתָּהּ		קפט	שֶׁלֹּא לְגַלּוֹת עֶרְוַת אָב
רו	שֶׁלֹּא לָבוֹא עַל שְׁתֵּי אֲחָיוֹת מֵחַיִּים		קצ	שֶׁלֹּא לְגַלּוֹת עֶרְוַת אֵם
רז	שֶׁלֹּא לָבוֹא עַל אִשָּׁה נִדָּה		קצא	שֶׁלֹּא לְגַלּוֹת עֶרְוַת אֵשֶׁת אָב וְאַף־עַל־פִּי שֶׁאֵינָהּ אִמּוֹ
רח	שֶׁלֹּא נִתֵּן מִזַּרְעֵנוּ לַמֹּלֶךְ		קצב	שֶׁלֹּא לְגַלּוֹת עֶרְוַת אָחוֹת בְּכָל צַד שֶׁהִיא אָחוֹת
רט	שֶׁלֹּא לָבוֹא עַל הַזְּכָרִים			
רי	שֶׁלֹּא לִשְׁכַּב עִם הַבְּהֵמוֹת		קצג	שֶׁלֹּא לְגַלּוֹת עֶרְוַת בַּת הַבֵּן
ריא	שֶׁלֹּא תִשְׁכַּבְנָה הַנָּשִׁים עִם הַבְּהֵמוֹת		קצד	שֶׁלֹּא לְגַלּוֹת עֶרְוַת בַּת הַבַּת
			קצה	שֶׁלֹּא לְגַלּוֹת עֶרְוַת הַבַּת
	קְדֹשִׁים		קצו	שֶׁלֹּא לְגַלּוֹת עֶרְוַת אָחוֹת מִן הָאָב וְהִיא בַּת אֵשֶׁת אָבִיו
ריב	מִצְוַת יִרְאַת אָב וָאֵם		קצז	שֶׁלֹּא לְגַלּוֹת עֶרְוַת אֲחוֹת אָב
ריג	שֶׁלֹּא לִפְנוֹת אַחַר עֲבוֹדָה זָרָה לֹא בְּמַחֲשָׁבָה וְלֹא בְדִבּוּר וְלֹא אֲפִלּוּ בְּהַבָּטָה		קצח	שֶׁלֹּא לְגַלּוֹת עֶרְוַת אֲחוֹת אֵם
			קצט	שֶׁלֹּא לָבוֹא עַל אֲחִי הָאָב

---

10. Scripture's expression for carnal relations in this and subsequent commandments.

11. I.e. with either a common father or a common mother.

⟨20⟩

[but only for the Temple service], and all the more certainly not a non-*kohen*

185. the precept of the Temple service on the Day of Atonement

186. not to ritually slay holy offerings outside the Sanctuary forecourt

187. the precept of covering the blood [in ritual slaying]

188. not to have pleasure with anyone among all those who are *'ervah* [forbidden consanguineous relations, married women, and so forth]

189. not to uncover the nakedness[10] of one's father

190. not to uncover one's mother's nakedness

191. not to uncover the nakedness of one's father's wife even if she is not his mother

192. not to uncover a sister's nakedness if she is his sister in any way[11]

193. not to uncover the nakedness of a son's daughter

194. not to uncover the nakedness of a daughter's daughter

195. not to uncover a daughter's nakedness

196. not to uncover the nakedness of a sister on one's father's side, who is the daughter of his father's wife

197. not to uncover the nakedness of a father's sister

198. not to uncover the nakedness of a mother's sister

199. not to have carnal relations with one's father's brother

200. not to be conjugally intimate with the wife of one's father's brother

201. not to be conjugally intimate with a son's wife

202. not to be conjugally intimate with a brother's wife

203. not to be conjugally intimate with both a woman and her daughter

204. not to uncover the nakedness of both a woman and the daughter of her son

205. not to uncover the nakedness of both a woman and her daughter's daughter

206. not to be conjugally intimate with two sisters while both are living

207. not to be conjugally intimate with a menstruous woman

208. that we should not give any of our progeny to Molech

209. not to have carnal connection with any male

210. not to have carnal connection with beasts

211. that women should not lie carnally with beasts

sidrah k'doshim (Leviticus 19–20)

212. the *mitzvah* of reverent fear for father and mother

213. not to turn astray after idol-worship, neither in thought nor in word, nor even by watching

THE LIST OF MITZVOTH

ריד	שֶׁלֹּא לַעֲשׂוֹת עֲבוֹדָה זָרָה לֹא לְעַצְמוֹ וְלֹא לְזוּלָתוֹ	רלג	שֶׁלֹּא לְעַוֵּל הַמִּשְׁפָּט
רטו	שֶׁלֹּא לֶאֱכֹל נוֹתָר	רלד	שֶׁלֹּא לְכַבֵּד גָּדוֹל בַּדִּין
רטז	מִצְוַת פֵּאָה	רלה	מִצְוַת שׁוֹפֵט שֶׁיִּשְׁפֹּט בְּצֶדֶק
ריז	שֶׁלֹּא לְכַלּוֹת הַפֵּאָה בַּשָּׂדֶה	רלו	שֶׁלֹּא לְרַגֵּל
ריח	מִצְוַת לֶקֶט	רלז	שֶׁלֹּא לַעֲמֹד עַל דַּם רֵעִים
ריט	שֶׁלֹּא לָקַחַת שִׁבֳּלִים הַנּוֹפְלִים בִּשְׁעַת הַקָּצִיר	רלח	שֶׁלֹּא לִשְׂנֹא אַחִים
		רלט	מִצְוַת תּוֹכָחָה לְיִשְׂרָאֵל שֶׁאֵינוֹ נוֹהֵג כַּשּׁוּרָה
רכ	מִצְוַת הַנַּחַת פְּאַת הַכֶּרֶם	רמ	שֶׁלֹּא לְהַלְבִּין פְּנֵי אָדָם מִיִּשְׂרָאֵל
רכא	שֶׁלֹּא לְכַלּוֹת פְּאַת הַכֶּרֶם		
רכב	מִצְוַת הַנַּחַת פֶּרֶט הַכֶּרֶם	רמא	שֶׁלֹּא לִנְקֹם
רכג	שֶׁלֹּא לִלְקֹט פֶּרֶט הַכֶּרֶם	רמב	שֶׁלֹּא לִנְטֹר
רכד	שֶׁלֹּא לִגְנֹב שׁוּם מָמוֹן	רמג	מִצְוַת אַהֲבַת יִשְׂרָאֵל
רכה	שֶׁלֹּא נְכַחֵשׁ עַל מָמוֹן שֶׁיֵּשׁ לְאַחֵר בְּיָדֵינוּ	רמד	שֶׁלֹּא לְהַרְבִּיעַ בְּהֵמָה עִם מִין שֶׁאֵינוֹ מִינוֹ
רכו	שֶׁלֹּא לִשָּׁבַע עַל כְּפִירַת מָמוֹן	רמה	שֶׁלֹּא לִזְרֹעַ כִּלְאֵי זְרָעִים [בְּשׁוּם מָקוֹם בָּאָרֶץ] וְלֹא נַרְכִּיב אִילָן (בְּשׁוּם מָקוֹם בָּאָרֶץ)
רכז	שֶׁלֹּא נִשָּׁבַע לַשֶּׁקֶר		
רכח	שֶׁלֹּא לַעֲשֹׁק		
רכט	שֶׁלֹּא לִגְזֹל	רמו	שֶׁלֹּא לֶאֱכֹל עָרְלָה
רל	שֶׁלֹּא נְאַחֵר שְׂכַר שָׂכִיר	רמז	מִצְוַת נֶטַע רְבָעִי
רלא	שֶׁלֹּא לְקַלֵּל אֶחָד מִיִּשְׂרָאֵל, בֵּין אִישׁ בֵּין אִשָּׁה	רמח	שֶׁלֹּא לֶאֱכֹל וְלִשְׁתּוֹת כְּדֶרֶךְ זוֹלֵל וְסוֹבֵא
רלב	שֶׁלֹּא לְהַכְשִׁיל תָּם בַּדֶּרֶךְ		

12. Literally, not to whiten any Jew's face—i.e. cause it to grow pale by making the blood drain away.

⟨22⟩

214. not to make an idol, neither for oneself nor for anyone else
215. not to eat left-over meat of sacrifices [after the permitted time]
216. the *mitzvah* of [leaving over] an end of the field [unreaped, for the poor]
217. not to reap the very last end of one's field
218. the precept of [leaving] gleanings [of the harvest for the poor]
219. not to gather stalks of grain that fell away during the harvest
220. the precept of leaving an end of a vineyard [unreaped, for the poor]
221. not to reap the very last end of a vineyard
222. the precept of leaving fallen grapes in a vineyard [for the poor]
223. not to gather the fallen grapes in a vineyard
224. not to steal anything of value
225. not to deny it when something of value that belongs to another is in our possession
226. not to swear over a false denial about something of value
227. that we should not swear falsely
228. not to wrongly retain another's property
229. not to commit robbery
230. that we should not delay payment of a hired man
231. not to curse a Jew, whether man or woman
232. not to make a trusting person stumble [by giving him misleading advice]
233. not to pervert justice in a civil judgment
234. not to honor an eminent person at a trial
235. the precept that a judge should pass judgment with righteousness
236. not to gossip slanderously
237. not to stand by idly over the blood of fellow-humans [as it is spilled]
238. not to hate one's brethren [fellow-Jews]
239. the religious duty to rebuke a Jew who does not conduct himself properly
240. not to shame a Jew [1,2]
241. not to take revenge
242. not to bear a grudge
243. the precept of love for a Jew
244. not to mate one beast with another which is not of the same species
245. not to sow different kinds of seed together, anywhere in the land [of Israel], nor should we graft a tree [onto another of a different species]
246. not to eat the first three years' produce of a tree
247. the precept of the fruit of a tree's fourth year
248. not to eat or drink in the manner of a glutton and guzzler

ספר החינוך — THE LIST OF MITZVOTH

רסד	מִצְוַת עִנְיַן טֻמְאַת הַכֹּהֲנִים לִקְרוֹבֵיהֶם, וּבִכְלָלָהּ שֶׁיִּתְאַבְּלוּ כָּל אֶחָד מִיִּשְׂרָאֵל עַל שִׁשָּׁה מְקֹרוֹבָיו הַיְדוּעִים		רמט	שֶׁלֹּא לְנַחֵשׁ
			רנ	שֶׁלֹּא לְעוֹנֵן
			רנא	שֶׁלֹּא לְהַקִּיף פַּאֲתֵי הָרֹאשׁ
			רנב	שֶׁלֹּא לְהַשְׁחִית פְּאַת זָקָן
רסה	שֶׁלֹּא יְשַׁמֵּשׁ כֹּהֵן טְבוּל יוֹם עַד שֶׁיַּעֲרִיב שִׁמְשׁוֹ		רנג	שֶׁלֹּא נִכְתֹּב בִּבְשָׂרֵנוּ כְּתֹבֶת קַעֲקַע
			רנד	מִצְוַת הַיִּרְאָה מִן הַמִּקְדָּשׁ
רסו	שֶׁלֹּא יִשָּׂא כֹהֵן אִשָּׁה זוֹנָה		רנה	שֶׁלֹּא לַעֲשׂוֹת [מַעֲשֵׂה] אוֹב
רסז	שֶׁלֹּא יִשָּׂא כֹהֵן אִשָּׁה חֲלָלָה		רנו	שֶׁלֹּא לַעֲשׂוֹת מַעֲשֵׂה יִדְּעוֹנִי
רסח	שֶׁלֹּא יִשָּׂא כֹהֵן אִשָּׁה גְרוּשָׁה		רנז	מִצְוַת כְּבוֹד חֲכָמִים
רסט	מִצְוַת קִדּוּשׁ זֶרַע אַהֲרֹן		רנח	שֶׁלֹּא לְהוֹנוֹת בַּמִּדּוֹת, וְכָל הַמִּדּוֹת בִּכְלָל
רע	שֶׁלֹּא יִכָּנֵס כֹּהֵן גָּדוֹל בְּאֹהֶל הַמֵּת		רנט	מִצְוַת צִדּוּק הַמֹּאזְנַיִם וְהַמִּשְׁקָלִים וְהַמִּדּוֹת
רעא	שֶׁלֹּא יִטַּמֵּא כֹּהֵן גָּדוֹל בְּשׁוּם טֻמְאָה בְּמֵת		רס	שֶׁלֹּא לְקַלֵּל אָב וָאֵם
רעב	מִצְוַת כֹּהֵן גָּדוֹל לִשָּׂא נַעֲרָה בְתוּלָה		רסא	מִצְוַת שֶׁיִּשָּׂרְפוּ מִי שֶׁיִּתְחַיֵּב שְׂרֵפָה
רעג	שֶׁלֹּא יִשָּׂא כֹּהֵן גָּדוֹל אַלְמָנָה		רסב	שֶׁלֹּא לָלֶכֶת בְּחֻקּוֹת הַגּוֹיִם
רעד	שֶׁלֹּא יִבְעַל כֹּהֵן גָּדוֹל אַלְמָנָה			אֱמֹר אֶל הַכֹּהֲנִים
רעה	שֶׁלֹּא יַעֲבֹד כֹּהֵן בַּעַל מוּם		רסג	שֶׁלֹּא יִטַּמֵּא כֹּהֵן הֶדְיוֹט בְּמֵת זוּלָתִי בַּקְּרוֹבִים הַמְבֹאָרִים בַּכָּתוּב
רעו	שֶׁלֹּא יַעֲבֹד כֹּהֵן בַּעַל מוּם עוֹבֵר			
רעז	שֶׁלֹּא יִכָּנֵס בַּעַל מוּם בַּהֵיכָל			
רעח	שֶׁלֹּא יַעֲבֹד כֹּהֵן טָמֵא			

---

13. I.e. who is not the *kohen gadol*.
14. I.e. whether they are obligated to attend to the burial of their close kin.

⟨24⟩

249. not to practice augury
250. not to conjure
251. not to round the corners [crop the hairs at the temples] of the head
252. not to mar the corners of the beard
253. that we should not inscribe in our flesh any tattoo
254. the precept of reverent awe for the Sanctuary
255. not to perform the act of an 'ov (a medium)
256. not to perform the act of a yid'oni (a kind of wizard)
257. the mitzvah of honoring the wise scholars
258. not to cheat with measures; and this includes all measures
259. the precept of making scales, weights and measures correct
260. not to curse one's father or mother
261. the precept that whoever deserves death by burning is to be burned
262. not to follow the customs of the nations

sidrah 'emor (Leviticus 21–24)
263. that an ordinary kohen[13] should not defile himself for any dead person other than the relatives stated clearly in Scripture
264. the precept regarding the defilement of kohanim for their near relatives;[14] included in this is [the mitzvah] that every Jew should mourn for the specific six among his relations [named in Scripture, at their death]
265. that a kohen defiled for a day who undergoes ritual immersion [to purify himself] should not serve [at the Sanctuary] till the sun sets
266. that a kohen should not marry a wanton
267. that a kohen should not marry a profaned woman
268. that a kohen should not marry a divorced woman
269. the precept of the sanctification of Aaron's descendants
270. that a kohen gadol[7] should not enter the tent of a dead man
271. that a kohen gadol should not defile himself with any ritual uncleanness for a dead man
272. the precept that a kohen gadol should marry a virgin
273. that a kohen gadol should not marry a widow
274. that a kohen gadol should not be conjugally intimate with a widow
275. that a kohen with a blemishing defect should not serve [at the Sanctuary]
276. that a kohen with a passing (temporary) blemish should not serve [at the Sanctuary]
277. that a kohen with a blemishing defect should not enter the holy Temple
278. that a ritually unclean kohen should not serve [at the Sanctuary]

ספר החינוך — THE LIST OF MITZVOTH

רעט	שלא יאכל כהן טמא תרומה	רצה	שלא לעשות דבר שיתחלל בו שם שמים בין בני־אדם
רפ	שלא יאכל שום זר תרומה	רצו	מצות קדוש השם
רפא	שלא יאכל תושב כהן ושכיר תרומה	רצז	מצות שביתה ביום ראשון של פסח
רפב	שלא יאכל ערל תרומה	רצח	שלא לעשות מלאכה ביום א' של פסח
רפג	שלא תאכל חללה מן הקדש		
רפד	שלא לאכל טבל	רצט	מצות קרבן מוסף כל שבעת ימי הפסח
רפה	שלא נקדיש בעלי מומין להקריבם למזבח		
רפו	מצות הקרבן להיות תמים	ש	מצות שביתה בשביעי של פסח
רפז	שלא נתן מום בקדשים	שא	שלא לעשות מלאכה ביום ז' של פסח
רפח	שלא נזרק דם בעל מום על המזבח		
		שב	מצות קרבן העמר של שעורים ביום שני של פסח
רפט	שלא נשחט בעלי מום לשם קרבן	שג	שלא לאכל מתבואה חדשה קדם כלות יום י"ו בניסן
רצ	שלא נקטיר אמורי בעלי מומין		
רצא	שלא לסרס אחד מכל המינין	שד	שלא לאכל קלי מתבואה חדשה עד היום ההוא
רצב	שלא להקריב קרבן בעל מום מיד הגוים	שה	שלא לאכל כרמל מתבואה חדשה עד הזמן הנזכר
רצג	מצות הקרבן שיהיה משמונה ימים ולמעלה	שו	מצות ספירת העמר
רצד	שלא לשחט בהמה ובנה ביום אחד	שז	מצות קרבן מנחה חדשה מן

⟨26⟩

279. that a ritually unclean *kohen* should not eat *t'rumah* [the *kohen*'s portion from produce]

280. that no non-*kohen* whatever should eat *t'rumah*

281. that neither the permanent worker nor the hired man of a *kohen* should eat *t'rumah*

282. that an uncircumcised person should not eat *t'rumah*

283. that a profaned woman should not eat of hallowed food

284. not to eat *tevel* (produce from which *t'rumah* and the tithes were not separated)

285. that we should not consecrate blemished, defective animals to offer them up on the altar

286. the precept that an animal offering is to be whole [without blemish or disfigurement]

287. that we should not make a blemishing defect in animals consecrated for holy offerings

288. that we should not sprinkle the blood of blemished, defective animals on the altar

289. that we should not ritually slay blemished, defective animals for holy offerings

290. that we should not burn the portions for the altar from blemished, defective animals

291. not to emasculate any creature out of all the animal species

292. not to offer up a blemished, defective offering received from non-Jews

293. the precept that an animal offering should be eight days old or more

294. not to ritually slay an animal and its young in one day

295. not to do anything through which the Name of Heaven [God] will be profaned among people

296. the *mitzvah* of sanctifying the Name [of God]

297. the precept of resting from work on the first day of Passover

298. not to do any work on the first day of Passover

299. the precept of the *musaf* (additional) animal offering all the seven days of Passover

300. the precept of resting from work on the seventh day of Passover

301. not to do any work on the seventh day of Passover

302. the precept of the offering of the 'omer (sheaf) of barley on the second day of Passover

303. not to eat [bread] from the new crop of cereal grains before the end of the 16th of Nissàn

304. not to eat parched kernels from the new crop until [the end of] that day

305. not to eat parched ears from the new crop until the aforementioned time

306. the precept of counting [forty-nine days from the offering] of the 'omer

307. the precept of the *minḥah* (meal-offering) of new wheat

⟨27⟩

ספר החינוך THE LIST OF MITZVOTH

שכא	מִצְוַת שְׁבִיתָה מִמְּלָאכָה בְּיוֹם שְׁמִינִי שֶׁל סֻכּוֹת	שח	הַחֲטִים בְּיוֹם עֲצֶרֶת
			מִצְוַת שְׁבִיתָה מִמְּלָאכָה בְּיוֹם עֲצֶרֶת
שכב	מִצְוַת קָרְבַּן מוּסָף בְּיוֹם שְׁמִינִי שֶׁל סֻכּוֹת, שֶׁהוּא נִקְרָא שְׁמִינִי עֲצֶרֶת	שט	שֶׁלֹּא לַעֲשׂוֹת מְלָאכָה בְּיוֹם חַג הַשָּׁבוּעוֹת
שכג	שֶׁלֹּא לַעֲשׂוֹת מְלָאכָה בְּיוֹם שְׁמִינִי בּוֹ	שי	מִצְוַת שְׁבִיתָה בְּיוֹם רֹאשׁ הַשָּׁנָה
שכד	מִצְוַת נְטִילַת לוּלָב	שיא	שֶׁלֹּא לַעֲשׂוֹת מְלָאכָה בְּיוֹם א' שֶׁל תִּשְׁרֵי
שכה	מִצְוַת יְשִׁיבַת סֻכָּה	שיב	מִצְוַת קָרְבַּן מוּסָף בְּיוֹם רֹאשׁ הַשָּׁנָה
	בְּהַר סִינַי	שיג	מִצְוַת תַּעֲנִית בְּיוֹם עֲשִׂירִי בְּתִשְׁרֵי
שכו	שֶׁלֹּא נַעֲבֹד הָאֲדָמָה בַּשָּׁנָה הַשְּׁבִיעִית	שיד	מִצְוַת קָרְבַּן מוּסָף בְּיוֹם עֲשִׂירִי בְּתִשְׁרֵי שֶׁהוּא נִקְרָא יוֹם הַכִּפּוּרִים
שכז	שֶׁלֹּא נַעֲשֶׂה עֲבוֹדָה גַם בְּאִילָנוֹת	שטו	שֶׁלֹּא לַעֲשׂוֹת מְלָאכָה בַּעֲשָׂרָה בְּתִשְׁרֵי
שכח	שֶׁלֹּא נִקְצֹר סְפִיחִים בַּשָּׁנָה הַשְּׁבִיעִית	שטז	שֶׁלֹּא לֶאֱכֹל וְלִשְׁתּוֹת בְּיוֹם הַכִּפּוּרִים
שכט	שֶׁלֹּא נֶאֱסֹף פֵּרוֹת הָאִילָן בַּשְּׁבִיעִית כְּדֶרֶךְ שֶׁאוֹסְפִין אוֹתָם בְּכָל שָׁנָה	שיז	מִצְוַת שְׁבִיתָה מִמְּלָאכָה בְּיוֹם הַכִּפּוּרִים
של	מִצְוַת סְפִירַת שֶׁבַע שַׁבָּתוֹת שָׁנִים	שיח	מִצְוַת שְׁבִיתָה מִמְּלָאכָה בְּיוֹם רִאשׁוֹן שֶׁל חַג הַסֻּכּוֹת
שלא	מִצְוַת תְּקִיעַת שׁוֹפָר בְּיוֹם הַכִּפּוּרִים שֶׁל יוֹבֵל	שיט	שֶׁלֹּא לַעֲשׂוֹת מְלָאכָה בְּיוֹם רִאשׁוֹן שֶׁל חַג הַסֻּכּוֹת
שלב	מִצְוַת קִדּוּשׁ שְׁנַת הַיּוֹבֵל	שכ	מִצְוַת קָרְבַּן מוּסָף בְּכָל יוֹם מִשִּׁבְעַת יְמֵי חַג הַסֻּכּוֹת
שלג	שֶׁלֹּא נַעֲבֹד הָאָרֶץ בִּשְׁנַת הַיּוֹבֵל		
שלד	שֶׁלֹּא נִקְצֹר סְפִיחֵי תְּבוּאוֹת שֶׁל שְׁנַת הַיּוֹבֵל		

⟨28⟩

on the day of the *Shavu'oth* festival

308. the precept of resting from work on the day of the *Shavu'oth* festival

309. not to do any work on the day of the *Shavu'oth* festival

310. the precept of resting from work on *Rosh haShanah*

311. not to do any work on the first day of Tishri [*Rosh haShanah*]

312. the precept of the *musaf* (additional) animal offering on *Rosh haShanah*

313. the precept of fasting on the tenth of Tishri

314. the precept of the *musaf* (additional) offering on the tenth of Tishri, which is called the Day of Atonement

315. not to do any work on the tenth of Tishri

316. not to eat or drink on the Day of Atonement

317. the precept of resting from work on the Day of Atonement

318. the precept of resting from work on the first day of the *Sukkoth* festival

319. not to do any work on the first day of the *Sukkoth* festival

320. the precept of the *musaf* (additional) offering on each of the seven days of the *Sukkoth* festival

321. the precept of resting from work on the eighth day of *Sukkoth*

322. the precept of the *musaf* (additional) offering on the eighth day of *Sukkoth*, which is called *Sh'mini 'Atzereth*

323. not to do any work on the eighth day [of *Sukkoth*]

324. the precept of taking the *lulav* (palm branch)

325. the *mitzvah* of dwelling in the *sukkah*

sidrah b'har (Leviticus 25–26:2)

326. that we should not work the earth in the seventh (sabbatical) year

327. that we should not do any work [then] in regard to trees either

328. that we should not harvest what grows wild in the seventh year

329. that we should not gather the fruit of the tree in the seventh year in the way that it is gathered every year

330. the precept of counting seven septennates (cycles of seven years)

331. the precept of sounding the *shofar* (ram's horn) on the Day of Atonement of the jubilee year

332. the precept of sanctifying the jubilee year

333. that we should not work the land in a jubilee year

334. that we should not harvest produce that grows wild in a jubilee year

ספר החינוך THE LIST OF MITZVOTH

שמז	מִצְוַת עֲבוֹדָה בְּעֶבֶד כְּנַעֲנִי לְעוֹלָם	שלה	שֶׁלֹּא לֶאֱסֹף פֵּרוֹת הָאִילָנוֹת בִּשְׁנַת הַיּוֹבֵל כְּדֶרֶךְ שֶׁאוֹסְפִין אוֹתָם בִּשְׁאָר שָׁנִים
שמח	שֶׁלֹּא לְהַנִּיחַ לְגוֹי לַעֲבֹד [בְּפֶרֶךְ] בְּעֶבֶד עִבְרִי הַנִּמְכָּר לוֹ	שלו	מִצְוַת עֲשִׂיַּת דִּין בֵּין לוֹקֵחַ וּמוֹכֵר
שמט	שֶׁלֹּא נִשְׁתַּחֲוֶה עַל אֶבֶן מַשְׂכִּית אֲפִלּוּ לַשֵּׁם	שלז	שֶׁלֹּא לְהוֹנוֹת בְּמִקָּח וּמִמְכָּר
	אם בחקתי	שלח	שֶׁלֹּא לְהוֹנוֹת אֶחָד מִיִּשְׂרָאֵל בִּדְבָרִים
שנ	מִצְוַת מַעֲרִיךְ אָדָם שֶׁיִּתֵּן דָּמָיו הַקְּצוּבִין בַּתּוֹרָה	שלט	שֶׁלֹּא נִמְכֹּר שָׂדֶה בְּאֶרֶץ יִשְׂרָאֵל לִצְמִיתוּת
שנא	שֶׁלֹּא נָמִיר הַקֳּדָשִׁים	שמ	מִצְוַת הֲשָׁבַת קַרְקַע לְבַעֲלֵיהֶן בַּיּוֹבֵל
שנב	מִצְוַת הַמֵּמִיר בְּהֶמַת קָרְבָּן בִּבְהֵמָה אַחֶרֶת, שֶׁתִּהְיֶינָה שְׁתֵּיהֶן קֹדֶשׁ	שמא	מִצְוַת פִּדְיוֹן הַנְּחָלוֹת שֶׁהֵן תּוֹךְ הָעִיר עַד הַשְׁלָמַת שָׁנָה
שנג	מִצְוַת מַעֲרִיךְ בְּהֵמָה שֶׁיִּתֵּן כְּפִי שֶׁיַּעֲרִיכֶנָּה הַכֹּהֵן	שמב	שֶׁלֹּא לִשְׁנוֹת מִגְרְשֵׁי עָרֵי הַלְוִיִּים וּשְׂדוֹתֵיהֶם
שנד	מִצְוַת מַעֲרִיךְ בָּתִּים שֶׁיִּתֵּן בָּעֵרֶךְ שֶׁיַּעֲרִיכֵם הַכֹּהֵן וְתוֹסֶפֶת חֹמֶשׁ	שמג	שֶׁלֹּא לְהָלְווֹת בְּרִבִּית לְיִשְׂרָאֵל
שנה	מִצְוַת מַעֲרִיךְ שָׂדֶה שֶׁיִּתֵּן בָּעֵרֶךְ הַקָּצוּב בַּפָּרָשָׁה	שמד	שֶׁלֹּא נַעֲבֹד בְּעֶבֶד עִבְרִי עֲבוֹדַת בִּזָּיוֹן כְּמוֹ עֲבוֹדַת כְּנַעֲנִי
שנו	שֶׁלֹּא לִשְׁנוֹת הַקֳּדָשִׁים מִקָּרְבָּן לְקָרְבָּן	שמה	שֶׁלֹּא נִמְכֹּר עֶבֶד עִבְרִי עַל אֶבֶן הַמִּקָּח
שנז	מִצְוַת דִּין מַחֲרִים מִנְּכָסָיו שֶׁהוּא לַכֹּהֲנִים	שמו	שֶׁלֹּא לַעֲבֹד בְּעֶבֶד עִבְרִי בַּעֲבוֹדַת פֶּרֶךְ

⟨30⟩

335. not to gather the fruit of trees in a jubilee year in the way that it is gathered in other years

336. the precept of effecting justice between buyer and seller

337. not to wrong [anyone by cheating] in buying and selling

338. not to oppress a Jew with words

339. that we should not sell a field in the land of Israel permanently

340. the precept of returning land to its original owners in the land of Israel in the jubilee year

341. the precept of redeeming inherited landed property which is within [an originally walled] city, until the completion of a year [from its sale]

342. not to alter the open land around the cities of the Levites, or their fields

343. not to lend at interest to a Jew

344. that we should not have a Hebrew manservant do contemptible work like a Canaanite slave

345. that we should not sell a Hebrew manservant at the selling-block [like all slaves]

346. not to work a Hebrew manservant at hard labor

347. the precept of keeping a heathen slave permanently

348. not to allow a non-Jew to work [severely] a Hebrew manservant who was sold to him

349. that we should not bow down to the ground (prostrate ourselves) on a figured stone, even [in worship] to the Eternal Lord

sidrah b'ḥukothai (Leviticus 26:3–27:34)

350. the precept of one who vows a man's valuation, that he should give his price that is set in the Written Torah

351. that we should not exchange (replace) animals consecrated for holy offerings

352. the precept of one who exchanges an animal [consecrated] for an offering, for another one, that both should be sacred

353. the precept of one who vows an animal's valuation, that he should give as the *kohen* values it

354. the precept of one who vows the valuation of a house, that he should give the value that the *kohen* sets on it, with the addition of one-fifth [of this value]

355. the precept of one who vows the valuation of a field, that he should give according to the value set in the *sidrah* (portion of Scripture)

356. not to change consecrated animals from one offering [for which they were consecrated] to another

357. the precept of the law about

THE LIST OF MITZVOTH   ספר החינוך

שעא	שֶׁלֹּא יֹאכַל הַנָּזִיר זֶרַע הָעֲנָבִים	שנח	שֶׁלֹּא יִמָּכֵר קַרְקַע שֶׁהָחֳרִים אוֹתָהּ בְּעָלָיו אֶלָּא תִּנָּתֵן לַכֹּהֲנִים
שעב	שֶׁלֹּא יֹאכַל הַנָּזִיר קְלִפַּת הָעֲנָבִים	שנט	שֶׁלֹּא יִגָּאֵל שְׂדֵה הַחֵרֶם
שעג	שֶׁלֹּא יְגַלַּח הַנָּזִיר שְׂעָרוֹ כָּל יְמֵי נִזְרוֹ	שס	מִצְוַת מַעֲשֵׂר בְּהֵמָה טְהוֹרָה בְּכָל שָׁנָה
שעד	מִצְוַת גִּדּוּל שְׂעַר הַנָּזִיר	שסא	שֶׁלֹּא לִמְכֹּר מַעֲשַׂר בְּהֵמָה אֶלָּא יֵאָכֵל בִּירוּשָׁלַיִם
שעה	שֶׁלֹּא יִכָּנֵס הַנָּזִיר לְאֹהֶל הַמֵּת		
שעו	שֶׁלֹּא יִטַּמֵּא הַנָּזִיר בְּמֵת וּבִשְׁאָר טֻמְאוֹת		נשא
שעז	מִצְוַת גִּלּוּחַ הַנָּזִיר וַהֲבָאַת קָרְבְּנוֹתָיו	שסב	מִצְוַת שִׁלּוּחַ טְמֵאִים חוּץ לְמַחֲנֵה שְׁכִינָה
שעח	מִצְוַת בִּרְכַּת כֹּהֲנִים בְּכָל יוֹם	שסג	שֶׁלֹּא יִכָּנֵס טָמֵא בְּכָל הַמִּקְדָּשׁ
שעט	מִצְוַת מַשָּׂא הָאָרוֹן בַּכָּתֵף	שסד	מִצְוַת וִדּוּי עַל הַחֵטְא
		שסה	מִצְוַת סוֹטָה, שֶׁיְּבִיאָהּ הַבַּעַל אֶל
	בהעלתך		הַכֹּהֵן וְיֵעָשֶׂה לָהּ כַּמִּשְׁפָּט הַכָּתוּב
שפ	מִצְוַת פֶּסַח שֵׁנִי בְּי״ד בְּאִיָּר	שסו	שֶׁלֹּא לִתֵּן שֶׁמֶן בְּקָרְבַּן סוֹטָה
שפא	מִצְוַת פֶּסַח שֵׁנִי שֶׁיֵּאָכֵל עַל מַצּוֹת וּמְרוֹרִים	שסז	שֶׁלֹּא לָשִׂים לְבוֹנָה בְּקָרְבַּן סוֹטָה
שפב	שֶׁלֹּא לְהוֹתִיר כְּלוּם מִבְּשַׂר פֶּסַח שֵׁנִי לְמָחֳרָתוֹ	שסח	שֶׁלֹּא יִשְׁתֶּה הַנָּזִיר יַיִן אוֹ כָל מִינֵי שֵׁכָר
שפג	שֶׁלֹּא לִשְׁבֹּר עֶצֶם מֵעַצְמוֹת פֶּסַח שֵׁנִי	שסט	שֶׁלֹּא יֹאכַל הַנָּזִיר עֲנָבִים לַחִים
		שע	שֶׁלֹּא יֹאכַל הַנָּזִיר צִמּוּקִים

15. I.e. when the period for which he vowed to be a *nazir* has ended (see Numbers 6:1–21).

⟨32⟩

one who vows a *ḥérem* on part of his property, that it goes to the *kohanim*

358. that land put by its owner under *ḥérem* is not to be sold, but rather given to the *kohanim*

359. that land under *ḥérem* is not to be redeemed

360. the precept of the tithe of clean [permissible] domestic animals, [to be given] every year

361. that the tithe of animals is not to be sold but only eaten in Jerusalem

sidrah naso (Numbers 4:21–7:89)

362. the precept of sending the ritually unclean outside the camp of the *shechinah*

363. that a ritually unclean person should not enter anywhere in the Sanctuary

364. the precept of confession over a sin

365. the precept of *sotah*, a straying woman [suspected of infidelity], that her husband should bring her to the *kohen*, and he should observe for her the rule of Scripture

366. not to put oil into the offering of a *sotah*

367. not to put frankincense in the offering of a *sotah*

368. that a *nazir* should not take wine or any strong drink [derived from grapes]

369. that a *nazir* should not eat fresh grapes

370. that a *nazir* should not eat raisins

371. that a *nazir* should not eat grape seeds

372. that a *nazir* should not eat grape skins

373. that a *nazir* should not shave his hair all his days as a *nazir*

374. the precept of letting a *nazir*'s hair grow long

375. that a *nazir* should not enter the tent of a dead person

376. that a *nazir* should not become defiled by a dead person or by any other uncleanness

377. the precept of shaving a *nazir*'s hair and bringing his offerings [15]

378. the precept of the blessing by the *kohanim*, [to be given] every day

379. the precept of carrying the holy ark on the shoulders

sidrah b'ha'aloth'cha (Numbers 8–12)

380. the precept of the "second Passover" offering on the fourteenth of Iyar

381. the precept of the "second Passover" offering, that it should be eaten with *matzah* and bitter herbs

382. not to leave anything over of the "second Passover" offering until the next day

383. to break none of the bones of the "second Passover" offering

THE LIST OF MITZVOTH

שפד	מִצְוַת תְּקִיעַת חֲצוֹצְרוֹת בַּמִּקְדָּשׁ וּבְמִלְחָמָה		

שְׁלַח לְךָ

שפה	מִצְוַת חַלָּה		
שפו	מִצְוַת צִיצִית		
שפז	שֶׁלֹּא לָתוּר אַחַר מַחְשֶׁבֶת הַלֵּב וּרְאִיַּת הָעֵינַיִם		

וַיִּקַּח קֹרַח

שפח	מִצְוַת שְׁמִירַת הַמִּקְדָּשׁ
שפט	שֶׁלֹּא יִתְעַסְּקוּ הַכֹּהֲנִים בַּעֲבוֹדַת הַלְוִיִּים וְלֹא הַלְוִיִּים בַּעֲבוֹדַת הַכֹּהֲנִים
שצ	שֶׁלֹּא יַעֲבֹד זָר בַּמִּקְדָּשׁ
שצא	שֶׁלֹּא לְבַטֵּל שְׁמִירַת הַמִּקְדָּשׁ
שצב	מִצְוַת פִּדְיוֹן בְּכוֹר אָדָם
שצג	שֶׁלֹּא לִפְדּוֹת בְּכוֹר בְּהֵמָה טְהוֹרָה
שצד	מִצְוַת עֲבוֹדַת הַלֵּוִי בַּמִּקְדָּשׁ
שצה	מִצְוַת מַעֲשֵׂר רִאשׁוֹן
שצו	מִצְוַת הַלְוִיִּים לָתֵת מַעֲשֵׂר מִן הַמַּעֲשֵׂר

זֹאת חֻקַּת

שצז	מִצְוַת פָּרָה אֲדֻמָּה
שצח	מִצְוַת טֻמְאָה שֶׁל מֵת
שצט	מִצְוַת מֵי נִדָּה, שֶׁמְּטַמְּאִין אָדָם טָהוֹר וּמְטַהֲרִין אָדָם טָמֵא מִטֻּמְאַת מֵת בִּלְבַד

פִּינְחָס

ת	מִצְוַת דִּינֵי נְחָלוֹת
תא	מִצְוַת תְּמִידִין בְּכָל יוֹם
תב	מִצְוַת קָרְבַּן מוּסָף שֶׁל שַׁבָּת
תג	מִצְוַת קָרְבַּן מוּסָף בְּכָל רֹאשׁ חֹדֶשׁ
תד	מִצְוַת קָרְבַּן מוּסָף בְּיוֹם חַג הַשָּׁבוּעוֹת
תה	מִצְוַת שׁוֹפָר בְּרֹאשׁ הַשָּׁנָה

רָאשֵׁי הַמַּטּוֹת

תו	מִצְוַת דִּין הֲפָרַת נְדָרִים
תז	שֶׁלֹּא נָחֵל דְּבָרֵינוּ בִּנְדָרִים

אֵלֶּה מַסְעֵי

תח	מִצְוַת יִשְׂרָאֵל לָתֵת עָרִים לַלְוִיִּם

---

16. To render it non-holy; it had to be presented as an offering at the Sanctuary.

⟨34⟩

384. the precept of sounding trumpets at the Sanctuary and in battle

sidrah sh'laḥ (Numbers 13–15)
385. the precept of *ḥallah* (a portion of dough set aside for the *kohen*)
386. the precept of *tzitzith* (tassels on a four-cornered garment)
387. not to go straying after the thoughts of the heart and the sight of the eyes

sidrah koraḥ (Numbers 16–18)
388. the precept of guarding the Sanctuary
389. that the *kohanim* should not engage in the Levites' sacred tasks, nor the Levites in the sacred tasks of the *kohanim*
390. that an outsider [who is not a *kohen*] should not work at the Sanctuary
391. not to cease the guarding of the Sanctuary
392. the precept of redeeming a firstborn child
393. not to redeem the firstling of a kosher domestic animal[16]
394. the precept of the Levite's service at the Sanctuary
395. the precept of the First Tithe
396. the obligation of the Levites to give a tithe of the tithe

sidrah ḥukath (Numbers 19–22:1)
397. the precept of the red heifer
398. the precept of the ritual uncleanness of the dead
399. the precept of the lustral water, that it defiles a ritually clean man, and purifies only a man defiled by the uncleanness of the dead

sidrah pinḥas (Numbers 25:10–30:1)
400. the precept of the laws of inheritance
401. the precept of the regular *'olah* (burnt) offerings [to be sacrificed] every day
402. the precept of the *musaf* (additional) offering of the Sabbath
403. the precept of the *musaf* (additional) offering every new-month-day
404. the precept of the *musaf* offering on the day of the Shavu'oth festival
405. the precept of [sounding] the *shofar* (ram's horn) on *Rosh haShanah*

sidrah mattoth (Numbers 30:2–32:42)
406. the precept of the law of nullifying vows
407. that we should not break our word in vows [that we make]

sidrah mas'é (Numbers 33–36)
408. the religious duty of the Israelites to give the Levites

ספר החינוך   THE LIST OF MITZVOTH

תיט	מִצְוַת תַּלְמוּד תּוֹרָה	תט	לָשֶׁבֶת בָּהֶן, וְהֵן קוֹלְטוֹת
תכ	מִצְוַת קְרִיַת שְׁמַע שַׁחֲרִית וְעַרְבִית		שֶׁלֹא לַהֲרֹג מְחֻיָּב קֹדֶם שֶׁיַּעֲמֹד בְּדִין
תכא	מִצְוַת תְּפִלִּין שֶׁל יָד	תי	מִצְוָה עַל בֵּית־דִין לְהַשְׁלִיךְ מַכֵּה
תכב	מִצְוַת תְּפִלִּין שֶׁל רֹאשׁ		נֶפֶשׁ בִּשְׁגָגָה מֵעִירוֹ לְעָרֵי
תכג	מִצְוַת מְזוּזָה		מִקְלָט, וְעַל הָרוֹצֵחַ בְּעַצְמוֹ
תכד	שֶׁלֹא לְנַסּוֹת נְבִיא אֱמֶת יוֹתֵר מִדַּאי		לָלֶכֶת שָׁם
		תיא	שֶׁלֹא יוֹרֶה הָעֵד שֶׁהֵעִיד בּוֹ בְּדִינֵי נְפָשׁוֹת
תכה	מִצְוַת הֲרִיגַת שִׁבְעָה עֲמָמִין		
תכו	שֶׁלֹא לָחֹן עַל עוֹבְדֵי עֲבוֹדָה זָרָה	תיב	שֶׁלֹא לָקַח כֹּפֶר לְהַצִּיל מִמָּוֶת הָרוֹצֵחַ
תכז	שֶׁלֹא לְהִתְחַתֵּן בְּעוֹבְדֵי עֲבוֹדָה זָרָה	תיג	שֶׁלֹא לָקַח כֹּפֶר מִמְּחֻיָּב גָּלוּת לְפָטְרוֹ מִן הַגָּלוּת

וְהָיָה עֵקֶב

אֵלֶּה הַדְּבָרִים

תכח	שֶׁלֹא לֵהָנוֹת מִצִּפּוּיֵי עֲבוֹדָה זָרָה	תיד	שֶׁלֹא לִמְנוֹת דַּיָּן אָדָם שֶׁאֵינוֹ חָכָם בְּדִינֵי תוֹרָה, אַף־עַל־פִּי שֶׁהוּא חָכָם בְּחָכְמוֹת אֲחֵרוֹת
תכט	שֶׁלֹא לְהַדְבִּיק שׁוּם דָּבָר מֵעֲבוֹדָה זָרָה עִם מָמוֹנֵנוּ וּבִרְשׁוּתֵנוּ לֵהָנוֹת בּוֹ		
תל	מִצְוַת בִּרְכַּת הַמָּזוֹן	תטו	שֶׁלֹא יִירָא הַדַּיָּן בַּדִּין מֵאָדָם רַע
תלא	מִצְוַת אַהֲבַת הַגֵּרִים		
תלב	מִצְוַת יִרְאַת הַשֵּׁם		וָאֶתְחַנַּן
תלג	מִצְוַת תְּפִלָּה	תטז	שֶׁלֹא לְהִתְאַוּוֹת מַה שֶּׁבְּיַד אָחִינוּ בְּנֵי יִשְׂרָאֵל
תלד	מִצְוַת הַחֶבְרָה וְהַדְּבִיקָה עִם חַכְמֵי הַתּוֹרָה	תיז	מִצְוַת אַחְדוּת הַשֵּׁם
		תיח	מִצְוַת אַהֲבַת הַשֵּׁם

⟨36⟩

cities to dwell in, which should give refuge [to the unintentional manslayer]
409. not to execute a guilty person who deserves death, before he stands trial
410. the religious duty of the court to impel a person who has killed someone unintentionally, to go from his city to the cities of refuge, and [the duty] of the manslayer himself to go there
411. that a witness who testifies in a trial for a capital crime should not speak in judgment
412. to take no ransom to save a killer from the death [he deserves]
413. to take no ransom from someone sentenced to banishment [to a city of refuge] to free him from the banishment

sidrah d'varim (Deuteronomy 1–3:22)

414. not to appoint any man as judge who is not learned in the laws of the Torah, even though he is learned in other wisdoms
415. that a judge presiding at a trial should not fear any evil man

sidrah va'eth-ḥanan (Deuteronomy 3:23–7:11)

416. not to desire what belongs to our fellow-Israelites
417. the precept of the oneness of the Eternal Lord
418. the precept of love for the Eternal Lord
419. the precept of Torah study
420. the *mitzvah* of reciting the *Sh'ma* (Deuteronomy 6:4) every morning and evening
421. the precept of the *t'fillin* (phylactery) of the hand
422. the precept of the *t'fillin* of the head
423. the precept of the *m'zuzah* [on the doorpost]
424. not to test a true prophet unduly
425. the precept of killing out the seven nations
426. to show no mercy to idol-worshippers
427. to form no marital bonds with idol-worshippers

sidrah 'ékev (Deuteronomy 7:12–11:25)

428. not to derive benefit from any ornamentation of an idol
429. not to attach any object whatsoever from idolatry to our possessions and our ownership, to derive benefit from it
430. the precept of blessing [the Almighty] for food
431. the precept of love for converts to Judaism
432. the precept of reverent awe for the Eternal Lord
433. the precept of prayer
434. the *mitzvah* of associating with and adhering to Torah scholars

THE LIST OF MITZVOTH ספר החינוך

תמה	שֶׁלֹּא לֶאֱכֹל בִּבְכוֹר תָּמִים חוּץ לִירוּשָׁלַיִם	תלה	מִצְוַת עַל כָּל הַצָּרִיךְ לִשָּׁבַע שֶׁיִּשָּׁבַע בְּשֵׁם הַשֵּׁם

רְאֵה אָנֹכִי

תמו	שֶׁלֹּא לֶאֱכֹל בְּשַׂר חַטָּאת וְאָשָׁם חוּץ לַקְּלָעִים, וַאֲפִלּוּ הַכֹּהֲנִים	תלו	מִצְוָה לְאַבֵּד עֲבוֹדָה זָרָה וּמְשַׁמְּשֶׁיהָ
תמז	שֶׁלֹּא לֶאֱכֹל בְּשַׂר הָעוֹלָה	תלז	שֶׁלֹּא לִמְחוֹת סִפְרֵי הַקֹּדֶשׁ וְהַשֵּׁמוֹת שֶׁל הַקָּדוֹשׁ־בָּרוּךְ־הוּא הַכְּתוּבִים שָׁם, וְכֵן בָּתֵּי עֲבוֹדַת הַקֹּדֶשׁ
תמח	שֶׁלֹּא לֶאֱכֹל בְּשַׂר קָדָשִׁים קַלִּים קֹדֶם זְרִיקַת דָּמִים		
תמט	שֶׁלֹּא יֹאכְלוּ כֹּהֲנִים בִּכּוּרִים קֹדֶם הַנָּחָתָם בָּעֲזָרָה	תלח	מִצְוָה לְהַקְרִיב כָּל הַקָּרְבָּנוֹת שֶׁיֵּשׁ עַל הָאָדָם בְּחוֹבָה אוֹ בִּנְדָבָה בְּרֶגֶל רִאשׁוֹן שֶׁפּוֹגֵעַ בּוֹ
תנ	שֶׁלֹּא לַעֲזֹב אֶת הַלְוִיִּם מָלֶּתֶת לָהֶם מַתְּנוֹתֵיהֶם וּמְלְשַׂמְּחָם בָּרְגָלִים	תלט	שֶׁלֹּא לְהַעֲלוֹת קָדָשִׁים בַּחוּץ
תנא	מִצְוַת שְׁחִיטָה		
תנב	שֶׁלֹּא לֶאֱכֹל אֵבֶר מִן הַחַי	תמ	מִצְוַת לְהַקְרִיב כָּל הַקָּרְבָּנוֹת בְּבֵית הַבְּחִירָה וְלֹא בַחוּץ
תנג	מִצְוָה לְהַשְׁפִּיל בַּהֲבָאַת הַקָּרְבָּן מִחוּצָה לָאָרֶץ לְבֵית הַבְּחִירָה	תמא	מִצְוַת פְּדִיַּת קָדָשִׁים שֶׁנָּפַל בָּהֶן מוּם, וְאַחַר־כָּךְ מֻתָּרִין בַּאֲכִילָה
תנד	שֶׁלֹּא לְהוֹסִיף עַל מִצְווֹת הַתּוֹרָה	תמב	שֶׁלֹּא לֶאֱכֹל מַעֲשֵׂר שֵׁנִי שֶׁל דָּגָן חוּץ לִירוּשָׁלַיִם
תנה	שֶׁלֹּא לִגְרֹעַ מִמִּצְווֹת הַתּוֹרָה		
תנו	שֶׁלֹּא לִשְׁמֹעַ מִמִּתְנַבֵּא בְּשֵׁם עֲבוֹדָה זָרָה	תמג	שֶׁלֹּא לֶאֱכֹל מַעֲשֵׂר שֵׁנִי שֶׁל תִּירוֹשׁ חוּץ לִירוּשָׁלַיִם
תנז	שֶׁלֹּא לֶאֱהֹב הַמֵּסִית	תמד	שֶׁלֹּא לֶאֱכֹל מַעֲשֵׂר שֵׁנִי שֶׁל יִצְהָר חוּץ לִירוּשָׁלַיִם
תנח	שֶׁלֹּא לַעֲזֹב הַשִּׂנְאָה מִן הַמֵּסִית		

---

17. Literally, outside the hangings, or curtains. As hangings formed the boundaries of the *mishkan* (Tabernacle) in the wilderness, this became the idiom for the limits of the holy Temple area in Jerusalem.

⟨38⟩

435. the precept that whoever must take an oath should swear by the name of the Eternal Lord

sidrah r'ēh (Deuteronomy 11:26–16:17)

436. the precept to destroy an idol and all objects in its service

437. not to erase holy writings or [written] names of the Holy One, blessed is He; this applies equally to houses of sacred worship [whatever bears His name]

438. the religious obligation to present all obligatory or voluntary offerings which a man is to bring, at the first pilgrimage festival that comes along

439. not to sacrifice holy offerings outside the Sanctuary

440. the precept to sacrifice all offerings at the Sanctuary, and not [anywhere] outside it

441. the precept to redeem animals consecrated for offerings which have become blemished, defective; and afterward they are permitted to be eaten

442. not to eat the Second Tithe of grain outside Jerusalem

443. not to consume the Second Tithe of wine outside Jerusalem

444. not to consume the Second Tithe of oil outside Jerusalem

445. not to eat an unblemished firstborn animal outside Jerusalem

446. not to eat the flesh of the *ḥattath* (sin-offering) and *'asham* (guilt-offering) beyond the boundaries[17] [of the Sanctuary precincts]—not even the *kohanim*

447. not to eat the flesh of the *'olah* (burnt-offering)

448. not to eat the flesh of offerings of lesser holiness before the sprinkling of their blood [on the altar]

449. that the *kohanim* should not eat *bikkurim* (first-fruits) before they are set down [before the Lord] in the Sanctuary forecourt

450. not to neglect the Levites by failing to give them their gifts and make them happy on the pilgrimage festivals

451. the precept of *sheḥittah* (ritual slaying)

452. not to eat a limb [or part taken] from a living animal

453. the precept to attend to bringing an animal offering from outside the land [of Israel] to the Sanctuary

454. not to add to the precepts of the Torah

455. not to diminish (take anything away from) the precepts of the Torah

456. to pay no heed to anyone prophesying in the name of an idol

457. to have no affection for an enticer [to idolatry]

458. not to relinquish hatred for an enticer [to idolatry]

ספר החינוך — THE LIST OF MITZVOTH

תעג	מִצְוַת מַעֲשֵׂר שֵׁנִי	תנט	שֶׁלֹּא לְהַצִּיל הַמַּסִּית
תעד	מִצְוַת מַעֲשֵׂר עָנִי, פַּעַם מַעֲשֵׂר שֵׁנִי בְּשָׁנָה שְׁלִישִׁית	תס	שֶׁלֹּא יְלַמֵּד הַמּוּסָת זְכוּת עַל מֵסִית
תעה	שֶׁלֹּא לִתְבֹּעַ הַהַלְוָאָה שֶׁעָבַר עָלֶיהָ שְׁבִיעִית	תסא	שֶׁלֹּא יִשְׁתֹּק הַמּוּסָת מִלְּלַמֵּד חוֹבָה עַל הַמֵּסִית
תעו	מִצְוָה לִנְגֹּשׂ אֶת הַנָּכְרִי	תסב	שֶׁלֹּא לְהָסִית אֶחָד מִיִּשְׂרָאֵל אַחַר עֲבוֹדָה זָרָה
תעז	מִצְוַת הַשְׁמָטַת כְּסָפִים בְּשָׁנָה שְׁבִיעִית	תסג	מִצְוַת חֲקִירַת הָעֵדִים הֵיטֵב
תעח	שֶׁלֹּא לִמְנֹעַ מִלְּהַחֲיוֹת הֶעָנִי וּמִלְּתֵן לוֹ מַה שֶּׁהוּא צָרִיךְ	תסד	מִצְוַת שְׂרֵפַת עִיר הַנִּדַּחַת וְכָל אֲשֶׁר בָּהּ
תעט	מִצְוַת צְדָקָה	תסה	שֶׁלֹּא לִבְנוֹת עִיר הַנִּדַּחַת לִכְמוֹת שֶׁהָיְתָה
תפ	שֶׁלֹּא נִמָּנַע מִלְּהַלְווֹת לֶעָנִי מִפְּנֵי הַשְּׁמִטָּה	תסו	שֶׁלֹּא לֵהָנוֹת בְּמָמוֹן עִיר הַנִּדַּחַת
תפא	שֶׁלֹּא לְשַׁלַּח עֶבֶד עִבְרִי רֵיקָם כְּשֶׁיֵּצֵא חָפְשִׁי	תסז	שֶׁלֹּא לְהִתְגּוֹדֵד כְּמוֹ עוֹבְדֵי עֲבוֹדָה זָרָה
תפב	מִצְוַת הַעֲנָק עֶבֶד עִבְרִי	תסח	שֶׁלֹּא לַעֲשׂוֹת קָרְחָה עַל מֵת
תפג	שֶׁלֹּא לַעֲבֹד בְּעֶבֶד בִּקְדֻשִּׁים	תסט	שֶׁלֹּא לֶאֱכֹל פְּסוּלֵי הַמֻּקְדָּשִׁין
תפד	שֶׁלֹּא לִגְזֹז אֶת הַקֳּדָשִׁים	תע	מִצְוַת בְּדִיקַת סִימָנֵי הָעוֹף
תפה	שֶׁלֹּא לֶאֱכֹל חָמֵץ אַחַר חֲצוֹת	תעא	שֶׁלֹּא לֶאֱכֹל חָגָב טָמֵא, וְכֵן כָּל שֶׁרֶץ הָעוֹף
תפו	שֶׁלֹּא לְהוֹתִיר מִבְּשַׂר קָרְבַּן הַחֲגִיגָה שֶׁנַּקְרִיב בְּיוֹם י״ד בְּנִיסָן עַד יוֹם הַשְּׁלִישִׁי	תעב	שֶׁלֹּא לֶאֱכֹל בָּשָׂר בִּבְהֵמָה וְחַיָּה וָעוֹף שֶׁמֵּתוּ מֵאֲלֵיהֶם

18. Of every three-year cycle, there being two such cycles between one *sh'mittah* (seventh, sabbatical) year and another.

⟨40⟩

459. not to rescue an enticer [to idol-worship from the death-penalty]
460. that someone enticed [to idolatry] should not speak in favor of the enticer
461. that a person enticed [to idol-worship] should not be silent [and refrain] from speaking out against the enticer
462. not to entice an Israelite toward idol-worship
463. the precept of examining witnesses thoroughly
464. the precept of burning a city gone astray [into idolatry], with all it contains
465. not to rebuild a city gone astray [into idolatry] to its former condition
466. not to derive any benefit from the wealth of a city gone astray [into idolatry]
467. not to gash oneself as idol-worshippers do
468. not to cause baldness [tearing the hair in grief] over the dead
469. not to eat holy offerings that became disqualified
470. the religious duty of examining the signs of a fowl [if it may be eaten]
471. not to eat unclean [non-kosher] locusts, nor any winged insects
472. not to eat the flesh of any domestic or wild beasts, or fowl, that died of themselves

473. the precept of the Second Tithe
474. the precept of the tithe for the poor, [given] in place of the Second Tithe in the third year[18]
475. not to demand payment of a loan over which the seventh year [sh'mittah] has passed
476. the precept of exacting a loan rigorously from a heathen
477. the precept of relinquishing money [owed] in the seventh year [sh'mittah]
478. not to refrain [hard-heartedly] from sustaining a poor man and giving him what he needs
479. the *mitzvah* of charity
480. that we should not refrain from lending money to the poor on account of [the arrival of] sh'mittah (the seventh year)
481. not to send away a Hebrew bondservant, when he goes free, empty-handed
482. the precept of giving a bonus to a Hebrew bondservant [at his discharge]
483. to do no work with animals consecrated for offerings
484. not to shear animals consecrated for offerings
485. not to eat *ḥamétz* after midday [on the day before Passover]
486. not to leave over till the third day any flesh of the festival offering (*korban ḥagigah*) that we sacrifice on the fourteenth day of Nissan

ספר החינוך   THE LIST OF MITZVOTH

תק	שֶׁלֹּא לִשְׁכֹּן בְּאֶרֶץ מִצְרַיִם לְעוֹלָם	תפז	שֶׁלֹּא לְהַקְרִיב קׇרְבַּן פֶּסַח בְּבָמַת יָחִיד
תקא	שֶׁלֹּא יַרְבֶּה לוֹ הַמֶּלֶךְ נָשִׁים	תפח	מִצְוָה לִשְׂמֹחַ בָּרְגָלִים
תקב	שֶׁלֹּא יַרְבֶּה לוֹ הַמֶּלֶךְ כֶּסֶף וְזָהָב לְבַד מַה שֶּׁצָּרִיךְ לוֹ	תפט	מִצְוָה לְהֵרָאוֹת בָּרְגָלִים בְּבֵית הַמִּקְדָּשׁ
תקג	מִצְוָה עַל הַמֶּלֶךְ לִכְתֹּב סֵפֶר תּוֹרָה אַחַת יְתֵרָה עַל שְׁאָר בְּנֵי יִשְׂרָאֵל	תצ	שֶׁלֹּא לַעֲלוֹת לָרֶגֶל בְּלֹא קׇרְבָּן שֶׁיִּהְיֶה עִמָּנוּ שֶׁנַּקְרִיב שָׁם
			שׁוֹפְטִים
תקד	שֶׁלֹּא יִהְיֶה לְשֵׁבֶט לֵוִי נַחֲלָה בָּאָרֶץ	תצא	מִצְוַת מִנּוּי שׁוֹפְטִים וְשׁוֹטְרִים בְּכָל קָהָל וְקָהָל מִיִּשְׂרָאֵל
תקה	שֶׁלֹּא יִטֹּל שֵׁבֶט לֵוִי חֵלֶק בַּבִּזָּה בִּשְׁעַת כִּבּוּשׁ הָאָרֶץ	תצב	שֶׁלֹּא לָטַעַת אִילָן בַּמִּקְדָּשׁ
תקו	מִצְוַת מַתְּנוֹת זְרוֹעַ לְחָיַיִם וְקֵבָה לַכֹּהֵן	תצג	שֶׁלֹּא לְהָקִים מַצֵּבָה
		תצד	שֶׁלֹּא לְהַקְרִיב קׇרְבָּן בַּעַל מוּם עוֹבֵר
תקז	מִצְוַת הַפְרָשַׁת תְּרוּמָה גְדוֹלָה	תצה	מִצְוָה לִשְׁמֹעַ מִכָּל בֵּית־דִּין הַגָּדוֹל שֶׁיַּעַמְדוּ לָהֶן לְיִשְׂרָאֵל בְּכָל זְמַן
תקח	מִצְוַת רֵאשִׁית הַגֵּז שֶׁיִּנָּתֵן לַכֹּהֵן		
תקט	מִצְוָה לִהְיוֹת הַכֹּהֲנִים עוֹבְדִים בַּמִּקְדָּשׁ מִשְׁמָרוֹת מִשְׁמָרוֹת, וּבַמּוֹעֲדִים עוֹבְדִים כְּאֶחָד	תצו	שֶׁלֹּא לְהַמְרוֹת עַל פִּי בֵית־דִּין הַגָּדוֹל שֶׁיַּעַמְדוּ לְיִשְׂרָאֵל
		תצז	מִצְוַת מִנּוּי מֶלֶךְ עָלֵינוּ
תקי	שֶׁלֹּא לִקְסֹם	תצח	שֶׁלֹּא לְמַנּוֹת מֶלֶךְ עַל יִשְׂרָאֵל כִּי־אִם מִבְּנֵי יִשְׂרָאֵל
תקיא	שֶׁלֹּא לְכַשֵּׁף		
תקיב	שֶׁלֹּא לַחֲבֹר חֶבֶר	תצט	שֶׁלֹּא יַרְבֶּה הַמֶּלֶךְ סוּסִים
תקיג	שֶׁלֹּא לִשְׁאֹל בְּאוֹב		

⟨42⟩

487. not to offer up a Passover offering on the provisional altar of an individual
488. the precept to rejoice on the pilgrimage festivals
489. the precept to appear on the pilgrimage festivals at the Temple
490. not to go up [to Jerusalem] for a pilgrimage festival without [provision for] an offering, that we would offer up there

sidrah shof'tim (Deuteronomy 16:18–21:9)

491. the precept of appointing judges and officers in every single community in Jewry
492. not to plant any tree in the Sanctuary
493. not to erect [any idolatrous type of] pillar
494. not to present as an offering an animal with a passing (temporary) blemishing defect
495. the religious duty to hearken to every great *beth din* that will arise to the Israelites in every period [i.e. any authoritative masters of tradition]
496. not to disobey the word of the great *beth din* that arises for the Israelites
497. the precept of appointing a king over us
498. not to appoint anyone king over Israel except a native Israelite
499. that the king should not amass horses [beyond his needs]
500. not to ever dwell in the land of Egypt
501. that the king should not take himself an unduly large number of wives
502. that the king should not amass gold and silver inordinately, but only what he finds necessary
503. the religious duty of the king to write one Torah scroll more than [the one that] the rest of the Israelites [are required to write]
504. that the tribe of Lévi should have no inheritance [of land] in the land [of Israel]
505. that the tribe of Lévi should take no share of the booty during the conquest of the land
506. the precept of giving the shoulder, two cheeks and stomach [of an offering] to the *kohen*
507. the religious duty of separating the "great *t'rumah*" [the *kohen*'s portion from produce]
508. the precept of the first of the fleece, that it should be given to the *kohen*
509. the precept that the *kohanim* should work at the Sanctuary in watches (turns of duty), and at festival times they should work in unison [all together]
510. not to practice divination
511. not to practice sorcery
512. not to employ charms
513. not to consult an *'ov* (a kind of medium

⟨43⟩

ספר החינוך — THE LIST OF MITZVOTH

תקיד שלא לשאל בידעוני
תקטו שלא לדרש אל המתים
תקטז מצוה לשמע מכל נביא ונביא שיהיה בכל דור דור אם לא יוסיף ולא יגרע במצוות התורה
תקיז שלא להתנבאות בשקר
תקיח שלא להתנבאות בשם עבודה זרה
תקיט שלא נמנע מהריגת נביא שקר ולא נגור ממנו
תקכ מצוה להכין שש ערי מקלט
תקכא שלא לרחם על המזיק בדיני נפשות
תקכב שלא להשיג גבול
תקכג שלא לחתך הדין על פי עד אחד
תקכד מצוה לעשות לעדים זוממים כמו שזממו לעשות
תקכה שלא לערץ מפני האויב במלחמה
תקכו מצוה למשח כהן למלחמה
תקכז מצוה לעשות במלחמת הרשות כמשפט הכתוב

תקכח שלא להחיות אחד מכל שבעה עממין
תקכט שלא להשחית אילני מאכל במצור, וכן כל השחתה בכלל הלאו
תקל מצות עריפת העגלה בנחל
תקלא שלא לעבד ולזרע בנחל איתן

כי תצא

תקלב מצות דין יפת תאר
תקלג שלא למכר אשת יפת תאר
תקלד שלא להעביד באשת יפת תאר אחר שבא עליה, כמו בשפחה
תקלה מצות דין תליה למי שיתחיב לתלות
תקלו שלא ילין הצלוב על העץ, וכן המת בביתו אלא לכבודו
תקלז מצות קבורה לנהרג על פי בית דין, וכן לכל מת
תקלח מצות השבת אבדה
תקלט שלא להתעלם מן האבדה

---

19. So reads the Hebrew text, *b'di-né n'fashoth*, according to the oldest manuscript. The other manuscripts and the first edition read instead, *b'di-né k'nasoth*, "in the cases (or sentences) of fines." While the penalties imposed on an attacker for wounds that he inflicts are regarded in the Talmud as fines, the term is not mentioned in the discussion of the *mitzvah* within the *Séfer haHinnuch*, and thus would seem to be an early scribal error.

⟨44⟩

514. not to consult a *yid'oni* (a kind of wizard)
515. not to seek contact with the dead
516. the precept to heed every single prophet who will be in every generation, provided he does not add anything to or take anything away from the precepts of the Torah
517. not to prophesy falsely
518. not to prophesy in the name of an idol
519. that we should not refrain from putting a false prophet to death, and not be afraid of him
520. the precept to prepare six cities of refuge
521. to have no mercy on a person who inflicts [mortal] injury, in the [ensuing] capital trial[19]
522. not to overreach one's boundary [to falsely claim another's property]
523. not to pass judgment on the word of one witness
524. the precept to do to false, scheming witnesses as they intended to do [to their victim through their testimony]
525. not to quail in fear before an enemy in battle
526. the precept to anoint a *kohen* for war
527. the precept to act in a voluntary war according to the rules of Scripture
528. to let no one in the seven nations [that originally inhabited the Land of Israel] stay alive
529. not to destroy fruit-bearing trees in setting siege; and so is every kind of [purposeless] destruction included in this ban
530. the precept of beheading the heifer in a riverbed
531. not to plow or sow in the coursing riverbed [where the heifer's neck was broken]

sidrah ki thétzé (Deuteronomy 21:10–25:19)

532. the precept of the law of a beautiful woman [taken captive in war]
533. not to sell a beautiful woman [taken captive in war]
534. not to make a beautiful [captive] woman work as a slave after one has been conjugally intimate with her
535. the precept of the law of hanging someone [after his execution] when it is required
536. that someone hung should not be left overnight on the gallows; nor [should] any dead man [be left overnight] in his house, unless it is for his honor
537. the precept of burial [the same day, speedily] for anyone put to death by court sentence, and so for every deceased person
538. the religious duty of returning something lost [to its owner]
539. not to turn a blind eye to a lost object

⟨45⟩

ספר החינוך   THE LIST OF MITZVOTH

תקמ   שֶׁלֹּא לְהַנִּיחַ בְּהֵמַת חֲבֵרוֹ רוֹבֶצֶת תַּחַת מַשָּׂאָהּ
תקמא   מִצְוַת הֲקָמַת מַשָּׂא לְיִשְׂרָאֵל
תקמב   שֶׁלֹּא תַעֲדֶה אִשָּׁה עֲדִי אִישׁ
תקמג   שֶׁלֹּא יַעֲדֶה הָאִישׁ עֲדִי אִשָּׁה
תקמד   שֶׁלֹּא לָקַח הָאֵם עַל הַבָּנִים
תקמה   מִצְוַת שִׁלּוּחַ הַקֵּן
תקמו   מִצְוַת מַעֲקֶה
תקמז   שֶׁלֹּא לְהַנִּיחַ מִכְשׁוֹל
תקמח   שֶׁלֹּא לִזְרֹעַ כִּלְאַיִם בְּכֶרֶם בְּאֶרֶץ יִשְׂרָאֵל, דְּאוֹרַיְתָא
תקמט   שֶׁלֹּא לֶאֱכֹל כִּלְאֵי הַכֶּרֶם בְּאֶרֶץ יִשְׂרָאֵל
תקנ   שֶׁלֹּא לַעֲשׂוֹת מְלָאכָה בִּשְׁנֵי מִינֵי בְּהֵמָה
תקנא   שֶׁלֹּא לִלְבֹּשׁ שַׁעַטְנֵז
תקנב   מִצְוַת קִדּוּשִׁין בְּאִשָּׁה
תקנג   מִצְוָה שֶׁתֵּשֵׁב אֵשֶׁת מוֹצִיא שֵׁם רַע תַּחְתָּיו לְעוֹלָם
תקנד   שֶׁלֹּא יְגָרֵשׁ מוֹצִיא שֵׁם רַע אֶת אִשְׁתּוֹ
תקנה   מִצְוָה עַל בֵּית־דִּין לִסְקֹל בָּאֲבָנִים מִי שֶׁיִּתְחַיֵּב סְקִילָה

תקנו   שֶׁלֹּא לַעֲנֹשׁ הָאָנוּס
תקנז   מִצְוָה עַל הָאוֹנֵס שֶׁיִּשָּׂא אֲנוּסָתוֹ לְאִשָּׁה
תקנח   שֶׁלֹּא יְגָרֵשׁ הָאוֹנֵס אֶת אֲנוּסָתוֹ
תקנט   שֶׁלֹּא יִקַּח סָרִיס בַּת יִשְׂרָאֵל
תקס   שֶׁלֹּא יִשָּׂא מַמְזֵר בַּת יִשְׂרָאֵל
תקסא   שֶׁלֹּא יִשָּׂא עַמּוֹנִי וּמוֹאָבִי בַּת יִשְׂרָאֵל
תקסב   שֶׁלֹּא לִקְרֹא שָׁלוֹם לְעַמּוֹן וּמוֹאָב
תקסג   שֶׁלֹּא לְהַרְחִיק זֶרַע עֵשָׂו מֵהִתְחַתֵּן עִם זֶרַע יִשְׂרָאֵל אַחַר שֶׁיִּתְגַּיְּרוּ אֶלָּא עַד ג׳ דּוֹרוֹת
תקסד   שֶׁלֹּא לְהַרְחִיק מִצְרִי כְּמוֹ־כֵן אֶלָּא עַד דּוֹר שְׁלִישִׁי, וְלֹא שְׁלִישִׁי בִּכְלָל
תקסה   שֶׁלֹּא יִכָּנֵס טָמֵא לְמַחֲנֵה לְוִיָּה
תקסו   מִצְוָה לְהַתְקִין יָד בַּמַּחֲנֶה
תקסז   מִצְוָה לְהַתְקִין יָתֵד בַּמַּחֲנֶה
תקסח   שֶׁלֹּא לְהַחֲזִיר עֶבֶד שֶׁבָּרַח מֵאֲדוֹנָיו מִחוּצָה לָאָרֶץ לָאָרֶץ יִשְׂרָאֵל
תקסט   שֶׁלֹּא לְהוֹנוֹת עֶבֶד זֶה הַבּוֹרֵחַ

⟨46⟩

540. not to leave a fellow-man's beast lying under its burden
541. the precept of lifting up a load for an Israelite (Jew)
542. that a woman should not wear a man's finery
543. that a man should not wear a woman's finery
544. not to take the mother-bird with the young [in a nest]
545. the precept of sending away [the mother-bird from] the nest
546. the religious duty of [building] a parapet
547. not to leave a stumbling-block (keep a dangerous object) about
548. not to sow mixed kinds of seeds in a vineyard in the land of Israel, by the Torah's law
549. not to eat the produce of mixed kinds of seeds grown in a vineyard in the land of Israel
550. not to do work with two kinds of animals [together]
551. not to wear cloth of wool and linen
552. the precept of the marriage rite in [taking] a wife
553. the precept that the wife of one who spreads an evil report [that she was immoral] is to remain with him permanently
554. that one who spreads an evil report [that she was immoral] is not to divorce his wife
555. the duty of the court to have anyone who merits stoning stoned to death
556. not to punish anyone compelled [to transgress]
557. the duty of a rapist to take his victim for a wife
558. that a rapist is not ever to divorce his victim
559. that an emasculated man is not to take any Israelite woman in marriage
560. that a bastard from an adulterous or incestuous union should not marry any [native] daughter of Israel
561. that no Ammonite or Moabite may marry a daughter of Israel
562. not to ever offer peace to Ammon or Moab [before a war]
563. not to exclude the progeny of Esau from intermarrying with the progeny of Israel, after they have been converted to Judaism, past two generations
564. similarly, to exclude an Egyptian only up to the third generation, but not including the third generation
565. that a ritually unclean person should not enter the camp of the Levites [the Temple Mount]
566. the precept to prepare a place [of easement] in a camp
567. the precept to prepare a boring-stick [spade, for easement] in a camp
568. not to return a slave who fled from his master, from outside the land to the land of Israel
569. not to oppress this slave who

ספר החינוך   THE LIST OF MITZVOTH

תקע שֶׁלֹּא תִהְיֶה קְדֵשָׁה מִבְּנוֹת יִשְׂרָאֵל

מֵאֲדוֹנָיו, מִחוּצָה לָאָרֶץ לְאֶרֶץ יִשְׂרָאֵל

תקעא שֶׁלֹּא לְהַקְרִיב אֶתְנַן זוֹנָה וּמְחִיר כֶּלֶב

תקעב שֶׁלֹּא לִלְוֹות בְּרִבִּית מִיִּשְׂרָאֵל

תקעג מִצְוַת הַלְוָאָה לְנָכְרִי בְּרִבִּית אִם יִצְטָרֵךְ לִלְווֹת, מַה שֶּׁאֵינוֹ כֵן בְּיִשְׂרָאֵל

תקעד שֶׁלֹּא לְאַחֵר הַנְּדָרִים וְהַנְּדָבוֹת

תקעה מִצְוַת קִיּוּם מוֹצָא שְׂפָתַיִם

תקעו מִצְוָה עָלֵינוּ לְהַנִּיחַ הַשָּׂכִיר לֶאֱכֹל בִּזְמַן שְׂכִירוּתוֹ מִדְּבָרִים יְדוּעִים

תקעז שֶׁלֹּא יָנִיף הַשָּׂכִיר חֶרְמֵשׁ עַל קָמַת חֲבֵרוֹ

תקעח שֶׁלֹּא יֹאכַל הַשָּׂכִיר בִּשְׁעַת מְלָאכָה

תקעט מִצְוָה עַל הָרוֹצֶה לְגָרֵשׁ אֶת אִשְׁתּוֹ שֶׁיְּגָרְשֶׁנָּה בִּשְׁטָר

תקפ שֶׁלֹּא יַחֲזִיר הַמְגָרֵשׁ גְּרוּשָׁתוֹ אַחַר שֶׁנִּשֵּׂאת

תקפא שֶׁלֹּא לְהוֹצִיא חָתָן מִבֵּיתוֹ כָּל שָׁנָה רִאשׁוֹנָה

תקפב מִצְוָה שֶׁיִּשְׂמַח חָתָן עִם אִשְׁתּוֹ שָׁנָה רִאשׁוֹנָה

תקפג שֶׁלֹּא לַחֲבֹל כֵּלִים שֶׁעוֹשִׂין בָּהֶן אֹכֶל נֶפֶשׁ

תקפד שֶׁלֹּא לִתְלֹשׁ סִימָנֵי צָרַעַת

תקפה שֶׁלֹּא לְמַשְׁכֵּן בַּעַל חוֹב בִּזְרוֹעַ

תקפו שֶׁלֹּא לִמְנֹעַ עֲבוֹט מִבְּעָלָיו בְּעֵת שֶׁצָּרִיךְ לוֹ

תקפז מִצְוַת הֲשָׁבַת מַשְׁכּוֹן לִבְעָלָיו בְּעֵת שֶׁהוּא צָרִיךְ לוֹ

תקפח מִצְוַת נְתִינַת שְׂכַר שָׂכִיר בְּיוֹמוֹ

תקפט שֶׁלֹּא יָעִיד קָרוֹב

תקצ שֶׁלֹּא לְהַטּוֹת מִשְׁפַּט גֵּר אוֹ יָתוֹם

תקצא שֶׁלֹּא לְמַשְׁכֵּן אַלְמָנָה

תקצב מִצְוָה לְהַנִּיחַ עֹמֶר הַשִּׁכְחָה

תקצג שֶׁלֹּא לָקַח עֹמֶר הַשִּׁכְחָה מִתְּבוּאָה אוֹ מֵאִילָנוֹת

⟨48⟩

flees from his master, from outside the land to the land of Israel

570. that there should be no "harlot" in Jewry (no woman conjugally intimate out of wedlock)

571. not to bring the wage of a harlot or the exchange-price of a dog as an offering [at the Sanctuary]

572. not to borrow at interest from an Israelite

573. the precept of lending to a heathen at interest if he needs to borrow money, which is not the case with an Israelite

574. not to be overly tardy with vowed and voluntary offerings

575. the religious duty of fulfilling whatever goes out from one's lips (mouth) [as a vow]

576. the duty [that lies] upon us to allow a hired worker to eat certain things [produce] while he is under hire [to work on it]

577. that a hired man should not raise a sickle to his fellow-man's [employer's] standing grain [to save it for himself]

578. that a hired man should not eat [from his employer's crops] at the time of [his actual] work

579. the precept that one who wants to divorce his wife should do so with a proper document

580. that a divorced man should not take back his ex-wife after she has been wed [and again divorced, or widowed]

581. that a bridegroom is not to be taken out of his house [for any lengthy purpose] the entire first year [of his marriage]

582. the precept that a bridegroom should rejoice with his wife the first year [of their marriage]

583. not to take in pledge (pawn) any objects with which sustaining food is prepared

584. not to pluck out signs of a *tzara'ath* infection

585. [that a private individual is] not to take an object in pledge from a debtor by force

586. not to withhold a pledged (pawned) object from its owner at the time he needs it

587. the religious duty of returning a pledged object to its owner at the time he needs it

588. the precept of giving a hired man his pay on the same day [when he has earned it]

589. that a near relation [of a person involved in a trial] should not give testimony

590. not to pervert justice in regard to a convert (proselyte) or an orphan

591. not to take anything in pledge from a widow

592. the precept of leaving forgotten sheaves [on the field, for the poor]

593. not to take a forgotten sheaf of grain or [forgotten fruit] from trees

THE LIST OF MITZVOTH ספר החינוך

	וְהָיָה כִּי תָבוֹא		תקפד	מִצְוַת מַלְקוֹת לָרְשָׁעִים
תרו	מִצְוַת קְרִיאָה עַל הַבִּכּוּרִים		תקפה	שֶׁלֹּא לְהוֹסִיף בְּמַלְקוֹת הַמְחֻיָּב
תרז	מִצְוַת וִדּוּי מַעֲשֵׂר			מַלְקוֹת, וּבִכְלָלָהּ שֶׁלֹּא נַכֶּה נֶפֶשׁ יִשְׂרָאֵל
תרח	שֶׁלֹּא לֶאֱכֹל מַעֲשֵׂר שֵׁנִי בַּאֲנִינוּת		תקפו	שֶׁלֹּא לַחְסֹם בְּהֵמָה בִּשְׁעַת מְלָאכָה
תרט	שֶׁלֹּא לֶאֱכֹל מַעֲשֵׂר שֵׁנִי בְּטֻמְאָה		תקפז	שֶׁלֹּא תִנָּשֵׂא הַיְבָמָה לְאַחֵר חוּץ מִן הַיָּבָם
תרי	שֶׁלֹּא לְהוֹצִיא דְמֵי מַעֲשֵׂר שֵׁנִי בִּשְׁאָר דְּבָרִים שֶׁאֵינָם מַאֲכִילָה וּשְׁתִיָּה		תקפח	מִצְוַת יִבּוּם
			תקפט	מִצְוַת חֲלִיצָה
תריא	מִצְוָה לְהִדַּמּוֹת בִּדְרָכָיו הַשֵּׁם הַטּוֹבִים וְהַיְשָׁרִים		תר	מִצְוָה לְהַצִּיל הַנִּרְדָּף
			תרא	שֶׁלֹּא לָחוּס עַל הָרוֹדֵף
	אַתֶּם נִצָּבִים		תרב	שֶׁלֹּא נַשְׁהֶה מֹאזְנַיִם וּמִשְׁקָלִים חֲסֵרִים עִמָּנוּ, וְאַף־עַל־פִּי שֶׁלֹּא נִשָּׂא וְנִתֵּן בָּהֶן
תריב	מִצְוַת הַקְהֵל בְּמוֹצָאֵי שְׁבִיעִית			
תריג	מִצְוָה לִכְתֹּב כָּל אֶחָד מִיִּשְׂרָאֵל סֵפֶר תּוֹרָה לְעַצְמוֹ, שֶׁנֶּאֱמַר: וְעַתָּה כִּתְבוּ לָכֶם אֶת הַשִּׁירָה הַזֹּאת וְלַמְּדָהּ אֶת בְּנֵי יִשְׂרָאֵל וְכוּ׳		תרג	מִצְוָה לִזְכֹּר מַה שֶּׁעָשָׂה עֲמָלֵק לְיִשְׂרָאֵל בְּצֵאתָם מִמִּצְרַיִם
			תרד	מִצְוָה לְהַכְרִית זַרְעוֹ שֶׁל עֲמָלֵק
			תרה	שֶׁלֹּא נִשְׁכַּח מַעֲשֵׂה עֲמָלֵק שֶׁעָשָׂה עִם אֲבוֹתֵינוּ בְּצֵאתָם מִמִּצְרַיִם
	סָלִיקוּ הַסִּימָנִים			

20. The period between the death and the burial of close kin.

21. In our author's original, this is given as *sidrah nitzavim*, which in the tradition generally followed today is Deuteronomy 29:9–30:20. In the tradition that our author knew, however, this *sidrah* evidently comprised Deuteronomy 29:9–31:30, i.e. our *sidroth nitzavim* and *va-yélech* combined into one, since the two precepts which follow are in what we know as *sidrah va-yélech*. (As he divides *sidrah mishpatim* into two—see note 4—he thus remains with the same number of *sidroth* as in our tradition.) Rambam MT *séfer 'ahavah*, end, dealing with the *haftaroth* (portions from the Books of the Prophets to follow the Sabbath Torah readings) equally fails to mention *va-yélech* in the list of *sidroth*. Somewhat similarly, in *Séfer ha'Oreh*, from the school of Rashi, we read that *sidrah nitzavim* is split into two portions in certain years, but there is no mention of a *sidrah va-yélech* (ed. Buber, p. 81).

⟨50⟩

594. the precept of whiplashes [flogging] for the wicked
595. not to add to the whiplashes due someone who merits flogging; included in this is [the injunction] that we should not strike any Jew
596. not to muzzle a domestic animal during [its] work
597. that a *y'vamah* (childless widow) should not marry anyone other than the *yavam* (her husband's brother)
598. the precept of levirate marriage
599. the precept of *ḥalitzah* [to release a childless widow from the obligation of levirate marriage]
600. the religious duty to save a person pursued [by a killer—by attacking *him*]
601. to have no mercy on a pursuer [with intent to kill]
602. that we should not keep deficient scales or weights with us, even if we will not use them in trading
603. the religious duty to remember what Amalek did to the Israelites when they came out of Egypt
604. the precept to eradicate the progeny of Amalek
605. that we should not forget the deed of Amalek that he wrought upon our forefathers when they came out of Egypt

sidrah ki thavo (Deuteronomy 26–29:8)
606. the precept of the recital over *bikkurim* (first-fruits)
607. the precept of the avowal over the tithes
608. not to eat of the Second Tithe while in *'aninuth*,[20] grief [over the death of close kin]
609. not to eat of the Second Tithe in ritual uncleanness
610. not to spend the money for [which] Second Tithe [was exchanged] on any things other than food or drink
611. the precept to emulate the good and right ways of the Eternal Lord

sidrah va-yélech (Deuteronomy 31)[21]
612. the precept to assemble [the entire people to hear the Torah read] directly after the seventh year [*sh'mittah*]
613. the religious duty for every Jew to write a Torah scroll for himself, as it is stated, *Now therefore write this song for yourselves, and teach it to the Israelites*, etc. (Deuteronomy 31:19)

[הֶעָרַת הַמְחַבֵּר]

כָּל מִצְוָה מִתַּרְי"ג מִצְוֹת אֵלּוּ שֶׁיִּהְיֶה עָלֶיהָ רֹשֶׁם נוֹהֶגֶת בַּזְּמַן הַזֶּה, וְהֵן בֵּין כֻּלָּם שְׁלֹשׁ־מֵאוֹת וְשִׁשִּׁים וְתִשְׁעָה. וְיֵשׁ מֵאֵלּוּ הַנּוֹהֲגוֹת שֶׁלֹּא יִתְחַיֵּב בָּהֶן הָאָדָם כִּי אִם בְּסִבָּה, וּפְעָמִים שֶׁלֹּא תָבֹא הַסִּבָּה לוֹ לָאָדָם בְּכָל יָמָיו וְנִמְצָא שֶׁלֹּא יַעֲשֶׂה אוֹתָהּ הַמִּצְוָה לְעוֹלָם, כְּגוֹן מִצְוַת נְתִינַת שְׂכַר בְּיוֹמוֹ, שֶׁיֵּשׁ מִבְּנֵי אָדָם שֶׁלֹּא יִשְׂכֹּר שָׂכִיר בְּיָמָיו, וְכָל כַּיּוֹצֵא בָהּ.

וְכֵן מִן הַלָּאוִין יֵשׁ קְצָת מֵהֶן שֶׁלֹּא יִתְחַיֵּב עֲלֵיהֶן הָאָדָם כִּי אִם מֵרְצוֹנוֹ וְעַל יְדֵי סִבַּת מַעֲשָׂיו, וּבְהִמָּנְעוֹ מֵאוֹתוֹ הַמַּעֲשֶׂה לֹא יִהְיֶה עָלָיו חֵטְא וְלֹא יֶחְסַר אֵלָיו דָּבָר, כְּגוֹן מוֹצִיא שֵׁם רַע, וְכֵן לָאו דְּלָא תְאַחֵר בַּנְּדָרִים הוּא גַם־כֵּן גּוֹרֵם אוֹתוֹ, שֶׁמִּי שֶׁיֶּחְדַּל לִנְדֹּר לֹא יִהְיֶה בּוֹ חֵטְא, וְכֵן כָּל כַּיּוֹצֵא בָזֶה, וְהֵן בֵּין כֻּלָּם צ"ט, מֵהֶן ע"ח עֲשֵׂה, וְאֶחָד וְעֶשְׂרִים לָאוִין.

אֲבָל אוֹתָם מִצְווֹת שֶׁחַיָּבִין בָּהֶן כָּל אָדָם מִיִּשְׂרָאֵל מִבְּלִי שֶׁיִּתְחַדֵּשׁ בּוֹ סִבָּה בָּעוֹלָם הֵן בֵּין כֻּלָּם מָאתַיִם וְשִׁבְעִים, סִימָנָם אֲ‍‌נִ‍‌י יָ‍‌שֵׁ‍‌נָ‍‌ה וְלִ‍‌בִּ‍‌י עֵ‍‌ר, מֵהֶן שְׁמוֹנֶה וְאַרְבָּעִים עֲשֵׂה וּשְׁנַיִם וְעֶשְׂרִים וּמָאתַיִם לָאוִין, וְתִמָּצֵא כָּל אַחַת בַּסֵּדֶר שֶׁלָּהּ בְּתוֹךְ הַסֵּפֶר, וְיֵשׁ עֲלֵיהֶם רֹשֶׁם עָגֹל. וְהַחִיּוּב שֶׁל אֵלּוּ לַעֲשׂוֹתָן אֵינוֹ בְּכָל עֵת רַק בִּזְמַנִּים יְדוּעִים מִן הַשָּׁנָה אוֹ מִן הַיּוֹם, חוּץ מִשִּׁשָּׁה מִצְווֹת מֵהֶן שֶׁחִיּוּבָן

---

1. Obviously our author made an identifying mark in his original manuscript both here and at every appropriate precept. In one old manuscript (MS Casanatense 134), dated 1345, the precept numbers appear (as usual in the old manuscripts) in the outer margins; and over a good many of them there is indeed a small circular mark. Similarly, in ed. Chavel the editor notes that in MS Vatican 163/1 (his notation of MS Vatican 190 is to be corrected) such a sign appears for instance at §§45, 46, 48. However, no attempt was ever made to show such a mark in the printed editions. (R. Chavel's date for the MS must also be corrected from 1313 to 1333, stated in its colophon; hence it is not, as he asserts, the oldest extant manuscript of the work: MS Parma, de Rossi 928, bears a date of 1327, evidently written by the original owner.)

2. Every Hebrew letter also denotes a number. The letters of 'ér are 'ayin = 70, résh = 200.

3. Like the mark mentioned at the beginning (see note 1) this sign too was never reproduced in the printed editions.

[Author's Note]

Every *mitzvah* of these 613 precepts on which there is a mark[1] remains in force at the present time, these [*mitzvoth*] being 369 out of the total. Among those which remain in effect, there are some which a man becomes obligated to observe only under particular circumstances, and it may happen that the circumstances will not come about for a person during his entire life, the result being that he will never observe this *mitzvah* at all: for instance, the precept (§ 588) of giving a hired man his pay on his day [when it is due]—for there are people who will never hire a worker in their lives—and so any similar instance.

So too, among the negative precepts (prohibitions) there are a few which a man does not become obligated to observe except by his own will and through the circumstances of his deeds; and should he refrain from or avoid that particular deed [which obligates him to keep the corresponding negative precept] he will incur no guilt and will be missing nothing [in his observance of the Torah]. For example, there is [the obligation of] one who gives [his wife] a bad name [of immorality] (§ 554), that he may never divorce his wife. He is himself the cause of becoming bound by this negative precept, because he spread a bad name [about her]. So also the negative precept of *you shall not be tardy* (Deuteronomy 23:22) in regard to [keeping] vows (§ 574)—a person likewise brings it on himself; for whoever *shall forbear to vow, it shall be no sin in him* (ibid. 23); and so everything similar. Altogether there are ninety-nine [such precepts], seventy-eight of them positive, and twenty-one negative.

However, those precepts which every Jew is required to observe without any particular circumstance ever having to come about, are 270 in number out of the total. The mnemonic sign for them is *I sleep, but my heart is 'ér, awake* (Song of Songs 5:2) [the numerical value of '*ér* being 270].[2] Of them, forty-eight are positive precepts, and 222 are negative; you will find each one in its proper *sidrah* (portion of Scripture) within the book, with a circular mark on them.[3] Yet the obligation to observe these [precepts] does not apply constantly, but only for certain times of the year or the day. The following six precepts,

תְּמִידִי, לֹא יִפְסַק מֵעַל הָאָדָם אֲפִלּוּ רֶגַע בְּכָל יָמָיו, וְאֵלּוּ הֵן: א. לְהַאֲמִין בַּשֵּׁם.
ב. שֶׁלֹּא לְהַאֲמִין זוּלָתוֹ.   ג. לְיַחֲדוֹ.   ד. לְאַהֲבָה אוֹתוֹ.   ה. לְיִרְאָה אוֹתוֹ.
ו. שֶׁלֹּא לָתוּר אַחַר מַחְשֶׁבֶת הַלֵּב וּרְאִיַּת הָעֵינַיִם.
סִמָּנָם שֵׁשׁ עָרֵי מִקְלָט תִּהְיֶינָה לָכֶם.

though, are an exception: their obligation *is* constant; it is not interrupted or removed from a person for even one moment in all his days. These are:

(1) to believe in the Eternal Lord (§ 25);
(2) not to believe in any other deity (§ 26);
(3) to have faith that He is one (§ 417);
(4) to love Him (§418);
(5) to fear-revere Him (§ 432);
(6) not to go astray following after the thought of the heart or the sight of the eyes (§ 387).

A mnemonic for them is, *there shall be for you* six *cities of refuge* (Numbers 35:13).

הַקְדָּמָה

🕎 🕎 🕎

הָאֱמֶת הַבָּרוּר בְּמִין הָאֱנוֹשִׁי הוּא מַה שֶׁהִסְכִּימָה עָלָיו דַּעַת רֹב בְּנֵי אָדָם שֶׁבָּעוֹלָם. וּכְבָר הִסְכִּימָה דַּעַת כֻּלָּם לְהַאֲמִין עֵדוּת אֲנָשִׁים, וּבְרִבּוֹת הַמְעִידִים עַל הַדָּבָר שֶׁיָּעִידוּ עָלָיו אָז יִתְאַמֵּת הָעִנְיָן יוֹתֵר בְּעֵינֵי שׁוֹמְעָיו, וּבִהְיוֹת הַמְעִידִים מוּעָטִים יִפֹּל קְצָת סָפֵק בַּדָּבָר לַפִּקְחִים. וְהָעִנְיָן הַזֶּה נִתְחַזֵּק כָּל־כָּךְ אֵצֶל בְּנֵי־אָדָם עַד שֶׁקָּבְעוּ בְּנִמוּסֵיהֶם כָּל אֻמָּה וְאֻמָּה לְהָמִית אִישׁ אֶחָד עַל פִּי שְׁנַיִם עֵדִים אוֹ שְׁלֹשָׁה, וְאִם מִן הַשְּׁלֹשָׁה הָכִי נִכְבָּד;[1] גַּם תּוֹרַת מֹשֶׁה הַשְּׁלֵמָה צִוְּתָה כֵן.

וְגַם־כֵּן הִסְכִּימָה דַּעַת הַכֹּל מִטַּעַם זֶה לְקַבֵּל מִפִּי אֲבוֹתֵיהֶם וְזִקְנֵיהֶם עֵדוּתָם, בְּמֶה שֶׁמְּסַפְּרִים לָהֶם שֶׁאֵרַע בִּימֵיהֶם אוֹ בִּימֵי אֲבוֹת אֲבוֹתֵיהֶם. וְאֵין סָפֵק כִּי בִּהְיוֹת הָאָבוֹת הַמְעִידִים רַבִּים וְאוֹתָם שֶׁאֵרַע בִּימֵיהֶם הַמַּעֲשֶׂה וְרָאוּ אוֹתוֹ בְּעֵינֵיהֶם רַבִּים, יִתְחַזֵּק הַדָּבָר בְּלֵב הַבָּנִים הַשּׁוֹמְעִים. עַל־כֵּן כְּשֶׁרָצָה הָאֱלֹהִים לָתֵת תּוֹרָה לְעַמּוֹ יִשְׂרָאֵל נְתָנָהּ לָהֶם לְעֵינֵי שֵׁשׁ מֵאוֹת אֶלֶף אֲנָשִׁים גְּדוֹלִים מִלְּבַד טַף וְנָשִׁים רַבִּים, לִהְיוֹת כֻּלָּם עֵדִים נֶאֱמָנִים עַל הַדְּבָרִים.[2]

גַּם לְמַעַן תִּהְיֶה הָעֵדוּת יוֹתֵר חָזָק וְנֶאֱמָן וְזַךְ כֻּלָּם לְמַעֲלַת הַנְּבוּאָה, לְפִי שֶׁאֵין בַּמֶּה שֶׁיִּוָּדַע מִצַּד הַנְּבוּאָה נוֹפֵל סָפֵק לְעוֹלָם. וְזֶהוּ שֶׁאָמַר הַשֵּׁם יִתְבָּרַךְ לְמֹשֶׁה: בַּעֲבוּר יִשְׁמַע הָעָם בְּדַבְּרִי עִמָּךְ וְגַם בְּךָ יַאֲמִינוּ לְעוֹלָם, כְּלוֹמַר הֵם וּבְנֵיהֶם לְעוֹלָם יַאֲמִינוּ בְךָ וּבִנְבוּאָתֶךָ, כִּי אָז יֵדְעוּ יְדִיעָה נֶאֱמָנָה כִּי יְדַבֵּר אֱלֹהִים אֶת הָאָדָם וָחַי, וְשֶׁכָּל נְבוּאָתְךָ אֱמֶת.

וְלוּלֵי שֶׁזָּכוּ לִנְבוּאָה בְּכָל הָאוֹתוֹת שֶׁעָשָׂה מֹשֶׁה לְעֵינֵי פַרְעֹה וּלְעֵינֵיהֶם, הָיָה

---

1. Expression from Deuteronomy 17:6.
2. A similar point is made in R. Judah haLévi, *Kuzari*, I §87—that the Almighty had the people purify themselves for two days (Exodus 19:10, 14–15) to be ready for the state of prophecy; then, after great wonders of thunder and lightning, fire continued burning about Mount Sinai forty days. They all saw Moses going back and forth through it, and they heard the Ten Commandments clearly.... Hence, thereafter they believed in Moses as a prophet. So too Ramban, commentary, Exodus 19:9: It seems to me that He said, *I am coming to you in a thick cloud* [meaning] that you should come close to the thick darkness in order *that the people may hear My words, and they themselves will* [thus] *be prophets in regard to My words, and not believe by the report of others.*

Preface

Clear, indisputable truth among mankind is what the minds of most human beings in the world have agreed upon. Now, the thinking of all has long agreed to believe human testimony; and the more the witnesses who attest to a matter, the more convincingly true it becomes to the ears of its hearers; while, if the witnesses are few, a bit of doubt about the matter may enter the intelligent mind. This concept became so firmly entrenched among humankind that every single nation made it a firm policy in its ways of law to put a person to death by the word of two or three witnesses,[1] it being more estimable if there are three. The perfect Torah of Moses too has so ordained.

Furthermore, the minds of all are unanimous, for this reason, in accepting from their fathers [and] elders their testimony in which they recount to them what occurred in their day or in the times of their own grandfathers. Beyond any doubt, when the fathers who so bear witness are numerous, when those in whose time the event occurred and who saw it with their own eyes are many, the matter becomes most strongly confirmed in the heart of the sons who listen. Therefore, when God wished to give the Torah to His people Israel, He gave it to them in sight of 600,000 grown men, not to mention the great number of children and women, that all might be faithful witnesses about the things [that happened then].

Moreover, in order that the testimony might be all the stronger and more faithful and trustworthy, they all were permitted to attain the level of prophecy—for doubt can never affect what becomes known through the medium of prophecy. This is why the Eternal Lord (be He blessed) said to Moses, [*Lo, I am coming to you in a thick cloud*] *that the people may hear when I speak with you, and may also believe in you forever* (Exodus 19:9). He meant by this, "they and their children will forever believe in you and in your prophecy; for then they will know with absolute affirmation *that God speaks with a man, and he lives* (Deuteronomy 5:21), and [therefore] your prophecy is truth."[2]

Had they not attained the state of prophecy during all the wonders that Moses wrought before Pharaoh's eyes and theirs, an objector

ספר החינוך   PREFACE

יָכוֹל בַּעַל הַדִּין לַחֲלֹק וְלוֹמַר: מִי יוֹדֵעַ אִם עָשָׂה הַכֹּל בְּתַחְבּוּלוֹת חָכְמַת הַשֵּׁדִים אוֹ בְכֹחַ שְׁמוֹת הַמַּלְאָכִים. וְאַף־עַל־פִּי שֶׁחַכְמֵי מִצְרַיִם וְכָל חַרְטֻמֶּיהָ, שֶׁהָיוּ בְקִיאִים בְּחָכְמַת הַשֵּׁדִים וְהַכִּשּׁוּף יוֹתֵר מִכָּל שְׁאָר הָעוֹלָם, הוֹדוּ בְעַל כָּרְחָם לְמֹשֶׁה וְאָמְרוּ לְפַרְעֹה כִּי בְכֹחַ הַשֵּׁם עָשָׂה, כְּמוֹ שֶׁכָּתוּב: אֶצְבַּע אֱלֹהִים הִיא, אַף־עַל־פִּי־כֵן הָרוֹצֶה לְהִתְעַקֵּשׁ יֹאמַר בְּיִתְרוֹן חָכְמָתוֹ מֵהֶם עָשָׂה וְהוֹדוּ לוֹ. אֲבָל אַחֲרֵי הַנְּבוּאָה לֹא נִשְׁאַר לָהֶם שׁוּם פִּקְפּוּק עַד עִנְיָן וְיָדְעוּ בְּבֵרוּר כִּי כָל הַמַּעֲשִׂים נַעֲשׂוּ בִּמְצִיאַת אֲדוֹן הָעוֹלָם וּמִיָּדוֹ הִגִּיעַ אֲלֵיהֶם הַכֹּל.

וְהֵם שֶׁרָאוּ בְעֵינֵיהֶם וְיָדְעוּ הַדָּבָר יְדִיעָה אֲמִתִּית שֶׁאֵין לִבְנֵי־אָדָם אֱמֶת חָזָק יוֹתֵר מִזֶּה, הֵעִידוּ לִבְנֵיהֶם אֲשֶׁר יָלְדוּ אַחֲרֵי־כֵן כִּי כָל דִּבְרֵי הַתּוֹרָה אֲשֶׁר קִבְּלוּ עַל יַד מֹשֶׁה מִ"בְּרֵאשִׁית" עַד "לְעֵינֵי כָּל יִשְׂרָאֵל" אֱמֶת וּבָרוּר בְּלִי שׁוּם סָפֵק בָּעוֹלָם, וּבְנֵיהֶם הֵעִידוּ לִבְנֵיהֶם גַּם־כֵּן, וּבְנֵיהֶם לִבְנֵיהֶם עָדֵינוּ.

נִמְצֵאת תּוֹרָתֵנוּ בְּיָדֵינוּ תּוֹרַת אֱמֶת מִפִּי שֵׁשׁ מֵאוֹת אֶלֶף עֵדִים נֶאֱמָנִים, שֶׁהוּא חֶשְׁבּוֹן הַכּוֹלֵל כָּל דֵּעוֹת בְּנֵי־אָדָם, מִלְּבַד טַף וְנָשִׁים.

וְעַתָּה אִם יִטְעֶה עָלֵינוּ מֵסִית אֲשֶׁר לְבָבוֹ פוֹנֶה מֵעִם יְיָ אֱלֹהֵינוּ וְיֹאמַר: מַה לְּךָ אִישׁ יְהוּדִי וְקַבָּלָתֶךָ, וּמַה לְּךָ לִשְׁאֹל אָבִיךָ וּזְקֵנֶיךָ, חֲקֹר וּדְרֹשׁ בְּדַעְתְּךָ הַטּוֹב וְהַעֲמֵק סְבָרוֹתֶיךָ, פְּקַח עֵינֶיךָ וּרְאֵה מַה בְּעוֹלָמְךָ, תְּנוּעַת הַגַּלְגַּל וְאַרְבַּע הַיְסוֹדוֹת שֶׁבָּאֲדָמָה, בָּהֶם תִּרְאֶה וְתָבִין תַּעֲלוּמוֹת חָכְמָה, וּבְשִׂכְלְךָ חֲקֹר וְתִלְמַד הָאֶחָד אֵיךְ יֵחַד—נָשִׁיב אֵלָיו כִּי מִצַּד חֲקִירָתֵנוּ לֹא נוּכַל לְהַשִּׂיג לָעוֹלָם בְּדָבָר אֱלֹהִים כְּלוּם, כִּי גַם בְּעִנְיְנֵי הָעוֹלָם הַשָּׁפָל לֹא יָכְלוּ כָּל חַכְמֵי הַטֶּבַע לָבוֹא עַד תַּכְלִיתָם, כִּי מִי

3. Cf. Rambam MT *hilchoth y'sodé torah* viii 1: The Israelites did not believe in Moses our master on account of the wonders he wrought; for he who believes on the basis of wonders has misgivings in his heart, that perhaps the wonders were done through spells and magic.... Why did they believe in him? Standing at Mount Sinai, our eyes saw—not others; our ears heard—not others—the fire, *the thunderings and lightnings* (Exodus 20:15). *He went close to the dark thickness* (ibid. 18), and the voice was speaking to him, and we heard it: "Moses, Moses, go tell them thus and thus."... And how do we know that the experience at Mount Sinai was the only proof that his prophecy was true past any doubts or qualms? For it is stated, *Lo, I am coming to you in a thick cloud, that the people may hear when I speak to you, and may also believe in you forever* (ibid. 19:9). Hence, before this they did not believe in him with with an enduring trust but with a faith that left room for reflections and afterthoughts.

4. Similarly R. Judah haLévi, *Kuzari*, I §27:... I and the entire community of Israel (Jewry) are obligated by Him because that experience [of the Israelites at Sinai] became confirmed truth for them through the sight of their eyes; afterward there was the continuing [chain of] tradition concerning that sight.

5. This idea is to be found in a sermon by Ramban (R. Moses b. Naḥman) titled *torath ha-shem t'mimah*: It is a tradition of the Sages (of blessed memory) that no more than 600,000 were created with different characters [of different types]; this number includes all [types of] minds; therefore the Torah was given [at Sinai]

⟨58⟩

would be able to argue and say, "Who knows? Perhaps he did everything through trickery by the knowledge of demons, or by the power of the names of angel-spirits." It is true that the wise men of Egypt and all its sorcerers, who were more expert in knowledge of demons and magic than all the rest of the world, conceded to Moses against their will and said to Pharaoh that he worked with the power of the Eternal Lord, as it is written, [*the magicians said to Pharaoh*] "*This is the finger of God*" (Exodus 8:15). Nevertheless, one who wants to be obstinate can say that he worked with the superiority of his wisdom over theirs, and [therefore] they yielded to him. However, after the state of prophecy [that the Israelites attained] no trace of skepticism was left for them in the matter: they knew with a clear certainty that all the deeds were wrought by the order of the Lord of the world, and by His power everything had happened to them.[3]

Now they, who saw it with their eyes and knew the matter with a true knowledge, beyond which people can have no firmer, more certain truth—they bore witness to the children who were born to them afterward, that all the words of the Torah which they received through Moses, from the first letter of *In the beginning* (Genesis 1:1) to the last letter of *in the sight of all Israel* (Deuteronomy 34:12), are true and certain past any doubt in the world. Then their sons bore witness to their children in turn, and their children to their children, and so until our time.[4]

Hence our Torah that we have is a Torah of truth, by the word of 600,000 faithful witnesses—which is the number that includes all the various personalities of human beings[5]—not counting the children and women.

Now, a person who might mislead us, *whose heart turns away from the Lord our God* (Deuteronomy 29:17), might argue with us and say, "What need have you, O Jew, of your received tradition? Why should you ask your father and your elders?[6] Search and ponder with your own good mind, and think deeply for yourself. Open your own eyes and see what there is in your world: the movement of the heavenly sphere, and the four elements found on earth.[7] By them you will perceive and understand the secrets of wisdom; and so probe with your intelligence, and you will learn how the one [God] could create but one nature." We can answer him that from our own delving we will never be able to grasp a thing about the word of God. Even in matters of this lowly world, all the learned students of nature could

ספר החינוך PREFACE

יִגַּלֶּה בְחָכְמַת הַמַּחְקָר סְגֻלַּת הָעֲשָׂבִים וְהַפֵּרוֹת וּסְגֻלַּת אֲבָנִים טוֹבוֹת וִיקָרוֹת וְסִבַּת תְּנוּעַת הַבַּרְזֶל בְּאֶבֶן תַּחְתִּיוֹת, כִּי שָׁם עָמְדוּ מַתְמִיהִים כָּל חַכְמֵי הַטֶּבַע וְכָל אַנְשֵׁי תְבוּנוֹת.

אַף כִּי נֹאמַר לְהָבִין מֵהֶם חָכְמוֹת נִכְבָּדוֹת וְדַעַת אֱלֹהִים נִמְצָא, חָלִילָה לָנוּ חָלִילָה לָבוֹא אַחֲרֵי הַמֶּלֶךְ בִּגְבֹהֵנוּ וּלְהָרִים יָד וְלַחְשֹׁב מַחֲשָׁבוֹת בַּמֶּה שֶׁלְּמַעְלָה מִמַּחְשְׁבוֹתֵינוּ וְאֵין צֹרֶךְ אֵלֵינוּ, כִּי הִנֵּה אֲבוֹתֵינוּ זִכְרוֹנָם לִבְרָכָה הֵמָּה סִדְּרוּ שֻׁלְחָן לְפָנֵינוּ, הֵם הֶעֱמִיקוּ שְׁאֵלָה וּבָאוּ אֶל תַּכְלִית הַיְדִיעָה הָאֲמִתִּית וְהִשִּׂיגוּ לָדַעַת כִּי יְדַבֵּר אֱלֹהִים אֶת הָאָדָם וָחָי. וּמַה לָּנוּ אַחֲרֵי זֹאת לַחְקֹר וּלְחַטֵּט אַחַר דִּבְרֵיהֶם. הָאֱמֶת אִתָּם, רַק לִשְׁתּוֹת בַּצָּמָא אֶת דִּבְרֵיהֶם כִּכְתָבָם וְכִלְשׁוֹנָם.

וְהַמָּשָׁל בָּזֶה מִי שֶׁהֵעִידוּ לוֹ אֶלֶף אַלְפֵי אֲנָשִׁים שֶׁלֹּא לִשְׁתּוֹת מֵימֵי נַחַל אֶחָד, לְפִי שֶׁרָאוּ אוֹתָם הַמַּיִם מְמִיתִים שׁוֹתָיו, וְנִסּוּ זֶה אֶלֶף פְּעָמִים בִּזְמַנִּים שׁוֹנִים וּבִאֲנָשִׁים מָחְלָקִים בָּאֲרָצוֹת; וְאָמַר אֵלָיו חָכָם אֶחָד רוֹפֵא מֻבְהָק: אַל תַּאֲמֵן לְכֻלָּם כִּי אֲנִי מוֹדִיעֲךָ מִצַּד חָכְמָה שֶׁאֵין אוֹתָם הַמַּיִם רְאוּיִים לְהָמִית, לְפִי שֶׁהֵם זַכִּים וְקַלִּים וְהֶעָפָר שֶׁעוֹבְרִים עָלָיו טוֹב, שְׁתֵה מֵהֶם כְּנַפְשְׁךָ שָׂבְעֶךָ—הֲטוֹב לָזֶה לְהַנִּיחַ עֵדוּת הַכֹּל הַמְפֻרְסָם וְלַעֲשׂוֹת כִּדְבַר הֶחָכָם? בֶּאֱמֶת לֹא טוֹב הַדָּבָר, וְאִישׁ מַשְׂכִּיל לֹא יִשְׁמַע אֵלָיו, וְכִדְבָרָיו לֹא יַעֲשֶׂה.

הוּא הַדָּבָר אֲשֶׁר הִקְדַּמְנוּ כִּי אֲמִתַּת עִנְיְנֵי הָעוֹלָם נוֹדַעַת מִפִּי רֻבֵּי בְנֵי־אָדָם הַמְּעִידִים עַל אוֹתָהּ אֱמֶת יוֹתֵר מֵהַמַּכְרִיחִים דִּבְרֵיהֶם מִצַּד שִׂכְלָם וְחַקִירָתָם, כִּי בִּהְיוֹת הָאָדָם חֲסַר הַשְּׁלֵמוּת אֵין שִׂכְלוֹ מַשִּׂיג אֶל תַּכְלִית הַדְּבָרִים. וְעַל־כֵּן הַדֶּרֶךְ הַנִּבְחָר לָאָדָם לַעֲשׂוֹת בְּכָל דִּבְרֵי הַתּוֹרָה הַמְקֻבֶּלֶת מִן הָעֵדִים הַנֶּאֱמָנִים אֲשֶׁר נָתַן אֲדוֹן הַחָכְמָה לִבְנֵי־אָדָם, וּבָהּ נִכְלָל כָּל דַּעַת יָקָר וְכָל חָכְמָה מְפֹאָרָה.

וְאִם יִשְׁאַל הַשּׁוֹאֵל: מַהוּ הָעִנְיָן שֶׁנִּתַּן הַשֵּׁם תּוֹרָה יְקָרָה כָזוֹ לִבְנֵי־אָדָם? הֲלֹא

---

to this number (see Exodus 12:37; *Kithvé Ramban*, ed. Chavel, I, 162). Similarly R. Baḥya, commentary, Genesis 46:27.

6. An allusion to Deuteronomy 32:7.

7. Fire, wind, water, earth; it is an ancient teaching that these are the fundamental elements of life on earth.

8. Expression based on Ecclesiastes 2:22, *for what is man, to come after the king?* (literal translation).

8a. Similarly Rashba, Responsa, I §9.

⟨60⟩

not achieve their purpose. For who is to reveal, through the wisdom of philosophical search, the special properties of grasses and fruits, the singular qualities of gems and precious stones, or the reason why iron is drawn by a magnet. There [before these questions] all the learned experts of nature and all the people of wisdom have stood still in wonder.

Even if we should propose to understand worthy wisdoms through them and [thus] find knowledge of God, far, far be it from us to come [seeking about] after the King[8] in our haughtiness, to raise a hand [in arrogance] and conceive thoughts about what is above our thought and of which we have no need. For here our forefathers of blessed memory arranged the table before us. They delved deeply in their quest and arrived at the utmost true knowledge, arriving at the certainty *that God can speak with man, and he lives* (Deuteronomy 5:21). After this, what business have we to search and probe beyond their words of truth? [We need] only drink in their words thirstily, as they were written and phrased.

Here is a parable to illustrate it: There was a man whom thousands upon thousands of people adjured not to drink the water of a certain stream, as they saw that water kill those who drank it. They tested this matter a thousand times, at various periods, and with persons from different countries. Yet one wise person, an expert physician, told this man, "Do not believe them all: for I tell you from the vantage-point of wisdom that this water is not lethal, because it is pure and swift-running, and the earth over which it passes is good. Drink to your heart's desire." Would it be good for that man to forget the widely-known testimony of all and do as this wise person said? Of course it would not be good; an intelligent person would not listen to him nor do as he advised.[8a]

This is the point we stated previously: the truth about the nature of the world is ascertained by the word of the far greater number of people who attest to that truth than the number of those who prove their words by their reasoning and keen probing thought. For since man falls short of perfection, his mind does not perceive the ultimate nature of things. For that reason, the choicest way for a man is to act according to all the words of the Torah, received from those faithful witnesses that the Lord of wisdom gave to mankind. It includes all precious knowledge and the entirety of splendid wisdom.

Yet someone might ask: What is the reason why the Eternal

לַשֵּׁם בָּרוּךְ הוּא הַכֹּל, וּלְמַעֲלָתוֹ וְלִכְבוֹדוֹ וּבִידִיעַת בְּנֵי־אָדָם בְּכֹחַ מַעֲשָׂיו אֵין תּוֹסֶפֶת לִכְבוֹדוֹ, כִּי לְתַכְלִית הַכָּבוֹד וְהַהוֹד לֹא יִהְיֶה תּוֹסֶפֶת וְגֵרוּעַ בִּשְׁבִיל דָּבָר.

תְּשׁוּבָתוֹ שֶׁל זֶה פְּשׁוּטָה, שֶׁאֵין דַּעַת בְּנֵי אִישׁ מַשִּׂיג בְּדַרְכֵי יוֹצְרוֹ לָדַעַת טַעַם מַעֲשָׂיו לָמָּה, כִּי גָבְהוּ דְרָכָיו מִדַּרְכֵיהֶם וּמַחְשְׁבוֹתָיו מִמַּחְשְׁבוֹתֵיהֶם. וְאַף־עַל־פִּי שֶׁאֵין טַעַם הַדָּבָר נִגְלֶה לָנוּ, יֵשׁ לָנוּ לְהַאֲמִין כִּי אַב הַחָכְמוֹת אֲדוֹן הַכֹּל, כָּל אֲשֶׁר עָשָׂה לְצֹרֶךְ עָשָׂה וּלְעִנְיָן מְחֻיָּב.

וּמִכָּל־מָקוֹם אֶפְשָׁר לָנוּ לִמְצֹא בַדָּבָר קְצָת טַעַם וְלוֹמַר כִּי יְדִיעַת בְּנֵי־אָדָם דַּרְכֵי הַשֵּׁם מְחַיֶּבֶת לְמַעֲלָתוֹ יִתְעַלֶּה, שֶׁאַחַר שֶׁעָלָה בְמַחֲשָׁבָה לְפָנָיו לִבְרֹאת עוֹלָם רָאוּי לִהְיוֹתוֹ בְתַכְלִית הַשְּׁלֵמוּת, כִּי הַשָּׁלֵם כָּל מַעֲשָׂיו שְׁלֵמוֹת, וְכֵן הוּא הָאֱמֶת שֶׁהוּא בָרוּךְ הוּא הִשְׁלִימוֹ בַכֹּל, כִּי לֹא חָסֵר מִמֶּנּוּ דָּבָר שֶׁיְּהֵא אָדָם יָכוֹל לוֹמַר עָלָיו: לָמָה לֹא עָשָׂה בְעוֹלָמוֹ כֵן שֶׁיִּוָּדַע מִמֶּנּוּ יִתְרוֹן חָכְמָה.

כִּי הִנֵּה בָּרָא בְעוֹלָמוֹ שְׂכָלִים נִבְדָּלִים, וְהֵם הַמַּלְאָכִים, וְכֵן בָּרָא שְׂכָלִים בְּגוּף קַיָּם, וְהֵם הַשָּׁמַיִם וְכָל צְבָאָם, וּבָרָא בָּאָרֶץ בְּרִיּוֹת גּוּפָנִיּוֹת בְּלִי שֵׂכֶל כְּלָל, וְהֵם הַבְּהֵמוֹת וְהָעוֹפוֹת וּשְׁאָר הַמִּינִים כַּיּוֹצֵא בָם, וְעוֹד בָּרָא בָאָרֶץ בְּרִיּוֹת גּוּפָנִיּוֹת בְּשֵׂכֶל, וְהוּא מִין הָאָדָם, לְהוֹדִיעַ כִּי לֹא נִמְנַע לְפָנָיו כָּל דָּבָר, שֶׁאַף־עַל־פִּי שֶׁהַחֹמֶר וְהַשֵּׂכֶל הֲפָכִים גְּמוּרִים עֵרְבָם יַחַד בְּגֹדֶל חָכְמָתוֹ וְעָשָׂה בָהֶם אֶת הָאָדָם. וְאִם־כֵּן עַל־כָּל־פָּנִים יִתְחַיֵּב שֶׁיִּהְיֶה אוֹתוֹ שֵׂכֶל הַמְעֹרָב בְּחֹמֶר, וְהוּא הָאָדָם, יוֹדֵעַ יוֹצְרוֹ וּמַכִּירוֹ, כְּדֵי לְהַשְׁלִים הַכַּוָּנָה בִּבְרִיאָתוֹ.

וְאִם לֹא הַתּוֹרָה שֶׁנָּתַן לוֹ יִמְשֹׁךְ הַשֵּׂכֶל אַחַר הַחֹמֶר בְּכָל תַּאֲוֺתָיו לְגַמְרֵי וְנִמְשַׁל כַּבְּהֵמוֹת נִדְמוּ, וּבְכֵן לֹא תִשְׁלַם הַמְּלָאכָה, לְפִי שֶׁיִּהְיֶה גּוּף הָאָדָם וְגוּף

---

9. Expression from Isaiah 55:9.

Lord gave so precious a Torah to human beings? Does not the Eternal Lord, blessed is He, possess everything? There are no bounds to His eminence and glory. Then by having human beings know the might of His deeds, nothing is added to His glory. Where there is ultimate, absolute glory and majesty, what can add to it or subtract from it?

The answer to this is simple: The human mind cannot grasp the ways of its Creator, to know the reason, the "why" of His deeds. "For His ways are higher than their ways, and His thoughts than their thoughts."[9] Yet even if the reason for something is not apparent to us, we must nevertheless believe that the Father of wisdoms, the Lord of all, wrought everything He did for a purpose, for some necessary objective.

However, even so we can find some bit of reason for the matter and say that human knowledge of the ways of the Eternal Lord follows necessarily from His eminence. For since the thought arose before Him to create the world, it is fitting that it should achieve ultimate perfection. When one is whole, perfect, all his works are perfection. And this indeed is the truth—that He (blessed is He) made it perfect, complete in everything, not leaving anything lacking in it, so that a man might be able to say about it, "Why did He not make it so in His world, so that yet more of [His] superior wisdom could be known from it?"

For now, He created in His world discarnate spirits of intelligence—the angels; and He equally created spirits of intelligence in enduring physical form, these being the heavens and all their host. Then he created on earth physical creatures without any intelligence, these being beasts and birds and the other species like them. Then He also created on earth physical beings with intelligence, i.e. the human species—all to let it be known that nothing is beyond Him. For even though matter and intelligence are total opposites, He merged them into one by His great wisdom and thereby made man. In all events, it would be inevitable that this intelligence merged with matter, i.e. man, should know his Maker and acknowledge Him, in order to complete the [Divine] intention in his creation.

Now, if not for the Torah that He gave him, man's intelligence would be completely drawn after his material nature, with all its cravings; he would be *like the beasts that perish* (Psalms 49:21); and thus the work [of his creation] would not be completed—for then the human body and the animal body would be one and the same practical-

PREFACE — ספר החינוך

הַבְּהֵמָה אֶחָד בְּעִנְיָן אַף־עַל־פִּי שֶׁאֵינוֹ אֶחָד בְּצוּרָה, וְנִמְצָא בַּיְצִירָה חִסָּרוֹן.

נִמְצָא לְפִי דְבָרֵינוּ שֶׁנְּתִינַת הַתּוֹרָה לְהַשְׂכִּיל לְבוֹת בְּנֵי־אָדָם מְחֻיֶּבֶת לְתַשְׁלוּם הַיְצִירוֹת. וְאִם יִשָּׁאֵל עוֹד: אַחַר שֶׁהִיא תַשְׁלוּם הַיְצִירוֹת לָמָּה נִתְּנָה לְעַם אֶחָד מֵעַמֵּי הָעוֹלָם וְלֹא לְכֻלָּם?

גַּם בָּזֶה הָיְתָה תְשׁוּבָתוֹ פְּשׁוּטָה לְהָשִׁיב שֶׁאֵין דַּעַת הַנּוֹצָר מַשִּׂיג כַּוָּנַת יוֹצְרוֹ. אֲבָל מִכָּל־מָקוֹם גַּם לָזֶה אֶפְשָׁר לִמְצֹא בּוֹ קְצָת טַעַם לְפִי מִנְהָגוֹ שֶׁל עוֹלָם. הֲלֹא יָדוּעַ כִּי בְּכָל דִּבְרֵי הָעוֹלָם הַשָּׁפָל פְּסֹלֶת מְרֻבָּה בּוֹ עַל הָעִקָּר, גַּם בָּעִקָּר חֵלֶק מִמֶּנּוּ נִבְחָר בּוֹ מִן הַכֹּל, כְּאִלּוּ תֹאמַר רֹב קַרְקָעוֹת שֶׁבָּעוֹלָם אֵינָם עֲדִית אֶלָּא מְעוּטָם, וְגַם בָּעֲדִית חֵלֶק מִמֶּנּוּ עֲדֵי עֲדָיִית, וְכֵן הַדָּבָר גַּם בְּפֵרוֹת הָעוֹלָם וּבְמִינֵי הַבְּהֵמוֹת וְהָעוֹפוֹת.

וְאִם־כֵּן גַּם בַּמִּין הָאֱנוֹשִׁי נִהְיָה הַדָּבָר כֵּן, לְדַמּוֹתוֹ לְמִינֵי הָעוֹלָם הַשָּׁפָל, אַחַר שֶׁהוּא מְשֻׁתָּף עִמָּהֶם בִּקְצָתוֹ, שֶׁהוּא בַעַל גּוּף נִפְסָד כָּהֶם, אֵין תֵּמַהּ בַּדָּבָר. וְעַל־כֵּן נִבְחַר מִמִּין הָאָדָם חֵלֶק אֶחָד וְהוּא יִשְׂרָאֵל, וְהוּא הַמְעַט מִכָּל הָעַמִּים, וּבָרוּךְ הַשֵּׁם שֶׁיּוֹדֵעַ כִּי הֵם מֻבְחַר הַמִּין הָאֱנוֹשִׁי וּבְחָרָם לִהְיוֹת נִקְרָאִים עַמּוֹ וְנָתַן לָהֶם כָּל עִקְּרֵי הַחָכְמָה.

וְאוּלָם גַּם לְכָל שְׁאָר מִין הָאָדָם נָתַן דֶּרֶךְ לְהַבְדִּילָם מִן הַבְּהֵמוֹת, וְהֵם שֶׁבַע מִצְוֹת שֶׁנִּצְטַוּוּ בָהֶם כָּל בְּנֵי הָעוֹלָם בִּכְלָל, כְּמוֹ שֶׁנִּכְתַּב עַל כָּל אַחַת מֵהֶם בְּעֶזְרַת הַשֵּׁם. וְגַם בְּעַם יִשְׂרָאֵל בְּעַצְמוֹ חֵלֶק מֵהֶם נִבְחָר יוֹתֵר, וְהוּא שֵׁבֶט הַלֵּוִי שֶׁנִּבְחַר לַעֲבוֹדָתוֹ תָּמִיד.

וְכֵן הַדָּבָר גַּם־כֵּן בְּכַדּוּר הָאָרֶץ, שֶׁיֵּשׁ בָּהּ חֵלֶק נִבְחָר מִן הַכֹּל, וְיָדַע הַשֵּׁם כִּי הַמֻּבְחָר שֶׁבָּהּ הוּא אֶרֶץ־יִשְׂרָאֵל וְהָיָה בָּהּ מִבְחָר מִין הָאָדָם. גַּם בְּאוֹתוֹ מִבְחָר הָאָרֶץ, הַטּוֹב שֶׁבּוֹ הוּא יְרוּשָׁלַיִם, וְעַל־כֵּן נִבְחֲרָה לִהְיוֹת מְשַׁכַּן הַתּוֹרָה וּמְקוֹם הָעֲבוֹדָה וּמִמֶּנָּה יִתְבָּרֵךְ כָּל כַּדּוּר הָאָרֶץ, כִּי שָׁם צִוָּה יְיָ אֶת הַבְּרָכָה.

---

10. Expression from Deuteronomy 7:7. The same question and essentially the same answer are to be found in R. Judah haLévi, *Kuzari*, I §§102–03.

11. The same thought is to be found in *ibid.* II §§10–12; cf. also Midrash T'hillim 24, 3: The Land of Israel is the *t'rumah*, the chosen part of all the lands.

⟨64⟩

ly, though they are not the same in form [and purpose]. The result would be a defect in the Divine formation of the world. Thus from our words we see that the giving of the Torah, to make the hearts of men wise, was essential for the perfection of humankind.

Yet one might further ask, "Since it is [for] the perfection of human beings, why was it given to but one people among the nations of the world, and not to all?" Here again it would be simple to give the answer that the mind of a created person cannot grasp the intent of his Maker. Nevertheless, though, for this too a bit of a reason can be found, derived from the nature of the world. It is well known that in everything in this lowly world, the waste matter is greater than the principal part; and even of the principal part, only a portion is chosen out of the whole. Thus you could say [for certain]: Most fields in the world are not prime, fertile land, but only a small part; and of the prime land, a fraction is the prime of the prime. The same is true of the produce of the world, and species of domestic animals and birds.

This being so, the same must be true about the human race, as man is comparable to the other species in this lowly world. And since he shares some characteristics with them, being possessed like them of a mortal, perishable body, there should be nothing surprising in this. Hence one part of the human race was chosen, this being the Israelites, the fewest of all peoples.[10] And blessed be the Eternal Lord who knows that they are the choice part of the human race, and who selected them to be called His people, giving them all the main principles of wisdom.

However, to all the rest of the human race He also gave a pathway to separate them from the animal level. This way comprises the seven precepts which all the people in the world were together commanded, as we will mention about each of them, with the Lord's help. And even of the Israelite people itself, one part is the more select—the tribe of Lévi, which was chosen to serve Him continually.

The same holds true in regard to the earthly globe: one part is more select than the rest. And knowing this select part to be the land of Israel, the Eternal Lord made it His wish to settle in it the choicest part of the human species.[11] Then, of that choice part of the earth itself, the very best region is Jerusalem. Therefore it was picked to be the dwelling-place of the Torah and the center of Divine service; and from it the entire earthly globe was to be blessed, *for there the Lord commanded the blessing* (Psalms 133:3).

ספר החינוך · PREFACE

וְאִם יִשְׁאַל עוֹד: אַחַר שֶׁאָמַרְתָּ כִּי עִקַּר הַכֹּל וְהַחֵלֶק הַנִּבְחָר הֵם עַם יִשְׂרָאֵל, אֵיךְ הַדָּבָר שֶׁהֵם סוֹבְלִים הַגָּלוּת וְהַצָּרוֹת מֵעוֹלָם?

הַתְּשׁוּבָה: יָדוּעַ הַדָּבָר וּמְפֻרְסָם בֵּין בְּנֵי הָעוֹלָם כִּי אֲדוֹן הַכֹּל בָּרָא שְׁנֵי עוֹלָמוֹת, עוֹלָם הַגּוּפוֹת וְעוֹלָם הַנְּשָׁמוֹת, וְעוֹלָם הַגּוּפוֹת כְּאֶפֶס וָתֹהוּ נֶחְשָׁב כְּנֶגֶד עוֹלָם הַנְּשָׁמוֹת, שֶׁזֶּה כְּצֵל עוֹבֵר וְזֶה קַיָּם לַעֲדֵי עַד. וְעַל־כֵּן בִּהְיוֹת הַנֶּפֶשׁ עִקַּר הָאָדָם וְהַדָּבָר הַקַּיָּם שֶׁבּוֹ וְנִשְׁאָר בִּלְתִּי כָלֶה לָעַד, וְהַגּוּף כְּלִי לַנֶּפֶשׁ, מְשַׁמֵּשׁ אֵלֶיהָ זְמַן מוּעָט וְאַחַר כֵּן נִפְסָד וְנֶאֱלָח, הִנְחִיל יְיָ לְעַמּוֹ עוֹלָם הַנְּשָׁמוֹת, שֶׁהוּא עוֹלָם נִצְחִי וְלַתַּעֲנוּג שֶׁבּוֹ אֵין שִׁעוּר.

וְאִם יִשְׁאַל הַשּׁוֹאֵל עוֹד: וְלָמָּה לֹא נָתַן הָאֵל לְעַמּוֹ אֲשֶׁר בָּחַר שְׁנֵי מָנוֹת, תַּעֲנוּג עוֹלָם הַגּוּפוֹת וְעוֹלָם הַנְּשָׁמוֹת? הַתְּשׁוּבָה, כִּי יָדוּעַ לְכָל בַּעַל שֵׂכֶל שֶׁאִי אֶפְשָׁר לְבַעַל חֹמֶר לְעוֹלָם בְּלִי שֶׁיֶּחֱטָא, וּמִמִּדּוֹת הָאֵל בָּרוּךְ הוּא הַקְּבוּעוֹת עֲדֵי עַד הִיא מִדַּת הַדִּין; וְהִיא תְחַיֵּב כָּל בַּעַל שֵׂכֶל לָלֶכֶת בְּדֶרֶךְ הַשֵּׂכֶל וּבִנְטוֹתוֹ לְהִתְחַיֵּב לַמֶּלֶךְ; וְאַחַר שֶׁחִיְּבָה מִדַּת הַדִּין, לִפְטֹר בְּלֹא כְלוּם אִי אֶפְשָׁר שֶׁכְּבָר יָצָא חַיָּב מִבֵּית מִדַּת הַדִּין, וְעַל־כֵּן מֵחַסְדֵי הַשֵּׁם עָלֵינוּ שָׁם חֶלְקֵנוּ לִצְרֹף הַחֵטְא מִמֶּנּוּ בָּעוֹלָם הַזֶּה הַנִּפְסָד לִהְיוֹת נַפְשׁוֹתֵינוּ נְקִיּוֹת וְקַיָּמוֹת בְּעוֹלָם הַנְּשָׁמוֹת, שֶׁיָּפָה שָׁם שָׁעָה אַחַת מִכָּל חַיֵּי הָעוֹלָם הַזֶּה.

וְאוּלָם יֵשׁ לְהַאֲמִין שֶׁיַּגִּיעַ זְמַן שֶׁנִּזְכֶּה לִשְׁנֵי הַמָּנוֹת, וְהֵם יְמוֹת הַמָּשִׁיחַ. וְהַטַּעַם, אָז בַּיָּמִים הָהֵם, לְפִי שֶׁלֹּא נִהְיֶה צְרִיכִים לְצֵרוּף הַגּוּפִים כְּלָל כִּי יִבָּטֵל מִמֶּנּוּ יֵצֶר הָרָע, כְּדִכְתִיב: וַהֲסִרֹתִי אֶת לֵב הָאֶבֶן מִבְּשַׂרְכֶם. וְאִם גַּם בָּעֵת הַהִיא מְעַט סִיג חֵטְא יִשָּׁאֵר, יִפֹּל הַחִיּוּב עַל רֹאשׁ הַשָּׂעִיר כַּאֲשֶׁר בַּתְּחִלָּה.

וְזֶהוּ שֶׁכָּתוּב בַּתּוֹרָה: אִם בְּחֻקֹּתַי תֵּלֵכוּ אַנְחִיל אֶתְכֶם טוּב הָעוֹלָם הַזֶּה,

---

12. This concept can be found in B'réshith Rabbah 12, 15: [This can be likened] to a king who had thin, delicate goblets. Said the king, "If I put hot liquids in them, they will crack; if I put cold liquids in them, they will buckle, warp." What did the king do? He mixed hot liquids with cold, and poured [that mixture] into them, and they held firm. So the Holy One, blessed is He, said: If I create the world with the quality of mercy, sin will abound; if with the quality of justice, how will the world endure? Then let Me create it with the qualities of both justice and mercy—and would that it stands firm!"

13. Mishnah, Avoth iv 17.

Someone might still ask, though, "In view of what you said, that the main part of all, the chosen portion, is the Israelite people, how can it be that since olden times they endure exile and troubles?"

The answer is that it is common knowledge, widespread among all the world's people, that the Lord of all created two worlds, a physical and a spiritual realm; and the physical world is reckoned as a worthless nothing in comparison with the spiritual realm: for this [earthly life] is as a passing shadow (Psalms 144:4), whereas that [realm] endures forever and ever. Therefore, since the soul is the important part of man, the enduring element in him that remains forever, while the body is only a vessel for the soul, which serves it a short time and then perishes and decomposes, the Lord gave His people the spiritual realm for their inheritance, as it is an eternal world, and its delight is beyond measure.

Someone might yet ask, "But why did God not give two portions to this people whom He chose: the pleasure of both the physical and the spiritual worlds?" The answer is that every intelligent person knows that a physical person cannot remain forever without sinning; and among the timeless attributes of God, blessed is He, is the quality of justice.[12] This is what impels every thinking being to go in an intelligent path [of life]. And should he stray, to become guilt-laden toward the [Divine] King, inasmuch as the quality of justice condemns him, it is impossible to let him off scot-free, since he has been deemed guilty by the court of the quality of justice. Therefore, in the Eternal Lord's loving-kindness toward us, He has made it our lot to be purified from the sin within us in this perishable, non-lasting world, so that our souls may be pure and everlasting in the spiritual world. For "one hour there is finer, better than all life on this world."[13]

However, we can trust that the time will come when we will attain the two portions, this being the time of the Messiah. The reason is that then, in those days, we will no longer need to have our bodies refined and purified at all—for the evil inclination will be made void in us, as it is written, *I will take away the stony heart out of your flesh* (Ezekiel 36:26). Even if some small impurity of sin will then remain, the guilt will be transferred onto the head of the scapegoat [sacrificed on the Day of Atonement] as in the early times [when the Holy Temple stood].

Hence it is written in the Torah, *If you will walk in my statutes* (Leviticus 26:3), I will have you inherit the good of this world. In

כְּלוֹמַר, אִם תִּהְיוּ שְׁלֵמִים וְלֹא תִהְיוּ צְרִיכִים לְצֵרוּף הַגּוּף תִּזְכּוּ אַף לְטוֹבַת הָעוֹלָם הַזֶּה. וְזֶהוּ שֶׁכָּתַב בְּאַבְרָהָם אָבִינוּ עָלָיו הַשָּׁלוֹם שֶׁבֵּרְכוֹ הַשֵּׁם בַּכֹּל אַף בְּטוֹבַת הָעוֹלָם הַזֶּה, שֶׁלֹּא נִצְטָרֵךְ בָּעֵת הַהִיא לְצֵרוּף הַגּוּף כְּלָל.

וְאַחֲרֵי זֹאת אֵין לִתְמֹהַּ בְּצַעֲרָן שֶׁל יִשְׂרָאֵל בַּגָּלֻיּוֹת יוֹתֵר מִכָּל הָאֻמּוֹת, כִּי הַכֹּל לְטוֹבָתָם וְלִכְבוֹדָם.

וְאַתָּה הַשּׁוֹאֵל, תֵּן עֵינֶיךָ וְלִבְּךָ עַל זֶה, כִּי דָבָר גָּדוֹל הוּא, לֹא יְבִינוּ אוֹתוֹ כָל רְשָׁעִים, וְהַמַּשְׂכִּילִים יָבִינוּ, כִּי הַרְבֵּה מִן הַיְּהוּדִים עֲנִיִּים בְּרֹב הַצָּרוֹת הַגְּדוֹלוֹת אֲשֶׁר תְּכָפוּם בַּגָּלֻיּוֹת, וְהֵם לֹא יָדְעוּ וְלֹא הֵבִינוּ אֶת טוּב עוֹלָם הַנְּשָׁמוֹת, כִּמְעַט נָטָיוּ רַגְלֵיהֶם בְּרֹב הַדְּאָגוֹת, וְלִבָּם לֹא נָכוֹן עִמָּם בְּרֹב רַעְיוֹנוֹת. הַשֵּׁם בַּחֲסָדָיו יַעֲבִיר מִלִּבֵּנוּ מַחְשְׁבוֹת אָוֶן וְיַשְׁפִּיעַ עָלֵינוּ שֵׂכֶל טוֹב וְדֵעוֹת נְכוֹנוֹת לְהַשְׁלִים חֶפְצוֹ, אָמֵן כֵּן יַעֲשֶׂה.

וְאִם יִשְׁאַל עוֹד: אַחַר שֶׁאָמַרְתָּ שֶׁעִקַּר הַכֹּל הוּא עוֹלָם הַנְּשָׁמוֹת וְסוֹף שְׂכַר הַמִּצְווֹת בּוֹ, לָמָּה לֹא יַזְכִּירֵנוּ בַּתּוֹרָה וְיֹאמַר: בַּעֲשׂוֹתְכֶם מִצְווֹתַי אַנְחִילְכֶם הָעוֹלָם הַבָּא? הַתְּשׁוּבָה, מִפְּנֵי שֶׁעִנְיַן הָעוֹלָם הַבָּא יָדוּעַ וְנִגְלֶה לְכָל בַּעַל שֵׂכֶל וּבָרוּר כַּשֶּׁמֶשׁ, אֵין כָּל אֻמָּה וְלָשׁוֹן שֶׁלֹּא יַסְכִּימוּ כִּי יֵשׁ לַנְּפָשׁוֹת הַשָּׁאֲרוּת אַחַר כְּלוֹת הַגּוּפִים, וְאֵין חוֹלֵק גַּם-כֵּן כִּי לְפִי טוֹבָתָהּ שֶׁל נֶפֶשׁ וְחָכְמָתָהּ וְכֹשֶׁר פְּעָלֶיהָ תַּעֲנוּגָהּ יוֹתֵר, כִּי מַחֲצָב הַנֶּפֶשׁ הַשִּׂכְלִית מִמּוֹצָא הַשֵּׂכֶל, וְכָל שֶׁמִּתְקָרֵב יוֹתֵר אֶל טִבְעוֹ, מָקוֹם שֶׁחֻצַּב מִמֶּנּוּ, תַּעֲנוּגוֹ יוֹתֵר.

אֵלֶּה הַדְּבָרִים אֵין צְרִיכִין חִזּוּק בִּרְאָיוֹת וְעֵדִים, הֵן הֵן עֵדֵיהֶם וּרְאָיוֹתֵיהֶם, מִשְׂכַל רִאשׁוֹן הֵן. וְעַל-כֵּן לֹא תַּאֲרִיךְ הַתּוֹרָה לְעוֹלָם בַּמֶּה שֶׁהוּא יָדוּעַ מִן הַסְּבָרָא

---

14. E.g. TB B'rachoth 35a, Shabbath 96b.

other words, if you will be perfect and will not require refining-purification of the body, you will attain the goodness of this world too. This is the significance of what Scripture writes of Abraham our father (peace be upon him), that the Eternal Lord blessed him "with everything" (Genesis 24:1): the Eternal Lord blessed him even with the good of this world, so that he had no need then of physical refinement [through suffering] at all.

Now, after this [explanation] one need not wonder at the suffering of Jewry in its exiles, more than all other nations. For it is all for their good and for their glory. And you, O questioner, set your eyes and heart [to meditate] on this, for it is an important matter which none among the wicked can understand, but only intelligent thinkers will grasp. Many among the Jews are poor and wretched amid all the multitude of great troubles that befall them continually in their exiles, and they have neither known nor understood the goodness of the spiritual world. Their feet have almost collapsed under the great mass of worries, and their heart (understanding) is not steadfast with them (Psalms 78:37), in their welter of troubling thoughts. May the Eternal Lord, in His kindness, remove evil, distressing thoughts from our heart and bestow upon us a flow of good intelligence and accurate views, to achieve His desire toward perfection. *Amen*, may He so do.

Now, someone might ask further, "Considering what you have said, that the most important thing is the spiritual world, and the ultimate reward for *mitzvoth* (religious good deeds) is [given] there, why does He not mention it in the Written Torah and say: If you observe My precepts, I will have you inherit [a share in] the world-to-come?" The answer is that the matter of the world-to-come is known and apparent to every intelligent person, being as clear as the sun. There is not one nation or people with a common language which is not in accord that there is survival for the soul after the body is gone; nor does anyone disagree that the greater the goodness of a soul, the greater its wisdom and the worthiness of its deeds, the greater is its [ultimate] pleasure. For the origin of the intelligent soul is from the source of intelligence, and the closer it gets to its natural habitat, from which it originated, the greater is its delight.

These concepts need no support by evidence and witnesses. They are their own witness and proof, being elementary. And so the Torah never adds words about what can be known by human reasoning, just as the Sages of blessed memory said in so many instances,[14] "This

הָאֱנוֹשִׁית, וְזֶהוּ אָמְרָם זִכְרוֹנָם לִבְרָכָה בְּכָל מָקוֹם, סְבָרָא הוּא, כְּלוֹמַר, וְאֵין צָרִיךְ קְרָא בְּמַה שֶּׁהַסְּבָרָא נוֹתֶנֶת.

וְעַל־כֵּן הִבְטִיחַתְנוּ הַתּוֹרָה בְּקִיּוּם הַמִּצְוֹת בָּעוֹלָם הַזֶּה, כְּלוֹמַר, שֶׁלֹּא נִהְיֶה טְרוּדִים בִּמְזוֹנוֹת וּבְמִלְחֶמֶת הָאוֹיְבִים, וְנוּכַל לְהִשְׁתַּדֵּל בַּעֲבוֹדַת הָאֵל וְנַשִּׂיג רְצוֹנוֹ. וְאֵין צָרִיךְ לְהַאֲרִיךְ עוֹד וְלוֹמַר: וּכְשֶׁתַּשִּׂיגוּ רְצוֹנוֹ תִּזְכּוּ לְתַעֲנוּג הָעוֹלָם הַבָּא, כִּי יָדוּעַ הַדָּבָר מֵאֵלָיו שֶׁכָּל נִבְרָא אֲשֶׁר יַשִּׂיג רְצוֹן בּוֹרְאוֹ יִתְעַלֶּה, יִתְקָרֵב אֵלָיו וְיִתְעַנֵּג בְּזִיווֹ.

וְעוֹד טַעַם אַחֵר, שֶׁאִלּוּ הִבְטִיחָה הַתּוֹרָה בִּגְמוּל הָעוֹלָם הַבָּא וְלֹא בָזֶה לֹא תִהְיֶה הַהַבְטָחָה נִרְאֵית בַּחַיִּים וְיִהְיֶה אוּלַי לֵב קְטַנֵּי אֲמָנָה נוֹקֵף בַּדְּבָרִים.

הַתּוֹרָה הַזֹּאת שֶׁאָמַרְנוּ שֶׁנִּתַּן הַשֵּׁם לְעַמּוֹ עַל־יַד מֹשֶׁה נְבִיאוֹ, מֵעִקָּרֶיהָ לָדַעַת כִּי הַשֵּׁם הָאֱלֹהִים אֲשֶׁר בַּשָּׁמַיִם מִמַּעַל שֶׁנָּתַן זֹאת הַתּוֹרָה לְיִשְׂרָאֵל, הוּא הַמָּצוּי הָרִאשׁוֹן שֶׁאֵין הַתְחָלָה וְתַכְלִית לִמְצִיאוּתוֹ בָּרוּךְ הוּא, וְשֶׁהוּא הַמַּמְצִיא וּבָרָא בִרְצוֹנוֹ וּבִיכָלְתּוֹ יֵשׁ מֵאַיִן כָּל הַנִּבְרָא, וְשֶׁיַּעֲמֹד קַיָּם כָּל מַה שֶּׁבָּרָא הַזְּמַן שֶׁיִּרְצֶה הוּא וְלֹא יוֹתֵר אֲפִלּוּ רֶגַע, וְשֶׁאֵין נִמְנָע לְפָנָיו לַעֲשׂוֹת כָּל דָּבָר; וּלְהַאֲמִין כִּי הוּא אֶחָד בְּלִי שׁוּם שִׁתּוּף; וּלְהַאֲמִין כִּי בְקִיּוּם הָאָדָם מַה שֶּׁכָּתוּב בָּהּ תִּזְכֶּה בָּהּ נַפְשׁוֹ לְתַעֲנוּג גָּדוֹל לְעוֹלָמִים וּלְהַאֲמִין כִּי הָאֵל מַשְׁגִּיחַ בְּמַעֲשֵׂה בְּנֵי־אָדָם וְיוֹדֵעַ כָּל פְּרָטֵי מַעֲשֵׂיהֶם וּמְשַׁלֵּם לְכָל אֶחָד לְפִי פְּעֻלָּתוֹ.

וּמֵעִקָּרֵי הַתּוֹרָה גַּם־כֵּן לְהַאֲמִין כִּי פֵּרוּשׁ הַתּוֹרָה הָאֲמִתִּי הוּא הַפֵּרוּשׁ הַמְקֻבָּל בְּיָדֵינוּ מֵחַכְמֵי יִשְׂרָאֵל הַקַּדְמוֹנִים, וְכָל שֶׁיְּפָרֵשׁ בָּהּ דָּבָר הֵפֶךְ כַּוָּנָתָם הוּא טָעוּת וְדָבָר בָּטֵל לְגַמְרֵי, לְפִי שֶׁחֲכָמֵינוּ קִבְּלוּ פֵּרוּשׁ הַתּוֹרָה מִמֹּשֶׁה רַבֵּנוּ עָלָיו הַשָּׁלוֹם,

---

15. Our author echoes here the frequent saying of Rav in TB B'rachoth 17a: In the world-to-come there will be no eating or drinking, no procreation or trading, no envy, hatred or rivalry, but only the righteous sitting, their crowns on their heads, and enjoying, thriving on the luster of the *shechinah*, the Divine Presence.
16. There would be nothing in this life to show it is true.

is a logical, reasonable tenet," meaning, there is no need for words of Scripture about what logic and reason dictate.

Therefore the Torah assured us about observing the precepts in this world: i.e. that we will not be harassed in [the earning of our] food or by war with enemies, and we will be able to strive in the worship of God and so achieve His will. But there was no need [for the Torah] to continue on and say, "and when you achieve His will you shall merit to attain the delight of the world-to-come." It is obvious that every created person who perceives the will of his Creator (be He exalted) will be drawn near to Him and will have pleasure in His splendor.[15]

Another reason [for Scripture's silence on the subject] is that if the Written Torah assured us of reward in the world-to-come and not [of reward] in this world, the assurance would not be realized in this life,[16] and the heart of those of small faith would perhaps have misgivings about these matters.

This Torah, which we said the Eternal Lord gave to His people through Moses His prophet, has as one of its main principles that we should know that the Lord God who is in heaven above, who gave this Torah to the Israelites, is the "first existent": there is no beginning or end to His existence (be He blessed). He brought all creation into existence, forming it by His will and His power, *creatio ex nihilo*, substance out of nothing. All that He created will stand and endure for as long as He wishes, and not an instant more. Nothing is withheld from Him, it is not beyond Him to do anything at all. And it is for us to believe that He is one; nothing, no entity in the world is joined to Him. It is for us to believe too, that by a man's fulfillment of what is written in it [in the Torah] his soul will merit great pleasure for eternity. It is for us to believe, further, that God observes the conduct of mankind and knows all the details of their deeds, and He rewards everyone according to his actions.

Among the main principles of the Torah is also [the requirement] to believe that the true sense of the Torah is the traditional, transmitted meaning (interpretation) that we possess, received of yore from the early Sages of Jewry. Anything in it which is explained in contradiction to their interpretation is erroneous and utterly worthless: For our Sages received the meaning of the Torah from Moses our master (peace be upon him), who received it in turn from the Eternal Lord,

שֶׁקִּבְּלוּ מֵאֵת הַשֵּׁם בָּרוּךְ הוּא כְּשֶׁעָמַד בַּשָּׁמַיִם אַרְבָּעִים יוֹם. וְאַף־עַל־פִּי שֶׁבִּזְמַן מוּעָט מִזֶּה הָיָה אֶפְשָׁר לִלְמֹד בְּכֹחַ הַמְלַמֵּד, רָצָה הַשֵּׁם לִרְמֹז לַלּוֹמְדִים שֶׁיִּלְמְדוּ בְּמָתוּן.

וְהַפֵּרוּשׁ הָאֲמִתִּי שֶׁאָמַרְנוּ הוּא הַפֵּרוּשׁ הַכָּתוּב בַּתַּלְמוּד הַבַּבְלִי וְהַיְרוּשַׁלְמִי שֶׁחִבְּרוּ חֲכָמֵינוּ הַקַּדְמוֹנִים, שֶׁקִּבְּלוּהוּ דּוֹר אַחַר דּוֹר מִמֹּשֶׁה רַבֵּנוּ עָלָיו הַשָּׁלוֹם. וְהַבַּבְלִי הוּא יוֹתֵר אָרֹךְ וּמְבֹאָר, וְעָלָיו אָנוּ סוֹמְכִים יוֹתֵר, וְהוּא עָשׂוּי לְשִׁשָּׁה סְדָרִים וְיֵשׁ בּוֹ שִׁשִּׁים מַסֶּכְתּוֹת לְפִי חִלּוּק הָעִנְיָנִים, סִימָנָם: שִׁשִּׁים הֵמָּה מְלָכוֹת, וְתקכ"ב פְּרָקִים. וְכֵן יִתְבָּאֵר פֵּרוּשׁ הַתּוֹרָה הָאֲמִתִּי מִסְּפָרִים אֲחֵרִים שֶׁחִבְּרוּ קְצָת מֵחֲכָמֵינוּ הַקַּדְמוֹנִים, וְנִקְרָאִים סִפְרָא וְסִפְרֵי וְתוֹסֶפְתָּא וּמְכִלְתָּא; כָּל אֵלֶּה סְפָרִים שֶׁכָּל יִשְׂרָאֵל מַאֲמִינִים בָּהֶם וְסוֹמְכִים עַל דִּבְרֵיהֶם בְּמַה שֶׁיִּהְיֶה שָׁם בְּלִי מַחֲלֹקֶת. וּבְמַה שֶׁיֵּשׁ בּוֹ מַחֲלֹקֶת כְּבָר פֵּרְשׁוּ הֵם גַּם־כֵּן הַהֶכְרֵעַ שֶׁנִּקַּח מֵהֶם, הַכֹּל מְבֹאָר יָפֶה בְּלִי שׁוּם סָפֵק וְעִרְבּוּב לַמְּבִינִים. וְכָל מִי שֶׁלִּבּוֹ נוֹקְפוֹ בְּעִנְיָנִים אֵלֶּה אֵינֶנּוּ בִּכְלָל עַם הַקֹּדֶשׁ, לְפִי שֶׁמִּפְשַׁט כּוֹתְבֵי הַתּוֹרָה בִּלְתִּי פֵּרוּשֵׁיהֶם וְקַבָּלָתָם הָאֲמִתִּיּוֹת לֹא נַסְכִּים אֶל הָאֱמֶת לְעוֹלָם, כִּי יֵשׁ כַּמָּה כְתוּבִים בַּתּוֹרָה נִרְאִים כְּסוֹתְרִים זֶה אֶת זֶה, וְיוֹדֵעַ פֵּרוּשָׁם יָבִין וְיִרְאֶה כִּי יְשָׁרִים דַּרְכֵי הַשֵּׁם.

הֲרֵי שֶׁכָּתוּב בַּתּוֹרָה: וּמוֹשַׁב בְּנֵי יִשְׂרָאֵל אֲשֶׁר יָשְׁבוּ בְמִצְרַיִם שְׁלֹשִׁים שָׁנָה וְאַרְבַּע מֵאוֹת שָׁנָה, וּמָצִינוּ בִּקְהָת בֶּן לֵוִי שֶׁהָיָה מִיּוֹרְדֵי מִצְרַיִם, וְאִם אַתָּה מוֹנֶה כָּל שְׁנֵי חַיָּיו וּשְׁנֵי חַיֵּי עַמְרָם בְּנוֹ וּשְׁמוֹנִים שָׁנָה שֶׁל מֹשֶׁה—שֶׁהָיָה בֶּן שְׁמֹנִים בְּעָמְדוֹ לִפְנֵי פַרְעֹה לְדַבֵּר אֵלָיו לְהוֹצִיא אֶת בְּנֵי יִשְׂרָאֵל מִמִּצְרַיִם—לֹא יַעֲלוּ כֻלָּם כִּי אִם ש"נ שָׁנָה; אֶלָּא שֶׁבָּא הַפֵּרוּשׁ עַל זֶה דְּמִשָּׁעָה שֶׁנֶּאֱמַר לְאַבְרָהָם "כִּי גֵר יִהְיֶה זַרְעֲךָ" מַתְחִיל חֶשְׁבּוֹן הַת"ל שָׁנָה, וּפֵרוּשׁ הַפָּסוּק כֵּן: וּמוֹשַׁב בְּנֵי יִשְׂרָאֵל

---

17. *Mechilta* is an early Midrash on the Book of Exodus, containing much material on Jewish law. On the other works, see "A foreword by the author," note 3.

18. When the stay of the Israelites in Egypt began.

19. Kohath lived 133 years (Exodus 6:18), and his son Amram 137 years (*ibid.* 20). Thus 133 plus 137 plus 80 total 350. This assumes that Kohath was born when Jacob and his sons entered Egypt, and thus lived all his life there. But even so, the calculation is unrealistically maximal, for as Rashi to Exodus 12:40 and TB Megillah 9a (s.v. *u-vish'ar*) points out, Amram was not born the day Kohath died, nor Moses the day Amram died. Hence many of the years of their lives overlapped. The calculation merely proves that the verse cannot be taken at face value.

be He blessed, when he stayed in heaven forty days (Exodus 24:18). Even though it was possible to learn [it all] in less time than that through the power of the [Divine] Teacher, the Eternal Lord wished to indicate to [future] students that they should learn [the Torah] slowly, patiently. This true meaning that we have mentioned is the interpretation written in the Babylonian and Jerusalem Talmuds, which our early Sages composed, having received it, through generation after generation, from Moses our master (peace be upon him).

The Babylonian Talmud is larger and clearer [than the Jerusalem Talmud], and on it we rely the more. It is arranged in six orders, and contains sixty tractates, according to divisions by their subject matter. The mnemonic sign for them is the verse, *There are sixty queens* (Song of Songs 6:8). And [they contain] 522 chapters.

The true meaning of the Torah also becomes clear from other works, which some of our early Sages composed, known as the *Sifra*, *Sifre*, *Tosefta*, and *Mechilta*.[17] These are works which all Jewry accepts as true, relying on their words in all matters that they contain about which there is no division of opinion. Where there are opposing views, they [the Sages] explained what conclusion we must derive from them, all being splendidly clarified, with no doubt or confusion left for those with understanding.

Anyone whose heart is troubled with misgivings or qualms about these matters is not to be included in this holy people. For by the simple, literal meaning of the verses of the Written Torah, without their interpretations and true traditions, we can never reach conclusions of truth. There are many verses in Scripture which appear to contradict one another; yet one who knows their true interpretation understands and sees that *the ways of the Lord are right* (Hosea 14:10).

Thus it is written in the Torah, *the time that the children of Israel dwelt in Egypt was four hundred and thirty years* (Exodus 12:40). Yet we find that Kohath the son of Levi was among those who went down [from Canaan to Egypt][18] (Genesis 46:11), and if you count all the years of his life and the years of his son Amram's life, and the eighty years of Moses [Amram's son]—for he was eighty when he stood before Pharaoh to speak to him to send the Israelites out of Egypt (Exodus 7:7)—they will all total no more than 350 years.[19] The explanation given for this, however, is that from the time Abraham was told, *Know, O know that your progeny will be alien sojourners in a land that is not theirs* (Genesis 15:13), the reckoning of the 430 years

ספר החינוך PREFACE

אֲשֶׁר יָשְׁבוּ בְּמִצְרַיִם וּבִשְׁאָר אֲרָצוֹת, כְּלוֹמַר שֶׁהִתְחִילוּ לִגְלוֹת, ת"ל שָׁנָה, דְּמִשָּׁעָה שֶׁנֶּאֱמַר לוֹ לְאַבְרָהָם "כִּי גֵר יִהְיֶה זַרְעֲךָ" וְגוֹ' הִתְחִיל עָלָיו הַצַּעַר, וּמִשָּׁם הַתְחָלַת הַחֶשְׁבּוֹן.

וְאַל יַקְשֶׁה עָלֶיךָ אָמְרוֹ "בְּנֵי יִשְׂרָאֵל", שֶׁהֲרֵי אָמְרוּ בַּמִּדְרָשׁ: אַבְרָהָם נִקְרָא יִשְׂרָאֵל, שֶׁנֶּאֱמַר: וּמוֹשַׁב בְּנֵי יִשְׂרָאֵל. וּמַה שֶּׁאָמַר בְּנֵי יִשְׂרָאֵל, כְּלוֹמַר בְּנֵי יִשְׂרָאֵל וְיִשְׂרָאֵל, אֲבָל מִפְּנֵי שֶׁהִתְחִיל לָאָב הַצַּעַר בִּבְשׂוֹרַת גָּלוּת הַבָּנִים הוֹצִיאוּ הַכָּתוּב בְּלָשׁוֹן זֶה.

וּמַה שֶּׁאָמַר "בְּמִצְרַיִם" גַּם כֵּן לָאו דַּוְקָא, אֶלָּא כְּלוֹמַר בַּגָּלוּת, וּמַה שֶּׁהוֹצִיא הַכֹּל בִּלְשׁוֹן מִצְרַיִם לְפִי שֶׁשָּׁם הָיָה עִקַּר הַגָּלוּת, וְאַחַר הָעִקָּר הַכֹּל הוֹלֵךְ וְעָלָיו נִקְרָא לְעוֹלָם.

וְכֵן כְּתִיב בַּתּוֹרָה: בְּשִׁבְעִים נֶפֶשׁ יָרְדוּ אֲבֹתֶיךָ מִצְרָיְמָה, וּכְשֶׁאַתָּה מוֹנֶה פְּרָטָן תִּמְצָא ס"ט נְפָשׁוֹת: אֶלָּא שֶׁבָּא הַפֵּרוּשׁ שֶׁיּוֹכֶבֶד נוֹלְדָה בֵּין הַחוֹמוֹת וְלֹא נֶחְשְׁבָה בִּפְרָט.

וְכֵן כָּתוּב אֶחָד אוֹמֵר: שִׁבְעַת יָמִים תֹּאכַל מַצּוֹת, וְכָתוּב אֶחָד אוֹמֵר: שֵׁשֶׁת יָמִים, וְכָאֵלֶּה יֵשׁ רַבִּים, לֹא יִתְבָּאֵר פִּתְרוֹנָם לְעוֹלָם כִּי אִם בְּפֵרוּשׁ הַתּוֹרָה הַמְּקֻבָּל בְּיָדֵינוּ מִמֹּשֶׁה רַבֵּינוּ עָלָיו הַשָּׁלוֹם שֶׁנְּתָנָהּ לָנוּ.

וְעַתָּה דַּע לְךָ לְפִי מַה שֶּׁקִּבַּלְנוּ מֵחֲכָמֵינוּ לִבְרָכָה וּמִפֵּרוּשֵׁיהֶם, כִּי חֶשְׁבּוֹן הַמִּצְוֹת הַנּוֹהֲגוֹת לְדוֹרוֹת שֶׁנִּכְלְלוּ בְּסֵפֶר הַתּוֹרָה שֶׁנָּתַן לָנוּ הַשֵּׁם יִתְעַלֶּה עוֹלֶה תרי"ג מִצְוֹת, בֵּין אוֹתָן שֶׁצִּוָּה לָנוּ לַעֲשׂוֹת וְאוֹתָן שֶׁהִזְהִירָנוּ שֶׁלֹּא לַעֲשׂוֹת, כִּי הַכֹּל נִקְרָאִים מִצְוֹת וְאוֹתָן שֶׁצִּוָּה לַעֲשׂוֹת עוֹלֶה חֶשְׁבּוֹנָן רמ"ח, וְשֶׁלֹּא לַעֲשׂוֹת עוֹלֶה שס"ה.

וּמֵהֶן שֶׁחַיָּבִין בָּהֶן כָּל יִשְׂרָאֵל בִּכְלָלָם זְכָרִים וּנְקֵבוֹת בְּכָל מָקוֹם וּבְכָל זְמַן,

20. A *baraitha* (external tannaitic teaching) in TB Megillah 9a recounts that this is how seventy Jewish scholars translated the verse for King Ptolemy—so that he should not think Scripture erroneous (and it is indeed so rendered in the Septuagint). The verse is similarly interpreted in Mechilta; TJ Megillah i 9; Tanḥuma ed. Buber, *sh'moth* 19; etc.

21. B'réshith Rabbah 63, 3: Abraham was called Israel. R. Nathan said: This is a profound thought [derived reconditely from the verse] *And the time that the children of Israel dwelt in Egypt* and in the land of Canaan and in the land of Goshen *was four hundred and thirty years.*

22. So Midrash haḤéfetz (MS): *And the time that the children of Israel dwelt*: its meaning is "and in other places"—the land of the Philistines and the land of Goshen. In that case, why does it say "in Egypt"?—because that was the hard, difficult greatest part [of the exile] (*Torah Shelemah*, Exodus 12 §601 note).

23. TB Bava Bathra 123b; B'réshith Rabbah 94, 15; Bamidbar Rabbah 13, 20; P'sikta d'R. Kahana 10 (86b); Midrash Sh'muel 32, 3. (The difficulty resolved here is that Jacob left Canaan with sixty-nine people, listed in Genesis 46:8–27; yet the last verse concludes that he arrived in Egypt with seventy.)

⟨74⟩

was begun. Then the meaning of the verse is this: *the time that the children of Israel dwelt in Egypt* and in other lands—i.e. [from the time] that they began to be exiled—*was four hundred and thirty years*.[20] For from the time Abraham was told that *your progeny will be alien sojourners*, etc. the pain [of this edict] began for him; and so the beginning of the reckoning is from that point.

Nor should it be a difficulty for you that the verse states "the children of *Israel*": for it is asserted in the Midrash,[21] "Abraham was called Israel, for it is stated: *the time that the children of Israel dwelt*." Scripture's words "the children of Israel" denote the Israelites and Israel [Jacob, their ancestor]; but because the anguish began for the Patriarch [Abraham] with the [Divine] prediction of the exile of the children, Scripture used this expression particularly to allude to him.

As to the phrase "in Egypt," it is not meant rigorously, exclusively, but in the sense of exile. The reason for conveying the entire [exile] by the term "Egypt" is that there the main part of the exile was spent, and the whole is included under the main part, always being called by its name.[22]

Thus too it is written in the Torah, *With seventy souls (persons) your forefathers went down to Egypt* (Deuteronomy 10:22); yet when you count them in detail, you find sixty-nine souls. But the explanation is given that Yocheved [Moses' mother] was born between the walls [the outer and inner wall of Egypt] and was not listed individually.[23]

So too, one verse of Scripture states, *Seven days shall you eat matzah, unleavened bread* (Exodus 12:15), and one verse states, *Six days* (Deuteronomy 16:8);[24] and there are many such instances, whose solution could never become clear except by the traditional body of interpretation of the Torah transmitted to us from Moses our master (peace be upon him), who gave it to us.

Now know that according to the tradition we have received from our Sages of blessed memory, and from their interpretations, the sum of the *mitzvoth* (precepts) which remain in effect for all generations, that are included in the Torah scroll which the Eternal Lord (be He exalted) gave us, amounts to 613 precepts, including both those which He commanded us to do and those which He warned us not to do—for all are called *mitzvoth*. Those things which He commanded us to do total 248 in number, and [what He commanded us] not to do total 365.[25]

There are those among them which every Jew generally, man

ספר החינוך PREFACE

וּמֵהֶן שֶׁאֵין חַיָּבִין בָּהֶם אֶלָּא יִשְׂרְאֵלִים בְּכָל מָקוֹם וּבְכָל זְמַן וְלֹא כֹהֲנִים וּלְוִיִּם. וְיֵשׁ שֶׁאֵין חַיָּבִין בָּהֶם אֶלָּא לְוִיִּם לְבַד, וְיֵשׁ שֶׁאֵין חַיָּבִין בָּהֶם אֶלָּא כֹהֲנִים לְבַד בְּכָל מָקוֹם וּבְכָל זְמַן. וְיֵשׁ שֶׁאֵין חַיָּב בָּהֶן אֶלָּא מֶלֶךְ יִשְׂרָאֵל לְבַד. וּמֵהֶן שֶׁאֵין חַיָּב בָּהֶן יָחִיד לְבַד אֶלָּא הַצִּבּוּר כֻּלָּם. וּמֵהֶן מִצְווֹת שֶׁאֵין חַיָּבִין בָּהֶן יִשְׂרָאֵל אֶלָּא בְּמָקוֹם יָדוּעַ וּבִזְמַן יָדוּעַ, וְהוּא אֶרֶץ יִשְׂרָאֵל וּבִזְמַן שֶׁרֹב יִשְׂרָאֵל שָׁם. וּבְאוֹתוֹ מָקוֹם וּבְאוֹתוֹ זְמַן יֵשׁ חִלּוּק גַּם-כֵּן בְּמִצְווֹת יְדוּעוֹת בֵּין אֲנָשִׁים לְנָשִׁים וּבֵין יִשְׂרְאֵלִים לְכֹהֲנִים וּלְוִיִּם.

וּמִן הַמִּצְווֹת אֵלּוּ יֵשׁ שֶׁאָדָם חַיָּב בָּהֶן לָקוּם וְלַעֲשׂוֹתָן בְּהַתְמָדָה, כְּגוֹן מִצְוַת אַהֲבַת הַשֵּׁם וְיִרְאָתוֹ וְכַיּוֹצֵא בָם. וְיֵשׁ שֶׁחַיָּב לָקוּם וְלַעֲשׂוֹתָן בִּזְמַן יָדוּעַ וְלֹא קֹדֶם לָכֵן, כְּגוֹן מִצְוַת סֻכָּה וְלוּלָב וְשׁוֹפָר וּשְׁבִיתַת הַמּוֹעֲדִים וּקְרִיאַת שְׁמַע, וְכָל כַּיּוֹצֵא בָהֶן, שֶׁיֵּשׁ לָהֶן זְמַן קָבוּעַ לַעֲשׂוֹתָן בַּשָּׁנָה אוֹ בַיּוֹם.

וְיֵשׁ מֵהֶן שֶׁאֵין אָדָם חַיָּב לַעֲשׂוֹתָן לְעוֹלָם אֶלָּא-אִם-כֵּן תִּהְיֶה סִבָּה שֶׁתָּבוֹא לְיָדוֹ עִנְיָן שֶׁיִּצְטָרֵךְ לַעֲשׂוֹת בּוֹ אוֹתָהּ מִצְוָה הָרְאוּיָה לְאוֹתוֹ עִנְיָן, כְּאִלּוּ תֹּאמַר שֶׁנְּתִינַת שָׂכָר שָׂכִיר בִּזְמַנּוֹ מִצְוָה אַחַת, וּבְוַדַּאי אֵין אָדָם חַיָּב לִשְׂכֹּר פּוֹעֲלִים כְּדֵי לְקַיֵּם מִצְוָה זוֹ, וְכֵן קְצָת כַּיּוֹצֵא בָהּ כְּמוֹ שֶׁנִּתְבָּרֵר הַכֹּל בְּעֶזְרַת הַשֵּׁם עַל כָּל מִצְוָה וּמִצְוָה שֶׁנִּכְתֹּב.

וְאַחַת מִן הַמִּצְווֹת וְהִיא עִקָּר וִיסוֹד שֶׁכֻּלָּן נִשְׁעָנוֹת עָלָיו הִיא מִצְוַת לִמּוּד הַתּוֹרָה, כִּי בַלִּמּוּד יֵדַע הָאָדָם הַמִּצְווֹת וִיקַיֵּם אוֹתָן. וְעַל-כֵּן קָבְעוּ לָנוּ חֲכָמֵינוּ זִכְרוֹנָם לִבְרָכָה לִקְרוֹת חֵלֶק אֶחָד מִסֵּפֶר הַתּוֹרָה בִּמְקוֹם קִבּוּץ הָעָם שֶׁהוּא בֵּית הַכְּנֶסֶת לְעוֹרֵר לֵב הָאָדָם עַל דִּבְרֵי הַתּוֹרָה וְהַמִּצְווֹת בְּכָל שָׁבוּעַ וְשָׁבוּעַ עַד שֶׁיִּגָּמְרוּ כָּל הַסֵּפֶר. וּלְפִי מַה שֶּׁשָּׁמַעְנוּ רֹב יִשְׂרָאֵל נוֹהֲגִים הַיּוֹם לִקְרוֹתוֹ כֻלּוֹ בְּשָׁנָה אֶחָת.

24. Mechilta on the first verse, which continues: How can both these verses be reconciled? This seventh day [of Passover] was included, and then was excluded [from the rule]—in order to teach us about the rule as a whole: Just as on the seventh day it is a voluntary matter [to eat *matzah*, not obligatory, since the day is excluded in the second verse] so are all [the seven days of Passover] a voluntary period [when *matzah* may be eaten or not]. (So too a *baraitha* in TB P'saḥim 120a. Mechilta adds that the first evening of Passover is an exception: Exodus 12:18 makes it obligatory to eat *matzah* then. In the introduction to Midrash Sifra, R. Ishmael lists thirteen rules or ways by which Scripture may be interpreted to understand its precepts; the eighth way is: Whatever is first included in a rule and then taken out of the rule to teach [us something about it], it was taken out to teach not only about itself, but about the rule as a whole.)

These three difficulties in Scripture and their resolutions in the Oral Tradition are given earlier in the Preface to R. Moses of Couçy, *Séfer Mitzvoth Gadol*.

25. See "The order and reckoning of the *mitzvoth*," note 1.

26. Cf. Rambam MT *hilchoth t'fillah* xiii 1: The common, widespread custom in all Jewry is that the Torah [reading] is completed in one year. . . . There are those

⟨76⟩

and woman, is duty-bound to observe, in every place and every time, but not *kohanim* or Levites. There are those which Levites alone are required to keep; there are some which none but *kohanim* are required to keep—in every place and every time. And there are others whose obligation is imposed on the king of Israel alone. Then there are some which an individual alone is not required to observe, but only the community as a whole. Among them [the 613 precepts] there are also some which a Jew is obligated to observe only in a certain place and at a certain time—i.e. in the land of Israel, and at the time when most of the Israelites (Jewry) are there. Then again, in any one place and one time, there is a difference in the obligation of certain precepts between man and woman, and between ordinary Israelites and *kohanim* and Levites.

Among these precepts, too, there are some which a man is required to arise and observe with constancy, such as the *mitzvah* of loving the Eternal Lord (§418), and reverently fearing Him (§432), and so on. Others require that we arise and do them at a certain time and not before—such as the precept of *sukkah* (§ 325), the *lulav* (palm branch, § 324), *shofar* (ram's horn, § 405), resting from work on the holy days (§§ 297, 300, etc.), reciting the *Sh'ma* (§ 420), and so on—which have a set time for observing them during the year or the day.

There are still others which a man is never required to do, unless some special circumstance comes to hand, some situation in which a particular *mitzvah*, appropriate to that situation, needs to be done. Thus we say that giving a hired man his pay at its proper time (§ 230) is one precept [of the 613]; but certainly a person is not duty-bound to hire workers in order to fulfill this precept; and so too some others, as we will clarify completely, with the Eternal Lord's help, at each and every precept that we will write.

One of the *mitzvoth*, which is a main principle and foundation on which all [the precepts] rest, is the *mitzvah* of learning Torah (§ 419). For by study, a man will know the precepts and will fulfill them. For this reason our Sages of blessed memory made it a rule for us to read one portion of the Torah scroll in a place where the people gather, i.e. the synagogue, to awaken a man's heart over the Torah's words and the precepts—so every single week [on the Sabbath], until the entire scroll is completed. According to what we have heard, most of Jewry have the custom nowadays of reading it in entirety in one year.[26]

ספר החינוך   PREFACE

וְעוֹד חִיְּבוּנוּ חֲכָמֵינוּ זִכְרוֹנָם לִבְרָכָה לִקְרוֹתוֹ כָּל אֶחָד וְאֶחָד מִיִּשְׂרָאֵל בְּבֵיתוֹ בְּכָל שָׁבוּעַ וְשָׁבוּעַ כְּמוֹ שֶׁקּוֹרִין אוֹתוֹ בִּמְקוֹם הַקִּבּוּץ, וְזֶהוּ אָמְרָם זִכְרוֹנָם לִבְרָכָה: לְעוֹלָם יַשְׁלִים אָדָם פָּרָשִׁיּוֹתָיו עִם הַצִּבּוּר, כְּדֵי שֶׁיַּשְׂכִּיל בַּדְּבָרִים יוֹתֵר בְּקָרְאוֹ אוֹתוֹ בְּבֵיתוֹ.

וְעַתָּה בִּהְיוֹת תרי״ג מִצְוֹת שֶׁבַּסֵּפֶר מְפֻזָּרוֹת בְּתוֹכוֹ הִנֵּה וָהֵנָּה בְּתוֹךְ סִפּוּרִים אֲחֵרִים שֶׁנִּכְתְּבוּ בַסֵּפֶר לְעִקָּר גָּדוֹל וּלְצֹרֶךְ שֶׁיֵּשׁ לִמְצֹא בָהֶם, אוּלַי לֹא יִתֵּן לִבּוֹ הַקּוֹרֵא בְחֶמְדּוֹ לִרְאוֹת כַּמָּה מִצְווֹת קָרָא בְּאוֹתוֹ שָׁבוּעַ וְלֹא יָעִיר לִבּוֹ לְזָרֵז עַצְמוֹ בָּהֶם. עַל־כֵּן רָאִיתִי טוֹב אֲנִי הַדַּל בְּאַלְפֵי תַּלְמִידֵי הַתַּלְמִידִים שֶׁבִּזְמַנִּי, אִישׁ יְהוּדִי מִבֵּית לֵוִי, בַּרְצְלוֹנִי, לִכְתֹּב הַמִּצְווֹת עַל דֶּרֶךְ הַסְּדָרִים וְכַסֵּדֶר שֶׁנִּכְתְּבוּ בַּתּוֹרָה זוֹ אַחַר זוֹ לְעוֹרֵר לֵב הַנַּעַר בְּנִי וְהַיְלָדִים חֲבֵרָיו בְּכָל שָׁבוּעַ וְשָׁבוּעַ, אַחַר שֶׁיִּלְמְדוּ הַסֵּדֶר, בְּחֶשְׁבּוֹן הַמִּצְווֹת, וּלְהַרְגִּיל אוֹתָם בָּהֶן וּלְהִתְפִּיס מַחְשְׁבוֹתָם בְּמַחֲשֶׁבֶת טְהוֹרָה וְחֶשְׁבּוֹן שֶׁל עִקָּר טֶרֶם שֶׁיַּכְנִיסוּ בְלִבָּם חֶשְׁבּוֹנוֹת שֶׁל שְׂחוֹק וְשֶׁל מַה־לְּךָ וּמַה־בְּכָךְ, וְגַם כִּי יַזְקִינוּ לֹא יָסוּרוּ מִמֶּנּוּ.

וְדַעְתִּי לִכְתֹּב עַל כָּל אַחַת רֶמֶז אֶחָד מִשָּׁרְשֵׁי הַמִּצְווֹת, הַנִּגְלֶה בַּכָּתוּב אֶכְתֹּב כְּמוֹת שֶׁהוּא, וּבַסָּתוּם אַגִּיד מַה שֶּׁשָּׁמַעְתִּי בּוֹ מִפִּי חֲכָמִים וּמַה שֶׁאָבִינָה בַדְּבָרִים. וְאֵינֶנִּי חוֹשֵׁב וְגוֹזֵר לְהַגִּיעַ אֶל הָאֱמֶת עַל־כָּל־פָּנִים, כִּי מִי כָמוֹנִי תּוֹלַעַת וְלֹא אִישׁ שֶׁלֹּא רָאִיתִי מְאוֹרוֹת חָכְמָה כָּל הַיָּמִים לְהָרִים יָד בַּמֶּה שֶׁלֹּא הִשִּׂיגוּ חֲכָמִים מְחֻכָּמִים. אָמְנָה לֹא חָסַרְתִּי דַעַת כִּי הַגְּמַלִּים לֹא יוּכְלוּן שְׂאֵת מַשָּׂא הַגְּמַלִּים, וְקָטָן שֶׁאֵינוֹ יוֹדֵעַ לְמִי מְבָרְכִין לֹא יִדְרֹשׁ בְּמַעֲשֵׂה מֶרְכָּבָה וְסוֹד חַשְׁמַלִּים, אֶלָּא שֶׁרַב חִשְׁקִי לִטְבֹּל קְצֵה הַמַּטֶּה בְּיַעֲרַת דְּבַשׁ הַמִּצְווֹת דִּתְחַקְנִי לִפְנֵס בְּיַעַר שֶׁאֵין לוֹ

---

who complete the Torah [reading once] in three years, but it is not a widespread practice. (According to TB Bava Kamma 82a, Torah reading on the Sabbath was instituted by the prophets.)

27. TB B'rachoth 8a.

28. I.e. keep pace with the congregational reading in his private study. As R. Yonah explains in his commentary, one should finish each *sidrah* at home before it is read in the synagogue.

29. The author echoes here two passages from the Talmud: (1) A child who knows to whom the benedictions of grace are said, may be included in a group saying grace (TB B'rachoth 48a). (2) A certain child was holding forth about the electrum [in Ezekiel's vision], and a fire came out of electrum and consumed him (TB Hagigah 13a).

30. Expression based on I Samuel 14:27.

⟨78⟩

In addition, our Sages of blessed memory have given us the obligation that every single person in Jewry should read it in his house every week, as it is read in the place of assembly.[27] This is what they meant when they said, "A man should ever complete his portions [of the Torah] with the congregation"[28]—so that he will gain more understanding of the words, as he reads it in his house.

Now, the 613 precepts in the scroll are scattered through it, here and there, amid other narratives that were written in the Book for the great doctrine and essential lessons that can be found in them. Hence in his innocent unawareness, perhaps the reader will not give his attention to see how many precepts he has read in that week, and may not bestir his heart to become alert and zealous about them. Therefore have I seen fit—I, the least of my group, a pupil of the students of my time, a Jew of the house of Lévi [a Levite] of the city of Barcelona [Spain]—to write the precepts according to the *sidroth* (the weekly portions) and in their sequence as they are written in the Torah, consecutively, in order to arouse (attract) the heart of my young son and the youngest [who are] his friends—every single week, after they learn the *sidrah*—in the reckoning of the precepts, in order to make them familiar with them and to fasten their thinking onto pure (holy) thought and the reckoning of important things, before they gather into their hearts reckonings of foolery, triviality and insignificance. For then even when they are old, they will not depart from it (Proverbs 22:6).

It is my intention to write about each *mitzvah* one implication or thought out of the root reasons for the precepts. What is revealed in the Holy Writ, I will set down in writing as it is [explained in Scripture]; and about whatever was left unrevealed, I will relate what I have heard from the mouths of Torah scholars, and what I understand of these matters. I do not intend or wish imperiously to arrive at the indisputable truth. For who am I, *a worm and not a man* (Psalms 22:7), who have not seen the radiances of wisdom all the days [of my life], to raise a hand [arrogantly] toward what learned scholars failed to grasp? In truth I have not failed to realize that ants cannot carry the burden of camels, and a child who does not know to whom the benedictions are said should not hold forth about the theme of the chariot (Ezekiel 1) and the secret of the electrums (e.g. *ibid.* 4).[29] It is only that my abounding desire to "dip the end of the staff in the honeycomb"[30] of the precepts has impelled me to enter the boundless forest, with

תְּחוּמִין, עִם דַּעְתִּי שֶׁהַרְבֵּה גְּדוֹלִים נִכְנְסוּ שָׁם וְהוֹצִיאוּ פְּחָמִין. אַךְ אָמַרְתִּי: מִי יִתֵּן וּתְהִי מַחֲשַׁבְתִּי נִטְרֶדֶת בָּזֶה כָּל הַיָּמִים, וְלֹא תִפָּסֵל וְתִפָּגֵם בִּמְזִמּוֹת עָמָל וָאָוֶן כְּמוֹ רְשָׁעִים אֲשֵׁמִים, וְכַחוֹתָם עַל יַד יָמִינִי אֲשִׂים אוֹתָן, וְכָל מַעְיָנַי אָשִׂים כָּל הַיּוֹם בַּעֲבוֹדָתָן, אֶעֱשֶׂה לָהֶן בִּלְבָבִי בַּיִת נֶאֱמָן מוֹשָׁב אֵיתָן, וְיֶתֶר מַעֲשַׂי כֻּלָּן אֲכִילָה וּשְׁתִיָּה וְעֵסֶק אֲנָשִׁים וְנָשִׁים דַּיָּן שְׁעָתָן.

הֲלֹא כֻלָּן צְרוּפוֹת וּטְהוֹרוֹת, כָּל אֶבֶן יְקָרָה מְסֻכָּתָן. [וְ]אִם בַּמֶּה שֶׁיִּכָּתֵב בְּפֵרוּשָׁן פְּסֹלֶת נִמְצָא לְעִתִּים, יִתְבָּרֵר הָאֹכֶל מִתּוֹכוֹ לְשָׁמְעָן, וְהוּא חוֹזֵר לְבֵית הַבְּעָלִים. וְהָרוֹצֶה לִסְעֹד אֶצְלִי יֹאכַל הַבָּשָׂר וְיַנִּיחַ בַּשֻּׁלְחָן עֲצָמוֹת וּקְלִפִּין.

וְרֹאשׁ דְּבָרַי אֲנִי מַזְכִּיר עָלַי לִזְכוּת מַה שֶּׁאָמְרוּ עָלַי רַבּוֹתַי: כָּל פְּטָטַיָּא בִּישִׁין וּפְטָטְיָא דְּאוֹרָיְתָא טָבִין. וְעוֹד דָּרְשׁוּ רַבּוֹתֵינוּ זִכְרוֹנָם לִבְרָכָה לְחַזֵּק לֵב הַלָּמֵד: וְדִגְלוֹ עָלַי אַהֲבָה, לְגִלְגּוּלוֹ עָלַי אַהֲבָה.

---

31. After Ezekiel 28:13.

32. TJ B'rachoth, end. *P'né Mosheh* comments: for as long as one meditates on them [the Torah's words] he will find meaning in them. (In quoting this passage, our author had a precedent to follow: It was quoted earlier by R. Z'raḥyah haLévi at the close of his introduction to his *Séfer haMe'oroth*.)

33. The letter *da-leth* being considered interchangeable with the *la-med*, R. Issachar in the Midrash finds in the word *diglo* a suggestion of *liglugo*, "his ludicrous babbling." Hence he interprets: If a child reads *Musheh* (or *Masheh*) for *Mosheh* (Moses), *Aharun* (or *Haran*) for Aaron, or *Efrun* for Efron—the Holy One, blessed is He, says, "his babbling is precious to me" (Shir haShirim Rabbah 2:4).

⟨80⟩

[despite] my knowing that many great men entered there and brought forth [mere] charcoal.

I but thought, "How I wish my mind would be occupied with this all the days [of my life], and should not become spoiled and blemished by schemes of evil and wrongdoing, like [the minds of] the wicked laden with guilt. *As a signet-ring on my right hand* (Jeremiah 22:24) will I set them [the precepts], and all my wellsprings [of energy] will I put at their service the entire day. In my heart I will make for them a sure, trusty home, a firm, enduring dwelling-place. For the rest of my activities—eating and drinking, business with men and women—whatever time is spent on them is enough for them.

Certainly [the precepts] are all refined and pure; "every precious stone is their covering."[31] If any "rubbish" should be found at times in what will be written in their explanation, the "good food" [useful parts, written] aptly, should be selected out, and let the rest return to its owner's home. Anyone who wishes to dine at my home can eat the meat and leave on the table the bones and shells.

In this preface of mine let me mention, to justify myself, what my Torah masters said: All prattle is bad, but the prattle of Torah is good.[32] Our Sages of blessed memory taught further, to encourage and hearten the student: *v'diglo* (his banner) *over me is love* (Song of Songs 2:4)— *liglugo*, his [a child's] babbling [of Scripture's words] is beloved to Me.[33]

סֵפֶר בְּרֵאשִׁית

וְאֵלֶּה סִדְרֵי הַשָּׁנָה שֶׁהַמִּצְוֹת בָּהֶן לְפִי חֶשְׁבּוֹן הָרַב הַגָּדוֹל נוֹדַע לְרֹב חָכְמָה וּמַעֲלָה בְּעַצְמוֹ רַבֵּנוּ מֹשֶׁה בַּר מַיְמוֹן זִכְרוֹנוֹ לִבְרָכָה

בְּרֵאשִׁית

[מִצְוַת פְּרִיָּה וּרְבִיָּה]

א יֵשׁ בָּהּ מִצְוַת עֲשֵׂה אַחַת, וְהִיא מִצְוַת פְּרִיָּה וּרְבִיָּה, שֶׁנֶּאֱמַר: וַיְבָרֶךְ אֹתָם אֱלֹהִים וַיֹּאמֶר לָהֶם אֱלֹהִים פְּרוּ וּרְבוּ.

מִשָּׁרְשֵׁי מִצְוָה זוֹ כְּדֵי שֶׁיִּהְיֶה הָעוֹלָם מְיֻשָּׁב, שֶׁהַשֵּׁם בָּרוּךְ הוּא חָפֵץ בְּיִשּׁוּבוֹ, כְּדִכְתִיב: לֹא תֹהוּ בְרָאָהּ לָשֶׁבֶת יְצָרָהּ. וְהִיא מִצְוָה גְּדוֹלָה שֶׁבִּסְבָתָהּ מִתְקַיְּמוֹת כָּל הַמִּצְוֹת בָּעוֹלָם, כִּי לִבְנֵי אָדָם נִתְּנוּ וְלֹא לְמַלְאֲכֵי הַשָּׁרֵת.

דִּינֵי הַמִּצְוָה מָתַי חַיָּב אָדָם לַעֲסֹק בָּהּ, וְכַמָּה בָנִים יִהְיוּ לוֹ וְיִפָּטֵר, וּמֵאֵי זֶה מִצְוֹת הוּא פָטוּר בְּעָסְקוֹ בָזוֹ, וְיֶתֶר פְּרָטֶיהָ, מְבֹאָרִים בִּיבָמוֹת בְּפֶרֶק שִׁשִּׁי וּבִבְרָכוֹת. וְנוֹהֶגֶת בְּכָל מָקוֹם וּבְכָל זְמַן, וְחַיָּב אָדָם לְהִשְׁתַּדֵּל בָּהּ מִשֶּׁהוּא רָאוּי לָהּ, וְהוּא הַזְּמַן שֶׁנָּתְנוּ חֲכָמִים זִכְרוֹנָם לִבְרָכָה לִשָּׂא אִשָּׁה. וּמִצְוָה זוֹ אֵינָהּ מֻטֶּלֶת

---

* See "A foreword by the author," note 10.

§1 1. Expression derived from TB B'rachoth 25b; i.e. without marriage and the birth of children, there would soon be no people to maintain and continue the settlement of the world, and to keep the precepts of the Torah.

2. When he has turned 17, and is then in his eighteenth year (Mishnah, Avoth v 21; MT *hilchoth 'ishuth* xv 2).

3. A son and a daughter, from whom issue will survive in turn (*ibid.* 4).

4. A bridegroom is not obligated to say the *Sh'ma* in the evening from the time of his marriage until its consummation (Mishnah, B'rachoth ii 5). Similarly TB Sukkah 25b declares a bridegroom (along with his escorts and all closely linked to the wedding) free of the obligation of *sukkah* (§286) the entire seven days after the wedding.

5. The basic principle that determines this here and throughout the work, is

GENESIS

THESE ARE THE *sidroth* [PORTIONS OF THE WRITTEN TORAH READ IN THE synagogue on the Sabbaths] of the year, in which are the *mitzvoth*, according to the reckoning of the great master, renowned for his vast wisdom and distinguished stature among his people, R. Moses b. Maimon of blessed memory.*

sidrah b'réshith
(Genesis 1–6:8)

[TO "BE FRUITFUL AND MULTIPLY"]

1 There is one positive precept in it: the *mitzvah* of procreation—as it is stated, *Then God blessed them, and God said to them: Be fruitful and multiply* (Genesis 1:28).

As regards root purposes of this precept, it is in order that the world should be settled, inhabited. For the Eternal Lord, blessed is He, desires its settlement, as it is written: *He did not create it a chaos; He formed it to be inhabited* (Isaiah 45:18). This is an important *mitzvah*, by virtue of which all the *mitzvoth* in the world are fulfilled: For to human beings were they given, not to the ministering angels.[1]

The laws of this precept—when a man is duty-bound to devote himself to it,[2] how many children he should have in order to have acquitted himself [fulfilled it],[3] and from which *mitzvoth* (religious obligations) he is left free while occupied with this,[4] as well as its other details—are explained in [the Babylonian Talmud] tractate *Yevamoth* chapter 6 and tractate *B'rachoth* (16a). It remains in force in every place[5] and every time,[6] and a man is obligated to strive for it from the time he is suited for it, this being the age that the Sages of blessed memory set for taking a wife [i.e. at eighteen].[2] This religious obligation is not imposed on women.[7] Anyone who fails to fulfill it [in his life] disobeys a positive precept, and his punishment is

§1–2: TO "BE FRUITFUL & MULTIPLY"/CIRCUMCISION

עַל הַנָּשִׁים. וְהַמְבַטְּלָהּ בְּטֵל עֲשֵׂה, וְעָנְשׁוֹ גָּדוֹל מְאֹד שֶׁמַּרְאֶה בְּעַצְמוֹ שֶׁאֵינוֹ רוֹצֶה לְהַשְׁלִים חֵפֶץ הַשֵּׁם לְיַשֵּׁב עוֹלָמוֹ.

פָּרָשַׁת אֵלֶּה תּוֹלְדֹת נֹחַ אֵין בָּהּ מִצְוָה

🕮 לֶךְ לְךָ

[מִצְוַת מִילָה]

ב יֵשׁ בָּהּ מִצְוַת עֲשֵׂה אַחַת, וְהִיא מִצְוַת מִילָה, שֶׁנֶּאֱמַר "זֹאת בְּרִיתִי אֲשֶׁר תִּשְׁמְרוּ בֵּינִי וּבֵינֵיכֶם וּבֵין זַרְעֲךָ אַחֲרֶיךָ הִמּוֹל לָכֶם כָּל זָכָר", וְנִכְפְּלָה בְּסֵדֶר אִשָּׁה כִּי תַזְרִיעַ דִּכְתִיב "וּבַיּוֹם הַשְּׁמִינִי יִמּוֹל בְּשַׂר עָרְלָתוֹ". וְהַרְבֵּה מִצְוֹת כְּמוֹ כֵן נִכְפְּלוּ בִּמְקוֹמוֹת הַרְבֵּה בַּתּוֹרָה, וְכֻלָּן לְצֹרֶךְ, כְּמוֹ שֶׁפֵּרְשׁוּם חֲכָמִים זִכְרוֹנָם לִבְרָכָה.

וְעִנְיָן מִצְוָה זוֹ הוּא שֶׁשּׁוֹחֲטִין הָעָרְלָה הַמְחַפָּה רֹאשׁ הַגְּוִיָּה וּפוֹרְעִין קְרוּם רַךְ שֶׁלְּמַטָּה מִמֶּנָּה כְּדֵי שֶׁתִּתְגַּלֶּה רֹאשׁ הָעֲטָרָה שֶׁבְּאוֹתוֹ אֵבֶר, כִּי יָדוּעַ לַמְּבִינִים שֶׁתַּשְׁלוּם צוּרַת הָאָדָם בְּהָסִיר מִמֶּנּוּ אוֹתָהּ עָרְלָה שֶׁהִיא תּוֹסֶפֶת בּוֹ.

מִשָּׁרְשֵׁי מִצְוָה זוֹ, לְפִי שֶׁרָצָה הַשֵּׁם יִתְבָּרַךְ לִקְבֹּעַ בָּעָם אֲשֶׁר הִבְדִּיל לִהְיוֹת נִקְרָא עַל שְׁמוֹ אוֹת קָבוּעַ בְּגוּפָם לְהַבְדִּילָם מִשְּׁאָר הָעַמִּים בְּצוּרַת גּוּפָם כְּמוֹ שֶׁהֵם מֻבְדָּלִים מֵהֶם בְּצוּרַת נַפְשׁוֹתָם אֲשֶׁר מוֹצָאָם וּמוֹבָאָם אֵינֶנּוּ שָׁוֶה, וְנִקְבַּע הַהֶבְדֵּל בְּגִלּוּי הַזָּהָב לְפִי שֶׁהוּא סִבָּה לְקִיּוּם הַמִּין, מִלְּבַד שֶׁיֵּשׁ בּוֹ תַּשְׁלוּם צוּרַת הַגּוּף, כְּמוֹ שֶׁאָמַרְנוּ. וְהָעָם הַנִּבְחָר חָפֵץ הַשֵּׁם יִתְבָּרַךְ לְהַשְׁלִים תְּכוּנָתוֹ, וְרָצָה לִהְיוֹת הַהַשְׁלָמָה עַל יְדֵי הָאָדָם וְלֹא בְּרָאוֹ שָׁלֵם מִבֶּטֶן, לִרְמֹז אֵלָיו כִּי כַּאֲשֶׁר תַּשְׁלוּם צוּרַת גּוּפוֹ עַל יָדוֹ כֵּן בְּיָדוֹ לְהַשְׁלִים צוּרַת נַפְשׁוֹ בְּהֶכְשֵׁר פְּעֻלּוֹתָיו.

דִּינֵי הַמִּצְוָה, עַל מִי מֻטֶּלֶת מִילַת הַקְּטַנִּים, וְכֵן מִילַת הָעֲבָדִים, יְלִיד בַּיִת

---

stated in Mishnah, Kiddushin i 9: *Every precept connected with the land [of Israel] is in force nowhere but in the land. What is not connected with the land, remains in effect both within and outside it.*

6. That the precepts of the Torah were given for all time is apparent from such teachings of the Sages as these: *Command Aaron* (Leviticus 6:2)—the verb "command" denotes encouragement [of a precept's observance] both at once and for all generations (Sifra). *Say to them: Throughout your generations* (Leviticus 22:3)—"Say to them" refers to those who stood before Mount Sinai; "throughout your generations": [this means] that the matter should remain in force for all generations (Sifra).

7. They are not required to take the initiative and strive to marry at all costs. If they refuse to marry, they violate no precept, for the obligation is on the male. In *Meshech Hochmah*, R. Meir Simhah of Dvinsk writes on Genesis 9:1: It is not unlikely that the Torah freed the woman from the religious obligation to "be fruitful and multiply," and imposed it only on the man, because... the woman endangers her life in pregnancy and childbirth [and hence it could not be made her religious duty].... But only for the preservation of the species did He so form her nature that her yearning to have children is stronger than the man's....

very great; for he shows personally[8] that he does not want to fulfill the wish of the Eternal Lord to settle His world.

In *sidrah noaḥ* (Genesis 6:9–11:32) there are no precepts.

sidrah lech l'cha
(Genesis 12–17)

2 [THE PRECEPT OF CIRCUMCISION]

There is one positive precept in it: the *mitzvah* of circumcision—as it is stated, *This is My covenant, which you shall keep, between Me and you and your descendants after you: Every male among you shall be circumcised* (Genesis 17:10). It is repeated in *sidrah thazri'a*, where it is written, *And on the eighth day the flesh of his foreskin shall be circumcised* (Leviticus 12:3). Many precepts are similarly repeated in numerous places in the Torah, and all for a necessary purpose, as our Sages of blessed memory explained them.[1]

The substance of this precept is that one cuts away the foreskin covering the head of the membrum, and uncovers the tender membrane beneath it, so that the head of the corona in that organ should be revealed. For it is known to the learned[2] that the perfection of the human form [is achieved] by removing that foreskin from it, as it is an accretion.

One root reason for this precept is that the Eternal Lord, be He blessed, wished to affix in the people that He set apart to be called by His name, a permanent sign in their bodies to differentiate them from the other nations in their bodily form,[2a] just as they are differentiated in their spiritual form, their very "exits and entrances"[3] [their pupose and way in the world] not being the same. This [physical] differentiation was set in the *golden orb* (Ecclesiastes 12:6)[4] as it is the causal source of the existence of the [human] species—apart from the fact that this constitutes the perfection of the physical form, as we have stated. The Eternal Lord (be He blessed) desired to perfect the [physical] character of the Chosen People; and He wished that this perfection be effected by man. He did not create him complete and perfect from the womb, in order to hint to him that just as the perfection of his physical form is by his own hand, so does it lie in his hand (within his means and power) to complete his spiritual form by the worthiness of his actions.

Some laws of the precept are: on whom lies the obligation to

§2: THE PRECEPT OF CIRCUMCISION

וּמִקְנַת כֶּסֶף, וְהַחִלּוּק שֶׁבֵּינֵיהֶם, וּבְאֵי זֶה עִנְיָן דּוֹחִין בִּשְׁבִילָהּ שַׁבָּת וְיוֹם טוֹב, וְאֵי זֶה קָטָן מַשְׁהִין מִילָתוֹ יוֹתֵר מִשְּׁמוֹנָה יָמִים, וְיֶתֶר פְּרָטֶיהָ, מְבֹאָרִים בְּפֶרֶק י"ט מְשַׁבָּת, וּבְפֶרֶק ד' מִיבָמוֹת. וְשָׁם בְּשַׁבָּת יִתְבָּאֵר כִּי הַמָּל מְבָרֵךְ: בָּרוּךְ אַתָּה ד' אֱלֹהֵינוּ מֶלֶךְ הָעוֹלָם אֲשֶׁר קִדְּשָׁנוּ בְּמִצְוֹתָיו וְצִוָּנוּ עַל הַמִּילָה, וַאֲבִי הַבֵּן, אוֹ בֵּית דִּין בְּמָקוֹם שֶׁאֵין אָב, מְבָרְכִין: בָּרוּךְ אַתָּה ד' אֱלֹהֵינוּ מֶלֶךְ הָעוֹלָם אֲשֶׁר קִדְּשָׁנוּ בְּמִצְוֹתָיו וְצִוָּנוּ לְהַכְנִיסוֹ בִּבְרִיתוֹ שֶׁל אַבְרָהָם אָבִינוּ; וְהָעוֹמְדִים שָׁם עוֹנִין, כְּשֵׁם שֶׁנִּכְנַס לַבְּרִית כֵּן יִזָּכֶה הָאֵל לְתוֹרָה וּלְחֻפָּה וּלְמַעֲשִׂים טוֹבִים.

וְנוֹהֶגֶת בְּכָל מָקוֹם וּבְכָל זְמָן. וְאֵין הַנָּשִׁים חַיָּבוֹת בְּמִילַת בְּנֵיהֶן, אֶלָּא הָאָב אוֹ בֵּית דִּין בְּמָקוֹם שֶׁאֵין אָב. וְעוֹבֵר עַל מִצְוָה זוֹ וְלֹא מָל עַצְמוֹ מִשֶּׁהִגִּיעַ לִכְלַל עֳנָשִׁין, שֶׁהוּא י"ג שָׁנָה וְיוֹם אֶחָד, בְּכָל יוֹם שֶׁיַּעֲבֹר עָלָיו מִשֶּׁיִּגְדַּל וְלֹא יָמוּל עַצְמוֹ מְבַטֵּל מִצְוַת עֲשֵׂה. וְאִם מֵת וְהוּא עָרֵל בְּמֵזִיד חַיָּב כָּרֵת, אֲבָל אֵין לָאָב חִיּוּב כָּרֵת בְּמִילַת בְּנוֹ אֶלָּא שֶׁעוֹבֵר עַל עֲשֵׂה. וְאֵין בְּכָל הַתּוֹרָה מִצְוַת עֲשֵׂה שֶׁחַיָּבִין בְּבִטּוּלָהּ כָּרֵת כִּי אִם זוֹ וּשְׁחִיטַת הַפֶּסַח.

פָּרָשַׁת וַיֵּרָא אֵלָיו וּפָרָשַׁת וַיִּהְיוּ חַיֵּי שָׂרָה [וּפָרָשַׁת תּוֹלְדֹת יִצְחָק] וּפָרָשַׁת וַיֵּצֵא יַעֲקֹב, אֵין בָּהֶן מִצְווֹת.

---

8. Literally, in himself. These lines somewhat recall a Talmudic teaching: Until he is twenty, the Holy One sits waiting in hope for a man [saying] "When will he take a wife?" Once he has reached twenty and not married, He says, "May his bones rot!" (TB Kiddushin 29b).

§2 1. Thus in TB Shabbath 132a-b we find: *And on the eighth day*—circumcision is to be performed at its proper time, even [if it be] on a Sabbath; *the flesh of his foreskin shall be circumcised*—even if there is a bright spot on it [indicating possible leprosy] it is to be cut. (Throughout Talmud and Midrash the principle holds that nothing in the Written Torah is to be considered redundant or unnecessary. If anything seems so, it is questioned, and a reason or purpose for it is determined.)

2. Literally, to those who understand. Cf. Rambam MT *hilchoth milah* iii 8 (quoting TB N'darim 31b): The foreskin is abhorrent, for so the heathen are contemned —as it is stated, *for all the nations are uncircumcised* (Jeremiah 9:25); and great is circumcision, since Abraham our father was not called whole, perfect, until he was circumcised—for [as the Almighty was to give him this commandment] He said, *Walk before Me and be whole; and I will set My covenant between Me and you* (Genesis 17:1-2).

2a. This thought is found in Rambam, *Guide* III 49.

3. Phrase based on Ezekiel 43:11.

4. See Rashi *ad loc.* that this denotes the organ of masculinity.

5. The circumcision of a child is his father's obligation (TB Kiddushin 29a); of a slave born or bought into Jewish ownership, his master's obligation. Upon the absence or refusal of the father or owner, the duty lies upon the *beth din* (religious court; Rambam MT *hilchoth milah* i 1). A slave born into Jewish ownership must be cir-

circumcise the very young, and so too the circumcision of slaves *born into the household or purchased for money* (Genesis 17:12), and the difference [in law] between them; in which circumstances the observance of the Sabbath and Festivals is set aside on its account; for which child the circumcision is delayed beyond the eight days [after his birth].[5] [These] and its other details are explained in chapter 19 of the Talmud tractate *Shabbath*, and chapter 4 of the tractate *Yevamoth*. There, in the tractate *Shabbath* (137b), it is explained that the man performing the circumcision says the benediction, "Blessed art Thou, Lord our God, King of the world, who hallowed us with His *mitzvoth* and commanded us about circumcision"; and the father of the child, or the religious court where there is no father, says the benediction, "Blessed art Thou, Lord our God, King of the world, who hallowed us with His *mitzvoth* and commanded us to bring him into the covenant of Abraham our father." Those standing there respond, "As he merited to [enter] the covenant, so may God grant him to attain Torah learning, the wedding canopy, and good deeds."[6]

[This precept] remains in force in every place and every time. Women have no obligation regarding the circumcision of their sons;[7] only the father does, or the *beth din* where there is no father. If someone transgresses this precept and does not have himself circumcised once he reaches the age of liability to punishment—this being thirteen years and a day—then every day that passes from the time he is grown and does not have himself circumcised, he disobeys [thereby] a positive precept. And if he dies while yet uncircumcised through deliberate will,[8] he has incurred *karéth*, that his soul should be cut off from eternal life (Genesis 17:14). A father, however, does not incur the punishment of *karéth* over the circumcision of his son, although he disobeys a positive precept.[9] In all the Torah there is no positive precept (command of something to do) which if ignored deliberately brings a punishment of *karéth*, other than this and the ritual slaughter of the Passover sacrifice (§5).[10]

As to the *sidroth va-yéra* (Genesis 18–22), *ḥayyé sarah* (ibid. 23–25:18), *tol'doth* (ibid. 25:19–28:9), and *va-yétzé* (ibid. 28:10–32:3)—there are no precepts in them.

וַיִּשְׁלַח יַעֲקֹב

[שֶׁלֹּא לֶאֱכֹל גִּיד הַנָּשֶׁה]

א יֵשׁ בָּהּ מִצְוַת לֹא תַעֲשֶׂה אַחַת, וְהִיא אַזְהָרַת גִּיד הַנָּשֶׁה, שֶׁנֶּאֱמַר "עַל כֵּן לֹא יֹאכְלוּ בְנֵי יִשְׂרָאֵל אֶת גִּיד הַנָּשֶׁה", וְהַאי לֹא יֹאכְלוּ לֹא נֶאֱמַר דֶּרֶךְ סִפּוּר, כְּלוֹמַר מִפְּנֵי שֶׁאֵרַע דָּבָר זֶה בָּאָב נִמְנָעִים הַבָּנִים מִלֶּאֱכֹל אוֹתוֹ גִּיד, אֶלָּא אַזְהָרַת הַשֵּׁם שֶׁלֹּא יֹאכְלוּהוּ.

מִשָּׁרְשֵׁי מִצְוָה זוֹ כְּדֵי שֶׁתִּהְיֶה רֶמֶז לְיִשְׂרָאֵל שֶׁאַף עַל פִּי שֶׁיִּסְבְּלוּ צָרוֹת רַבּוֹת בַּגָּלֻיּוֹת מִיַּד הָעַמִּים וּמִיַּד בְּנֵי עֵשָׂו, שֶׁיִּהְיוּ בְּטוּחִים שֶׁלֹּא יֹאבְדוּ, אֶלָּא לְעוֹלָם יַעֲמֹד זַרְעָם וּשְׁמָם וְיָבוֹא לָהֶם גּוֹאֵל וְיִגְאָלֵם מִיַּד צַר, וּבְזָכְרָם תָּמִיד עִנְיָן זֶה עַל יַד הַמִּצְוָה שֶׁתִּהְיֶה לְזִכָּרוֹן יַעַמְדוּ בֶּאֱמוּנָתָם וּבְצִדְקָתָם לְעוֹלָם. וְרֶמֶז זֶה הוּא לְפִי שֶׁאוֹתוֹ מַלְאָךְ שֶׁנִּלְחַם עִם יַעֲקֹב אָבִינוּ, שֶׁבָּא בַּקַּבָּלָה שֶׁהָיָה שָׂרוֹ שֶׁל עֵשָׂו, רָצָה לְעָקְרוֹ לְיַעֲקֹב מִן הָעוֹלָם הוּא וְזַרְעוֹ וְלֹא יָכֹל לוֹ, וְצִעֲרוֹ בִּנְגִיעַת הַיָּרֵךְ, וְכֵן זֶרַע עֵשָׂו מְצַעֵר לְזֶרַע יַעֲקֹב, וּלְבַסּוֹף תִּהְיֶה לָהֶם יְשׁוּעָה מֵהֶם, כְּמוֹ שֶׁשָּׁמַעְנוּ בָּאָב שֶׁזָּרְחָה לוֹ הַשֶּׁמֶשׁ לְרַפְּאָתוֹ וְנוֹשַׁע מִן הַצַּעַר כֵּן יִזְרַח לָנוּ הַשֶּׁמֶשׁ שֶׁל מָשִׁיחַ וִירַפְּאֵנוּ מִצַּעֲרֵנוּ וְיִגְאָלֵנוּ אָמֵן בִּמְהֵרָה בְּיָמֵינוּ.

דִּינֵי הַמִּצְוָה, מַהוּ הַגִּיד הָאָסוּר, וְהַחִטּוּט שֶׁאָנוּ חַיָּבִין לְחַטֵּט אַחֲרָיו, וּבְאֵי זוֹ בְּהֵמָה נוֹהֵג, וּמִי נֶאֱמָן עַל נִקּוּרוֹ, וְיֶתֶר פְּרָטֶיהָ, מְבֹאָרִים בְּפֶרֶק ז' מֵחֻלִּין. וְנוֹהֶגֶת בְּכָל מָקוֹם וּבְכָל זְמַן בִּזְכָרִים וּבִנְקֵבוֹת. וְעוֹבֵר עָלֶיהָ וְאָכַל גִּיד אֶחָד אֲפִלּוּ הוּא פָּחוֹת מִכְּזַיִת, אוֹ שֶׁאָכַל כְּזַיִת מִגִּיד הַנָּשֶׁה גָּדוֹל לוֹקֶה.

---

cumcised when eight days old; if bought into Jewish ownership, on the day of his purchase (*ibid.* 3, from TB Shabbath 135b). Circumcision at its proper time, on the eighth day, is performed even on a Sabbath or festival day; once delay beyond the eighth day has become necessary, it may not take place on these holy days (*ibid.* 9). An ill child is not circumcised until he is well; a child of yellowish tinge is not circumcised until his color is normal (*ibid.* 16–17).

6. In our custom the response is, "As he entered the covenant, so may he enter to Torah," etc.

7. TB Kiddushin 29a.

8. From "then every day" to here is not in the oldest manuscripts, but it clearly belongs here, following MT *hilchoth milah* i 2.

9. TB Shabbath 133a.

10. So the Mishnah, K'rithuth i 1.

§3 1. This is in keeping with TB Hullin 101b: This [injunction] was stated at Sinai, but it was written in its place [in Genesis] that one might know for what reason it was forbidden them. Rambam, Commentary to Mishnah, Hullin vii end, is most emphatic on this point: Note well the great principle included (implicit) in this Mishnah—that it was declared on Sinai to be forbidden. To you it was shown that you might know that everything we abstain from or do today, we do only by the commandment of the Holy One, blessed is He, through Moses our master.... Thus in regard to the sinew of the thigh-bone, we do not follow an injunction of Jacob our father but a precept of Moses our master....

sidrah va-yishlaḥ
(Genesis 32:4–36:43)

3 [NOT TO EAT THE SINEW OF THE THIGH-VEIN]
There is one negative precept in it: the admonition about the sinew of the thigh-vein—as it is stated, *Therefore the children of Israel do not eat the sinew of the thigh-vein* (Genesis 32:33). This phrase, "do not eat," is not stated merely by way of narrative, as part of a story—i.e. because this happened with the father, the children refrain from eating the sinew; it is rather an admonition of the Eternal Lord that they should not eat it.[1]

At the root of this precept lies the purpose that Jewry should have a hint that even though they will endure great tribulations in the exiles at the hands of the nations and the descendants of Esau,[2] they should remain assured that they will not perish, but their progeny and name will endure forever, and a redeemer will come and deliver them from the oppressor's hand. Remembering this matter always through the precept, which will serve as a reminder, they will stand firm in their faith and righteousness forever.

Now, this [serves as such a] hint because we find in our [Midrashic] tradition[3] that the angel who fought with Jacob our father (Genesis 32:25) was the celestial prince (guardian angel) of Esau:[4] He wanted to extirpate Jacob from the world, both him and his progeny; unable to prevail against him (Jacob), he pained him by touching his thigh (*ibid.* 26). Thus the descendants of Esau inflict pain and suffering on the descendants of Jacob; but ultimately they will be rescued from them—even as we find regarding the father (our ancestor Jacob), that *the sun shone for him* (*ibid.* 32) to heal him,[5] and he was delivered from the pain. So will the sun of the Messiah shine for us: he will heal us from our suffering and redeem us—*amen*, soon, in our days.[5a]

As to the laws of this precept—which is the forbidden sinew; the porging (removing) and scraping that we are required to do to clean out all around it; to which animals this applies; who can be trusted with its porging;[6] and its other details—they are explained in chapter 7 of the Talmud tractate *Ḥullin*. It remains in force in every place and time, applying to both men and women.[7] If one transgresses it and eats one [whole] sinew, even if it be less than the amount of an olive, or if he eats the amount of an olive from a large sinew of the thigh-vein, he is punishable by flogging.[8]

ספר החינוך END OF BOOK OF GENESIS

פָּרָשַׁת וַיֵּשֶׁב יַעֲקֹב וּפָרָשַׁת וַיְהִי מִקֵּץ וּפָרָשַׁת וַיִּגַּשׁ אֵלָיו וּפָרָשַׁת וַיְחִי יַעֲקֹב אֵין בָּהֶן מִצְוֹת

נִשְׁלַם סֵפֶר בְּרֵאשִׁית, תְּהִלָּה לָאֵל

2. The Sages taught that the Romans, who inaugurated the final exile when they destroyed the second Sanctuary, were descended from Esau: e.g. TB Gittin 56b, 57b.

3. B'réshith Rabbah 77, 3 and 78, 3; Tanḥuma, va-yishlaḥ 8; Shir haShirim Rabbah 3:10.

4. It is a tradition of the Sages that every major nation has a celestial prince, a patron angel, in the heavenly realm who champions its cause (while the "celestial prince" of Jewry is the Almighty Himself; so e.g. Sh'moth Rabbah 32, 6); and Esau was the founder of a major nation (see note 2).

5. B'réshith Rabbah 78, 5 teaches that this shining of the sun was to heal him of his injury. This root idea behind the precept was given by R. Aaron haLévi in *P'kudath haLévi*, 93, in the name of R. Aha: ... the forbiddance of the thigh-bone sinew is to make us aware of the [Divine] assurance which the descendants from the thigh (loins) of Jacob have, that they will not be wiped out in exile, even if they suffer tribulations. Hence *he touched the hollow of his thigh* (Genesis 32:26), but could not vanquish him—and this was the guardian angel of Esau. Then *there shone for him the sun* (ibid. 32) of healing in the days of the Messiah, *as he passed over Penuel* (ibid.), as the troubles *panu*, went away.

5a. Similarly Ramban to Genesis 32:26.

6. The sinews of both the right and left thigh-bones are forbidden (Mishnah, Ḥullin vii 1); there is an inner sinew near the bone, whose consumption is forbidden by the law of the Torah, and hence punished; and an outer sinew near the flesh, which is forbidden only by the restriction of the Sages, and hence its consumption is not punished (TB Ḥullin 91a). Every last trace, and all about it, must be removed and scraped out; its fat is permitted, but the people Israel (Jewry), being holy, treat it as forbidden (*baraitha*, ibid. 92b). The prohibition applies to all kosher domestic and wild animals, but not to fowl (Mishnah, Ḥullin vii 1 and 6). In Talmud times the Sages considered all butchers trustworthy about porging (removing) the sinew (ibid. 1); in the *Shulḥan Aruch*, R. Joseph Caro found it necessary to limit this trust to observant butchers known and held in good repute in regard to keeping kosher, etc. (*Yoreh Dé'ah* 65, 14).

7. This derives from the principle in the Mishnah, Kiddushin i 7: All negative precepts, whether or not their observance is connected with any specific time, both men and women are required to keep....

8. Mishnah, Ḥullin vii 3.

⟨90⟩

As to the *sidroth va-yéshev* (Genesis 37–40), *mikkétz* (ibid. 41–44:17), *va-yiggash* (ibid. 44:18–47:27) and *va-y'ḥi* (ibid. 47:28–50:26), there are no precepts in them.

THE BOOK OF GENESIS HAS BEEN COMPLETED, PRAISE GOD.

סֵפֶר וְאֵלֶּה שְׁמוֹת

פָּרָשַׁת וְאֵלֶּה שְׁמוֹת וּפָרָשַׁת וָאֵרָא אֵין בָּהֶן מִצְוֹת

בֹּא אֶל פַּרְעֹה

יֵשׁ בָּהּ תֵּשַׁע מִצְוֹת עֲשֵׂה וְאַחַת עֶשְׂרֵה מִצְוֹת לֹא תַעֲשֶׂה

[מִצְוַת קִדּוּשׁ הַחֹדֶשׁ]

לְקַדֵּשׁ חֳדָשִׁים וּלְעַבֵּר שָׁנִים בְּבֵית דִּין גָּדוֹל בְּחָכְמָה סָמוּךְ בָּאָרֶץ, וְלִקְבֹּעַ מוֹעֲדֵי הַשָּׁנָה עַל פִּי אוֹתוֹ קִדּוּשׁ, שֶׁנֶּאֱמַר "הַחֹדֶשׁ הַזֶּה לָכֶם רֹאשׁ חֳדָשִׁים", כְּלוֹמַר, כְּשֶׁתִּרְאוּ חִדּוּשָׁהּ שֶׁל לְבָנָה תִּקְבְּעוּ לָכֶם רֹאשׁ חֹדֶשׁ, אוֹ אֲפִלּוּ לֹא תִרְאוּהָ מִכֵּיוָן שֶׁהִיא רְאוּיָה לְהֵרָאוֹת עַל פִּי הַחֶשְׁבּוֹן הַמְקֻבָּל.

וְכֵן תִּכְלֹל מִצְוָה זוֹ מִצְוַת עִבּוּר הַשָּׁנָה, לְפִי שֶׁיְּסוֹד מִצְוַת קִדּוּשׁ הַחֹדֶשׁ כְּדֵי שֶׁיַּעֲשׂוּ יִשְׂרָאֵל מוֹעֲדֵי הַשֵּׁם בְּמוֹעֲדָם, וּכְמוֹ כֵן מִצְוַת עִבּוּר הַשָּׁנָה מִזֶּה הַיְסוֹד הִיא. וְאוּלָם מִלְּבַד זֶה הַמִּקְרָא בָּאוּ הָעֵדוּת בְּכִתְבֵי הַתּוֹרָה יוֹרוּ עַל מִצְוַת הָעִבּוּר, וְהוּא מַה שֶּׁכָּתוּב: וְשָׁמַרְתָּ אֶת הַחֻקָּה הַזֹּאת לְמוֹעֲדָהּ, וְכֵן: שָׁמוֹר אֶת חֹדֶשׁ הָאָבִיב.

וְעִנְיַן הַמִּצְוָה כֵּן, שֶׁבָּאִים שְׁנֵי יִשְׂרָאֵלִים כְּשֵׁרִים לִפְנֵי הַבֵּית דִּין וּמְעִידִין בִּפְנֵיהֶם שֶׁרָאוּ הַלְּבָנָה בְּחִדּוּשָׁהּ, וְקוֹבְעִים רֹאשׁ חֹדֶשׁ עַל פִּיהֶם שֶׁאוֹמְרִים "הַיּוֹם מְקֻדָּשׁ". וְטַעַם שֶׁאֵין מִצְוָה זוֹ אֶלָּא בִסְמוּכִין, לְפִי שֶׁבָּא בְּפֵרוּשׁ הַחֹדֶשׁ הַזֶּה לָכֶם,

§4

1. This interpretation of the verse is implicit in the Talmud (TB Rosh haShanah 20a) and Midrash Mechilta, etc. So too Rashi on the verse. It is based on the fact that the Hebrew for "month," *hodesh*, is linked with the word *hadash*, "new."

2. Since each festival and holy day occurs, by the Torah's laws, on a particular day of a particular month, when the beginnings of the months are determined the holy days are automatically set with them.

3. I.e. Passover must always be observed in the spring (TB Rosh haShanah 21a), the season when the Israelites left Egypt. The normal Jewish year is twelve lunar months, approximately eleven days shorter than the solar year. Hence if Passover, set for the 15th to the 21st of Nissan, occurs one year in the spring, each subsequent year it will arrive about eleven days earlier in the solar calendar, until it would be observed well in the winter. It is therefore necessary, every few years, to add an extra (thirteenth) month—a second Adar—before Nissan, to keep Passover in the spring. This is known as *'ibbur*, intercalation, which the author explains below.

EXODUS

As regards the *sidroth sh'moth* (Exodus 1–6:1) and *va'éra* (*ibid.* 6:2–9:35), there are no precepts in them.

sidrah bo
(Exodus 10–13:16)

It contains nine positive and eleven negative precepts.

4 [THE PRECEPT OF ESTABLISHING THE MONTHS] to sanctify months and intercalate years at the *beth din* (religious court) that is greatest in wisdom [and] ordained with authority in the Land [of Israel], and to set the dates of the year's festivals according to that sanctification. For it is stated, *This month shall be for you the beginning of months* (Exodus 12:2): In other words, when you see the renewal of the moon, you will establish for yourselves the beginning of the month;[1] and thus [do] even if you do not see it, once it is due to be seen according to the accepted reckoning.

This precept also includes the religious obligation to intercalate the year [by adding a lunar month when necessary]. For the fundamental reason for the precept of sanctifying each month is that the Israelites might observe the holy days of the Eternal Lord at their proper times;[2] and the intercalation of the year is for the same fundamental reason. Indeed, apart from this verse, there is evidence in other verses of the Torah which points to the precept of intercalation. Thus it is written, *You shall therefore keep this ordinance* [of observing Passover] *at its season* [of spring] (Exodus 13:10); and so too, *Observe the month of* aviv, *the spring* (Deuteronomy 16:1).[3]

This is the substance of the precept: Two reputable Israelites come before the *beth din* and testify before them [the judges of the court] that they saw the moon in its renewal. They [the judges] set the beginning of the month according to their word, by saying, "The day is hallowed!" The reason why this precept is only for the ordained

§ 4: ESTABLISHING THE MONTHS ספר החינוך

גְּדוֹלִים וּסְמוּכִים כְּמוֹתְכֶם, כִּי לְמֹשֶׁה וְאַהֲרֹן נֶאֱמַר. וְעוֹד דָּרְשׁוּ הַדָּבָר מִדְּסָמַךְ לוֹ "דַּבְּרוּ אֶל כָּל עֲדַת יִשְׂרָאֵל", כְּלוֹמַר שֶׁיְּהֵא לָהֶם לְאוֹתָן שֶׁיְּקַדְּשׁוּ הַחֹדֶשׁ רְשׁוּת כָּל יִשְׂרָאֵל, כְּלוֹמַר חֲכָמִים גְּדוֹלִים שֶׁבְּיִשְׂרָאֵל, כְּגוֹן בֵּית דִּין הַגָּדוֹל. וְכֵן כָּל מִי שֶׁהוּא חָכָם גָּדוֹל בְּיִשְׂרָאֵל וְנִסְמַךְ בְּאֶרֶץ יִשְׂרָאֵל, וְהַסְּמִיכוּת יָדוּעַ אֵיךְ עוֹשִׂין אוֹתוֹ, יֵשׁ לוֹ רְשׁוּת לַעֲשׂוֹת מִצְוָה זוֹ אֲפִלּוּ בְחוּצָה לָאָרֶץ, וְהוּא שֶׁלֹּא הִנִּיחַ כְּמוֹתוֹ בָּאָרֶץ. וְכֵן מָצִינוּ שֶׁעָשׂוּ כֵּן חֲנַנְיָה בֶּן אֲחִי רַבִּי יְהוֹשֻׁעַ וַעֲקִיבָא בֶּן יוֹסֵף שֶׁהָיוּ בְּעִנְיָן זֶה. אֲבָל בִּלְתִּי תַּנָּאִים אֵלּוּ אֵין רְשׁוּת לְשׁוּם אָדָם מִיִּשְׂרָאֵל לִקְבֹּעַ חֳדָשִׁים וּלְעַבֵּר שָׁנִים.

וְאִם תִּשְׁאַל: אִם כֵּן הֵיאַךְ אָנוּ עוֹשִׂים הַיּוֹם שֶׁאֵין לָנוּ חֲכָמִים סְמוּכִים? דַּע שֶׁכָּךְ קִבַּלְנוּ שֶׁרַבִּי הִלֵּל הַנָּשִׂיא בְּנוֹ שֶׁל רַבִּי יְהוּדָה הַנָּשִׂיא שֶׁהָיָה גָּדוֹל בְּדוֹרוֹ וְנִסְמַךְ בָּאָרֶץ וְהוּא הֶחָכָם שֶׁתִּקֵּן לָנוּ חֶשְׁבּוֹן הָעִבּוּר, הוּא קִדֵּשׁ חֳדָשִׁים וְעִבֵּר שָׁנִים הָעֲתִידִים לָבוֹא עַד שֶׁיָּבוֹא אֵלִיָּהוּ, וְעַל זֶה אָנוּ סוֹמְכִים הַיּוֹם.

זֶה שֶׁאָמַרְנוּ הוּא עַל דַּעַת הָרַמְבָּ"ם זִכְרוֹנוֹ לִבְרָכָה. וְהָרַמְבָּ"ן זִכְרוֹנוֹ לִבְרָכָה יַחְשֹׁב קִדּוּשׁ הַחֹדֶשׁ מִצְוָה אַחַת וְעִבּוּר שָׁנִים מִצְוָה אַחַת, וּרְאָיוֹתָיו בְּסֵפֶר הַמִּצְוֹת שֶׁלּוֹ, וְכֵן בַּעַל הֲלָכוֹת גַּם כֵּן. וְהַפָּסוּק הַמּוֹרֶה עַל מִצְוַת הָעִבּוּר, כְּלוֹמַר שֶׁנַּחְשֹׁב הַתְּקוּפוֹת כְּדֵי שֶׁנַּעֲשֶׂה הַמּוֹעֲדִים בִּזְמַן קָבוּעַ לָהֶם הוּא: וְשָׁמַרְתָּ אֶת הַחֻקָּה הַזֹּאת לְמוֹעֲדָהּ, וְכֵן: שָׁמוֹר אֶת חֹדֶשׁ הָאָבִיב, כְּמוֹ שֶׁכְּתַבְנוּ.

מִשָּׁרְשֵׁי מִצְוָה זוֹ כְּדֵי שֶׁיַּעֲשׂוּ יִשְׂרָאֵל מוֹעֲדֵי הַשֵּׁם בִּזְמַנָּן, שֶׁהַשֵּׁם צִוָּה שָׁנָה לַעֲשׂוֹת

---

4. This interpretation is in keeping with the majority view of the Sages in TB Rosh haShanah 22a and Rashi's comment. Similarly Mechilta on the second part of the verse, "it shall be the first *for you*."

5. The person is addressed as *Rabbi* (by those who were themselves ordained) and he is told (by them), "Behold, you are ordained, and you have the right to judge even cases involving fines." (Rambam MT *hilchoth sanhedrin* iv 2).

6. In TB B'rachoth 63a.

7. I.e. a fixed system by which we can know which years to enlarge by adding a thirteenth month (see note 3). This R. Hillel lived thirteen generations after his renowned forebear of the same name, Hillel the Elder. In his *Séfer Zakkuth*, *gittin* chapter 4 (Leghorn 1745, 43a) Ramban records the tradition mentioned here: "From the time of R. Hillel ... in the year ... 4118 [= 358] the Sanhedrin (supreme court) in the land of Israel came to an end, and it ceased to have learned experts. It was he who regulated the order of intercalation, reckoned the years, and fixed the months for the generations to come." (A similar tradition is quoted in *Séfer ha'Ibbur* by R. Abraham b. Ḥiyya—ed. Filipowski, 97—in the name of R. Hai Ga'on.) Our author's question and answer can also be found in Ramban, commentary to Rambam ShM positive precept § 153.

8. I.e. in his commentary to Rambam's work of this name, generally printed alongside it. He makes this point in his commentary on root principle 1.

[rabbinic authorities to fulfill] is that it is stated explicitly, *This month shall be for you* [to sanctify]—for those as great and as ordained, invested with authority as you—for this was said [by the Almighty] to Moses and Aaron.[4] This point was also derived [in Midrash *Mechilta*] from the fact that directly after this comes the verse, *Speak to all the community of Israel* (Exodus 12:3), as much as to say that those who would sanctify the new month must have the authority of all Israel—meaning the greatest sages in Israel, such as the supreme *beth din* [the members of the Sanhedrin]. So likewise, any great scholar in Jewry who was ordained in the land of Israel—the way in which ordination is conferred is known[5]—has the authority to fulfill this precept even outside the land of Israel—but only if he did not leave anyone in the Land who is his equal. And so we find that R. Joshua's nephew Ḥananyah and Akiva b. Joseph acted,[6] for they were involved in this matter [of sanctifying the new month outside the land of Israel]. However, without all these conditions, no person whatever in Jewry has the right to determine months and intercalate years.

Then you might ask: In that case, what do we do today, when we have no properly ordained, authorized sages? Know [however] that this is the tradition we have received: R. Hillel *haNassi* (the patriarch), the son of R. Judah *haNassi*, was the outstanding scholar of his generation, and he was properly ordained in the Land; and he was the Sage who prepared for us the reckoning of [the cycle of] intercalation;[7] he sanctified the months and intercalated the years that were destined to come until Elijah would arrive [to herald the advent of the Messiah]. And on that we rely today.

What we have stated [here] follows the view of Rambam (R. Moses b. Maimon) of blessed memory. Ramban (R. Moses b. Naḥman) of blessed memory reckons the sanctification of the month as one precept, and the intercalation of the years as another, his proofs [for this being given] in his *séfer ha-mitzvoth* (Book of Precepts).[8] So too the author of *halachoth g'doloth*. The verse of Scripture which indicates the precept of intercalation, i.e. that we should calculate the seasons in order to observe the holy days at the times set for them, is: *You shall therefore keep this ordinance* [of observing Passover] *at its season* (Exodus 13:10); and so too: *Observe the month of* aviv, *spring* (Deuteronomy 16:1)—as we have written.

At the root of this precept lies the purpose that the Israelites should keep the holy days of the Eternal Lord at their proper time: For the

פֶּסַח בִּזְמַן שֶׁהַתְּבוּאָה בָּאָבִיב, כְּמוֹ שֶׁכָּתוּב: "שָׁמוֹר אֶת חֹדֶשׁ הָאָבִיב וְעָשִׂיתָ פֶּסַח", וְחַג הַסֻּכּוֹת בִּזְמַן הָאָסִיף, כְּמוֹ שֶׁכָּתוּב "וְחַג הָאָסִיף תְּקוּפַת הַשָּׁנָה". וְאִלּוּלֵי עִבּוּר הַשָּׁנִים יָבוֹאוּ הַמּוֹעֲדִים שֶׁלֹּא בִּזְמַנִּים אֵלּוּ: לְפִי שֶׁיִּשְׂרָאֵל מְחַשְּׁבִים חָדְשֵׁיהֶם וּמוֹעֲדֵיהֶם לִימֵי שְׁנַת הַלְּבָנָה, שֶׁהֵם שנ"ד יוֹם, ח' שָׁעוֹת, תתע"ו חֲלָקִים, וְהִיא חֲסֵרָה מִשְּׁנַת הַחַמָּה י' יָמִים, כ"א שָׁעוֹת, ר"ד חֲלָקִים, סִימָן יכ"א ר"ד, וּבִשְׁבִיל הַתְּבוּאוֹת וְהַפֵּרוֹת בְּכֹחָהּ שֶׁל חַמָּה, נִמְצָא שֶׁאִלּוּלֵי הָעִבּוּר שֶׁאָנוּ מַשִׂימִים בּוֹ שְׁנוֹת הַלְּבָנָה בִּשְׁנוֹת הַחַמָּה לֹא יָבוֹא פֶּסַח בִּזְמַן הָאָבִיב וְהַסֻּכּוֹת בִּזְמַן הָאָסִיף. וְנִתְקַן הַדָּבָר לְהֵעָשׂוֹת בִּגְדוֹלֵי הַדּוֹר, לְפִי שֶׁהוּא עִנְיָן חָכְמָה גְדוֹלָה, גַּם יֹאמְרוּ כִּי מִמֶּנּוּ יוּדַע מִקְרֵה הַשָּׁנָה בַּתְּבוּאוֹת, וְאֵין רָאוּי לְמָסְרוֹ אֶלָּא לִגְדוֹלִים וַחֲסִידִים.

דִּינֵי הַמִּצְוָה, כְּגוֹן חֲקִירַת עֵדוּת הַחֹדֶשׁ, וְאִיּוּם הָעֵדִים לִפְעָמִים, וְדִין חִלּוּל שַׁבָּת בְּעֵדוּת זוֹ כֵּיצַד, וְעַל מָה מְעַבְּרִין אֶת הַשָּׁנָה וְעַל מָה אֵין מְעַבְּרִין אוֹתָהּ, וְאֵי זֶה חֹדֶשׁ הָיוּ מְעַבְּרִין וְהוּא אֲדָר, וּכְמוֹ שֶׁדָּרְשׁוּ זִכְרוֹנָם לִבְרָכָה: וְשָׁמַרְתָּ אֶת הַחֻקָּה הַזֹּאת לְמוֹעֲדָהּ, מְלַמֵּד שֶׁאֵין מְעַבְּרִין אֶת הַשָּׁנָה אֶלָּא בְּפֶרֶק הַסָּמוּךְ לַמּוֹעֵד. וְעוֹד דָּרְשׁוּ זִכְרוֹנָם לִבְרָכָה בְּפָסוּק זֶה, מִנַּיִן שֶׁאֵין מְעַבְּרִין אֶת הַחֹדֶשׁ אֶלָּא בַּיּוֹם, [וְאֵין מְקַדְּשִׁין אֶת הַחֹדֶשׁ אֶלָּא בַּיּוֹם] — תַּלְמוּד לוֹמַר "מִיָּמִים יָמִימָה". וְעוֹד דָּרְשׁוּ זִכְרוֹנָם לִבְרָכָה: "לְחָדְשֵׁי הַשָּׁנָה", חֳדָשִׁים אַתָּה מְחַשֵּׁב לְשָׁנָה וְאִי אַתָּה מְחַשֵּׁב יָמִים. וְעוֹד אָמְרוּ בְּעִנְיָן זֶה: "חֹדֶשׁ יָמִים", יָמִים אַתָּה מְחַשֵּׁב לְחֹדֶשׁ וְאִי אַתָּה מְחַשֵּׁב שָׁעוֹת. וְיֶתֶר פְּרָטֶיהָ, מְבֹאָרִים בְּמַסֶּכֶת רֹאשׁ הַשָּׁנָה, וּבְרֹאשׁוֹן שֶׁל סַנְהֶדְרִין, וּבִבְרָכוֹת כְּמוֹ כֵן.

וְנוֹהֶגֶת בְּכָל מָקוֹם וּבְכָל זְמַן שֶׁיִּהְיוּ לָנוּ חֲכָמִים סְמוּכִים בַּתְּנָאִים שֶׁכָּתַבְנוּ.

9. So interpreted in TB Sanhedrin 13a.

10. A "part" (*ḥélek*) is three and a third seconds; there are 1080 parts in an hour, 18 in a minute.

11. In the Hebrew original a mnemonic device is now added: two groups of letters whose respective numerical values are 10, 20, 1 ; 200, 4.

12. See MT *hilchoth kiddush ha-ḥodesh* ii 2–7.

13. See *ibid.* iii 15.

14. This is based on Mishnah, Rosh haShanah i 4: "In regard to two months the Sabbath may be violated: Nissan and Tishri; for in those [months] the messengers [of the *beth din*] go out to Syria, and in them [those months] the holy days are determined." If two saw the new moon of these months on a Friday evening, they might violate the Sabbath to reach the supreme *beth din* in Jerusalem and testify in time to have the months properly set; for Passover begins the fifteenth of Nissan; *Yom Kippur*, the tenth of Tishri; and *Sukkoth*, the fifteenth. The messengers of the *beth din* would not set out until those months were properly sanctified, and they had to reach Syria before the holy days, to inform the Jewish communities when to observe them.

15. This is answered in TB Sanhedrin 11b: For three causes the year may be intercalated: on account of spring [if spring crops will not ripen by Passover], on account of the fruit of the trees [if they will not ripen by *Shavu'oth*], and on account of the summer solstice [if it will fall too late in the year] (bracketed additions after Rashi).

Eternal Lord ordered Passover celebrated when the grain is in the *aviv* stage, newly ripened—as written, *Observe the month of* aviv, *and keep Passover* (ibid.); and the festival of *Sukkoth* [is to be celebrated] at harvest-time, as it is written, *and the festival of ingathering (harvest) at the turn of the year* (Exodus 34:22).[9] If not for intercalation of the years, the holy days would not occur at these times [of the year].

For the Jewish people reckon their months and holy days according to the days of the lunar year, which are 354 days, eight hours, and 876 parts (=48 minutes and 40 seconds).[10] It is less than the solar year by ten days, 21 hours and 204 parts (=11 minutes and 20 seconds).[11] But now, the ripening of grain and produce [in farm and orchard] is by the power of the sun. The result is that without intercalation, by which we make the lunar years come equal with the solar years, Passover would not occur in the spring, nor *Sukkoth* at harvest-time. The matter was worked out, to be carried into effect, by the great, outstanding scholars of their generation: for it is a matter of profound wisdom. It is even said that how crops will fare in a given year can be known from it. Then it is not fitting to transmit this [knowledge of the method of intercalation] to any but great and pious scholars.

The laws of this precept [concern] for example: the examination of testimony on the month [the new moon];[12] the solemn warning of witnesses at times;[13] the law of violating the Sabbath for the sake of this testimony—when it may be done;[14] for what cause the year is intercalated and for what it is not;[15] which extra month is added— this being [a second] Adar, as our Sages of blessed memory interpreted: *You shall therefore keep this ordinance at its season* (Exodus 13:10) —this teaches us that the year is to be intercalated only at the period close to the season [of Passover].[16] Our Sages of blessed memory derived more from this verse: How do we know that the month is not to be intercalated except by day, nor is the [new] month to be sanctified except by day?[17]—for it is stated, *mi-yamim yamimah*, "from days to days" (ibid.).[18] Our Sages further interpreted: *it shall be the first of the months of the year for you* (Exodus 12:2)—you may reckon months to a year, but you may not reckon days.[19] They said, too, in this regard: *a month of days* (Numbers 11:21, literal translation): you may account days to a month, but not hours.[20] The rest of its details are explained in the Talmud tractate *Rosh haShanah*, the first chapter of *Sanhedrin*, and likewise in *B'rachoth*.

It is in force at every place and time that we shall have ordained,

וְעוֹבֵר עָלֶיהָ וְלֹא עֲשָׂאָהּ, אִם הוּא חָכָם שֶׁרָאוּי לָהּ בִּטֵּל עָשָׂה וְעָנְשׁוֹ גָּדוֹל מְאֹד שֶׁגּוֹרֵם קִלְקוּל הַמּוֹעֲדוֹת. וְעַכְשָׁיו בַּעֲווֹנוֹתֵינוּ שֶׁאֵין אָנוּ מְעַבְּרִין שָׁנִים עַל פִּי סְמוּכִים אָנוּ סוֹמְכִים בְּחֶשְׁבּוֹנֵנוּ עַל הַחֶשְׁבּוֹן הַמְּקֻבָּל מֵרַבִּי הִלֵּל כְּמוֹ שֶׁאָמַרְנוּ.

[מִצְוַת שְׁחִיטַת הַפֶּסַח]

ה לִשְׁחֹט בְּיוֹם י״ד בְּנִיסָן בֵּין הָעַרְבַּיִם שֶׂה תָמִים זָכָר בֶּן שָׁנָה, אוֹ גְדִי, בְּבֵית הַבְּחִירָה, וְזֶה נִקְרָא קָרְבַּן הַפֶּסַח, שֶׁנֶּאֱמַר: וְשָׁחֲטוּ אֹתוֹ כֹּל קְהַל עֲדַת יִשְׂרָאֵל בֵּין הָעַרְבָּיִם. וְעִנְיַן הַמִּצְוָה הוּא שֶׁמִּתְקַבְּצִין אֲנָשִׁים מִיִּשְׂרָאֵל לַחֲבוּרוֹת, וְלוֹקְחִין מִן הַשּׁוּק אוֹ מִבֵּיתָם גְּדִי אֶחָד אוֹ שֶׂה בֶּן שָׁנָה תָמִים זָכָר וְשׁוֹחֲטִין אוֹתוֹ בַּעֲזָרַת בֵּית הַמִּקְדָּשׁ בְּיוֹם י״ד בְּנִיסָן בֵּין הָעַרְבָּיִם, וְאַחַר כָּךְ לָעֶרֶב אוֹכְלִין בֵּין כֻּלָּם אַחַר מַאֲכָלָם, שֶׁמִּצְוָתוֹ לְאָכְלוֹ עַל הַשֹּׂבַע.

מִשָּׁרְשֵׁי מִצְוָה זוֹ כְּדֵי שֶׁיִּזְכְּרוּ הַיְּהוּדִים לְעוֹלָם הַנִּסִּים הַגְּדוֹלִים שֶׁעָשָׂה לָהֶם הַשֵּׁם בִּיצִיאַת מִצְרַיִם.

דִּינֵי הַמִּצְוָה, כְּגוֹן זְמַן שְׁחִיטָתוֹ בַיּוֹם אֵימָתַי, וְשֶׁהוּא נִשְׁחָט בְּשָׁלֹשׁ כִּתּוֹת בָּעֲזָרָה, וְכִי דּוֹחֶה שַׁבָּת עָלָיו, וְדִינֵי מְנוּיָיו, וּקְרִיאַת הַהַלֵּל עָלָיו, וּתְקִיעַת חֲצוֹצְרוֹת, וְיֶתֶר פְּרָטֶיהָ, מְבֹאָרִים בְּמַסֶּכֶת פְּסָחִים.

וְנוֹהֶגֶת בִּזְכָרִים וּבִנְקֵבוֹת בִּזְמַן הַבַּיִת, וְהָעוֹבֵר עָלֶיהָ בְּמֵזִיד וְלֹא עָשָׂה פֶּסַח חַיָּב כָּרֵת. בְּשׁוֹגֵג אֵינוֹ מֵבִיא קָרְבָּן, לְפִי שֶׁהוּא אֶחָד מִשְּׁלֹשָׁה חֲטָאִים שֶׁבִּזְדוֹנָן כָּרֵת וְאֵין בְּשִׁגְגָתָן חַטָּאת, וְהֵן זֶה, וּמְגַדֵּף, וּמְבַטֵּל מִילָה.

16. I.e. directly before Nissan; Mechilta d'R. Shim'on b. Yoḥai (MdRSbY) *ad loc*. TB Sanhedrin 12a: No month may be doubled for intercalation other than Adar.

17. An omission in the Hebrew (evidently an early scribal oversight between identical phrases) has been corrected according to ShM positive precept §153.

18. MdRSbY on Exodus 13:10 (p. 42 lines 6-8); ShM *loc. cit.* Cf. TB Rosh haShanah 25b and Sanhedrin 11b.

19. I.e. to intercalate a year, only a whole month may be added, not some number of days; TB Megillah 5a, Nazir 7a (where cf. *tosafoth*).

20. A month may be started only a whole day earlier or later; TB Megillah 5a.

21. Literally, "nullified" or "made nought of," and so throughout the work.

§5   1. Literally "between the evenings," which the Sages explain to mean between noon and evening (Mechilta; MdRSbY; TJ P'saḥim v 1); generally translated "at dusk" or "in the evening." As MH notes, the precept actually concerns not the ritual slaying but the further details of the sacrifice, particularly the sprinkling of the bood. (An Israelite was permitted to slay it—though not to sprinkle the blood; Mishnah, P'saḥim v 6—but in actual practice he relegated the task to a *kohen*.)

2. So Tosefta, P'saḥim v 3; TJ 33c; TB 70a, 119b; Mechilta, Exodus 12:8.

3. Psalms 113–118.   4. See Mishnah, P'saḥim v 1, 5, 8; viii 3; v 7.

authorized sages under the conditions that we have written. Should someone transgress this [precept] and not carry it out, if he is a sage who is fit and worthy for it, he has disobeyed[21] a positive precept, and his punishment is very great, for he causes distortion in [the observance of] the holy days. But nowadays that, for our sins, we do not intercalate the years through ordained authorities, we rely for our reckoning on the calculation received in tradition from R. Hillel, as we have stated.

5 [THE RITUAL SLAYING OF THE PASSOVER OFFERING]

to slay ritually at the Sanctuary, on the fourteenth of Nissan in the afternoon, a male sheep without blemish, in its first year, or a goat, which is called the Passover offering—as it is stated, *and the whole assembly of the community of Israel shall slay it in the afternoon*[1] (Exodus 12:6). The substance of this precept is that people of Israel would unite into groups and take from the market or from their home either a male goat or sheep, unblemished, in its first year; and they would have it slain ritually in the forecourt of the Holy Temple on the fourteenth of Nissan in the afternoon. Afterward, in the evening, they would eat it among all of them after their meal: for its law is that it be eaten in satiety [after the meal].[2]

At the root of this precept lies the purpose that Jewry should remember forever the great miracles which the Eternal Lord did for them at the exodus from Egypt.

The laws of this precept concern, for example: when is the proper time of day for its ritual slaying; that it is thus slain for three assemblies in the Temple forecourt; that observance of the Sabbath is set aside for it; the laws of those counted and registered for it; the reading of *hallél* (psalms of praise)[3] over it; and the sounding of trumpets [for every reading of *hallél*].[4] The rest of its details are explained in the Talmud tractate *P'saḥim*.

It is in force for both men and women[5] at the time the Sanctuary is in existence. Whoever disobeys it deliberately and does not offer up a Passover offering, incurs *karéth*[6] [Divine severance of existence; Numbers 9:13]. If someone transgresses unintentionally (by an oversight), he does not bring an offering [in atonement]. For this is one of three sins whose intentional violation is punished by *karéth*, but whose unintentional violation does not require a *ḥattath* (sin-offering)—these being this precept, vilification of the Divine name (§70), and deliberately ignoring the precept of circumcision (§2).[7]

§6–7: ABOUT EATING THE PASSOVER OFFERING

[מִצְוַת אֲכִילַת בְּשַׂר הַפֶּסַח]

ו לֶאֱכֹל בְּשַׂר הַפֶּסַח בְּלֵיל חֲמִשָּׁה עָשָׂר בְּנִיסָן עַל פִּי תְּנָאִים שֶׁבַּכָּתוּב, שֶׁנֶּאֱמַר: וְאָכְלוּ אֶת הַבָּשָׂר בַּלַּיְלָה הַזֶּה.

וּמִשָּׁרְשֵׁי מִצְוָה זוֹ מַה שֶּׁכָּתַבְנוּ בִּשְׁחִיטָתוֹ, כְּדֵי לִזְכֹּר הַנִּסִּים הַגְּדוֹלִים שֶׁעָשָׂה לָנוּ הָאֵל שֶׁהוֹצִיאָנוּ מֵעַבְדוּת.

דִּינֵי הַמִּצְוָה, כַּמָּה חַיָּב כָּל אֶחָד לֶאֱכֹל מִמֶּנּוּ לְכָל הַפָּחוֹת, וְהַנִּמְנִין עָלָיו אֵיךְ יִתְנַהֲגוּ עַד שֶׁיֹּאכְלוּהוּ, שֶׁלֹּא לָצֵאת מִן הַחֲבוּרָה, וְשֶׁלֹּא יְשַׁנּוּ, וְיֶתֶר פְּרָטֶיהָ, מְבֹאָרִים בִּפְסָחִים.

וְנוֹהֶגֶת בִּזְכָרִים וּנְקֵבוֹת. וְעוֹבֵר עָלֶיהָ בִּטֵּל עֲשֵׂה. וּכְלָל גָּדוֹל בְּכָל הַתּוֹרָה לְכָל שֶׁאוֹמֵר שֶׁיְּבַטֵּל מִצְוַת עֲשֵׂה שֶׁכּוֹפִין אוֹתוֹ בֵּית דִּין אִם יֵשׁ כֹּחַ בְּיָדָם עַד שֶׁיְּקַיְּמֶנּוּ.

[שֶׁלֹּא לֶאֱכֹל הַפֶּסַח נָא וּמְבֻשָּׁל]

ז שֶׁלֹּא לֶאֱכֹל בְּשַׂר הַפֶּסַח נָא וּבָשֵׁל כִּי אִם צְלִי אֵשׁ, שֶׁנֶּאֱמַר: אַל תֹּאכְלוּ מִמֶּנּוּ נָא וּבָשֵׁל מְבֻשָּׁל בַּמָּיִם כִּי אִם צְלִי אֵשׁ. הָעִנְיָן הַזֶּה שֶׁלֹּא יֹאכַל אוֹתוֹ קֹדֶם גְּמַר בִּשּׁוּלוֹ אֲפִלּוּ בְצָלִי, וְזֶהוּ פֵּרוּשׁ נָא, שֶׁהַבָּשָׂר שֶׁהִתְחִיל בּוֹ מַעֲשֶׂה הָאוּר וְנִצְלָה מְעַט וְאֵינוֹ רָאוּי לַאֲכִילַת אָדָם עֲדַיִן נִקְרָא נָא, אֲבָל כְּשֶׁהוּא חַי לְגַמְרֵי שֶׁלֹּא הִתְחִיל בּוֹ הָאוּר כְּלָל, אֵין בִּכְלַל לָאו דְּנָא לִלְקוֹת עָלָיו מִשּׁוּם אַל תֹּאכְלוּ מִמֶּנּוּ נָא, אֲבָל אָסוּר מִדְּאוֹרַיְתָא שֶׁכָּל שֶׁאֵינוֹ צְלִי אֵשׁ אָסְרָה הַתּוֹרָה דֶּרֶךְ כְּלָל. וּפֵרוּשׁ בָּשֵׁל שֶׁבִּשְּׁלוֹ בַּמַּיִם אוֹ בְכָל מַשְׁקֶה אוֹ בְמֵי פֵּרוֹת, שֶׁנֶּאֱמַר "וּבָשֵׁל מְבֻשָּׁל", רִבָּה הַכֹּל.

מִשָּׁרְשֵׁי מִצְוָה זוֹ מַה שֶּׁכָּתוּב בִּשְׁחִיטָתוֹ, לִזְכֹּר נֵס יְצִיאַת מִצְרַיִם. וְזֶהוּ שֶׁנִּצְטַוֵּינוּ לְאָכְלוֹ צְלִי דַוְקָא, לְפִי שֶׁכֵּן דֶּרֶךְ בְּנֵי מְלָכִים וְשָׂרִים לֶאֱכֹל בָּשָׂר צְלִי

---

5. TB P'saḥim 91b.

6. I.e. if he does not bring a "second Passover" offering on the fourteenth of Iyar (Rambam MT *hilchoth korban pesaḥ* v 2).

7. No *ḥattath* need be brought for inadvertent vilification of the Divine name, because it is a negative precept whose violation involves no action—merely speech (Mishnah, K'rithoth i 1). Circumcision and the Passover offering are positive precepts (commands to be fulfilled, not prohibitions), and a *ḥattath* is required only for a negative precept that was inadvertently transgressed (*ibid.*).

§6   1. I.e. the night after the fourteenth, as in the Jewish reckoning the day always begins at the previous evening.

2. The bulk of an olive (Mishnah, P'saḥim viii 3).

3. See TB P'saḥim 86a and Mishnah x 8.

4. Since both are included in precept §5, and it is apparent from Exodus 12:8 that all who are included in that are also required to take part in the eating.

5. Literally, has nullified, or made nought of.

6. So TB K'thuboth 86a, Ḥullin 132b.

⟨100⟩

[EATING THE PASSOVER OFFERING]

6 to eat the flesh of the Passover offering on the evening of the fifteenth of Nissan,[1] under the conditions given in Scripture—as it is stated, *And they shall eat the flesh on that night* (Exodus 12:8).

At the root of this precept lies what we have written about its ritual slaying: It is in order to remember the great miracles which God wrought for us when he took us out from slavery.

As to the laws of the precept—the very least amount that one is required to eat of it;[2] how those registered for it should behave until they eat it: not to leave the group [registered for it], and not to go to sleep [until it is completely eaten];[3] and its other details—they are explained in the Talmud tractate *P'saḥim*.

It applies to both men and women.[4] He who transgresses it has disobeyed[5] a positive precept. And it is a general rule throughout the Torah about anyone who says that he will not keep a positive precept, that the *beth din* coerces him, if it has the power, until he fulfills it.[6]

[NOT TO EAT THE PASSOVER OFFERING SLIGHTLY ROASTED OR COOKED]

7 not to eat the flesh of the Passover offering raw or cooked, but only roasted by fire—as it is stated, *Do not eat any of it na (under-roasted) or boiled at all with water, but roast with fire* (Exodus 12:9). The nub of the matter is that it should not be eaten before its preparation for eating, even by roasting, is completed—for this is the meaning of *na*: flesh on which the action of the fire has begun to take effect, and it is slightly roasted, but is not yet fit for a person to eat, is called *na*. When it is completely raw, however, the fire not having started to affect it at all, it is not included in the prohibition of *na*, so that a man should receive lashes of the whip on account of the verse, *Do not eat any of it na*. It is prohibited, though, by the law of the Written Torah: For whatever is not roasted by fire, the Torah forbade as part of a general rule.[1] The term "boiled" applies if it was cooked with water or any beverage, or with fruit juice: for the verb is doubled (literally, *and boiling, boiled with water*), which enlarges the precept to include all [forms of cooking].[2]

At the root of this precept lies the purpose written about its [the Passover offering's] ritual slaying (§5): that we should remember the miracle of the exodus from Egypt. This is why we were commanded to eat it specifically roasted: for this is the way of royal princes and rulers,

§7: NOT TO EAT THE PASSOVER OFFERING UNDERROASTED, ETC.

שֶׁהוּא מַאֲכָל טוֹב וּמִטְעָם, אֲבָל שְׁאָר הָעָם אֵינָם יְכוֹלִים לֶאֱכֹל מְעַט בָּשָׂר שֶׁתַּשִּׂיג יָדָם כִּי אִם מְבֻשָּׁל כְּדֵי לְמַלֵּא בִטְנָם. וְאָנוּ שֶׁאוֹכְלִים הַפֶּסַח שֶׁיְּצָאָנוּ לְחֵרוּת לִהְיוֹת מַמְלֶכֶת כֹּהֲנִים וְעַם קָדוֹשׁ וַדַּאי רָאוּי לָנוּ לְהִתְנַהֵג בַּאֲכִילָתוֹ דֶּרֶךְ חֵרוּת וְשָׂרוּת, מִלְּבַד שֶׁאֲכִילַת הַצָּלִי יוֹרֶה עַל הַחִפָּזוֹן שֶׁיָּצְאוּ מִמִּצְרַיִם וְלֹא יָכְלוּ לִשְׁהוֹת עַד שֶׁיִּתְבַּשֵּׁל בִּקְדֵרָה.

דִּינֵי הַמִּצְוָה, כְּגוֹן אִם עָשָׂהוּ צְלִי קְדֵרָה אוֹ סָכוֹ בְמַשְׁקִין אוֹ בְמֵי פֵרוֹת אוֹ בְמַיִם אוֹ בְשֶׁמֶן תְּרוּמָה מַה דִּינוֹ, וְיֶתֶר פְּרָטֶיהָ, מְבֹאָרִים בִּפְסָחִים. וְנוֹהֶגֶת בִּזְכָרִים וּנְקֵבוֹת בִּזְמַן הַבַּיִת. וְהָעוֹבֵר עָלֶיהָ וְאָכַל נָא אוֹ מְבֻשָּׁל לוֹקֶה. וְכֵן אִם אָכַל שְׁנֵיהֶם כְּאַחַת לוֹקֶה מַלְקוּת אַחַת, שֶׁשְּׁנֵיהֶם לָאו אֶחָד, לְדַעַת הָרַמְבַּ"ם זִכְרוֹנוֹ לִבְרָכָה.

וְהָרַמְבַּ"ן זִכְרוֹנוֹ לִבְרָכָה מָנָה אוֹתָן שְׁנֵי לָאוִין, וְכָתַב שֶׁלּוֹקִין עֲלֵיהֶן עַל כָּל אֶחָד וְאֶחָד, דְּכֵיוָן דִּכְתִיב לֹא תֹאכְלוּ כִּי אִם צְלִי אֵשׁ, מְפָרֵט בָּנָא וּמְבֻשָּׁל לָמָּה לִי, שְׁמַע מִנַּהּ לִלְקוֹת עַל כָּל אֶחָד וְאֶחָד מִן הַפְּרָטִים.

וְאָמַר זִכְרוֹנוֹ לִבְרָכָה כִּי בְכָל הַמִּצְוֹת יִהְיֶה הַמִּנְיָן כֵּן, שֶׁכָּל הַנִּפְרָטִים בַּתּוֹרָה אֶחָד אֶחָד וְהֵם דְּבָרִים חֲלוּקִים נִמְנֶה כָּל אֶחָד לְמִצְוָה אַחַת בְּחֶשְׁבּוֹן הַמִּצְוֹת, כְּגוֹן זֶה דְּנָא וּמְבֻשָּׁל, וְכֵן אֶתְנָן וּמְחִיר, וּשְׂאוֹר וּדְבַשׁ וְחֶלְבָּם. וְאָמְנָם בְּעִנְיָנִים הַמַּלְקוֹת יֵשׁ חִלּוּק בָּהֶם, שֶׁכָּל הַנִּפְרָטִים בְּלָאו אֶחָד אֵין לוֹקִין עֲלֵיהֶם אֶלָּא מַלְקוּת אַחַת, כְּגוֹן אֶתְנַן זוֹנָה וּמְחִיר כֶּלֶב, וּשְׂאוֹר וּדְבַשׁ, מִשְׁפַּט גֵּר יָתוֹם, וְכַיּוֹצֵא בָהֶן כֻּלָּן, אֲבָל הַלָּאוִין שֶׁיֵּשׁ בָּהֶן כְּלָל וּפְרָטִים בַּתְּחִלָּה אוֹ בַסּוֹף, כְּגוֹן זֶה הַלָּאו שֶׁפֵּרֵט "נָא

---

§7 1. The *mitzvah* (positive precept) to eat it roasted implies that anything else is forbidden.

2. From "The nub of the matter" to here derives from TB P'saḥim 41a; cf. also Rambam MT *hilchoth korban pesaḥ* viii 6–7.

3. This reason is given in Rambam, *Guide* III 46.

4. I.e. roasted in a pot, in nothing but its own juice; TB P'saḥim 41a and Rashi.

5. Mishnah, P'saḥim ii 8, vii 3.

6. MT *hilchoth korban pesaḥ* viii 4; ShM root 9.

7. In his commentary (*hassagoth*, "objections") to Rambam ShM root 9.

⟨102⟩

to eat roast meat, since it is a good and savory food. The rest of the people, however, must eat the little bit of meat which they manage to afford, in no other way but boiled, so as to fill their stomachs. But we would eat the Passover offering to commemorate that we went out into freedom to become *a kingdom of kohanim and a holy nation* (Exodus 19:6). Then it is certainly fitting for us to behave, while eating it, in the manner of freedom and lordship. Moreover, eating [it as] roast meat recalls the haste with which they [our ancestors] left Egypt (Exodus 12:11, Deuteronomy 16:3),[3] when they could not wait until it [the meat of their Passover offering] would boil in the pot.

As to the laws of the precept—for instance, if one prepared it as pot-roast[4] or smeared it with a beverage, fruit juice, water, or oil which is *t'rumah* (the *kohen*'s hallowed portion): what is its law;[5] and the rest of its details—these are clarified in the Talmud tractate *P'saḥim*. It applies to both man and woman, at the time of the Holy Temple [when the Sanctuary stands]. Whoever violates it and eats it *na* (under-roasted) or boiled, receives whiplashes. So too, if one ate both of them together, he receives one lashing; for both are one negative precept, in the view of Rambam of blessed memory.[6]

However, Ramban of blessed memory counts them as two negative precepts,[7] and he writes that whiplashes are given for each one separately: For since it is written, *Do not eat of it . . . but only roast with fire* (Exodus 12:9), what need was there to specify "*na* or boiled"? Hence we learn from this that for each and every one of the specified [forbidden] kinds, whiplashes are to be given.

He wrote further (be his memory for a blessing) that in all precepts the reckoning will be so: Whatever is detailed in the Torah one by one, if they are separate subjects, each one [item] is to be reckoned a separate precept in the sum of *mitzvoth*—for instance, this case of "*na* and boiled," *the hire of a harlot or the barter of a dog* (Deuteronomy 23:19; §571), *no leaven and no honey* (Leviticus 2:11; §117), and others. In regard to punishment by whiplashes, however, there is a different [rule] for them: when all are detailed under one [inclusive] prohibition, one is not punished for them by more than one whipping; for example, *the hire of a harlot or the barter of a dog; no leaven and no honey; you shall not pervert the justice due the stranger or the orphan* (Deuteronomy 24:17; §590); and so for all similar instances. But at times, prohibitions have a general statement and the details are specified before or after it: for instance, this injunction, which specifies "*na* and boiled" and gives a general

וּמְבֻשָּׁל" וְכוֹלֵל "אַל תֹּאכְלוּ... כִּי אִם צְלִי אֵשׁ" וְכֵן בְּנָזִיר כּוֹלֵל "מִכֹּל אֲשֶׁר יֵעָשֶׂה מִגֶּפֶן הַיַּיִן... לֹא יֹאכֵל", וְאַחַר כָּךְ פּוֹרֵט חַרְצַנִּים וְזָג וַעֲנָבִים לַחִים וִיבֵשִׁים, בְּאֵלּוּ וְכַיּוֹצֵא בָּהֶן לוֹקִין עֲלֵיהֶן עַל כָּל אֶחָד וְאֶחָד, כִּי רִבּוּי הַפְּרָט שֶׁלֹּא הָיָה צָרִיךְ יוֹרֶה עַל הַמַּלְקוֹת עַל כָּל אֶחָד וְאֶחָד, כְּמוֹ שֶׁאָמַרְנוּ. וְהִרְבָּה הָרַב רְאָיוֹתָיו עַל זֶה בָּעִקָּר הַתְּשִׁיעִי בְּסֵפֶר הַמִּצְוֹת שֶׁלּוֹ שֶׁאֵין חֶשְׁבּוֹן הַלָּאוִין כְּחֶשְׁבּוֹן הַמַּלְקִיּוֹת.

וְזֶה שֶׁאָמַרְתִּי שֶׁהָרַמְבַּ"ן זִכְרוֹנוֹ לִבְרָכָה יִמְנֶה כָּל הַפְּרָטִים בְּשָׁמָם אֶחָד אֶחָד מִצְוָה בִּפְנֵי עַצְמָהּ, דַּוְקָא כְּשֶׁהֵם חֲלוּקִים בָּעִנְיָן כְּמוֹ שֶׁכָּתַבְנוּ, כְּגוֹן שְׂאוֹר וּדְבַשׁ אֶתְנָן וּמְחִיר, אֲבָל בִּמְקוֹם שֶׁהָעִנְיָן אֶחָד אַף עַל פִּי שֶׁנִּפְרָטִין בְּשֵׁמוֹת חֲלוּקִים לֹא נִמְנֶה זֶה כִּי אִם מִצְוָה אַחַת, כְּגוֹן "כָּל הַבְּכוֹר אֲשֶׁר יִוָּלֵד בִּבְקָרְךָ וּבְצֹאנְךָ", שֶׁאֵין זֶה אֶלָּא צַוָּאָה אַחַת לְהַקְדִּישׁ כָּל בְּכוֹר, וְהַפְּרָט אֵינוֹ אֶלָּא בֵאוּר. וְכֵן "וְכָל מַעְשַׂר בָּקָר וָצֹאן", שֶׁאֵין זֶה אֶלָּא צַוָּאָה לְהַפְרִישׁ וְלָתֵת מַעֲשֵׂר מִבְּהֵמוֹת אִלּוּ. וְכֵן "שֹׁפְטִים וְשֹׁטְרִים" שֶׁאֵין זֶה אֶלָּא שֶׁנַּעֲשֶׂה דִין עַל פִּי אֲנָשִׁים אֵלֶּה, וְצַוָּאָה אַחַת הִיא. וְכֵן "מֹאזְנֵי צֶדֶק אַבְנֵי צֶדֶק אֵיפַת צֶדֶק וְהִין צֶדֶק", שֶׁהַכֹּל צַוָּאָה אַחַת שֶׁלֹּא נְשַׁקֵּר הַמִּדּוֹת.

[שֶׁלֹּא לְהוֹתִיר מִבְּשַׂר הַפֶּסַח]

יא. שֶׁלֹּא לְהוֹתִיר כְּלוּם מִבְּשַׂר הַפֶּסַח לְמָחֳרָתוֹ שֶׁהוּא יוֹם חֲמִשָּׁה עָשָׂר בְּנִיסָן, שֶׁנֶּאֱמַר: וְלֹא תוֹתִירוּ מִמֶּנּוּ עַד בֹּקֶר.

מִשָּׁרְשֵׁי מִצְוָה זוֹ מַה שֶּׁכָּתוּב בִּשְׁחִיטָתוֹ, לְזֵכֶר נִסֵּי מִצְרַיִם. וְזֶה שֶׁנִּצְטַוִּינוּ שֶׁלֹּא לְהוֹתִיר מִמֶּנּוּ, הָעִנְיָן הוּא כְּדֶרֶךְ מְלָכִים וְשָׂרִים שֶׁאֵינָם צְרִיכִים לְהוֹתִיר

rule, *Do not eat . . . but only roast with fire.* So too about the Nazirite: there is a general rule, *of all that is made of the grapevine . . . he shall not eat* (Numbers 6:4), then particular details [are proscribed]: pressed grapes, grape seeds, fresh and dried grapes (*ibid.* 3–4). In these and similar instances, whiplashes are given for each one separately: for the unneeded addition of the detail indicates whiplashes as punishment for each separately, as we have stated. The master [Ramban] arrayed his many proofs for this in the ninth Principle of his *Book of Precepts*—that the number of negative precepts is not identical with the number of misdeeds punishable by whipping.

Now, this point that I have stated, that Ramban of blessed memory counts all particular details listed individually [in Scripture], each as a separate injunction—this is only when they are disparate in content, as we have written: for example, leaven and honey, a harlot's hire and a dog's barter. But where the subject is one, even though particular instances are listed separately, it is counted as no more than one precept. For example, *All the firstling males that are born of your herd and flock, you shall consecrate to the Lord your God* (Deuteronomy 15:19). This is but one commandment to consecrate every firstborn animal, and the particulars are merely a clarification [of that commandment]. So also, *All the tithe of the herd and the flock* (Leviticus 27:32), for this is only a commandment (§351) to separate out and give a tithe (a tenth) from these animals. So too, *Justice and officers shall you appoint* (Deuteronomy 16:18; §491), as this is only [an injunction] that we shall effect justice through these people, and it is but one commandment. So also, *Just scales, just weights, a just éphah and a just hin shall you have* (Leviticus 19:36; §258): it is all one commandment, that we should not falsify the measures.

8 [TO LEAVE OVER NO FLESH OF THE PASSOVER OFFERING] not to leave over anything from the flesh of the Passover offering for the morrow, which is the fifteenth of Nissan—as it is stated, *you shall let nothing of it remain till the morning* (Exodus 12:10).

At the root of this precept lies the reason written in regard to its ritual slaying (§5): to [have us] remember the miracles of Egypt. As for the reason why we were commanded to let nothing of it remain, this conduct is like the way of kings and noblemen, who need not leave over any prepared food of theirs from one day to the next.

§8–9: ON THE PASSOVER OFFERING / TO REMOVE HAMÉTZ

מְתַבְּשִׁילִם מִיּוֹם אֶל יוֹם, וְעַל כֵּן אָמַר שֶׁאִם יִוָּתֵר מִמֶּנּוּ יִנָּתֵן כְּדָבָר שֶׁאֵין חֵפֶץ בּוֹ כְּדֶרֶךְ מַלְכֵי אֲדָמָה, וְכָל זֶה לִזְכֹּר וְלִקְבֹּעַ בַּלֵּב שֶׁבְּבוֹאוֹ זְמַן גְּאֻלָּנוּ הַשֵּׁם מֵעַבְדוּת וְנַעֲשִׂינוּ בְּנֵי חוֹרִין וְזָכִינוּ לְמַלְכוּת וְלִגְדֻלָּה.

דִּין הַמִּצְוָה בִּפְסָחִים. וְנוֹהֶגֶת בִּזְכָרִים וּנְקֵבוֹת בִּזְמַן הַבַּיִת. וְעוֹבֵר עָלֶיהָ וְהוֹתִיר עָבַר עַל לָאו, אֲבָל אֵין לוֹקִין עַל לָאו זֶה, לְפִי שֶׁהוּא נִתָּק לַעֲשֵׂה, שֶׁנֶּאֱמַר "וְהַנֹּתָר וְגוֹ' בָּאֵשׁ תִּשְׂרֹפוּ", וַהֲלָכָה הִיא לָאו שֶׁנִּתַּק לַעֲשֵׂה אֵין לוֹקִין עָלָיו.

[מִצְוַת הַשְׁבָּתַת חָמֵץ]

ט לְהָסִיר כָּל לֶחֶם חָמֵץ מִמִּשְׁכְּנוֹתֵינוּ בְּיוֹם אַרְבָּעָה עָשָׂר בְּנִיסָן, שֶׁנֶּאֱמַר "אַךְ בַּיּוֹם הָרִאשׁוֹן תַּשְׁבִּיתוּ שְּׂאֹר מִבָּתֵּיכֶם", וּפֵרוּשׁוֹ רִאשׁוֹן קֹדֶם לַפֶּסַח.

מִשָּׁרְשֵׁי מִצְוָה זוֹ כְּדֵי שֶׁנִּזָּכֵר הַנִּסִּים שֶׁבְּמִצְרַיִם, כְּמוֹ שֶׁכָּתוּב בְּקָרְבַּן פֶּסַח.

דִּינֵי הַמִּצְוָה, כְּגוֹן שְׁעַת בִּעוּרוֹ מִן הַיּוֹם מָתַי, וּמַה הִיא הַשְׁבָּתָתוֹ, וּבְאֵי זֶה מָקוֹם צָרִיךְ לְחַפְּשׂוֹ, וּבְאֵי זֶה מָקוֹם אֵינוֹ צָרִיךְ, וּמֵאֵימָתַי מֻטֶּלֶת הַמִּצְוָה עָלָיו אִם יוֹצֵא לַדֶּרֶךְ, וְאִם חָל אַרְבָּעָה עָשָׂר בְּנִיסָן בְּשַׁבָּת אֵיךְ יִהְיֶה דִּינוֹ, וְהַבִּטּוּל בַּפֶּה שֶׁצָּרִיךְ לַעֲשׂוֹת נוֹסָף עַל הַבִּעוּר, וְיֶתֶר פְּרָטֶיהָ, מְבֹאָרִים בְּפֶסַח רִאשׁוֹן.

וְנוֹהֶגֶת בְּכָל מָקוֹם וּבְכָל זְמַן בִּזְכָרִים וּנְקֵבוֹת. וְהָעוֹבֵר עָלֶיהָ וְלֹא הִשְׁבִּיתוֹ בִּטֵּל עֲשֵׂה דְּתַשְׁבִּיתוּ. וְאִם יֵשׁ חָמֵץ בְּמִשְׁכְּנוֹתָיו עוֹבֵר גַּם כֵּן עַל לֹא תַעֲשֶׂה, שֶׁנֶּאֱמַר "שְׂאֹר לֹא יִמָּצֵא בְּבָתֵּיכֶם", אֲבָל אֵין לוֹקִין עַל לָאו זֶה אִם לֹא עָשָׂה בּוֹ מַעֲשֶׂה, שֶׁהֲלָכָה הִיא: לָאו שֶׁאֵין בּוֹ מַעֲשֶׂה אֵין לוֹקִין עָלָיו.

---

1. Also in MT *hilchoth korban pesah* ix.
2. MT *ibid.* x 11, *hilchoth p'sulé ha-mukdashin* xviii 9.
3. TB Makkoth 13b (cited in Rashi to Deuteronomy 25:1).

1. So explained in TB P'sahim 5a.
2. See Mishnah, P'sahim i 1, 3; ii 1.
3. *Ibid.* i 1.
4. I.e. he will not be at home at the standard time to search and remove all *hamétz*; TB P'sahim 6a.
5. I.e. the day before Passover, when the last traces of *hamétz* must ordinarily be gathered and burnt; Mishnah, P'sahim iii 6, TB 13a.
6. *Ibid.* 6b.
7. I.e. if he did no act to bring *hamétz* into his house during Passover, but merely failed to remove it.
8. TB P'sahim 63b, 84a; Sanhedrin 63b; etc.

Therefore He stated that if anything remains of it, it should be burnt like something for which there is no need—in the manner of the kings of the earth. All this is to [make us] remember and to fix in our heart that at this time [of year] the Eternal Lord rescued us from slavery and we became free men and attained majesty and grandeur.

The law of this precept is in the Talmud tractate *P'saḥim* (102b).[1] It applies to both man and woman in the time of the Temple. He who transgresses it and leaves [meat] over, violates a negative precept. But no whiplashes are given for this, because it is connected onto a positive precept, as it is stated, *and what remains*, etc. *you shall burn with fire* (Exodus 12:10);[2] and it is a rule [that for violating] a negative precept which is connected with a positive precept, no lashes are given.[3]

9 [THE PRECEPT OF REMOVING ḤAMÉTZ]

to remove all leavened bread, *ḥamétz*, from our dwellings on the fourteenth day of Nissan—as it is stated, *however, on the first day you shall put away leaven out of your houses* (Exodus 12:15); and its meaning is "the first day" *before* Passover.[1]

At the root of this precept lies the purpose that we should remember the miracles that occurred in Egypt, as written [above] about the Passover sacrifice (§5).

As to the laws of the precept—for instance, what is the time of day by which it [*ḥamétz*] must be all cleared away; what it means to "put it away";[2] where one must search for it [to remove it], and where one need not;[3] from which time [how early] the obligation devolves upon him [to search and remove *ḥamétz*] if he is leaving on a journey;[4] what should the rule be if the fourteenth of Nissan falls on a Sabbath;[5] making *ḥamétz* null and void by one's spoken word, which needs to be done in addition to clearing it away;[6] and its other details—these are explained in the first part (chapters 1–4) of Talmud tractate *P'saḥim*.

This precept remains in force in every time and place, for both man and woman. If someone transgresses it and does not clear it [his *ḥamétz*] away, he has disobeyed the positive commandment to "put away leaven out of your houses." And if there is *ḥamétz* in his dwelling, he also violates a negative precept: for it is stated, *For seven days no leaven shall be found in your houses* (Exodus 12:19); but one is not punished by whipping over this negative precept if he has done no action:[7] for it is a rule regarding a negative precept that if there was no action [done to violate it] one is not whipped for it.[8]

§10–11: TO EAT MATZAH / HAVE NO HAMÉTZ IN ONE'S POSSESSION

[מִצְוַת אֲכִילַת מַצָּה]

י לֶאֱכֹל לֶחֶם מַצָּה בְּלֵיל חֲמִשָּׁה עָשָׂר בְּנִיסָן הֶעָשׂוּי מִמִּין דָּגָן, שֶׁנֶּאֱמַר "בָּעֶרֶב תֹּאכְלוּ מַצֹּת", וּפֵרוּשׁוֹ לֵיל חֲמִשָּׁה עָשָׂר בְּנִיסָן, בֵּין בִּזְמַן שֶׁיִּהְיֶה שָׁם פֶּסַח אוֹ בִּזְמַן שֶׁלֹּא יִהְיֶה שָׁם.

מִשָּׁרְשֵׁי מִצְוָה זוֹ מַה שֶּׁכָּתוּב בְּקָרְבַּן הַפֶּסַח.

דִּינֵי הַמִּצְוָה, כְּגוֹן שִׁמּוּר הַצָּרִיךְ לַמַּצּוֹת וְעִנְיָנֵי לִישָׁתָן, וּבְאֵי זֶה מַיִם נִלּוֹשׁוֹת, וְשִׁעוּר אֲכִילָתָן לְכָל הַפָּחוֹת, וְיֶתֶר פְּרָטֶיהָ, מְבֹאָרִים בְּפֶסַח רִאשׁוֹן. וְנוֹהֶגֶת בְּכָל מָקוֹם וּבְכָל זְמַן בִּזְכָרִים וּנְקֵבוֹת. וְעוֹבֵר עָלֶיהָ בִּטֵּל עֲשֵׂה. וּכְבָר אָמַרְנוּ שֶׁבֵּית דִּין כּוֹפִין עַל בִּטּוּל עֲשֵׂה.

[שֶׁלֹּא יִמָּצֵא חָמֵץ בִּרְשׁוּתֵנוּ בַּפֶּסַח]

יא שֶׁלֹּא יִמָּצֵא חָמֵץ בִּרְשׁוּתֵנוּ כָּל יְמֵי הַפֶּסַח, שֶׁנֶּאֱמַר: שִׁבְעַת יָמִים שְׂאֹר לֹא יִמָּצֵא בְּבָתֵּיכֶם. וּבֵאֲרוּ חֲכָמֵינוּ זִכְרוֹנָם לִבְרָכָה: לָאו דַּוְקָא בֵּיתוֹ, אֶלָּא כָּל שֶׁבִּרְשׁוּתוֹ. וְלָאו דַּוְקָא שְׂאוֹר שֶׁהוּא מְחַמֵּץ, דְּהוּא הַדִּין לְחָמֵץ, דִּשְׂאוֹר וְחָמֵץ חַד הוּא לְעִנְיָן אִסּוּרוֹ.

מִשָּׁרְשֵׁי הַמִּצְוָה כְּדֵי שֶׁנִּזְכֹּר לְעוֹלָם הַנִּסִּים שֶׁנַּעֲשׂוּ לָנוּ בִּיצִיאַת מִצְרַיִם, כְּמוֹ שֶׁכָּתוּב בְּשֶׂה הַפֶּסַח. וְנִזְכֹּר שֶׁאֵרַע לָנוּ כָּעִנְיָן זֶה שֶׁמִּתּוֹךְ חִפָּזוֹן הַיְצִיאָה אָפִינוּ הָעִיסָה מַצָּה כִּי לֹא יָכְלוּ לְהִתְמַהְמֵהַּ עַד שֶׁיַּחֲמִיץ, כְּמוֹ שֶׁכָּתוּב, וַיֹּאפוּ אֶת הַבָּצֵק וְגוֹמֵר.

דִּינֵי הַמִּצְוָה, כְּגוֹן אִם הִפְקִיד חֲמֵצוֹ בְּיַד אֲחֵרִים מַה דִּינוֹ, אוֹ אֲחֵרִים בְּיָדוֹ,

---

1. See §6 note 1.
2. I.e. wheat, spelt, barley, oats or rye (Rambam MT *hilchoth hamétz u-matzah* v 1).
3. I.e. whether or not the holy Temple in Jerusalem is in existence; TB P'sahim 120a.
4. I.e. of the dough from which they are made; TB P'sahim 40a, 42a, 48a. The term *shimmur* (watchful care) also—and primarily—denotes keeping them at every stage, from wheat to finished *matzoth*, specifically for this *matzah* which will be eaten that evening by the Torah's commandment.
5. About the water see *ibid.* 42a; the least amount: as of an olive (Mishnah, Hallah i 2).

1. TB P'sahim 5b.
2. TB Bétzah 7b.
3. *Tur 'Orah Hayyim* §440 cites differing views; see also *Shulhan 'Aruch ibid.*

[THE PRECEPT OF EATING MATZAH ON PASSOVER]

10 to eat unleavened bread, *matzah*, on the evening of the fifteenth of Nissan,[1] made of a species of cereal grain[2]—as it is stated, *at evening you shall eat unleavened bread* (Exodus 12:18), meaning the evening of the fifteenth of Nissan, whether it is a time when there is a Passover sacrifice there, or a time when there is not.[3]

At the root of this precept lies the purpose written [above] about the Passover sacrifice (§5).

As to the laws of the precept—such as the watchful care needed in regard to *matzoth* and the manner of their kneading;[4] with what water they should be kneaded; the very least amount that must be eaten,[5] and its other details—these are explained in the first part (chapters 1–4) of Talmud tractate *P'saḥim*. It remains in effect at every time and place, for both man and woman. One who transgresses it has disobeyed a positive precept. And we have already stated (§6) that the *beth din* applies coercion to prevent the disobedience of a positive *mitzvah*.

[TO HAVE NO ḤAMÉTZ IN OUR POSSESSION DURING PASSOVER]

11 that no *ḥamétz* should be found in our possession during all the days of Passover—as it is stated, *For seven days no leaven shall be found in your houses* (Exodus 12:19); and our Sages of blessed memory explained [that this means] not particularly in one's house, but anywhere in one's possession;[1] and not particularly leaven [e.g. yeast] which causes leavening, as the law is the same for *ḥamétz*; for leaven and *ḥamétz* are all one as regards the prohibition.[2]

At the root of the precept lies the purpose that we should forever remember the miracles that were wrought for us in [connection with] the departure from Egypt, as was written about the Passover lamb (§5), and we should remember that something like this happened to us: that amid the haste of the departure we baked the dough as *matzah*, since they could not delay until it became leavened (rose); as it is written, *they baked unleavened cakes of the dough which they had brought out of Egypt, for it was not leavened; because they were thrust out of Egypt and could not tarry, neither had they prepared for themselves any provisions* (Exodus 12:39).

As to the laws of the precept—for instance, what is the law if one left his *ḥamétz* in the care of others, or others left theirs in his care;[3]

§11-12: ABOUT ḤAMÉTZ DURING PASSOVER

וְכֵן חָמֵץ הֶקְדֵּשׁ בְּיָדוֹ אוֹ שֶׁל גּוֹי בְּאַחֲרָיוּת וְשֶׁלֹּא בְּאַחֲרָיוּת, וְדִין גּוֹי אַלֵּם שֶׁהִפְקִיד לוֹ חָמֵץ, וְדִין תַּעֲרֹבֶת חָמֵץ אִם עוֹבְרִין עָלָיו, וְהַפַּת שֶׁעִפְּשָׁה מַה דִּינוֹ. וְיֶתֶר פְּרָטֶיהָ, מְבֹאָרִים בְּפֶסַח רִאשׁוֹן.

וְנוֹהֶגֶת בִּזְכָרִים וּנְקֵבוֹת בְּכָל מָקוֹם וּבְכָל זְמַן. וְעוֹבֵר עָלֶיהָ וְנִמְצָא חָמֵץ בִּרְשׁוּתוֹ בְּמֵזִיד עָבַר עַל שְׁנֵי לָאוִין מִשּׁוּם בַּל יֵרָאֶה וּבַל יִמָּצֵא, וְלוֹקֶה כָּל זְמַן שֶׁעָשָׂה בוֹ מַעֲשֶׂה, כְּגוֹן שֶׁחִמֵּץ עִסָּה וְהִנִּיחַ בְּבֵיתוֹ, אוֹ שֶׁלָּקַח חָמֵץ וְהִצְנִיעוֹ בְּבֵיתוֹ. אֲבָל אִם לֹא עָשָׂה בּוֹ שׁוּם מַעֲשֶׂה אֶלָּא שֶׁנִּשְׁאַר בַּבַּיִת מִקֹּדֶם הַפֶּסַח אֵין לוֹקֶה עָלָיו, שֶׁהֲלָכָה הִיא לָאו שֶׁאֵין בּוֹ מַעֲשֶׂה אֵין לוֹקִין עָלָיו, כְּמוֹ שֶׁאָמַרְנוּ.

[שֶׁלֹּא לֶאֱכֹל מִכָּל דָּבָר שֶׁיֵּשׁ בּוֹ חָמֵץ]

יב שֶׁלֹּא לֶאֱכֹל מִדְּבָרִים שֶׁיֵּשׁ בָּהֶן חָמֵץ וְאַף עַל פִּי שֶׁאֵין עִקַּר הַדָּבָר חָמֵץ. כְּגוֹן כֻּתָּח הַבַּבְלִי וְכַיּוֹצֵא בּוֹ, שֶׁנֶּאֱמַר: כָּל מַחְמֶצֶת לֹא תֹאכֵלוּ. וּפֵרְשׁוּ זִכְרוֹנָם לִבְרָכָה שֶׁעִנְיָן הַכָּתוּב הַזֶּה יוֹרֶה בָזֶה, שֶׁכָּךְ קִבְּלוּ הַפֵּרוּשׁ בּוֹ.

וְדַעַת הָרַמְבַּ״ם זִכְרוֹנוֹ לִבְרָכָה שֶׁאִם יֵשׁ בַּמַּאֲכָלִים אֵלּוּ כַּזַּיִת חָמֵץ בִּכְדֵי אֲכִילַת פְּרָס אָסוּר מִן הַתּוֹרָה בְּלָאו, כְּלוֹמַר לְמַלְקוֹת, אֲבָל לֹא לְכָרֵת, מִבֵּינָן שֶׁנִּתְעָרֵב בְּרֹב. וְאִם לֹא יִהְיֶה בָּהֶם כַּזַּיִת חָמֵץ בִּכְדֵי אֲכִילַת פְּרָס לֹא יִהְיֶה בּוֹ מַלְקוֹת אֶלָּא מַכַּת מַרְדּוּת, לְפִי שֶׁאֵינוֹ אָסוּר מִן הַתּוֹרָה אֶלָּא מִדְּרַבָּנָן, וְכֵן כָּתַב בְּחִבּוּרוֹ הַגָּדוֹל. וְאִם כֵּן לְדַעְתּוֹ יָבוֹא הַלָּאו הַזֶּה דְּכָל מַחְמֶצֶת לְהֵיכָא שֶׁנִּתְעָרַב

---

4. This refers to a man who will force him to pay should the *hamétz* be lost or stolen, whether or not it is his fault; hence it is considered under his responsibility, as if in his possession, and he must remove it from his domain before Passover (Rambam MT *hilchoth hamétz u-matzah* iv 4).

5. Rambam *ibid*; Mishnah, P'sahim iii 1; Rashi *ad loc.* (TB 42a).

6. I.e. it is no longer fit to eat—not even for dogs: TB P'sahim 42b; R. Isaac Alfasi (Rif) *ad loc.*

7. So Rambam MT *hilchoth hamétz u-matzah* i 2–3.

1. Made of sour milk, old (moldering) bread crusts and salt, for dipping food into it (TB P'sahim 43a).

2. *Ibid*.

3. Literally, within an amount of food that can be eaten in the same time as *p'ras*, half a loaf. Rambam MT *hilchoth hamétz u-matzah* i 6 defines this as the bulk of three eggs; Rashi to TB P'sahim 42b, four eggs. As our author avowedly follows Rambam, the term has been rendered throughout as "the amount of three eggs." Rambam's view is to be found in ShM negative precept §198.

4. MT *Ibid*. "Punishment for disobedience" is also a whipping; but while it is always thirty-nine lashes of the whip when ordained by the Torah, here (in Rambam's view) the amount is at the *beth din*'s discretion.

so too if *hamétz* consecrated [to the Sanctuary] is in his possession, or the *hamétz* of a non-Jew, either under his responsibility, or not under his responsibility;[1] the law when a powerful non-Jew left his *hamétz* with him;[4] the law of food mixed with *hamétz*, if this causes violation of the precept;[5] what is the law about bread that decayed;[6] and its other details—these are explained in the first part (chapters 1–4) of the Talmud tractate *P'sahim*.

It applies to both man and woman, in every place, in every time. If one violates it deliberately and *hamétz* is to be found in his possession, he transgresses two negative precepts: that it should not be seen (§20) and not be found in his possession; and he receives whiplashes, provided he did it by some action: e.g., if he leavened dough and left it in his house; or if he acquired *hamétz* and put it away in his house. But if he did no action whatever with it but it merely remained in his house from before Passover, he is not punished for it. For the rule is: for violating a negative precept where no action is involved, one is not punished by whiplashes[7]—as we have stated (§9).

12 [TO EAT NOTHING CONTAINING HAMÉTZ DURING PASSOVER]

not to eat anything which has *hamétz* in it, even though the main element of the food is not *hamétz*: for instance, Babylonian sauce,[1] and anything similar—for it is stated, *You shall eat nothing leavened* (Exodus 12:20), and our Sages of blessed memory explained[2] that the content of this verse is meant to teach [us] this, for so they received the meaning of it [in the Oral Tradition].

The ruling of Rambam of blessed memory is that if these foods contain an amount of *hamétz* equal to an olive, within an amount equal to three eggs,[3] the negative precept is transgressed; in other words, it is punishable by whiplashes, but not by *karéth* [Divine severance of existence], since it [the *hamétz*] was mixed into a greater part [of other food]. If there is not *hamétz* in the amount of an olive in food of the amount of three eggs, the standard punishment of whiplashes is not given, but rather a flogging for disobedience; for it is not forbidden by the Written Torah, but by the law of the Sages. And so he [Rambam] wrote in his great work.[4]

Thus, by his view, this negative precept, *You shall eat nothing leavened*, applies where an olive's amount of *hamétz* was mixed into

§12: TO EAT NOTHING ON PASSOVER CONTAINING HAMÉTZ

כְּזַיִת חָמֵץ בִּכְדֵי אֲכִילַת פְּרָס שֶׁיִּהְיֶה בּוֹ לָאו, כְּלוֹמַר מַלְקוּת וְלֹא כָרֵת.

וְהָרַמְבְּ"ן זִכְרוֹנוֹ לִבְרָכָה כָּתַב הֶפֶךְ מִזֶּה, וְאָמַר שֶׁהַלָּאו הַזֶּה אֵינֶנּוּ נֶחְשָׁב בִּכְלַל הַלָּאוִין, אֶלָּא שֶׁהוּא מִן הַלָּאוִין הָרַבִּים שֶׁבָּאוּ בְּחָמֵץ וּבִשְׂאוֹר. וְזֶה הַלָּאו בָּא לְהוֹרוֹת עַל מַה שֶּׁאָמְרוּ חֲכָמִים בַּגְּמָרָא: [מַחְמֶצֶת] — אֵין לִי אֶלָּא שֶׁנִּתְחַמֵּץ מֵאֵלָיו; חִמְּצוֹ עַל יְדֵי דָבָר אַחֵר מִנַּיִן — תַּלְמוּד לוֹמַר כָּל מַחְמֶצֶת.

אֲבָל בְּעִנְיָן חָמֵץ שֶׁנִּתְעָרֵב, כָּל זְמַן שֶׁיִּהְיֶה בּוֹ כְזַיִת בִּכְדֵי אֲכִילַת פְּרָס, בָּזֶה אֵין צָרִיךְ לָאו בִּפְנֵי עַצְמוֹ, דַּהֲרֵי הוּא כְּאִלּוּ הוּא בְעֵינָיו וְיֵשׁ בּוֹ כָרֵת כְּמוֹ בְּכָל חָמֵץ שֶׁהוּא בְעֵינוֹ, וְאִם לֹא יִהְיֶה בַּתַּעֲרֹבֶת כְּזַיִת בִּכְדֵי אֲכִילַת פְּרָס הָאוֹכְלוֹ פָּטוּר, אֲבָל אָסוּר, שֶׁהֲלָכָה כְּדִבְרֵי חֲכָמִים שֶׁאָמְרוּ עַל חָמֵץ דָּגָן גָּמוּר עָנוּשׁ כָּרֵת, וְכֹל שֶׁהוּא כְזַיִת בִּכְדֵי אֲכִילַת פְּרָס דָּגָן גָּמוּר נִקְרָא, וְעַל עֵרוּבוֹ, כְּלוֹמַר שֶׁהוּא פָּחוֹת מִכְּזַיִת בִּכְדֵי אֲכִילַת פְּרָס, בְּלֹא כְלוּם, וּדְלֹא כְּרַבִּי אֱלִיעֶזֶר דְּפָלִיג עֲלַיְהוּ בַּגְּמָרָא וְאָמַר עַל עֵרוּבוֹ בְּלָאו.

מִשָּׁרְשֵׁי מִצְוָה זוֹ מַה שֶּׁכָּתַבְנוּ בִּשְׂאוֹר. וְאוּלָם לְחַזֵּק הַדָּבָר בְּלִבֵּנוּ הִרְחִיקָתְנוּ הַתּוֹרָה מִמֶּנּוּ כָּל כָּךְ.

דִּינֵי הַמִּצְוָה, כְּגוֹן הַדְּבָרִים שֶׁנִּכְלְלוּ בְּאִסּוּר זֶה מַה הֵן וּמָה שָּׁם, וְיֶתֶר פְּרָטֶיהָ, בִּפְסָחִים. וְנוֹהֶגֶת בַּזְּכָרִים וּנְקֵבוֹת בְּכָל מָקוֹם וּבְכָל זְמַן. וְהָעוֹבֵר עָלֶיהָ לוֹקֶה, וּבִתְנַאי שֶׁיִּהְיֶה בָּהֶן כְּזַיִת בִּכְדֵי אֲכִילַת פְּרָס, כְּמוֹ שֶׁאָמַרְנוּ, אֲבָל אֵין בּוֹ כָרֵת לְדַעַת הָרַמְבְּ"ם זִכְרוֹנוֹ לִבְרָכָה, וּלְדַעַת הָרַמְבְּ"ן זִכְרוֹנוֹ לִבְרָכָה יֵשׁ בּוֹ כָרֵת.

---

5. In his commentary to ShM negative precept §198.

6. TB P'saḥim 28b. The bracketed word that follows in the Hebrew is not in our editions of the Talmud, but is found in three early manuscripts (*Dikduké Sof'rim*).

7. E.g. by the sediment (lees) of wine that became dried in an oven (*tosafoth, ibid.* s.v. *maḥamath*). The word *ḥim'tzo* (if it was made leavened) is not in our Talmud editions, but is present likewise in Ramban's citation in his *hassagoth* (commentary) to ShM, negative precept §198 (ed. Chavel, p. 340).

8. Ibid. 43a.

9. See Mishnah, P'saḥim iii 1, and TB 42a.

10. Cf. also *Shulḥan 'Aruch 'Orah Ḥayyim* §446.

three eggs' amount of food; then a negative precept is transgressed; i.e. one becomes punishable by whiplashes, but not by *karéth*.

Ramban of blessed memory, however, wrote the very opposite of this:[5] He stated that this prohibition is not to be reckoned in the general list of the negative precepts, for it is included under the many prohibitions given [in the Torah] about *hamétz* and leaven. This negative precept, though, was written to instruct us on what the Sages said in the Talmud:[6] *mahmetzeth, anything leavened* (Exodus 12:20) — thus I know only what that became leavened of itself [is banned]; how do I know this [applies also] if it was leavened by something else?[7] Scripture writes, *kol mahmetzeth, anything leavened whatever.*

Furthermore, [Ramban holds] concerning *hamétz* mixed [into other food] that as long as there is an olive's amount of it in three eggs' amount of food, there is no need for a separate negative precept for this: for it is as if the *hamétz* were intact (in its original state), and it incurs the punishment of *karéth* [Divine severance of existence], as any *hamétz* in its original, natural state does. And if the mixture does not contain an olive's amount of *hamétz* in three eggs' amount of food, one who eats it is not punished, although it is forbidden: For the law follows the ruling of the Sages,[8] who said that for pure [unadulterated] *hamétz*, of grain, the punishment is *karéth*, and whatever has an olive's amount of *hamétz* in three eggs' amount of food is considered as pure grain [*hamétz*]; but for its mixture, i.e. with less than an olive's amount in three eggs' amount of food, there is no punishment at all. We thus do not follow R. Eli'ezer, who differs with them in the Talmud[8] and says that over its mixture one violates a negative precept.

At the root of this precept lies the point we wrote about leaven (§ 11); indeed, to confirm the matter in our heart, the Torah removed us from it [leaven] even to this great extent.

As to the laws of the precept—such as what matters are included under this prohibition: what are they and what are their names;[9] and its other details—[these are to be found] in the Talmud tractate *P'sahim*.[10] It applies to both man and woman, in every place and every time. He who transgresses it receives whiplashes, but this on condition that there is [at least] an olive's amount [of *hamétz*] in three eggs' amount of the food [he ate], as we have stated. There is, though, no punishment of *karéth* [Divine severance of existence] for it, according to Rambam of blessed memory; while according to Ramban of blessed memory, there is *karéth* for it. If there is not an olive's amount

וְאִם אֵין בּוֹ כְזַיִת בִּכְדֵי אֲכִילַת פְּרָס אֵין בּוֹ חִיּוּב מַלְקוֹת אֶלָּא דִינוֹ כְּדִין חֲצִי שִׁעוּר שֶׁאָסוּר מִן הַתּוֹרָה, וְאֵין לוֹקִין עָלָיו, וּבָזֶה יוֹדוּ שְׁנֵיהֶם זִכְרוֹנָם לִבְרָכָה.

[שֶׁלֹּא נַאֲכִיל מִן הַפֶּסַח לְיִשְׂרָאֵל מְשֻׁמָּד]

יג שֶׁלֹּא נַאֲכִיל מִן הַפֶּסַח לְיִשְׂרָאֵל מְשֻׁמָּד, שֶׁנֶּאֱמַר "כָּל בֶּן נֵכָר לֹא יֹאכַל בּוֹ", וּבָא הַפֵּרוּשׁ עָלָיו בֶּן יִשְׂרָאֵל שֶׁנִּתְנַכְּרוּ מַעֲשָׂיו לְאָבִיו שֶׁבַּשָּׁמַיִם, וְכֵן תִּרְגֵּם אוֹנְקְלוֹס.

מִשָּׁרְשֵׁי מִצְוָה זוֹ מַה שֶּׁכָּתוּב בִּשְׁחִיטָתוֹ, לִזְכֹּר נִסֵּי מִצְרַיִם, וְעַל כֵּן רָאוּי שֶׁלֹּא יֹאכַל בּוֹ מְשֻׁמָּד, אַחַר שֶׁאָנוּ עוֹשִׂין אוֹתוֹ לְאוֹת וּלְזִכָּרוֹן שֶׁבָּאנוּ בְּאוֹתוֹ הַזְּמָן לַחֲסוֹת תַּחַת כַּנְפֵי הַשְּׁכִינָה וְנִכְנַסְנוּ בִּבְרִית הַתּוֹרָה וְהָאֱמוּנָה, אֵין רָאוּי שֶׁנַּאֲכִיל מִמֶּנּוּ לְמִי שֶׁהוּא הֵפֶךְ מִזֶּה שֶׁיָּצָא מִן הַכְּלָל וְכָפַר בָּאֱמוּנָה. וְעַל כַּיּוֹצֵא בָּזֶה נֶאֱמַר בַּתַּלְמוּד לִפְעָמִים "סָבְרָא הוּא", כְּלוֹמַר וְאֵין צָרִיךְ רְאָיָה אַחֶרֶת. וְנוֹהֶגֶת בִּזְכָרִים וּנְקֵבוֹת בִּזְמַן הַבַּיִת שֶׁיֵּשׁ שָׁם פֶּסַח. וְעוֹבֵר עָלֶיהָ וְהֶאֱכִיל מִמֶּנּוּ לְבֶן נֵכָר עוֹבֵר עַל לָאו. וְאֵין בּוֹ מַלְקוֹת לְפִי שֶׁאֵין בּוֹ מַעֲשֶׂה.

[שֶׁלֹּא נַאֲכִיל מִן הַפֶּסַח לְגֵר וְתוֹשָׁב]

יד שֶׁלֹּא לְהַאֲכִיל מִבְּשַׂר הַפֶּסַח לְגֵר וּלְתוֹשָׁב וְשָׂכִיר: תּוֹשָׁב, שֶׁנֶּאֱמַר לֹא יֹאכַל בּוֹ. וְהַתּוֹשָׁב הוּא אָדָם מִן הָאֻמּוֹת שֶׁקִּבֵּל עָלָיו שֶׁלֹּא לַעֲבֹד עֲבוֹדָה זָרָה וְאוֹכֵל נְבֵלוֹת. וְשָׂכִיר הוּא גֵּר שֶׁמָּל וְלֹא טָבַל, שֶׁכֵּן פֵּרְשׁוּ חֲכָמִים זִכְרוֹנָם לִבְרָכָה.

מִשָּׁרְשֵׁי מִצְוָה זוֹ מַה שֶּׁכָּתַבְנוּ בַּאֲחֵרוֹת לִזְכֹּר יְצִיאַת מִצְרָיִם. וּבַעֲבוּר שֶׁקּוֹרְבָּן

13

1. In Mechilta and MdRSbY.

2. "Any Israelite who turns apostate shall not eat of it." MH notes, however, that this precept applies for certain only to an idol-worshipping apostate. To any other apostate, it is a matter of doubt if the precept applies.

3. I.e. we became the Almighty's own people.

4. TB Shabbath 96b, etc.

5. So Rambam MT *hilchoth korban pesaḥ* ix 7.

6. MH tentatively postulates that although the precept applies only where a person gave the apostate bodily some of the Passover offering to eat, i.e. he put it into the man's mouth, and hence he did a physical act, the core action that makes the precept be violated is the eating of it, and to this the person contributed no physical act; his deed was only a prelude. See also *Kessef Mishneh* to MT *hilchoth korban pesaḥ* (cited in ed. Chavel).

14

1. The "resident" is so defined in Sifra to Leviticus 25:35 (*parashah* 5); *ibid.* to *ibid.* 47 (*perek* 8). The "hired servant" is thus defined in TB Yevamoth 71a.

[of *hamétz*] in three eggs' amount of the food, it brings no punishment of whiplashes, but its law is rather like the rule for "half a measure" [of something prohibited]: It is forbidden by the Written Torah's law, but no whipping is given for it. In this matter both [Rambam and Ramban] of blessed memory concur.

13 [TO GIVE AN APOSTATE NO PART OF A PASSOVER OFFERING TO EAT]

that we should give an apostate Jew nothing of the Passover offering to eat—as stated, *no alien shall eat of it* (Exodus 12:43); and the meaning given for this [alien] through the tradition[1] is: an Israelite whose ways have become estranged, alien to his Father in heaven. And so Onkelos rendered it [in his Aramaic translation].[2]

At the root of this precept lies what was written about its ritual slaying (§5): that we should remember the miracles of Egypt. It is therefore fitting that an apostate should not eat of it, since we prepare it as a sign and a commemoration that at that time we came to shelter under the wings of the *shechinah* (Divine Presence)[3] and we entered the covenant of Torah and faith. So it is not fitting that we should give someone who has turned against this, leaving the community and denying our faith, any of it to eat. About something like this it is sometimes said in the Talmud,[4] "It is logical, reasonable"; i.e. it needs no other proof.

This applies to both man and woman, at the time the Holy Temple stands, where the Passover offering is [sacrificed]. Whoever transgresses it and gives an "alien" any of it to eat, violates a negative precept; but no whiplashes are given for it,[5] since it involves no [personal] action.[6]

14 [TO GIVE NO PART OF A PASSOVER OFFERING TO "A PARTIAL PROSELYTE AND RESIDENT"]

not to have any [partial] proselyte or "resident" eat of the Passover offering—as it is stated, *A resident and a hired servant shall not eat of it* (Exodus 12:45). A "resident" is a member of the nations who has resolved not to worship idols, but eats carcasses (non-kosher food). A "hired servant" is a partial convert who has undergone circumcision but not ritual immersion. For so the Sages of blessed memory explained.[1]

At the root of this precept lies the point we have written of the

§14–15: RESTRICTIONS ABOUT THE PASSOVER OFFERING

זֶה לִזְכֹּר חֵרוּתֵנוּ וּבוֹאֵנוּ בִּבְרִית נֶאֱמָנָה עִם הַשֵּׁם (יִתְבָּרַךְ) רָאוּי שֶׁלֹּא יֵהָנוּ בּוֹ רַק אוֹתָם שֶׁהִשְׁלִימוּ בֶּאֱמוּנָה, וְהֵם יִשְׂרְאֵלִים גְּמוּרִים וְלֹא אֵלּוּ שֶׁעֲדַיִן לֹא בָּאוּ עִמָּנוּ בִּבְרִית שָׁלֵם. וְעִנְיַן הַרְחָקַת הֶעָרֵל מֵאֲכִילָתוֹ גַּם כֵּן מִזֶּה הַשֹּׁרֶשׁ.

וְנוֹהֶגֶת בִּזְמַן הַבַּיִת בִּזְכָרִים וּנְקֵבוֹת. וְעוֹבֵר עָלֶיהָ וְהֶאֱכִיל לְאֵלּוּ עוֹבֵר עַל לָאו, וְאֵין לוֹקִין עָלָיו שֶׁאֵין בּוֹ מַעֲשֶׂה.

[שֶׁלֹּא לְהוֹצִיא מִבְּשַׂר הַפֶּסַח חוּצָה]

טו שֶׁלֹּא לְהוֹצִיא מִבְּשַׂר הַפֶּסַח מִמְּקוֹם הַחֲבוּרָה, שֶׁנֶּאֱמַר: לֹא תוֹצִיא מִן הַבַּיִת מִן הַבָּשָׂר חוּצָה.

מִשָּׁרְשֵׁי מִצְוָה זוֹ מַה שֶּׁכָּתַבְנוּ, לִזְכֹּר נִסֵּי מִצְרַיִם, וּמִפְּנֵי שֶׁנַּעֲשֵׂינוּ אֲדוֹנִים בָּאָה הַמִּצְוָה עָלָיו שֶׁיִּהְיֶה נֶאֱכָל בִּמְקוֹם הַחֲבוּרָה וְלֹא נוֹצִיאֵהוּ לַחוּץ, כְּדֶרֶךְ מַלְכֵי אֶרֶץ, שֶׁכָּל הַמּוּכָן לָהֶם נֶאֱכָל בְּהֵיכָלָם בְּרֹב עַם שְׁלָהֶם, וְדַלַּת הָאָרֶץ בְּעֵת יָכִינוּ סְעֻדָּה גְּדוֹלָה יִשְׁלְחוּ מִמֶּנָּה לַחוּץ מָנוֹת לִרְעֵיהֶם לְפִי שֶׁהוּא חִדּוּשׁ אֶצְלָם.

דִּינֵי הַמִּצְוָה, כְּגוֹן מַה דִּינוֹ שֶׁל בָּשָׂר כְּשֶׁיּוֹצֵא חוּץ, וְהַהֶקֵּף שֶׁצְּרִיכָה הַחֲבוּרָה לַעֲשׂוֹת, וְדִין מְחִצָּה שֶׁנִּפְרְצָה בֵּין הַחֲבוּרוֹת, וְיֶתֶר הַפְּרָטִים, מְבֹאָרִים בִּפְסָחִים. וְנוֹהֶגֶת בִּזְמַן הַבַּיִת בִּזְכָרִים וּנְקֵבוֹת. וְעוֹבֵר עָלֶיהָ וְהוֹצִיא מִן הַבַּיִת הַבָּשָׂר לַחוּץ עָבַר עַל לָאו וְלוֹקִין עָלָיו, וְהוּא שֶׁיַּעֲשֶׂה בָּהּ עֲקִירָה מִן הַבַּיִת וְהַנָּחָה לַחוּץ, כַּדִּין הַיָּדוּעַ בְּהוֹצָאָה שֶׁל שַׁבָּת.

---

2. See §13, note 6, which applies here equally.

15   1. Targum Jonathan translates this "outside the group," i.e. of people registered to eat of one Passover offering; Mechilta, MdRSbY, Tosefta P'saḥim vi 9, TB 85b, TJ vii 13 all interpret that the prohibition regarding the house means or includes the group registered for one offering.
    2. TB P'saḥim 85a.
    3. See Rambam MT *hilchoth korban pesaḥ* ix 3 and *Kessef Mishneh*, ad loc.
    4. TB P'saḥim 86b (with Rashi); Rambam *ibid.* 1
    5. TB P'saḥim 85b; Rambam *ibid.* 1.

⟨116⟩

others: that we should remember the departure from Egypt. And because this offering is to [provide] a remembrance of our liberation and our entry into the faithful covenant with the Eternal Lord (be He blessed), it is proper that only those should enjoy it who have entirely accepted the faith, i.e. complete Israelites, and not those who have not wholly entered the covenant with us. The matter of keeping an uncircumcised person away from eating it (§17) is also for this root reason.

It is in force at the time the Holy Temple stands, applying to both man and woman. If someone transgresses it and gives these [kinds of people of the Passover offering] to eat, he violates a negative precept. But no whiplashes are given for it, since it involves no [personal] action.[2]

15 [TO CARRY NO FLESH OF THE PASSOVER OFFERING OUTSIDE THE HOME]

not to take any flesh of the Passover offering outside the place of the group—as it is stated, *you shall not carry forth any of the flesh outside the house* (Exodus 12:46).[1]

At the root of this precept lies the aim we have written: that we should remember the miracles of Egypt. Because we were made lords and masters, the religious obligation was given that it should be eaten in the location of the group [which sacrificed it], and we should not take it outside—this in the manner of kings of the land: For all that is prepared for them is eaten in their palaces, amid their great retinue. But when the poor commoners of the land prepare a great meal, they send portions out to their friends, as it is a rare experience for them.

The laws of the precept are, for example: what is the law about meat that is taken outside;[2] the boundary that a group [with a Passover offering] needs to make;[3] the law of a partition between two groups that was broken through;[4] the further details are clarified in the Talmud tractate *P'saḥim*. It applies when the Holy Temple exists, for both man and woman. He who transgresses it and takes some of the meat outside, has violated a negative precept, and one is whipped (given lashes) for it—but this only if he removes it from the house and brings it to rest outside, as in the known law about taking something out on the Sabbath.[5]

§16: TO BREAK NO BONE OF THE PASSOVER OFFERING

[שֶׁלֹּא לִשְׁבֹּר עֶצֶם מִן הַפֶּסַח]

טז שֶׁלֹּא לִשְׁבֹּר עֶצֶם מִכָּל עַצְמוֹת הַפֶּסַח, שֶׁנֶּאֱמַר: וְעֶצֶם לֹא תִשְׁבְּרוּ בוֹ.

מִשָּׁרְשֵׁי הַמִּצְוָה לִזְכֹּר נִסֵּי מִצְרַיִם, כְּמוֹ שֶׁכָּתַבְנוּ בָּאֲחֵרוֹת. וְגַם זֶה גִּזְעוֹ מִן הַשֹּׁרֶשׁ הַנִּזְכָּר, שֶׁאֵין כָּבוֹד לִבְנֵי מְלָכִים וְיוֹעֲצֵי אֶרֶץ לִגְרֹר הָעֲצָמוֹת וּלְשָׁבְרָם כִּכְלָבִים, לֹא יֵאוֹת לַעֲשׂוֹת כָּכָה כִּי אִם לַעֲנִיֵּי הָעָם הָרְעֵבִים. וְעַל כֵּן בִּתְחִלַּת בּוֹאֵנוּ לִהְיוֹת סְגֻלַּת כָּל הָעַמִּים מַמְלֶכֶת כֹּהֲנִים וְעַם קָדוֹשׁ, וּבְכָל שָׁנָה וְשָׁנָה בְּאוֹתוֹ הַזְּמַן, רָאוּי לָנוּ לַעֲשׂוֹת מַעֲשִׂים הַמַּרְאִים בָּנוּ הַמַּעֲלָה הַגְּדוֹלָה שֶׁעָלִינוּ לָהּ בְּאוֹתָהּ שָׁעָה. וּמִתּוֹךְ הַמַּעֲשֶׂה וְהַדִּמְיוֹן שֶׁאֲנַחְנוּ עוֹשִׂין נִקְבַּע בְּנַפְשׁוֹתֵינוּ הַדָּבָר לְעוֹלָם.

וְאַל תַּחְשֹׁב בְּנִי לִתְפֹּשׂ עַל דְּבָרַי וְלוֹמַר, וְלָמָּה יְצַוֶּה אוֹתָנוּ הַשֵּׁם (יִתְבָּרַךְ) לַעֲשׂוֹת כָּל אֵלֶּה לְזִכָּרוֹן אוֹתוֹ הַנֵּס, הֲלֹא בְזִכָּרוֹן אֶחָד יַעֲלֶה הַדָּבָר בְּמַחְשַׁבְתֵּנוּ וְלֹא יִשָּׁכַח מִפִּי זַרְעֵנוּ? כִּי לֹא מֵחָכְמָה תִּתְפְּשֵׂנִי עַל זֶה, וּמַחְשֶׁבֶת הַנַּעַר יַשִּׂיאֲךָ לְדַבֵּר כֵּן.

וְעַתָּה בְּנִי אִם בִּינָה שְׁמָעָה זֹּאת וְהַטֵּה אָזְנְךָ וּשְׁמַע, אֲלַמֶּדְךָ לְהוֹעִיל בַּתּוֹרָה וּבַמִּצְוֹת. דַּע כִּי הָאָדָם נִפְעָל כְּפִי פְּעֻלּוֹתָיו, וְלִבּוֹ וְכָל מַחְשְׁבוֹתָיו תָּמִיד אַחַר מַעֲשָׂיו שֶׁהוּא עוֹסֵק בָּהֶם אִם טוֹב וְאִם רַע, וַאֲפִלּוּ רָשָׁע גָּמוּר בְּלִבּוֹ וְכָל יֵצֶר מַחְשְׁבוֹת לִבּוֹ רַק רַע כָּל הַיּוֹם, אִם יְעוֹרֵר רוּחוֹ וְיָשִׂים הִשְׁתַּדְּלוּתוֹ וְעִסְקוֹ בְּהַתְמָדָה בַּתּוֹרָה וּבַמִּצְוֹת, וַאֲפִלּוּ שֶׁלֹּא לְשֵׁם שָׁמַיִם, מִיַּד יִנְטֶה אֶל הַטּוֹב וּבְכֹחַ מַעֲשָׂיו יָמִית הַיֵּצֶר הָרָע, כִּי אַחֲרֵי הַפְּעֻלּוֹת נִמְשָׁכִים הַלְּבָבוֹת.

וַאֲפִלּוּ אִם יִהְיֶה אָדָם צַדִּיק גָּמוּר וּלְבָבוֹ יָשָׁר וְתָמִים, חָפֵץ בַּתּוֹרָה וּבַמִּצְוֹת, אִם אוּלַי יַעֲסֹק תָּמִיד בִּדְבָרִים שֶׁל דֹּפִי, כְּאִלּוּ תֹּאמַר דֶּרֶךְ מָשָׁל שֶׁהִכְרִיחוֹ הַמֶּלֶךְ וּמִנָּהוּ בְּאֻמָּנוּת רָעָה, בֶּאֱמֶת אִם כָּל עִסְקוֹ תָּמִיד כָּל הַיּוֹם בְּאוֹתוֹ אֻמָּנוּת, יָשׁוּב

---

16   1. Cf. these commentaries on Scripture, to Exodus 12:46: R. Anselme Astruc, *Midr'shé haTorah* (p. 108): "and you shall not break a bone of it"—this implies that they ate it in a jaunty, mocking manner, as an addition to their fill of food, their thought being only to show them [the Egyptians] that while the Egyptians intended harm for them if they ritually slew it [the Passover lamb], it brought them rescue. *Moshav Z'kénim* (so too *Pa'ané-aḥ Raza* and R. Ashér in *Hadar Z'kénim*): For the Passover offering was to be eaten 'al ha-sova (after a full meal); and when one breaks a bone to eat what it contains [the marrow] he appears to be hungry. R. Joseph b. David of Saragossa (disciple of R. Nissim): He commanded us that it should be eaten in a manner showing disdain. For with choice, valued food [meat] a man settles down to eat it slowly, gnawing the bones clean and breaking them to eat their marrow; and if he can stint and leave some over, he will put it away where it will keep. Yet here he does the opposite: *you shall let none of it remain till the morning* (Exodus 12:10); *and you shall not break a bone of it.*

 1a. Expression from Deuteronomy 31:21.
 2. Expressions from Job 34:16 and Proverbs 22:17.
 3. Expression from Genesis 6:5.

⟨118⟩

16 [NOT TO BREAK ANY BONE OF THE PASSOVER OFFERING] not to break any one of the bones of the Passover offering: as it is stated, *you shall not break a bone of it* (Exodus 12:46).

At the root of the precept lies the purpose to have us remember the miracles of Egypt, as we have written of the others. This is also a branch [corollary] of the above root purpose: For it is not a way of honor for royal princes and counsellors of the land to scrape the bones and break them like dogs. This is fit only for the hungry poor of the people to do. Therefore, at the beginning of our emergence to become the treasured choice of all the nations, *a kingdom of kohanim and a holy nation* (Exodus 19:6), and again every year at the same time, it is fitting for us to perform deeds which reflect the great degree of excellence to which we rose at that hour.[1] Through the action and the symbol that we perform, we set this matter in our souls permanently.

Now, do not think, my son, to seize upon my words and ask, "But why should the Eternal Lord (be He blessed) command us to do all these things in order to commemorate that miracle? Would the matter not have entered our consciousness through one commemoration, and thus not be forgotten out of the mouths of our descendants?[1a] For not out of wisdom would you pounce on me about this, but rather childish thinking would move you to speak so.

And now, my son, if you have understanding, hear this; incline your ear and hearken.[2] I will teach you of the Torah and the precepts, for your benefit.

Know that a man is influenced in accordance with his actions. His heart and all his thoughts are always [drawn] after his deeds in which he is occupied, whether [they are] good or bad. Thus even a person who is thoroughly wicked in his heart, and every imagination of the thoughts of his heart is only evil the entire day[3]—if he will arouse his spirit and set his striving and his occupation, with constancy, in the Torah and the *mitzvoth*, even if not for the sake of Heaven, he will veer at once toward the good, and with the power of his good deeds he will deaden his evil impulse. For after one's acts is the heart drawn.

And even if a man should be thoroughly righteous, his heart upright and honest, desiring the Torah and the *mitzvoth*, should he but engage constantly in impure matters—as we might say by way of example, if the king forcefully appointed him to an evil vocation—then in truth, if his entire occupation, constantly, all the day, will be in that vocation, at some point in time he will turn from the righteousness

§16: TO BREAK NO BONE OF THE PASSOVER OFFERING

לִזְמַן מִן הַזְּמַנִּים מְצַדֶּקֶת לִבּוֹ לִהְיוֹת רָשָׁע גָּמוּר, כִּי יָדוּעַ הַדָּבָר וֶאֱמֶת שֶׁכָּל אָדָם נִפְעָל כְּפִי פְּעֻלּוֹתָיו, כְּמוֹ שֶׁאָמַרְנוּ.

וְעַל כֵּן אָמְרוּ חֲכָמִים זִכְרוֹנָם לִבְרָכָה: רָצָה הַמָּקוֹם לְזַכּוֹת יִשְׂרָאֵל לְפִיכָךְ הִרְבָּה לָהֶם תּוֹרָה וּמִצְוֹת, כְּדֵי לְהַתְפִּיס בָּהֶן כָּל מַחְשְׁבוֹתֵינוּ וְלִהְיוֹת בָּהֶן כָּל עִסְקֵנוּ, לְהֵטִיב לָנוּ בְּאַחֲרִיתֵנוּ, כִּי מִתּוֹךְ הַפְּעֻלּוֹת הַטּוֹבוֹת אֲנַחְנוּ נִפְעָלִים לִהְיוֹת טוֹבִים וְזוֹכִים לְחַיֵּי עַד. וְרָמְזוּ זִכְרוֹנָם לִבְרָכָה עַל זֶה בְּאָמְרָם כָּל מִי שֶׁיֵּשׁ לוֹ מְזוּזָה בְּפִתְחוֹ וְצִיצִית בְּבִגְדוֹ וּתְפִלִּין בְּרֹאשׁוֹ מֻבְטָח לוֹ שֶׁלֹּא יֶחֱטָא, לְפִי שֶׁאֵלּוּ מִצְוֹת תְּמִידִיּוֹת וְנִפְעָל בָּהֶן תָּמִיד.

לָכֵן אַתָּה רְאֵה גַם רְאֵה מַה מְּלַאכְתְּךָ וְעִסְקְךָ כִּי אַחֲרֵיהֶם תִּמָּשֵׁךְ וְאַתָּה לֹא תִמְשְׁכֵם. וְאַל יַבְטִיחֲךָ יִצְרְךָ לוֹמַר, "אַחֲרֵי הֱיוֹת לִבִּי שָׁלֵם וְתָמִים בֶּאֱמוּנַת אֱלֹהִים מָה הֶפְסֵד יֵשׁ כִּי אֶתְעַגֵּג לִפְעָמִים בְּתַעֲנוּגֵי אֲנָשִׁים לָשֶׁבֶת בַּשְּׁוָקִים וּבָרְחוֹבוֹת, לְהִתְלוֹצֵץ עִם הַלֵּצִים וּלְדַבֵּר צָחוֹת, וְכַיּוֹצֵא בְאֵלּוּ הַדְּבָרִים שֶׁאֵין מְבִיאִין עֲלֵיהֶם אֲשָׁמוֹת וְחַטָּאוֹת, הֲלֹא גַם לִי לֵבָב כְּמוֹ הֵם, קְטַנֵּי עָבָה מִמָּתְנֵיהֶם, וּמַדּוּעַ יִמְשְׁכוּנִי הֵם אַחֲרֵיהֶם". אַל בְּנִי, הִשָּׁמֶר מִפְּנֵיהֶם פֶּן תִּלָּכֵד בְּרִשְׁתָּם, רַבִּים שָׁתוּ מִתּוֹךְ כָּךְ כּוֹס תַּרְעֵלָתָם, וְאַתָּה אֶת נַפְשְׁךָ תַּצִּיל.

וְאַחַר דַּעְתְּךָ זֶה אַל יִקְשֶׁה עָלֶיךָ מֵעַתָּה רִבּוּי הַמִּצְוֹת בְּעִנְיָן זְכִירַת נִסֵּי מִצְרַיִם שֶׁהֵן עַמּוּד גָּדוֹל בְּתוֹרָתֵנוּ, כִּי בְרַבּוֹת עִסְקֵנוּ בָּהֶם נִתְפָּעֵל אֶל הַדָּבָר, כְּמוֹ שֶׁאָמַרְנוּ.

דִּינֵי הַמִּצְוָה, כְּגוֹן שׁוֹבֵר עֶצֶם מִמֶּנּוּ אֲפִלּוּ אַחַר זְמַן אֲכִילָתוֹ, וְדִין אִם יֵשׁ כְּזַיִת בָּשָׂר עָלָיו מַה דִּינוֹ, וְדִין הַסְּחוּסִים וְגִידִים הָרַכִּים שֶׁסּוֹפָן לְהַקְשׁוֹת, וְיֶתֶר פְּרָטֶיהָ, מְבֹאָרִים בִּפְסָחִים. וְנוֹהֶגֶת בִּזְכָרִים וּנְקֵבוֹת בִּזְמַן הַבַּיִת. וְעוֹבֵר עָלֶיהָ וְשָׁבַר עֶצֶם בְּפֶסַח טָהוֹר לוֹקֶה.

---

4. TB Makkoth 23b.
5. TB M'nahoth 43b.
6. Rambam MT *hilchoth m'zuzah* vi 13 quotes the same passage and adds, "because he has several [constant] reminders."
7. Expression based on I Kings 12:10.
8. TB P'sahim 84a; Rambam MT *hilchoth korban pesah* x 1.
9. *Ibid.* 84b; Rambam *ibid.* 3.
10. *Ibid.* 84a.

of his heart to become completely wicked. For it is a known and true matter that every man is influenced in accordance with his actions, as we have stated.

For this reason the Sages of blessed memory said:[4] The omnipresent God wished to make the Israelites meritorious; therefore He gave them an ample, abundant Torah and a multitude of *mitzvoth*. [It was] in order to fasten all our thoughts onto them, that all our preoccupation should be with them—and thus to do us good in our afterlife. For by the good actions we are acted upon to become good (virtuous), meriting eternal life. Our Sages of blessed memory hinted at this when they said:[5] Whoever has a *m'zuzah* at his entrance, *tzitzith* in his garment, and *t'fillin* on his head, he is assured that he will not sin.[6] For these are uninterrupted *mitzvoth* [to be observed constantly] and one is constantly affected by them.

Therefore look you carefully to what your work and your occupation are: for after them will you be drawn, and you will not draw them [to you]. And let not your imagination make you confident, so that you say, "Now that my heart is entire and whole with faith in God, what loss (harm) is there if I will enjoy occasionally the pleasures of men, to stay in the markets and streets, to jest with the frivolous and speak sparkling wit? and so other, similar pursuits that do not bring guilt and sins [directly] in their wake? Surely I have a heart as stout as theirs. My little finger is thicker than their loins.[7] Then why would they pull me along with them?" Do not proceed so, my son. Beware of them, that you should not be caught in their net. Many have drunk, as a result, the cup of their poison. Then you must save your life.

And now that you are aware of this, you should not find it hard to understand, henceforth, the multiplication of precepts in connection with remembering the miracles of Egypt, as they are a major pillar in our Torah. For as we become increasingly occupied with them, so are we affected by the matter, as we have stated.

As for the laws of the precept—for instance, if someone breaks one of its bones even after the permitted time for eating it;[8] what the law is if there is an olive's amount of meat on it;[9] the law about cartilages and soft sinews which eventually harden;[10] and its other details—these are explained in the Talmud tractate *P'saḥim*. It applies to both man and woman, at the time the Holy Temple is extant. One who transgresses it and breaks a bone of a ritually pure[10] Passover offering, is punished by whiplashes.

§17–18: ON THE PASSOVER OFFERING / SANCTIFYING THE FIRSTBORN

[שֶׁלֹּא יֹאכַל עָרֵל מִן הַפֶּסַח]

יז שֶׁלֹּא יֹאכַל הֶעָרֵל מִן הַפֶּסַח, שֶׁנֶּאֱמַר: וְכָל עָרֵל לֹא יֹאכַל בּוֹ, וְהוּא הֶעָרֵל שֶׁמֵּתוּ אֶחָיו מֵחֲמַת מִילָה, וְאֵין צָרִיךְ לוֹמַר מְשֻׁמָּד לָעַרְלוּת, וּבוֹ הוּא דְּאֵינוֹ אוֹכֵל אֲבָל אוֹכֵל הוּא בְּמַצָּה וּמָרוֹר, וְכֵן תּוֹשָׁב וְשָׂכִיר גַּם כֵּן.

מִשָּׁרְשֵׁי מִצְוָה זוֹ מַה שֶּׁכָּתַבְנוּ בְּתוֹשָׁב וְשָׂכִיר.

דִּינֵי הַמִּצְוָה כְּגוֹן מִילַת בָּנָיו וַעֲבָדָיו אִם מְעַכְּבִין אוֹתוֹ לִשְׁחֹט וְלֶאֱכֹל הַפֶּסַח, וְיֶתֶר פְּרָטֶיהָ, בִּפְסָחִים. וְנוֹהֶגֶת בִּזְמַן הַבַּיִת. וְעוֹבֵר עָלֶיהָ כְּגוֹן עָרֵל שֶׁאָכַל כְּזַיִת מִמֶּנּוּ לוֹקֶה.

[מִצְוַת קִדּוּשׁ בְּכוֹרוֹת בְּאֶרֶץ יִשְׂרָאֵל]

יח לְקַדֵּשׁ הַבְּכוֹרוֹת, כְּלוֹמַר שֶׁיִּהְיוּ כָּל הַוְּלָדוֹת הַנּוֹלָדִים בָּרִאשׁוֹנָה, כְּלוֹמַר יוֹצֵא רִאשׁוֹן מֵרֶחֶם הַנְּקֵבָה בֵּין בָּאָדָם בֵּין בַּבְּהֵמָה הַזְּכָרִים קֹדֶשׁ לַשֵּׁם, שֶׁנֶּאֱמַר: קַדֶּשׁ לִי כָל בְּכוֹר פֶּטֶר כָּל רֶחֶם בִּבְנֵי יִשְׂרָאֵל בָּאָדָם וּבַבְּהֵמָה לִי הוּא, וְדָוְקָא בְּהֵמָה, דְּהַיְנוּ שׁוֹר וְכֶשֶׂב וָעֵז, אֲבָל לֹא חַיָּה, וּמִכָּל בְּהֵמָה טְמֵאָה חֲמוֹר לְבַד בְּמִצְוָה זוֹ.

וְעִנְיַן הַמִּצְוָה בִּבְהֵמָה טְהוֹרָה כֵּן, שֶׁמִּצְוָה עַל הַבְּעָלִים לְהַקְדִּישׁוֹ וְלוֹמַר "הֲרֵי זֶה קֹדֶשׁ", וְחַיָּבִים לָתֵת אוֹתוֹ בְּכוֹר לַכֹּהֲנִים וְיַקְרִיבוּ חֶלְבּוֹ וְדָמוֹ עַל הַמִּזְבֵּחַ וְהֵם אוֹכְלִים הַבָּשָׂר בִּירוּשָׁלַיִם. וְאֵינוֹ נוֹתְנוֹ לוֹ מִיָּד שֶׁיִּוָּלֵד אֶלָּא מְטַפֵּל בּוֹ, בִּבְהֵמָה דַּקָּה שְׁלֹשִׁים יוֹם וּבְגַסָּה חֲמִשִּׁים יוֹם.

---

17 1. Hence by law he remains uncircumcised until there can be no doubt of his ability to survive circumcision. This follows Rashi to Exodus 12:48 and to TB Yevamoth 70a, s.v. *he'orél*.

2. TB Yevamoth 71a.

3. They too may eat *matzah* and *maror*, though the Passover offering is forbidden them.

4. TB Yevamoth 70b–71a.

18 1. TB B'choroth 6a.

2. TB 'Arachin 29a; Rambam MT *hilchoth b'choroth* i 4.

3. TB B'choroth 26b.

⟨122⟩

[NO UNCIRCUMCISED PERSON SHOULD EAT OF THE PASSOVER OFFERING]

17 that an uncircumcised person is not to eat of the Passover offering—as it is stated, *no uncircumcised person shall eat of it* (Exodus 12:48). This means an uncircumcised person whose brothers died on account of [their] circumcision;[1] and there is no need to add [that it also applies to] a heretic regarding circumcision. It is only this [the Passover offering] that he may not eat, however; but he may eat of the *matzah* and the *maror* (bitter herbs).[2] And the same holds true for a "resident" and a "hired servant" (§14).[3]

At the root of this precept lies the reason we have written about the "resident" and the "hired servant" (§14).

The laws of the precept are, for instance: if the circumcision of his sons and servants is a necessary condition to permit a person to ritually slay and eat the Passover offering.[4] Further details are to be found in the Talmud tractate *P'saḥim*. It is in effect at the time the Holy Temple exists. One who transgresses it—for example, an uncircumcised person who eats an olive's amount of it [the Passover offering]—is punished with whiplashes.

[SANCTIFYING THE FIRSTBORN AND FIRSTLINGS IN THE LAND OF ISRAEL]

18 to sanctify the firstborn: i.e. that of all young that are born first—every newborn that is the first to have emerged from a womb, whether human or animal—the males are holy to the Eternal Lord; as it is stated, *Consecrate to me every firstborn; whatever is the first to leave the womb among the Israelite people, both of man and of* b'hémah *(beast), it is mine* (Exodus 13:2)—which means only domestic animals, i.e. the ox, sheep and goat, but not wild species. And out of all the unclean (non-kosher) domestic animals, only the donkey is included in this precept.[1]

The substance of the precept on [kosher] domestic animals is this: There is a religious obligation on the owner to consecrate it and say, "This is now holy."[2] One is then duty-bound to give this firstborn to the *kohanim*; they offer up its fat and blood on the altar, and they eat its flesh within Jerusalem. Now, he [the owner] does not give it to him [the *kohen*] so soon as it is born, but rather takes care of a small domestic animal (sheep or goat) thirty days and a large domestic animal (ox) fifty days.[3]

§18: SANCTIFYING FIRSTBORN & FIRSTLINGS IN ERETZ ISRAEL

וּבְחוּצָה לָאָרֶץ שֶׁאֵין לָנוּ מִקְדָּשׁ, נוֹעֵל דֶּלֶת בְּפָנָיו וּמֵת מֵאֵלָיו, כְּדַעַת קְצָת הַמְּפָרְשִׁים. וּמֵהֶן שֶׁאָמְרוּ שֶׁמַּמְתִּין לוֹ לְעוֹלָם, וְאִם נָפַל בּוֹ מוּם יֵאָכֵל בַּמּוּם בְּכָל מָקוֹם וּלְכָל אָדָם שֶׁיִּרְצֶה הַכֹּהֵן לִתְּנוֹ, דְּכְחָלִּין הוּא נֶחְשָׁב, וּכְמוֹ שֶׁכָּתוּב, "תֹּאכְלֶנּוּ הַטָּמֵא וְהַטָּהוֹר יַחְדָּו כַּצְּבִי וְכָאַיָּל". וְכֵן כָּתַב הָרַמְבַּ״ן זִכְרוֹנוֹ לִבְרָכָה בְּהִלְכוֹת בְּכוֹרוֹת שֶׁלּוֹ.

וּבְכוֹר אָדָם וּפֶטֶר חֲמוֹר נִפְרָשׁ עִנְיָנָם בְּמִצְוַת הַפְּדִיָּה שֶׁבְּכָל אֶחָד בְּעֶזְרַת הַשֵּׁם, וְהֵם בְּסֵדֶר זֶה עָשָׂה ח׳ וּבְסֵדֶר וַיִּקַּח קֹרַח עָשָׂה ב׳.

מִשָּׁרְשֵׁי מִצְוָה זוּ שֶׁרָצָה הַשֵּׁם לְזַכּוֹתֵנוּ לַעֲשׂוֹת מִצְוָה בְּרֵאשִׁית פְּרָיֵנוּ לְמַעַן דַּעַת כִּי הַכֹּל שֶׁלּוֹ וְאֵין לוֹ לְאָדָם דָּבָר בָּעוֹלָם רַק מַה שֶׁיֶּחֱלַק לוֹ הַשֵּׁם בַּחֲסָדָיו, וְיָבִין זֶה בִּרְאוֹתוֹ כִּי אַחַר שֶׁיִּגַע הָאָדָם כַּמָּה יְגִיעוֹת וְטָרַח כַּמָּה טְרָחִים בְּעוֹלָמוֹ וְהִגִּיעַ לַזְּמַן שֶׁעָשָׂה פְּרִי, וְחָבִיב עָלָיו רֵאשִׁית פִּרְיוֹ כְּבָבַת עֵינוֹ, מִיָּד נוֹתְנוֹ לְהַקָּדוֹשׁ בָּרוּךְ הוּא וּמִתְרוֹקֵן רְשׁוּתוֹ מִמֶּנּוּ וּמַכְנִיסוֹ לִרְשׁוּת בּוֹרְאוֹ.

וְעוֹד לִזְכֹּר הַנֵּס הַגָּדוֹל שֶׁעָשָׂה לָנוּ הַשֵּׁם בִּבְכוֹרֵי מִצְרַיִם שֶׁהֲרָגָם וְהִצִּילָנוּ מִיָּדָם.

דִּינֵי הַמִּצְוָה, בְּאֵי זֶה מָקוֹם נִשְׁחָט וְנֶאֱכָל, וְעַד אֵי זֶה זְמַן מִצְוָה לָהֶם לְאָכְלוֹ, וְעִנְיַן הַמּוּמִין הַפּוֹסְלִין בּוֹ, וְאֵי זֶה מוּם קָבוּעַ אוֹ מוּם עוֹבֵר וְהַחִלּוּק שֶׁבֵּינֵיהֶם, וּמִי נֶאֱמָן עַל מוּמָיו, וְאִם נָפְלוּ בוֹ אוֹ נַעֲשׂוּ בוֹ לְדַעַת, וְאֵי זֶה חָכָם רָאוּי לְהוֹרוֹת בְּמוּמָיו, וְדִין בְּכוֹר הַשֻּׁתָּפִין יִשְׂרְאֵלִים אוֹ שֻׁתָּף גּוֹי, וּבְאֵי זֶה עִנְיָן נִפְטָרָה הַבְּהֵמָה

---

4. I.e. where a *kohen* might offer up a firstborn animal as a sacrifice; hence what follows applies equally in Israel today, as long as the Sanctuary is not rebuilt.

5. R. Eli'ezer of Metz, quoted in *Mord'chai* to TB 'Avodah Zarah i.

6. Rambam MT *hilchoth b'choroth* i 10.

7. It would then be unfit to offer up at the altar if the Sanctuary were standing (Leviticus 22:20).

8. Chapter 5, end.

9. See Exodus 13:15, Numbers 3:13, 8:17.

10. Respectively TB Z'vahim 56b, B'choroth 26b.

11. The blemishes are defined in TB B'choroth chapters 6–7, and Rambam MT *hilchoth bi'ath ha-mikdash* vii, *hilchoth 'issuré mizbé-ah* ii. On the difference in law between temporary and permanent ones see TB B'choroth 41a and Rambam *ibid. hilchoth b'choroth* ii 2.

12. TB B'choroth 35a–b.

13. *Ibid.* 36b.

14. TB Hullin 135a–b; Mishnah, B'choroth i 1.

15. TB B'choroth 15b.

However, outside the land of Israel, where we have no Sanctuary,[4] he [the owner] locks the door upon it, and it subsequently dies of itself —this according to the view of some authorities.[5] There are others, though,[6] who say that he waits indefinitely regarding it, and if it becomes blemished[7] it may be eaten anywhere, by any person to whom the *kohen* would wish to give it, for it is considered desanctified (non-holy) food; as it is written, *you shall eat it, the unclean and the clean equally, like the gazelle and the hart* (Deuteronomy 15:22). So Ramban (R. Moses b. Naḥman) of blessed memory wrote in his *hilchoth b'choroth* (Laws of the Firstborn).[8]

About a human firstborn and the firstling of a donkey, we will explain (with the Lord's help) in the precepts of each one's redemption. They are the eighth positive precept in this *sidrah* (§22) and the second in *sidrah koraḥ* (§392).

At the root of the precept lies the reason that the Eternal Lord wished to grant us the merit to perform a *mitzvah* with the "first of our fruit," in order to know that everything is His and a man has nothing in the world but what the Eternal Lord allots him in His kindness. This will be understood when one sees that after a man has toiled through many labors and gone through many troubles in his world, and the time has come when fruit is yielded—and the first of his fruit is beloved to him as the apple of his eye—he gives it at once to the Holy One, blessed is He; he deprives himself of his possession, making it the possession of his Creator.

It is also [given us to observe] in order to remember the great miracle that the Eternal Lord did for us in relation to the firstborn of Egypt—that He slew them and saved us from their hand.[9]

Some laws of this precept are: at which place it [a firstborn animal] is to be ritually slain and eaten; until which time it is a religious duty to eat it;[10] the matter of blemishes (defects) which disqualify it [as a sacrifice], what is a permanent blemish or a temporary one, and the difference [in law] between them;[11] who is believed [in testimony] about its defects, whether they occurred by chance or were deliberately inflicted;[12] which learned scholar is fit to render decisions about its blemishes;[13] the law of a firstborn animal belonging to two Israelite (Jewish) partners, or [to one Jewish and] one non-Jewish partner;[14] in which instance a domestic animal is freed of the obligation of the firstborn and in which instance not;[15] what is the law when there is doubt if a firstborn was truly first;[15] the question of a firstborn by Caesarian

§18–19: ON FIRSTBORN, ETC. / TO EAT NO ḤAMETZ ON PASSOVER

מן הבכורה או לא נפטרה, ובכור ספק מה דינו, ובכור שענין יוצא דפן, וטמטום ואנדרוגינוס, ויתר פרטיו, מבארים במסכת בכורות.

ונוהגת מצוה זו של קדוש בכור בהמה טהורה מדאוריתא בארץ ישראל בלבד בכל זמן, וכמו שדרשו רבותינו זכרונם לברכה: מדכתיב "ואכלת לפני יי אלהיך [וגו'] מעשר דגנך תירשך ויצהרך. ובכרת בקרך", מקיש, וכו': [מקום שאתה מביא מעשר דגן, אתה מביא בכורות; מחוצה לארץ, שאין אתה מביא מעשר דגן, אי אתה מביא בכורות]. ומדרבנן, אף בחוצה לארץ, ובזכרים ובנקבות בין ישראלים בין בכהנים ולויים.

ואף על פי שהבכור שנולד לכהן שלו הוא, מכל מקום חיב להקריב חלבו ודמו ולאכל הבשר בתורת בכור. ובכור אדם ופטר חמור אינו נוהג בכהן ולוי, כמו שנכתוב בעזרת השם. וזאת מן המצות שחיובה בסבת דבר.

[שלא לאכל חמץ בפסח]

יט שלא לאכל חמץ בפסח, שנאמר: ולא יאכל חמץ. משרשי מצוה זו מה שכתבנו בשאר מצות הפסח.

דיני המצוה, כגון מה הם הדברים שנאסר בהן חמץ, והן ה' מיני דגן, ודין הלש אותן במי פרות, ודין לתיתה, ותבשיל שנמצא בו חמץ, ודין כלים שנשתמש בהן חמץ בחמין או בצונן, ויתר פרטיה, מבארים בפסחים. ונוהגת בכל מקום ובכל זמן בזכרים ונקבות. ועובר עליה ואכל כזית חמץ בפסח במזיד חיב כרת, בשוגג חיב חטאת קבועה.

---

16. Ibid. 19a, 41a.
17. Midrash Sifre, Deuteronomy §110.
18. I.e. if a firstling is born to the domestic animal of a Jew; but see further, p. 434.
19. As stated in Scripture: *For all the firstborn among the Israelites, both of man and of beast, are Mine: On the day that I struck down every firstborn in the land of Egypt, I consecrated them to Me* (Numbers 8:17). I.e. as it were, when all the firstborn in Egypt died in the last of the ten plagues, the Israelite firstborn (man and beast) were kept safe by Divine grace, and they were thus placed for all time in a special relationship of sanctification to Him.

1. See §10, note 2 (derived from Mishnah, P'saḥim ii 5).
2. TB P'saḥim 35b; see also *tosafoth* there, s.v. *mé péroth*.
3. Ibid. 40a–b; see also Rambam MT *hilchoth ḥamétz u-matzah* v 7.
4. Ibid. 40a (Rambam *ibid.* 8).
5. Ibid. 30b (Rambam *ibid.* 21–26).
6. In §108 our author explains that this means a specific animal offering which all, rich or poor, must bring alike—in contrast to another type of sin-offering, for which the wealthy must bring a more expensive sacrifice, and the poor something less costly.

SIDRAH BO

birth, a firstborn of uncertain sex, or a hermaphrodite.[16] [These] and its other details are clarified in the Talmud tractate *B'choroth*.

This precept, to sanctify the firstling of a kosher domestic animal, stays in force, by law of the Written Torah, in the land of Israel alone, at all times. As our Sages of blessed memory taught:[17] Since it is written, *you shall eat before the Lord your God ... the tithe of your grain, your wine and your oil, and the firstlings of your herd and flock* (Deuteronomy 14:23), the Torah equates the firstling with the tithe: From a place where you bring the tithe of grain [i.e. in the land of Israel] you are to bring the firstling; from outside the land [abroad], where you do not bring the tithe of grain, you need not bring the firstling. By enactment of the Sages, though, it is in effect outside the land as well.[18] And it applies to both man and woman, both ordinary Israelites and *kohanim* and Levites.

Although a firstling born to a *kohen* belongs to him, he is nonetheless obligated to offer up its fat and blood [on the altar] and eat its flesh under the law of the firstling. The obligations about a human firstborn and the firstling of a donkey do not apply to a *kohen* or a Levite, as we will write with the Lord's help (§§22, 392).

This is one of the precepts that became obligatory because of a specific circumstance.[19]

19 [TO EAT NO ḤAMÉTZ ON PASSOVER]

not to eat *hamétz* on Passover—as it is stated, *no leavened bread shall be eaten* (Exodus 13:3). At the root of this precept lies the aim we have written in regard to the other precepts of Passover.

The laws of the precept are, for example: which products can become forbidden as *hamétz*—these being the five species of cereal grain;[1] the law if one kneads them with fruit juices;[2] the law about moistening [the grain before grinding it];[3] [the law on] a cooked dish in which *hamétz* was found;[4] and the law on dishes and utensils that were used for leavened food, hot or cold.[5] [These] and other details are clarified in the Talmud tractate *P'sahim*. It is in force in every place and time, for both man and woman. If someone transgresses it and eats an olive's bulk of *hamétz* during Passover—if he does it deliberately, he incurs the punishment of *karéth* [Divine severance of existence]; if it is unintentional, he incurs an obligation to bring a standard, unvarying *hattath* (sin-offering).[6]

§20–21: NO ḤAMÉTZ TO BE SEEN / TO TELL OF THE EXODUS

[שֶׁלֹּא יֵרָאֶה לָנוּ חָמֵץ בְּפֶסַח]

כ שֶׁלֹּא יֵרָאֶה חָמֵץ בְּכָל מוֹשְׁבוֹתֵינוּ כָּל שִׁבְעַת יְמֵי הַפֶּסַח, שֶׁנֶּאֱמַר: וְלֹא יֵרָאֶה לְךָ חָמֵץ וְלֹא יֵרָאֶה לְךָ שְׂאוֹר בְּכָל גְּבֻלֶךָ. וְאֵין אֵלֶּה שְׁנֵי לָאוִין בִּשְׁנֵי עִנְיָנִים, אֲבָל הֵם בְּעִנְיָן אֶחָד, כְּמוֹ שֶׁאָמְרוּ זִכְרוֹנָם לִבְרָכָה, פָּתַח הַכָּתוּב בְּחָמֵץ וְסִיֵּם בִּשְׂאוֹר, לוֹמַר לְךָ הוּא חָמֵץ הוּא שְׂאוֹר, כְּלוֹמַר אֵין הֶפְרֵשׁ בֵּין הֶחָמֵץ עַצְמוֹ וּבֵין דָּבָר הַמַּחְמִיץ.

מִשָּׁרְשֵׁי הַמִּצְוָה מַה שֶּׁכָּתַבְנוּ בִּשְׁאָר מִצְוֹת הַפֶּסַח. דִּינֶיהָ מְבֹאָרִים בִּפְסָחִים. וְנוֹהֶגֶת בְּכָל מָקוֹם וּבְכָל זְמַן בִּזְכָרִים וּנְקֵבוֹת. וְעוֹבֵר עָלֶיהָ וְלָקַח חָמֵץ בְּפֶסַח וְהִנִּיחוֹ בִרְשׁוּתוֹ לוֹקֶה, אֲבָל אִם לֹא הוֹצִיאוֹ מִקֹּדֶם הַפֶּסַח מִבֵּיתוֹ אֵינוֹ לוֹקֶה עָלָיו לְפִי שֶׁאֵין בּוֹ מַעֲשֶׂה, וְאֵין לוֹקִין עָלָיו, כְּמוֹ שֶׁאָמַרְנוּ.

[מִצְוַת סִפּוּר יְצִיאַת מִצְרָיִם]

כא לְסַפֵּר בְּעִנְיַן יְצִיאַת מִצְרַיִם בְּלֵיל חֲמִשָּׁה עָשָׂר בְּנִיסָן כָּל אֶחָד כְּפִי צַחוּת לְשׁוֹנוֹ, וּלְהַלֵּל וּלְשַׁבֵּחַ הַשֵּׁם עַל כָּל הַנִּסִּים שֶׁעָשָׂה לָנוּ שָׁם, שֶׁנֶּאֱמַר: וְהִגַּדְתָּ לְבִנְךָ וְגוֹ'. וּכְבָר פֵּרְשׁוּ חֲכָמִים דְּמִצְוַת הַגָּדָה זוֹ הִיא בְּלֵיל חֲמִשָּׁה עָשָׂר בְּנִיסָן בִּשְׁעַת אֲכִילַת מַצָּה. וּמַה שֶּׁאָמַר הַכָּתוּב "לְבִנְךָ" לָאו דַּוְקָא בְּנוֹ אֶלָּא אֲפִלּוּ עִם כָּל בְּרִיָּה.

וְעִנְיַן הַמִּצְוָה שֶׁיִּזְכֹּר הַנִּסִּים וְהָעִנְיָנִים שֶׁאֵרְעוּ לַאֲבוֹתֵינוּ בִּיצִיאַת מִצְרַיִם וְאֵיךְ לָקַח הָאֵל יִתְבָּרַךְ נִקְמָתֵנוּ מֵהֶן. וַאֲפִלּוּ בֵּינוֹ לְבֵין עַצְמוֹ אִם אֵין שָׁם אֲחֵרִים חַיָּב לְהוֹצִיא הַדְּבָרִים מִפִּיו, כְּדֵי שֶׁיִּתְעוֹרֵר לִבּוֹ בַּדָּבָר, כִּי בַדִּבּוּר יִתְעוֹרֵר הַלֵּב.

מִשָּׁרְשֵׁי מִצְוָה זוֹ מַה שֶּׁכָּתוּב בְּקָרְבַּן הַפֶּסַח. וְאֵין מִן הַתֵּמַהּ אִם בָּאוּ לָנוּ מִצְוֹת רַבּוֹת עַל זֶה, מִצְוֹת עֲשֵׂה וּמִצְוֹת לֹא תַעֲשֶׂה, כִּי הוּא יְסוֹד גָּדוֹל וְעַמּוּד חָזָק

---

§20   1. Evidently by a scribal error, under the influence of Deuteronomy 16:4, "seven days" is added here; in this verse, "seven days" occurs in the first part.
  2. TB Bétzah 7b, version of ShM negative precept §200.

§21   1. See §6 note 1.
  2. In Mechilta on the verse.
  3. TB P'saḥim 116a (*baraitha*); *ibid*. This paragraph is essentially a summary of Rambam ShM, positive precept §157.
  4. Literally, between him and himself (*ibid., ibid.*)

⟨128⟩

SIDRAH BO

20 [NO ḤAMÉTZ IS TO BE SEEN WITH US DURING PASSOVER] that no *ḥamétz* should be seen in any of our dwelling-places during the seven days of Passover—as it is stated, *and no leavened bread shall be seen with you, neither shall leaven be seen with you, within all your borders*[1] (Exodus 13:7). Now, these are not two negative precepts, about two [separate] matters, but rather one subject, as our Sages of blessed memory said:[2] The verse begins with *ḥamétz*, leavened food, and concludes with *s'or*, leaven—to tell you that *ḥamétz* is the same as *s'or* [in this law]. In other words, there is no [legal] difference between actual leavened food and the leavening agent.

At the root of the precept lies what we have written about the other *mitzvoth* of Passover. Its laws are explained in the Talmud tractate *P'saḥim*. And it remains in effect in every time and every place, for both man and woman. If one transgresses it, acquiring *ḥamétz* during Passover and leaving it on his premises, he receives whiplashes. If, however, he [merely] did not remove it before Passover from his house, he receives no whipping for it—for no action was involved, and therefore no lashes are given for it, as we have stated (§9).

21 [THE PRECEPT OF RECOUNTING THE EXODUS FROM EGYPT] to tell about the departure from Egypt, on the evening of the fifteenth of Nissan,[1] each person according to his eloquence, and to laud and praise the Eternal Lord for all the miracles He wrought for us there—as it is stated, *you shall tell your son on that day, saying: It is because of what the Lord did for me when I came out of Egypt* (Exodus 13:8). Long ago the Sages explained[2] that the religious duty of telling [about the exodus] is [to be fulfilled] on the evening of the fifteenth of Nissan, at the time the *matzah* is eaten. As to Scripture's expression, "your son," it does not mean necessarily one's son, but actually any person.[3]

The substance of the precept is that one should remember the miracles and the events that occurred for our forefathers in [connection with] the exodus from Egypt, and how God (be He blessed) took revenge upon them for us. Even when alone,[4] if no others are present, a person is obligated to speak the words with his mouth, so that his heart will be inspired about the matter; for by speech the heart is aroused.

At the root of this precept lies what was written about the Passover offering (§5). And we need not wonder that we have received so many precepts for this [purpose], both positive (to do) and negative (to refrain

בְּתוֹרָתֵנוּ וּבֶאֱמוּנָתֵנוּ. וְעַל כֵּן אָנוּ אוֹמְרִים לְעוֹלָם בְּבִרְכוֹתֵינוּ וּבִתְפִלּוֹתֵינוּ "זֵכֶר לִיצִיאַת מִצְרַיִם", לְפִי שֶׁהוּא לָנוּ אוֹת וּמוֹפֵת גָּמוּר בְּחִדּוּשׁ הָעוֹלָם, וְכִי יֵשׁ אֱלוֹהַּ קַדְמוֹן חָפֵץ וְיָכוֹל פּוֹעֵל כָּל הַנִּמְצָאוֹת, אֶל הַיֵּשׁ שֶׁהֵם [תְּלוּיִים] עָלָיו וּבְיָדוֹ לְשַׁנּוֹתָם — אֶל הַיֵּשׁ — [כְּפִי] שֶׁיַּחְפֹּץ בְּכָל זְמַן מִן הַזְּמַנִּים כְּמוֹ שֶׁעָשָׂה בְּמִצְרַיִם שֶׁשִּׁנָּה טִבְעֵי הָעוֹלָם בִּשְׁבִילֵנוּ, וְעָשָׂה לָנוּ אוֹתוֹת מְחֻדָּשִׁים גְּדוֹלִים וַעֲצוּמִים, הֲלֹא זֶה מְשַׁתֵּק כָּל כּוֹפֵר בְּחִדּוּשׁ הָעוֹלָם וּמְקַיֵּם הָאֱמוּנָה בִּידִיעַת הַשֵּׁם, וְכִי הַשְׁגָּחָתוֹ וִיכָלְתּוֹ בַּכְּלָלִים וּבַפְּרָטִים כֻּלָּם.

דִּינֵי הַמִּצְוָה, כְּגוֹן הַסֵּדֶר שֶׁחַיָּבִין יִשְׂרָאֵל לַעֲשׂוֹת בַּלַּיְלָה הַזֶּה בְּעִנְיַן סְעֻדָּתָן, וְהַכּוֹסוֹת שֶׁל יַיִן שֶׁחַיָּבִין לִשְׁתּוֹת וְשִׁעוּרָן, וּמְזִיגָתָן, וְסִדּוּרָן. וְהִנְנִי כּוֹתֵב לְךָ בְּנֵי הַסֵּדֶר בִּקְצָרָה כַּאֲשֶׁר שְׁמַעְתִּיו מִפִּי חַכְמֵי הַדּוֹר בְּדִיּוּק:

בַּתְּחִלָּה מְבִיאִין מַיִם וְנוֹטְלִין יָד אַחַת בִּשְׁבִיל כּוֹס שֶׁל קִדּוּשׁ שֶׁצְּרִיכִין לִטּוֹל, וְהָכֵי אִיתָא בִּבְרָכוֹת פֶּרֶק כֵּיצַד, שֶׁבַּכּוֹס מַסְפִּיק נְטִילַת יָד אַחַת, וְאֵין מְבָרְכִין עַל נְטִילָה זוֹ. וְאִם רָצָה לִטּוֹל שְׁתֵּי יָדָיו לַכּוֹס נוֹטֵל בְּלֹא בְרָכָה.

וְאַחַר כָּךְ מְבָרֵךְ עַל הַיַּיִן וּמְקַדֵּשׁ וְאֵינוֹ מְבָרֵךְ עַל הַיַּיִן לְאַחֲרָיו. וְאַחַר כָּךְ נוֹטֵל שְׁתֵּי יָדָיו וּמְבָרֵךְ עַל נְטִילַת יָדַיִם וּמְטַבֵּל בְּיֶרֶק וּמְבָרֵךְ עָלָיו "בּוֹרֵא פְּרִי הָאֲדָמָה" לְפָנָיו, וּלְאַחֲרָיו אֵינוֹ מְבָרֵךְ "בּוֹרֵא נְפָשׁוֹת" וְכוּ', לְפִי שֶׁיַּמְתִּין עַד שֶׁיֹּאכַל הַמָּרוֹר וְאָז יְבָרֵךְ "בּוֹרֵא נְפָשׁוֹת" עַל הַמָּרוֹר וְעַל הַיֶּרֶק. וְאֵין כָּל מַה שֶּׁעָשָׂה בֵּינְתַיִם הַפְסָקָה כְּמוֹ שֶׁנִּפְרָשׁ.

וְאַחַר שֶׁאָכְלוּ מִן הַיֶּרֶק בַּחֲרֹסֶת מוֹזְגִין כּוֹס שֵׁנִי, וְקוֹרִין הַהַגָּדָה עִם שְׁנֵי

---

5. Cf. Rambam, *Guide*, II §25: And know that with belief in the creation of the world out of nought all the wonders then become possible. Ramban, commentary, Exodus 20:2: For should the world be pre-existent [since time eternal] then nothing of its nature could ever change. Our author generally echoes Ramban *ibid.* here.

6. Wines in earlier times (including the Talmudic period) were stronger and were diluted before drinking.

7. See the author's Preface (toward the end) that he wrote this work as a guide for his young son. He now follows R. Sh'lomoh ibn 'Adreth, who may have been our author's master teacher (Rashba, *Responsa ascribed to Ramban*, §202; *Responsa*, I §§72, 241). Our procedure at the *séder* today, following other authorities, differs somewhat. Cf. R. Ḥayyim b. Sh'mu'él b. David of Toledo (disciple of Rashba), *Tz'ror haḤayyim* (Jerusalem 1966), pp. 127–30.

8. According to other authorities, whom we follow in our practice, this is not done (Rama, *Shulḥan 'Aruch 'Oraḥ Ḥayyim*, 473, 1).

9. In our practice this is not said (*ibid.* 6); see R. Menaḥem M. Kasher, *Haggadah Shelemah*, 97–101.

10. So our author specifies below. This is a mixture of chopped apples, nuts, cinnamon, wine, etc. intended to resemble the mud in which our ancestors toiled in slavery in Egypt. In our practice, though, it is dipped in salt water, etc. (*Shulḥan 'Aruch ibid.*); see R. Kasher *ibid.* 101–04.

from doing)—as it is a great foundation and a mighty pillar in our Torah and our faith. For this reason we always say in our benedictions and our prayers, "a commemoration for the departure from Egypt": because it is a full indication and proof of the creation of the world out of non-existence, and that there is a pre-existent God with will and power who gives all created things their being—the existent God on whom they [utterly] depend, in whose power it lies to change them as He may wish, at any particular time [whatever, just] as He did in Egypt, when He altered the world's ways of nature for our sake, and wrought for us great and mighty unprecedented signs. Surely this must silence everyone who denies the creation of the world out of non-existence, and must permanently affirm human faith in the knowledge of the Eternal Lord, and [the faith] that His watchful control and power extend to all groups and individuals.[5]

The laws of this precept pertain, for instance, to the *séder* ("order") which Jews are required to make on this night, which includes the festive meal, the four cups of wine that one is required to drink, their proper measure, their proper mixture [with water],[6] and their proper order. Here, my son, I will write out for you the *séder* in brief, precisely as I heard it from the great scholars of the generation:[7]

At first water is brought, and one hand is washed for the cup of [wine for] *kiddush* ("sanctification");[8] it requires hand-washing, but we find in the sixth chapter of the Talmud tractate *B'rachoth* (43a) that for the wine-cup, it is enough to wash one hand. No benediction is said over this washing. If one wishes to wash both hands for the wine-cup, he may do so, without a benediction.

Then one says the blessing over the wine and recites the *kiddush*, but says no benediction over the wine after [drinking] it. After this he washes both hands and says, "Blessed are Thou, Lord . . . who hallowed us with his *mitzvoth* and commanded us about washing the hands."[9] He dips a vegetable [into *ḥaroseth*][10] and says over it before [eating] it, "Blessed art Thou . . . who dost create the fruit of the earth." After it he does not say [the general benediction after food] "Blessed art Thou . . . Creator of all life and its needs," etc. for he should wait until he eats the *maror* (bitter herbs) and then recite this blessing over both the *maror* and this vegetable;[11] and what he does in between the two does not constitute an interruption, as we will explain.

Having eaten of the vegetable [dipped] in *ḥaroseth*, one pours[12] the second cup [of wine] and reads the *haggadah* [the traditional account of

§21: TO RETELL ABOUT THE EXODUS   ספר החינוך

פְּרָקִים מִן הַהַלֵּל, וְנוֹטְלִין הַיָּד אַחַת, וּמְבָרֵךְ "אֲשֶׁר גְּאָלָנוּ" וכו' עַל כּוֹס הַשֵּׁנִי וְשׁוֹתִין אוֹתוֹ, וְאֵין מְבָרְכִין עָלָיו "בּוֹרֵא פְּרִי הַגֶּפֶן" וְלֹא אַחֲרָיו "עַל הַגֶּפֶן".

וְאַחַר שֶׁשָּׁתוּ כּוֹס שֵׁנִי נוֹטְלִין לַיָּדַיִם וּמְבָרְכִין עַל נְטִילַת יָדַיִם, וְנוֹטְלִין חֲצִי מַצָּה וּמַנִּיחִין אוֹתָהּ עַל שְׁלֵמָה וּמְבָרְכִין עַל הַחֲצִי הַמּוֹצִיא וְלֶאֱכֹל מַצָּה, וְנוֹטְלִין חֲזֶרֶת וּמְבָרְכִין לֶאֱכֹל מָרוֹר וְאוֹכְלִין מִמֶּנּוּ בִּטְבוּל בַּחֲרֹסֶת, וְאֵין מְבָרְכִין עָלֶיהָ בּוֹרֵא פְּרִי הָאֲדָמָה לְפִי שֶׁנִּפְטָרָה בִּבְרָכָה שֶׁבֵּרְכוּ בַּיֶּרֶק תְּחִלָּה, דְּהָכֵי מִתּוֹכַח בַּגְּמָרָא דְּלָא הֲוֵי הַפְסָקָה לְעוֹלָם שֶׁנִּצְטָרֵךְ לַחֲזֹר וּלְבָרֵךְ אֶלָּא אִם כֵּן יֵשׁ בַּדָּבָר שְׁנֵי עִנְיָנִים, שֶׁיַּעֲקֹר הָאָדָם דַּעְתּוֹ מִן הָעִנְיָן, כְּגוֹן דְּאָמְרֵי "הַב וְנִבְרִיךְ", וְכַיּוֹצֵא בָּזֶה, וְכֵן שֶׁלֹּא יְהֵא בְּאֶפְשָׁר לַעֲשׂוֹת שְׁנֵי הַדְּבָרִים בְּיַחַד, כְּגוֹן מַה שֶּׁאָמְרוּ זִכְרוֹנָם לִבְרָכָה: מִשְׁתֵּי וּבְרוּכֵי בַּהֲדֵי הֲדָדֵי לָא אֶפְשָׁר.

וְאַחַר שֶׁאוֹכְלִין מִן הַמָּרוֹר בִּטְבוּל מִמֶּנּוּ כּוֹרְכִין עַל גַּבֵּי מַצָּה וְאוֹכְלִין, וְאַחַר כָּךְ אוֹכְלִין סְעֻדָּתָן, וְאַחַר כָּךְ אוֹכֵל כָּל אֶחָד וְאֶחָד מְעַט מַצָּה זֵכֶר לַפֶּסַח שֶׁהָיָה נֶאֱכָל עַל הַשּׂבַע, וְאֵין אוֹכְלִין עוֹד כָּל הַלַּיְלָה שֶׁלֹּא לְסַלֵּק טַעַם הַמַּצָּה מִן הַפֶּה, דִּכְתִיב "מִדְּבַשׁ לְפִי", אֲבָל מַיִם וַדַּאי שׁוֹתִין שֶׁאֵין הַמַּיִם מְפִיגִין הַטַּעַם. וְכֵן שׁוֹתִין גַּם כֵּן תְּרֵי כָּסֵי דְמִצְוָה כִּי לֹא נִדְחָה מִצְוָה מִטַּעַם זֶה.

וְאַחַר כָּךְ נוֹטְלִין לַיָּדַיִם, וְאֵין מְבָרְכִין עַל נְטִילַת יָדַיִם, וּמוֹזְגִין כּוֹס שְׁלִישִׁי, וּמְבָרֵךְ עָלָיו בִּרְכַּת הַמָּזוֹן וּבוֹרֵא פְּרִי הַגֶּפֶן, אֲבָל לֹא לְאַחֲרָיו עַל הַגֶּפֶן. וְאַחַר כָּךְ

---

11. In our practice this blessing is not said then either (*Turé Zahav* to *Shulhan 'Aruch ibid.* §475, 8).

12. Literally, mixes; see note 6.

13. In preparation for drinking the second cup; see note 8.

14. In our practice the blessing *is* said (Rama, *ibid.* §474, 1).

15. In our practice the first blessing is said over the half *matzah* held between two whole ones; the second blessing, over the upper whole *matzah* and the half; then pieces from both are eaten (*ibid.* §475, 1; *Hok Ya'akov* to *ibid.* 2).

16. Literally, freed, i.e. of the obligation to say the blessing over it.

17. TB P'sahim 103b.

18. TB Hullin 87a. (The term *hav v'nivréch*, "Come, let us say grace," is the reading of MS Munich II (*Dikduké Sof'rim*) and Rashi in TB P'sahim 103b.)

19. Literally, in a state of satiety.

20. The last two sentences derive from R. Z'rahyah haLévi, *Séfer haMa'or*, P'sahim, end.

21. In preparation for saying grace.

22. Literally, mixed; see note 6.

⟨132⟩

SIDRAH BO

the liberation from Egypt] along with two paragraphs of the *hallél* (Psalms 113–114). Then he washes one hand[13] and says over the second cup of wine, "Blessed art Thou, Lord ... who redeemed us and redeemed our fathers from Egypt," etc. and he drinks it. One does not say before it the benediction "who dost create the fruit of the vine,"[14] nor after it the blessing "for the vine and the fruit of the vine."

After the second cup of wine is drunk, the hands are washed, with the benediction "and commanded us on the washing of the hands." Half a *matzah* is taken and placed on a whole one; and one recites over the half-*matzah*, "Blessed art Thou ... who dost bring forth bread from the earth," then the benediction, "and commanded us to eat *matzah*."[15] Then one takes bitter herbs and says the benediction "who commanded us to eat *maror*"; and he eats of it, dipping it into *ḥaroseth*. One does not say over it the blessing "who dost create the fruit of the earth," since it is covered[16] by the benediction recited earlier over the vegetable. For so is it evident from the Talmud,[17] that an interruption requiring us to repeat a benediction is never considered to occur unless another subject is involved in the matter [of the interruption], through which a man turns his mind away completely from the [first] subject: for instance, if [in between] it was said, "Come, let us say grace," and so on. So too if [the act which was interrupted] would be impossible to do together [with the interruption]: for example, as the Sages of blessed memory said:[18] To drink and say grace at the same time is impossible.

Having eaten of the *maror* dipped [in *ḥaroseth*], one makes a sandwich of some of it with *matzah* and eats it. Then the meal is eaten. After that, each and every one takes a bit of *matzah* in commemoration of the Passover offering, which used to be eaten after the meal.[19] Nothing more is to be eaten the entire night, so as not to remove the taste of the *matzah* from the mouth—as it is written, *sweeter than honey to my mouth* (Psalms 119:103). Water, however, may certainly be drunk, for water will not remove the taste. So also are two obligatory cups of wine yet to be drunk, since a religious duty is not to be set aside for this reason.[20]

Then the hands are washed,[21] without the benediction "on the washing of the hands." The third cup of wines is poured;[22] grace is recited over it, then the blessing, "who dost create the fruit of the vine." But the blessing after it, "Blessed art Thou ... for the vine and the fruit of the vine," is not said. Thereafter the fourth cup is poured, and

⟨133⟩

§21–22: TO RETELL THE EXODUS / REDEEM A FIRSTBORN DONKEY

מוֹזְגִין כּוֹס רְבִיעִי וְגוֹמְרִים עָלָיו אֶת הַהַלֵּל, וְאֵין מְבָרְכִין עָלָיו בּוֹרֵא פְּרִי הַגֶּפֶן, אֲבָל אַחֲרָיו מְבָרְכִין עַל הַגֶּפֶן, וְהוּא שֶׁלֹּא יְהֵא דַעְתָּם לִשְׁתּוֹת עוֹד כּוֹס חֲמִישִׁי.

נִמְצָא לְפִי זֶה שֶׁאֵין מְבָרְכִין בּוֹרֵא פְּרִי הַגֶּפֶן אֶלָּא תְּרֵי זִמְנֵי, עַל כּוֹס הַקִּדּוּשׁ וְעַל כּוֹס הַבְּרָכָה, וְעַל הַגֶּפֶן פַּעַם אַחַת אַחַר כָּל הַכּוֹסוֹת. וְאַרְבַּע הַכּוֹסוֹת וּמַצָּה דְּמִצְוָה צְרִיכִין הֲסִבָּה.

וְיֶתֶר הַפְּרָטִים מְבֹאָרִים בְּסוֹף פְּסָחִים. וְנוֹהֶגֶת בִּזְכָרִים וּנְקֵבוֹת בְּכָל מָקוֹם וּבְכָל זְמַן, וְעוֹבֵר עָלֶיהָ בְּטֵל עֲשֵׂה.

[מִצְוַת פִּדְיוֹן פֶּטֶר חֲמוֹר]

כב לִפְדּוֹת וְלַד חֲמוֹר זָכָר שֶׁנּוֹלַד רִאשׁוֹן, שֶׁנֶּאֱמַר: וְכָל פֶּטֶר חֲמֹר תִּפְדֶּה בְשֶׂה. וְעִנְיָנָהּ הוּא שֶׁלּוֹקֵחַ הַיִּשְׂרָאֵל שֶׂה אֶחָד וְנוֹתְנוֹ לַכֹּהֵן בְּפִדְיוֹן בְּכוֹר הַחֲמוֹר, שֶׁהוּא לָשֵׁם מִן הַטַּעַם שֶׁכְּתַבְנוּ לְמַעְלָה, וְהוּא בָרוּךְ הוּא נְתָנוֹ לַכֹּהֵן, וּלְפִיכָךְ פּוֹדֵהוּ הַיִּשְׂרָאֵל מִמֶּנּוּ, כִּי הַשֵּׁם רָצָה שֶׁיִּהְיֶה לוֹ פִּדְיוֹן בְּשֶׂה.

וְאִם אֵין לוֹ שֶׂה פּוֹדֵהוּ בְּדָמָיו שֶׂה, וּלְפִי שֶׁאֵין דְּמֵי הַשֵּׂיּוֹת שָׁוִין אָמְרוּ זִכְרוֹנָם לִבְרָכָה: עַיִן יָפָה בְּסֶלַע, רָעָה בַּחֲצִי סֶלַע, וּבֵינוֹנִית בִּשְׁלֹשָׁה זוּזִים, וּזְמַן הַפִּדְיוֹן עַד שְׁלֹשִׁים יוֹם. וְהַשֶּׂה חֻלִּין בְּיַד כֹּהֵן, וְהַחֲמוֹר בְּיַד יִשְׂרָאֵל.

מִשָּׁרְשֵׁי מִצְוָה זוֹ כְּדֵי שֶׁיִּזְכְּרוּ הַיְּהוּדִים לְעוֹלָם הַנֵּס שֶׁעָשָׂה לָהֶם הָאֵל בִּיצִיאַת מִצְרַיִם שֶׁהָרַג כָּל בְּכוֹרֵיהֶם שֶׁנִּמְשְׁלוּ לַחֲמוֹרִים, כְּמוֹ שֶׁכָּתוּב.

דִּינֵי הַמִּצְוָה כְּגוֹן שֶׁתָּפוּת הַנָּכְרִי אוֹ מְקַבֵּל חֲמוֹר מִמֶּנּוּ לְהַשְׁפִּיל בּוֹ, וְדִין גּוֹי

---

23. See note 14.

24. Rambam MT *hilchoth hametz u-matzah* viii 10 lists it as something to be done, though it is not obligatory (based on TB P'sahim 118a); Rabad (R. Abraham b. David) on *Séfer haMa'or* §794 considers it praiseworthy. However, *Shulhan 'Aruch 'Orah Hayyim* §481, 1 forbids it (see also gloss of Rema and *Mishnah B'rurah* there). For a recent further discussion see R. Menahem M. Kasher, *Haggadah Shelemah*, 94–95.

25. Mishnah, P'sahim x 1; Tosefta *ibid*.; TJ *ibid*. See R. Kasher, *ibid*. 68 ff.

26. I.e. chapter 10.

1. TB B'choroth 11a. A *sela* was made of 19.2 grams of silver, and was worth four *zuzim* (*dinarim, denarii*).

2. Ibid. 13a, 9b.

3. Cf. Tanhuma ed. Buber, *bamidbar* 24: Said the Holy One: On account of My love of the people Israel, I changed the order of things. How? I wrote in My Torah that a donkey should be redeemed with a lamb—as it is stated, *the firstling of a donkey you shall redeem with a lamb* (Exodus 34:20); and I did not do so, but redeemed a lamb with a donkey: The Egyptians are likened to donkeys, as it is stated, *whose flesh is as the flesh of donkeys*; and the Israelites are called a lamb—as it is stated, *Israel is a scattered sheep* (Jeremiah 50:17); and I slew the firstborn of the Egyptians and consecrated the firstborn of the Israelites—as it is stated, *For all the firstborn among the*

over it the *hallél* is completed (Psalms 115–118). One does not say over it [the wine] "Blessed art Thou ... who dost create the fruit of the vine,"²³ but after it the benediction "for the vine and the fruit of the vine" is recited—that is, if one does not have in mind to drink yet a fifth cup.²⁴

We thus find that the blessing "who dost create the fruit of the vine" is said no more than twice: on the cup of *kiddush* and the cup of the grace. And the [second] blessing, "for the vine and the fruit of the vine," is said but once, after all the cups [are drunk]. The four cups of wine and the *matzah* [eaten] by religious obligation require reclining [that one should recline while taking them].²⁵

Other details [of the precept] are clarified toward the end of the Talmud tractate *P'saḥim*.²⁶ It applies to both man and woman, in every place and at every time. He who transgresses it disobeys a positive precept.

22 [THE PRECEPT OF REDEEMING A FIRSTBORN DONKEY] to redeem the male young of a donkey that was the first to be born—as it is stated, *every firstling of a donkey you shall redeem with a lamb* (Exodus 13:13). Substantially it means that an Israelite would take a lamb and give it to a *kohen* as redemption (ransom) for a firstling of a donkey. For it belongs [originally] to the Eternal Lord, for the reason we have written above (§18), and He (be He blessed) gave it to the *kohen*. Therefore the Israelite redeems it from him—for the Eternal Lord wanted it to be ransomed for a lamb.

If someone has no lamb, he may redeem it for the price of a lamb. And since the prices of lambs are not all the same [so that there is no fixed rate], our Sages of blessed memory said: A generous person [redeems it] for a *sela;* a niggardly person, for half a *sela;* and a middle-range person, for three *zuzim*.[1] The time for its redemption is [from its birth] until thirty days. The lamb is then the non-holy property of the *kohen*, and the donkey the property of the Israelite.[2]

At the root of this precept lies the purpose that the Jews should remember forever the miracle which God wrought for them at the departure from Egypt—that He slew all their [the Egyptians'] firstborn, who were likened to donkeys [in Scripture: ... *in the land of Egypt ... whose flesh is as the flesh of donkeys* (Ezekiel 23:19–20)][3]—as it is written (Exodus 13:14–15).

The laws of the precept are, for instance, the case of partnership

§22–24: ABOUT A FIRSTBORN DONKEY / THE SABBATH LIMITS

שֶׁהִפְרִישׁ פֶּטֶר חֲמוֹר מַה דִּינוֹ, וְדִין חֲמוֹר שֶׁיְּלָדָה כְּמִין סוּס, וְדִין לוֹקֵחַ חֲמוֹר מִגּוֹי, וְעִנְיָן סָפֵק אִם בְּכוֹרָה מַה דִּינוֹ, וְדִין נוֹתֵן הַחֲמוֹר בְּעַצְמוֹ לַכֹּהֵן, וְיֶתֶר פְּרָטֶיהָ, מְבֹאָרִים בְּמַסֶּכֶת בְּכוֹרוֹת. וְנוֹהֶגֶת בְּכָל מָקוֹם וּבְכָל זְמַן, בִּזְכָרִים וּנְקֵבוֹת יִשְׂרְאֵלִים, וְלֹא בְּכֹהֲנִים וּלְוִיִּם. וְעוֹבֵר עַל זֶה בִּטֵּל עֲשֵׂה.

[מִצְוַת עֲרִיפַת פֶּטֶר חֲמוֹר]

כג לַעֲרֹף פֶּטֶר חֲמוֹר אִם לֹא רָצָה לִפְדּוֹתוֹ, שֶׁנֶּאֱמַר: וְאִם לֹא תִפְדֶּה וַעֲרַפְתּוֹ. עִנְיָנָהּ שֶׁהוֹרְגֹ וְלַד הַחֲמוֹר אִם לֹא רָצָה לִפְדּוֹתוֹ, וְגָזַר הַשֵּׁם שֶׁלֹּא יֵהָנֶה בּוֹ מִכֵּיוָן שֶׁלֹּא פָדָהוּ, וַאֲפִלּוּ הַנְּבֵלָה אֲסוּרָה לוֹ בַּהֲנָאָה.

מִשָּׁרְשֵׁי מִצְוָה זוֹ מַה שֶּׁכָּתוּב בִּפְדִיָּה.

מִדִּינֵי הַמִּצְוָה, מַה שֶּׁאָמְרוּ דְּמִצְוַת פְּדִיָּה קוֹדֶמֶת לַעֲרִיפָה, וְשֶׁאָסוּר בַּהֲנָאָה אִם מֵת קֹדֶם פִּדְיוֹן וְיִקָּבֵר, וְכִי מִצְוָה לְהָרְגוֹ בְּקוֹפִיץ וְלֹא בְּדָבָר אַחֵר; וְיֶתֶר פְּרָטֶיהָ, מְבֹאָרִים גַּם כֵּן בִּבְכוֹרוֹת. וְנוֹהֶגֶת [בַּכֹּל] כְּמוֹ הַפְּדִיָּה.

וַיְהִי בְּשַׁלַּח

[שֶׁלֹּא נֵצֵא בְּשַׁבָּת חוּץ לַתְּחוּם]

כד יֵשׁ בָּהּ מִצְוַת לֹא תַעֲשֶׂה אַחַת, וְהִיא שֶׁנִּמְנַעְנוּ שֶׁלֹּא לָלֶכֶת בְּשַׁבָּת חוּץ לִגְבוּלִים יְדוּעִים, שֶׁנֶּאֱמַר: אַל יֵצֵא אִישׁ מִמְּקֹמוֹ בַּיּוֹם הַשְּׁבִיעִי, וּבָא הַפֵּרוּשׁ עָלָיו שֶׁמְּקוֹמוֹ נִקְרָא כָּל שֶׁאֵינוֹ מַרְחִיק יוֹתֵר מִשְּׁלֹשׁ פַּרְסָאוֹת חוּץ לָעִיר. וְהַפַּרְסָה ד' מִילִין, וְהַמִּיל אַלְפַּיִם אַמָּה. וּמוֹדְדִין מִשְּׂפַת הַבַּיִת הַחִיצוֹן שֶׁבָּעִיר אֲפִלּוּ הָיְתָה

Israelites are Mine, both of man and of beast; on the day that I smote all the firstborn in the land of Egypt I consecrated them for Myself (Numbers 8:17). So too Bamidbar Rabbah 4, 5.

4. Mishnah, B'choroth i 1.
5. TB M'nahoth 67a.
6. Mishnah, B'choroth i 2.
7. TB B'choroth 11a.
8. Mishnah, B'choroth i 5; MT *hilchoth b'chorim* xii 4.
9. Mishnah, B'choroth ii 1.

1. Mishnah, B'choroth i 7. (As explained there, the "beheading" is actually breaking the animal's neck with a hatchet from behind.)
2. I.e. it should rather be redeemed; *ibid.*
3. Cf. Rambam MT *hilchoth b'chorim* xii 4.

1. Rambam MT *hilchoth shabbath* xxvii 1–2.
2. In general, though not in all instances, a cubit ('*ammah*) is considered to be 18.9 inches (48 centimeters) according to one view, 22.7 inches (57.6 centimeters) according to another. Hence a mil would be 3149.6 feet (0.518 miles; 960 meters) by the first view, and 3779.5 feet (0.625 miles; 1.15 kilometers) by the second view. And a parasang (Hebrew, *parsah*; plural, *parsa'oth*) 2.1 miles (3.84 kilometers) by the

⟨136⟩

with a non-Jew, or if one receives a donkey from him to take care of it;[4] what the law is if a non-Jew consecrates [to the Temple] the firstling of a donkey;[5] the law of a donkey that bore offspring resembling a kind of horse;[6] the law for a man who buys a donkey from a non-Jew;[4] the problem when there is doubt if [a donkey] has produced a firstling—what is its law;[7] and the law when someone gives the donkey itself to a *kohen*.[8] [These] and further details are clarified in the Talmud tractate *B'choroth*. It is in effect everywhere and at all times, for Israelites, both man and woman, but not for *kohanim* and Levites.[9] If someone transgresses it, he has disobeyed a positive precept.

[TO BREAK THE NECK OF AN UNREDEEMED FIRSTBORN DONKEY]

23 to behead a firstling donkey if one does not want to redeem it—as it is stated, *and if you will not redeem it, then you shall behead it* (Exodus 13:13). In substance it means that one kills the [firstborn] young of a donkey if he does not wish to ransom it. The Eternal Lord decreed that he should have no benefit from it, since he did not redeem it; even any benefit from the carcass is forbidden him.[1]

At the root of this precept lies what is written [above] about redemption.

Regarding the laws of the precept—what the Sages said, that the *mitzvah* of redemption takes priority over beheading;[2] that all benefit from it is forbidden if it dies before being redeemed, and it is to be buried;[3] and that the religious obligation is to kill it with a butcher's hatchet and not anything else;[1] and its other details—these too are explained in the Talmud tractate *B'choroth*. It is in force wherever [the precept of] redemption (§22) is in force.

sidrah b'shallah

(Exodus 13:17–17:16)

[NOT TO GO BEYOND PERMITTED LIMITS ON THE SABBATH]

24 There is one negative precept in this [*sidrah*], which is that we are restricted from going on the Sabbath beyond the known bounds—as it is stated, *let no man go out of his place on the seventh day* (Exodus 16:29); and the explanation given for it[1] is that "his place" means whatever is not more than three parasangs away from the city. A parasang is four mils, a mil being 2,000 cubits.[2] [This distance] is measured from the edge of

§24: NOT TO GO BEYOND THE PERMITTED SABBATH LIMITS

גְּדוֹלָה כְּנִינְוֵה. זֶהוּ לְדִין תּוֹרָה, אֶלָּא שֶׁחֲכָמִים גָּדְרוּ גֶּדֶר וְאָסְרוּ שֶׁלֹּא יֵלֵךְ יוֹתֵר מֵאַלְפַּיִם אַמָּה חוּץ לָעִיר.

מִשָּׁרְשֵׁי מִצְוָה זוֹ שֶׁנִּזְכֹּר וְנֵדַע שֶׁהָעוֹלָם מְחֻדָּשׁ לֹא קַדְמוֹן, כְּמוֹ שֶׁכָּתוּב בְּפֵרוּשׁ בְּמִצְוַת שַׁבָּת: כִּי שֵׁשֶׁת יָמִים עָשָׂה יְיָ אֶת הַשָּׁמַיִם וְאֶת הָאָרֶץ אֶת הַיָּם וְאֶת כָּל אֲשֶׁר בָּם וַיָּנַח בַּיּוֹם הַשְּׁבִיעִי. עַל כֵּן לְזֵכֶר הַדָּבָר רָאוּי לָנוּ שֶׁנָּנוּחַ בְּמָקוֹם אֶחָד, כְּלוֹמַר שֶׁלֹּא נֵלֵךְ בְּדֶרֶךְ רָחוֹק רַק דֶּרֶךְ טִיּוּל וְעֹנֶג, וּבַהֲלִיכַת י״ב מִילִין אֵין בּוֹ טֹרַח רַב.

דִּינֵי הַמִּצְוָה, כְּגוֹן שׁוֹבֵת בַּמִּדְבָּר אוֹ בִּמְעָרָה מַה דִּינוֹ, וְכֵן מִי שֶׁיָּצָא חוּץ לַתְּחוּם לִרְצוֹנוֹ אוֹ לְאָנְסוֹ אוֹ בִּרְשׁוּת בֵּית דִּין, וְאִם הַקַּף בְּמֶחֱצָה בְּשַׁבָּת מַה דִּינוֹ, וּבַיִת הַיּוֹצֵא יוֹתֵר מִשְּׁאָר בָּתֵּי הָעִיר שִׁבְעִים אַמָּה וּשְׁיָרַיִם, וּבֵית הַכְּנֶסֶת שֶׁיֵּשׁ בּוֹ דִּירָה לְחַזָּנִים, וּבֵית עֲבוֹדָה זָרָה שֶׁיֵּשׁ בָּהּ דִּירָה לִכְמָרִים, וְאוֹצָרוֹת שֶׁיֵּשׁ בָּהֶן דִּירָה, וְשָׁלֹשׁ מְחִצּוֹת שֶׁאֵין עֲלֵיהֶן תִּקְרָה וּמַעֲזִיבָה מַה דִּינָן עִם הָעִיר, וְעִיר אֲרֻכָּה, מְרֻבַּעַת, עֲגֻלָּה, עֲשׂוּיָה כְּמִין גַּם אוֹ כְּקֶשֶׁת, מֵהֵיכָן מוֹדְדִין לָהּ, וּבָאֵי זֶה חֶבֶל מוֹדְדִין, וְכַמָּה שִׁעוּרוֹ שֶׁל חֶבֶל, וְהִגִּיעַ לְגַיְא אוֹ לְהַר אוֹ לְכֹתֶל כֵּיצַד מוֹדֵד, וּבְכַמִּי סוֹמְכִין בִּמְדִידָה, וּמִי נֶאֱמָן לְהָעִיד עַל הַתְּחוּמִין, וְיֶתֶר פְּרָטֶיהָ, מְבֹאָרִים בְּמַסֶּכְתָּא הַבְּנוּיָה עַל זֶה וְהִיא עֵרוּבִין.

וְנוֹהֶגֶת בְּכָל מָקוֹם וּבְכָל זְמַן בַּזְּכָרִים וּנְקֵבוֹת. וְעוֹבֵר עָלֶיהָ וְהָלַךְ אֲפִלּוּ אַמָּה אַחַת יוֹתֵר מִשָּׁלֹשׁ פַּרְסָאוֹת לוֹקֶה, וְכֵן אִם הָלַךְ אֲפִלּוּ אַמָּה אַחַת יוֹתֵר חוּץ לְאַלְפַּיִם אַמָּה סָמוּךְ לָעִיר לוֹקֶה מַכַּת מַרְדּוּת דְּרַבָּנָן. וְהָרַמְבָּ״ן זִכְרוֹנוֹ לִבְרָכָה כָּתַב כִּי מַה שֶּׁאָמַר הָרַמְבָּ״ם זִכְרוֹנוֹ לִבְרָכָה בְּסֵפֶר הַמִּצְוֹת שֶׁלּוֹ דְּאִסּוּר תְּחוּמִין

first view, 2.5 miles (4.61 kilometers) by the second. According to the Oral Tradition, three parasangs was the length of the Israelite camp in the wilderness.

3. See Jonah 1:2, 3:2, 4:11.

4. By resting on the Sabbath, the Jew affirms his faith that the world was created by Divine will and did not exist independently through an infinite past, since the Sabbath is linked in Scripture with His rest on the seventh day.

5. TB 'Eruvin 61b (Rambam MT *hilchoth shabbath* xxvii 2).

6. *Ibid.* 52b, 41b, 44b (Rambam *ibid.* 13, 16). On the permission of the *beth din* see §4, note 14.

7. *Ibid.* 42a (Rambam *ibid.* 14).

8. Literally, seventy cubits and a remnant; *ibid.* 52b, 55b (Rambam *ibid.* xxviii 1).

9. *Ibid.* 55b (Rambam *ibid.* 2–4).

10. *Ibid.* 55a (Rambam *ibid.* 6–8).

11. *Ibid.* 57b–58a (Rambam *ibid.* 11).

12. *Ibid.* (Mishnah); Rambam *ibid.* 13–15.

13. *Ibid.* 55b (Rambam *ibid.* 17).

14. When a person violates a negative precept, he receives thirty-nine lashes; when he is punished for disobedience, the number of lashes is at the discretion of the *beth din* according to Rambam, whom our author generally (and avowedly) follows.

the furthermost house of the city, even if it is as large as Nineveh[3]—this by the law of the [Written] Torah. The Sages, however, made a "fence" (a precautionary measure) and forbade walking more than 2,000 cubits outside the city.[1]

At the root of this precept lies the aim that we should remember and know that the world was engendered out of non-existence and was not pre-existent, as it is written explicitly about the *mitzvah* of [observing] the Sabbath: *for in six days the Lord made heaven and earth, the sea, and all that is in them; and He rested on the seventh day* (Exodus 20:11).[4] Therefore, in remembrance of this, it is fitting for us that we should rest in one place, which means that we should not go on any lengthy journey but only walk for strolling and pleasure; and in walking twelve mils there is no great exertion.

The laws of the precept are, for example: what the law is for one who rests, observing the Sabbath, in the desert or a cave;[5] so too one who went beyond the limit of his own free will, under compulsion, or by permission of the *beth din*;[6] if one was surrounded by a partition on the Sabbath, what his law is;[7] a house which is further out than the other houses of a city by slightly more than seventy cubits;[8] a synagogue which contains a dwelling for the stewards and sextons;[9] a house of idol-worship which contains a dwelling for the priests;[9] storehouses (warehouses) which contain a dwelling;[9] three partitions without a roof with a paved covering, what their law is in relation to the city;[9] an elongated, square or round city;[10] a city shaped like the Greek letter *gamma* or like a bow—from which point one measures outward from it;[10] with which sort of rope the measure is taken, and what the length of the rope should be;[11] when a valley, a hill or a wall is reached, how the measure is to be taken;[12] on whom one relies for the measurement;[13] who is reliable to testify about the limits.[13] [These] and its further details are clarified in the Talmud tractate built about this [theme], i.e., '*Eruvin*.

It remains in force in every place, in every time, for both man and woman. If someone violates it and goes even one cubit beyond three parasangs, he is given whiplashes. Similarly, if he walks even one extra cubit beyond the 2,000 cubits near a city, he is whipped in punishment for disobedience, by law of the Sages.[14]

Ramban of blessed memory has written[15] that when Rambam of blessed memory states in his *Book of Precepts* [negative §321] that the prohibition of [going beyond] the limits by law of the Written Torah

§24–25: THE SABBATH LIMITS / TO BELIEVE IN GOD

דְּאוֹרַיְתָא הוּא בְּיוֹתֵר מֵאַלְפַּיִם אַמָּה, וְכֵן מַה שֶּׁאָמַר בְּחִבּוּרוֹ הַגָּדוֹל שֶׁחָזַר מִזֶּה וְכָתַב שֶׁהַשִּׁעוּר שֶׁל תּוֹרָה הוּא שָׁלֹשׁ פַּרְסָאוֹת, כִּי הַכֹּל טָעוּת, שֶׁאֵין לָנוּ אִסּוּר תְּחוּמִין דְּאוֹרַיְתָא כְּלָל, וְכֵן מְתֹבָאֵר בִּמְקוֹמוֹת הַרְבֵּה מִן הַגְּמָרָא שֶׁלָּנוּ שֶׁהִיא גְּמָרַת בָּבֶל שֶׁאָנוּ סוֹמְכִין עָלֶיהָ בְּכָל דְּבָרֵינוּ. וְהִרְבָּה הָרַב רְאָיוֹתָיו עַל זֶה בְּמִצְוַת שי"ג מִן הַלָּאוִין. וְהוּא יְפָרֵשׁ "אַל יֵצֵא" כְּמוֹ "אַל יוֹצִיא", כְּמוֹ שֶׁיֵּשׁ בְּמַסֶּכֶת עֵרוּבִין מַאן דְּמַשְׁמַע לֵיהּ הָכִי.

שש וישמע יתרו

יֵשׁ בָּהּ שָׁלֹשׁ מִצְוֹת עֲשֵׂה וְי"ד מִצְוֹת לֹא תַעֲשֶׂה

[מִצְוַת הָאֱמָנָה בִּמְצִיאוּת הַשֵּׁם יִתְבָּרַךְ]

כה לְהַאֲמִין שֶׁיֵּשׁ לָעוֹלָם אֱלוֹהַּ אֶחָד שֶׁהִמְצִיא כָּל הַנִּמְצָא, וּמִכֹּחוֹ וְחֶפְצוֹ הָיָה כָּל מַה שֶּׁהוּא, וְשֶׁהָיָה וְשֶׁיִּהְיֶה לַעֲדֵי עַד, וְכִי הוּא הוֹצִיאָנוּ מֵאֶרֶץ מִצְרַיִם וְנָתַן לָנוּ אֶת הַתּוֹרָה, שֶׁנֶּאֱמַר בִּתְחִלַּת נְתִינַת הַתּוֹרָה: אָנֹכִי יְיָ אֱלֹהֶיךָ אֲשֶׁר הוֹצֵאתִיךָ מֵאֶרֶץ מִצְרַיִם וְגוֹ'. וּפֵרוּשׁוֹ כְּאִלּוּ אָמַר, "תֵּדְעוּ וְתַאֲמִינוּ שֶׁיֵּשׁ לָעוֹלָם אֱלוֹהַּ", כִּי מִלַּת אָנֹכִי תּוֹרָה עַל הַמְּצִיאוּת. וַאֲשֶׁר אָמַר "אֲשֶׁר הוֹצֵאתִיךָ" וְכוּלֵּי לוֹמַר שֶׁלֹּא יִפְתֶּה לְבַבְכֶם לָקַחַת עִנְיַן צֵאתְכֶם מֵעַבְדוּת מִצְרַיִם וּמַכּוֹת הַמִּצְרִים דֶּרֶךְ מִקְרֶה, אֶלָּא דְּעוּ שֶׁאָנֹכִי שֶׁהוֹצֵאתִי אֶתְכֶם בְּחֵפֶץ וּבְהַשְׁגָּחָה, כְּמוֹ שֶׁהִבְטִיחַ לַאֲבוֹתֵינוּ אַבְרָהָם יִצְחָק וְיַעֲקֹב.

שֹׁרֶשׁ מִצְוָה זוֹ אֵין צָרִיךְ בֵּאוּר, יָדוּעַ הַדָּבָר וְנִגְלֶה לַכֹּל כִּי הָאֱמוּנָה הַזּוֹ יְסוֹד הַדָּת, וַאֲשֶׁר לֹא יַאֲמִין בָּזֶה כּוֹפֵר בָּעִקָּר וְאֵין לוֹ חֵלֶק וּזְכוּת עִם יִשְׂרָאֵל.

---

15. In his commentary to Rambam ShM, negative precept §321.
16. Rambam MT *hilchoth shabbath* xxvii 1.

1. This is somewhat based on ShM and *Séfer Mitzvoth Gadol*, positive precepts §1.

⟨140⟩

means beyond 2,000 cubits, and so too when he states in his great work,[16] where he retracts this and writes [instead] that the limit by the Torah's law is three parasangs—it is all in error: For by the Written Torah's law, we have no prohibition at all in regard to limits. This is made clear in many places in our Talmud, the Babylonian, on which we rely in all our matters [of Jewish life]. The master [Ramban] has amassed his many proofs for this in precept §313 [321] of the negative precepts. And he would then interpret the verse *let no man go out*, al yétzé, *of his place on the seventh day* as meaning *al yotzi*, "let no man take out" [any object from his place]—as there is one Sage in the tractate *'Eruvin* (17b) for whom it has this meaning.

sidrah yithro
(Exodus 18–20)

There are three positive and fourteen negative precepts in it.

25 [TO BELIEVE IN THE EXISTENCE OF GOD]
to believe that the world has one God, who brought all existence into being; by His power and His will does everything come about—all that was, that is, and that will be for time eternal; and that He brought us out from the land of Egypt and gave us the Torah. For it is stated at the beginning of the giving of the Torah [at Mount Sinai], *I am the Lord your God who brought you out of the land of Egypt, out of the house of bondage* (Exodus 20:2);[1] and its meaning is as if He said, "You shall know and believe that the world has a God"; for the word "I" implies [His very real] existence. And when He said, "who brought you out," etc. He meant that "your heart should not be led astray to take the matter of your emergence (liberation) from the slavery of Egypt and the plagues [that afflicted] the Egyptians [as something that happened] by way of chance. Know rather that it is I who took you out through [My] desire and watchful care"—as He had promised our Patriarchs, Abraham, Isaac and Jacob.

The root purpose of this precept needs no explanation. It is a known matter, apparent to all, that this belief is the foundation of the religion; whoever would not believe in it denies the main principle [of the one God in our faith], and he has no portion or merit within Jewry.

§25–26: TO BELIEVE IN GOD / AND IN NO OTHER DIVINITY

וְעִנְיָן הָאֲמָנָה הוּא שֶׁיִּקָּבַע בְּנַפְשׁוֹ שֶׁהָאֱמֶת כֵּן וְשֶׁאִי אֶפְשָׁר חִלּוּף זֶה בְּשׁוּם פָּנִים. וְאִם יִשָּׁאֵל עָלָיו, יָשִׁיב לְכָל שׁוֹאֵל שֶׁזֶּה יַאֲמִין לִבּוֹ וְלֹא יוֹדֶה בְּחִלּוּף זֶה אֲפִלּוּ יֹאמְרוּ לְהָרְגוֹ, שֶׁכָּל זֶה מַחֲזִיק וְקוֹבֵעַ הָאֲמָנַת הַלֵּב כְּשֶׁמּוֹצִיא הַדָּבָר מִן הַכֹּחַ אֶל הַפֹּעַל, רְצוֹנִי לוֹמַר כְּשֶׁיְּקַיֵּם בְּדִבְרֵי פִיו מַה שֶׁלִּבּוֹ גּוֹמֵר. וְאִם יִזְכֶּה לַעֲלוֹת בְּמַעֲלוֹת הַחָכְמָה וְלִבּוֹ יָבִין וּבְעֵינָיו יִרְאֶה בְּמוֹפֵת נֶחְתָּךְ שֶׁהָאֲמָנָה הַזֹּאת שֶׁהֶאֱמִין אֱמֶת וּבָרוּר, אִי אֶפְשָׁר לִהְיוֹת דָּבָר בִּלְתִּי זֶה, אָז יְקַיֵּם מִצְוַת עֲשֵׂה זוֹ מִצְוָה מִן הַמֻּבְחָר.

דִּינֵי מִצְוָה זוֹ, כְּגוֹן מַה שֶׁמְּחֻיָּב עָלֵינוּ לְהַאֲמִין עָלָיו שֶׁכָּל הַיְכֹלֶת וְכָל הַגְּדֻלָּה וְהַגְּבוּרָה וְהַתִּפְאֶרֶת וְכָל הַהוֹד וְכָל הַבְּרָכָה וְכָל הַקִּיּוּם בּוֹ, וְשֶׁאֵין בָּנוּ כֹּחַ וְשֵׂכֶל לְהַשִּׂיג וּלְהַגִּיד גָּדְלוֹ וְטוּבוֹ, כִּי לָרֹב מַעֲלָתוֹ וְהוֹדוֹ לֹא יַשִּׂיג רַק לְעַצְמוֹ, וְלִשְׁלֹל מִמֶּנּוּ בְּכָל כֹּחֵנוּ כָּל חִסָּרוֹן וְכָל מַה שֶׁהוּא הֵפֶךְ כָּל שְׁלֵמוּת וְכָל מַעֲלָה, וְהָעִנְיָנִים הַיּוֹצְאִים מִזֶּה כְּגוֹן לָדַעַת שֶׁהוּא נִמְצָא, שָׁלֵם, בִּלְתִּי גּוּף וְלֹא כֹחַ בְּגוּף, כִּי הַגּוּפִים יַשִּׂיגוּם הַחֶסְרוֹנוֹת, וְהוּא בָּרוּךְ הוּא לֹא יַשִּׂיגֵהוּ מִין מִמִּינֵי הַחִסָּרוֹן, כְּמוֹ שֶׁאָמַרְנוּ; וּשְׁאָר דְּבָרִים רַבִּים הַנֶּאֱמָרִים בְּעִנְיָן זֶה, כֻּלָּם מְבֹאָרִים בְּסִפְרֵי יוֹדְעֵי חָכְמַת הָאֱלֹהוּת. אַשְׁרֵי הַדּוֹכִים אֵלֶיהָ כִּי אָז יְקַיְּמוּ מִצְוָה זוֹ עַל בֻּרְיָהּ.

וְנוֹהֶגֶת בְּכָל מָקוֹם וּבְכָל זְמַן בִּזְכָרִים וּנְקֵבוֹת. וְעוֹבֵר עָלֶיהָ אֵין לוֹ חֵלֶק וּזְכוּת עִם יִשְׂרָאֵל, כְּמוֹ שֶׁאָמַרְנוּ. וְזֹאת מִן הַמִּצְוֹת שֶׁאֵין לָהֶם זְמַן יָדוּעַ שֶׁכָּל יְמֵי הָאָדָם חַיָּב לִחְיוֹת בְּמַחֲשָׁבָה זוֹ.

[שֶׁלֹּא נַאֲמִין אֱלֹהוּת בִּלְתִּי הַשֵּׁם לְבַדּוֹ]

כו שֶׁלֹּא נַאֲמִין אֱלֹהִים זוּלָתִי הַשֵּׁם לְבַדּוֹ, שֶׁנֶּאֱמַר "לֹא יִהְיֶה לְךָ אֱלֹהִים אֲחֵרִים עַל פָּנָי", וּפֵרוּשׁוֹ לֹא תַאֲמִין אַחֵר אֱלוֹהַּ זוּלָתִי. וְכָתַב הָרַמְבַּ"ן זִכְרוֹנוֹ

---

2. So Rambam, *Guide*, I 59; see Job 42:2, I Chronicles 29:11.
3. Cf. *ibid.* 55–59.

⟨142⟩

SIDRAH YITHRO

The substance of this faith is that a person should determine in his mind that this is the truth, and nothing else of any sort is possible instead. And should it be questioned, let him answer every questioner that this he believes in his heart and will never acknowledge anything else in its stead, even if others should purpose to kill him [for it]. For all this strengthens and sets the heart's belief firmly, when one transforms the potential [of faith] into something actual, i.e. when he affirms with the words of his mouth what his heart has decided. Then if he should merit to rise in levels of wisdom so that with his heart he understands and with his eyes he sees, by clearcut proof, that this belief which he holds is absolutely true—it could not be otherwise—then he shall have fulfilled this *mitzvah* in the very best way.

The laws of this precept are, for example, that it is incumbent upon us to believe about Him that all ability, all grandeur, power and splendor, all eminence, all blessing, all existence—are through Him; and we have neither the power nor the intelligence to conceive and relate His greatness and benevolence; for on account of His immense degree of eminence and glory He can be apperceived by none but Himself alone. [2] [It is for us] to ascribe to him, with all our ability, no shortcoming whatsoever and nothing which is in any way the opposite of total perfection and total excellence. [3] Then there are those matters which derive from it, such as to know that He is immanent, wholly perfect, without any body or physical power of a body: for physical bodies are ultimately subject to deficiencies and shortcomings, while He (be He blessed) is not subject to any kind of deficiency or shortcoming whatever, as we stated. [These] and many other concepts which were expressed on this theme are all explained in the works of those learned in the wisdom of the Divinity. Fortunate are those who attain this [wisdom], for then they will fulfill this *mitzvah* thoroughly.

It is in force in every place, at every time, for both man and woman. Anyone who transgresses it has no portion or merit with the people Israel, as we have stated. This is one of the precepts for which there is no set time, since all the days of a man's life he is required to live with this concept.

26 [TO BELIEVE IN NO DIVINITY BUT GOD] that we should not believe [in] any god other than the Eternal Lord alone—as it is stated, *You shall have no other gods before Me* (Exodus

§26: TO BELIEVE IN NO DIVINITY BUT GOD

לִבְרָכָה: לֹא תִמְצָא לְעוֹלָם שֶׁיֹּאמַר הַכָּתוּב אֱלֹהִים אֲחֵרִים רַק עַל הַאֲמָנַת הַלֵּב אֲבָל עַל הָעֲשִׂיָּה לֹא יֹאמַר לְעוֹלָם "לֹא תַעֲשֶׂה אֱלֹהִים אֲחֵרִים" כִּי לֹא תִפֹּל בִּלְשׁוֹן עֲשִׂיָּה אֲחֵרִים. וְיָפֶה דִּקְדֵּק זִכְרוֹנוֹ לִבְרָכָה, דִּבְרֵי פִי חָכָם חֵן.

וְזֹאת הַמִּצְוָה הִיא הָעִקָּר הַגָּדוֹל שֶׁבַּתּוֹרָה שֶׁהַכֹּל תָּלוּי עָלָיו, כְּמוֹ שֶׁאָמְרוּ זִכְרוֹנָם לִבְרָכָה: כָּל הַמּוֹדֶה בַּעֲבוֹדָה זָרָה כְּאִלּוּ כָּפַר בְּכָל הַתּוֹרָה כֻּלָּהּ. וְאֶחָד הַמְקַבֵּל בֶּאֱלוֹהַּ לְשׁוּם דָּבָר זוּלָתִי הַשֵּׁם לְבַדּוֹ, אוֹ הָעוֹבֵד אוֹתוֹ דָּבָר כְּדֶרֶךְ עֲבוֹדָתוֹ כְּלוֹמַר כְּדֶרֶךְ שֶׁעוֹבְדִין אוֹתוֹ הַמַּאֲמִינִים בּוֹ, אוֹ אֲפִלּוּ שֶׁלֹּא כְּדֶרֶךְ עֲבוֹדָתוֹ אַךְ יַעֲבְדֶנּוּ בְּאַרְבַּע עֲבוֹדוֹת יְדוּעוֹת שֶׁהֵן זִבּוּחַ וְקִטּוּר וְנִסּוּךְ וְהִשְׁתַּחֲוָיָה, עָבַר עַל לֹא יִהְיֶה לְךָ. וְנִסּוּךְ וְזוֹרֵק דָּבָר אֶחָד הוּא, וּמִתְחַיְּבִין בִּזְרִיקָה כְּמוֹ בְנִסּוּךְ.

שֹׁרֶשׁ מִצְוָה זוֹ נִגְלֶה וְיָדוּעַ. פְּרָטֶיהָ, כְּגוֹן מַה שֶּׁאָמְרוּ שֶׁאִם קִבֵּל בֶּאֱלֹהַּ בְּאֶחָד מִכָּל הַנִּבְרָאִים, וַאֲפִלּוּ מוֹדֶה שֶׁהַקָּדוֹשׁ בָּרוּךְ הוּא שׁוֹלֵט עָלָיו וְעַל אֱלוֹהוֹ, עָבַר עַל לֹא יִהְיֶה. וּמָה הַדָּבָר שֶׁנִּקְרָא דֶּרֶךְ עֲבוֹדָתוֹ וְשֶׁלֹּא כְּדֶרֶךְ עֲבוֹדָתוֹ, וְאִם עֲבָדָהוּ דֶּרֶךְ בִּזּוּי עֲבוֹדָתוֹ בְכָךְ מַה דִּינוֹ, וְאַרְבַּע עֲבוֹדוֹת הָאֲסוּרוֹת בְּכָל הָאֱלוֹהוּת עַד הֵיכָן מִתְפַּשֵּׁט אִסּוּרָן, בְּעִנְיַן מַה שֶּׁאָמְרוּ זִכְרוֹנָם לִבְרָכָה דְּשָׁבַר מַקֵּל לְפָנֶיהָ בִּכְלָל זִבּוּחַ הוּא. וְכֵן מַה שֶּׁאָסְרוּ זִכְרוֹנָם לִבְרָכָה לִקְרוֹת בְּסִפְרֵי עוֹבְדֵי עֲבוֹדָה זָרָה הַמְחַבְּרִים בְּעִנְיְנֵי עֲבוֹדוֹתֶיהָ אוֹ בִדְבָרִים אֲחֵרִים שֶׁלָּהּ כָּל שֶׁגּוֹרְמִין לְהַאֲמִין בָּהּ בְּשׁוּם צַד, וְאִסּוּר הִרְהוּר הַלֵּב אַחֲרֶיהָ, וְדִין יִשְׂרָאֵל שֶׁעֲבָדָהּ אֲפִלּוּ פַּעַם אַחַת מַה דִּינוֹ, וְאִם קִבְּלוּ בֶאֱלוֹהַּ וְחָזַר תּוֹךְ כְּדֵי דִבּוּר חַיָּב, שֶׁלֹּא נֶאֱמַר בָּזֶה תּוֹךְ כְּדֵי דִבּוּר כְּדִבּוּר,

---

1. In his commentary to Pentateuch, Exodus 20:3.
2. For essentially, it is not the mere making of something in the form of an idol, unaccompanied by any forbidden intention or belief, which constitutes an act of idolatry. Only belief in it (or associated with it), that it represents a heathen deity with independent heavenly powers to affect human life and fortune, in response to its worship—only that brings it into the severely forbidden domain of idolatry.
3. Sifre, Numbers §111.
4. I.e. by saying to it, "thou art my god"; cf. Exodus 32:4.
5. I.e. having the body touch the ground in abject veneration. See TB Sanhedrin 60
6. Ibid.
7. Ramban, commentary, Exodus 20:3.
8. TB Sanhedrin 60b; see also Rambam MT hilchoth 'avodah zarah iii 2.
9. Ibid. (Rambam ibid. 5).
10. I.e. if the stick was used in the worship of the idol (e.g. to beat with it in rhythm) then breaking it is equated with breaking the neck of an animal in offering it up as a sacrifice; TB 'Avodah Zarah 51a.
11. Derived perhaps from the law in TB Shabbath 149a that it is forbidden to gaze at ikons and images of idolatry (MY).
12. TB Shabbath 149a.   13. TB Hullin 39a.
14. More precisely, within the time it takes to say (in Hebrew), "Peace upon you, my master."

⟨144⟩

20:3), which means, "You shall believe [in] no other god but Me. Ramban of blessed memory has written:[1] You will never find Scripture saying *other gods* except in reference to the heart's belief; but in regard to action it is never stated in Scripture, "You shall make no other gods" for the term "other" does not fit with the verb of doing.[2] This is a point well taken by him (be his memory for a blessing); *the words of a wise man's mouth are a grace* (Ecclesiastes 10:12).

This precept is *the* great principle of the Torah, on which all depends. As the Sages of blessed memory said,[3] whoever accepts idol-worship, it is as though he denied the entire Torah. If a person accepts as a god anything whatever other than the Eternal Lord,[4] or if he worships that thing in its manner of service, i.e., in the way that those who believe in it serve and relate to it religiously; or even if not in its manner of worship, if he venerates it with the four known ways of worship, i.e. ritually slaying a sacrifice, burning [any ritual substance on an altar], pouring a libation [of wine], and prostration,[5] he has violated the precept, *You shall have no other gods before Me*. Pouring a libation and sprinkling [blood on an altar], though, are one and the same thing [one way of worship], and sprinkling blood brings as much guilt as pouring [wine on the altar].[6]

The root reason for this precept is obvious and known. Its particulars are, for instance, what they [the Sages] said, that if someone accepts as a god any one out of all the entities that were created, then even if he acknowledges that the Holy One, blessed is He, rules over him and his god, he violates the commandment, *You shall have no other gods before Me;*[7] which is the service that is called the way of its worship, and which is not the way of its worship;[8] if one worshipped it [an idol] in a disgraceful way, but such is its [mode of] worship, what is the law;[9] regarding the four services which are forbidden for all divinities, how far does their prohibition extend—for example, the teaching of the Sages of blessed memory, that if someone broke a stick before it [an idol], this is included under the ban on ritually slaying a sacrifice.[10]

So too, there is the prohibition which they (of blessed memory) placed on reading books by idol-worshippers written about its [their idol's] ways of religious service, or about other matters concerning it[11] —whatever may cause one to believe in it from any aspect;[12] the ban on reflection, meditation of the heart about it;[12] what the law is if a Jew worshipped it even once.[13] If he accepted it as a god but retracted within the time it takes to speak [three or four words][14]—then he is guilty,

§26: TO BELIEVE IN NO DIVINITY BUT GOD

וְהוּא הַדִּין בְּעִנְיָן קִדּוּשִׁין. וְהָעוֹבְדָהּ מֵאַהֲבָה שֶׁחִבֵּב אוֹתָהּ צוּרָה לְרֹב יָפְיָהּ אוֹ מִיִּרְאָה שֶׁלֹּא תָּרַע לוֹ וְלֹא שֶׁיְּקַבְּלָהּ בֶּאֱלוֹהַּ, וְכֵן הָעוֹשֶׂה לָהּ כְּבוֹדוֹת כְּגוֹן חִבּוּק נִשּׁוּק סָךְ מַלְבִּישׁ מַנְעִיל מַהוּ דִּין אִסּוּרוֹ. וְדִינֵי בִּטּוּלֵי עֲבוֹדָה זָרָה כֵּיצַד, וְהַחִלּוּק שֶׁבֵּין עֲבוֹדָה זָרָה דְּיִשְׂרָאֵל לַעֲבוֹדָה זָרָה דְּגוֹי בְּעִנְיַן בִּטּוּלָהּ, וְאִסּוּרֵי הֲנָאָה שֶׁל עֲבוֹדָה זָרָה עַד הֵיכָן, וְהַחִלּוּק שֶׁבֵּין תָּלוּשׁ הַנֶּעֱבָד לִמְחֻבָּר מֵעִקָּרוֹ, וּמֵאֵימָתַי הִיא נַעֲשֵׂית עֲבוֹדָה זָרָה, וְדִינֵי מְשַׁמְּשֵׁי עֲבוֹדָה זָרָה, וְאִם בָּטֵל הִיא מַה יְּהֵא בְּמִשְׁמְּשֶׁיהָ, וְתִקְרֹבֶת שֶׁלָּהּ מַה דִּינוֹ. וַעֲבוֹדָה זָרָה שֶׁהִנִּיחוּהָ עוֹבְדֶיהָ, וְהַהַרְחָקָה מֵעוֹבְדֶיהָ בְּיוֹם עֲבוֹדָתָהּ וְסָמוּךְ לוֹ, וְהַדְּבָרִים הָאֲסוּרִים לָנוּ לִמְכֹּר לָהֶם לְעוֹלָם מִפְּנֵי חֲשָׁשׁ קְלוֹנָהּ, וְהַהַרְחָקָה עִיר שֶׁיֵּשׁ עֲבוֹדָה זָרָה בְּתוֹכָהּ, וְיֶתֶר רֹב פְּרָטֶיהָ, מְבֹאָרִים בַּמַּסֶּכְתָּא הַבְּנוּיָה עַל זֶה וְהִיא עֲבוֹדָה זָרָה.

וְנוֹהֶגֶת בִּזְכָרִים וּבִנְקֵבוֹת בְּכָל מָקוֹם וּבְכָל זְמַן. וְהָעוֹבֵר עָלֶיהָ וְעָבַד עֲבוֹדָה זָרָה כְּדֶרֶךְ עֲבוֹדָתָהּ, אוֹ שֶׁלֹּא כְּדֶרֶךְ עֲבוֹדָתָהּ בְּאַרְבַּע עֲבוֹדוֹת שֶׁכָּתַבְנוּ, בְּעֵדִים וְהַתְרָאָה נִסְקָל, וּבְשִׁגְגָה, חַיָּב לְהָבִיא הַטָּאת קְבוּעָה.

וְזֹאת הַמִּצְוָה הִיא מִכְּלַל הַשֶּׁבַע מִצְווֹת שֶׁנִּצְטַוּוּ כָּל בְּנֵי הָעוֹלָם בִּכְלָלָן. אֲבָל מִכָּל מָקוֹם חִלּוּקִין יֵשׁ בִּפְרָטִים בֵּין יִשְׂרָאֵל לִשְׁאָר הָאֻמּוֹת, וְהַכֹּל מְבֹאָר שָׁם בַּעֲבוֹדָה זָרָה. וּמִן הַחִלּוּקִין שֶׁבֵּין יִשְׂרָאֵל לִשְׁאָר הָאֻמּוֹת בְּעִנְיַן הַמִּצְווֹת הַמֻּטָּלוֹת עַל הַכֹּל הוּא שֶׁיִּשְׂרָאֵל לֹא יִתְחַיֵּב לְעוֹלָם בְּלֹא עֵדִים וְהַתְרָאָה, וּשְׁאָר הָאֻמּוֹת

15. TB Bava Bathra 129b.
16. TB Sanhedrin 61b.
17. In the Middle East and the orient it was a general custom to smear the body with oil; it was thus a way of honoring the idol.
18. TB Sanhedrin 60b.
19. TB 'Avodah Zarah 52b–53a.
20. Ibid. 52b (Rambam MT hilchoth 'avodah zarah viii 8–9).
21. Ibid. 34b.
22. Ibid. 45a (Rambam ibid. viii 1).
23. Ibid. 51b.
24. Ibid. 51b, 52b.
25. E.g. meat, wine, fruit; ibid. 29b, 32b, 50a.
26. Ibid. 53b.
27. Ibid. 2a, 6b (Rambam ibid. ix 10).
28. Literally, out of suspicion of its disgrace (a euphemism); ibid. 13b–14a (Rambam ibid. ix 6).
29. Ibid. 11b.
30. I.e. two or more people warn him beforehand that the penalty for his act will be death, and with a defiant answer he commits the deed in their sight.
31. See §19, note 6.
32. TB Sanhedrin 56a; these are: idolatry, blasphemy, murder, incestuous and consanguineous relations; robbery, just civil law, eating a limb torn from a living animal (Rambam MT hilchoth m'lachim ix 1).

for in this the rule does not hold that "within the time it takes to speak" is as if while still speaking [to cancel or undo the original words][15]—and the law is the same in regard to marrying. [Then there is law for] one who serves it out of love, as he cherishes that figure [the idol] for its great beauty;[16] or [if he serves it] out of fear, that it should not harm him, but [in either case] he did not accept it as a god;[16] so, too, if one shows it forms of respect and honor, such as embracing or kissing it, smearing it with oil,[17] putting clothing or shoes on it—what is the law of its forbiddance.[18]

[We have, further] laws of making an idol null and void;[19] the difference between the idol of an Israelite and the idol of a heathen, in regard to making it null and void;[20] how far the ban goes on having any benefit from an idol or idolatry;[21] the difference [in law] between a detached object which is worshipped and one which from its original state is attached [to the earth];[22] from which time it is considered an idol;[23] the law for objects which are used in idol-worship, and if one makes an idol null and void, what of the objects which have served it;[24] what is the law for offerings brought to it;[25] [what of] an idol whose worshippers have abandoned it;[26] keeping distant from its worshippers before and on the day of its religious service;[27] the things we are forbidden ever to sell them, out of suspicion that they will offer them up to the idol;[28] and keeping well away from a city within which there is idol-worship.[29] [These] and the remaining many details [of the precept] are clarified in the Talmud tractate built about this [subject], i.e. 'Avodah Zarah.

It applies to both man and woman, in every time and in every place. If someone transgresses it and worships an idol in the [accepted] way of its veneration, or if not in its way of veneration, then in the four modes of worship that we have written—this with witnesses and a warning[30]— he is stoned to death. If it was done unintentionally, he is required to bring a standard, unvarying *hattath*.[31]

This precept is also one of the group of seven precepts which all people in the world generally were commanded to keep.[32] There are, however, differences in detail between [the duty of] Jewry and [that of] the other nations.[33] This is all explained there, in the tractate 'Avodah Zarah. Among the differences between Israelites and the other nations in regard to the precepts imposed as duties upon all, there are these: An Israelite never incurs punishment without witnesses and a warning,[34] while the other nations require no warning: for it

אֵין צְרִיכִין הַתְרָאָה, לְפִי שֶׁאֵין חִלּוּק בָּהֶן בֵּין שׁוֹגֵג לְמֵזִיד. וְכֵן יִתְחַיְּבוּ גַם כֵּן בְּהוֹדָאַת פִּיהֶם, מַה שֶּׁאֵין כֵּן בְּיִשְׂרָאֵל שֶׁצָּרִיךְ עֵדִים. וְעוֹד יֵשׁ חִלּוּק אַחֵר, כִּי הָאֻמּוֹת בְּעָבְרָם עַל כָּל אַחַת מִמִּצְווֹתָם יִתְחַיְּבוּ לְעוֹלָם מִיתָה, וְזֶהוּ אָמְרָם זִכְרוֹנָם לִבְרָכָה, אַזְהָרָתָן זוֹ הִיא מִיתָתָן, וְיִשְׂרָאֵל יִתְחַיֵּב קָרְבָּן, פְּעָמִים מַלְקוּת, פְּעָמִים מִיתָה, וּפְעָמִים אֵינוֹ מִתְחַיֵּב בְּכָל אֵלֶה אֶלָּא שֶׁהוּא כְּעוֹבֵר עַל מִצְוַת מֶלֶךְ וְנָשָׂא עֲוֹנוֹ.

[שֶׁלֹּא לַעֲשׂוֹת פֶּסֶל]

כז שֶׁלֹּא נַעֲשֶׂה צְלָמִים שֶׁיַּעַבְדוּ, וַאֲפִלּוּ לֹא עֲבָדָם הָעוֹשֶׂה, הָעֲשִׂיָּה לְבַד אֲסוּרָה לְהַרְחִיק הַמִּכְשׁוֹל, וְאֵין הֶפְרֵשׁ בֵּין שֶׁיַּעֲשֶׂה בְּיָדוֹ אוֹ יְצַוֶּה לַעֲשׂוֹת, שֶׁנֶּאֱמַר: לֹא תַעֲשֶׂה לְךָ פֶסֶל וְכָל תְּמוּנָה, וְהַמְצַוֶּה לַעֲשׂוֹתָהּ הוּא הַגּוֹרֵם הָעֲשִׂיָּה, זֶהוּ דַּעַת הָרַמְבַּ״ם זִכְרוֹנוֹ לִבְרָכָה. וְדַעַת הָרַמְבַּ״ן זִכְרוֹנוֹ לִבְרָכָה שֶׁאֵין הָאַזְהָרָה בְּכַאן אֶלָּא שֶׁלֹּא יַעֲשֶׂה צְלָמִים עַל דַּעַת לְעָבְדָם. גַּם כָּתַב שֶׁאֵין לָנוּ לִמְנוֹת לָאו זֶה מִן הַמִּקְרָא הַזֶּה, כִּי לֹא יַזְהִיר בָּזֶה הַכָּתוּב רַק בְּאִסּוּר עֲבוֹדָה זָרָה שֶׁהוּא בְּמִיתָה, וּבַעֲשִׂיַּת צְלָמִים כָּל זְמַן שֶׁלֹּא עֲבָדָם אֵין בַּדָּבָר אֶלָּא מַלְקוּת. וְהוּא זִכְרוֹנוֹ לִבְרָכָה כָּתַב שֶׁכָּל פָּסוּק זֶה דְּלֹא יִהְיֶה לְךָ נֶחְשָׁב לְלָאו אֶחָד, יַזְהִיר שֶׁלֹּא נוֹדֶה הָאֱלֹהוּת לְזוּלָתוֹ בֵּין שֶׁיְּקַבְּלֶנּוּ בֶּאֱלוֹהַּ, כְּלוֹמַר שֶׁיֹּאמַר לוֹ אֵלִי אַתָּה אוֹ שֶׁיִּשְׁתַּחֲוֶה לוֹ אוֹ יַעַבְדֵנוּ בְּאַחַת מֵאַרְבַּע עֲבוֹדוֹת אֲסוּרוֹת אוֹ בַּעֲבוֹדָתוֹ הַמְיֻחֶדֶת לוֹ. אֲבָל הַמַּנִּיעָה בַּעֲשִׂיַּת הַצְּלָמִים וְקִיּוּמָם כָּתַב הוּא דְּנָפְקָא לָן מִפָּסוּק דְּאַל תִּפְנוּ אֶל הָאֱלִילִים וֵאלֹהֵי מַסֵּכָה לֹא תַעֲשׂוּ לָכֶם.

---

33. See TB Sanhedrin 56b, 'Avodah Zarah 52b.

34. I.e. for a deliberate transgression, which is punished far more severely than an inadvertent violation.

35. TB Sanhedrin 57b; Rashi to Makkoth 9a, s.v. l'fichach; Rambam ibid. x 1.

36. Cf. R. Juda b. Pazzi's teaching in TJ Kiddushin i 1, and Korban 'Edah ad loc. (R. Yeruham Leiner in fifth ed. Chavel, p. 766).

37. TB Sanhedrin 57a.

§27 1. ShM negative precept §§2, 4, MT hilchoth 'avodah zarah iii 9.

2. In his hassagoth ("objections") to ShM negative precept §5.

3. I.e. Exodus 20:3–4.

4. Ritually slaying a sacrifice, burning any ritual substance on an altar, pouring a libation of wine, and prostration (§26).

makes no difference in their law whether a transgression occurred unintentionally or deliberately.[35] So, too, do they become guilty by their own confession,[36] which is not the case with a Jew: for him witnesses are required [to convict him]. And there is one other difference: When [citizens of] the nations transgress one of their precepts, they always incur the penalty of death; this is the meaning of what the Sages of blessed memory said,[37] "Their prohibition is their death warrant." An Israelite, though, can become required sometimes to bring an offering, sometimes to receive whiplashes, and sometimes to be put to death; and sometimes he incurs none of these penalties, but is as one who has violated the commandment of the king, and he bears [the burden] of his guilt.

27 [NOT TO MAKE A GRAVEN IMAGE] that we should not make images to be worshipped; and even if the one who makes it does not worship it, the manufacture is itself forbidden, in order to keep such "stumbling-blocks" [to our religiosity] far removed. It makes no difference whether one makes it by his own hand or orders it made: for it is stated, *You shall not make yourself a graven image, or any likeness of anything* (Exodus 20:4), and one who orders it made causes it to be produced. This is the view of Rambam of blessed memory.[1]

However, the view of Ramban of blessed memory[2] is that the injunction is solely that one should not make images with the aim to worship them. He wrote further that we are not to reckon this negative precept as derived from this verse of Scripture. For in this verse He warns us only of the ban against idol-worship, which brings on the death penalty; whereas the manufacture of images, as long as we do not worship them, is a matter involving only whiplashes. And he (of blessed memory) wrote that this entire verse of *You shall have no other gods*, etc.[3] is considered as one negative precept, warning us that we should accept no god other than Him, whether by acknowledging it as a divinity—i.e. by saying to it, "You are my god"—or by bowing down to it, or by venerating it in one of the four forbidden ways of worship[4] or in its own particular way of worship. But the restraint [which the Torah imposes] on making idols and keeping them, he writes, derives from the verse, *Do not turn to the idols, or make for yourselves molten gods* (Leviticus 19:4).

§27–28: NO GRAVEN IMAGE / NO PROSTRATION IN IDOL-WORSHIP

וְתָמֵהַּ אֲנִי עַל הָרַמְבָּ"ם זִכְרוֹנוֹ לִבְרָכָה שֶׁכָּתַב שֶׁאֵין הֶפְרֵשׁ בֵּין שֶׁיַּעֲשֵׂם בְּיָדוֹ אוֹ יְצַוֶּה לַעֲשׂוֹתָם, שֶׁהֲרֵי מִצְוָה מְשֻׁלַּחַת הוּא וְקַיְמָא לָן מְשַׁלֵּחַ פָּטוּר.

שֹׁרֶשׁ מִצְוָה זוֹ יָדוּעַ שֶׁהוּא לְהַרְחִיק עֲבוֹדָה זָרָה.

דִּינֵי הַמִּצְוָה כְּגוֹן הָעוֹשֶׂה צוּרוֹת אֵי זוֹ צוּרָה אֲסוּרָה לַעֲשׂוֹת וְאֵי זוֹ מֻתֶּרֶת, וְהַחִלּוּק שֶׁבֵּין בּוֹלֶטֶת לְשׁוֹקַעַת, וְדִין טַבַּעַת שֶׁיֵּשׁ עָלֶיהָ חוֹתָם, וְיֶתֶר פְּרָטֶיהָ מְבֹאָרִים בְּמַסֶּכֶת עֲבוֹדָה זָרָה.

וְנוֹהֶגֶת בְּכָל מָקוֹם וּבְכָל זְמַן בִּזְכָרִים וּנְקֵבוֹת. וְעוֹבֵר עָלֶיהָ וְעָשָׂה צְלָמִים הַנֶּעֱבָדִים בְּמֵזִיד לוֹקֶה.

[שֶׁלֹּא לְהִשְׁתַּחֲווֹת לַעֲבוֹדָה זָרָה]

כח שֶׁלֹּא לְהִשְׁתַּחֲווֹת לַעֲבוֹדָה זָרָה, וַעֲבוֹדָה זָרָה הִיא כָּל מַה שֶּׁיַּעֲבֹד זוּלָתִי הָאֵל בָּרוּךְ הוּא, שֶׁנֶּאֱמַר: לֹא תִשְׁתַּחֲוֶה לָהֶם וְלֹא תָעָבְדֵם. וְאֵין פֵּרוּשׁ הַכָּתוּב לֹא תִשְׁתַּחֲוֶה עַל מְנָת לַעֲבֹד, שֶׁנִּלְמַד מִמֶּנּוּ שֶׁהַהִשְׁתַּחֲוָאָה לְבַד שֶׁלֹּא לְכַוָּנַת עֲבוֹדָה שֶׁלֹּא יְהֵא אָסוּר, שֶׁהֲרֵי בְּמָקוֹם אַחֵר נֶאֱמַר בַּתּוֹרָה "כִּי לֹא תִשְׁתַּחֲוֶה לְאֵל אַחֵר", שֶׁאָסְרָה הַהִשְׁתַּחֲוָאָה בִּלְבַד בְּשׁוּם צַד. וְאָמְנָם סָמַךְ אֵלֶיהָ "וְלֹא תָעָבְדֵם" לוֹמַר שֶׁהַהִשְׁתַּחֲוָאָה הִיא אַחַת מִדַּרְכֵי הָעֲבוֹדָה, וְלָמַדְנוּ מִכָּאן עִם סִיּוּעַ כְּתוּבִים אֲחֵרִים שֶׁאַרְבַּע עֲבוֹדוֹת הֵם שֶׁהִקְפִּידָה הַתּוֹרָה בָּהֶן בְּכָל עֲבוֹדָה זָרָה שֶׁבָּעוֹלָם, וַאֲפִלּוּ אֵין דֶּרֶךְ עֲבוֹדָתָהּ בְּכָךְ חַיָּבִין עֲלֵיהֶן, וְאַחַת מֵהֶן הַהִשְׁתַּחֲוָאָה.

שֹׁרֶשׁ מִצְוָה זוֹ יָדוּעַ.

דִּינֵי הַמִּצְוָה, כְּגוֹן מָה הִיא הִשְׁתַּחֲוָאָה אִם בִּפְשׁוּט יָדַיִם וְרַגְלַיִם אוֹ מַשֶּׁהוּ שֶׁיְּכַבֵּשׁ פָּנָיו בַּקַּרְקַע, וְהֶרְחֵק הָעִנְיָן, כְּגוֹן מַה שֶּׁאָמְרוּ כְּגוֹן שֶׁאִם יָשַׁב לוֹ קוֹץ בְּרַגְלוֹ אוֹ

---

5. "There are no agents, messengers, for a matter of transgression" (TB Kiddushin 42b): whoever commits a wrong is himself punished, not whoever employed or sent him. *Minhath Hinnuch* answers, though, that Rambam evidently considers an employer equally guilty with an artisan who makes the idol, not because he appoints an agent or delegates another to make it, but because this is the decree of the Torah: it is included in the precept, *You shall not make yourself a graven image*, etc. (See also *Torah Shelemah*, Exodus 20, §134 and note.)

6. TB 'Avodah Zarah 43b (Ramban cited in *Tur Yoreh Dēʿah* §141; MT *hilchoth 'avodah zarah* iii 10–11).

7. I.e. in the image of a man; TB *ibid*.

§28 1. Although rendered above, "or serve them," this is the Hebrew's literal meaning.

2. From the beginning to here is derived from Rambam ShM negative precept §5.

3. TB Horayoth 4a; see *Torah Shelemah*, Exodus 20, §145 and note.

4. TB 'Avodah Zarah 12a.

⟨150⟩

Now, I wonder at Rambam of blessed memory, that he wrote that it makes no difference whether one makes them by his own hand or orders them made: For one who gives an order is appointing an agent, and we have an established rule that one who appoints an agent [to do a wrong] is free of punishment.[5]

The root purpose of this precept is known (evident): It is to keep idol-worship well removed.

The laws of the precept are, for instance: for one who makes images, which image is it forbidden to make, and which permitted;[6] the difference [in law] between one which protrudes and one that is sunk into the surface;[6] the law for a ring which has a seal on it.[7] [These] and its other details are explained in the Talmud tractate *Avodah Zarah*.

It remains in force in every place and every time, for both man and woman. If someone transgresses it and intentionally makes images which are worshipped, he is given whiplashes.

28 [NOT TO PROSTRATE ONESELF IN IDOL-WORSHIP]

not to bow down to the ground in idol-worship; and it is idol-worship whenever one venerates anything at all other than God, blessed is He; as it is stated, *you shall not prostrate yourself before them or serve them* (Exodus 20:5). Now, the meaning of the verse is not "you shall not prostrate yourself in order (with the intention) to worship," so that we would learn from it that merely bowing down to touch the ground without the intention of worship is not forbidden: because elsewhere it is stated in the Torah, *For you shall not prostrate yourself to any other god* (Exodus 34:14), which forbids merely bowing down to the ground, in any way. Here, however, "and you shall not serve them"[1] follows immediately, to indicate that prostration is one of the [standard] ways of worship.[2] From this we learn, with the aid of other verses in Scripture, that there are four modes of worship to which the Torah strictly objects in regard to any idol in the world; even if it is not generally worshipped so, one incurs guilt through them. And one of them is bowing down to prostrate oneself.

The root of this precept is known. The laws of the precept are, for instance: what is prostration: is it when hands and feet are spread on the ground, or from the time that the face is buried in the ground;[3] and keeping well away from this matter: for example, the teaching of the Sages[4] that if a thorn lodged in a person's foot or if money of his was scattered before an idol, it is not permitted to prostrate oneself and take

נִתְפַּזְּרוּ לוֹ מָעוֹת בִּפְנֵי עֲבוֹדָה זָרָה שֶׁאֵין רַשַּׁאי לָשׁוּחַ וְלִטְּלָם מִפְּנֵי שֶׁנִּרְאֶה כְּמִשְׁתַּחֲוֶה, וְיֶתֶר פְּרָטֶיהָ, מְבֹאָרִים בְּמַסֶּכֶת עֲבוֹדָה זָרָה.

וְנוֹהֶגֶת בְּכָל מָקוֹם וּבְכָל זְמַן בִּזְכָרִים וּנְקֵבוֹת. וְעוֹבֵר עָלֶיהָ וְהִשְׁתַּחֲוָה לְשׁוּם עֲבוֹדָה זָרָה בָּעוֹלָם אוֹ זָבַח וְקִטֵּר וְנִסֵּךְ אוֹ זָרַק בְּמֵזִיד, חַיָּב כָּרֵת, וּבְעֵדִים נִסְקָל, וּבְשׁוֹגֵג חַיָּב חַטָּאת. וּבֵאוּר מִשְׁפְּטֵי הָעֹנֶשׁ בְּפֶרֶק ז׳ מִסַּנְהֶדְרִין.

[שֶׁלֹּא לַעֲבֹד עֲבוֹדָה זָרָה בְּמַה שֶּׁדַּרְכָּהּ לְהֵעָבֵד]

כט שֶׁלֹּא נַעֲבֹד שׁוּם עֲבוֹדָה זָרָה בָּעוֹלָם בִּדְבָרִים שֶׁדַּרְכָּהּ שֶׁעוֹבְדִים אוֹתָהּ הַמַּאֲמִינִים בָּהּ, וְאַף עַל פִּי שֶׁאֵין עֲבוֹדָתָהּ בְּאַחַת מֵאַרְבַּע עֲבוֹדוֹת שֶׁאָמַרְנוּ לְמַעְלָה, מִכֵּיוָן שֶׁעֲבָדָהּ בְּמַה שֶּׁדַּרְכָּהּ לְהֵעָבֵד חַיָּב, וְאַף עַל פִּי שֶׁעֲבוֹדָתָהּ דֶּרֶךְ בִּזָּיוֹן, כְּגוֹן הַפּוֹעֵר לִפְעוֹר וְזוֹרֵק אֶבֶן לְמַרְקוּלִיס וּמַעֲבִיר שְׂעָרוֹ לִכְמוֹשׁ, שֶׁנֶּאֱמַר "וְלֹא תָעָבְדֵם", כְּלוֹמַר בְּמַה שֶּׁדַּרְכָּן לְהֵעָבֵד אֵי זוֹ עֲבוֹדָה שֶׁתִּהְיֶה.

שָׁרְשָׁהּ יָדוּעַ. דִּינֶיהָ, כְּגוֹן מִי שֶׁעוֹבְדָהּ דֶּרֶךְ עֲבוֹדָתָהּ לְכַוָּנַת בִּזָּיוֹן מַה דִּינוֹ, וּשְׁאָר פְּרָטֶיהָ, מְבֹאָרִים בְּמַסֶּכֶת עֲבוֹדָה זָרָה.

וְנוֹהֶגֶת בְּכָל מָקוֹם וּבְכָל זְמַן בִּזְכָרִים וּנְקֵבוֹת. וְעוֹבֵר עָלֶיהָ בְּמֵזִיד וְיֵשׁ עֵדִים נִסְקָל. וּמְבֹאָר דִּין זֶה גַּם כֵּן בְּפֶרֶק ז׳ מִסַּנְהֶדְרִין.

שְׁתֵּי מִצְווֹת אֵלּוּ שֶׁיִּמְנֶה הָרַמְבַּ״ם זִכְרוֹנוֹ לִבְרָכָה שֶׁהֵן הִשְׁתַּחֲוָאָה לַעֲבוֹדָה זָרָה וְכֵן שֶׁלֹּא לְעָבְדָהּ בְּמַה שֶּׁדַּרְכָּהּ לְעָבְדָהּ יְכַלְּלֵם הָרַמְבַּ״ן זִכְרוֹנוֹ לִבְרָכָה בְּלָאו דְּלֹא יִהְיֶה לְךָ, כְּמוֹ שֶׁכְּתַבְנוּ לְמַעְלָה. נִמְצָא שֶׁיִּסְתַּלֵּק שְׁתֵּי מִצְווֹת בְּכָאן מֵחֶשְׁבּוֹנוֹ שֶׁל הָרַב רַבִּי מֹשֶׁה בֶּן מַיְמוֹן זִכְרוֹנוֹ לִבְרָכָה.

---

§29   1. Rambam MT *hilchoth 'avodah zarah* iii 5.
   2. Paragraph derived from Rambam ShM negative precept §6; cf. *Torah Shelemah*, Exodus 20, §152 (from Midrash haGadol) and Addenda p. 233.
   3. TB Sanhedrin 64a.

⟨152⟩

them, for he would seem to be prostrating himself in worship. [These] and its further details are clarified in the Talmud tractate '*Avodah Zarah*.

It is in force in every time and place, for both man and woman. If someone violates it and prostrates himself before any idol in the world, or offers a sacrifice, burns incense, pours a libation or sprinkles [the blood of an offering]—deliberately, intentionally—he incurs *karéth* [Divine severance of existence]. If there were witnesses, he is stoned to death. If it was done unintentionally, he is obligated to bring a *ḥattath* (sin-offering). The explanation of the rules of punishment [will be found] in chapter 7 of the tractate *Sanhedrin*.

[NOT TO WORSHIP AN IDOL IN ITS USUAL WAY OF VENERATION]

29 that we should worship no idol whatever in the world by such means as those who believe in it customarily serve it. Even if its service is not in one of the four modes of worship that we mentioned above (§26), once a person worships it in the way it is usually venerated, he incurs guilt—and this even if its worship is by something disgraceful:[1] for example, if one uncovers [to evacuate] to Pe'or, or throws a stone at Merculis (Mercurius), or brings his hair as an offering to Chemosh. For it is stated, *and you shall not serve them* (Exodus 20:5, literal translation), which means in the way that it is usual to serve them, whatever that mode of worship might be.[2]

Its root purpose is known (evident). Its laws—such as: if one serves it [an idol] in its way of worship, [but] with the intention of [showing] contempt, how should he be judged?[3]—and its other details, are explained in the tractate '*Avodah Zarah*.

It is in effect in every place, at every time, for both man and woman. If one violates it deliberately and there are witnesses, he is stoned to death. This law is explained too in the seventh chapter of the tractate *Sanhedrin*.

These two precepts which Rambam of blessed memory lists—prostration to an idol, and not to serve it in the way it is customarily worshipped—Ramban of blessed memory includes in the negative precept, *You shall have no other gods before Me* (Exodus 20:3), as we have written above (§27). As a result, he removes two precepts here from the reckoning of R. Moses b. Maimon [Rambam] of blessed memory.

§30: NOT TO TAKE AN OATH IN VAIN

[שֶׁלֹּא לִשָּׁבַע לַשָּׁוְא]

לֹ שֶׁלֹּא נִשָּׁבַע לְבַטָּלָה, שֶׁנֶּאֱמַר: לֹא תִשָּׂא אֶת שֵׁם ה' אֱלֹהֶיךָ לַשָּׁוְא. וְעִנְיַן הַבַּטָּלָה הוּא בְּאַרְבַּע צְדָדִין, כְּגוֹן שֶׁנִּשְׁבַּע עַל דָּבָר יָדוּעַ שֶׁאֵינוֹ כֵן, כְּגוֹן עַל עַמּוּד שֶׁל שַׁיִשׁ שֶׁהוּא שֶׁל זָהָב וְכֵן כָּל כַּיּוֹצֵא בָּזֶה. הַצַּד הַשֵּׁנִי, כְּגוֹן שֶׁנִּשְׁבַּע עַל הַיָּדוּעַ שֶׁהוּא כֵן, כְּגוֹן עַל הָאֶבֶן שֶׁהוּא אֶבֶן וְעַל הָעֵץ שֶׁהוּא עֵץ וְכֵן כָּל כַּיּוֹצֵא בָּזֶה. הַשְּׁלִישִׁי שֶׁנִּשְׁבַּע לְבַטֵּל מִצְוָה זוֹ אוֹ מִצְווֹת שֶׁחִיְּבָנוּ הַשֵּׁם בָּרוּךְ הוּא, שֶׁגַּם זֶה לְבַטָּלָה לְגַמְרֵי הוּא שֶׁאֵין בְּיָדוֹ לִשָּׁבַע עַל מַה שֶּׁכְּבָר חִיְּבוֹ הָאֵל, וּכְמִי שֶׁנִּשְׁבַּע בְּדָבָר יָדוּעַ שֶׁאֵינוֹ כֵן הוּא. הָרְבִיעִי, שֶׁנִּשְׁבַּע לַעֲשׂוֹת דָּבָר שֶׁאֵין בּוֹ כֹּחַ לַעֲשׂוֹתוֹ כְּגוֹן שֶׁלֹּא יִישַׁן שְׁלֹשָׁה יָמִים רְצוּפִים אוֹ שֶׁלֹּא יֹאכַל שִׁבְעָה יָמִים רְצוּפִים וְכֵן כָּל כַּיּוֹצֵא בָּזֶה.

מִשָּׁרְשֵׁי מִצְוָה זוֹ לָדַעַת בְּנֵי אָדָם וְלִקְבֹּעַ בְּנַפְשׁוֹתָם וּלְחַזֵּק הָאֱמוּנָה בְּלִבּוֹתָם כִּי הָאֵל בָּרוּךְ הוּא אֲשֶׁר בַּשָּׁמַיִם מִמַּעַל חַי וְקַיָּם לָעַד, אֵין קִיּוּם כְּקִיּוּמוֹ, וְרָאוּי וּמְחֻיָּב עָלֵינוּ בְּזָכְרֵנוּ שְׁמוֹ הַגָּדוֹל עַל מַעֲשֵׂינוּ וְעַל דְּבָרֵינוּ לְזָכְרוֹ בְּאֵימָה בְּיִרְאָה בְּרֶתֶת וּבְזִיעַ, לֹא כְּמִתְהַתְּלִים וּמְדַבְּרִים בְּדָבָר קַל כְּמוֹ הַדְּבָרִים הַהוֹוִים וְנִפְסָדִים וְאֵינָם נִשְׁאָרִים בְּקִיּוּמָם כָּמוֹנוּ אֲנַחְנוּ בְּנֵי אָדָם וּשְׁאָר דִּבְרֵי הָעוֹלָם הַשָּׁפָל, עַל כֵּן רָאוּי לִקְבֹּעַ הָעִנְיָן הַזֶּה בְּלִבֵּנוּ וְלִהְיוֹת יִרְאָתוֹ עַל פָּנֵינוּ לְחַיּוֹתֵנוּ וּלְזַכּוֹתֵנוּ חִיְּבָנוּ בַּמִּצְוָה הַזֹּאת לְבַל נַזְכִּיר שְׁמוֹ הַקָּדוֹשׁ לְבַטָּלָה, וְעֹנֶשׁ מַלְקוֹת עַל הַמֵּקֵל וְעוֹבֵר עָלֶיהָ.

וּמִזֶּה הַשֹּׁרֶשׁ בְּעַצְמוֹ הוּא עִנְיַן שְׁבוּעַת שֶׁקֶר, כְּלוֹמַר נִשְׁבַּע לְקַיֵּם דָּבָר וְלֹא קִיְּמוֹ שֶׁהִיא נִקְרֵאת שְׁבוּעָה בְּטוּי, שֶׁבָּא עָלֶיהָ לָאו אַחֵר בִּפְנֵי עַצְמוֹ בְּסֵדֶר קְדשִׁים תִּהְיֶה, כְּמוֹ שֶׁנֶּאֱמַר "וְלֹא תִשָּׁבְעוּ בִשְׁמִי לַשָּׁקֶר", כִּי הַנִּשְׁבָּע בַּשֵּׁם הַגָּדוֹל לְאַמֵּת

---

§30
1. TB Sh'vu'oth 29a.
2. TJ Sh'vu'oth iii 8 end.
3. TB Sh'vu'oth 25a. The paragraph is based on Rambam MT *hilchoth sh'vu'oth* i 4–6.
4. A Talmudic expression: TB B'rachoth 22a.
5. TB Sh'vu'oth 20b.

⟨154⟩

[NOT TO SWEAR IN VAIN]

30 that we should not swear in vain [to no valid purpose], for it is stated, *You shall not take the name of the Lord your God in vain* (Exodus 20:7). Now this matter of "in vain" (purposelessness) is in four possible ways: [1] for instance, if someone swears about something known, that it is not so: for example, about a marble pillar, that it is of gold;[1] and so anything similar. The second way: for example, if one swears about something known, that it *is* so:[2] for instance, about stone that it is stone, or about wood that it is wood; and so anything similar. The third way: if someone swears to violate "this precept" or precepts [in general] which the Eternal Lord, blessed is He, has bound us to observe.[1] This, too, is entirely in vain, purposeless: for it is not in his power to take an oath about [violating] something to which God already bound and obligated him. So this is like swearing about something known, that it is not so. The fourth way: if someone swears to do something which he has not the power or strength to do — for instance, that he will not sleep for three days in a row,[3] or that he will not eat seven days in a row, and so anything similar.

At the root of this precept lies the aim that human beings should know and affirm in their minds, and strengthen the faith in their hearts, that there is no existence like that of God, blessed is He, who is in heaven above, living and enduring forever. So is it fitting and required of us, when we mention His great name in connection with our actions and our words, that we should mention Him in awe and fear, quivering and trembling[4] — not like mockers who speak of light, trivial matters, e.g. things which exist [fleetingly] and then are lost to oblivion, not enduring in their original state, such as us human beings and other entities in this lowly world. Therefore it is fitting to set this matter firmly in our hearts and to have His awe before us, that we may find life and merit. [For this reason] He obligated us to observe this precept, that we should not mention His holy name in vain, purposelessly; and He set the punishment of whiplashes for one who takes it lightly and transgresses it.

Out of this root purpose itself comes the matter of swearing falsely: i.e. if someone swore to fulfill something and he did not fulfill it, which is called "an oath of expression"; this is another, separate negative precept (§227) in *sidrah k'doshim*, as it is stated, *And you shall not swear by My name falsely* (Leviticus 19:12).[5] For if someone swears by the great name [of God] to affirm as true something that

§30: NOT TO TAKE AN OATH IN VAIN	ספר החינוך

דָּבָר שֶׁהָיָה וְהוּא יוֹדֵעַ שֶׁשֶּׁקֶר בְּפִיו, הִנֵּה הוּא מֵקֵל בְּיִרְאַת אֱלֹהִים כְּאוֹמֵר בְּלִבּוֹ שֶׁאֵין אֱמֶת, תֵּאָלַמְנָה שְׂפָתָיו.

וְכֵן הַנִּשְׁבָּע לַעֲשׂוֹת דָּבָר וְאַחַר כָּךְ לֹא יַעֲשֵׂנוּ, הִנֵּה הוּא גַם כֵּן בְּמוֹרְדֵי אוֹר מַכְחִישֵׁי הָאֱמֶת, כִּי פֵּרוּשׁ נִשְׁבָּע הוּא לְפִי דַּעְתִּי שֶׁאוֹמֵר הָאָדָם בְּלִבּוֹ וְאוֹמֵר בְּפִיו לִהְיוֹת מְקֻיָּם אוֹתוֹ דָּבָר שֶׁנִּשְׁבַּע עָלָיו וְלֹא יְשַׁנֵּהוּ לְעוֹלָם, כְּמוֹ שֶׁהַשֵּׁם בָּרוּךְ הוּא קַיָּם וְלֹא יִשְׁתַּנֶּה לַעֲדֵי עַד. וְזֶהוּ שֶׁלְּשׁוֹן שְׁבוּעָה יָבוֹא לְעוֹלָם בִּלְשׁוֹן נִפְעָל, כְּלוֹמַר שֶׁנִּפְעָל בִּדְבָרָיו לִהְיוֹתוֹ קַיָּם בְּמַה שֶּׁאָמַר בְּקִיּוּמוֹ בָּרוּךְ הוּא.

וּבְעִנְיַן הַנֶּדֶר דֶּרֶךְ אַחֶרֶת יֵשׁ בּוֹ, שֶׁהוּא כְּמַכְנִיס דָּבָר בְּגֶדֶר הָאָסוּר וּכְאִלּוּ יֹאמַר דָּבָר פְּלוֹנִי שֶׁהוּא מֻתָּר יְהֵא אָסוּר עָלַי כְּקָרְבָּן שֶׁאָסַר הַשֵּׁם יִתְבָּרֵךְ וְאָמְרוּ זִכְרוֹנָם לִבְרָכָה, דְּדַוְקָא כְּשֶׁהוּא נוֹדֵר בְּדָבָר הַנִּדָּר יְהֵא חָל הַנֶּדֶר וְלֹא בְעִנְיָן אַחֵר, שֶׁאִם יֹאמַר הֲרֵי דָּבָר פְּלוֹנִי אָסוּר עָלַי כְּקָרְבָּן, כְּמוֹ שֶׁאָמַרְנוּ, בָּזֶה יָחוּל הַנֶּדֶר, אֲבָל אִם יֹאמַר כְּבָשָׂר חֲזִיר אֵין זֶה נֶדֶר, שֶׁהַתּוֹרָה אָמְרָה כִּי יִדֹּר נֶדֶר כְּלוֹמַר כִּי יִדֹּר בְּדָבָר הַנִּדָּר.

וְכֵן מִי שֶׁיֶּאֱסֹר דָּבָר לַחֲבֵרוֹ אוֹ עַל עַצְמוֹ (כְּמוֹ הַדְּבָרִים שֶׁל קָרְבָּן שֶׁאָסַר לָנוּ הַשֵּׁם יִתְבָּרֵךְ) כְּעִנְיָן זֶה הוּא, שֶׁהוּא כְּאִלּוּ אוֹמֵר דָּבָר פְּלוֹנִי יְהֵא אָסוּר עָלָיו אוֹ עַל חֲבֵרוֹ כְּמוֹ הַדְּבָרִים שֶׁל קָרְבָּן שֶׁאָסַר לָנוּ הַשֵּׁם (יִתְבָּרֵךְ). וְזֶה הָעִנְיָן שֵׁשׁ בָּנוּ כֹּחַ לֶאֱסֹר הַמֻּתָּר, לְפִי שֶׁהַתּוֹרָה לִמְּדַתְנוּ בְּכָךְ, מִדִּכְתִיב "לֶאֱסֹר אִסָּר... לֹא יַחֵל דְּבָרוֹ". וְעִנְיָן זֶה הוּא דּוֹמֶה לְהַקְדֵּשׁ שֶׁמָּצָאנוּ בַתּוֹרָה שֶׁיֵּשׁ כֹּחַ בָּאָדָם לְהַקְדִּישׁ אֶת

6. And thus he scorns a fundamental Divine principle and attribute; cf. TB Shabbath 55a: "the seal of the Holy One, blessed is He, is truth."

7. Expression based on Psalms 31:19, *Let the lying lips be mute*.

8. I.e. against the Almighty, who is the source of light for all the celestial luminaries (so Ibn Ezra on the verse).

9. TB N'darim 14a.

10. *Ibid.* 13a–b. When a person vows that something should be as forbidden to him as another object banned by a *neder*, i.e. a vowed object, his words take effect, because the first vowed object, e.g. the animal, became forbidden by virtue of a verbal declaration which dedicates and consecrates it [in the case of a sacrifice, for an offering]; hence the object of the present vow becomes equally forbidden by the verbal declaration. A pig's flesh, however, is initially and constantly forbidden by Torah law. No vow can be valid to impose the same ban, imposed by the Torah, on another object.

11. Here our author refers to a case where a man does not *transfer* a specific existing consecration but merely states that this object should be forbidden as sacrifices are forbidden. (From "like anything" to here is not in the oldest manuscripts, and is thus evidently a later addition.)

⟨156⟩

happened, yet he knows a lie is in his mouth, then here he treats the fear of God with scorn, as one who says in his heart that there is no [such thing as] truth.[6] Then let his lips be mute.[7]

So too if someone swears he will do something, and afterward he does not do it: you see, he is also *of those that rebel against the light* (Job 24:13), denying the truth. For the significance of taking an oath to my mind, is that the man determines in his heart and says with his mouth that he will fulfill the particular matter about which he swears and will never change or veer from it—just as the Eternal Lord, blessed is He, enduringly exists and will never change until the end of time. This is why the Hebrew verb for swearing is always in *nif'al*, the passive form, as though to say that he is affected by his own words, that it [his oath] must endure as valid on account of his reference to His enduring existence, blessed is He.

As for *neder*, the vow, that is a different way [of obligation]: for by that a person brings a permitted matter within the boundary of the forbidden. It is as though he said, "This thing which is permissible should be as forbidden to me as an animal offering, which the Eternal Lord, blessed is He, has prohibited." As our Sages of blessed memory said,[9] when a person takes a vow by referring to a vowed object, [intending to transfer the holiness of that object to the item he wants to forbid] then his vow takes effect, but not by some other way of wording. Thus, if he says, "Let that thing be as forbidden to me as this animal offering"—as we stated—so the vow takes effect; but if he says, "[as forbidden to me] as the flesh of a pig," it is no vow: because the Torah said, *When a man vows a* neder (Numbers 30:3), which implies, when he vows by reference to a *neder*, a vowed object.[10]

So too if a person makes something forbidden to his fellow-man or to himself, like anything brought as an offering—which the Eternal Lord (be He blessed) banned to us[11]—just so is this matter. It is as though he said that this particular thing should be forbidden to him or to his fellow like the contents of offerings which the Eternal Lord (be He blessed) banned to us. In substance it means that we have the power to make forbidden what is originally permitted. For so the Torah taught us, since it is written, *to tie a bond* [a ban] *about himself, he shall not profane his word* (Numbers 30:3, literal translation). Thus the matter is similar to *hekdesh*, consecration, about which we find in the Torah that a man has the power to consecrate what belongs to him, by the words of his mouth, and then it becomes forbidden at once

§30: NOT TO TAKE AN OATH IN VAIN

שֶׁלּוֹ בִּדְבָרָיו פִּיו וְיִהְיֶה אָסוּר מִיָּד לוֹ וּלְכָל הָעוֹלָם, כְּדִכְתִיב, וְאִישׁ כִּי יַקְדִּשׁ אֶת בֵּיתוֹ קֹדֶשׁ.

וּכְמוֹ כֵן יֵשׁ לוֹ כֹּחַ עַל עַצְמוֹ לֶאֱסֹר דְּבָרִים עַל גּוּפוֹ. וְזֶהוּ אָמְרָם זִכְרוֹנָם לִבְרָכָה לְעוֹלָם בִּלְשׁוֹן הַנְּדָרִים "הֲרֵי עָלַי" אוֹ "פִּי לַדִּבּוּר", כְּלוֹמַר שֶׁהוּא מַרְחִיק אוֹתוֹ דָּבָר מִמֶּנּוּ, וְכֹחַ יֵשׁ לוֹ לִקְשֹׁר עַצְמוֹ בְּאִסּוּר אוֹתוֹ דָּבָר כְּמוֹ שֶׁיֵּשׁ לוֹ כֹּחַ בִּנְכָסָיו לְאָסְרָם.

וְזֶהוּ הַדִּין וְהַטַּעַם בְּעַצְמוֹ שֶׁהַשְּׁבוּעָה חָלָה עַל דָּבָר שֶׁיֵּשׁ בּוֹ מַמָּשׁ וְעַל שֶׁאֵין בּוֹ מַמָּשׁ, כִּי עַל גּוּף הָאָדָם תִּפֹּל הַשְּׁבוּעָה, כְּלוֹמַר שֶׁגּוּפוֹ נִתְקַיֵּם לַעֲשׂוֹת אוֹתוֹ דָבָר וַהֲרֵי הַגּוּף יֵשׁ לוֹ מַמָּשׁ. אֲבָל הַנֶּדֶר אֵינוֹ חָל אֶלָּא עַל דָּבָר שֶׁיֵּשׁ בּוֹ מַמָּשׁ לְפִי שֶׁהוּא כְּמַכְנִיס דָּבָר בִּגְדֵר אִסּוּר שְׁאָר דְּבָרִים, כְּלוֹמַר דָּבָר פְּלוֹנִי יְהֵא (אָסוּר) עָלַי כְּגֶדֶר קָרְבָּן שֶׁהוּא אָסוּר עָלָיו, וְאִם אֵין מַמָּשׁ בַּמֶּה שֶׁהוּא מַכְנִיס תּוֹךְ הַגֶּדֶר לֹא עָשָׂה וְלֹא כְלוּם.

וְכֵן מִן הַטַּעַם הַזֶּה אֵין שְׁבוּעָה חָלָה עַל שְׁבוּעָה וְנֶדֶר חָל עַל גֶּדֶר, שֶׁהֲרֵי בִּשְׁבוּעָה כֵּיוָן שֶׁנִּכְנַס הָאָדָם בְּעַצְמוֹ בְּמֶחֱצַת הַקִּיּוּם כְּמוֹ שֶׁאָמַרְנוּ אֲפִלּוּ יִכְפֹּל הַדִּבּוּר אֶלֶף פְּעָמִים שֶׁהוּא נִכְנָס שָׁם, כְּנִיסַת גּוּפוֹ בְּמָקוֹם אֶחָד בְּפַעַם אַחַת הִיא נַעֲשֵׂית, וְאֵין זֶה אַחַר מִכֵּן אֶלָּא כְּכוֹפֵל דְּבָרִים לְבַטָּלָה, אֲבָל הַנֶּדֶר שֶׁהוּא כִּמְקַבֵּל עַל עַצְמוֹ לִהְיוֹת לוֹ דָבָר הַמֻּתָּר כְּאִלּוּ נֶאֱסָר, בְּכָל עֵת שֶׁהוּא שׁוֹנֶה בְקַבָּלָתוֹ מוֹסִיף עַל עַצְמוֹ אִסּוּר אִם יְבַטֵּל קַבְּלוֹתָיו, וּלְפִיכָךְ הוּא חַיָּב עַל כָּל אַחַת וְאַחַת.

וְזֶהוּ הָעִנְיָן בְּעַצְמוֹ שֶׁהַשְּׁבוּעָה אֵינָהּ חָלָה עַל דְּבַר מִצְוָה וְהַנֶּדֶר חָל אֲפִלּוּ עַל דְּבַר מִצְוָה, שֶׁהַנִּשְׁבָּע מְדַבֵּר עַל גּוּפוֹ וְגוּפוֹ כְּבָר נִתְקַיֵּם בְּאוֹתוֹ עִנְיָן מֵהַר סִינַי,

---

12. TB N'darim 13b.
13. *Ibid.* 13a, 17a.
14. I.e. it is as though he clothes himself with one restricting garment upon another, and should he break his word, it is as if he tears through them with a knife: each and every one is slashed.
15. I.e. a vow to ignore a *mitzvah* and treat it as nought; TB N'darim 16a.
16. I.e. from the time our people received the Torah and became committed to it by solemn covenant, for all generations; Rambam MT *hilchoth n'darim* iii 7.

both to him and to all the world—as it is written, *when a man shall consecrate (dedicate) his house to be holy* (Leviticus 27:14).

In the same way, a man has power over himself, to make things forbidden to his person. In this regard the Sages of blessed memory gave [as an example of] the proper expressions for taking a vow: "Let this [ban] be upon me," or "Let my mouth [be forbidden] for my talking [with you]";[12] i.e. he causes that thing [about which he vows] to be "removed" from him [banned to him]. And he has the power to make a prohibition about these objects binding on him, just as he has power to make his property forbidden [like *hekdesh*].

For the very same reason the law is that an oath is binding about both matters of substance and matters without substance[12]—for over the body of a man does an oath establish its hold. In other words, his body exists and has the ability to do that deed [which he swore to do], and the body is a matter of substance.

A vow, however, can take effect only for something which has substance, for it is as though he [who takes the vow] brings something [permitted] within the bounds (the domain) of the forbidden—i.e. that this particular object should be as forbidden to him as the category of offerings which are forbidden him. Then if the thing which he wishes to bring into the domain of the forbidden has no substance, he has in effect done nothing at all.

Similarly, for the same reason, one oath cannot take effect over another oath, while one vow can go into effect over another.[13] For with an oath, since the man himself enters the boundaries of the extant range of the oath, as we have stated, even if he should repeat the statement a thousand times that he enters there, the ingress of his person into a single area can occur only once, and afterward he is only like a person who repeats words in vain (purposelessly). However, with a *neder*, a vow, where it is as though he accepts upon himself that something permissible should be as if forbidden him, every time he repeats his acceptance [of this] a person adds for himself another prohibition, [which he transgresses] should he then ignore his acceptances; and therefore he incurs punishment for each and every one.[14]

This is the very nub of the reason why an oath cannot take effect over the subject of a precept, while a *neder*, a vow, takes hold even of the subject-matter of a precept:[15] For the person swearing an oath speaks in reference to his person, and his person was already committed [bound in duty] about that subject-matter from Mount Sinai.[16] With a *neder*,

§30: NOT TO TAKE AN OATH IN VAIN

אֲבָל בְּנֶדֶר אֵינוֹ מְדַבֵּר אֶלָּא עַל הַדָּבָר שֶׁרוֹצֶה לְהַכְנִיס בִּגְדֵר הָאִסוּר וְעַל אוֹתוֹ הַדָּבָר מַמָּשׁ לֹא נִתְקַיֵּם הוּא מֵעוֹלָם, וּלְפִיכָךְ חָל עָלָיו הָאִסּוּר, וְאֵין מַאֲכִילִין לוֹ לְאָדָם דָּבָר הָאָסוּר לוֹ, וְזֶה שֶׁאָמְרוּ זִכְרוֹנָם לִבְרָכָה שֶׁהַנִּשְׁבָּע אָסַר נַפְשׁוֹ עַל הַחֵפֶץ וְהַנּוֹדֵר אָסַר הַחֵפֶץ עַל נַפְשׁוֹ.

וְאִם תִּשְׁאַל, מִי שֶׁנָּדַר שֶׁלֹּא לֶאֱכֹל דָּבָר שֶׁהוּא מִצְוָה עָלָיו לְאָכְלוֹ, אֵיךְ לֹא יֹאכְלֶנּוּ, שֶׁהֲרֵי אוֹתוֹ דָּבָר מְצֻוֶּה הוּא עָלָיו בַּעֲשֵׂה וְיָבֹא עֲשֵׂה וְיִדְחֶה לֹא תַעֲשֶׂה דְּלֹא יַחֵל, כִּי כֵן יֹאמְרוּ חֲכָמִים בְּכָל מָקוֹם אֲתֵי עֲשֵׂה וְדָחֵי לֹא תַעֲשֶׂה? תְּשׁוּבָתְךָ שֶׁהַנֶּדֶר עֲשֵׂה וְלָאו יֵשׁ בּוֹ, לָאו דְּלֹא יַחֵל וַעֲשֵׂה דְּכָל הַיּוֹצֵא מִפִּיו יַעֲשֶׂה.

וּמִן הַטַּעַם הַזֶּה שֶׁאָמַרְנוּ שֶׁעַם הַשְּׁבוּעָה גּוּפוֹ נִפְעָל, אָמְרוּ הַמַּתְפִּיס בִּשְׁבוּעָה פָּטוּר וּבִנְדָרִים חַיָּב. כֵּיצַד, שָׁמַע שֶׁנָּדַר חֲבֵרוֹ וְאָמַר "אַף אֲנִי כָּמוֹךְ" בְּתוֹךְ כְּדֵי דִּבּוּר הֲרֵי זֶה אָסוּר, לְפִי שֶׁכַּוָּנָתוֹ שֶׁל זֶה לוֹמַר כְּמוֹ שֶׁאַתָּה אָסוּר בְּזֶה הַדָּבָר כֵּן אֶהְיֶה אֲנִי אָסוּר בּוֹ, וּבְכָךְ יַסְפִּיק אֵלָיו. אֲבָל בִּשְׁבוּעָה שֶׁאָנוּ מְדַמִּים הָרִאשׁוֹן כְּאִלּוּ הִפְעִיל גּוּפוֹ בִּדְבָרָיו כְּמוֹ שֶׁאָמַרְנוּ, לֹא שֶׁהִרְחִיק דָּבָר אַחֵר מִגּוּפוֹ, לֹא רָאוּ זִכְרוֹנָם לִבְרָכָה שֶׁיִּהְיֶה זֶה הָאַחֲרוֹן בִּכְלַל הַפְּעֻלּוֹת זֶה בְּאָמְרוֹ אַף אֲנִי כָּמוֹךָ, עַד שֶׁיּוֹצִיא מִפִּיו מַמָּשׁ לְשׁוֹן הַפְּעֻלּוֹת עַל עַצְמוֹ, כְּגוֹן שֶׁיֹּאמַר אַף אֲנִי כָּמוֹךְ נִשְׁבָּע, אוֹ שֶׁיִּשְׁמַע מִפִּי אַחֵר שֶׁיַּפְעִילֵהוּ לְאוֹתוֹ דָּבָר וְהוּא יְקַיֵּם וְיוֹדֶה שֶׁחָפֵץ בְּאוֹתָן הַפְּעֻלּוֹת, כְּגוֹן שֶׁאָמַר לוֹ אָדָם אַחֵר "מַשְׁבִּיעֲךָ אֲנִי" וְהוּא יַעֲנֶה אָמֵן.

כְּלָלוֹ שֶׁל דָּבָר, לְשׁוֹן הַשְּׁבוּעָה צָרִיךְ לוֹמַר בְּפִיו עַל עַצְמוֹ אוֹ שֶׁיַּזְכִּירֶנּוּ אַחֵר

---

17. Thus, for example, if he vowed to eat no *matzah* on the first night of Passover, the ban falls in turn on each piece of *matzah* he may pick up and wish to eat. The Torah's obligation to eat it remains binding upon him, but he has made all *matzah* unavailable to him.

18. TB N'darim 2b.

19. E.g. TB Shabbath 132b, Bêtzah 8b. I.e. if a positive precept conflicts with a negative, we are to violate the negative precept in order to fulfill the positive one.

20. TB Sh'vu'oth 20a, view of Rava; Rif, Sh'vu'oth iii; MT *hilchoth n'darim* iii 1.

though, he speaks only in reference to that object which he wishes to include in the boundary of the forbidden; and in regard to that particular object he was never committed [bound in duty].[17] Hence the ban takes effect upon him, and a man may not be allowed to eat something forbidden to him. In this sense our Sages of blessed memory said[18] that one who swears an oath has placed a ban on himself in regard to the object, while a person who vows a *neder* has put a ban on the object in regard to himself.

Now, you may ask: If someone vows a *neder* not to eat something which it is a *mitzvah*, a Divine duty to consume, how shall he not eat it? Here the *mitzvah* is an obligation of a positive precept which falls upon him; then let the positive precept come and thrust aside the negative precept, *he shall not break his word* (Numbers 30:3). For so the Sages say everywhere:[19] the positive precept comes and thrusts the negative one aside.

Your answer is that the *neder* (the vow) involves both a positive and a negative precept: the negative duty, *he shall not break his word* (§407), and the positive obligation, *he shall do according to all that comes out of his mouth* (ibid.— §575).

It is also for this reason which we stated, that with an oath the person himself is bound, that the Sages said:[20] Whoever attaches himself to an oath is free of obligation; but with a *neder* he is under obligation. How so? If he heard his fellow-man vowing a *neder* and he said immediately after the other's words, "I too, as you," he is forbidden, bound [by the vow]; for his intention was to say, "As you are bound, forbidden in this regard, so let me be forbidden in regard to it"; thus it suffices for him. With an oath, however, we conceive the first person as though he had affected his body by his words, as we said—not that he put something else beyond the reach of his person. Therefore the Sages of blessed memory did not find that this latter person could be included in the effect of the first person's words by saying, "I too, as you"—not until he uttered with his mouth an expression clearly causing himself to be affected; for instance, if he said, "I too swear like you"; or if he hears another expressing such a thing about him and he confirms and acknowledges that he desires this consequence. For instance, another man will say, "I impose this oath on you," and he answers *Amen* (so be it).

This is the crux of the matter: With the expression of an oath, a person must say it with his mouth about himself, or another should

§30: NOT TO TAKE AN OATH IN VAIN

עָלָיו מַמָּשׁ וְהוּא יְקַבֵּל, אֲבָל מִכֹּחַ הַפְּעֻלּוֹת אָדָם אַחֵר אֵינֶנּוּ נִפְעָל מִכֵּיוָן שֶׁגּוּפוֹ צָרִיךְ הַפְּעֻלּוֹת, מַה שֶּׁאֵין כֵּן בְּנֶדֶר. אוֹ אֶפְשָׁר לוֹמַר כִּי מֵחֹמֶר הַגֶּדֶר שֶׁהוּא חָמוּר מִן הַשְּׁבוּעָה, שֶׁהֲרֵי דִּמּוּ אוֹתוֹ לְחַיֵּי הַמֶּלֶךְ, הֶחְמִירוּ בוֹ לִהְיוֹת נִתְפָּשׂ בַּהֲתָרָה יוֹתֵר מִן הַשְּׁבוּעָה.

וּמִן הַטַּעַם הַזֶּה שֶׁכָּתַבְנוּ בִּשְׁבוּעָה שֶׁעִנְיָנָהּ הוּא שֶׁאָדָם גּוֹמֵר לְקַיֵּם דְּבָרָיו וּלְאַמֵּת כְּמוֹ שֶׁהוּא מַאֲמִין בְּקִיּוּם אֱלֹהַי, הָיָה לָנוּ לִלְמֹד שֶׁלֹּא תִתְבַּטֵּל שְׁבוּעָה בְּשׁוּם צַד, אֶלָּא שֶׁהָיָה מֵחַסְדֵי הָאֵל עָלֵינוּ בְּדַעְתּוֹ חֻלְשַׁת בִּנְיַן גּוּפֵנוּ וּמְעוּט דַּעְתֵּינוּ וְהִתְמָדַת שִׁנּוּי רְצוֹנֵנוּ לָתֵת לָנוּ עֵצָה לָצֵאת מִמַּאֲסַר הַשְּׁבוּעָה בְּהִתְחַדֵּשׁ עָלֵינוּ הָרָצוֹן בְּכָל עֵת שֶׁאֶפְשָׁר לָנוּ לִתְלוֹת בְּעִנְיַן הַשְּׁבוּעָה טַעֲנַת אֹנֶס אוֹ שְׁגָגָה, כְּמוֹ שֶׁמְּפֹרָשׁ בִּמְקוֹמוֹ בִּשְׁבוּעוֹת וּנְדָרִים.

וְאוּלָם לֹא הִרְשָׁנוּ לָצֵאת מִמֶּנּוּ בְּשָׁאַט בְּנֶפֶשׁ רַק בְּתַחְבּוּלָה וּבַעֲצַת חָכָם, שֶׁיָּבוֹא הַנִּשְׁבָּע לִפְנֵי אִישׁ חָכָם וְנָבוֹן בְּדַרְכֵי הַתּוֹרָה וְיִתְוַדֶּה אֵלָיו כִּי מֵחֶסְרוֹן יְדִיעָתוֹ שֶׁלֹּא הָיָה יוֹדֵעַ בְּשָׁעָה שֶׁנִּשְׁבַּע דָּבָר שֶׁיָּדַע אַחַר כָּךְ הוּא רוֹצֶה לְבַטֵּל מַה שֶּׁנִּשְׁבַּע עָלָיו, וְכִי הוּא מַכִּיר כִּי הַבִּטּוּל מֵעוּט דַּעְתּוֹ וְחֶסְרוֹנוֹ גּוֹרֵם אוֹתוֹ, לֹא דָבָר אַחֵר וּמַחְשָׁבָה חִיצוֹנִית שֶׁיִּהְיֶה בְּלִבּוֹ חָלִילָה. וְאַחַר הוֹדָאַת פִּיו עַל זֶה וְיַכִּיר הֶחָכָם וְיִרְאֶה כִּי יֵשׁ מַמָּשׁ בִּדְבָרָיו שֶׁנִּתְחַדֵּשׁ אֵלָיו דָּבָר שֶׁאִלּוּ הַסְכִּים עָלָיו בְּשָׁעָה שֶׁנִּשְׁבַּע לֹא הָיָה כֵן מִתְחָרֵט, יְקַבֵּל וִדּוּיוֹ וְיַתִּירֶנּוּ מִשְּׁבוּעָתוֹ. וְזֶהוּ אָמְרָם זִכְרוֹנָם לִבְרָכָה הוּא אֵינוֹ מוֹחֵל אֲבָל אֲחֵרִים מוֹחֲלִין לוֹ.

עַל כֵּן לְעוֹלָם אִי אֶפְשָׁר לְהַתִּיר שְׁבוּעָה כִּי אִם בְּסִבַּת שׁוּם חִדּוּשׁ לַנִּשְׁבָּע,

---

21. I.e. by the life of the Almighty; Sifre, Numbers §153. There, though, the oath is apparently held to be more serious, since it continues, "with oaths, it is as if one swore by the King Himself"; Zohar II 115b, however (also III 255a), states clearly that this means vows rank higher; and so also Ramban to Numbers 30:3, end—for kabbalistic reasons. For a thorough discussion see *Emek N'tziv* to Sifre, Numbers §153, II 278–79.

22. TB Sh'vu'oth 26a, N'darim 20b.

23. So e.g. TB N'darim 78b, that a single learned expert may dissolve a vow.

24. TB B'rachoth 32a, Ḥagigah 10a.

⟨162⟩

utter it about him specifically, and he should accept it [by answering *Amen*]. But by the force of [the oath] that another enacts [for himself] he is not affected, since his own person needs a direct enactment—which is not the case with a *neder*, a vow. Or it might be said that because of the stringency of a *neder*—for it is more severe than an oath, since it is likened to "the life of the King" [as though he vowed by that][21]—it is taken more strictly, that it should take hold more swiftly [easily] than an oath.

Now, from this reason that we have written about an oath—that in substance it means a man commits himself to keep his word and make it true, even as he believes in the enduring Divine existence—we should infer that an oath should never be able to become void in any way. However, it was one of the kindnesses of God toward us, knowing as He does the weakness of our physical structure, the paucity of our intelligence, and the constancy with which we change our wishes, to give us a plan by which to go free from the constraint of an oath when our wish [in its regard] becomes something new. [We can be released from it] whenever it is possible to bring in, concerning the oath, a claim of compulsion or error (mistakenness)—as it is explained in its proper place in the Talmud tractates *Sh'vu'oth* and *N'darim*.[22]

We were not permitted, however, to go free of it [simply] with an air of disdain, but only through the plan and counsel of a wise scholar. The one who took the oath comes before a wise scholar who is knowledgeable in the ways of the Torah,[23] and he confesses before him that on account of his lack of knowledge, something he did not know when he took the oath but learned afterward, he wishes to make null and void this oath which he swore; and he acknowledges that the limitation and lack of his awareness [now] causes him [to seek its] nullification, not any other matter or extraneous [ulterior] thought that might be in his heart, Heaven forbid. After his oral confession about this, and after the wise scholar recognizes and sees that his words have substance—that something new entered his awareness, and had he known of it when he swore, he would not have taken the oath, and therefore he is now sorry—he accepts his confession and absolves him of his oath. Hence the Sages of blessed memory said:[24] He cannot grant himself forgiveness [for the oath], but others can absolve him.

For this reason it is never possible to undo an oath except on

§30: NOT TO TAKE AN OATH IN VAIN

כְּגוֹן שֶׁיֹּאמַר "אִלּוּ הָיִיתִי יוֹדֵעַ דָּבָר פְּלוֹנִי לֹא הָיִיתִי נִשְׁבָּע מֵעוֹלָם", שֶׁזֶּה כְּעֵין אֹנֶס הוּא. אֲבָל אִם יֹאמַר "הַתִּירוּנִי מִשְּׁבוּעָתִי" בְּלֹא טַעֲנָה אֵין כֹּחַ בְּאָדָם לְהַתִּירוֹ. וּמִכֹּחַ זֶה הָעִנְיָן אָמְרוּ זִכְרוֹנָם לִבְרָכָה שֶׁאֵין פּוֹתְחִין בְּנוֹלָד שֶׁאֵינוֹ מָצוּי, לְפִי שֶׁאֵינוֹ אוֹמֵר לְהֶדְיָא שֶׁהוּא נִחָם כְּשֶׁנִּשְׁבַּע שֶׁנַּחְשְׁבֵהוּ כְּאָנוּס אֶלָּא שֶׁרְצוֹנוֹ הַיּוֹם כְּמוֹ שֶׁהָיָה תְּחִלָּה אֶלָּא שֶׁרוֹצֶה עַכְשָׁיו בְּהֶתֵּר.

כֵּיצַד, נִשְׁבַּע שֶׁלֹּא יֶהֱנֶה בִּפְלוֹנִי וְנַעֲשָׂה סוֹפֵר הָעִיר אוֹ טַבָּח, וְהוּא אוֹמֵר "רְצוֹנִי קַיֶּמֶת שֶׁלֹּא הָיִיתִי חָפֵץ לֵהָנוֹת בּוֹ, וְלֹא הָיִיתִי רוֹצֶה שֶׁיֵּעָשֶׂה סוֹפֵר אוֹ טַבָּח", אֵין מַתִּירִין לוֹ עַד שֶׁיֹּאמַר "אַחַר שֶׁאֲנִי רוֹאֶה שֶׁזֶּה הָאִישׁ נַעֲשָׂה סוֹפֵר מִתְנַחֵם אֲנִי עַל שֶׁנִּשְׁבַּעְתִּי עַל הֲנָאָתוֹ מֵעוֹלָם, וּמִי יִתֵּן שֶׁלֹּא נִשְׁבַּעְתִּי", בְּעִנְיָן זֶה מַתִּירִין לוֹ שֶׁהֲרֵי מוֹדֶה שֶׁנִּשְׁתַּנָּה חֶפְצוֹ וּמִתְחָרֵט עַל מַעֲשָׂיו לְגַמְרֵי בְּחֶסְרוֹן יְדִיעָתוֹ, שֶׁאִלּוּ יָדַע בְּעֵת הַשְּׁבוּעָה מַה שֶּׁהוּא יוֹדֵעַ הַיּוֹם לֹא הָיָה נִשְׁבָּע מֵעוֹלָם וּכְאָנוּס הוּא, וְדָרְשִׁינָן הָאָדָם בִּשְׁבוּעָה, פְּרָט לְאָנוּס.

וּמִזֶּה הַיְסוֹד גַּם כֵּן כְּשֶׁתִּפּוֹלָה שְׁבוּעָתוֹ בְּדַעַת אֲחֵרִים קָשֶׁה לְהַתִּירוֹ, דְּמִכֵּיוָן שֶׁסִּלֵּק דַּעְתּוֹ מִן הַדָּבָר וְנִתְלָה בְּדַעַת אֲחֵרִים אֵין טַעֲנַת אֹנֶס וּשְׁגָגָה מְצוּיָה אֶצְלוֹ אַחַר כֵּן. וְזֶהוּ שֶׁאָמְרוּ שֶׁהַנִּשְׁבָּע עַל דַּעַת אֲחֵרִים אֵין לוֹ הֲפָרָה, וּמִכָּל מָקוֹם לִדְבַר מִצְוָה הִסְכִּימוּ חֲכָמִים לְהַתִּיר, לְפִי שֶׁכָּל שֶׁיַּעֲשֶׂה הָאָדָם וְהוּא דָּבָר גּוֹרֵם לִבְטוּל מִצְוָה אוֹ שֶׁתֵּעָשֶׂה מִצְוָה בְּהַמְּנַע אוֹתוֹ מַעֲשֶׂה, לֵב כָּל יִשְׂרָאֵל הוּא שֶׁיְּבֻטַּל הַמַּעֲשֶׂה שֶׁל הֶדְיוֹט וְתֵעָשֶׂה מִצְוָה, וְאָנוּ רוֹאִים כְּאִלּוּ בָּאוּ כָּל הָרַבִּים שֶׁנִּשְׁבַּע עַל דַּעְתָּם עִמּוֹ (לפניו) [לְפָנֵינוּ] וְאָמְרוּ שֶׁאִלּוּ יָדְעוּ הֵם בִּשְׁבוּעָתוֹ בִּטּוּל מִצְוָה לֹא

---

25. I.e. a proper argument for release; TB N'darim 64a.
26. Rambam MT *hilchoth sh'vu'oth* vi 12.
27. TB Sh'vu'oth 26a.
28. TB Gittin 36a.
29. So R. Jacob Tam in *tosafoth ibid.* s.v. 'aval.

⟨164⟩

account of something new in [the awareness of] the one who swor[e] it: for instance, if he says, "Had I known this particular thing, I would never have sworn"; for then it is akin to compulsion. If he says, however, "Set me free of my oath," without any plea (reason), no human power can free him. And by the force of this rule, the Sages of blessed memory said that [the wise scholar, in guiding the man to find a plea][2] does not open with an unlikely "born" situation which did not exist [at the time he took the oath]. For then he does not say explicitly that he was sorry when he swore the oath, that we should regard him as compelled [to it against his will]; rather, his will today is as it was originally, but he now merely wants a release.

What then is the procedure? If someone swore not to have any benefit from so-and-so, and that person became the town's scribe or butcher, and [now] he says, "My wish stands, that I wanted to have no benefit from him; but I did not want him to become the town's scribe or butcher," he is not freed [of his vow—not] until he says "Now that I see that this man became the scribe, I regret that I ever took an oath about any benefit from him. How I wish I had not sworn." In this case he is absolved,[26] because he now admits that his desire has changed, and he completely regrets what he did in his lack of knowledge—for had he known at the time of the oath what he knows today, he would never have sworn. Then he is as one who was compelled, and we interpret,[27] *whatever a man shall utter with an oath* (Leviticus 5:4)—"a man" [i.e. with free will], not someone compelled.

From this same basis comes also [the law] that when someone lets his oath depend on the mind (will) of others, it is difficult to release him. For since he removed his own mind from the matter and became dependent on the mind of others, a claim of compulsion or error is not likely to be found for him afterward. This is why the Sages said[28] that if someone swears an oath [that will depend] on the mind of others, there is no way of making it null and void for him. If it was for a matter of a *mitzvah* (a religious duty), though, the Sages agreed to grant him a release:[28] For whatever a man does, if it is something which can cause a *mitzvah* to remain undone, or if the *mitzvah* can be observed by removing that matter, it would be the heart's wish of any Jew that the action of the individual should be undone, become void, and the *mitzvah* should be done.[29] Then we regard it as though the many others on whose responsibility he swore the oath now came before us and said that had they known that in his oath lay the voiding

תַּסְכִּים דַּעְתָּם עִמּוֹ, וַהֲרֵי יֵשׁ לָנוּ טַעֲנַת אֹנֶס וּשְׁגָגָה, וּלְפִיכָךְ אָמְרוּ רַבּוֹתֵינוּ זִכְרוֹנָם לִבְרָכָה: אֲבָל לִדְבַר מִצְוָה יֵשׁ לוֹ הֲפָרָה.

וְאַל תַּחְשֹׁב לְהַקְשׁוֹת עָלַי עַל הַנַּחַת טַעַם זֶה שֶׁאָמַרְתִּי שֶׁעִקַּר הַהֶתֵּר בְּהִתְחַדֵּשׁ בָּאָדָם דָּבָר שֶׁאִלּוּ הָיָה בּוֹ יוֹדֵעַ לֹא מִתְּחִלָּה לֹא הָיָה נִשְׁבָּע, שֶׁהֲרֵי הוּא כְּעֵין אָנוּס אוֹ מֻטְעֶה, וְתֹאמַר וַהֲרֵי מָצִינוּ לְגַבֵּי שְׁבוּעַת הַשֵּׁם הֶתֵּר, כְּמוֹ שֶׁדָּרְשׁוּ זִכְרוֹנָם לִבְרָכָה בְּוַיְחַל מֹשֶׁה כִּבְיָכוֹל שֶׁהִתִּירוֹ מִן הַשְּׁבוּעָה, וְעַל עִנְיָן זְרֻבָּבֶל בֶּן שְׁאַלְתִּיאֵל שֶׁאָמְרוּ זִכְרוֹנָם לִבְרָכָה שֶׁנִּשְׁאַל אֶל מִשְׁבּוּעָתוֹ, וְחָלִילָה לִהְיוֹת שִׁנּוּי רָצוֹן אִתּוֹ? כִּי יֵשׁ לַהֲשִׁיבְךָ, וְהַדִּין דִּין אֱמֶת, כִּי כָּל מַה שֶּׁבָּא בַּכְּתוּבִים בָּעִנְיָנִים כָּיוֹצֵא אֵלּוּ הַכֹּל נֶאֱמַר עַל צַד הַמְקַבְּלִים שֶׁהֵם בְּנֵי אָדָם, כִּי חָלִילָה לָאֵל וּמִלְּבָבֵנוּ לְהַאֲמִין שֶׁיִּצְטָרֵךְ אֲדוֹן הַכֹּל לְהִשָּׁבַע בְּדָבָר אַף כִּי לְהַתִּירוֹ וּלְבַטְּלוֹ אַחֲרֵי כֵן; אֲבָל יֵאָמֵר אוֹתוֹ דָּבָר עַל צַד קַבָּלַת הָעֹנֶשׁ הַנּוֹפֵל עַל הַגֶּנֶעֱשׁ, שֶׁאִם נִתְחַיֵּב הָאָדָם לְגֹדֶל חֶטְאוֹ לְהַעֲנִישׁוֹ עַל כָּל פָּנִים עַד שֶׁאֵין רָאוּי לָתֵת לוֹ מָקוֹם לִתְשׁוּבָה, יִפֹּל עַל עִנְיָן הָאִישׁ הַלָּזֶה שְׁבוּעָה אֵצֶל הַשֵּׁם, כְּלוֹמַר חֹזֶק עָנְשׁוֹ וּגְזֵרָתוֹ עָלָיו כְּאִלּוּ יֵשׁ שְׁבוּעָה בַּדָּבָר.

וְכֵן לְעִנְיַן הַטּוֹבָה, אִם זָכָה הָאָדָם מֵרֹב חֲשִׁיבוּתוֹ לְקַבֵּל טוֹבָה הוּא וְזַרְעוֹ יֹאמַר הַכָּתוּב גַּם כֵּן כִּי הַשֵּׁם נִשְׁבַּע לְהֵיטִיב לוֹ. וְעַל זֶה וְכַיּוֹצֵא בּוֹ אָמְרוּ זִכְרוֹנָם לִבְרָכָה "כְּדֵי לְשַׁבֵּר אֶת הָאֹזֶן מַה שֶּׁהִיא יְכוֹלָה לִשְׁמֹעַ", שֶׁאֵין לְדַמּוֹת לִבְנֵי אָדָם חֹזֶק דָּבָר וְקִיּוּמוֹ רַק בְּמַה שֶּׁהֵם מַחֲזִיקִים וּמְקַיְּמִים דִּבְרֵיהֶם.

30. TB B'rachoth 32a: the verb *va-y'hal* (and besought) is linked with *yahel* in Numbers 30:3, "he shall not break, profane his word"—i.e. Moses prevailed on the Almighty to profane and break His oath, by releasing Him from it, as it were. His oath was in His words, *and I will consume them* (Exodus 32:10; Rashi to B'rachoth 32a). Sh'moth Rabbah 43, 5 has an elaborate, detailed version.

31. I.e. not to grant Shealtiel's father any children; briefly in TB Sanhedrin 38a, more fully in Va-yikra Rabbah 10, 5—that the Lord asked the heavenly court (of angels) to release Him from the vow. There is apparently a scribal error in our text: it should be Shealtiel the son of Jeconiah (I Chronicles 3:17).

32. Mechilta, *bahodesh* 4 (Exodus 19:18), etc.

of a religious duty [on account of the oath he could not observe it] their mind would not have agreed with him. Here, then, we have the plea of compulsion and error. Therefore our Sages of blessed memory said:[28] But for a matter of *mitzvah*, a religious duty, it can be made null and void for him.

Now, do not think to query me about the hypothesis of this reason I have given, that the main way of release from an oath is when something new becomes known to the man, such that had he known it originally, he would not have taken the oath—for then he is akin to someone who was compelled or in error. Do not say: Yet we find a release in connection with the oath of the Eternal Lord—as our Sages of blessed memory taught on the verse, *And Moses besought the Lord* (Exodus 32:11), that so to speak, he released Him from the oath.[3] So too in connection with Zerubbabel the son of Shealtiel, the Sages of blessed memory said that God asked [to be released] from His oath.[31] Yet Heaven forfend [to think] there could be any change of will with Him.

There is this to answer you, and it is a premise of truth: All that is found in Scripture of this nature—all was stated with regard to those who receive [a *subjective* awareness of Divine response, as it were]— human beings. For far be it from God, or from our heart to believe that the sovereign Ruler of all should need to swear about anything or to undo it and nullify it afterward. This theme was stated however, in regard to receiving the punishment due the person to be punished: For if a man becomes so guilty, through the enormity of his sin, that he must be punished under all circumstances, to such an extent that he is not fit to be granted any scope for repentance—then about this man, the term "oath" in connection with the Eternal Lord fits well: i.e. so strongly is his punishment and sentence set for him, as though an oath had been taken about the matter.

So too about a good reward: If a man has merited, by his great worthiness, to receive a good reward [for] both himself and his descendants, Scripture will say likewise that the Eternal Lord swore to grant him good reward. About this and similar matters our Sages used the expression, "in order to make the ear accept calmly [with comprehension] what it is able to hear (understand)."[32] For the intensity and permanence of a matter cannot be described to human beings except in the way that they characterize their own matters as strong, intense and lasting.

§30: NOT TO TAKE AN OATH IN VAIN   ספר החינוך

וְעַל הַדֶּרֶךְ הַזֶּה בְּעַצְמוֹ דָּרְשׁוּ זִכְרוֹנָם לִבְרָכָה הֶתֵּר עַל שְׁבוּעַת הַשֵּׁם, רְצוֹנָ
לוֹמַר כִּי חַנּוּן וְרַחוּם הוּא אֶרֶךְ אַפַּיִם וְרַב חֶסֶד וּמְכַפֵּר עַל הַחוֹטְאִים, וְאַף עַל
שֶׁגָּדַל חֶטְאָם וְחָזָק עַד שֶׁרָאוּי שֶׁאִם יֶחֱטָא אִישׁ כָּל כָּךְ לְאִישׁ שֶׁלֹּא יִשָּׁבַע שֶׁלֹּא לְמָ
לְעוֹלָם. וְעַל הַדֶּרֶךְ הַזֶּה אָמְרוּ זִכְרוֹנָם לִבְרָכָה כִּי מֹשֶׁה הִתִּירוֹ, כְּלוֹמַר שֶׁבִּזְכוּ
תְּפִלָּתוֹ הַטּוֹבָה גָּרַם שֶׁהַשֵּׁם (יִתְבָּרַךְ) שֶׁהוּא שׁוֹמֵעַ תְּפִלָּה סָלַח לַעֲוֹנָם.

וְזֶהוּ שֶׁלֹּא תִמְצָא לְרַבּוֹתֵינוּ זִכְרוֹנָם לִבְרָכָה שֶׁיִּדְרְשׁוּ עִנְיָן הַהֶתֵּר אֶ
שְׁבוּעָתוֹ בָּרוּךְ הוּא כִּי אִם בְּחֵטְא גָּדוֹל, שֶׁכָּל הַשּׁוֹמֵעַ יִגְזֹר שֶׁאֵינוֹ נִתָּן לְכַפָּרָ
כְּלוֹמַר וְרָאוּי לִשָּׁבַע עָלָיו שֶׁלֹּא לְכַפֵּר אוֹתוֹ, וְרַחֲמָיו בָּרוּךְ הוּא גָּדְלוּ עַל כָּ
מַחְשְׁבוֹתֵינוּ וּמְכַפֵּר אֶל כָּל הַשָּׁבִים אֵלָיו בְּכָל לֵב, וְאִם רַב עֲוֹנָם מִנְּשׂוֹא לְ
דַעְתֵּנוּ.

וְהָרְאָיָה לִדְבָרֵינוּ אֵלֶּה מַה שֶּׁאָמְרוּ בְּרֹאשׁ הַשָּׁנָה גַּבֵּי גְזַר דִּין שֶׁיֵּשׁ עִ
שְׁבוּעָה, דְּמַסִּיק רָבָא הָתָם דְּזֶבַח וּבְמִנְחָה אֵינוֹ מִתְכַּפֵּר אֲבָל מִתְכַּפֵּר הוּא בְּדִבְ
תוֹרָה, וְאֵין זֵכֶר שָׁם שֶׁיִּצְטָרֵךְ הָאֵל לְשָׁאֵל עָלֶיהָ, כִּי יְדוּעִים וּבְרוּרֵ
הַדְּבָרִים לְכָל רוֹאֵי הַשֶּׁמֶשׁ שֶׁהַכֹּל נֶאֱמַר עַל צַד הַמָּשָׁל אֶל הַמְּקַבְּלִים. וּמִפְּנֵי
הֶאֱרַכְתִּי בָזֶה עַד הֵנָּה לִפְנוֹת לְךָ הַדֶּרֶךְ בִּמְקוֹמוֹת רַבִּים.

וּמַה שֶּׁאָמַרְתִּי לְךָ שֶׁיִּכְּנוּ חֲכָמִים זִכְרוֹנָם לִבְרָכָה לְשׁוֹן הֶתֵּר בִּשְׁבוּעַת הַשֵּׁ
לֹא תִמְצָא זֶה לְעוֹלָם אֶלָּא בְּמָקוֹם שֶׁכִּנּוּ לוֹ הַשְּׁבוּעָה לְחַיָּב בְּרִיָּה, אֲבָל בְּמָקוֹ
שֶׁכִּנּוּ לוֹ שְׁבוּעָה לִזְכוּת בְּרִיָּה לֹא יַזְכִּירוּ שָׁם לְעוֹלָם הֶתֵּר, כִּי רַב הַחֶסֶד מַטֶּה כְּלַ
חֶסֶד וְלֹא יָשִׁיב דְּבָרוֹ הַטּוֹב רֵיקָם, רְצוֹנִי לוֹמַר כִּי מֵאַחַר שֶׁנִּרְאָה הָאָדָם שָׁע
אַחַת זַכַּאי לִפְנֵי הַמָּקוֹם רָאוּי לְקַבֵּל הַטּוֹבָה כָּל כָּךְ שֶׁהוּא כְּאִלּוּ הַקָּדוֹשׁ בָּרוּךְ הוּ

---

33. I.e. (as one might say today) it is as clear as daylight.
34. So TB Rosh haShanah 17a.
35. Expression echoing Isaiah 55:11, *so shall My word be that goes forth from My
outh: it shall not return to Me empty.*

⟨168⟩

Now, in the very same sense, our Sages of blessed memory taught of a release for the oath of the Eternal Lord, meaning by this that *He is gracious and compassionate, slow to anger, abounding in loving-kindne* (Joel 2:13), and He grants sinners atonement—and this even if their si had grown so great and immense that it would be fitting, should a ma sin toward another man to such an extent, that the other should swea never to forgive. In this vein the Sages of blessed memory said tha Moses released Him [from His oath]:[30] i.e. with the merit of his goo prayer he brought it about that the Eternal Lord (be He blessed), wh hearkens to prayer, forgave their iniquity.

This is the reason why you will never find our Sages of blesse memory teaching about a release in regard to an oath of His (blesse is He) except in connection with an enormous sin, about which who ever heard of it would declare flatly that it is unforgivable, which mear that it deserves to have an oath taken about it never to forgive it. Y His mercies (blessed is He) go beyond all our thoughts, and He gran atonement to all who return to Him in repentance with the whol heart, even if, to our mind, their iniquity became too much to bea

The proof for these words of ours is what the Sages said in th Talmud tractate *Rosh haShanah* (18a) about a Divine decree tha carries an oath with it. Rava concludes there that with an animal o meal offering it will not be forgiven, but it can be granted atoneme: through words of Torah—and there is no mention there that Go should have any need to ask about it [for a release]. For these matte are known and clear to all who see the sun,[33] that it was all said b way of metaphor for those who receive [a subjective awareness o Divine will]. For this reason have I been lengthy about it till here, pave the way for you [to grasp this point] in many instances.

Now, this theme which I have related to you, that the Sages o blessed memory use the expression of release about the oath of th Eternal Lord—you will never find it except in an instance where the ascribed to Him an oath to impose punishment on some creature; bu where they ascribed to Him an oath to grant someone reward, the will never mention a release there. For the One who abounds i loving-kindness tips [the scales of justice] toward the side of loving kindness,[34] and He will not let His good word return empty,[35] withou meaning. By this I mean that once a man appears for even one brie while [so] virtuous before the omnipresent God, so worthy of receivin good reward, that it is as if the Holy One, blessed is He, swore an oat

§30: NOT TO TAKE AN OATH IN VAIN

נִשְׁבַּע עָלָיו עַל הַגְּמוּל הַטּוֹב, כְּעִנְיָן שֶׁנֶּאֱמַר "נִשְׁבַּע יי לְדָוִד" וְכַיּוֹצֵא בּוֹ לֹא יִסְתַּלֵּק מִמֶּנּוּ הַזְּכוּת עוֹד, גַּם כִּי יֶחֱטָא הַרְבֵּה, וְזֶה מִמִּדּוֹתָיו הַיְקָרוֹת בָּרוּךְ הוּא.

דִּינֵי הַמִּצְוָה, כְּגוֹן כִּנּוּיֵי שְׁבוּעָה שֶׁאָמְרוּ זִכְרוֹנָם לִבְרָכָה שֶׁהֵן כִּשְׁבוּעָה וּפֵרוּשׁ כִּנּוּיָיו הוּא לְשׁוֹנוֹת הַרְבֵּה שֶׁהֵן בֵּין בְּנֵי אָדָם לְפִי הַמְּקוֹמוֹת, כְּעֵין מַה שֶּׁאָמְרוּ זִכְרוֹנָם לִבְרָכָה, "שְׁבוּתָה שְׁקוּקָה" וְכוּלֵּי. וְכֵן דִּין אָלָה וְאָרוּר אִם הֵן כִּשְׁבוּעָה, וְהָאוֹמֵר לָאו בְּהַזְכָּרַת שֵׁם, וְכֵן יָמִין וּשְׂמֹאל, וְדִין פִּיו וְלִבּוֹ שָׁוִין, וּמַה שֶּׁלִּמְדוּנוּ מִדִּין זֶה דְּפִיו וְלִבּוֹ שָׁוִין שֶׁעוֹדְרִין לְהַרְגִּין וּלְחָרָמִין, כְּגוֹן שֶׁיֹּאמַר יֵאָסֵר כָּל פֵּרוֹת שֶׁבָּעוֹלָם עָלַי אִם יִהְיֶה כֵן וְכֵן, וְיִהְיֶה בְּלִבּוֹ שֶׁלֹּא יֵאָסְרוּ כִּי אִם הַיּוֹם וְאַף עַל פִּי שֶׁמִּן הַסְּתָם מַשְׁמָע לְעוֹלָם. וּכְגוֹן זֶה דַוְקָא שֶׁאֵין דִּבְרֵי פִיו סוֹתְרִין לְגַמְרֵי מַחֲשֶׁבֶת לִבּוֹ הֻתַּר לָנוּ שֶׁנִּדּוֹר לְהַרְגִּין וּלְחָרָמִין וְלֹא בְּצַד אַחֵר; וְיֶתֶר רֹב פְּרָטֶיהָ, בִּשְׁבוּעוֹת וּבִנְדָרִים.

וְנוֹהֶגֶת בְּכָל מָקוֹם וּבְכָל זְמַן בִּזְכָרִים וּנְקֵבוֹת. וְעוֹבֵר עָלֶיהָ וְנִשְׁבַּע עַל עַמּוּד שֶׁל שַׁיִשׁ שֶׁהוּא שֶׁל זָהָב אוֹ עַל שֶׁל זָהָב שֶׁהוּא שֶׁל זָהָב, אוֹ לְבַטֵּל מִצְוָה זוֹ, א לַעֲשׂוֹת דָּבָר שֶׁאֵין כֹּחַ אָדָם יָכוֹל לַעֲשׂוֹתוֹ, בְּמֵזִיד לוֹקֶה, וְאַף עַל פִּי שֶׁאֵין שָׁנ מַעֲשֶׂה, לְרֹב חֹמֶר הָעִנְיָן חִיְּבַתּוּ הַתּוֹרָה מַלְקוֹת. וּבְשׁוֹגֵג פָּטוּר בְּזוֹ מִקָּרְבָּן, אֲבָ בִּשְׁבוּעַת שֶׁקֶר, וְהוּא הַנִּקְרָא שְׁבוּעַת בִּטּוּי, חִיְּבָה הַתּוֹרָה קָרְבָּן לְשׁוֹגֵג, כְּמ שֶׁנִּכְתֹּב בְּעֶזְרַת הַשֵּׁם.

36. This theme is similarly to be found in TJ Sanhedrin x 2 and Tanḥuma, a-yéra 15–17. Cf. also TB Shabbath 55a: Never did a good measure [promising good] ssue from the Holy One, blessed is He, and He then retracted toward evil.

37. Mishnah, N'darim i 1.

38. *Ibid.* 2; i.e. local idiomatic expressions for swearing oaths, native to particular laces or regions.

39. TB Sh'vu'oth 36a.

40. *Ibid.* and Nazir 3b; Rambam MT *hilchoth sh'vu'oth* ii 6.

41. TB Sh'vu'oth 26b.

42. I.e., they wish to take his possessions, and he claims they are *t'rumah*, con- ecrated property, and thus forbidden to ordinary men; he may then take this vow: "Let all the fruit, etc. if these goods are not *t'rumah*"; TB N'darim 27b–28a.

43. There is a Talmudic rule that "words which are in the heart are no words" TB Kiddushin 49b) —of no matter legally; in cases of compulsion and duress, how- ver, the circumstances make his true meaning obvious, and it is as if he had said so xplicity (TB N'darim 28a and R. Nissim there).

44. TB N'darim 28a, and R. Nissim *ad loc.*

45. See notes 1–3.

46. And the rule is that for violating a negative precept that involves no action, vhiplashes are not given (TB Sanhedrin 63b). See §13, note 6.

47. Mishnah, Sh'vu'oth iii 11.

48. *Ibid.* 10.

⟨170⟩

over him about that good recompense—in the vein of the verse, *The Lord swore to David* (Psalms 132:11), and other such [verses]—that merited reward will never depart from him, even if he should sin greatly. This is one of His precious attributes.[36]

The laws of the precept concern, for instance, substitute forms of oaths, about which the Sages of blessed memory said[37] that they are as oaths. The term "substitute forms" means the many expressions [for swearing] which are current among people according to the regions—such as the examples which they of blessed memory gave:[38] *sh'vuthah, sh'kukah*, etc. So too there is the law of *'alah* ("oath") and *'arur* ("cursed be"), if they are the same as a regular oath;[39] so too, if one says "No" with the mention of a Divine name, and also [if he thus said] "Right" or "Left";[40] the law that his mouth and heart must be equal [together in expressing the oath or vow];[41] and what we learned in regard to this law—that one may take a vow before killers and bandits [in order to go free]: for instance, that he should say, "Let all fruit and produce in the world be forbidden to me if this is so,"[42] and in his heart he means they should be forbidden him only that day, although by itself, generally [his vow] implies forever.[43] But in such an instance, it is only if the words of the mouth do not entirely contradict the thoughts of the heart that we are permitted to take a vow for killers and bandits, but not in any other way.[44] [These] and the rest of its multitude of details are [to be found] in the Talmud tractates *Sh'vu'oth* and *N'darim*.

It applies in every place, at every time, for both man and woman. If someone transgresses it and swears about a pillar of marble that it is of gold, or of gold that it is gold; or [if he swears] to violate a particular precept, or to do something which human power cannot do[45]—if [he did this] deliberately, he is given whiplashes. Even though there is no action involved here,[46] because of the immense gravity of the matter [because it is so serious] the Torah imposed the punishment of whipping.[47] If [it was done] inadvertently, he is free in this instance of the obligation to bring an animal offering.[47] For an oath over a falsehood, however, which is called "an expressed oath," the Torah imposed the duty for someone who transgressed inadvertently to bring an animal offering[48]—as we will write (§227), with the Eternal Lord's help.

§31: TO HALLOW THE SABBATH IN WORDS

[מִצְוַת קִדּוּשׁ שַׁבָּת בִּדְבָרִים]

לא לְדַבֵּר דְּבָרִים בְּיוֹם שַׁבָּת בִּכְנִיסָתוֹ וְכֵן בִּיצִיאָתוֹ שֶׁיִּהְיֶה בָּהֶם זֵכֶר גְּדֻלַּת הַיּוֹם וּמַעֲלָתוֹ, וְהַבְדָּלָתוֹ לְשֶׁבַח מִשְּׁאָר הַיָּמִים שֶׁלְּפָנָיו וְאַחֲרָיו, שֶׁנֶּאֱמַר "זָכוֹר אֶת יוֹם הַשַּׁבָּת לְקַדְּשׁוֹ", כְּלוֹמַר זָכְרֵהוּ זֵכֶר קְדֻשָּׁה וּגְדֻלָּה. וּבְפֵרוּשׁ אָמְרוּ לָנוּ חֲכָמֵינוּ שֶׁדְּבָרִים אֵלֶּה מְצֻוִּים אָנוּ לְאָמְרָם עַל הַיַּיִן, שֶׁכֵּן בָּא הַפֵּרוּשׁ זָכְרֵהוּ עַל הַיַּיִן.

וְהָעִנְיָן הוּא שֶׁנּוֹתְנִין בְּכוֹס רְבִיעִית יַיִן חַי אוֹ מָזוּג אוֹ יוֹתֵר מֵרְבִיעִית אֲבָל לֹא פָחוֹת מִזֶּה, וְהַמְזִינָה יְדוּעָה שֶׁהִיא עַל חֵלֶק אֶחָד שֶׁל יַיִן חַי נָטוּל שְׁלֹשָׁה חֶלְקֵי מַיִם, וּמְבָרְכִין עָלָיו קִדּוּשׁ שַׁבָּת כְּמוֹ שֶׁיָּדוּעַ הַנֹּסַח בֵּין הַיְּהוּדִים. וְכֵן בִּיצִיאַת שַׁבָּת גַּם כֵּן מְבָרְכִין עַל הַיַּיִן לִכְבוֹד הַיּוֹם, וְאוֹתָהּ בְּרָכָה שֶׁל מוֹצָאֵי שַׁבָּת נִקְרֵאת הַבְדָּלָה.

מִשָּׁרְשֵׁי מִצְוָה זוֹ כְּדֵי שֶׁנִּתְעוֹרֵר מִתּוֹךְ מַעֲשֶׂה זֶה לִזְכֹּר גְּדֻלַּת הַיּוֹם וְנִקְבַּע בְּלִבֵּנוּ אֱמוּנַת חִדּוּשׁ הָעוֹלָם כִּי שֵׁשֶׁת יָמִים עָשָׂה הַשֵּׁם וְגוֹמֵר. וְעַל כֵּן נִתְחַיַּבְנוּ לַעֲשׂוֹת הַמַּעֲשֶׂה עִם הַיַּיִן לְפִי שֶׁטֶּבַע הָאָדָם מִתְעוֹרֵר בּוֹ הַרְבֵּה שֶׁהוּא סוֹעֵד וּמְשַׂמֵּחַ, וּכְבָר אָמַרְתִּי לְךָ כִּי לְפִי הִתְעוֹרְרוּת הָאָדָם וּמַעֲשֵׂהוּ יִתְפָּעֵל אֶל הַדְּבָרִים לְעוֹלָם.

וּמִזֶּה הַשֹּׁרֶשׁ אָמְרוּ בַּגְּמָרָא לְבָרְכָם זִכְרוֹנָם לִבְרָכָה שֶׁאִם הַפַּת חָבִיב עַל אָדָם יוֹתֵר שֶׁיְּקַדֵּשׁ עַל הַפַּת, כִּי אָז מִתְעוֹרֵר טִבְעוֹ יוֹתֵר לְמַה שֶּׁהוּא תָאֵב, וְאַף עַל פִּי שֶׁבִּיצִיאַת הַיּוֹם לֹא אָמְרוּ כֵן אֶלָּא שֶׁחִיְּבוּ לְהַבְדִּיל בַּיַּיִן עַל כָּל פָּנִים, גַּם בָּזֶה צָדְקוּ, כִּי הֵם זִכְרוֹנָם לִבְרָכָה, גַּם הַתּוֹרָה הַשְּׁלֵמָה, יִבָּחֲרוּ לְעוֹלָם בָּרֹב, וּבֶאֱמֶת כִּי רֹב הָעוֹלָם יִתְאַוּוּ אֶל הַשְּׁתִיָּה בְּמוֹצָאֵי שַׁבָּת יוֹתֵר מִן הָאֲכִילָה, לְפִי שֶׁכְּבָר קָבְעוּ סְעֻדָּה גְדוֹלָה בַּיּוֹם לִכְבוֹד הַשַּׁבָּת.

וְאֵין צֹרֶךְ לָתֵת טַעַם עַל חִיּוּבָם אוֹתָנוּ בְּכוֹס רְבִיעִית שֶׁיִּהְיֶה, דְּפָחוֹת מִזֶּה

---

§31   1. TB P'saḥim 106a (cf. ShM positive precept §155).

2. A *log* is 11.7 liquid ounces (345.6 cubic centimeters) in one view, 20.2 liquid ounces (597 cubic centimeters) in another. The fourth, *r'vi'ith*, would be 2.9 liquid ounces (86.4 cubic cm) by the first view, 5.0 liquid ounces (149.3 cubic cm) by the second. On the wine see §21, note 6.

3. TB P'saḥim 108b (see Rashbam there).

4. TB Shabbath 77a.

5. TB B'rachoth 52a, P'saḥim 102b; similarly Rambam ShM positive precept §155.

6. See §24, note 4.

7. See TB B'rachoth 35b.

8. TB P'saḥim 106b.

9. *Ibid.* 107a.

⟨172⟩

[TO HALLOW THE SABBATH IN WORDS]

31 to speak words on the Sabbath day as it arrives and again as it leaves, in which there is a remembrance of the day's greatness and exalted level, and of its being set apart from the days before and after it as a laudable time—as it is stated, *Remember the sabbath day to keep it holy* (Exodus 20:8)—i.e. remember it by recalling [its] holiness and greatness. In their explanation our Sages told us we are commanded to say these words over [a cup of] wine—for thus the interpretation came [down to us in our tradition]:[1] Remember it over wine.

In substance it means that a fourth [of a *log*][2] of full-strength or diluted wine is poured into a cup, or more than a fourth, but not less.[3] How to dilute it is known: to one part of full-strength wine, three parts of water [are added].[4] And the blessing of *kiddush*, the sanctification of the Sabbath, is said over it, with the [standard] text that is known among the Jews. So too, as the Sabbath leaves, a blessing is again said over [a cup of] wine in honor of the day, this benediction at the departure of the Sabbath being called *havdalah*.[5]

At the root of this *mitzvah* lies the purpose that we should be stirred, as a result of this deed, to remember the greatness of the day and affirm in our heart our enduring faith in the creation of the world out of non-existence: *for in six days the Lord made heaven and earth, the sea, and all that is in them; and He rested on the seventh day* (Exodus 20:11).[6] Therefore were we commanded to perform this deed with the wine, for a man's nature is greatly stirred[7] by it, as it sustains and gives joy. And I have already told you (§16) that to the degree that a man is moved and inspired by his deed, so is he always influenced.

In view of this root purpose, our Sages of blessed memory said in the Talmud[8] that if a man loves bread more [than wine], he should say the blessing of *kiddush* (sanctification) over the loaves of bread—for then his nature will be stirred the more by what he desires. For the day's departure, though, they did not say so, but imposed the obligation to say *havdalah* over wine in every case.[9] Even in this, however, they are justified: for they (be their memory for a blessing) like our perfect Torah, always choose [the way of] the majority; and in truth, most people have a greater desire to drink than to eat when the Sabbath leaves, having already had a large meal during the day in honor of the Sabbath.

Now, there is no need to give a reason why they required of us that the cup should contain [at least] a fourth [of a *log*], for a smaller

§31–32: HALLOW THE SABBATH IN WORDS / DO NOT WORK THAT DAY

הַשִּׁעוּר אֵינוֹ רָאוּי וְלֹא יִתְעוֹרֵר לֵב אָדָם עָלָיו. וַאֲשֶׁר חִיְּבוּנוּ בַּהַדָּחַת הַכּוֹס, וְשֶׁלֹּא לִטְעֹם כְּלוּם עַד שֶׁיְּקַדֵּשׁ, וְשֶׁיְּקַדֵּשׁ בִּמְקוֹם סְעֻדָּה, כָּל זֶה עַנְפֵי שֹׁרֶשׁ הַתְּעוֹרְרוּת שֶׁאָמַרְתִּי.

דִּינֵי הַמִּצְוָה, כְּגוֹן נֹסַח הַקִּדּוּשׁ וְהַהַבְדָּלָה אֵי זֶהוּ, וְאֵי זֶה יַיִן רָאוּי לְקַדֵּשׁ עָלָיו וְאֵי זֶה אֵינוֹ רָאוּי, וְאִם מְקַדְּשִׁין אוֹ מַבְדִּילִין בְּשֵׁכָר, וְהָאוֹכֵל בְּעֶרֶב שַׁבָּת וְקִדֵּשׁ עָלָיו שַׁבָּת, אוֹ בְּשַׁבָּת וְיָצָא שַׁבָּת, וְכֵן נֹסַח קִדּוּשׁ יָמִים טוֹבִים וְהַהַבְדָּלָתָן, וְדִינֵי הַבְּרָכָה שֶׁאָנוּ חַיָּבִין לְבָרֵךְ עַל הַנֵּר בְּמוֹצָאֵי שַׁבָּת וְיוֹם הַכִּפּוּרִים, וְדִינֵי הַבְּרָכָה שֶׁאָנוּ חַיָּבִים לְבָרֵךְ עַל הַבְּשָׂמִים בְּמוֹצָאֵי שַׁבָּת וְאֵיזוֹ בְשָׂמִים הֵן הָרְאוּיִין לְבָרֵךְ עֲלֵיהֶן אוֹ שֶׁאֵינָם רְאוּיִין, וְיֶתֶר פְּרָטֶיהָ, מְבֹאָרִים בְּסוֹף פְּסָחִים וּבִמְקוֹמוֹת מְפֻזָּרוֹת וְשַׁבָּת.

וְנוֹהֶגֶת בְּכָל מָקוֹם וּבְכָל זְמַן בִּזְכָרִים וּבִנְקֵבוֹת, וְאַף עַל פִּי שֶׁהִיא מִן הַמִּצְוֹת שֶׁהַזְּמַן גְּרָמָא, שֶׁכֵּן לִמְּדוּנוּ רַבּוֹתֵינוּ זִכְרוֹנָם לִבְרָכָה שֶׁהַנָּשִׁים חַיָּבוֹת בְּקִדּוּשׁ וְהַבְדָּלָה. וְעוֹבֵר עָלֶיהָ וְלֹא קִדֵּשׁ הַשַּׁבָּת בִּדְבָרִים בִּטֵּל מִצְוַת עֲשֵׂה. וְאִם קִדְּשׁוֹ בִּדְבָרִים בְּלֹא יַיִן אוֹ בְלֹא פַת דְּיָעֲבַד יָצָא יְדֵי תוֹרָה.

[שֶׁלֹּא לַעֲשׂוֹת מְלָאכָה בְּשַׁבָּת]

לב שֶׁלֹּא לַעֲשׂוֹת מְלָאכָה בְּיוֹם הַשַּׁבָּת אֲנַחְנוּ, וְלֹא נַנִּיחַ לַעֲשׂוֹת לְבָנֵינוּ וַעֲבָדֵינוּ וּבְהֶמְתֵּנוּ, שֶׁנֶּאֱמַר: לֹא תַעֲשֶׂה כָל מְלָאכָה, וְגוֹמֵר. וְאֵין סָפֵק כִּי אַף־עַל־פִּי שֶׁהַכָּתוּב הוֹצִיא הַמְּלָאכָה אִסּוּר בָּנוּ וּבְבָנִים וּבַעֲבָדִים וּבַבְּהֵמוֹת בְּלָאו אֶחָד שֶׁאֵין הָעִנְיָן שָׁוֶה, כִּי הָעוֹשֶׂה מְלָאכָה בְּגוּפוֹ יִתְחַיֵּב מִיתַת בֵּית דִּין אִם הוּא

---

10. It is too insignificant to leave any great impression.
11. TB B'rachoth 51a.
12. TB P'sahim 105a.
13. *Ibid.* 101a.
14. TB Bava Bathra 96a, 97a–b (Rambam MT *hilchoth shabbath* xxix 15, 17).
15. TB P'sahim 107a.
16. *Ibid.* 100a.
17. *Ibid.* 105a.
18. TB B'rachoth 43a–b.
19. *Ibid.* 51b.
20. *Ibid.* 20b.
21. I.e. after the fact, although it is not the proper way; see R. Moses of Coucy, *Séfer Mitzvoth Gadol*, positive precept §29.

amount is not a fit (respectable) measure, and a man's heart will not be stirred over it.[10] As for the obligation they [the Sages] imposed on us to wash the cup [before pouring the wine into it],[11] to taste no food before one says the blessing of *kiddush*,[12] and to recite the *kiddush* at the place (setting) of the meal[13] — these are all branches [details] of the root purpose of arousal [of the soul] that I have conveyed.

The laws of the precept are, for instance: What is the proper text for *kiddush*, and what for *havdalah*? Which wine is suitable for reciting the *kiddush* over it, and which is not?[14] May *kiddush* or *havdalah* be said over beer?[15] What if one sets to eating before the Sabbath and the onset of the Sabbath in its holiness comes upon him;[16] or if he ate on the Sabbath and the Sabbath departed [what is the law regarding *havdalah*]?[17] So too, [what is] the proper text of *kiddush*, and *havdalah*, for festival days? Then there are the laws of the blessing we are required to recite over a candle at the end of the Sabbath and the Day of Atonement; the laws of the blessing we are required to say over fragrant spices (at the Sabbath's end);[18] which spices are suitable for saying the benediction over them, and which not.[19] [These] and further details are clarified toward the end of the Talmud tractate *P'sahim* and in certain places in the tractates *B'rachoth* and *Shabbath*.

It applies in every place and every time, for both man and woman —even though it is one of the precepts whose observance is dependent upon time; for so our Sages of blessed memory taught us[20]—that women are obligated to observe *kiddush* and *havdalah*. He who transgresses it and does not hallow the Sabbath with words, disobeys a positive precept. And if someone sanctifies it with words but without wine or bread, since it is done,[21] he has fulfilled the Torah's requirement.

32 [NOT TO DO ANY WORK ON THE SABBATH]

that we should not do work on the Sabbath day, and not allow our children, servants or domestic animals to work—as it is stated, *you shall not do any work at all: you or your son or your daughter, your manservant or your maidservant, or your cattle* (Exodus 20:10). There can be no doubt, however, that even though Scripture expressed the ban on work for us, our children, servants, and domestic animals all in one negative precept—the matter is not the same [for all]. For if someone does work with his own body, he incurs death by sentence of the *beth din*, if he has done it deliberately. For the work of others,

§32: NOT TO DO ANY WORK ON THE SABBATH   ספר החינוך

מֵזִיד, וּבִמְלֶאכֶת אֲחֵרִים אַף עַל פִּי שֶׁמֻּזְהָר עֲלֵיהֶם בְּלָאו לֹא יִתְחַיֵּב עֲלֵיהֶן אֲפִלּוּ מַלְקוּת, שֶׁאֵין מַלְקוּת לְעוֹלָם בְּמַעֲשֵׂה אֲחֵרִים.

וּמִלְּשׁוֹן הָרַמְבַּ״ם זִכְרוֹנוֹ לִבְרָכָה מַשְׁמַע שֶׁהוּא סוֹבֵר כִּי הַלָּאו הַזֶּה דְּלֹא תַעֲשֶׂה כָל מְלָאכָה אַתָּה... וּבְהֶמְתֶּךָ יָבוֹא לְמַאֲמָר אַחַר בְּהֶמְתּוֹ, וּכְגוֹן שֶׁחוֹרֵשׁ בָּהּ וּכְלֵי הַמַּחֲרֵשָׁה בְּיָדוֹ, דְּאִלּוּ בְמַאֲמָר לְבַד לְפִי דַעְתּוֹ אֵין בּוֹ אֶלָּא אִסּוּר עֲשֵׂה, וְעַל כֵּן אָמְרוּ בַּגְּמָרָא לְפִי דַעְתּוֹ שֶׁזֶּה הַלָּאו דְּמַאֲמָר הוּא שֶׁנִּתַּן לְאַזְהָרַת מִיתַת בֵּית דִּין, כְּלוֹמַר שֶׁאָדָם שֶׁנֶּהֱרַג עַל זֶה וְאֵין לוֹקִין עָלָיו.

וְהָרַמְבַּ״ן זִכְרוֹנוֹ לִבְרָכָה יִתְפֹּשׂ עָלָיו הַרְבֵּה בְּפֵרוּשׁוֹ זֶה, וְאָמַר כִּי לָאו כִּי זֶה שֶׁל מַאֲמָר אֵינוֹ אֶלָּא בְּהוֹלֵךְ אַחַר בְּהֶמְתּוֹ הַטְּעוּנָה מַשּׂוֹי אֲבָל הָאָדָם לֹא יַעֲשֶׂה שׁוּם מַעֲשֶׂה בְּיָדָיו, וְלָכֵן לֹא יָבוֹא עָלָיו לְעוֹלָם לֹא מַלְקוֹת וְלֹא מִיתָה, וְכִדְקַיְמָא לָן כָּל לָאו שֶׁאֵין בּוֹ מַעֲשֶׂה אֵין לוֹקִין עָלָיו. וּכְמוֹ שֶׁדְּרָשׁוּהוּ זִכְרוֹנָם לִבְרָכָה, "אַתָּה... וּבְהֶמְתֶּךָ", לִכְתוּב קְרָא לֹא תַעֲשֶׂה כָל מְלָאכָה וּבְהֶמְתֶּךָ, אַתָּה לָמָּה לִי, הוּא נִיהוּ דְּכִי עָבֵיד מְלָאכָה מְחַיֵּב, אֲבָל עַל מְלֶאכֶת בְּהֶמְתּוֹ לָא מְחַיֵּב עָלֶיהָ בְּלָאו כְּמוֹ בִּמְלֶאכֶת בְּנוֹ הַקָּטָן וַעֲבָדָיו הַכְּנַעֲנִי, אֲבָל בִּמְלֶאכֶת עַצְמוֹ מַמָּשׁ בָּזֶה לֹא הָיָה צָרִיךְ לוֹמַר שֶׁחַיָּב, שֶׁהֲרֵי עָנְשׁוֹ מְפֹרָשׁ: כָּל הָעוֹשֶׂה בוֹ מְלָאכָה יוּמָת.

וּמַה שֶּׁאָמְרוּ בַּגְּמָרָא בְּלָאו דְּמַאֲמָר שֶׁהוּא לָאו שֶׁנִּתַּן לְאַזְהָרַת מִיתַת בֵּית דִּין, פֵּרוּשׁוֹ לְפִי דַעַת הָרַמְבַּ״ן זִכְרוֹנוֹ לִבְרָכָה כִּי מִפְּנֵי שֶׁהוּא כּוֹלֵל שְׁאָר מַלְאֲכוֹת גַּם כֵּן שֶׁהֵן בְּאַזְהָרַת מִיתַת בֵּית דִּין, אַף־עַל־גַּב דְּבִמְאַמָּר וַדַּאי אֵין בּוֹ אֶלָּא לָאו

---

1. MT *hilchoth shabbath* xx 2.
2. I.e. *that your ox and your donkey may have rest* (Exodus 23:12); and for violating a prohibition which is inferred from a positive precept, one is not given whiplashes.
3. TB Shabbath 154a.
4. I.e. an act done in violation of this precept does incur the death penalty. According to Ramban, whose view follows, if an act can involve a death penalty in at least one aspect of the precept, it is not punished by whiplashes even where it does not bring a death penalty.
5. In his commentary on Rambam ShM, root principle 14.
6. TB Sanhedrin 63b, etc.
7. TB Shabbath 154b.
8. Up to the age of thirteen, when he becomes obligated to observe the Sabbath in his own right.
9. I.e. those done by a man himself.

⟨176⟩

however, even though he is adjured about them [to prevent them] by a negative precept, over them he incurs not even the punishment of whiplashes: For lashes are never given for the action of others.

From the language of Rambam of blessed memory,[1] it is to be inferred that he believes this negative precept [in regard to domestic animals], *you shall not do any work at all . . . or your cattle*, to refer to one who drives his beast while walking behind it, thus plowing with it with the plowshare in his hand. For if one merely walks behind his domestic animal to drive it, in his view only a positive precept is involved.[2] Therefore it was stated in the Talmud,[3] according to his view, that this ban on driving an animal while walking behind it is a negative precept which brings a warning of death by sentence of the *beth din:*[4] in other words, a man deserves to be put to death for it, but one is not whipped with lashes for it.

Ramban of blessed memory, though, is very critical of him in his explanation of this;[5] and he said that this negative precept about one who drives his animal walking behind it applies only to one who thus drives a beast laden with a burden, while the man, however, does no deed at all with his hands. And therefore neither whiplashes nor a death sentence will ever be given him—as it follows the rule established for us:[6] for violating any negative precept which involves no [personal] action, no whiplashes are given.

Then this is as our Sages of blessed memory interpreted:[7] *you . . . and your cattle:* let Scripture write, *you shall do no work at all . . . and your cattle;* why do I need [the extra] "you"? It is to indicate that when [a man himself] does work, he is punishable [by death], but for the work of his animal he is not punishable; he is merely adjured about it by the negative precept, as [he is] about the work of his small son[8] and his non-Jewish bondservant. As to his very own work, however, there is no need for Scripture to state that he is punishable: for his penalty is expressly stated: *whoever does any work on the Sabbath day, he shall surely be put to death* (Exodus 31:15).

Now, it is stated in the Talmud[3] about the ban on walking behind an animal to drive it, that it is a negative precept about which a warning of death sentence by the *beth din* can be given. Its explanation, though, according to the view of Ramban of blessed memory, is that because it includes other kinds of work as well,[9] it can thus involve a warning of death at the hands of the *beth din*. Even though about driving an animal while walking behind it there is no more than a mere negative precept

גְּרִידָא דַּאֲפִלּוּ מַלְקוּת נַמֵּי אֵין בּוֹ, אַף־עַל־פִּי־כֵן נִקְרָא הַלָּאו הַזֶּה לָאו שֶׁנִּתַּן לְאַזְהָרַת מִיתַת בֵּית דִּין מִפְּנֵי אוֹתָן דְּבָרִים שֶׁהוּא כּוֹלֵל שֶׁיֵּשׁ בָּהֶן מִיתַת בֵּית דִּין.

וּכְעֵין זֶה אָמְרוּ זִכְרוֹנָם לִבְרָכָה בְּרִאשׁוֹן שֶׁל עֵרוּבִין בְּלָאו דְּאַל יֵצֵא אִישׁ מִמְּקוֹמוֹ, דְּכֵינָן שֶׁהוּא כּוֹלֵל אַף מוֹצִיא מֵרְשׁוּת לִרְשׁוּת כַּדְּרָשָׁא שֶׁדָּרְשׁוּ בּוֹ "אַל יוֹצִיא", דַּהֲוָה לֵיהּ מֵעַתָּה לָאו שֶׁנִּתַּן לְאַזְהָרַת מִיתַת בֵּית דִּין בְּמִקְצָת עִנְיָנוֹ, וְכֵינָן שֶׁכֵּן אִית לָן לְמֵימַר בָּזֶה בְּכָל עִנְיָנָיו שֶׁאֵין לוֹקִין עָלָיו. וְעַל הַדֶּרֶךְ הַזֶּה בְּעַצְמוֹ נִפְרָשׁ בְּלָאו דִּמְחַמֵּר בְּכָאן.

מִשָּׁרְשֵׁי מִצְוָה זוֹ שֶׁנִּהְיֶה פְּנוּיִים מֵעֲסָקֵינוּ לִכְבוֹד הַיּוֹם לִקְבֹּעַ בְּנַפְשׁוֹתֵינוּ אֱמוּנַת חִדּוּשׁ הָעוֹלָם שֶׁהִיא חֶבֶל הַמּוֹשֶׁכֶת כָּל יְסוֹדֵי הַדָּת, וְנִזְכֹּר בְּיוֹם אֶחָד בְּכָל שָׁבוּעַ וְשָׁבוּעַ שֶׁהָעוֹלָם נִבְרָא בְּשִׁשָּׁה יָמִים חֲלוּקִים וּבַשְּׁבִיעִי לֹא נִבְרָא דָּבָר, וּבְכָל יוֹם וָיוֹם נִבְרְאוּ עִנְיָנִים חֲלוּקִים לְהוֹרוֹת עַל הָרָצוֹן הַפָּשׁוּט, שֶׁלֹּא כְדַעַת הַמִּתְפַּלְסְפִים הַנִּמְאָסִים לָנוּ בְדַעְתָּם זֶה שֶׁחוֹשְׁבִין לֵאמֹר שֶׁעִם הֱיוֹתוֹ בָּרוּךְ הוּא הָיָה הַכֹּל. וּבִמְנוּחָתֵנוּ בַּשְּׁבִיעִי זֵכֶר לָנוּ בְּחִדּוּשׁוֹ שֶׁל עוֹלָם, כִּי כְשֶׁיִּשְׁבְּתוּ בְּנֵי אָדָם כֻּלָּם בְּיוֹם אֶחָד בַּשָּׁבוּעַ וְיִשְׁאַל כָּל שׁוֹאֵל מַה עִלַּת זֹאת הַמְּנוּחָה, וְתִהְיֶה הַמַּעֲנֶה "כִּי שֵׁשֶׁת יָמִים עָשָׂה יְיָ" וְגוֹמֵר, כָּל אֶחָד יִתְחַזֵּק כָּךְ בֶּאֱמוּנָה הָאֲמִתִּית.

וּמִלְּבַד זְכִירַת חִדּוּשׁ הָעוֹלָם יֵשׁ בּוֹ זְכִירַת נֵס מִצְרַיִם, שֶׁהָיִינוּ עֲבָדִים שָׁם וְלֹא הָיִינוּ יְכוֹלִים לָנוּחַ בְּעֵת חֶפְצֵנוּ בִּמְנוּחָה, וְהָאֵל הִצִּילָנוּ מִיָּדָם וְצִוָּנוּ לָנוּחַ בַּשְּׁבִיעִי,

---

10. I.e. this is why it is referred to in TB Shabbath 154a as a negative precept that does not bring a penalty of whiplashes.

11. I.e. through an infinite past; cf. Rambam, *Guide* II 19.

12. The paragraph is based on *ibid.* 32.

which involves not even whiplashes for its violation, nevertheless it is called a negative precept that involves death through the *beth din*—because of those matters that it includes for which death through the *beth din* can be given.

Our Sages of blessed memory said something quite similar in the first chapter of the Talmud tractate '*Eruvin* (17b) about the negative precept, *let no man go out of his place* (Exodus 16:29): Since it includes also taking something out from one domain to another [on the Sabbath], in keeping with the exposition given about it [there], which interprets *al yétzé* (let not go out) as *al yotzi* (let not carry out), it thus becomes a negative precept which involves death through the *beth din* in regard to [one aspect] of its subject matter. This being the case, we can then say of it in regard to its entire subject matter, that no whiplashes are given for its violation.[10] In the very same way can we explain here about the negative precept regarding one who drives his domestic animal while walking behind it.

At the root of this precept lies the purpose that we should remain away from our normal occupations, in honor of the day, in order to affirm in our souls our belief in the creation of the world out of non-existence—which is a cord that pulls [along with it] all the basic tenets of the religion. And so we ought to remember on one day every single week that the world was created in six separate days, and on the seventh nothing was created; and each and every day something separate, distinct was created, demonstrating the simple pure [Divine] will—in contradiction to the theory of the philosophizers, who are abhorrent to us with their hypothesis, thinking that along with His existence (blessed is He) everything existed.[11]

By resting on the seventh day we will recall the creation of the world out of non-existence: For when people will all rest from work on one day of the week, and whoever wonders at it will ask, "What is the reason for this rest?"—then the answer will be, *for in six days the Lord made heaven and earth, the sea, and all that is in them; and on the seventh day He rested* (Exodus 20:11). Everyone will be strengthened and confirmed in the true faith by this.[12]

Furthermore, apart from recalling the creation of the world out of non-existence, it leads to the remembrance of the miracle of Egypt: For we were slaves there, and could not rest when we desired repose; and God rescued us from their hand (their power), and commanded us to rest on the seventh day. So Scripture mentions in the *Book of Deuteron-*

§32–33: DO NO WORK ON THE SABBATH / HONOR FATHER & MOTHER

וְעַל־כֵּן זָכַר בְּמִשְׁנֶה תוֹרָה זֶה הַשֹּׁרֶשׁ הַשֵּׁנִי שֶׁיֵּשׁ לָנוּ בִּמְנוּחָה, וְאָמַר שָׁם בְּמִצְוַת שַׁבָּת: וְזָכַרְתָּ כִּי עֶבֶד הָיִיתָ בְּאֶרֶץ מִצְרָיִם . . . עַל כֵּן צִוְּךָ יְיָ אֱלֹהֶיךָ לַעֲשׂוֹת אֶת יוֹם הַשַּׁבָּת.

דִּינֵי הַמִּצְוָה, כְּגוֹן כַּמָּה הֵן הַדְּבָרִים שֶׁנִּקְרָאִים עִקַּר מְלָאכוֹת לְחַיֵּב בָּהֶן הָעוֹשֶׂה אוֹתָן, כְּגוֹן אַרְבָּעִים מְלָאכוֹת חָסֵר אַחַת שֶׁמָּנוּ חֲכָמִים וְתוֹלְדוֹתֵיהֶן, וְהַמְּלָאכוֹת הַקַּלּוֹת שֶׁאָסְרוּ הֵם לְגֶדֶר, וְהַדְּבָרִים גַּם כֵּן הַנִּקְרָאִים שְׁבוּתִים, וּמַה שֶּׁלָּמְדוּ זִכְרוֹנָם לִבְרָכָה מִן הַכָּתוּב כִּי דוֹחִין הַכֹּל לְהַצָּלַת נְפָשׁוֹת, וְכִי הַנָּדְרִי לְחַלֵּל אֶת הַשַּׁבָּת בִּשְׁבִיל הַצָּלַת נְפָשׁוֹת מְשֻׁבָּח. וְהַטַּעַם לְפִי שֶׁשַּׁבָּת עֲשִׂיַּת הַמִּצְוָה הוּא וְקִיּוּם הַסִּבָּה הוּא קִיּוּם הַכֹּל. וּמִפְּנֵי כֵן אָמְרוּ זִכְרוֹנָם לִבְרָכָה שֶׁנֶּאֱמַן כָּל חוֹלֶה לוֹמַר צָרִיךְ אֲנִי שֶׁיִּתְחַלְּלוּ שַׁבָּת עָלַי, וְכָל חוֹלֶה בְּקָדַּחַת שׁוֹכֵב עַל עֶרֶשׂ דְּוָי בִּכְלַל סַכָּנָה הוּא לְחַלֵּל עָלָיו אֶת שַׁבָּת. וְיֶתֶר רַבֵּי פְרָטֶיהָ מְבֹאָרִים בְּמַסֶּכֶת שַׁבָּת וְיוֹם טוֹב.

וְנוֹהֶגֶת בְּכָל מָקוֹם וּבְכָל זְמַן בִּזְכָרִים וּנְקֵבוֹת. וְעוֹבֵר עָלֶיהָ בְּמֵזִיד נִסְקָל, וְהוּא שֶׁיִּהְיוּ שָׁם עֵדִים וְהַתְרָאָה. שֶׁכְּלָל זֶה [יִהְיֶה] בְּיָדְךָ לְעוֹלָם, שֶׁאֵין מִיתָה אוֹ מַלְקוֹת אֶלָּא בְעֵדִים וְהַתְרָאָה, וְהַהַתְרָאָה לְעוֹלָם לְהַבְחִין בֵּין שׁוֹגֵג לְמֵזִיד. וְדַע זֶה הָעִקָּר בְּכָל מָקוֹם, וְלֹא תִשְׁאַל מִמֶּנִּי לְהַחֲזִירוֹ. וְאִם עָשָׂה מְלֶאכֶת מַחֲשֶׁבֶת בְּשׁוֹגֵג מֵבִיא חַטָּאת קְבוּעָה.

[מִצְוַת כִּבּוּד אָב וָאֵם]

לג לְכַבֵּד הָאָב וְהָאֵם, שֶׁנֶּאֱמַר "כַּבֵּד אֶת אָבִיךָ וְאֶת אִמֶּךָ" וְגוֹמֵר, וּבָא הַפֵּרוּשׁ: אֵי זֶהוּ כִבּוּד מַאֲכִיל וּמַשְׁקֶה, מַלְבִּישׁ וּמְכַסֶּה, מַכְנִיס וּמוֹצִיא.

מִשָּׁרְשֵׁי מִצְוָה זוֹ שֶׁרָאוּי לוֹ לָאָדָם שֶׁיַּכִּיר וְיִגְמֹל חֶסֶד לְמִי שֶׁעָשָׂה עִמּוֹ טוֹבָה

---

13. TB Shabbath 73a, in the Mishnah, and discussed (with the forms of work that constitute their derivatives) in the *g'mara* which follows.

14. TB Yoma 84b–85b (derived from Leviticus 18:5, *You shall therefore keep My statutes and My ordinances, that a man may do them and live by them*—"live," not die by them. Hence all precepts are set aside, as a rule, to save human life).

15. *Ibid.* 83a; and see Ramban, *Torath ha'Adam, sha'ar ha-sakkanah*, s.v. *b'perek 'en ma'amidin*, end.

16. TB 'Avodah Zarah 28a (Rambam MT *hilchoth shabbath* ii 5).

17. See §26, note 30.

18. From "There can be" to here derives from Rambam ShM negative precept §61, end; similarly Rambam MT *hilchoth sanhedrin* xii 2.

19. I.e. he was aware of the work he was doing, but forgot it was the Sabbath, or did not realize that such work is forbidden then. Cf. e.g. TB Bétzah 13b.

20. See §19, note 6.

§33   1. I.e. escort and attend upon them; TB Kiddushin 31b.

omy this second root purpose that we find in resting, and it states there about the precept of the Sabbath: *And you shall remember that you were a servant in the land of Egypt ... therefore the Lord your God commanded you to keep the sabbath day* (Deuteronomy 5:15).[12]

The laws of the precept are, for instance: which kinds are called actual labors, for which whoever does them will be punished—for example, the thirty-nine kinds of labor which the Sages listed,[13] and their derivatives; the light, minor labors which the Sages forbade as a "fence," a precaution; so too those matters which are called *sh'vuthim* (abstentions in keeping with the Sabbath spirit); and [the rule] which the Sages of blessed memory derived from Scripture, that everything is thrust aside in order to save human life, and whoever is alert and quick to violate the Sabbath in order to save human life, is praiseworthy.[14] The reason is that the key factor in the observance of a *mitzvah* is the human being, and to sustain the key factor is to sustain all. For this reason the Sages of blessed memory said[15] that every ill person is to be believed if he says, "It is necessary that you should violate the Sabbath on my behalf." So too, every ill person with fever who lies on a sickbed is in the category of danger, so that the Sabbath is to be violated for him.[16] [These] and further details are clarified in the Talmud tractates *Shabbath* and *Yom-tov* (*Bétzah*).

It remains in force in every place and every time, for both man and woman. One who transgresses it intentionally is stoned to death, provided there were witnesses and a warning.[17] You should always have this rule with you: There can be no death penalty or whiplashes except where there were witnesses and a warning. The warning always serves to differentiate between the intentional and the unintentional sinner. Keep this principle everywhere in mind, and do not ask of me to repeat it.[18] And if someone did conscious work [on the Sabbath] inadvertently,[19] he should bring a standard, unvarying *ḥattath* (sin-offering).[20]

33 [THE PRECEPT OF HONORING FATHER AND MOTHER] to honor one's father and mother, as it is stated, *Honor your father and your mother*, etc. (Exodus 20:12). The explanation is given [in our Oral Tradition]: What constitutes [this] honor?—to provide food and drink, clothing and raiment, and to take them in and lead them out.[1]

At the root of this *mitzvah* lies the thought that it is fitting for a man to acknowledge and treat with loving-kindness the person who

§33 : ON HONORING FATHER AND MOTHER

וְלֹא יִהְיֶה נָבָל וּמִתְנַכֵּר וּכְפוּי טוֹבָה, שֶׁזּוּ מִדָּה רָעָה וּמְאוּסָה בְּתַכְלִית לִפְנֵי אֱלֹהִים וַאֲנָשִׁים. וְשֶׁיִּתֵּן אֶל לִבּוֹ כִּי הָאָב וְהָאֵם הֵם סִבַּת הֱיוֹתוֹ בָּעוֹלָם, וְעַל כֵּן בֶּאֱמֶת רָאוּי לוֹ לַעֲשׂוֹת לָהֶם כָּל כָּבוֹד וְכָל תּוֹעֶלֶת שֶׁיּוּכַל, כִּי הֵם הֱבִיאוּהוּ לָעוֹלָם, גַּם יָגְעוּ בּוֹ כַּמָּה יְגִיעוֹת בְּקַטְנוּתוֹ.

וּכְשֶׁיִּקְבַּע זֹאת הַמִּדָּה בְּנַפְשׁוֹ יַעֲלֶה מִמֶּנָּה לְהַכִּיר טוֹבַת הָאֵל בָּרוּךְ הוּא, שֶׁהוּא סִבָּתוֹ וְסִבַּת כָּל אֲבוֹתָיו עַד אָדָם הָרִאשׁוֹן, וְשֶׁהוֹצִיאוֹ לַאֲוִיר הָעוֹלָם וְסִפֵּק צָרְכּוֹ כָּל יָמָיו וְהֶעֱמִידוֹ עַל מַתְכֻּנְתּוֹ וּשְׁלֵמוּת אֵבָרָיו, וְנָתַן בּוֹ נֶפֶשׁ יוֹדַעַת וּמַשְׂכֶּלֶת, שֶׁאִלּוּלֵי הַנֶּפֶשׁ שֶׁחֲנָנוּ הָאֵל יִהְיֶה כְּסוּס כְּפֶרֶד אֵין הָבִין, וְיַעֲרֹךְ בְּמַחְשַׁבְתּוֹ כַּמָּה וְכַמָּה רָאוּי לוֹ לְהִזָּהֵר בַּעֲבוֹדָתוֹ בָּרוּךְ הוּא.

דִּינֵי הַמִּצְוָה, כְּגוֹן כִּבּוּד זֶה מִנִּכְסֵי מִי חַיָּב לַעֲשׂוֹתוֹ אִם מִשֶּׁל אָב אוֹ מִשֶּׁל עַצְמוֹ, וַהֲלָכָה מִשֶּׁל אָב אִם יֵשׁ לוֹ נְכָסִים לָאָב, וְאִם לָאו יְחַזֵּר הַבֵּן אֲפִלּוּ עַל הַפְּתָחִים וְיַאֲכִיל אָבִיו, וְכִבּוּד אָב וָאֵם אֵי זֶה קוֹדֵם, וְעַד הֵיכָן כְּבוֹד אָב וָאֵם, וְאִם מָחַל עַל כְּבוֹדוֹ אִם יִהְיֶה מָחוּל, וְאִם יִרְאֶנּוּ עוֹבֵר עַל דִּבְרֵי תוֹרָה בְּאֵי זֶה לָשׁוֹן יְמָנְעֶנּוּ, וְאִם יְצַוֵּהוּ (אָבִיו) לַעֲבֹר עַל דִּבְרֵי תוֹרָה שֶׁלֹּא יַאֲמִינֵהוּ בָזֶה, וְכִי חַיָּב לְכַבְּדוֹ בְּחַיָּיו וּבְמוֹתוֹ, וְכֵיצַד הוּא הַכִּבּוּד בְּמוֹתוֹ, וְיֶתֶר פְּרָטֶיהָ, מְבֹאָרִין בְּקִדּוּשִׁין, וּקְצָת מֵהֶן בִּמְקוֹמוֹת מֵהַתַּלְמוּד.

וְנוֹהֶגֶת בְּכָל מָקוֹם וּבְכָל זְמַן בִּזְכָרִים וּבִנְקֵבוֹת כָּל זְמַן שֶׁאֶפְשָׁר לָהֶן, כְּלוֹמַר בְּכָל עֵת שֶׁלֹּא יִמְנְעוּ אוֹתָן בַּעֲלֵיהֶן. וְעוֹבֵר עָלֶיהָ בִּטֵּל עֲשֵׂה, וְעָנְשׁוֹ גָּדוֹל מְאֹד,

2. Literally, into the air of the world.
3. Literally, property, or goods.
4. TB Kiddushin 32a, TJ i 7.
5. Ibid. 31a.
6. Ibid. 31a, 32a; Rambam MT *hilchoth mamrim* vi 7.
7. Ibid. 32a. Literally, is [his honor] forgiven?
8. Ibid.
9. TB Bava M'tzi'a 32a.
10. TB Kiddushin 31b.
11. Ibid. 30b.

⟨182⟩

treated him with goodness, and he should not be a scoundrel, an ingrate who turns a cold shoulder [to him]—for this is an evil quality, utterly vile before God and mankind. It is for a person to realize that his father and mother are the cause of his being in the world; hence in very truth it is proper for him to give them every honor and every benefit that he can, since they brought him into the world and then, too, labored through many troubles over him in his early years.

When he sets this quality firmly in his character, a person will rise from this to recognize the goodness of God, blessed is He, who is the primary Cause of his existence and the existence of all his forebears, back to Adam, the first man. And [he will realize] that He brought him forth into the light of day,[2] provided for his needs all his days [on earth], brought him to his proper estate with all his limbs whole, and gave him a cognitive and intelligent spirit—and if not for this spirit with which God endowed him, he would be *like a horse, like a mule, without understanding* (Psalms 32:9). Then let him reckon in his mind how very, very right it is for him to take care about serving and worshipping Him, be He blessed.

The laws of the *mitzvah* are for example: this honoring [of the parents], out of whose money[3] it is to be done, one's father's or one's own—the law being:[4] at the father's expense if the father has property, and if he has not, the son is to make the rounds of doors [to beg for charity, if necessary] and so support his father. Then, in honoring one's father and mother, which of them takes precedence?[5] How far does honoring the father and mother go (to what limits)?[6] If a parent is willing to forego his honor (overlook it), is it then permitted [to ignore his honor]?[7] If someone sees him [his father] transgressing the words of the Torah, in what terms he may speak to deter him;[8] if his father should order him to transgress the words of the Torah, that he should not heed him about this;[9] that one is duty-bound to honor him both in life and in death, and how [a parent] is honored in death.[10] [These] and further details are explained in the tractate *Kiddushin*, and some of them elsewhere in the Talmud.

It applies in every place and every time, to both man and woman, as long as it is possible for them [women] to observe it—i.e. at such time as their husbands do not restrain them.[11] Anyone who transgresses it disobeys a positive precept, and his punishment is very great, for he becomes as a stranger (one who turns a cold shoulder) to his Father in heaven. If the *beth din* has the power, it compels him [to obey it], as we

שֶׁנַּעֲשָׂה כְּמִתְנַכֵּר לְאָבִיו שֶׁבַּשָּׁמַיִם. וְאִם יֵשׁ כֹּחַ בְּבֵית דִּין כּוֹפִין אוֹתוֹ, כְּמוֹ שֶׁכָּתַבְנוּ לְמַעְלָה שֶׁבְּבִטּוּל עֲשֵׂה כּוֹפִין בֵּית דִּין.

[שֶׁלֹּא לַהֲרֹג נָקִי]

לד שֶׁלֹּא לַהֲרֹג נֶפֶשׁ, שֶׁנֶּאֱמַר: לֹא תִרְצָח.

שֹׁרֶשׁ מִצְוָה זוֹ יָדוּעַ וְנִגְלֶה לְכָל רוֹאֵי הַשֶּׁמֶשׁ, כִּי הַשֵּׁם בָּנָה הָעוֹלָם וְצִוָּנוּ לִפְרוֹת וְלִרְבּוֹת כְּדֵי לְיַשְּׁבוֹ לְפָנָיו, וּמְנָעָנוּ שֶׁלֹּא נַחֲרִיבֵהוּ בְּיָדֵינוּ לַהֲרֹג וּלְאַבֵּד הַבְּרִיּוֹת שֶׁהֵן הַמְיַשְּׁבוֹת הָעוֹלָם.

וְאוּלָם הָרְשָׁעִים הַגְּמוּרִים כְּגוֹן הַמִּינִין וְהַמַּלְשִׁינִים אֵינָן מְיַשְּׁבֵי עוֹלָם, וַעֲלֵיהֶם אָמַר הַכָּתוּב "וּבַאֲבֹד רְשָׁעִים רִנָּה", לְפִי שֶׁהֵן לֹא יוֹשִׁיבוּ הָעוֹלָם אֲבָל יַחֲרִיבוּהוּ בְּכָל כֹּחָם. וְזֶהוּ מַה שֶּׁאָמַר חָכָם מֵחֲכָמֵינוּ זִכְרוֹנָם לִבְרָכָה בְּאָבְדוֹ הָרְשָׁעִים, "קוֹצִים אֲנִי מְכַלֶּה מִן הַכֶּרֶם", כְּלוֹמַר בְּאָבְדָן אֵלֶּה יִתְיַשֵּׁב הָעוֹלָם יוֹתֵר, כְּמוֹ שֶׁפֵּרוֹת הַכֶּרֶם מִתְרַבִּים וְטוֹבִים יוֹתֵר בְּסִלּוּק הַקּוֹצִים מִמֶּנּוּ.

מִדִּינֵי הַמִּצְוָה מַה שֶּׁאָמְרוּ זִכְרוֹנָם לִבְרָכָה שֶׁאֶחָד הַהוֹרֵג אֶת הַבָּרִיא אוֹ אֶת הַחוֹלֶה נָטוּי לָמוּת, וַאֲפִלּוּ הַגּוֹסֵס בְּחֹלִי בִּידֵי שָׁמַיִם נֶהֱרָג עָלָיו. וְדִין מִשְׁפַּט הָרוֹצֵחַ כֵּיצַד, וְיֶתֶר פְּרָטֶיהָ, מְבֹאָרִין בְּפֶרֶק ט׳ מִסַּנְהֶדְרִין וְשֵׁנִי מִמַּכּוֹת.

וְנוֹהֶגֶת בְּכָל מָקוֹם וּבְכָל זְמַן בִּזְכָרִים וּנְקֵבוֹת. וְעוֹבֵר עָלֶיהָ וְרָצַח בְּמֵזִיד וְיֵשׁ עֵדִים שֶׁהִתְרוּ בוֹ הוֹרְגִין אוֹתוֹ בְּסַיִף. בְּשׁוֹגֵג לְמַטָּה נִכְתֹּב דִּינוֹ בְּעֶזְרַת הַשֵּׁם בְּסֵדֶר אֵלֶּה מַסְעֵי.

[שֶׁלֹּא לְגַלּוֹת עֶרְוַת אֵשֶׁת אִישׁ]

לה שֶׁלֹּא לָבוֹא עַל אֵשֶׁת אִישׁ, שֶׁנֶּאֱמַר "לֹא תִנְאָף", וּבָא הַפֵּרוּשׁ שֶׁלְּשׁוֹן

---

§34
1. See §30, note 33.
2. I.e. harmonious, productive members of the community.
3. Hebrew, *minim*; Rambam defines five types in MT *hilchoth t'shuva* iii 7.
4. R. 'El'azar b. R. Simeon, in TB Bava M'tzi'a 83b.
5. TB Sanhedrin 88a.

have written above (§6), that when a positive precept is deliberately ignored, the *beth din* is to apply force.

34 [NOT TO PUT AN INNOCENT MAN TO DEATH]
not to kill any person, as it is stated, *You shall not kill* (Exodus 20:13).

The root reason for this precept is known and obvious to all who see the sun.[1] For the Eternal Lord structured the world and commanded us to be fruitful and multiply (Genesis 1:28), so that we should inhabit and settle it before Him; and He enjoined us not to destroy it with our hands by killing and annihilating human beings, who are the inhabitants and settlers of the world.[2]

Those who are thoroughly wicked, however, such as sectarian heretics[3] and slanderous informers, are not [considered] inhabitants and settlers of the world; and of them Scripture said, *when the wicked perish, there is joy* (Proverbs 11:10)—for they will not settle the world but rather desolate it with all their power. This is why one of our Sages of blessed memory[4] said about His decimation of the wicked, "Weeds do I [the Almighty] remove from the vineyard": i.e. by the elimination of these, the world becomes the more settled, even as the fruit of the vine increases and improves the more by the removal of weeds from it.

Among the laws of the precept there is what the Sages of blessed memory said:[5] that if someone kills a healthy person or a sick man on the verge of death, or even a person breathing his last from an illness sent by Heaven, he is put to death for it; and the law how the trial of a killer is carried out. [These] and the rest of its details are explained in the ninth chapter of the Talmud tractate *Sanhedrin* and the second chapter of *Makkoth*.

It is in effect in every place and every time, for both man and woman. If someone transgresses it and kills deliberately, and there are witnesses who warned him, he is to be slain by the sword. As to one who kills inadvertently, we will write the law for him below with the help of the Eternal Lord, in the *sidrah mas'é* (§410).

35 [NOT TO BE IMMORAL WITH ANOTHER'S WIFE]
not to be conjugally intimate with a married woman, for it is stated, *lo tin'af, You shall not commit adultery* (Exodus 20:13), and the

§35: NOT TO BE IMMORAL WITH ANOTHER'S WIFE

נָאוּף סְתָם מַשְׁמַע בְּאֵשֶׁת אִישׁ, כְּמוֹ שֶׁאָמְרוּ זִכְרוֹנָם לִבְרָכָה, אֵין נָאוּף אֶלָּא בְּאֵשֶׁת אִישׁ. וְנִכְפַּל זֶה הַלָּאו בְּסֵדֶר אַחֲרֵי מוֹת שֶׁכָּתוּב שָׁם בְּפֵרוּשׁ: וְאֶל אֵשֶׁת עֲמִיתְךָ לֹא תִתֵּן שְׁכָבְתְּךָ לְזָרַע לְטָמְאָה בָהּ.

מִשָּׁרְשֵׁי מִצְוָה זוֹ כְּדֵי שֶׁיִּתְיַשֵּׁב הָעוֹלָם כַּאֲשֶׁר חָפֵץ הַשֵּׁם, וְהַשֵּׁם בָּרוּךְ הוּא רָצָה שֶׁיִּהְיוּ כָּל עִנְיְנֵי עוֹלָמוֹ עוֹשִׂין פֵּרוֹתֵיהֶן כָּל אֶחָד וְאֶחָד לְמִינֵהוּ וְלֹא שֶׁיִּתְעָרְבוּ מִין בְּמִין אַחֵר, וְכֵן רָצָה שֶׁיִּהְיֶה זֶרַע הָאֲנָשִׁים יָדוּעַ שֶׁל מִי הוּא וְלֹא יִתְעָרְבוּ זֶה עִם זֶה.

וְעוֹד יִמָּצְאוּ הֶפְסֵדִין כַּמָּה בַּנָּאוּף שֶׁתִּהְיֶה סִבָּה לְבַטֵּל כַּמָּה מִמִּצְוֹת הָאֵל עָלֵינוּ שֶׁצִּוָּנוּ בִּכְבוֹד הָאָבוֹת וְלֹא יַכִּירוּ בָנִים עִם הַנָּאוּף. וְעוֹד יִהְיֶה כְּשָׁלוֹן בַּמֶּה שֶׁנִּצְטַוִּינוּ גַּם-כֵּן שֶׁלֹּא לָבוֹא עַל הָאָחוֹת וְעַל הַרְבֵּה נָשִׁים, וְהַכֹּל יֵעָקֵר בְּסִבַּת הַנָּאוּף, שֶׁלֹּא יַכִּירוּ בְּנֵי אָדָם קְרוֹבוֹתֵיהֶן, מִלְּבַד שֶׁיֵּשׁ בְּעִנְיָן הַנָּאוּף עִם אֵשֶׁת אִישׁ צַד גֶּזֶל שֶׁהוּא דָּבָר בָּרוּר שֶׁהַשֵּׂכֶל מַרְחִיקוֹ, גַּם כִּי הוּא סִבָּה לְאִבּוּד נְפָשׁוֹת, כִּי יָדוּעַ הַדָּבָר בְּטֶבַע בְּנֵי אִישׁ שֶׁמְּקַנְּאִים עַל נָאוּף וְגַם בַּת זוּגָם עִם אֲחֵרִים, וְיוֹרְדִין עִם הַנּוֹאֵף עַד לְחַיָּיו, וְכַמָּה תַקָּלוֹת מִלְּבַד אֵלֶּה.

דִּינֵי הַמִּצְוָה, כְּגוֹן הַרְחָקַת הָעִנְיָן שֶׁלֹּא לְהִתְיַחֵד עִמָּהֶן, וּמִשְׁפַּט הַנּוֹאֵף וְהַנּוֹאֶפֶת גַּם כֵּן, שֶׁגַּם הִיא בְּאִסּוּר וּבְדִין, וְיֶתֶר פְּרָטֶיהָ, מְבֹאָרִים בְּמַסֶּכֶת סַנְהֶדְרִין וּבִמְקוֹמוֹת בַּתַּלְמוּד.

וְשָׁם בְּסַנְהֶדְרִין מְתֹבָאַר שֶׁהַנּוֹאֵף עִם אֵשֶׁת אִישׁ גְּמוּרָה שְׁנֵיהֶם בְּחֶנֶק, וְהַנּוֹאֵף עִם נַעֲרָה מְאֹרָסָה שְׁנֵיהֶם בִּסְקִילָה, וְאִם נַעֲרָה מְאֹרָסָה בַּת כֹּהֵן הִיא תִּשָּׂרֵף וְהוּא יֵחָנֵק.

וְאִסּוּר אֵשֶׁת אִישׁ הוּא מִן הַמִּצְוֹת שֶׁהֵן עַל כָּל בְּנֵי הָעוֹלָם בִּכְלָל בֵּין יִשְׂרָאֵל

35
1. Cited by Rashi on the verse, in keeping with Mechilta that here the Torah gives the warning, while the penalty is stated in Leviticus 20:10, which expressly concerns a married woman.

2. I.e. who is its father.

3. Similarly R. Saadyah Ga'on, *Emunoth v'De'oth*, iii 2.

4. TB Kiddushin 80b.

5. As expressly stated in Leviticus 20:10.

6. TB Sanhedrin 84b.

7. See note 8.

8. A betrothed girl (*m'orasah*) was legally the wife of her man, and thus forbidden to any other. For Jewish marriage took place in two stages: *'érusin* (generally translated as betrothal), which bound the two as man and wife, and *n'su'in* ("marriage"), generally a year later, whereupon they began living together. (The interim period, when the couple, though legally married, did not live together, was to allow the woman to prepare what she would need in her new life.) Today *'érusin* and *n'su'in* take place together under the wedding canopy.

9. TB Sanhedrin 66b (Rambam MT *hilchoth 'issuré bi'ah* iii 4).

10. Leviticus 21:9; ibid. 50b (Rambam *ibid.* 5).

explanation was given [in the Oral Tradition] that the term *ni'uf* (adultery) by itself generally connotes a married woman—as our Sages of blessed memory said: *ni'uf* means with none but a married woman.[1] This prohibition was reiterated in the *sidrah aḥaré moth*, where it is written distinctly, *And to your neighbor's wife you shall not give your conjugal intimacy, to defile yourself with her* (Leviticus 18:20).

At the root of this precept lies the purpose that the world should be settled as the Eternal Lord desired; and the Lord (blessed is He) wished that everything in his world should produce its fruit (offspring), each according to its species, and no one species should become intermingled with another. And so did He wish that about a human child it should always be known whose it is,[2] and they should not become intermingled with one another.

Quite a few other harmful results will also be found to follow from adultery: for it will be the cause of transgression of several obligations which God imposed on us. Thus, He commanded us about honoring parents, and they will not be recognized by the children where there was adultery. There will be a further disaster about what we were equally commanded, not to be conjugally intimate with a sister and with many other women [relatives]: All will be uprooted, overturned, on account of adultery, for people will not recognize their female relatives.[3] And this apart from the fact that there is in adultery with a married woman an aspect of theft, which is something that, clearly, the intelligence should spurn. Moreover, it is a cause of the loss of human life: for it is a known fact about human nature that people grow jealous over the adulterous relations of their wives with others, and they settle accounts with the adulterer even to the death. And there are so many other misfortunes in addition to these [as a result].

The laws of the precept—such as keeping well away from this matter by not being alone with them;[4] the sentence of the adulterer, and the adulteress as well, for she too is subject to the prohibition and the punishment[5]—[these] and its other details are explained in the tractate *Sanhedrin* and in various places elsewhere in the Talmud.

There, in the tractate *Sanhedrin*,[6] it is explained that if someone commits adultery with a completely married woman,[7] both are put to death by strangulation. If one commits adultery with a betrothed girl,[8] both are put to death by stoning;[9] and if the betrothed girl is a *kohen*'s daughter, she is given death by burning,[10] and he by strangulation.

The ban on a married woman is one of the religious precepts

§35–37: BANS ON ADULTERY, KIDNAPPING, FALSE TESTIMONY

בֵּין גּוֹי. אֲבָל יֵשׁ חִלּוּק קְצָת בָּעִנְיָן, שֶׁאֵין אִישׁוּת לְגוֹי אֶלָּא עַל יְדֵי בְּעִילָה וְיִשְׂרָאֵל קוֹנֶה אוֹתָהּ אֲפִלּוּ בְּקִדּוּשִׁין.

[שֶׁלֹּא לִגְנֹב נֶפֶשׁ מִיִּשְׂרָאֵל]

לו שֶׁלֹּא לִגְנֹב נֶפֶשׁ מִיִּשְׂרָאֵל, שֶׁנֶּאֱמַר "לֹא תִגְנֹב", וּבָא הַפֵּרוּשׁ שֶׁבְּגוֹנֵב נְפָשׁוֹת הַכָּתוּב מְדַבֵּר.

שֹׁרֶשׁ הַמִּצְוָה נִגְלֶה הוּא. דִּינֵי הַמִּצְוָה, כְּגוֹן מַה שֶּׁאָמְרוּ אֵין חִלּוּק בֵּין גָּדוֹל לְקָטָן וּבֵין אִישׁ לְאִשָּׁה, דְּנֶפֶשׁ מִכָּל מָקוֹם מַשְׁמַע, וְדִין הָאָב הַגּוֹנֵב בְּנוֹ אוֹ הָרַב אֶת תַּלְמִידוֹ, וְיֶתֶר פְּרָטֶיהָ, מְבֹאָרִים בְּפֶרֶק י"א מִסַּנְהֶדְרִין.

וְאִסּוּרָהּ נוֹהֶגֶת בְּכָל מָקוֹם בִּזְכָרִים וּנְקֵבוֹת. וְעוֹבֵר עָלֶיהָ וְגָנַב נֶפֶשׁ חַיָּב חֶנֶק, וְהוּא שֶׁמְּכָרוֹ אוֹתוֹ נֶפֶשׁ, שֶׁכֵּן בָּא הַפֵּרוּשׁ שֶׁאֵין הַחִיּוּב חָל עָלָיו עַד שֶׁיִּמְכְּרוֹ, שֶׁכָּתוּב אַחֵר מְגַלֶּה עָלָיו, דִּכְתִיב: וְגֹנֵב אִישׁ וּמְכָרוֹ . . . מוֹת יוּמָת.

[שֶׁלֹּא לְהָעִיד בְּשֶׁקֶר]

לז שֶׁלֹּא לְהָעִיד עֵדוּת שֶׁקֶר, שֶׁנֶּאֱמַר "לֹא תַעֲנֶה בְרֵעֲךָ עֵד שָׁקֶר", וְנִכְפַּל בְּמָקוֹם אַחֵר בְּלָשׁוֹן אַחֵר: עֵד שָׁוְא.

שֹׁרֶשׁ מִצְוָה זוֹ נִגְלֶה, כִּי הַשֶּׁקֶר נִמְאָס וְנֶאֱלָח לְעֵין כָּל מַשְׂכִּיל, גַּם כִּי בְּעֵדוּת אֱמֶת הָעוֹלָם עוֹמֵד, שֶׁכָּל דִּבְרֵי רִיבוֹת בְּנֵי אָדָם מִתְבַּטְּלִים בְּעֵדוּת אֲנָשִׁים, וְאִם כֵּן עֵדוּת שֶׁקֶר סִבָּה לְחָרְבַּן הַיִּשּׁוּב.

דִּינֵי הַמִּצְוָה, כְּגוֹן מִמִּי מְקַבְּלִין עֵדוּת וּמִמִּי אֵין מְקַבְּלִין, וּבַמֶּה יִפָּסְלוּ בְּנֵי

---

1. TB Sanhedrin 86a.
2. I.e. if either was kidnapped; *ibid.* 85b; Mechilta, Exodus 21:16.
3. If either was kidnapped; the proof in the verse that follows lies in the words "stealing a soul," which implies whichever kind of human being is the victim; *ibid.*
4. TB Sanhedrin 85b–86a (Rambam MT *hilchoth g'névah* ix 5).
5. *Ibid.* 84b.
6. I.e. into slavery; *ibid.* 85b. and Rashi.
7. *Ibid.*

37   1. See MT *hilchoth 'éduth* ix 1.

imposed on all people in the world generally, both Jewish and non-Jewish. There is a slight difference in the matter, though [between the two categories]: for marriage becomes binding for a heathen only through conjugal relations, while an Israelite makes a woman his wife even by *kiddushin*, sanctifying her to him.

36 [NOT TO KIDNAP ANY JEWISH PERSON]

not to kidnap any soul in Jewry—for it is stated, *You shall not steal* (Exodus 20:13), and the explanation was given [in the Oral Tradition][1] that the verse refers to the theft of persons (kidnapping).

The root reason of the precept is obvious. As to the laws of the precept, there is, for instance, the statement of the Sages: there is no difference [in law] between an adult and a child,[2] or between a man and a woman;[3] for "soul" [in the verse, *If a man is found stealing a soul among his brethren*—Deuteronomy 24:7] implies of any kind. Then there is the law for a father who kidnaps his son, or a teacher [who kidnaps] his pupil.[4] [These] and its further details are explained in chapter 11 of the tractate *Sanhedrin*.

Its prohibition is in force everywhere, for both man and woman. If someone transgresses it and kidnaps a person, he incurs death by strangulation[5]—but only if he sold that person.[6] For so the explanation was given [in the Oral Tradition],[7] that the punishment is not incurred until he sells [him]: because another verse makes this clear, as it is written, *And whoever steals a man and sells him ... shall be put to death* (Exodus 21:16).

37 [NOT TO BEAR FALSE WITNESS]

not to give false testimony—as it is stated, *You shall not bear false witness against your neighbor* (Exodus 20:13); and it was repeated in another place [in Scripture], with a different expression—[about bearing] "vain (invalid) witness" (Deuteronomy 5:17).

The root reason for this precept is apparent: because falsehood is vile and rotten in the sight of every person of intelligence, especially since the world endures through true testimony: For all matters of dispute between people are resolved through human testimony; hence false witness is a cause of ruin in a community.

The laws of the precept are, for example: from whom testimony is accepted, and from whom it is not accepted;[1] for what [reasons]

אָדָם לְהָעִיד, וְכֵיצַד קַבָּלַת הָעֵדוּת, וְכִי יֵשׁ בְּנֵי אָדָם שֶׁאֵין מְעִידִין לְכָל אָדָם מֵרֹב מַעֲלָתוֹ, וּדְרִישַׁת הָעֵדוּת וְהַחֲקִירָה, וְהַחִלּוּקִין שֶׁבֵּין עֵדוּת מָמוֹן לְעֵדוּת נְפָשׁוֹת, וְהַחִלּוּק שֶׁבֵּין דְּרִישָׁה לִבְדִיקָה, וְהַחִלּוּק שֶׁבֵּין עֵדוּת בִּשְׁטָר לְעַל פֶּה, וְיֶתֶר רַבֵּי פְּרָטֶיהָ, מְבֹאָרִין בְּסַנְהֶדְרִין וּבִמְקוֹמוֹת בַּתַּלְמוּד.

וְנוֹהֶגֶת בְּכָל מָקוֹם וּבְכָל זְמַן בִּזְכָרִים אֲבָל לֹא בִּנְקֵבוֹת, שֶׁאֵין הַנָּשִׁים בְּתוֹרַת עֵדוּת, שֶׁהָעֵדוּת צָרִיךְ כִּוּוּן וְיִשּׁוּב הַדַּעַת הַרְבֵּה. וְהָעוֹבֵר עַל לָאו זֶה וְהֵעִיד שֶׁקֶר בַּחֲבֵרוֹ, שָׁם הַכָּתוּב גְּבוּל עָנְשׁוֹ לַעֲשׂוֹת לוֹ כַּאֲשֶׁר חָשַׁב לַעֲשׂוֹת לַחֲבֵרוֹ, וְיֵשׁ בּוֹ מַלְקוֹת כְּמוֹ כֵן. וְשָׁם בְּסַנְהֶדְרִין גַּם כֵּן מִתְבָּאֵר.

[שֶׁלֹּא לַחְמֹד]

לח שֶׁלֹּא לְהַעֲלוֹת בְּמַחְשַׁבְתֵּנוּ לַעֲשׂוֹת תַּחְבּוּלָה לָקַחַת לָנוּ מַה שֶׁהוּא לְזוּלָתֵנוּ מֵאַחֵינוּ, שֶׁנֶּאֱמַר "לֹא תַחְמֹד בֵּית רֵעֶךָ" וְגוֹמֵר. וּכְבָר הוֹכִיחוּ זִכְרוֹנָם לִבְרָכָה מִפָּסוּק אַחֵר, דִּכְתִיב, "לֹא תַחְמֹד וְכוּ' וְלָקַחְתָּ לָךְ" שֶׁאָסוּר לָאו דְּלֹא תַחְמֹד אֵינוֹ נִגְמָר עַד שֶׁיַּעֲשֶׂה בּוֹ מַעֲשֶׂה. וַאֲפִלּוּ נָתַן הַדָּמִים לַחֲבֵרוֹ עַל הַחֵפֶץ גַּם כֵּן עַל לָאו דְּלֹא תַחְמֹד, שֶׁאֵין לָאו דְּלֹא תַחְמֹד נִתְקָן בִּנְתִינַת הַדָּמִים כָּל זְמַן שֶׁדֶּרֶךְ הֶכְרֵחַ לְקָחוֹ מִמֶּנּוּ, כֵּן הוּא הַפֵּרוּשׁ הָאֲמִתִּי לְרַבּוֹתֵינוּ זִכְרוֹנָם לִבְרָכָה.

מִשָּׁרְשֵׁי מִצְוָה זוֹ לְפִי שֶׁמַּחְשָׁבָה רָעָה הִיא זוֹ וְגוֹרֶמֶת לוֹ לְאָדָם תַּקָּלוֹת הַרְבֵּה, שֶׁאַחַר שֶׁיִּקָּבַע בְּמַחְשַׁבְתּוֹ לָקַחַת מִמֶּנּוּ אוֹתוֹ הַדָּבָר שֶׁחָמַד, מִתּוֹךְ אוֹתָהּ תַּאֲוָה רָעָה לֹא יַשְׁגִּיחַ בְּשׁוּם דָּבָר, וְאִם לֹא יִרְצֶה חֲבֵרוֹ לְמָכְרוֹ יֶאֱנֹס אוֹתוֹ מִמֶּנּוּ, וְאִם יַעֲמֹד כְּנֶגְדּוֹ אֶפְשָׁר שֶׁיַּהַרְגֶנּוּ, כַּאֲשֶׁר מָצִינוּ בְּנָבוֹת שֶׁנֶּהֱרַג עַל כַּרְמוֹ שֶׁחָמַד מִמֶּנּוּ אַחְאָב.

---

2. See *Shulḥan 'Aruch Ḥoshen Mishpat*, §28, 21.

3. I.e. kings are not to give evidence, and great scholars may refrain if they wish; TB Sanhedrin 18a, Sh'vu'oth 30b.

4. TB Sanhedrin 40a.

5. *Ibid.* 32a.

6. See MT *hilchoth 'éduth* iii 4.

7. TB Bava Kamma 88a.

8. I.e. where the punishment they wished to bring upon their victim may not be given them: e.g. if they testified falsely that someone's parents were a *kohen* and a divorced woman, so as to give him the status of a defective, disqualified *kohen*; even if the witnesses were *kohanim*, giving them this defective status would punish their sons and descendants as well, and this the Torah did not decree. Hence they are whipped (TB Makkoth 2b).

38

1. Mechilta, *baḥodesh* 8 end.

2. So Rambam MT *hilchoth g'zélah* i 9.

3. So *ibid.* 11.

people are disqualified to testify;[1] how testimony is taken;[2] that there are certain people who need not give evidence for everyone, on account of their high rank;[3] the investigation and searching scrutiny of the witnesses;[4] the differences between testimony in civil cases and testimony in capital cases;[5] the difference between investigation and examination;[4] and the difference between documented and oral testimony.[6] [These] and its many other details are explained in the tractate *Sanhedrin* and in various places in the Talmud.

It is in effect in every place and every time, for men but not for women—since women may not serve as witnesses:[7] for bearing witness requires great concentration and presence of mind. If someone violates this negative precept and bears false witness against his fellow, Scripture has set the extent of his punishment (Deuteronomy 19:19), that to him should be done what he thought to do to his fellow [through his testimony]; and he can also be punished by whiplashes.[8] There, in the tractate *Sanhedrin*, this too is explained.

38 [NOT TO COVET WHAT BELONGS TO ANOTHER]

not to entertain the thought of carrying out any scheme to take for ourselves what belongs to someone else of our brethren—as it is stated, *You shall not covet your neighbor's house*, etc. (Exodus 20:13); and long ago our Sages of blessed memory deduced from another verse, *you shall not covet . . . or take for yourselves* (Deuteronomy 7:25), that the ban *You shall not covet* is not truly, finally broken until some action is taken about it.[1] But even if one gives his fellow-man money for the object [which he craves and means to take by force] he too already transgresses the negative precept, *You shall not covet:* for the forbidden act of coveting is not made right by giving money [for the desired object] so long as he takes it from him by force.[2] This is the true interpretation [as given] by our Sages of blessed memory.

At the root of this precept lies the reason that this is an evil thought and causes a man many misfortunes: For after he firmly decides in his mind to take from the other that object which he craves out of an evil desire, he will take no notice of anything [and will stop at nothing]; and should his fellow-man not wish to sell it to him, he will wrest it from him by force; and if the other should stand up against him, he may kill him—as we find in the case of Naboth, who was murdered over his vineyard, which Ahab craved [to get] from him (I Kings 21).[3]

דִּינֵי הַמִּצְוָה, אֵיךְ רָאוּי לְהִתְרַחֵק הַרְבֵּה מִן הַמִּדָּה הָרָעָה הַזֹּאת, מְבֹאָרִים בִּמְקוֹמוֹת בַּתַּלְמוּד בְּפִזּוּר וּבַמִּדְרָשׁוֹת.

וְנוֹהֶגֶת בְּכָל מָקוֹם וּבְכָל זְמַן בִּזְכָרִים וּנְקֵבוֹת. וְעוֹבֵר עָלֶיהָ וְחָמַד, וַאֲפִלּוּ עָשָׂה בּוֹ שׁוּם מַעֲשֶׂה, אֵינוֹ חַיָּב מַלְקוֹת, לְפִי שֶׁהוּא דָּבָר שֶׁנִּתָּן לְהִשָּׁבוֹן, שֶׁהֲרֵי אֲפִלּוּ אֲנָסוֹ מִמֶּנּוּ לְהִשָּׁבוֹן נִתָּן. וּמִכָּל מָקוֹם הֲרֵי הוּא כְּעוֹבֵר עַל מִצְוַת מֶלֶךְ יִתְעַלֶּה, וְכַמָּה שְׁלוּחִים יֵשׁ לַמֶּלֶךְ יִתְעַלֶּה לִטֹּל נִקְמָתוֹ מִמֶּנּוּ.

[שֶׁלֹּא לַעֲשׂוֹת צוּרוֹת אֲפִלּוּ לְנוֹי]

לט שֶׁלֹּא לַעֲשׂוֹת צוּרַת אָדָם מִשּׁוּם דָּבָר, הֵן מִמַּתָּכוֹת הֵן מֵעֵץ וָאֶבֶן וְזוּלָתָם, וַאֲפִלּוּ לְנוֹי, שֶׁנֶּאֱמַר "לֹא תַעֲשׂוּן אִתִּי", וְדָרְשׁוּ זִכְרוֹנָם לִבְרָכָה לֹא תַעֲשׂוּן אוֹתִי, כְּלוֹמַר לֹא תַעֲשׂוּן דִּמְיוֹן אוֹתָהּ צוּרָה דְּהַיְנוּ גּוּף אָדָם שֶׁפְּתַחְתִּי עָלֶיהָ בְּתוֹרָתִי: נַעֲשֶׂה אָדָם בְּצַלְמֵנוּ.

וְהַכַּוָּנָה בַּכָּתוּב מִצַּד הַשֵּׂכֶל שֶׁנִּתַּן בּוֹ. וּמַה שֶּׁנֶּאֱמַר בְּצַלְמֵנוּ עַל חֵלֶק הַשֵּׂכֶל שֶׁבָּאָדָם, מִפְּנֵי שֶׁהַשֵּׂכֶל כֻּלּוֹ הוּא בָּרוּךְ הוּא, אֲבָל אֵין שׁוּם דִּמְיוֹן אַחֵר בֵּינוֹ בָּרוּךְ הוּא וּבֵין שׁוּם בְּרִיָּה בִּבְרִיַּת מִבְּרוּאָיו חָלִילָה.

וְלָאו דְּלֹא תַעֲשֶׂה לְךָ פֶסֶל, שֶׁקָּדַם עִנְיָנוֹ, שֶׁלֹּא נַעֲשָׂה שׁוּם צוּרָה שֶׁתִּעָבֵד, וְזֶה הַלָּאו מְיֻחָד לְצוּרַת אָדָם שֶׁלֹּא נַעֲשָׂה אוֹתוֹ כְּלָל אֲפִלּוּ לְנוֹי, וְזֶה לְהַרְחִיק עֲבוֹדָה זָרָה.

דִּינֵי הַמִּצְוָה, כְּגוֹן הָעוֹשֶׂה צוּרַת אָדָם חֲסַר אֵבֶר אֶחָד אוֹ יוֹתֵר מַה דִּינוֹ, וְיֶתֶר פְּרָטֶיהָ, מְבֹאָרִים בְּפֶרֶק שְׁלִישִׁי מֵעֲבוֹדָה זָרָה. וּבְמַסֶּכֶת סַנְהֶדְרִין אָמְרוּ זִכְרוֹנָם לִבְרָכָה שֶׁהַלָּאו הַזֶּה הוּא כּוֹלֵל עִנְיָנִים אֲחֵרִים. אָמְנָם עִקַּר הַלָּאו בַּמֶּה שֶׁזְּכַרְנוּ, וְכֵן אָמְרוּ בַּמְּכִילְתָּא.

---

4. See *Shulḥan 'Aruch Hoshen Mishpat*, §359 end.
5. Cf. Rambam *ibid*. 9, and comment of Rabad.

§39
1. TB Rosh haShanah 24b.
2. Cf. Rambam, *Guide* I 1: "and because of this intellectual perception, it was said of him, *in the image of God He created him*" (Genesis 1:27).
3. E.g. a ban against appointing judges "through the power of silver and gold"—because money is paid for the appointments (TB Sanhedrin 7b); against making images of angels, sun, moon, stars, etc. (TB 'Avodah Zarah 43b).
4. Mechilta, *bahodesh* 10 beginning, view of R. Nathan (see *Torah Shelemah*, Exodus 20, §495 and note—where "499" should be "497").

⟨192⟩

The laws of the precept—how to keep far away from this evil quality—are explained in various scattered places in the Talmud, and in the Midrashim.[4] It applies in every place, at every time, for both man and woman. If someone transgressed it and coveted [something], even if he did some deed about it he does not incur a whipping (lashes). For you see, even if he took it by force, [the matter] is given to [rectification by his] returning it.[5] Nonetheless, he is as one who violates a command of the sovereign King; and the King has many messengers to exact His revenge from him.

[TO MAKE NO SCULPTURED HUMAN IMAGES, EVEN FOR ORNAMENTATION]

39 not to make a human figure out of anything, be it of metals, of wood, or anything else—even for [mere] ornamentation; for it is stated, *You shall not make 'itti, with Me* (Exodus 20:20), and our Sages of blessed memory interpreted it[1] as *You shall not make 'othi, Me*—meaning that "you are not to make anything resembling that form, i.e. the human figure, about which I wrote in My Torah, *Let us make man in our image*" (Genesis 1:26).

Actually, the meaning of the verse [in Genesis] is in regard to the intelligence given him [man]; the words "in our image" refer to the intelligent, mental part of man: for intelligence is entirely His [attribute].[2] But there is no other resemblance whatever between Him, blessed is He, and any created being whatever (perish the thought).

The negative precept, *You shall not make yourself a graven image* (Exodus 20:4), which was given before (§27), [means] that we should not make any image which will be worshipped; while this prohibition is specifically about the human form, that we should not make it at all, even for beauty (ornamentation)—this in order to keep idolatry well away.

The laws of the precept, such as: if someone makes a human figure lacking one limb or more—what the law is for him—and its other details, are explained in the third chapter of the Talmud tractate *'Avodah Zarah* (43a). In the tractate *Sanhedrin* (7b) our Sages of blessed memory taught that this negative precept includes other matters;[3] however, the principal intent of the prohibition is what we have mentioned; and so is it stated in the Midrash *Mechilta* (Exodus 20:20).[4]

It remains in force in every place and every time, for both man and

§39–40: BANS ON SCULPTURED HUMAN IMAGE & HEWN-STONE ALTAR

וְנוֹהֶגֶת בְּכָל מָקוֹם וּבְכָל זְמַן בִּזְכָרִים וּנְקֵבוֹת. וְעוֹבֵר עָלֶיהָ וְעָשָׂה צוּרַת אָדָם אֲפִלּוּ לְנוֹי עָבַר עַל מִצְוַת מֶלֶךְ כְּלוֹמַר וְאֵין בָּהּ חִיּוּב מַלְקוֹת.

[שֶׁלֹּא לִבְנוֹת אַבְנֵי מִזְבֵּחַ גָּזִית]

מ שֶׁלֹּא נִבְנֶה מִזְבֵּחַ מֵאֲבָנִים שֶׁיִּגַּע בָּהֶן בַּרְזֶל, שֶׁנֶּאֱמַר "לֹא תִבְנֶה אֶתְהֶן גָּזִית", פֵּרוּשׁ גָּזִית הוּא כְּשֶׁפּוֹסְלִין מִן הָאֶבֶן בִּכְלִי בַּרְזֶל. וְאִם נִבְנָה בְּאַבְנֵי גָזִית פָּסוּל.

מִשָּׁרְשֵׁי מִצְוָה זוֹ שֶׁנִּקְבַּע בְּנַפְשׁוֹתֵינוּ מִיּוֹם עֲשׂוֹתוֹ שֶׁבְּסִבָּתוֹ תָּבוֹא לָנוּ מְחִילַת הֶעָוֹן וְהַבְּרָכָה וְהַשָּׁלוֹם אַחֲרֵי כֵן, וְעַל כֵּן זֶה לְזִכָּרוֹן הַדָּבָר נִצְטַוֵּינוּ שֶׁלֹּא לַעֲשׂוֹת בּוֹ דָּבָר כְּלָל בְּכֵלִים הַמּוּכָנִים לְהַשְׁחָתָה, וְזֶהוּ הַבַּרְזֶל שֶׁדַּרְכּוֹ תָּמִיד וּמוּכָן לִשְׁפֹּךְ דָּם. וּכְבָר הִקְדַּמְתִּי לְךָ בִּתְחִלָּה כִּי הָאָדָם נִפְעָל כְּפִי פְּעֻלּוֹתָיו וּמַחְשְׁבוֹתָיו וְהוֹלְכוֹת לְעוֹלָם אַחֲרֵי מַעֲשָׂיו, עַל־כֵּן רָאוּי לָנוּ לַעֲשׂוֹת הַפְּעֻלּוֹת כְּפִי כַוָּנַת הַדְּבָרִים. וְהַסָּכָל הַמַּהְבִּיל הַשּׁוֹמֵעַ דְּבָרִים אֵלֶּה לֹא יֵדַע וְלֹא יָבִין.

דִּינֵי הַמִּצְוָה, כְּגוֹן מֵהֵיכָן הָיוּ מְבִיאִין אוֹתָן הָאֲבָנִים שֶׁבּוֹנִין בָּהֶן הַמִּזְבֵּחַ, שֶׁאָמְרוּ זִכְרוֹנָם לִבְרָכָה כִּי מִן בְּתוּלַת קַרְקַע אוֹ מִן הַיָּם הַגָּדוֹל הָיוּ מְבִיאִין אוֹתָן, וְדִין אִם נָגַע בַּרְזֶל בְּאֶבֶן אַחַר שֶׁנִּבְנֵית בַּמִּזְבֵּחַ אִם פּוֹסֶלֶת הַכֹּל אוֹ הִיא לְבַדָּהּ פְּסוּלָה, וּמַה שֶּׁאָמְרוּ זִכְרוֹנָם לִבְרָכָה כְּשֶׁמְּלַבְּנִין אֶת הַמִּזְבֵּחַ פַּעֲמַיִם בְּשָׁנָה שֶׁלֹּא יְלַבְּנוּהוּ בִּכְלִי שֶׁיְּהֵא בּוֹ בַּרְזֶל כְּדֵי שֶׁלֹּא יִגַּע הַבַּרְזֶל בָּאֶבֶן, וְיֶתֶר פְּרָטֶיהָ, מְבֹאָרִים בְּמַסֶּכֶת מִדּוֹת.

וְנוֹהֶגֶת בִּזְמַן הַבַּיִת בִּזְכָרִים וּנְקֵבוֹת. וְהָעוֹבֵר עָלֶיהָ וּבָנָה אֶבֶן שֶׁנָּגַע בָּהּ בַּרְזֶל בַּמִּזְבֵּחַ אוֹ בַּכֶּבֶשׁ לוֹקֶה.

---

5. Evidently because our author holds it to be an omnibus (composite) negative precept, applying also to other matters than its own text—since he mentioned "other matters" in the previous paragraph; and the rule is that for violating such a precept, whiplashes are not given. Rambam differs, though (MT *hilchoth 'avodah zarah* iii 10).

§40   1. So Mechilta, *bahodesh* 11, and Ramban on the verse.
2. So Mechilta *ibid.*: The altar was created to lengthen a man's life, and iron was created to shorten a man's life. It is not permitted to lift the "shortener" over the "lengthener."
3. Mishnah, Middoth iii 4; TB Z'vaḥim 54a.
4. Mishnah *ibid.*

woman. If someone transgresses it and makes a human figure, even for beauty (ornamentation), he violates the commandment of the King, although there is no penalty of whiplashes for it.[5]

40 [NOT TO BUILD AN ALTAR OF HEWN STONES]

that we should not build an altar of stones which have been touched by [any instrument of] metal—for it is stated, *you shall not build it* gazith (Exodus 20:22), the term *gazith* applying when [blocks] of stone are hewn by a metal tool.[1] And if it was built of hewn stones, it is unfit for use.

At the root of this precept lies the purpose that we should set firmly in our minds from the day it [the altar] is made, that because of it we will be granted forgiveness of iniquity, and afterward blessing and peace. Therefore, that this point should be remembered, we were charged not to fashion anything at all of it with instruments that were prepared for destruction, i.e. iron which cuts and is always ready to shed blood.[2] I already informed you earlier (§16) that a man is acted upon and influenced according to his actions and thoughts, which always follow his deeds. It is therefore fitting to have the connotations of our acts accord with their original intention. If a fool, however, will grope in confusion over these words, he will neither realize nor understand [this].

The laws of the precept are, for instance: from where they would bring those stones of which the altar was built; for the Sages of blessed memory said that out of virgin (unworked) earth or out of the great sea they would be brought.[3] Then there is the law if iron touched a stone after it was built into the altar: if it makes all [the stones] unacceptable, or it alone becomes unfit.[4] There is, further, what the Sages of blessed memory said: When the altar is whitened [with whitewash] twice a year, it should not be whitened with an instrument containing iron, so that the iron should not touch a stone.[4] [These] and its further details are explained in the Talmud tractate *Middoth*.

It applies at the time the Holy Temple is extant, for both man and woman. If someone transgressed it and built a stone which iron had touched into the altar, or into the ramp, he would receive whiplashes.

§41–42: NO STEPS UP TO ALTAR / ON THE HEBREW BONDSERVANT

[שֶׁלֹּא לִפְסֹעַ עַל הַמִּזְבֵּחַ]

מא שֶׁלֹּא לַעֲלוֹת עַל הַמִּזְבֵּחַ בְּמַדְרֵגוֹת כְּדֵי שֶׁלֹּא יַעֲשֶׂה פְּסִיעוֹת גַּסּוֹת בַּעֲלוֹתוֹ, שֶׁנֶּאֱמַר: וְלֹא תַעֲלֶה בְמַעֲלֹת עַל מִזְבְּחִי אֲשֶׁר לֹא תִגָּלֶה עֶרְוָתְךָ עָלָיו; אֶלָּא כְּשֶׁהוּא עוֹלֶה שָׁם מְהַלֵּךְ בְּנַחַת וּבְיִרְאָה, עָקֵב בְּצַד גּוּדָל, וְכֵן נֶאֱמַר בַּמְּכִילְתָּא.

מִשָּׁרְשֵׁי מִצְוָה זוֹ מַה שֶּׁכָּתַבְנוּ בַּמִּצְוָה הַקּוֹדֶמֶת לָהּ לִקְבֹּעַ בְּנַפְשׁוֹתֵינוּ יִרְאַת הַמָּקוֹם וַחֲשִׁיבוּתוֹ, וְעַל כֵּן הִזְהִירָנוּ שֶׁלֹּא לִנְהֹג שָׁם קַלּוּת רֹאשׁ בְּשׁוּם עִנְיָן. וְהַכֹּל יוֹדְעִין שֶׁהָאֲבָנִים לֹא יַקְפִּידוּ בְּשׁוּם בִּזָּיוֹן, שֶׁאֵינָן רוֹאוֹת וְלֹא שׁוֹמְעוֹת, אֶלָּא כָּל הָעִנְיָן לָתֵת צִיּוּר בְּלִבֵּנוּ בְּיִרְאַת הַמָּקוֹם וַחֲשִׁיבוּתוֹ וּכְבוֹדוֹ הַגָּדוֹל, כִּי מִתּוֹךְ הַפְּעֻלָּה הַלֵּב נִפְעָל, כְּמוֹ שֶׁכָּתַבְתִּי.

דִּינֵי הַמִּצְוָה, כֵּיצַד עוֹשִׂין הַכֶּבֶשׁ כְּדֵי שֶׁלֹּא יָבוֹאוּ לַעֲבֹר עָלָיו בְּלָאו זֶה, וְצוּרָתוֹ וְכָל עִנְיָנוֹ, מְבֹאָרִים בְּפֶרֶק שְׁלֹשָׁה מִדּוֹת. וְנוֹהֶגֶת בִּזְמַן הַבַּיִת בִּזְכָרִים וּנְקֵבוֹת. וְהָעוֹבֵר עָלֶיהָ וּפָסַע פְּסִיעָה גַּסָּה עַל הַמִּזְבֵּחַ עַד שֶׁנִּגְלָה עֶרְוָתוֹ בְּמֵזִיד לוֹקֶה, וַעֲנָוִים יִשְׁכְּנוּ אָרֶץ.

וְאֵלֶּה הַמִּשְׁפָּטִים

יֵשׁ בָּהּ עֶשְׂרִים וְשָׁלֹשׁ מִצְוֹת עֲשֵׂה וּשְׁלֹשִׁים מִצְוֹת לֹא תַעֲשֶׂה

[מִצְוַת דִּין עֶבֶד עִבְרִי]

מב לָדוּן בְּדִין עֶבֶד עִבְרִי כְּמוֹ שֶׁכָּתוּב בַּפָּרָשָׁה, שֶׁנֶּאֱמַר, "כִּי תִקְנֶה עֶבֶד עִבְרִי" וְגוֹמֵר, כְּלוֹמַר שֶׁנַּעֲשֶׂה לוֹ הַדְּבָרִים שֶׁנִּצְטַוֵּינוּ בָּהֶן, כְּגוֹן לְשַׁלְּחוֹ בַּשְּׁבִיעִית, אוֹ בְּתוֹךְ שֵׁשׁ אִם פָּגַע בּוֹ יוֹבֵל, אוֹ בְּגֵרָעוֹן כֶּסֶף, אוֹ בְּמִיתַת אָדוֹן שֶׁלֹּא הִנִּיחַ בֵּן

---

41 1. So Rambam ShM negative precept §80. On the root reason which follows, cf. Ramban on Exodus 21:23.

2. See Rambam MT *hilchoth béth ha-b'hirah* ii 13.

3. The law is the same even if trousers were worn (Mechilta, Exodus 20:23) since long strides are in any case seriously irreverent at the altar.

4. I.e. in contrast to those who might show arrogance by violating this precept. The expression echoes Psalms 37:11, 29.

42 1. Exodus 21:2.

2. I.e. from the sum which the owner paid for six years of the servant's labor (that being his maximum period of servitude); the amount the servant has earned by his labor is deducted, and the remainder, for the unfinished part of the six years, is refunded the owner. Thus, if he acquires money for the refund, the servant can leave before the six years are ended; TB Kiddushin 14b (Mishnah, i 2).

3. *Ibid.* 17a.

SIDRAH YITHRO

41 [NOT TO STRIDE BY STEPS TO THE ALTAR]
not to go up to the level of the altar by stairs, so that big, wide steps should not be taken in going up—as it is stated, *And you shall not go up by stairs to My altar, that your nakedness be not exposed on it* (Exodus 20:23). Instead, when one goes up there, he is to walk in tranquillity and reverent awe, heel next to toe; and thus is it stated in the Midrash *Mechilta* (*baḥodesh* 11).[1]

At the root of this *mitzvah* lies the purpose we have written about the precept before this: to set firmly in our minds a reverent awe for the place and its [supreme] eminence. Therefore were we adjured to behave there with no levity whatever, of any kind. Now, all know that the stones will not mind or object to any shaming insult; they neither see nor hear. The whole matter, then is rather to implant a conception in our heart of reverent awe for the location, its eminence and its supreme majesty. For out of one's action is the heart acted upon, as I have written (§16).

The laws of the precept—how the ramp was to be made so that none should be led to violating this prohibition;[2] its proper form; and its entire subject matter—are explained in chapter 3 of the tractate *Middoth*. It is in effect when the Holy Temple is extant, for both man and woman. If one transgressed it and trod with big, wide steps up to the level of the altar until his nakedness was exposed[3]—if it was deliberately done, he is given whiplashes. And the humble will dwell in the land.[4]

sidrah mishpatim
(Exodus 21–24)

It contains twenty-three positive and thirty negative precepts.

42 [THE LAW OF THE HEBREW BONDSERVANT]
to carry out the law of a Hebrew slave as it is written in the *sidrah* —for it is stated, *When you buy a Hebrew servant* (Exodus 21:2). This means that we should do for him all the things about which we were commanded: for example, to send him free in the seventh year [of his servitude],[1] or within the six years [of servitude] if the jubilee year occurred during the period, or by deducting money,[2] or through the death of an owner who did not leave a son [to inherit];[3] and to treat the servant with the bored earlobe (Exodus 21:6) also according to

§42–43 : ON THE HEBREW BONDSERVANT AND MAIDSERVANT

זָכָר, וְלִנְרְצָע גַּם־כֵּן כְּדִינוֹ הַכָּתוּב בּוֹ, הַכֹּל כְּמוֹ שֶׁלִּמְּדוּנוּ רַבּוֹתֵינוּ זִכְרוֹנָם לִבְרָכָה מִתּוֹךְ הַכָּתוּב, כְּמוֹ שֶׁמְּפֹרָשׁ בְּפֶרֶק רִאשׁוֹן מִקִּדּוּשִׁין.

מִשָּׁרְשֵׁי מִצְוָה זוֹ שֶׁרָצָה הָאֵל שֶׁיִּהְיֶה עַמּוֹ יִשְׂרָאֵל אֲשֶׁר בָּחַר בּוֹ עַם קָדוֹשׁ מָלֵא וּמְעֻטָּר בְּכָל מִדּוֹת טוֹבוֹת וּמְעֻלּוֹת, כִּי מִתּוֹךְ כָּךְ תָּחוּל הַבְּרָכָה עֲלֵיהֶם, וְהַחֶסֶד וְהָרַחֲמִים מִן הַמִּדּוֹת הַמְשֻׁבָּחוֹת שֶׁבָּעוֹלָם. וְעַל כֵּן הִזְהִירָנוּ לָרַחֵם עַל אֲשֶׁר הוּא תַחַת יָדֵינוּ וְלִגְמֹל לוֹ חֶסֶד, כַּאֲשֶׁר כָּתוּב בַּפָּרָשָׁה, וּכְמוֹ שֶׁיָּדַעְנוּ גַּם כֵּן בְּקַבָּלָה.

דִּינֵי הַמִּצְוָה, כְּגוֹן הַחִלּוּקִין שֶׁבֵּין מוֹכֵר עַצְמוֹ לִמְכָרוּהוּ בֵּית דִּין, וְהַדְּבָרִים שֶׁהוּא נִקְנֶה בָהֶם, וְשֶׁהוּא יוֹצֵא בָהֶן לְחֵרוּת, וּשְׁאָר דִּינָיו, מְבֹאָרִים שָׁם בְּקִדּוּשִׁין.

וְנוֹהֶגֶת מִצְוָה זוֹ בִּזְכָרִים אֲבָל לֹא בִנְקֵבוֹת, שֶׁאֵין הָאִשָּׁה קוֹנָה עֶבֶד עִבְרִי. וְדַוְקָא בִּזְמַן שֶׁיִּשְׂרָאֵל שְׁרוּיִין עַל אַדְמָתָן, שֶׁכֵּן בָּא הַפֵּרוּשׁ הַמְקֻבָּל שֶׁאֵין עֶבֶד עִבְרִי נוֹהֵג אֶלָּא בִּזְמַן שֶׁהַיּוֹבֵל נוֹהֵג, וּמְפֹרָשׁ הוּא שֶׁדִּין הַיּוֹבֵל אֵינוֹ אֶלָּא בָאָרֶץ.

וְעוֹבֵר עָלֶיהָ וְלֹא עָשָׂה לְעֶבֶד מַה שֶּׁכָּתוּב בּוֹ בִּטֵּל עֲשֵׂה, וְגַם מְלַמֵּד נַפְשׁוֹ לִהְיוֹת אַכְזָרִי, וְכִמְעַט שֶׁמֵּעִיד עַל עַצְמוֹ שֶׁאֵינוֹ מִבְּנֵי יִשְׂרָאֵל, כִּי הֵם רַחֲמָנִים בְּנֵי רַחֲמָנִים.

[מִצְוַת יִעוּד שֶׁל אָמָה עִבְרִיָּה]

מג לְיַעֵד אָמָה הָעִבְרִיָּה, כְּלוֹמַר שֶׁאוֹמְרוֹ לוֹמַר שֶׁיִּשְׂרָאֵל שֶׁקָּנָה אָמָה הָעִבְרִיָּה שֶׁיִּשָּׂאֶנָּה לוֹ לְאִשָּׁה אוֹ יִתְּנֶנָּה לִבְנוֹ לְאִשָּׁה, שֶׁנֶּאֱמַר "אִם רָעָה בְּעֵינֵי אֲדֹנֶיהָ אֲשֶׁר לוֹ יְעָדָהּ וְהֶפְדָּהּ", וְאָמְרוּ זִכְרוֹנָם לִבְרָכָה כָּאן רֶמֶז לְךָ שֶׁמִּצְוָה בְּיִעוּד, וּבְפֵרוּשׁ אָמְרוּ זִכְרוֹנָם לִבְרָכָה מִצְוַת יִעוּד קוֹדֶמֶת לְמִצְוַת פְּדִיָּה.

מִשָּׁרְשֵׁי מִצְוָה זוֹ שֶׁרִחֵם הָאֵל עַל הָעֲנִיָּה הַנִּמְכֶּרֶת וְעַל אָבִיהָ שֶׁנִּצְטָרֵךְ

---

4. Mishnah, Kiddushin i 2.

5. Sifra on Leviticus 25:40: "Let him [the Hebrew servant] be with you"— [equally] with you in regard to food, drink and bedding: that you should not eat refined bread and he coarse bread, you drink aged wine and he new wine; you sleep on soft cloth and he on straw. Similarly TB Kiddushin 20a.

6. TB Kiddushin 14b (Rambam MT *hilchoth 'avadim* iii 12).

7. Ibid. 14b, 16a, 17a.

8. So TB Bava M'tzi'a 71a.

9. TB 'Arachin 29a.

10. Ibid. 32b and Kiddushin 38b (see also below, §330).

11. So TB Yevamoth 79a and Bétzah 32b, that compassion is one of the identifying characteristics of Jewry.

1. So Rashi on the verse; for the language of Scripture implies that by her purchase she was already designated to become her master's wife, and he was expected to marry her. That he might give her to his son in marriage derives from verse 9.

2. Mishnah, B'choroth i 7 (TB 13a).

his law,[4] that is written [in the Torah] for him—all as our Sages of blessed memory taught us out of Scripture, as it is explained in the first chapter of the tractate *Kiddushin*.

At the root of this precept lies the reason that God wished His people Israel, whom He chose, to be a holy people filled and adorned with every good and noble quality; for as a result, blessing will be bestowed upon them. And kindness and mercy are among the most worthy qualities in the world. For this reason we were adjured to have mercy on someone who is under our ownership, and to treat him with kindness—as it is written in the *sidrah*, and as we know further by the Oral Tradition.[5]

As to the laws of the precept—such as the differences [in law] between one who sells himself [into servitude] and one who is sold by the *beth din*;[6] the ways by which he is bought [to become bound to his owner], and by which he goes free;[7] and its other laws—[these] are explained there, in the tractate *Kiddushin*.

This precept applies to a man, but not to a woman—for a woman may not buy a Hebrew servant[8]—and this only when the Israelites dwell in their land: for the traditional explanation is given that the law of the Hebrew servant is in force only at the time when the law of the jubilee year is observed;[9] and it was made quite explicit that the law of the jubilee is observed only in the Land.[10]

If someone violated it and did not treat a servant as it is written concerning him, he would thus disobey a positive precept and teach himself to be cruel, and would practically attest about himself that he is not a Jew, for they are the compassionate sons of compassionate fathers.[11]

43 [MARITAL DESIGNATION OF THE HEBREW MAIDSERVANT]

to designate a Hebrew maidservant for betrothal, i.e. that the very Israelite who purchases a Hebrew maidservant should take her for a wife or give her to his son for a wife—as it is stated, *If she does not please her master, who has designated her for himself, then he shall let her be redeemed* (Exodus 21:8); and our Sages of blessed memory noted[1] that here you have a hint that there is a *mitzvah* of designating [her] for betrothal; moreover, they (of blessed memory) said explicitly:[2] the *mitzvah* of designation for betrothal takes precedence over [is preferable to] the precept of redemption (§44).

At the root of this precept lies the reason that God had compassion

§43–44: LAWS OF THE HEBREW MAIDSERVANT ספר החינוך

לְמָכְרָהּ, וְצִוָּה הַקּוֹנֶה אוֹתָהּ לִשָּׂא אוֹתָהּ לְאִשָּׁה וְלַעֲשׂוֹתָהּ גְּבֶרֶת, כִּי אֵל חַנּוּן וְרַחוּם הוּא. וְאִם אֵין הַקּוֹנֶה חָפֵץ בָּהּ לְעַצְמוֹ שֶׁיַּשִּׂיאֶנָּה לִבְנוֹ, כִּי גַם עִם בֶּן אֲדוֹנֶיהָ תִּשְׂמַח וְתָגֵל, אוֹ שֶׁיִּגְרַע מִפִּדְיוֹנָהּ מִכָּל מָקוֹם וִיסַיְּעֶנָּה שֶׁתֵּצֵא מֵעַבְדוּת, וְלֹא שֶׁיִּגְרְמוּ עַל כָּל פָּנִים שֶׁתַּעֲמֹד תַּחַת יָדוֹ עַד זְמַן הַמֶּכֶר גַּם אִם יָשְׁרָה בְּעֵינָיו עֲבוֹדָתָהּ הַרְבֵּה. וְכָל זֶה מֵחַסְדֵי הָאֵל עַל בְּרוּאָיו וּמִמִּדּוֹתָיו הַמְעֻלּוֹת.

דִּינֵי הַמִּצְוָה, כְּגוֹן עַד מָתַי הַבַּת נִמְכֶּרֶת, וְשֶׁאֵינָהּ נִמְכֶּרֶת עַל יְדֵי אָדוֹן, כְּלוֹמַר דַּאֲפִלּוּ עָבַר וּמְכָרָהּ אֵין הַמְּכִירָה כְלוּם, וְשֶׁהָאָב יָכוֹל לְמָכְרָהּ כַּמָּה פְעָמִים, וְהַדְּבָרִים שֶׁהִיא נִקְנֵית בָּהֶן וְשֶׁהִיא יוֹצֵאת בָּהֶן לְחֵרוּת, וּבְכַמָּה יְצִיאוֹת הִיא יְתֵרָה עַל הָעֶבֶד, וְדִינֵי הַבּוֹגֶרֶת, וּזְמַן הָאַיְלוֹנִית, וְיֶתֶר פְּרָטֶיהָ, מְבֹאָרִים בָּרִאשׁוֹן שֶׁל קִדּוּשִׁין.

וְנוֹהֶגֶת בִּזְמַן שֶׁהַיּוֹבֵל נוֹהֵג דַּוְקָא. וְהָעוֹבֵר עַל זֶה, וְלֹא יְעָדָהּ לֹא לוֹ וְלֹא לִבְנוֹ וְלֹא סִיַּע בְּפִדְיוֹנָהּ לֹא קִיֵּם מִצְוָה זוֹ, אֲבָל אֵין לְכָפוֹ לְפִי הַדּוֹמֶה עַל קִיּוּם מִצְוָה זוֹ, שֶׁהֲרֵי כָּתוּב שָׁם בְּפֵרוּשׁ "וְאִם שְׁלָשׁ אֵלֶּה לֹא יַעֲשֶׂה לָהּ", מִכְּלָל שֶׁהַתּוֹרָה הִנִּיחָה הַדָּבָר בִּרְצוֹנוֹ. וּמִכָּל מָקוֹם אִם עָשָׂה כֵן קִיֵּם מִצְוָה וְעָשָׂה כָּרָאוּי, וְתָבוֹא עָלָיו בְּרָכָה, וּבָנִים טוֹבִים וּכְשֵׁרִים רְאוּיִים לָצֵאת מִזִּוּוּגָם.

[מִצְוַת פִּדְיוֹן אָמָה הָעִבְרִיָּה]

מד לִפְדּוֹת אָמָה הָעִבְרִיָּה שֶׁנֶּאֱמַר "וְהֶפְדָּהּ", וְזוֹ מִצְוַת עֲשֵׂה, כְּלוֹמַר שֶׁיְּסַיַּע הָאָדוֹן הַקּוֹנֶה אוֹתָהּ בְּפִדְיוֹנָהּ וְיִתֵּן לָהּ מָקוֹם לָשׁוּב לְבֵית אָבִיהָ, כְּמוֹ שֶׁאָמְרוּ זִכְרוֹנָם לִבְרָכָה שֶׁמְּגָרַע פִּדְיוֹנָהּ וְתֵצֵא, כְּלוֹמַר שֶׁאִם לְקָחָהּ בְּשִׁשִּׁים דִּינָרִים לְשֵׁשׁ שָׁנִים וַעֲבָדָהּ שָׁלֹשׁ וְקִבְּצָה שְׁלֹשִׁים דִּינָרִים שֶׁיִּקָּחֵם וִישַׁלְּחֶנָּה, וְלֹא יִטְעֹן עָלֶיהָ

---

3. Our author echoes here Rambam MT *hilchoth 'avadim* iv 2: A father is not permitted to sell his daughter [into servitude] unless he is poor and nothing is left him, neither land nor movable goods, nor even the clothing that covers him.

4. See §44.

5. TB K'thuboth 40b.

6. MdRSbY (Rambam MT *hilchoth 'avadim* iv 10); see also *Torah Shelemah*, Exodus 21, §184 and note.

7. TB Kiddushin 18a.

8. Mishnah, Kiddushin i 2; TB 14b, 16a.

9. Mishnah *ibid*. TB 17b.

10. I.e. at the age of twelve years and six months; TB Kiddushin 4a, etc.

11. *Ibid*.

12. I.e. when conditions are such that the jubilee year can be observed at its proper time; TB Gittin 65a.

1. TB Kiddushin 14b.

⟨200⟩

on the poor girl who was sold, and on her father who was compelled to sell her.³ So He commanded the one who purchased her to take her for a wife and to make her a mistress [in his home]: for He is a gracious and compassionate God. And if the purchaser does not desire her for himself, he is to marry her to his son: for with her master's son she will equally be happy and rejoice. Or else he is to deduct from her redemption price at least,⁴ and help her that she should go free of servitude; and he should not, at any rate, make her remain under his ownership until the [end of the full] period of the purchase, even if he finds her work very gratifying. All this derives from the loving-kindness of God for His creatures, and from His exalted noble qualities.

The laws of the precept are, for instance: till when [what age] a daughter may be sold;⁵ that she may not be sold [resold] by the master: which means that even if he acted wrongly and sold her, the sale amounts to nothing;⁶ that the father may sell her several times;⁷ the ways that make her purchase take effect;⁸ and [the ways] by which she can go free;⁸ how many more ways she has of going free than a Hebrew manservant;⁹ the laws of a *bogereth*, a girl who has come of age;¹⁰ and the time [when] a barren girl [may be sold].¹¹ [These] and further details are clarified in the first chapter of the Talmud tractate *Kiddushin*.

It is in effect only at the time that the jubilee year is in effect.¹² If someone transgresses it and designates her for betrothal neither to himself nor to his son, nor does he help achieve her redemption, then he has not observed this precept. Seemingly, however, he is not to be coerced to fulfill this precept: for here Scripture has phrased it explicitly, *And if he does not do these three things for her* (Exodus 21:11); hence the Torah has left the matter to his own free will. Nevertheless, if he did so, he has fulfilled a *mitzvah* and acted worthily; blessing shall come upon him; and good and worthy sons are due to issue from their marriage.

[THE REDEMPTION OF THE HEBREW MAIDSERVANT]

44 to redeem a Hebrew maidservant—as it is stated, *then he shall let her be redeemed* (Exodus 21:8). This is a positive precept, i.e. that the master who purchased her should assist in her redemption and give her a chance to return to her father's home. As our Sages of blessed memory said,¹ he reduces her redemption price and she goes free: i.e. if he acquired her for sixty dinars for a period of six years, and she worked three years and saved up thirty dinars, that he should take them and

⟨201⟩

שֶׁתַּשְׁלִים שְׁנוֹת עֲבוֹדָתָהּ עַל כָּל פָּנִים, אוֹ שֶׁיֹּאמַר "מְעוֹתַי הָיוּ בְטֵלוֹת אֶצְלָהּ,
תּוֹסִיף לִי רֶוַח אִם תִּרְצֶה לָצֵאת", שֶׁאֵין זֶה כִּי אִם רֹעַ לֵב, וְלִבְנֵי יִשְׂרָאֵל שֶׁהֵם
בְּנֵי מְלָכִים, רַחְמָנִים בְּנֵי רַחְמָנִים, רָאוּי לָהֶם לַעֲשׂוֹת חֶסֶד עִם הַבְּרִיּוֹת, אַף כִּי
לַאֲשֶׁר עֲבָדוּם, וַאֲפִלּוּ יוֹם אֶחָד.

מִשָּׁרְשֵׁי הַמִּצְוָה מַה שֶּׁכָּתַבְנוּ בְיִעוּד, וּפְרָטֶיהָ גַּם כֵּן שָׁם בְּקִדּוּשִׁין.

[שֶׁלֹּא יִמְכֹּר אָמָה עִבְרִיָּה הַקּוֹנֶה אוֹתָהּ מִיַּד הָאָב]

מה שֶׁכָּל מִי שֶׁיִּקְנֶה אָמָה עִבְרִיָּה לֹא יִמְכְּרֶנָּה לְאָדָם אַחֵר לְעוֹלָם, שֶׁנֶּאֱמַר:
לְעַם נָכְרִי לֹא יִמְשֹׁל לְמָכְרָהּ בְּבִגְדוֹ בָהּ. וּפֵרוּשׁוֹ כְּתַרְגּוּמוֹ, לִגְבַר אָחֳרָן, וּלְהַרְחִיק
הַדָּבָר נֶאֱמַר בְּלָשׁוֹן זֶה, כְּלוֹמַר שֶׁדּוֹמֶה לַעֲנָיָהּ הַקְּטַנָּה אִם מוּכְרָה לְאָדָם אַחֵר
שֵׁנִית כְּאִלּוּ יִמְכְּרֶנָּה לְעַם נָכְרִי.

מִשָּׁרְשֵׁי הַמִּצְוָה שֶׁרָצָה הָאֵל הָאֵל לְזַכּוֹתֵנוּ, וְצִוָּנוּ לְהִתְנַהֵג בְּמִדַּת הַחֶמְלָה הָאֲהוּבָה
לְפָנָיו.

דִּינֵי הַמִּצְוָה כָּתוּב לְמַעְלָה בְּמִצְוַת יִעוּד.

[שֶׁלֹּא לִגְרֹעַ שְׁאֵר כְּסוּת וְעוֹנָה]

מו שֶׁכָּל קוֹנֶה אָמָה הָעִבְרִיָּה וִיעָדָהּ שֶׁלֹּא יִגְרַע לָהּ שְׁאֵרָהּ כְּסוּתָהּ וְעוֹנָתָהּ.
וּפֵרוּשׁ שְׁאֵר, מָזוֹן, וּכְסוּת כְּמַשְׁמָעוֹ, וְעוֹנָה דֶּרֶךְ אֶרֶץ.

וּבִכְלָל לָאו זֶה כָּל בְּנוֹת יִשְׂרָאֵל גַּם כֵּן, שֶׁלֹּא לִגְרֹעַ לָהֶן דָּבָר מֵאֵלֶּה, וְקַל
וָחֹמֶר הַדְּבָרִים, אִם לָזוֹ לֹא יִגְרַע כָּל שֶׁכֵּן לַאֲחֵרוֹת בְּנוֹת חוֹרִין. וְזֶה שֶׁכָּתוּב

---

2. I.e. the money I paid for her future labor—which she will never give me, as she is going free now—has lain idle all this time (since the day I paid for six years of her labor). I could have invested this amount in something profitable and derived revenue. Alternately, were she to remain in my employment, that too would be profitable, since her labor is worth more to me than the price I paid. Under the present circumstances, her redemption and departure mean a loss of possible profit for me.

1. I.e. it would be the second time she is sold.

1. So TB K'thuboth 47b.

send her away, and he should not demand of her to complete her years of servitude no matter what; nor should he say, "My money remained useless with her;[2] let her add on something as my profit if she wishes to go free." For this is nothing but the heart's evil, and since the Israelites (Jews) are royal princes, compassionate sons of compassionate fathers, it is fitting for them to deal kindly with human beings, even with those who have been their servants even if for but one day.

At the root of the precept lies what we have written about designation for betrothal (§43). Its details are equally [to be found] there, in the tractate *Kiddushin*.

[THE BUYER OF A HEBREW MAIDSERVANT MAY NOT SELL HER]

45 that whoever purchases a Hebrew maidservant is not to sell her to any other man, ever—as it is stated, *he shall have no power to sell her to a foreign people, since he has dealt faithlessly with her* (Exodus 21:8). That means, as Onkelos translates it, "to another man"; but in order to convey the matter in a more emphatic way, this expression was used: In other words, to the poor child, if he sells her to another man, a second time,[1] it seems as if he sells her to a foreign people.

At the root of the precept lies the reason that God wished to make us meritorious, and He commanded us to behave with the quality of compassion, which is beloved before Him.

The laws of the precept were written above, with the *mitzvah* of designation for marriage (§43).

[NOT TO WITHOLD FROM ONE'S WIFE HER RIGHTFUL DUE]

46 that whoever purchases a Hebrew maidservant and accepts her in designation for marriage, is not to leave her short of her [rightful] *sh'ér*, *k'suth* and *'onah*. The meaning of *sh'ér* is food; *k'suth* has its plain meaning, clothing; and *'onah* means conjugal intimacy.[1]

Now, in this negative precept all Israelite (Jewish) daughters are equally included—that none of these things is to be diminished for them. It is a matter we learn by *kal va-ḥomer* (*a fortiori*), reasoning from the lesser to the greater: If for this [Hebrew maidservant] one should not diminish [any of these], how much more so for others, who are free women. This is why it is written, *he shall deal with her* [the maid-

§46–47: A WIFE'S RIGHTFUL DUE / EXECUTION BY STRANGULATION

"כְּמִשְׁפַּט הַבָּנוֹת יַעֲשֶׂה לָּהּ", אָמְרוּ בַּמְּכִילְתָּא שֶׁהוּא בָא לְלַמֵּד וְנִמְצָא לָמֵד, שֶׁהַבָּנוֹת לְמֵדוֹת מִמֶּנָּה.

מִדִּינֵי הַמִּצְוָה, מַה שֶּׁאָמְרוּ זִכְרוֹנָם לִבְרָכָה: הַמַּתְנֶה עִם אִשְׁתּוֹ "עַל מְנָת שֶׁאֵין לָךְ עָלַי שְׁאֵר כְּסוּת וְעוֹנָה" מַה דִּינוֹ, וּמַה שֶּׁאָמְרוּ שֶׁהָאִשָּׁה עוֹלָה עִם הַבַּעַל וְאֵינָהּ יוֹרֶדֶת, וּלְפִיכָךְ מְחַשְּׁבִין מְזוֹנוֹתֶיהָ וּכְסוּתָהּ לְפִי מַעֲלָתוֹ; וְעִנְיַן חִלּוּק הָעוֹנוֹת שֶׁהוּא לְפִי כֹּבֶד אֻמָּנוּת הָאִישׁ, עַד שֶׁאָמְרוּ לְבְרָכָה לְבְרָכָה שֶׁעוֹנַת הַסַּפָּן פַּעֲמַיִם בְּשָׁנָה, וְהַגַּמָּל פַּעַם בְּחֹדֶשׁ, וְתַלְמִיד חָכָם פַּעַם בְּשָׁבוּעַ וְרָאוּי לוֹ שֶׁתְּהֶא לֵיל שַׁבָּת, וְיֶתֶר פְּרָטֶיהָ, מְבֹאָרִים בְּסֵדֶר נָשִׁים בְּפִזּוּר.

וְנוֹהֶגֶת מִצְוָה זוֹ לְעִנְיַן בַּת חוֹרִין בְּכָל מָקוֹם וּבְכָל זְמָן בִּזְכָרִים. וְעוֹבֵר עָלֶיהָ וְגָרַע לְאִשְׁתּוֹ אַחַת מִשָּׁלֹשׁ אֵלֶּה מֵרְצוֹנוֹ עַל צַד שֶׁיְּכַוֵּן לְהַכְאִיבָהּ עָבַר עַל לָאו, וְהוּא כְּעוֹבֵר עַל אַזְהָרַת מֶלֶךְ, אֲבָל אֵין לוֹקִין עַל לָאו זֶה, לְפִי שֶׁאֵין בּוֹ מַעֲשֶׂה.

[מִצְוַת בֵּית דִּין לַהֲרֹג בְּחֶנֶק הַמְחֻיָּב]

מז שֶׁנִּצְטַוֵּינוּ לְהָמִית הָעוֹבְרִים עַל קְצָת מִצְוֹת שֶׁבַּתּוֹרָה בְּחֶנֶק, שֶׁנֶּאֱמַר "מַכֵּה אִישׁ וָמֵת מוֹת יוּמָת", וְזוֹ שֶׁל מַכֵּה אִישׁ אַחַת מֵהֶן שֶׁמִּיתָתוֹ בְחֶנֶק, שֶׁהֲרֵי כָּתוּב בּוֹ מוֹת יוּמָת, וּבְפֵרוּשׁ אָמְרוּ זִכְרוֹנָם לִבְרָכָה כָּל מִיתָה הָאֲמוּרָה בַּתּוֹרָה סְתָם אֵינָהּ אֶלָּא חֶנֶק. (לָמַדְנוּ לְחַיָּבֵי מִיתוֹת שֶׁאֵינָן בְּתַשְׁלוּמִין, שֶׁנֶּאֱמַר "אֵין כֶּסֶף מַכֵּה אִישׁ וָמֵת מוֹת יוּמָת"; מְכִילְתָּא.)

שֹׁרֶשׁ מִצְוָה זוֹ נִגְלֶה לַכֹּל, כִּי מֶלֶךְ בְּמִשְׁפָּט יַעֲמִיד אָרֶץ, שֶׁאִלּוּלֵי יִרְאַת

---

2. I.e. Scripture wishes to teach us about the maidservant, that she is to be treated in marriage like a free woman, but actually we learn from this the proper treatment of the free woman.
3. TB K'thuboth 56a.
4. If his standard of living, etc. was higher than hers.
5. TB K'thuboth 61b.
6. *Ibid.* 62b.
7. Similarly Rambam ShM negative precept §262.
8. See §7, end.

47 1. This seems to contradict our author's statement in §34 (last paragraph) that a murderer is to be executed by the sword (decapitation—the accepted ruling: TB Sanhedrin 76b, 84b; TJ vii 3). MY suggests that §34 refers to a case where the victim died instantly, or at least within twenty-four hours, while here the victim died later of his wounds. This seems difficult, however, as here our author goes on to state that the murderer is given a swift, easy death because he strove to kill his victim as

servant] *after the manner of daughters* (Exodus 21:9). So the Sages said in the Midrash *Mechilta* that this comes to teach us [about another matter] and the result is that we learn about *it*—we learn from this about the daughters [free women].[2]

Among the laws of the precept there is what our Sages of blessed memory said:[3] If a person makes a condition with his wife, "[I marry you] on condition that you have no food, clothing or conjugal rights due from me," what the law is for him. Then there is what they said, that a woman can rise in status with her husband, but not go down; therefore her food and clothing [due her] are reckoned according to his level.[4] There is, too, the subject of the difference in the various times of conjugal due, according to the arduousness of the husband's vocation, in keeping with what our Sages of blessed memory said,[5] that the conjugal frequency due from a sailor is twice a year; a camel driver, once a month; a Torah scholar, once a week, and it is fitting that this be Friday night.[6] [These] and its further details are clarified in the order *Nashim* of the Talmud, where they are scattered.

This precept in regard to a free daughter is in force in every place and every time, for men. If a person transgresses it and leaves his wife short of any of these three deliberately, of his free will, because so he intends to make her suffer,[7] he violates a negative precept. He is as one who violates a warning of the King, but no whipping of lashes is given for it, since it involves no act.[8]

[THE COURT IS TO EXECUTE BY STRANGULATION ANYONE WHO DESERVES IT]

47 that we were commanded to put to death by strangulation those who violate certain precepts of the Torah—for it is stated, *He that strikes a man so that he dies, shall surely be put to death* (Exodus 21:12); and this [precept] about one who strikes a man is one of those for which the punishment of death is by strangulation:[1] For it is written about it, *he shall surely be put to death*, and our Sages said explicitly:[2] Every death sentence which is not specified in the Torah[3] means nothing other than strangulation. [Thus too] we learn that those who incur death are not to have payments imposed on them: for it is stated, *without money. He that strikes a man so that he dies, he shall surely be put to death* (ibid. 11–12);[4] so Midrash *Mechilta* (*n'zikin* 3 end).

The root reason for this precept is obvious to all: for *the King by*

§47: ON EXECUTION BY STRANGULATION WHEN DESERVED

swiftly as possible (without prolonging his death agony). It hardly suggests that the murderer sought to complete his deed swiftly if the victim lingered on for more than twenty-four hours. And at any rate, if the criminal is executed by strangulation (an easier death, as our author states in §50) because he sought to dispatch his victim quickly, why does he deserve this consideration only when the dead man lingered on so long?

From the first Hebrew edition on, a note by an anonymous scholar has been added in many editions that this is simply an oversight by our author. While an error in a word or a phrase might be conceivable, how are we to understand an "oversight" of such length, in which our author explains (in the next paragraph) why the murderer should be thus executed?

Minhath Ḥinnuch would amend "strangulation" (*ḥenek*) to "decapitation" (*hereg*), considering it a copyist's error. But, as R. Menaḥem M. Kasher points out in *Torah Shelemah*, Exodus 21 §240, note, how could our author speak of decapitation and then go on (in the third paragraph) to describe strangulation!

Necessarily our author had a source or basis for this ruling—of which traces apparently exist. Here is a passage in Mechilta as found in our editions, and as given in *Séfer Vehizhir* (I, p. 131, without the editor's emendations):

מכילתא	ספר והזהיר
"מות יומת", בסייף. אתה אומר בסייף. או אינו אלא בחנק, הרי אתה דן: נאמר כאן מות יומת ונאמר להלן בנואף מות יומת (ויקרא כ י), מה להלן בחנק, אף כאן בחנק. אתה מקיש למנאף, אני מקישו למגדף: נאמר כאן מות יומת ונאמר במגדף מות יומת (ויקרא כד טז), מה להלן בסקילה אף כאן בסקילה. ת"ל אתה מקיש למגדף ואני מקישו למנאף. ת"ל שופך דם האדם וגומ' (בראשית ט ו).	"מות יומת", בחנק. אתה אומר בחנק, או אינו אלא בסייף, הרי אתה דן: נאמר כאן מות יומת ונאמר בנואף מות יומת (ויקרא כ י), מה להלן בחנק אף כאן בחנק. עד שאתה מקישו לנואף הקישו למגדף: נאמר כאן מות יומת ונאמר במגדף מות יומת (ויקרא כד טז), מה להלן בסקילה אף כאן בסקילה. ת"ל שופך דם האדם [באדם דמו ישפך] (בראשית ט ו).

There is some internal evidence that the version in *Vehizhir* is the older and more authentic; but this cannot be gone into here. The main point is that our Mechilta begins, "*he shall surely be put to death*—by the sword"; whereas *Vehizhir* has, "by strangulation." In our Mechilta attempts are made to show that he should rather be executed by strangulation or stoning, and these are refuted by the citation of Genesis 9:6, *Anyone who spills a man's blood, by man shall his blood be shed*; that is, executed in a manner that sheds his blood; of the four forms of death prescribed in the Torah, the only such form is decapitation. In *Vehizhir*'s version an attempt to establish the proper form of death as decapitation is refuted from Leviticus 20:10; and an attempt to establish stoning as the proper form is refuted by citing (like our Mechilta's passage) Genesis 9:6—for in TB Sanhedrin 57b it is interpreted to mean that a murderer's end should be by strangulation.

In both Vehizhir and our Mechilta editions, a passage (not cited above) then establishes decapitation as the proper sentence. In the Mechilta this has been the accepted view throughout. In Vehizhir it comes as a divergent view. Again, in his commentary Don Isaac Abarbanel likewise states, "*he shall surely be put to death*—by strangulation" (cited, like Vehizhir, in *Torah Shelemah, loc. cit.*).

Now, in a genizah fragment of MdRSbY (ed. Epstein-Melamed p. 169), after the derivation from Scriptural interpretation by two Sages that the murderer should undergo decapitation (as in TJ Sanhedrin vii 3), this follows: R. [the Sage's name is undecipherable] said: *You shall love your neighbor as yourself* (Leviticus 19:18)—choose an easy death for him. In TB (P'sahim 75a, Sanhedrin 52a) and TJ (Sanhedrin vi 4) this is found in the (later) teachings of the *g'mara*. In MdRSbY it is evidently an earlier, tannaitic teaching, which might well oppose the preceding rule of decapitation for all murderers, since in the prevailing view of the Talmud, strangulation is the easiest death that a court can impose (TB Sanhedrin 49b; MT *hilchoth sanhedrin* xiv 4).

Now, by his own statement, our author followed ShM in his listing of the 613 precepts. According to a list of correspondences between the *mitzvoth* in our work and those in ShM, this precept corresponds to ShM positive §227. There, however, we find only a brief statement that "He charged us to execute by strangulation those who violate certain commandments, as He (be He blessed) said, *he shall surely be put to death*." Further on in this work, though, we will find our author quoting things from ShM which are not in the editions we have. See e.g. §282, note 2 and §487, note 1. As MY writes in those instances, our author evidently had an earlier version of ShM, rendered from Arabic into Hebrew by R. Abraham b. Ḥisdai (no longer extant) which varied from the version we know (as attested by R. Moses ibn Tibbon in the introduction to his Hebrew translation). Possibly, then, having two views in the *halachah* on a murderer, with no clear indication as to which to follow, Rambam may have sought to apply each view where it logically fit best—that some murderers should be subject to decapitation (the view of the two Talmudim) and some to strangulation, following (perhaps) the texts of Mechilta and MdRSbY that he had. If he did so, he later retracted, of course.

What criterion might Rambam have set for dividing murderers into the two categories? The only clue lies in our author's words. In §34 (last paragraph) he states simply, "If someone transgresses it and kills deliberately..." This precept concerns one who "strikes a man," and we read in the second paragraph, "... it is a killer's intention to murder the victim swiftly; for fearing him, he would hasten his death with all his power." Here, then, it was not deliberate murder but an impulsive act during a clash.

2. TB Sanhedrin 52b.

3. I.e. the method of execution is not stated.

4. Although the first two words are part of the previous verse, referring to something else entirely, it is inferred from their proximity that anyone condemned to death cannot be required to pay damages too in connection with his crime. So also MdRSbY and *Lekah Tov* on the verse. (The last two sentences are not in the oldest manuscripts, and thus are evidently a later addition.)

§47: ON EXECUTION BY STRANGULATION WHEN DESERVED

הַמִּשְׁפָּט יַהַרְגוּ בְּנֵי אָדָם זֶה אֶת זֶה, עַל כֵּן צִוָּנוּ הָאֵל בָּרוּךְ הוּא לְהָמִית הָרוֹצֵחַ, וּבְחָכְמָתוֹ בָּרוּךְ הוּא רָאָה שֶׁרָאוּי לַעֲנֹשׁ אוֹתוֹ בְּמִיתַת חֶנֶק, וְהַדָּבָר נָאוֹת גַּם לְדַעְתֵּנוּ אָנוּ, כִּי כַּאֲשֶׁר עָשָׂה כֵּן יֵעָשֶׂה לּוֹ, וְהָרוֹצֵחַ כַּוָּנָתוֹ לְהָמִית הַנִּרְצָח בִּמְהֵרָה כִּי מִפַּחְדּוֹ אֵלָיו יְמַהֵר מִיתָתוֹ בְּכָל כֹּחוֹ, וּכְמוֹ כֵן הֵקֵלָה הַתּוֹרָה בְּמִשְׁפָּטוֹ לַהֲמִיתוֹ בְּחֶנֶק שֶׁהִיא מִיתָה מְמַהֶרֶת, וְלֹא בִּשְׂרֵפָה וּסְקִילָה שֶׁהֵן בְּצַעַר רַב. וְאוּלָם בְּמִשְׁפְּטֵי הַזֻּמָּה שֶׁנֶּהֱנוּ הָעוֹבְרִים בַּעֲבֵרָה וְנִמְשְׁכָה הֲנָאָתָן קְצָת, תָּבוֹא בָהֶן פְּעָמִים שְׂרֵפָה, פְּעָמִים סְקִילָה.

דִּינֵי הַמִּצְוָה כֵּיצַד, כְּגוֹן מַה שֶּׁאָמְרוּ לְבִרְכָה זִכְרוֹנָם שֶׁמַּשְׁקִיעִין אֶת הַמְחֻיָּב בְּזֶבֶל עַד אַרְכֻּבּוֹתָיו וְכוֹרְכִין סוּדָר קָשֶׁה [לְתוֹךְ הָרַכָּה] עַל צַוָּארוֹ, זֶה מוֹשֵׁךְ אֶצְלוֹ וְזֶה מוֹשֵׁךְ אֶצְלוֹ עַד שֶׁנַּפְשׁוֹ יוֹצְאָה, וְיֶתֶר פְּרָטֶיהָ, מְבֹאָרִים בְּפֶרֶק ז' מִסַּנְהֶדְרִין.

וּמִצְוָה זוֹ אֵינָהּ נוֹהֶגֶת אֶלָּא בָּאָרֶץ, שֶׁאֵין דִּינֵי דָּנִין נְפָשׁוֹת אֶלָּא בָּאָרֶץ. וּמִי שֶׁבְּיָדוֹ לַעֲשׂוֹת דִּין וְאֵינוֹ עוֹשֶׂה בָּטֵל עֲשֵׂה זֶה, וְעָנְשׁוֹ גָּדוֹל שֶׁאֵלְמָלֵא מוֹרָאַת הַדִּין אִישׁ אֶת רֵעֵהוּ חַיִּים בְּלָעָנוּ.

הָרַמְבַּ"ן זִכְרוֹנוֹ לִבְרָכָה לֹא יִמְנֶה זֹאת הַמִּצְוָה בְּחֶשְׁבּוֹנוֹ, וְכֵן כָּל אַרְבַּע מִיתוֹת שֶׁל בֵּית דִּין שֶׁהֵן סְקִילָה שְׂרֵפָה הֶרֶג וְחֶנֶק שֶׁיִּמְנֶה הָרַמְבַּ"ם זִכְרוֹנוֹ לִבְרָכָה לְאַרְבַּע מִצְוֹת לֹא יִמְנֶה הוּא אוֹתָן, וְאָמַר כִּי בְּפָסוּק שֶׁל "וּבִעַרְתָּ הָרָע מִקִּרְבֶּךָ" צִוַּתָה הַתּוֹרָה דֶּרֶךְ כְּלָל שֶׁנְּבַעֵר כָּל עוֹשֵׂי הָרַע מִבֵּינֵינוּ, וּבוֹ נִכְלְלוּ כָּל הַדִּינִין, וּכְשֶׁיְּפָרֵט הַכָּתוּב אַחֲרֵי כֵן חִלּוּק הַמִּשְׁפָּטִים לְפִי הָעֳנָשִׁין אֵין זֶה נֶחְשָׁב לְמִצְוָה שֶׁאֵינוֹ כִּי אִם בֵּאוּר עִנְיָן. וְהֶחָכָם יָבֹל לוֹ הַיָּשָׁר בְּעֵינָיו.

---

5. See §35 at notes 9–10.
6. Mishnah, Sanhedrin vii 3 (TB 52b).
7. This must be taken to mean only when capital cases can be judged in the holy land; and as MH notes, capital cases may be judged in the land of Israel when the holy Temple is extant and the *kohanim* are ministering properly there, and the great Sanhedrin of seventy-one judges is in its place (in the Chamber of Hewn Stone) at the Sanctuary. Other cases may be tried outside the holy land as long as there are properly ordained justices and authorized courts exist in the land; then they may be tried in other lands as well; for only judges who were ordained in the land of Israel may serve in a *beth din* outside the land. In §491 our author makes this point explicitly; here he evidently wished to be brief.
8. Expression derived from Mishnah, Avoth iii 2.
9. In his commentary (*hassagoth*) to Rambam ShM, root principle 14.

⟨208⟩

justice establishes the land (Proverbs 29:4). If not for the fear of justice, people would kill one another. Therefore God, blessed is He, charged us to put a killer to death; and in His wisdom He found it fitting to punish him with execution by strangulation. Now, the matter seems fitting to our mind as well: for *as he has done, so shall be done to him* (Leviticus 24:19), and it is a killer's intention to murder the victim swiftly; for fearing him, he would hasten his death with all his power. Similarly, the Torah lightened his sentence to have him executed by strangulation, which is a death that comes swiftly, and not burning or stoning, in which there is great suffering. However, in trials for forbidden conjugal intimacy, when those who committed the wrong derived enjoyment from the iniquity, and their enjoyment lasted a while, there can sometimes be death by burning, sometimes by stoning. [5]

How the laws of the precept are [carried out]—for instance, the teaching of the Sages of blessed memory that the guilty (sentenced) man is sunk into dung up to his knees and a stiff cloth is wrapped around his neck, and then one pulls [one end] toward him, and the other pulls [one end] toward him, until his life expires [6]—[this] and its other details are explained in chapter 7 of the Talmud tractate *Sanhedrin*.

This precept can be in effect only in the land [of Israel], for capital crimes are judged only in the land. [7] Whoever has it in his power to carry out this judgment and does not do so, has disobeyed this positive precept; and his penalty will be great, for if not for fear of the law, one man would swallow another alive. [8]

Ramban of blessed memory [9] does not list this precept in his reckoning; and so all the four means of death by sentence of the *beth din* (court), which are: stoning, burning, decapitation by the sword, and strangulation. While Rambam of blessed memory counts them as four precepts, he does not count them. He states [rather] that in the verse, *you shall purge the evil from your midst* (Deuteronomy 17:7), the Torah commanded in a general way that we should clear out all evildoers from our midst, and in this all the [capital] sentences are included. Then, when Scripture details afterward the difference between the [various] judgments according to the punishments, this is not to be reckoned [in each case] as a precept [by itself] but only a clarification of the topic. Then let the wise scholar choose [between them] what seems right in his eyes.

§48: NOT TO STRIKE ONE'S FATHER OR MOTHER

[שֶׁלֹּא לְהַכּוֹת אָב וָאֵם]

מח שֶׁלֹּא יַכֶּה הַבֵּן הָאָב וְהָאֵם, וַאֲפִלּוּ אִם הֵם יַכּוּ אוֹתוֹ הַכָּאָה רַבָּה בְּכָל זְמַן שֶׁלֹּא יִשָּׂאוּ נַפְשָׁם לַהֲמִיתוֹ, שֶׁנֶּאֱמַר: וּמַכֵּה אָבִיו וְאִמּוֹ מוֹת יוּמָת. וְאַף־עַל־פִּי שֶׁלֹּא הִזְהִיר הַכָּתוּב בְּפֵרוּשׁ עַל זֶה שֶׁיֹּאמַר "אַל תַּכּוּ הָאָבוֹת" אֶלָּא שֶׁכָּתַב עֹנֶשׁ הַמַּכֶּה אוֹתָם, דֶּרֶךְ הַתַּלְמוּד לְעוֹלָם לִשְׁאֹל בְּעִנְיָן כָּזֶה וְלוֹמַר עֹנֶשׁ שָׁמַעְנוּ אַזְהָרָה מִנַּיִן, גַּם בָּזֶה יֵשׁ לָנוּ אַזְהָרָה, שֶׁהֲרֵי אָנוּ מֻזְהָרִין עַל כָּל אִישׁ מִיִּשְׂרָאֵל שֶׁלֹּא לְהַכּוֹתוֹ, שֶׁכָּתוּב בְּמִי שֶׁנִּתְחַיֵּב מַלְקוֹת "אַרְבָּעִים יַכֶּנּוּ לֹא יֹסִיף", וְכָל שֶׁכֵּן לְמִי שֶׁלֹּא נִתְחַיֵּב, וְהָאָב בִּכְלַל יִשְׂרָאֵל הוּא, וְאַזְהָרָתוֹ מֵהָכָא.

וְאַף־עַל־פִּי שֶׁלָּאו שֶׁל לֹא יֹסִיף נֶחְשָׁב לָאו בִּפְנֵי עַצְמוֹ, מִכָּל מָקוֹם הֲרֵי כְּלָל בְּיָדֵינוּ שֶׁכָּל שֶׁיֵּשׁ בּוֹ כָּרֵת אוֹ מִיתָה יֵשׁ בּוֹ לָאו חוּץ מִפֶּסַח וּמִילָה, וּבַהֲכָאַת אָב וָאֵם הֲרֵי יֵשׁ בּוֹ כָּרֵת בְּלֹא עֵדִים וּמִיתָה בְּעֵדִים, וְעַל כֵּן יֵשׁ לָנוּ לוֹמַר עַל כָּל פָּנִים שֶׁנִּלְמַד הָאַזְהָרָה בּוֹ מִקְרָא דְּלֹא יֹסִיף אַחַר שֶׁלֹּא מְצָאנוּהָ בְּמָקוֹם אַחֵר, וְתִהְיֶה עִקַּר הָאַזְהָרָה לְיִשְׂרָאֵל וּבִכְלָלָהּ נִלְמַד לְמַכֵּה אָב וָאֵם.

וְעִנְיַן חִיּוּב מִיתָה בְּמַכֶּה אָמְרוּ זִכְרוֹנָם לִבְרָכָה שֶׁהוּא כְּשֶׁהוֹצִיא מֵהֶם דָּם דַּוְקָא, מַה שֶּׁאֵין כֵּן בִּשְׁאָר כָּל אָדָם שֶׁאֲפִלּוּ הוֹצִיא מֵהֶן דָּם נִתַּן לְחִיּוּב מָמוֹן.

מִשָּׁרְשֵׁי הַמִּצְוָה לְיַסֵּר הַנִּבְלִים וְהַמּוֹסֵרִים שֶׁהֱרִימוּ יָד בְּמִי שֶׁהֱבִיאָם לָעוֹלָם בִּרְצוֹן הָאֵל וְעָשָׂה לָהֶם כַּמָּה טוֹבוֹת, וּמֶלֶךְ בְּמִשְׁפָּט יַעֲמִיד אָרֶץ.

דִּינֵי הַמִּצְוָה, כְּגוֹן מַכֵּהוּ לְאַחַר מִיתָה שֶׁפָּטוּר, וְהִכָּהוּ עַל אָזְנוֹ וְחֵרְשׁוֹ שֶׁחַיָּב

---

§48 1. Evidently derived from R. Dimi's statement, TB Kiddushin 31a.

2. In which case all is permitted him to save his life.

3. E.g. TB Sanhedrin 54a; and on 56a the Talmud states that punishment is not given unless there was a warning (admonition) elsewhere in the Torah.

4. Listed in this work as §595, and it includes a ban on giving anyone a blow (TB Makkoth 9a); then how can the same precept be counted twice?

5. See §2, end.

6. Derived from TJ Sanhedrin vii 11 (see MY and ed. Chavel).

7. Similarly Rambam, ShM negative precept §26, writes that one negative statement (injunction) in the Torah may serve as a warning against several misdeeds, if there is a separate punishment written for each of them.

8. TB Sanhedrin 85b.

9. Literally, vile people and slanderers.

⟨210⟩

48 [NOT TO STRIKE ONE'S FATHER OR MOTHER]

that a son is not to strike his father or his mother, even if they give him a severe beating,[1] as long as they do not wish to kill him[2]—as it is stated, *And whoever strikes his father or his mother shall surely be put to death* (Exodus 21:15).

Now, Scripture gives no explicit admonition about this, to say, "Do not strike parents," but merely writes the punishment for one who beats them. Yet it is the way of the Talmud always to ask in such a case, "We have heard the penalty; from where do we learn the warning?"[3] However, about this too we have a warning: for you see, we are cautioned about every man in Jewry not to strike him. For it is written about a person who incurred a whipping, *Forty lashes he may give him, but he may not give more* (Deuteronomy 25:3). How much more would this apply to someone who did not merit a whipping at all; and a father is included with all Jews [in the admonition]. Hence the admonition is derived from here.

Now, even though this prohibition, "he may not give more," is considered a negative precept in its own right,[4] nevertheless we have a rule that whatever involves *karéth* [Divine severance of existence] or a death sentence is the subject of a negative precept, except for the Passover offering (§5) and circumcision (§2).[5] And for striking a father or a mother, *karéth* is incurred if there were no witnesses,[6] and the death penalty if witnesses were present. Therefore we must say, in any event, that the admonition about it is learned from the verse, *he may not give more*, since we do not find it anywhere else. The main admonition is then about [striking] Jews, and by extending it we apply it to one who strikes a father or mother.[7]

About the death penalty for one who strikes [a parent], our Sages of blessed memory said[8] that he incurs it specifically when he draws blood from [either of] them—which is not the case with all other human beings, where, even if he draws blood, he incurs a penalty of money (damages).

At the root of the precept lies the purpose of punishing the scoundrels and wretches[9] who have raised a hand against a person who brought them into the world by the will of God, and did them so many favors. And *the King by justice establishes the land* (Proverbs 29:4).

The laws of the precept are, for instance, about one who beats him [a parent] after [his] death—that he goes free;[8] if he struck him on his ear and deafened him, he incurs the death penalty, for it is impossible

§48–49: NOT TO STRIKE A PARENT / LAWS OF FINES—PENALTIES

מִיתָה שֶׁאִי אֶפְשָׁר שֶׁלֹּא יֵצֵא טִפַּת דָּם בְּפָנִים, וְהָעוֹשֶׂה בּוֹ חַבּוּרָה לִרְפוּאָה שֶׁפָּטוּר, וּלְכַתְּחִלָּה לֹא יַעֲשֶׂה לוֹ רְפוּאָה שֶׁמְּבִיאָה לְחַבּוּרָה אִם אֶפְשָׁר עַל יְדֵי אַחֵר, וְדִין שְׁתוּקִי שֶׁחַיָּב עַל אִמּוֹ וְלֹא עַל אָבִיו, וְדִין גֵּר שֶׁהוֹרָתוֹ שֶׁלֹּא בִּקְדֻשָּׁה שֶׁאֵין חַיָּב בִּשְׁנֵיהֶם, וְדִין גֵּר שֶׁאָסוּר לוֹ לְהַכּוֹת אָבִיו גּוֹי דְּרַבָּנָן, וְדִין מִי שֶׁהָיוּ אָבִיו וְאִמּוֹ רְשָׁעִים גְּמוּרִים מְפַרְסָמִים שֶׁפָּטוּר עַל הַכָּאָתָן עַד שֶׁיַּעֲשׂוּ תְּשׁוּבָה, אֲבָל אָסוּר הוּא מִכָּל מָקוֹם אֲפִלּוּ קֹדֶם תְּשׁוּבָה, וְלִכָּל אֵין הַבֵּן נַעֲשֶׂה שָׁלִיחַ בֵּית דִּין לְיַסֵּר אָבִיו חוּץ מִמֵּסִית, וְיֶתֶר פְּרָטֶיהָ, בְּסוֹף סַנְהֶדְרִין.

וְנוֹהֶגֶת בְּכָל מָקוֹם וּבְכָל זְמַן בִּזְכָרִים וּנְקֵבוֹת וְטֻמְטוּם וְאַנְדְּרוֹגִינוֹס. וְעוֹבֵר עָלֶיהָ וְהִכָּה אוֹתָם הַכָּאָה שֶׁיֵּשׁ בָּהּ חַבּוּרָה בְּעֵדִים וְהַתְרָאָה מִיתָתוֹ בְּחֶנֶק, וּבְלֹא חַבּוּרָה חַיָּב עֲלֵיהֶם כִּשְׁאָר כָּל אָדָם, שֶׁהַמַּכֶּה חֲבֵרוֹ הַכָּאָה שֶׁיֵּשׁ בָּהּ תַּשְׁלוּמִין שֶׁל שָׁוֶה פְּרוּטָה מְשַׁלֵּם וְאֵינוֹ לוֹקֶה, וְאִם אֵין בָּהּ שָׁוֶה פְּרוּטָה לוֹקֶה וְאֵינוֹ מְשַׁלֵּם, שֶׁהֲלָכָה הִיא אֵין אָדָם מֵת וּמְשַׁלֵּם, וְכֵן אֵין לוֹקֶה וּמְשַׁלֵּם.

[מִצְוַת דִּינֵי קְנָסוֹת]

מט שֶׁנִּצְטַוֵּינוּ בְּדִין חוֹבֵל בַּחֲבֵרוֹ לְעָנְשׁוֹ, כְּמוֹ שֶׁכָּתוּב בַּתּוֹרָה בְּפָרָשַׁת "וְכִי יְרִיבֻן אֲנָשִׁים", וְזֶה נִקְרָא דִּינֵי קְנָסוֹת. וּבְפָסוּק אַחֵר כּוֹלֵל מִשְׁפְּטֵי הַקְּנָסוֹת כֻּלָּם, וְהוּא שֶׁכָּתוּב, "כַּאֲשֶׁר עָשָׂה כֵּן יֵעָשֶׂה לוֹ", יִרְצֶה לוֹמַר שֶׁיֻּלְקַח מָמוֹנוֹ מַה שֶּׁיְּצַעֲרֵהוּ בִּכְדֵי מַה שֶּׁצִּעֵר הוּא אֶת חֲבֵרוֹ, כְּמוֹ שֶׁבָּאָה הַקַּבָּלָה בּוֹ. וַאֲפִלּוּ לֹא הִכָּהוּ אֶלָּא שֶׁבִּיְּשׁוֹ בִּלְבַד יְצַעֲרוּהוּ בֵּית דִּין בְּמָמוֹנוֹ שֶׁיְּשַׁלֵּם לַמִּתְבַּיֵּשׁ כְּפִי הַשִּׁעוּר הַהוּא.

10. TB Bava Kamma 86a.
11. TB Sanhedrin 84b.
12. Even if, on being questioned, his mother may have identified his father once; see Rambam MT *hilchoth mamrim* v 9.
13. I.e. his mother was non-Jewish when he was conceived; hence he is considered unrelated to his parents from the time of the conversion, even if his mother converted to Judaism during his gestation; MT *ibid.* (and see *Kessef Mishneh*).
14. So that people should not say he went from a more holy or noble state (in which he might not strike his parent) to a lower, ignoble state (in which he might); MT *ibid.* 11 (and see *Kessef Mishneh*).
15. TB Sanhedrin 85a–b.
16. Since Scripture writes of the man who incites to idolatry, *neither shall you spare or conceal him* (Deuteronomy 13:9); *ibid.* (MT *ibid.* 14).
17. So Rambam MT *ibid.* 5, based on TB Sanhedrin 27a (*Kessef Mishneh*).
18. In which case blood was shed beneath the skin.
19. TB Sanhedrin 84b.
20. So *ibid.* 85a, etc. (On the value of a *p'rutah* see §58, note 7.)
21. TB K'thuboth 36b.
22. TB Bava Kamma 71a, etc.

§49 1. TB Bava Kamma 83b–84a.

that a drop of blood should not have been shed within;[10] if someone makes a wound in him [a parent] in order to cure him, he goes free; but originally, at the start, he should not give him a cure that leads to a wound, if it can be done by someone else;[11] the law of a *sh'thuki*, an illegitimate son of uncertain fatherhood, that he is guilty over [striking] his mother but not over his father;[12] the law about a proselyte, who was not conceived in holiness, that he is guilty over neither of them [neither parent];[13] the law about a proselyte, that he is forbidden to strike his non-Jewish father, by decree of the Sages;[14] the law about a person whose father and mother are notorious, utterly wicked evildoers, that he bears no guilt for striking them, until they repent;[15] but in any event he is not permitted to do so even before [their] repentance; hence a son may not be made an emissary of the court to punish his father, except in the case of an inciter to idolatry.[16] [These] and its other details are [found] toward the end of the Talmud tractate *Sanhedrin*.

It is in effect in every place and every time, for both man and woman, a *tumtum* (one of unknown gender) and a hermaphrodite.[17] If someone transgressed it and struck them [either of the parents] a blow sufficient to cause a wound,[18] with witnesses and a [prior] warning, his death sentence is by strangulation.[19] If it was without [causing] a wound, he is guilty over them like any other person: For if someone strikes his fellow a blow that incurs damages of [at least] a *p'rutah*, he pays and is not given whiplashes; and if it does not involve damages of a *p'rutah*, he is whipped and does not pay.[20] For it is a rule: a man does not both die and pay money;[21] and so too, one does not both receive whiplashes and pay money.[22]

49 [THE LAWS OF FINES—PENALTIES]

that we were commanded about the law of one who wounds his fellow—to punish him—as it is written in the Torah in the section beginning, *And if men quarrel* (Exodus 21:18). This is called the laws of fines. In another sentence of Scripture all the rules about fines are summed up—this being the verse, *as he has done, so shall be done to him* (Leviticus 24:19)—which means that out of a person's money should be taken what will give him as much pain as he gave his fellow—as it was explained in the Oral Tradition.[1] Even if he did not strike the other but only shamed him, the *beth din* is to cause him pain through his money that he is to pay the shamed person, according to that amount [of pain which the shame caused the other].

§49: THE LAWS OF FINES—PENALTIES

וְאֵלֶּה הַדִּינִין שֶׁנִּקְרָאִין דִּינֵי קְנָסוֹת, כְּגוֹן נִזְקֵי אָדָם בְּאָדָם וְשׁוֹר בְּשׁוֹר וְשׁוֹר בְּאָדָם וְאָדָם בִּבְהֵמָה, אֵין דָּנִין אוֹתָן אֶלָּא בְּבֵית דִּין הַסְּמוּכִין בְּאֶרֶץ יִשְׂרָאֵל.

שֹׁרֶשׁ מִצְוָה זוֹ וּבִכְלָל כָּל מַה שֶּׁבָּא בַתּוֹרָה בְּעִנְיַן הַדִּין, אֵינִי צָרִיךְ לִנְגֹּעַ אַחַר טַעֲמוֹ שֶׁל דָּבָר, כִּי דָּבָר מֻשְׂכָּל הוּא, שֶׁאִם אֵין מִשְׁפָּט לֹא יִתְיַשְּׁבוּ בְּנֵי אָדָם וְלֹא יַעַמְדוּ יַחְדָּו לְעוֹלָם, וְאִי אֶפְשָׁר לָאָרֶץ בִּלְתִּי הַמִּשְׁפָּט.

דִּינֵי הַמִּצְוָה, כְּגוֹן הַחוֹבֵל בַּחֲבֵרוֹ שֶׁחַיָּב בַּחֲמִשָּׁה דְּבָרִים הַיְדוּעִים, וְכֵיצַד מְחַשְּׁבִין אוֹתָן, וְדִין הַבֹּשֶׁת שֶׁהַכֹּל לְפִי הַמְבַיֵּשׁ וְהַמִּתְבַּיֵּשׁ, וְדִין יָשֵׁן שֶׁבִּיֵּשׁ אוֹ שֶׁבִּיְּשׁוּהוּ, וְאִם מֵת מָתוֹךְ בָּשְׁתּוֹ מַה דִּינוֹ עִם יוֹרְשָׁיו, וּמְבַיֵּשׁ שׁוֹטֶה אוֹ חֵרֵשׁ אוֹ קָטָן מַה דִּינֵיהֶם, וּמְבַיֵּשׁ גֵּר וְעֶבֶד, וְהַמְבַיֵּשׁ בִּדְבָרִים, וְהַחִלּוּק שֶׁבֵּין תַּלְמִיד חָכָם לִשְׁאָר בְּנֵי אָדָם מַה דִּינֵיהֶם, וְדִין הַבּוֹעֵט בַּחֲבֵרוֹ בְּרֶגֶל אוֹ שֶׁתְּקָעוֹ בְכַפּוֹ, אוֹ סְטָרוֹ עַל פָּנָיו, צָרַם אָזְנוֹ, תָּלַשׁ שְׂעָרוֹ, רָקַק וְהִגִּיעַ לוֹ הָרָק, וְיֶתֶר פְּרָטֶיהָ, מְבֹאָרִים בְּבָבָא קַמָּא פֶּרֶק הַחוֹבֵל.

וְשָׁם מִתְבָּרֵר שֶׁיֵּשׁ חִלּוּק בְּדִינֵי קְנָסוֹת בֵּין מִלְתָּא דְּשְׁכִיחָא וְאִית בַּהּ חֶסְרוֹן כִּיס, דְּבְהָא עָבְדִינָן שְׁלִיחוּתַיְהוּ, לְמִלְתָּא דְּלָא שְׁכִיחָא וְאַף עַל גַּב דְּאִית בַּהּ חֶסְרוֹן כִּיס, אִי נַמִּי דְּשְׁכִיחָא וְלֵית בַּהּ חֶסְרוֹן כִּיס, דְּבְהָנֵי לָא עָבְדִינָן שְׁלִיחוּתַיְהוּ. וְכָתַב רַבֵּנוּ אַלְפָסִי זִכְרוֹנוֹ לִבְרָכָה: מִנְהַג שְׁתֵּי יְשִׁיבוֹת שֶׁאַף עַל פִּי שֶׁאֵין גּוֹבִין קְנָס מְנַדִּין לֵיהּ עַד שֶׁמְּפַיֵּס לְבַעַל דִּינֵיהּ, וְכַד יָהֵיב לֵיהּ שִׁעוּר מַאי דַּחֲזֵי לֵיהּ שָׁרוּ לֵיהּ לְאַלְתַּר בֵּין אַפֵּיס לֵיהּ מָרֵיהּ לְדִינָא בֵּין לָא אַפֵּיס.

---

2. See *ibid.* 84a–b; and see §47, note 7, which applies here as well.
3. Mishnah, Bava Kamma viii 1 (TB 83b).
4. I.e. how much pain the shame caused; *ibid.*
5. Mishnah *ibid.* (TB 86b).
6. TB *ibid.* and Sanhedrin 65a (Rambam MT *hilchoth ḥovél* iii 3).
7. TB Bava Kamma 86b.
8. *Ibid.* and 87a (Mishnah, viii 3).
9. *Ibid.* 91a.
10. TJ Bava Kamma viii 6 (Rambam *ibid.* iii 5; but see also Rama in *Shulḥan 'Aruch Yoreh Dé'ah*, §243, 6).
11. TB Bava Kamma 27b, 90b.
12. *Ibid.* 84b.
13. Rif, Bava Kamma viii beginning.
14. I.e. of Sura and Pumbeditha, the two main centers of Torah study and authority in the period of the *ge'onim*.

⟨214⟩

SIDRAH MISHPATIM

These cases which are called the judgments of fines, such as in injuries that one man inflicts on another, or one ox on another, or which an animal inflicts on a man, or a man on an animal, may be judged only by an ordained, authorized *beth din* in the land of Israel.[2]

As for a root purpose of this precept, and in general, regarding all that is conveyed in the Torah about judgment in law, I have no need to strive after a reason for it, as it is a reasonable, self-understood axiom that if there were no justice, human beings would not become settled in communal life and would not endure together permanently; a land cannot get along without justice.

The laws of the precept are for instance: that if someone wounds his fellow, he is required to pay the five known damages, and how they are reckoned;[3] the law of disgrace, that it all depends on who caused the shame and who was shamed;[4] the law of a sleeping person who causes or suffers shame;[5] if someone dies [in his sleep] while subjected to his shame, what the law is regarding his heirs;[6] if the person inflicting the shame is a witless fool, a deaf and dumb person, or a child, what the law is for them;[7] if someone shames a proselyte or a servant;[8] if someone inflicts shame with words;[9] the difference between a Torah scholar and other human beings—what the law is for them;[10] the law for one who kicked his fellow with his foot, struck him with his palm, slapped him in the face, pinched his ear, pulled out his hair, or expectorated so that the spittle reached the other.[11] [These] and further details are explained in the eighth chapter of the Talmud tractate *Bava Kamma*.

There[12] it is made clear that there is a difference in regard to the laws of fines between something usual, likely to happen, which involves monetary loss—in which cases we [the *beth din* in another land] carry out their mission [acting as deputies of the original authorized courts in the land of Israel]—and, on the other hand, something unusual, unlikely to happen, even if it involves monetary loss, or equally, something usual and likely, involving no monetary loss—in which cases we [the *beth din* in another land] do not carry out their mission [to act as their deputies]. However, R. Isaac Alfasi of blessed memory wrote:[13] It is the practice of the two academies[14] that even though fines are not imposed and collected, he [the guilty person who incurs them] is placed in excommunication until he pacifies his claimant; and when he gives him the proper amount due him, he is released [from the excommunication] at once, whether his claimant becomes mollified and reconciled with him or not.

ספר החינוך §49–50: LAWS OF FINES / ON COURT EXECUTION BY DECAPITATION

וְנוֹהֶגֶת מִצְוָה זוֹ שֶׁאָנוּ חַיָּבִין לָדוּן וְלַעֲנֹשׁ הַחוֹבֵל בִּזְכָרִים כִּי לָהֶם נִתַּן לַעֲשׂוֹת דִּין, וְלֹא בִנְקֵבוֹת שֶׁאֵינָן דָּנוֹת, אֲבָל הֵן מִכְּלַל מָקוֹם בִּכְלַל דִּין הַתַּשְׁלוּמִין, בֵּין שֶׁבְּיִישׁוּ אוֹ שֶׁנִּתְבַּיְּישׁוּ. וְגַם שָׁם מִתְבָּאֵר תַּשְׁלוּמֵי נֶזֶק הָאִשָּׁה הַנְּשׂוּאָה הֵיאַךְ נֶחֱלָקִים.

[מִצְוַת בֵּית דִּין לַהֲרֹג בְּסַיִף הַמְחֻיָּב]

נ שֶׁנִּצְטַוֵּינוּ לַהֲרֹג הָעוֹבְרִים עַל קְצָת מִצְווֹת הַתּוֹרָה בְּסַיִף, וְזֶה הַדִּין נִקְרָא לְרַבּוֹתֵינוּ זִכְרוֹנָם לִבְרָכָה הֶרֶג, וְהִיא מִיתָה קַלָּה, וּמִכָּל מָקוֹם חֶנֶק קַלָּה יוֹתֵר מִמֶּנָּה. וְאֶחָד מִן הַמּוּמָתִים בְּמִיתָה זוֹ, הַמַּכֶּה עַבְדּוֹ אֲפִלּוּ כְנַעֲנִי, וְהוּא שֶׁמֵּת תַּחַת יָדוֹ, שֶׁנֶּאֱמַר "נָקֹם יִנָּקֵם", וּבָא הַפֵּרוּשׁ שֶׁיֵּהָרֵג מַכֵּהוּ בְּסַיִף.

כְּבָר כָּתַבְתִּי לְמַעְלָה שֶׁהָרַמְבַּ"ן זִכְרוֹנוֹ לִבְרָכָה לֹא יִמְנֶה אַרְבַּע מִיתוֹת בֵּית דִּין לְאַרְבַּע מִצְווֹת כְּמוֹ הָרַמְבַּ"ם זִכְרוֹנוֹ לִבְרָכָה.

מִשָּׁרְשֵׁי מִצְוָה זוֹ שֶׁרָצָה הָאֵל לַעֲקֹר מִתּוֹךְ אֻמָּתוֹ הַקְּדוֹשָׁה רֹעַ הַלֵּב וְהָאַכְזָרִיּוּת הַגְּדוֹלָה, וְעַל כֵּן צִוְּתָה שֶׁכָּל מִי שֶׁיִּגְבַּר עָלָיו כַּעַס גָּדוֹל כָּל כָּךְ שֶׁיַּכֶּה הַכָּאַת מָוֶת עַבְדּוֹ שֶׁהוּא בְּבֵיתוֹ וְאֵין לוֹ מוֹשִׁיעַ, שֶׁיּוּמַת הָעוֹשֶׂה זֶה, אַף עַל פִּי שֶׁהָעֶבֶד קִנְיַן כַּסְפּוֹ וְאִבֵּד אֶת מָמוֹנוֹ בְּמוֹתוֹ, אַף עַל פִּי כֵן יֵהָרֵג אַחַר שֶׁהִגְבִּיר כַּעֲסוֹ עַל נַפְשׁוֹ כָּל-כָּךְ, וְדִין רָאוּי וְכָשֵׁר הוּא, מִשְׁפְּטֵי יי צְדְקוּ יַחְדָּו.

דִּינֵי הַמִּצְוָה, כְּגוֹן דִּין יוֹם אוֹ יוֹמַיִם, וְיֶתֶר פְּרָטֶיהָ, מְבֹאָרִים בְּבָבָא קַמָּא.

וְהָעוֹבֵר עָלֶיהָ וְלֹא עָשָׂה בּוֹ דִין, אִם יֵשׁ כֹּחַ בְּיָדוֹ בִּטֵּל עֲשֵׂה, וְעָנְשׁוֹ גָּדוֹל, שֶׁגּוֹרְמִים תַּקָּלוֹת לִבְנֵי אָדָם.

---

15. So TJ Sanhedrin iii 9.
16. TB Bava Kamma 15a, 47a.
17. See Mishnah, K'thuboth vi 1 (TB 65b), and Rambam MT *hilchoth hovél* iv 15.

§50 1. So TB Sanhedrin 49b, 50a, etc.
2. *Ibid.* 52b.
3. In contrast to the law that when a heathen slave dies, the master is to be consoled as for the loss of a domestic animal, "May the omnipresent God replenish your loss for you," but not as for the death of kin (TB B'rachoth 16b).
4. I.e. if the servant lingers on "a day or two" before dying, which Mechilta interprets to mean twenty-four hours, the master is not executed (Rambam MT *hilchoth rotzé-aḥ* ii 12).
5. I.e. for one who beat his servant to death.

⟨216⟩

This precept, that we are obligated to try and punish one who wounds and injures [another], applies to men, for to them was given [the duty] to effect justice, and not to women, who do not sit in judgment.[15] They are, however, included under the law of payments, whether they cause or suffer shame.[16]

There too the payments of damages to a married woman are explained—how they are divided [between her and her husband].[17]

50 [THE COURT SHOULD EXECUTE BY DECAPITATION ANYONE WHO DESERVES IT]

that we were commanded to put to death those who violate certain precepts of the Torah, by the sword. This penalty is called by our Sages of blessed memory *hereg* ("slaying"), and it is a light, easy death, although strangulation is yet easier.[1] One of those executed by this death is a person who smites his bondservant, even a former heathen, so that he dies under his hand. For it is stated [about this] *he shall surely be punished* (Exodus 21:20), and the traditional explanation[2] is that his attacker is to be killed by the sword.

I have written previously, above (§47), that Ramban of blessed memory does not reckon the four ways of death imposed by the *beth din* as four precepts, as Rambam of blessed memory does.

At the root of this precept lies the reason that God wished to eradicate from the midst of His holy people the heart's evil and great cruelty. Therefore [the Torah] commanded that if anyone becomes so overwhelmed by fierce anger that he beats to death his servant who is in his home and has no one to save him, then let the one who did this be put to death. Even though the servant was his purchased possession, and he lost his own property by the other's death, nevertheless he is to be slain,[3] since his rage prevailed over his spirit to such an extent. It is a fitting and eminently proper law; *the ordinances of the Lord are true, they are righteous altogether* (Psalms 19:10).

The laws of the precept, such as the law of *a day or two* (Exodus 21:21),[4] and its other details, are explained in the Talmud tractate *Bava Kamma*. If someone transgresses this precept and does not impose justice on him,[5] if it was in his power to do so, he has disobeyed a positive precept; and his punishment is great, for he is thus the cause of stumbling-blocks, misfortunes for people.

§51 : THE COURT TO JUDGE DAMAGE BY DOMESTIC ANIMALS

[מִצְוַת בֵּית דִּין לָדוּן בְּנִזְקֵי בְהֵמָה]

נא לָדוּן בְּדִין שׁוֹר הַמַּזִּיק, בֵּין שֶׁהִזִּיק אָדָם כְּמוֹ שֶׁכָּתוּב בַּפָּרָשָׁה "וְכִי יִגַּח", בֵּין שֶׁהִזִּיק מָמוֹן כְּמוֹ שֶׁכָּתוּב בַּפָּרָשָׁה "וְכִי יִגֹּף". וְעִקַּר פֵּרוּשׁוֹ שֶׁל יִגֹּף, יֶדְחֹף. וּמִיהוּ בֵּין שֶׁהִזִּיקוֹ בְגוּפוֹ אוֹ בְרַגְלָיו אוֹ נָשַׁךְ בְּשִׁנָּיו אוֹ אֲפִלּוּ הִזִּיק בְּקַרְנָיו כָּל כְּלָל לְשׁוֹן נְגִיפָה מַשְׁמַע, אֲבָל נְגִיחָה לֹא מַשְׁמַע אֶלָּא בְּקֶרֶן. וּכְבָר נִתְרַבּוּ נִזְקֵי שׁוֹר בְּאָדָם מִדִּכְתִיב בַּפָּרָשָׁה כִּי יִגַּח "וְהֵמִית" דְּמַשְׁמַע וְהֵמִית מִכָּל מָקוֹם בֵּין בִּנְגִיחָה בֵּין בִּשְׁאָר דְּבָרִים. וְלָאו דַּוְקָא שׁוֹר אֶלָּא אֲפִלּוּ כָּל בְּהֵמָה וְחַיָּה וָעוֹף שֶׁהִזִּיקוּ חַיָּבִין אֶלָּא שֶׁדִּבֵּר הַכָּתוּב בָּרָגִיל.

כְּבָר אָמַרְנוּ שֶׁכָּל הַמִּצְוֹת הַבָּאוֹת לָנוּ עַל דְּבַר הַמִּשְׁפָּט שֹׁרֶשׁ אֶחָד לָהֶן, וְדָבָר מֻשְׂכָּל הוּא, וְאֵינִי צָרִיךְ לַחֲזֹר אוֹתוֹ בְּכָל אַחַת וְאַחַת.

דִּינֵי הַמִּצְוָה, כְּגוֹן אֵי זֶהוּ הַמּוּעָד וְהַתָּם, וְהַחִלּוּק שֶׁבֵּינֵיהֶן, וּדְבָרִים שֶׁהַבְּהֵמָה מוּעֶדֶת בָּהֶן בִּתְחִלָּה וְשֶׁאֵינָהּ מוּעֶדֶת לָהֶן עַד שֶׁנִּדְרָאָה מַרְגֶּלֶת בָּהֶן, וְהַרְגֵּל זֶה בְּאֵי זֶה עִנְיָן יִהְיֶה שֶׁנַּחְזִיקֶנָּה בְּמוּעֶדֶת, וּבְאֵי זֶה עִנְיָן תַּנִּיחַ הַהַרְגֵּל שֶׁתַּחֲזֹר לְתַמּוּתָהּ, וַחֲמִשָּׁה מִינֵי חַיּוֹת הַמּוּעָדוֹת מִתְּחִלָּתָן, וְחִלּוּק הָרְשֻׁיּוֹת שֶׁתַּזִּיק שָׁם בְּתוֹכָן, וּמַה שֶּׁנִּקְרָא אָבוֹת בַּנְּזִיקִין וּמַה שֶׁנִּקְרָא תוֹלָדוֹת, וְהַחִלּוּק שֶׁבֵּינֵיהֶן בְּאַחַת, וְדִינֵי הַשְּׁמִירוֹת שֶׁאָדָם חַיָּב לְשָׁמְרָן כְּדֵי שֶׁלֹּא יַזִּיקוּ, וְכֵיצַד יִתְחַיֵּב אוֹ יִפָּטֵר בָּהֶן, וְיֶתֶר רֻבֵּי פְרָטֶיהָ, מְבֹאָרִים בְּשִׁשָּׁה פְרָקִים רִאשׁוֹנִים מִן בָּבָא קַמָּא.

וְאֵלֶּה הַדִּינִין הַנִּקְרָאִין דִּינֵי קְנָסוֹת כְּבָר אָמַרְנוּ דָּנִין דָּנִין אוֹתָן אֶלָּא בֵּית דִּין

---

§51 1. So Mechilta and Rashi on the verse.

2. So TB Bava Kamma 2b.

3. So Rashi on verse 28, based on Mechilta, *n'zikin* 10 beginning.

4. I.e. on whoever owned or used the creature; based on Mishnah, Bava Kamma v 7 (TB 54b).

5. *Ibid.* ii 4, TB 23a.

6. *Ibid.* i 4 (TB 15b).

7. Mishnah *ibid.*, TB *ibid.* (Rambam MT *hilchoth nizké mamon* i 5).

8. Mishnah, Bava Kamma ii 4 (TB 23b).

9. Even if they have been tamed; TB *ibid.* 15b (Rambam *ibid.* ix 6).

10. I.e. whether the damage occurred on the property of the owner of the injuring animal, or of the owner of the injured one; Mishnah *ibid.* 5 (TB 24b), etc.

11. *Ibid.* i 1, TB 2b, 3a, 4b.

12. If an animal does damage with its foot (by treading or trampling—a "main type" of damage), that is paid for in full; if in walking it causes chips or particles of matter to fly off and they do damage (a "derivative of foot") only half the damage is paid; TB Bava Kamma 3b.

13. Mishnah *ibid.* iv 9, TB 55b.

14. See §47, note 7, which applies here as well.

⟨218⟩

[THAT THE COURT SHOULD JUDGE DAMAGES BY DOMESTIC ANIMALS]

51 to judge the case of a damaging ox, whether it injured a man, as written in the section beginning *And if an ox gores a man* (Exodus 21:28), or it damaged property, as written in the section beginning *And if one man's ox* yiggof, *hurts another's* (ibid. 35). The main meaning of *yiggof* is "thrusts, butts"; however, whether it caused injury with its body or feet, bit with its teeth, or even caused damage with all its horns [not by goring], all are included under the range of meaning of *yiggof*.[1] The verb *yiggaḥ* (gores), though, denotes only [injury] with the horn.[2] Yet the list of injuries to a man by an ox [which are subject to this law] was enlarged [to include all], since in the section of "if an ox gores" it is written, *but it has killed* (ibid. 29)—i.e. in any way, whether by goring or by any other means.[3] Nor does it mean specifically an ox; rather, if any domestic or wild animal at all, or a bird, did damage, there is an obligation[4] to pay damages. It is only that Scripture spoke of what is usual.

We have stated before (§49) that all precepts given us concerning justice have one root purpose, and it is a reasonable, self-understood matter. I have no need to repeat this for each and every one.

Now as to the laws of the precept: for instance, which is a *mu'ad* (a habitually damaging animal) and which a *tam* (a newly damaging animal),[5] and the difference [in law] between them;[6] those matters in which an animal is regarded as a *mu'ad* from the beginning, and those in which it is not a *mu'ad* until we see it become habituated in them;[7] in what way it becomes thus habituated, that it should be considered a *mu'ad*;[8] in what way it can give up this habit, that it should return to its status of *tam*;[8] five wild animals which are considered *mu'ad* from the start;[9] the difference [in law] between the domains in which [the animal] does an injury;[10] what are called "fathers" (main types) of damages, and what "offspring" (derivative forms),[11] and the difference [in law] between them in one instance;[12] the laws of the ways in which a man is required to guard them that they should do no damage, and how he becomes obligated or freed from these requirements.[13] [These] and the rest of its many details are clarified in the first six chapters of the Talmud tractate *Bava Kamma*.

In regard to those judgments which are called cases of fines, we have stated earlier (§49) that they are judged only in an ordained, authorized *beth din*, and that in the land of Israel.[14] The damager,

הַסְּמוּכִין וּבְאֶרֶץ יִשְׂרָאֵל. אֲבָל הַמַּזִּיק חַיָּב לְשַׁלֵּם בְּדִינֵי שָׁמַיִם בְּכָל מָקוֹם, וְאִם תָּפַשׂ הַנִּזּוֹק אֵין מוֹצִיאִין מִיָּדוֹ בְשׁוּם מָקוֹם.

[שֶׁלֹּא לֶאֱכֹל שׁוֹר הַנִּסְקָל]

נב שֶׁלֹּא נֹאכַל בְּשַׂר שׁוֹר הַנִּסְקָל, אֲפִלּוּ נִשְׁחַט כָּרָאוּי, מִכֵּיוָן שֶׁנִּגְמַר דִּינוֹ בְּשָׂרוֹ אָסוּר, כֵּן מְפֹרָשׁ בַּמְּכִילְתָּא, שֶׁנֶּאֱמַר "וְלֹא יֵאָכֵל אֶת בְּשָׂרוֹ", וְלָאו דַּוְקָא שׁוֹר אֶלָּא אַף כָּל הַמַּזִּיקִין בִּבְהֵמָה חַיָּה וָעוֹף, אֶלָּא שֶׁיְּדַבֵּר בָּרָגִיל.

מִשָּׁרְשֵׁי הַמִּצְוָה כְּדֵי לְהַסְכִּים בְּדַעְתֵּנוּ שֶׁכָּל מִי שֶׁבָּאָה תַקָּלָה עַל יָדוֹ מְרֻחָק וְנִמְאָס עִם אֱלֹהִים וְעִם אֲנָשִׁים, וַאֲפִלּוּ שׁוֹגֵג כְּמוֹ הַבְּהֵמָה שֶׁאֵין לָהּ דַּעַת, וְכָל שֶׁכֵּן מֵזִיד. וּבִהְיוֹת דַּעְתֵּנוּ עַל דָּבָר זֶה יְבִיאֵנוּ לְהִזָּהֵר הַרְבֵּה בְּכָל מַעֲשֵׂינוּ עַד שֶׁלֹּא תֵצֵא תַקָּלָה מִתַּחַת יָדֵנוּ לְעוֹלָם.

מִדִּינֵי הַמִּצְוָה, מַה שֶּׁבֵּאֲרוּ זִכְרוֹנָם לִבְרָכָה שֶׁבֵּין תָּם בֵּין מוּעָד נִסְקָל עַל כָּל בְּרִיָּה שֶׁמֵּמִית, בֵּין אִישׁ אוֹ אִשָּׁה אוֹ קָטָן אוֹ עֶבֶד, וְשֶׁאֵין גּוֹמְרִין דִּינוֹ אֶלָּא בִּפְנֵי בְעָלָיו אִם יֵשׁ לוֹ בְעָלִים, וְכֵן מַה שֶּׁאָמְרוּ שֶׁיֵּשׁ צְדָדִין הַרְבֵּה שֶׁהַשּׁוֹר מֵמִית וְאֵינוֹ נִסְקָל, וְיֶתֶר פְּרָטֶיהָ, מְבֹאָרִים בְּקַמָּא.

וְנוֹהֶגֶת מִצְוַת אִסּוּר בְּשָׂרוֹ בִּזְכָרִים וּנְקֵבוֹת, וּבְאֶרֶץ יִשְׂרָאֵל דַּוְקָא נוֹהֵג דִּין שׁוֹר הַנִּסְקָל עַל פִּי סְמוּכִין, וּבְבֵית דִּין שֶׁל כ"ג. וְעוֹבֵר עָלֶיהָ וְאָכַל כְּזַיִת מִבְּשָׂרוֹ בְּמֵזִיד לוֹקֶה.

[מִצְוַת בֵּית דִּין לָדוּן בְּנִזְקֵי הַבּוֹר]

נג לָדוּן בְּדִינֵי הַפּוֹתֵחַ בּוֹר בְּמָקוֹם שֶׁהוּא כִּשְׁלוֹן לִבְנֵי אָדָם, שֶׁנֶּאֱמַר "וְכִי

---

15. So TB Bava Kamma 15b.

52 1. On the verse which follows; so too TB Bava Kamma 41a.
2. So MdRSbY on the verse; see also Mishnah, 'Eduyoth vi 1, and TB *ibid*.
3. TB Bava Kamma 41a.
4. So Exodus 21:28, 29, 31, 32.
5. TB Sanhedrin 79b; if it is a wild animal, etc. it is sentenced with no owner present (Rambam MT *hilchoth nizké mamon* x 6).
6. I.e. if it caused death unintentionally; TB Bava Kamma 44a.
7. See §47, note 7, in regard to capital cases, which applies here as well.

however, is required in any case to pay, by the laws of Heaven. And if the injured man [who suffered the damage] seized [the amount of his damages from the other] it is not taken out of his hand (possession) in any event.[15]

52 [NOT TO EAT ANY OX SENTENCED TO DEATH BY STONING] that we should not eat the flesh of an ox sentenced to stoning, even if it was properly ritually slain; for once its judgment was completed (sentence was passed), its flesh is forbidden. So is it explained in the Midrash *Mechilta:*[1] for it is stated, *and its flesh shall not be eaten* (Exodus 21:28). This does not mean specifically an ox, but any injuring creature, domestic or wild animal, or bird;[2] Scripture merely spoke of what is usual.

At the root of the precept lies the aim that we should realize in our thinking that whatever was the cause of a disaster or misfortune is to be scorned as something abhorrent to both God and humanity, even if it acted unintentionally, such as an animal which is witless, and all the more certainly a deliberate perpetrator of injury. As we reflect on this thought, it will influence us to be so very careful in all our deeds that no disaster or misfortune should ever issue from under our hands.

Among the laws of the precept there is what the Sages of blessed memory explained,[3] that whether it is a *tam* (an animal only beginning to cause fatal injury) or a *mu'ad* (a habitual killer), it is stoned to death for any person it kills, be it a man or a woman, a child, or a servant;[4] that its judgment is not to be completed (and sentence passed) except in its owner's presence, if it has an owner;[5] so also what the Sages said, that there are many ways in which an ox can kill and not be stoned to death.[6] [These] and its other details are explained in the Talmud tractate *Bava Kamma*.

The ban on eating its flesh applies to both man and woman; but only in the land of Israel can a case of an ox to be stoned be tried, by ordained, authorized persons[7]—and that in a *beth din* of twenty-three [judges]. If someone transgresses it and eats of its flesh the amount of an olive, deliberately, he is given whiplashes.

53 [THE OBLIGATION OF THE COURT TO JUDGE DAMAGES BY A PIT] to judge cases of those who open a pit in a place where it is a hazard, a cause of injury for people—as it is stated, *And if a man shall*

יִפְתַּח אִישׁ בּוֹר" וְגוֹמֵר, כְּמוֹ שֶׁכָּתוּב בַּפָּרָשָׁה. וְלָאו דַּוְקָא בוֹר אֶלָּא אֲפִלּוּ שִׁיחַ וּמְעָרָה, וְלֹא נֶאֱמַר בּוֹר אֶלָּא לְלַמֵּד שֶׁיְּהֵא בּוֹ כְּדֵי לְהָמִית דְּהַיְנוּ עֲשָׂרָה טְפָחִים.

שָׁרָשֶׁיהָ כְּבָר נִכְתָּב. דִּינֶיהָ, כְּגוֹן מַה שֶּׁאָמְרוּ שׁוֹר וְלֹא אָדָם, חֲמוֹר וְלֹא כֵלִים, חוֹפֵר בּוֹר בִּרְשׁוּתוֹ וְהִפְקִיר רְשׁוּתוֹ וְלֹא בוֹרוֹ, שֶׁחַיָּב, הִפְקִיר בּוֹרוֹ גַּם כֵּן פָּטוּר לְפִי שֶׁבִּרְשׁוּתוֹ חָפַר, מַה שֶּׁאֵין כֵּן בְּחוֹפֵר בִּרְשׁוּת הָרַבִּים שֶׁאֵינוֹ חוֹפֵר בִּרְשׁוּת מִתְּחִלָּה וּלְפִיכָךְ חַיָּב בּוֹ בְּכָל צַד. וְכֵן הַחוֹפֵר בּוֹר בִּרְשׁוּתוֹ סָמוּךְ לִרְשׁוּת הָרַבִּים מַמָּשׁ וְלֹא הִפְקִיר בּוֹרוֹ וְאֵין שׁוּם דָּבָר מַפְסִיק בֵּין הַבּוֹר וּרְשׁוּת הָרַבִּים, כְּגוֹן אֵלּוּ הַחוֹפְרִים לָאֻשִּׁין, פֵּרוּשׁ יְסוֹדוֹת לְכָתְלֵיהֶם, פָּטוּר. וּמִפְּנֵי כֵן פָּטוּר, אַף־עַל־פִּי שֶׁאִי אֶפְשָׁר לָרַבִּים לְהִשָּׁמֵר אַחַר שֶׁהוּא סָמוּךְ לַדֶּרֶךְ כָּל־כָּךְ, שֶׁאִי אֶפְשָׁר לְיִשּׁוּב הָאָרֶץ בִּלְתִּי שֶׁיַּעֲשׂוּ כָּל אֶחָד יְסוֹדוֹת לְבָתֵּיהֶם.

וְדִין הַמְגַלֶּה בּוֹר אַף עַל פִּי שֶׁלֹּא חֲפָרוֹ שֶׁאָמְרוּ זִכְרוֹנָם לִבְרָכָה שֶׁחַיָּב, דְּמִכָּל מָקוֹם בַּעַל הַתַּקָּלָה הוּא. וְחִלּוּק הַדִּינִין הַבָּאִין בְּעִנְיָן הַגִּלּוּי לְפִי כִּסּוּיוֹ שֶׁל בּוֹר בְּחָלְשׁוֹ וְחָזְקוֹ, וְדִין שֶׁל שֻׁתָּפִין בְּעִנְיָן הַכִּסּוּי, וְדִין בּוֹר שֶׁחֲפָרוּהוּ שְׁנַיִם זֶה אַחַר זֶה עַל מִי מֵהֶן חִיּוּבוֹ, וְדִינֵי חִיּוּב שֶׁיֵּשׁ לוֹ לָאָדָם בְּהַרְחָקַת הַנֵּזֶק כְּדֵי שֶׁלֹּא יָבוֹא הַנֵּזֶק לִבְנֵי אָדָם בְּמֵימָיו וְקוֹצָיו וּבְכוּכִיּוֹתָיו, וְיֶתֶר פְּרָטֶיהָ, מְבֹאָרִים בְּפֶרֶק ג' וְה' מְקַמָּא וּבַתְרָא.

וְנוֹהֶגֶת בִּזְכָרִים שֶׁעֲלֵיהֶם לַעֲשׂוֹת דִּין וְלֹא בִּנְקֵבוֹת שֶׁהֵן אֵינָן דַּנּוֹת, אֲבָל מִכָּל מָקוֹם בִּכְלָל דִּין הַתַּשְׁלוּמִין הֵן, בֵּין הִזִּיקוּ אוֹ הֻזְּקוּ.

§53 1. Mishnah, Bava Kamma v 5 (TB 50b).

2. The handbreadth (*tefah*) is 3.15 inches (8 centimeters) in one view, 3.78 inches (9.6 cm) by another ruling.

3. Exodus 21:33 reads, *and an ox or a donkey falls into it*; this is taken to mean that the death of a man or damages to inanimate objects by the pit need not be paid for; TB Bava Kamma 53b, etc. (From "what the Sages said" to here is not in the oldest manuscripts; but this seems to be part of the original.)

4. Ibid. 49b–50a.

5. Ibid. 49b.

6. E.g. if he placed a cover on it that could bear the weight of oxen but not of camels, then camels came and broke it in, after which oxen fell in—if camels did not usually come there, he has no liability, as this is considered an accident; *ibid.* 52a–b.

7. Mishnah, Bava Kamma v 6 (see reading of Rif and Rambam).

8. TB *ibid.* 51a.

9. *Ibid.* 30a.

10. TJ Sanhedrin iii 9.

open a pit, etc. (Exodus 21:33)—as written in the *sidrah*. This does not mean only, specifically a pit, but even a ditch or a cave;[1] "pit" was stated to convey that it should have the capacity to cause death [for the Torah's laws to apply], i.e. ten handbreadths.[2]

Its root purpose was written earlier (§49). It laws are, for instance, what the Sages said: *an ox* and not a man, *a donkey* and not utensils;[3] if someone digs a pit on his property and then leaves the property ownerless, but not the pit, that he pays damages;[4] if he made the pit ownerless also, he is free, quit of damages, because he dug it in his own property—which is not the case when someone digs a pit in the public domain, for he does not dig with permission (by right) originally, and he is therefore liable to pay damages for it in every respect.[4] So too, if someone digs a pit on his property right next to the public domain and does not leave his pit ownerless, and nothing whatever serves as a barrier between the pit and the public domain—for example, those who dig for *'ushin*, which means foundations for their walls—he is free of liability.[4] He has no liability for this reason, even though it is not possible for the public to guard itself [against injury], since it is so close to the road: for the settlement of the land cannot be achieved unless everyone sets foundations for his house.

[Then we have] the law of one who uncovers a pit, even though he did not dig it, about which our Sages of blessed memory said that he is liable for damages, since in any event he is responsible for the misfortunes [which it causes];[5] the difference in the laws which apply to the uncovering, depending on the cover of the pit—its weakness or strength;[6] the law for a pit of partners, in regard to covering it;[7] the law of a pit which two dug, one after the other: on which of them does the liability for its damage fall.[8] Then there are the laws of the duty a man has to remove [a potential source of] damage and injury to a [safe] distance, so that people should suffer no injury or damage through his water, his thorns, or his broken glassware.[9] [All these] and the rest of its details are explained in chapters 3 and 5 of *Bava Kamma*, and in *Bava Bathra*.

It applies to men, for on them lies the obligation to effect justice, and not to women, who do not judge cases.[10] They are, however, included under the law of the payments for damages, whether they caused or suffered injury.

§54: THE COURT TO IMPOSE PROPER PAYMENT ON A THIEF, ETC.

[מִצְוַת בֵּית דִּין לָדוּן גַּנָּב בְּתַשְׁלוּמִים אוֹ בְּמִיתָה]

נד לָדוּן בְּדִינֵי הַגַּנָּב כְּמוֹ שֶׁכָּתוּב בַּפָּרָשָׁה, "כִּי יִגְנֹב אִישׁ" וְגוֹמֵר. וְעִנְיַן הַגְּנֵבָה הוּא הַלּוֹקֵחַ דְּבַר מָמוֹן חֲבֵרוֹ מִבֵּיתוֹ אוֹ מִכִּיסוֹ בְּעֵת שֶׁלֹּא יִרְאֶה בַעַל הַבַּיִת וְלֹא יֵדַע, וְכָל כַּיּוֹצֵא בָזֶה.

שֹׁרֶשׁ מִצְוַת הַמִּשְׁפָּט יָדוּעַ. דִּינֶיהָ, כְּגוֹן תַּשְׁלוּמֵי כֶפֶל וְאַרְבָּעָה וַחֲמִשָּׁה, וְדִין הַהֲרוּג הַבָּא בַּמַּחְתֶּרֶת אוֹ לְמָכְרוֹ בִּגְנֵבָתוֹ, וְדִינֵי הַגְּנֵבָה שֶׁהִשְׁבִּיחָהּ בְּבֵית הַגַּנָּב מֵאֵלֶיהָ אוֹ מֵחֲמַת הוֹצָאָה, וְדִין גְּנֵבָה שֶׁהוּקְרָה שֶׁמְּשַׁלֵּם קֶרֶן כְּעֵין שֶׁגָּנַב וְתַשְׁלוּמֵי הַכְּפָלִים בִּשְׁעַת הָעֲמָדָה בְּדִין, וְדִין גַּנָּב שֶׁגָּנַב מִיַּד הַגַּנָּב שֶׁאֵין מְשַׁלֵּם כֶּפֶל לְאֶחָד מֵהֶן אֲפִלּוּ קֹדֶם יֵאוּשׁ, וְדִין גַּנָּב נִכְסֵי הֶקְדֵּשׁ אוֹ נִכְסֵי גּוֹי, אוֹ הַגּוֹנֵב עֲבָדִים וּשְׁטָרוֹת וְקַרְקָעוֹת, וְהַגּוֹנֵב בְּשַׁבָּת וּבָא עָלָיו חִיּוּב חִלּוּל שַׁבָּת וּגְנֵבָה כְּאֶחָד מַה דִּינוֹ לְעִנְיַן תַּשְׁלוּמִין, וּמֵאֵי זֶה מִנְּכָסָיו מַגְבִּין בֵּית דִּין דִּין מִמֶּנּוּ הַתַּשְׁלוּמִין, וְאִם נִמְכַּר בִּגְנֵבָתוֹ שֶׁצָּרִיךְ שֶׁיִּהְיוּ דָּמָיו כִּדְמֵי הַגְּנֵבָה אוֹ פָחוֹת, אֲבָל הָיוּ יוֹתֵר אֵינוֹ נִמְכַּר: וְדִינֵי שׁוֹמֵר שֶׁגָּנַב אוֹ שֶׁנִּגְנַב מִבֵּיתוֹ, וְדִין אָסוּר קְנִיַּת גְּנֵבָה מִיַּד גַּנָּב, וּמִי שֶׁקָּנָה מֵהֶן מַה דִּינוֹ עִם הַבְּעָלִים, וְיֶתֶר פְּרָטֶיהָ, מְבֹאָרִים בְּפֶרֶק ז' מִקַּמָּא, וּבְפֶרֶק ח' מִסַּנְהֶדְרִין, וּבַשְּׁלִישִׁי מִמְּצִיעָא וּבִמְקוֹמוֹת מְעַטִּים מִכְּתֻבּוֹת וְקִדּוּשִׁין וּשְׁבוּעוֹת.

וְנוֹהֶגֶת בִּזְכָרִים שֶׁעֲלֵיהֶם לַעֲשׂוֹת דִּין, וּבְכָל מָקוֹם שֶׁיֵּשׁ בֵּית דִּין סְמוּכִין בָּאָרֶץ מְחַיְּבִין לְשַׁלֵּם תַּשְׁלוּמֵי אַרְבָּעָה וַחֲמִשָּׁה, וְאִם אֵין סְמוּכִין אֵין לָהֶן כֹּחַ

---

§54   1. So Rambam MT *hilchoth g'névah* i 3.

2. Discussed respectively in TB Sanhedrin 72b, and Kiddushin 18a and MdRSbY.

3. I.e. if the thief went to expense to improve it; in either case, to whom does the gain in value belong? TB *ibid.* 65a.

4. A thief must pay twice the value of what he steals (Exodus 22:3); *ibid.*

5. I.e. either the owner or the first thief; Mishnah, Bava Kamma vii 1.

6. Which loss of hope might serve to let the stolen object become the second thief's property; see MY.

7. Mishnah, Bava M'tzi'a iv 9 (TB 56a); TB Bava Kamma 62b.

8. TB K'thuboth 31a.

9. TB Bava Kamma 5a.

10. TB Kiddushin 18a.

11. TB Sh'vu'oth 49a, Bava M'tzi'a 33b, 34a.

12. TB Bava Kamma 118b.

13. *Ibid.* 115a.

14. See §49, at note 15.

15. So, too "double payment." This rather means that if there is an ordained *beth din* in the land of Israel, the law may be carried out (see §47, note 7); MY so explains the Hebrew.

⟨224⟩

[THAT THE COURT SHOULD IMPOSE PROPER PAYMENT ON A THIEF, OR HE MAY INCUR DEATH]

54 to judge the cases of a thief, as it is written in the *sidrah*, *If a man steals*, etc. (Exodus 21:37). In substance, it is stealing (theft) when a person takes something of value from his fellow, from his house or from his purse, when the householder does not see and does not know; and so anything similar.[1]

The root purpose of the precepts of justice is known (evident). Its laws are, for example, the payment of double value (Exodus 22:3) and four and five times the value (*ibid.* 21:37); the law on killing a thief who breaks in (*ibid.* 22:1), or selling him [into servitude] for his theft (*ibid.* 2);[2] the law for something that improved, gained in value in the thief's house, either by itself or as a result of expenditure;[3] the law for a stolen object whose market value rose [of itself]—that he pays the principal according to its worth when he committed the theft, and the "double" (second) value according to its worth when he stands trial;[4] the law for a thief who steals from a thief, that he does not pay the "double" (second) value to either of them,[5] even before hope [of its recovery] is given up [by the owner];[6] the law for one who stole consecrated property, or the property of a non-Jew;[7] [the law] if one steals slaves, documents, or land;[7] if someone steals on the Sabbath, and he incurs together the penalties for violation of the Sabbath and for theft, what the law is for him regarding payment;[8] out of which kind of property of his does the *beth din* exact payment from him;[9] if he is sold [into servitude], that it is necessary for his monetary value to be either equal to the amount of the theft or less, but if it was more, he is not sold;[10] the laws of a custodian who stole [the object given him for safekeeping], or from whose house it was stolen;[11] the law that it is forbidden to buy a stolen object from a thief,[12] and if someone bought from them [thieves] what the law is for him in regard to the owner.[13] [These] and its further details are explained in chapter 7 of the tractate *Bava Kamma*, chapter 8 of *Sanhedrin*, chapter 3 of *Bava M'tzi'a*, and in a few other places in *K'thuboth*, *Kiddushin*, and *Sh'vu'oth*.

It applies to men, as it is for them to effect justice.[14] Wherever there is an ordained, authorized *beth din* in the land [of Israel], it can impose the payment of four and five [times the theft—Exodus 21:37];[15] and if [the judges] are not ordained and authorized, they do not have the power to impose [these sentences] but only to return the stolen object or its value in money. However, the practice of selling the thief himself

לְחַיָּב אֶלָּא לְהַחְזִיר הַגְּנֵבָה אוֹ דָמֶיהָ. אֲבָל מְכִירַת הַגַּנָּב עַצְמוֹ אֵינָהּ נוֹהֶגֶת וַאֲפִלּוּ בִּסְמוּכִין אֶלָּא בִּזְמַן שֶׁהַיּוֹבֵל נוֹהֵג.

[מִצְוַת בֵּית דִּין לָדוּן בְּנִזְקֵי הַבְּעֵר]

נה לָדוּן בְּנִזְקֵי שֵׁן וָרֶגֶל, כְּלוֹמַר מִי שֶׁהִזִּיק לַחֲבֵרוֹ נֶזֶק הַבָּא מֵחֲמַת הַשֵּׁן אוֹ מֵחֲמַת הָרֶגֶל, כְּגוֹן שֶׁהִכְנִיס בְּהֶמְתּוֹ בִּשְׂדֵה חֲבֵרוֹ וְאָכְלָה שָׁם אוֹ הִפְסִידָה יוֹנְקוֹתָיו בְּעָבְרָהּ שָׁם בְּרַגְלֶיהָ, יֵשׁ עָלֵינוּ לְחַיְּבוֹ בְּתַשְׁלוּמִין מִן הָעִדִּית שֶׁלּוֹ כָּל מַה שֶּׁהִפְסִיד, שֶׁנֶּאֱמַר "כִּי יַבְעֶר אִישׁ" וְגוֹמֵר, וּפֵרְשׁוּ זִכְרוֹנָם לִבְרָכָה דְּהַיְנוּ שֵׁן. וּמַה שֶּׁכָּתוּב אַחַר כֵּן "וְשִׁלַּח אֶת בְּעִירֹה" וְגוֹמֵר פֵּרְשׁוּ זִכְרוֹנָם לִבְרָכָה דְּהַיְנוּ רֶגֶל, וְנֶאֱמַר עַל שְׁנֵיהֶם "מֵיטַב שָׂדֵהוּ וּמֵיטַב כַּרְמוֹ יְשַׁלֵּם".

שֹׁרֶשׁ מִצְוַת הַמִּשְׁפָּט יָדוּעַ. דִּינֶיהָ, כְּגוֹן מָה הֵם הַמְּקוֹמוֹת שֶׁחַיָּבִין שָׁם עַל הַשֵּׁן וְהָרֶגֶל, וּמָה הֵן שֶׁאֵין חַיָּבִין בָּהֶן, וְחִלּוּק הַדִּין בְּאוֹכֶלֶת מַה שֶּׁרָאוּי לָהּ לֶאֱכֹל לְמַה שֶּׁאֵינוֹ רָאוּי, וְכֵן מַה שֶּׁרָאוּי לָהּ עַל יְדֵי הַדְּחָק, כְּגוֹן פָּרָה שֶׁאָכְלָה שְׂעוֹרִים וַחֲמוֹר שֶׁאָכַל כַּרְשִׁינִין אוֹ דָגִים, וַחֲזִיר שֶׁאָכַל בָּשָׂר, וְכֶלֶב שֶׁלִּקְלֵק אֶת הַשֶּׁמֶן, וְחָתוּל שֶׁאָכַל תְּמָרִים, וְאִם נֶהֱנֵית שֶׁמְּשַׁלֶּמֶת מַה שֶּׁנֶּהֱנֵית, וְיֶתֶר פְּרָטֶיהָ, בְּגִיטִּין וּבְקַמָּא. וְהָתָם אָמְרִינַן פֶּרֶק הַחוֹבֵל, כִּי קָא אָמַר רָבָא דְּשׁוֹר בְּשׁוֹר גּוֹבִין אוֹתוֹ בְּבָבֶל בְּשֵׁן וּבְרֶגֶל דְּמוּעָדִין מִתְּחִלָּתָן נִינְהוּ.

וְנוֹהֶגֶת בִּזְכָרִים שֶׁעֲלֵיהֶן לַעֲשׂוֹת הַדִּין, וּמִכָּל מָקוֹם בְּעִקְּבוֹת הַנְּקֵבוֹת בִּכְלַל דִּין הַתַּשְׁלוּמִין בֵּין הַמַּזִּיקוֹ אוֹ הַנִּזָּק. וּבֵית דִּין הָעוֹבֵר עָלֶיהָ וְלֹא דָן זֶה דִּין כְּמוֹ שֶׁכָּתוּב בִּטֵּל עֲשֵׂה.

---

16. Since the law of the Hebrew servant is observed only at that time (§42).

§55 1. TB Bava Kamma 2b.
2. *Ibid.* 19b (in the Mishnah).
3. I.e. the value of the food which the animal's owner thus saved, but not the cost of what was actually eaten; *ibid.* 19b, 20a. (If the animal ate unfit food, half the damages are to be paid; if the food was edible in an emergency, full damages—and the benefit—are to be paid if it happened in the public domain.)
4. Damages for such injuries are not considered fines; hence, because they are usual occurrences involving monetary loss, they should be imposed by the courts outside the land of Israel too (§49, at note 12), acting as deputies of the authorized courts in Israel. However, if a *tam*, an animal in its first or second such offense, gores

[into servitude] is in effect, even when there is an ordained, authorized *beth din*, only at the time that the law of the jubilee is in effect.[16]

[THE OBLIGATION OF THE COURT TO JUDGE DAMAGES BY A DOMESTIC ANIMAL'S GRAZING OR TRAMPLING]

55 to judge damages of Tooth and Foot: this means that if someone caused his fellow damage that occurred on account of teeth or feet—for instance, if he brought his domestic animal into his fellow's field and it grazed there, or it damaged the other's saplings by trampling them with its feet—it is for us to require him to pay out of his choice land all the loss that the other suffered. For it is stated, *If a man* yav'er *(causes grazing in) a field*, etc. (Exodus 22:4), and our Sages of blessed memory explained[1] that this means "the tooth" [damage by grazing]. As for the words after this, *and shall let his beast loose*, etc. (*ibid.*) our Sages of blessed memory explained[1] that it means "the foot"; and for both it is stated, *of the best of his field and the best of his vineyard shall he pay* (*ibid.*).

The root purpose of the precepts of civil justice is known (§49). As for its laws—for instance, which are the places where, if damage by tooth or foot occurs there, one is obligated to pay, and which, where one is not obligated;[2] the difference in law for a grazing animal, whether it consumes what is fit for it to eat or what is unfit, or again, what is fit for it to eat in emergency: for example, if a cow ate barley, a donkey ate vetch or fish, a pig ate meat, a dog lapped up oil, or a cat ate dates—and if it enjoyed or benefited from it, its benefit is to be paid for[3]—[these] and its other details are in the tractates *Gittin* and *Bava Kamma*. And there, in chapter 8 [of *Bava Kamma*] (84b) we learn: When Rava said that [damages caused by] one ox to another are to be collected in Babylonia, [he meant damages] by tooth or foot, for [in this respect] they are considered *mu'ad*, habitual offenders, from the start.[4]

It applies to men, as it is for them to carry out justice.[5] Women, however, are included under the law of payment for damages, whether they caused or suffered damage. If a *beth din* violates it and does not judge this kind of case as it is written in Scripture, it has disobeyed a positive precept.

§56–57: ON DAMAGE BY FIRE / CASES INVOLVING UNPAID CUSTODIAN

[מִצְוַת בֵּית דִּין לָדוּן בְּנִזְקֵי הָאֵשׁ]

נו לָדוּן וּלְחַיֵּב לְשַׁלֵּם מִי שֶׁהִזִּיק חֲבֵרוֹ בָּאֵשׁ, כְּגוֹן שֶׁהִדְלִיק אֶת גְּדִישׁוֹ אוֹ שָׂרַף לוֹ שׁוּם דָּבָר, שֶׁנֶּאֱמַר "כִּי תֵצֵא אֵשׁ" וְגוֹמֵר, פֵּרוּשׁ תֵּצֵא מַשְׁמַע אֲפִלּוּ יָצְאָה מֵעַצְמָהּ, וּבָא לְהַזְהִיר שֶׁאֲפִלּוּ הַמַּדְלִיק בְּתוֹךְ שֶׁלּוֹ וְיָצְאָה מֵעַצְמָהּ וְהִזִּיקָה שֶׁחַיָּב, לְפִי שֶׁלֹּא שָׁמַר גַּחַלְתּוֹ, שֶׁהָאָדָם חַיָּב לִשְׁמֹר אִשּׁוֹ שֶׁלֹּא תֵצֵא וְתַזִּיק, שֶׁדֶּרֶךְ הָאֵשׁ לָלֶכֶת מֵעַצְמָהּ אַף־עַל־פִּי שֶׁאֵינוֹ בַּעַל חַיִּים.

שָׁרְשָׁהּ יָדוּעַ כְּמוֹ שֶׁאָמַרְנוּ. דִּינֶיהָ כְּגוֹן שִׁעוּר הַהַרְחָקָה שֶׁמַּרְחִיקִין בְּעֶרְבָה מִן הַמֵּצֶר שֶׁהוּא לְפִי גָבְהָהּ שֶׁל דְּלֵקָה, וְדִין הַשְּׁלוּחָהּ בְּיַד חֵרֵשׁ שׁוֹטֶה וְקָטָן אוֹ פִּקֵּחַ, וְדִין הָרַבִּים, שֶׁאָדָם הֵבִיא הָאוּר וְאֶחָד הֵבִיא עֵצִים וְאֶחָד לִבָּה, וְלִבָּה וְלִבַּתּוּ הָרוּחַ, וְדִין כֵּלִים טְמוּנִים בְּגָדִישׁ אוֹ טְמוּנִים בְּבֵירָה, וְדִין גָּמָל עוֹבֵר טָעוּן פִּשְׁתָּן וְדָלְקָה בְּנֵר חֶנְוָנִי מַה דִּינוֹ, אוֹ בְּנֵר חֲנֻכָּה, וְיֶתֶר פְּרָטֶיהָ, מְבֹאָרִים בְּפֶרֶק שֵׁנִי וְשִׁשִּׁי מִן קַמָּא.

וְנוֹהֶגֶת בִּזְכָרִים כִּי לָהֶם לַעֲשׂוֹת דִּין, וּבֵית דִּין הָעוֹבֵר עָלֶיהָ וְלֹא דָן הַמַּזִּיק בְּתַשְׁלוּמִין כְּמוֹ שֶׁכָּתוּב בִּטֵּל עֲשֵׂה.

[מִצְוַת בֵּית דִּין לָדוּן בְּדִין שׁוֹמֵר חִנָּם]

נז לָדוּן בְּדִין שׁוֹמֵר חִנָּם, שֶׁנֶּאֱמַר "כִּי יִתֵּן אִישׁ אֶל רֵעֵהוּ כֶּסֶף אוֹ כֵלִים לִשְׁמֹר" וְגוֹמֵר, וּבָא הַפֵּרוּשׁ שֶׁפָּרָשָׁה זוֹ נֶאֶמְרָה בְּשׁוֹמֵר חִנָּם, וּלְפִיכָךְ פָּטַר בּוֹ אֶת הַגְּנֵבָה. וּפֵרוּשׁ חִנָּם הוּא שֶׁלֹּא הוּא קִבֵּל הַנִּפְקָד שׁוּם שָׂכָר עַל שְׁמִירַת הַפִּקָּדוֹן.

---

another animal, the payment of damages is a fine; hence judges outside the holy land do not try such cases, and consequently a goring animal can never be declared a *mu'ad*, a habitual offender (TB Bava Kamma 84b, Rashi s.v. *'en mu'ad*). Hence Rava taught that such cases, of damage by tooth or foot, may be tried in Babylonia, since for these an animal is always considered a *mu'ad*.

5. See §49, at note 15.

§56 1. So TB Bava Kamma 22b.
2. *Ibid.* 61b.
3. *Ibid.* 59b, 60a.
4. I.e. and the building then caught fire; Mishnah, Bava Kamma vi 6 (Rambam MT *hilchoth nizké mamon* xiv 13).
5. See §49, at note 15.

§57 1. TB Bava M'tzi'a 94b.

[THE OBLIGATION OF THE COURT TO JUDGE DAMAGE BY FIRE]

56 to judge and impose payment on one who has caused his fellow damage by fire—for example, if he set flame to his stacked grain, or burned anything of his—as it is written, *If fire breaks out*, etc. (Exodus 22:5). The sense of "breaks out" (*thétzé*) implies even if it broke out or spread by itself;[1] and so it comes to serve notice that even if a person kindled a fire within his own property and it spread by itself and caused damage, he is required to pay, because he did not watch his flame. For a man is duty-bound to watch his fire that it should not spread and do damage, since it is the way of fire to "travel" by itself, even though it is not a living creature.

Its root reason is known, as we have stated (§49). As to its laws —for instance, the distance that a fire is to be kept away from the boundary [of one's property], which is according to the height of the blaze;[2] the law for a person who sends it [flame] by the hand of a deaf-mute, a witless fool or a child, or with a normal, intelligent person;[3] the law of several people, one of whom brought the flame, one brought the wood, and one fanned the flame;[3] or if both a person and the wind fanned the flame;[3] the law if objects were hidden in stacked grain, or hidden in a building;[2] the case of a camel that passes by laden with flax and it catches fire from the lamp of a shopkeeper: what its law is—or [if it catches fire] from a Ḥanukkah candle[4]—[these] and its other details are explained in the second and sixth chapters of the Talmud tractate *Bava Kamma*.

It applies to men, as it is for them to effect justice.[5] If a *beth din* transgresses it and does not sentence the one who [thus] causes damage to make payment as it is written in Scripture, it has disobeyed a positive precept.

[THAT THE COURT SHOULD JUDGE CASES INVOLVING AN UNPAID CUSTODIAN]

57 to judge the case of an unpaid custodian, as it is stated, *If a man gives money or goods to his neighbor to guard*, etc. (Exodus 22:6). The explanation was given [in the Oral Tradition][1] that this section [of Scripture] deals with *shomér ḥinnom* (an unpaid keeper), and for this reason he is free of obligation in case of theft. The meaning of *ḥinnom* is that the recepient left in charge of it has received no recompense whatever for guarding the object in his care.

§57–58: CASES OF AN UNPAID CUSTODIAN / PLAINTIFF & DEFENDANT

הַשֹּׁרֶשׁ יָדוּעַ. דִּינֶיהָ, כְּגוֹן הַטּוֹעֵן טַעֲנַת גַּנָּב בְּפִקָּדוֹן וְנִשְׁבַּע וְאַחַר כָּךְ בָּאוּ עֵדִים בִּרְשׁוּתוֹ, וְחָזַר וְטָעַן טַעֲנַת גַּנָּב וְנִשְׁבַּע וְאַחַר כָּךְ בָּאוּ עֵדִים שֶׁהוּא בִּרְשׁוּתוֹ מַה דִּינוֹ; וְדִין טוֹעֵן טַעֲנַת אֲבֵדָה, וְדִין טוֹעֵן טַעֲנַת פִּקָּדוֹן, מַה דִּינוֹ; וְדִין טוֹעֵן וְחָזַר וְטָעַן טַעֲנַת גַּנָּב וְנִשְׁבַּע וְאַחַר כָּךְ בָּאוּ עֵדִים שֶׁהוּא בִּרְשׁוּתוֹ, וְדִין טוֹעֵן טַעֲנַת גַּנָּב בְּפִקָּדוֹן שֶׁל קָטָן, וְיֶתֶר פְּרָטֶיהָ, מְבֹאָרִים בְּפֶרֶק תְּשִׁיעִי מִן קַמָּא וּשְׁלִישִׁי מִמְּצִיעָא, וּשְׁמִינִי מִשְּׁבוּעוֹת.

וְנוֹהֶגֶת בְּכָל מָקוֹם וּבְכָל זְמַן, וּבֵית דִּין הָעוֹבֵר עָלֶיהָ בָּטֵל עָשָׂה.

[מִצְוַת בֵּית דִּין לָדוּן בְּדִין טוֹעֵן וְכוֹפֵר]

נח שֶׁנִּצְטַוֵּינוּ לָדוּן בְּדִין טוֹעֵן וְנִטְעָן, כְּלוֹמַר שֶׁנַּעֲשֶׂה דִין לְכָל מִי שֶׁתּוֹבֵעַ אֶת חֲבֵרוֹ בְּשׁוּם דָּבָר אוֹ שֶׁהִלְוָהוּ אוֹ הִפְקִידוֹ אוֹ גְּזָלוֹ אוֹ עֲשָׁקוֹ אוֹ חֲמָסוֹ, שֶׁנֶּאֱמַר "עַל כָּל דְּבַר פֶּשַׁע וְכוּ׳, אֲשֶׁר יֹאמַר כִּי הוּא זֶה".

וּבָא הַפֵּרוּשׁ עַל לְשׁוֹן זֶה שֶׁל "כִּי הוּא זֶה", שֶׁאֵין נִשְׁבָּעִין מִן הַתּוֹרָה אֶלָּא אִם כֵּן יוֹדֶה הַנִּתְבָּע בְּמִקְצָת הַהַלְוָאָה, אֲבָל אִם יֹאמַר "לֹא הָיוּ דְבָרִים מֵעוֹלָם" אוֹ "הֶחֱזַרְתִּי הַכֹּל בְּמִלְוָה", וַאֲפִלּוּ בְּפִקָּדוֹן, פָּטוּר מִשְּׁבוּעָה מִן הַתּוֹרָה. וְזֶהוּ שֶׁאָמְרוּ זִכְרוֹנָם לִבְרָכָה בַּגְּמָרָא דְּכִי כְתִיב "כִּי הוּא זֶה" אַמַּלְוֶה הוּא דִּכְתִיב, כְּלוֹמַר עַל טַעֲנַת מִלְוֶה שֶׁהִיא "פְּרַעְתִּיךָ" אוֹ "לֹא הָיוּ דְבָרִים מֵעוֹלָם", אֲבָל עַל

---

2. TB Bava Kamma 108a.

3. I.e. that the object given him for safekeeping (e.g. an ox) has been lost, and he actually took it for himself. It is a Scriptural decree that if he pleaded theft and his deceit was discovered, he must pay double the value; but if he pleaded loss, he needs pay only the value of the object (ibid.).

4. In this case he initially swears that the other's object, found in his possession, was given him for safekeeping (as a *pikkadon*), and then he admits his theft. Ordinarily a thief must pay double the value of his theft; but as this is a fine, because he admitted it he is free of the penalty. However, he swore falsely at first that it was a *pikkadon*, left in his care by the owner—which would have freed him from liability had the object been lost or stolen from him. Hence he must bring an offering (*korban sh'vu'ah*) to atone for the oath (TB Bava Kamma 105b).

5. I.e. that the object deposited with him was lost.

6. *Ibid.* 107b.

7. *Ibid.* 106b.

§58 1. And now he wishes to recover what is rightfully his.

2. Or refused to return the object given him for safekeeping (cf. Rambam MT hilchoth g'zelah i 4).

3. TB Bava Kamma 106b.

4. *Ibid.* 107a; even though the phrase is in the verse about a custodian given something for safekeeping, by the Sages' traditional rules of interpretation it is applicable to a plea generally used by a borrower.

The root reason [for the precept] is known (§49). Its laws are, for example: if someone states a plea of theft about an object left him for safekeeping, and swears to it, and afterward witnesses come to testify that it is in his possession, whereupon he repeats his plea of theft and swears to it, after which come witnesses testifying that it is in his possession: what is the law for him;[2] the case of one who states a plea of loss;[3] the case of one who argues that an object was deposited with him for safekeeping [while the owner argues that he stole it]: what the law is for him;[4] the case of one who states [another plea][5] then comes with a plea of theft, swearing to it, and afterward witnesses come to testify that it is in his possession;[6] and the case of one who gives a plea of theft about an object left him by a child for safekeeping.[7] [These] and its further details are clarified in chapter 9 of tractate *Bava Kamma*, chapter 3 of *Bava M'tzi'a*, and chapter 8 of *Sh'vu'oth*.

It applies in every place and every time. A *beth din* which transgresses it has disobeyed a positive precept.

[THE COURT'S OBLIGATION TO JUDGE THE CASE OF A PLAINTIFF AND A DEFENDANT]

58 that we were commanded to judge cases between a plaintiff and a defendant; in other words, that we should hold trial for any person who sues his fellow about any matter: if he either lent him money or left something with him for safekeeping,[1] or if the other robbed him, refused to pay him,[2] or bought something from him by force—as it is stated, *For every matter of injustice ... of which one says: This is it* (Exodus 22:8).

The interpretation was given [in the Oral Tradition][3] about this expression, "This is it," [that it teaches us] that an oath need not be taken by Torah law unless the defendant [in the case of a loan] admits to part of the loan; but if he says, "Nothing of the sort ever happened," or "I returned everything"—about a loan, or even about an object given him for safekeeping—he has no obligation to swear [to it] by Torah law. For this reason our Sages of blessed memory said in the Talmud that when "This is it" was written [in the Torah], it was written in allusion to a loan[4]—i.e. about a plea generally used over a loan, viz. "I paid you," or, "None of this ever happened." As regards the plea that custodians (keepers) would argue, however—a plea of accident or theft—even if he does not admit to part [of the claim] but says, "All was

§58: THE COURT TO JUDGE CASES OF PLAINTIFF AND DEFENDANT

טַעֲנַת שׁוֹמְרִים שֶׁהִיא טַעֲנַת אֹנֶס אוֹ גְּנֵבָה אֲפִלּוּ אִם לֹא יוֹדֶה אִם לֹא מִקְצָת אֶלָּא יֹאמַר הַכֹּל נֶאֱנָס חַיָּב לִשָּׁבַע.

וּבְפָסוּק זֶה נִכְלְלוּ כָּל הַתְּבִיעוֹת שֶׁבֵּין בְּנֵי אָדָם שֶׁיִּכָּנֵס בֵּינֵיהֶם הַהוֹדָאָה וְהַהַכְחָשָׁה.

שֹׁרֶשׁ הַדִּינִין יָדוּעַ.

דִּינֶיהָ, כְּגוֹן מִקְצָת מוֹדֶה שֶׁנִּשְׁבַּע מִדְּאוֹרַיְתָא, פֵּרוּשׁ מוֹדֶה בִּפְרוּטָה וְכוֹפֵר בִּשְׁתֵּי מָעִין כֶּסֶף, דְּפָחוֹת מִכֵּן אֵינוֹ נִשְׁבַּע דְּאוֹרַיְתָא אֶלָּא אִם כֵּן עֵד מֵעִיד כְּנֶגְדּוֹ, שֶׁנִּשְׁבַּע אֲפִלּוּ כְשֶׁכּוֹפֵר בִּפְחוֹת מִשְּׁתֵּי מָעִין, אֲבָל בִּפְחוֹת מִפְּרוּטָה אֵינוֹ נִשְׁבָּע לְעוֹלָם אֶלָּא אִם כֵּן טְעָנוֹ כֵלִים, דְּבְכֵלִים אֲפִלּוּ טְעָנוֹ שְׁתֵּי מְחָטִין וְהוֹדָה בְּאַחַת וְכָפַר בְּאַחַת נִשְׁבָּע. וּכְשֶׁנִּשְׁבָּע בְּהוֹדָאַת מִקְצָת בְּשֶׁטְּעָנוֹ בְדָבָר שֶׁבְּמִדָּה אוֹ מִנְיָן אוֹ מִשְׁקָל.

וְדִין כּוֹפֵר בַּכֹּל, וְהוֹדָאָה וְהוֹדָאַת הַטַּעֲנָה, וְהוֹדָאַת בַּעַל דִּין, וְדִינֵי שׁוֹמְרִים, וּמְחֻיַּב שְׁבוּעָה דְּאוֹרַיְתָא אוֹ דְרַבָּנָן, וְדִינֵי נִשְׁבָּע וְנִפְטָר, וְנִשְׁבַּע וְנוֹטֵל, וְדִין חָשׁוּד עַל הַשְּׁבוּעָה, וְהִפּוּכֵי הַשְּׁבוּעָה, וּבְאֵי זֶה עֲבֵרָה נַעֲשָׂה חָשׁוּד, וְאֵיזוֹ תְּשׁוּבָה יוֹצִיאֶנּוּ מִן הַחֲשָׁד.

וּמִי שֶׁלֹּא נוֹדַע שֶׁהוּא חָשׁוּד וְזָכָה בְּמָמוֹן בִּשְׁבוּעָתוֹ וְאַחַר כָּךְ בָּאוּ עֵדִים שֶׁחָשׁוּד הָיָה שֶׁחַיָּב לְהַחֲזִיר הַמָּמוֹן, וּמְחֻיָּב שְׁבוּעָה שֶׁאֵינוֹ יָכוֹל לִשָּׁבַע מַה דִּינוֹ, וְדִינֵי מִגּוֹ, וְדִינֵי בָּרִיא וְשֶׁמָּא, וְדִינֵי גִּלְגּוּל שְׁבוּעָה בֵּין בָּרִיא עַל בָּרִיא אוֹ עַל שֶׁמָּא, וַאֲפִלּוּ שֶׁמָּא עַל שֶׁמָּא, בְּכָל עִנְיַן שְׁבוּעָה מְגַלְגְּלִין, וּבְכָל שְׁבוּעָה יֵשׁ גִּלְגּוּל בֵּין דְּאוֹרַיְתָא אוֹ דְרַבָּנָן, וַאֲפִלּוּ שֶׁהִיא תַקָּנַת אַחֲרוֹנִים.

וְדִינֵי הַטְּעָנוֹת שֶׁאָנוּ דָנִין הַנִּתְבָּע כְּמֵשִׁיב אֲבֵדָה, וְהַדְּבָרִים שֶׁאֵין נִשְׁבָּעִין

5. And about this he was as helpless as in the case of accident; in this ruling our author follows Riva in *tosafoth*, TB Bava Kamma 107a, s.v. '*éruv*.

6. So Rambam ShM positive precept §246.

7. TB Sh'vu'oth 38b, 39b (view of Rav), 40a. A *m'ah* (singular of *m'oth*) was a coin weighing and worth 0.8 grams of silver (roughly equivalent to four cents); it was worth thirty-two times a *p'rutah*; i.e. thirty-two *p'rutoth* equalled one *m'ah*.

8. *Ibid.* 40b. 9. Mishnah, Sh'vu'oth vi 6 (TB 42b). 10. *Ibid.* 1 (TB 38b).

11. Thus, if one claims wheat, and the other admits owing him barley, this does not obligate him to take an oath on it; *ibid*.

12. That it is as good as the evidence of a hundred witnesses; TB K'rithoth 12a, etc. 13. Mishnah, Bava M'tzi'a vii 8 (TB 93a).

14. By Torah law: if the defendant admits part of the claim, if one witness testifies against him, or when the custodian of an object must clear himself of suspicion of negligence about it; see Mishnah, Sh'vu'oth vii; TB 44b–45a ff. 15. *Ibid*.

16. That he is capable of swearing falsely; *ibid*.

17. That instead of having the defendant take an oath that he speaks the truth, with which he goes free, the plaintiff so swears and receives his claim; *ibid*. and TB 41a. 18. Mishnah, Sh'vu'oth vii 4; TB 44b–45a. 19. TB Sanhedrin 25b.

SIDRAH MISHPATIM

lost by accident (or taken by force)," [5] he is obligated to swear [to it].

In this verse are included all claims between people which involve admission and denial. [6]

The root purpose of the [civil] laws is known (evident).

Its laws are, for instance, that one who admits part [of a claim] must take an oath by the Torah's law [that he does not owe the rest]. This means if he admits to a *p'rutah* and denies [owing] two silver *m'oth;*[7] for about less than this he need not take an oath by the Torah's law—unless a witness testifies against him, in which case he must swear even if he denies [owing] less than two *m'oth*. Over [the denial of] less than a *p'rutah*, though, one never needs to take an oath—unless the claim is for goods, objects: for over goods, even if the claim is for two needles and he admits about one, he takes an oath.[8] And when an oath is sworn over a partial admission, it is where the claim is about something measured, counted or weighed.[9]

Then [there is] the law for one who denies all;[10] that an admission on the subject of the claim [alone brings the obligation to swear];[11] [the law about] an admission by the person on trial;[12] the laws for custodians [of objects left for safekeeping];[13] when an oath is required by Torah law and when by the decree of the Sages;[14] the law of one who swears an oath and goes free, and one who swears an oath and takes [what he claims];[15] the law for one who is suspected about an oath;[16] the reversal (transferral) of an oath [from defendant to plaintiff];[17] through which transgression one becomes suspected [that he may swear falsely],[18] and which repentance will remove him from suspicion.[19]

[There is, further] the law for a person about whom it was not known that he was suspect, and so he won something of monetary value with his oath, and afterward witnesses came to testify that he was suspected [of dishonesty in oath-taking]—that he must return what he obtained;[20] a person obligated to swear who cannot take an oath: what is his law;[21] the laws of *miggo* [to believe a person's plea if he could equally have presented a better plea, which would have been believed];[22] the laws about pleas of certainty and doubt;[23] the laws of "rolling on" an oath about a plea of certainty onto another sure plea or onto a plea of doubt, and even [an oath] about one uncertain plea onto another—in every matter involving an oath, it can be "rolled on"; indeed, with every oath, whether by Torah law or the law of the Sages, there can be a "rolling on," even if it is an ordinance of late authorities.[24]

[Then we have] the laws about those claims in regard to which we

§58: THE COURT TO JUDGE CASES OF PLAINTIFF AND DEFENDANT

עֲלֵיהֶם דִּין תּוֹרָה, וּפֵרוֹת שֶׁהִגִּיעוּ לַכַּתָּפַיִם אִם דִּינָן כְּקַרְקַע לְעִנְיַן שְׁבוּעָה. וְהָאוֹמֵר לַחֲבֵרוֹ "שְׁטָר בְּיָדְךָ וּזְכוּת יֵשׁ לִי בּוֹ", אִם כּוֹפִין אוֹתוֹ לְהוֹצִיאוֹ, וְדִין הַבָּא לִפָּרַע שֶׁלֹּא בִּפְנֵי הַמַּלְוֶה, וְדִין מַלְוֶה עַל הַמַּשְׁכּוֹן וְאָבַד הַמַּשְׁכּוֹן אִם חוֹלְקִין זֶה עִם זֶה בְּמִנְיַן מְעוֹת הַמַּלְוָה, וְדִין הַמַּלְוֶה בִּישּׁוּב וְרָצָה לְפָרְעוֹ בַּמִּדְבָּר, וְדִין לוֹוֶה אוֹמֵר "פָּרַעְתִּי מֶחֱצָה" וְהָעֵדִים מְעִידִים שֶׁפְּרָעוֹ כֻּלּוֹ, וְדִין לוֹוֶה מוֹדֶה בִּשְׁטָר שֶׁכְּתָבוֹ וְטוֹעֵן שֶׁפְּרָעוֹ אִם צָרִיךְ לְקַיֵּם הַמַּלְוֶה, וְדִין שְׁטָר שֶׁלָּוָה בּוֹ וּפְרָעוֹ.

וְדִין שׁוֹלֵחַ מָנֶה בְּיַד שָׁלִיחַ לְמִי שֶׁנִּתְחַיֵּב לוֹ וּבָא לַחֲזוֹר בּוֹ, וְדִין טַעֲנַת פָּרוּעַ בִּשְׁטָר שֶׁבְּיַד שָׁלִישׁ, וְדִין שְׁטָר שֶׁאֵין בּוֹ מָקוֹם אוֹ זְמַן אִם כָּשֵׁר, וְדִין אַחֲרָיוּת טָעוּת סוֹפֵר בְּכָל הַשְּׁטָרוֹת חוּץ מִשִּׁטְרֵי מַתָּנָה, וְדִין מְשֻׁעְבָּד מְשַׁלְטְלִין שֶׁלּוֹ, וְהָעוֹשֶׂה שָׂדֵהוּ אוֹ עֲבָדָיו אַפּוֹתִיקֵי סְתָם אוֹ מְפֹרָשׁ, וְדִין טְרֵיפַת שֶׁבַח וּפֵרוֹת בֵּין בְּנִגְזָל בֵּין בְּבַעַל חוֹב, וְדִין מִי שֶׁאָבַד שְׁטָרוֹ אוֹ נִמְחַק, וְדִין מִי נוֹתֵן שָׂכָר כְּתִיבַת הַשְּׁטָר, וְדִין שׁוּמָא דְּהַדְרָא לְעוֹלָם אֶלָּא אִם כֵּן זַבְּנָהּ אוֹ אוֹרְתָהּ אוֹ יַהֲבָהּ בְּמַתָּנָה.

וְדִין הַדְּבָרִים שֶׁאֵין שְׁבוּעָה בָּהֶם אֶלָּא חֵרֶם סְתָם, וְשֶׁאֵין נִשְׁבָּעִין עַל טַעֲנַת חֵרֵשׁ שׁוֹטֶה וְקָטָן, וְהַדַּיָּנִין הַיּוֹצְאִין מֵהֶם עִם הַגְּדוֹלִים, וְשֶׁאֵין מְקַבְּלִין עֵדוּת אֶלָּא בִּפְנֵי בַעַל דִּין, וְקָטָן אֲפִלּוּ בְּפָנָיו כְּאִלּוּ אֵינוֹ, וְהַסּוּמָא שֶׁהוּא כְּבָרִיא לְכָל דָּבָר

---

20. See Rambam MT *hilchoth to'én v'nit'an* ii 9.
21. He must then fulfill the plaintiff's demands; TB Bava Bathra 34a, etc.
22. TB K'thuboth 12b, etc.
23. E.g. the plaintiff says, "You owe me this amount," and the defendant replies, "I do not know; perhaps"; TB Bava Kamma 118a, etc.
24. I.e. where a person is legally not required to swear a certain oath, if at the same time he becomes obligated to take a different oath, then he must swear the first one as well; it is "rolled on" to the second one; Mishnah, Sh'vu'oth vii 8, TB 48b.
25. E.g. if the plaintiff argued, "You have this amount of my [late] father's money," and the defendant admitted owing half the amount; the defendant is believed, for were he a liar, he could have denied it altogether; hence it is as though the amounts were argued about money found ("You really found twice as much and returned only the half to me"), in which case the defendant need not swear to his plea; Mishnah, Sh'vu'oth vi 1 (TB 38b); TB Bava M'tzi'a 4b; and see Gittin 48b. It should be noted that the Sages established a rule *mip'né tikkun ha'olam*, "for the sake of social harmony," that a person returning a lost object need not swear that he did not find more and is withholding the rest, no matter what the loser may contend—for otherwise nobody would be willing to return anything he found. The principle applies in any similar situation.   26. Mishnah, Sh'vu'oth vi 5 (TB 42b).
27. E.g. wheat which has grown its full height (Rashi, TB Bava Kamma 95b, s.v. *maggi'a*); ibid. 6 (TB 42b); and see Rambam MT *hilchoth to'én v'nit'an* v 4).
28. See Rambam *ibid.* v 7; *Maggid Mishneh*'s reference is to TB Bava Bathra 168a.
29. Mishnah, Sh'vu'oth vii 7 (TB 45a).
30. *Ibid.* vi 7 (TB 43a).   31. TB Bava Kamma 118a.
32. I.e. if the borrower need take an oath about the half to which he does not admit; TB Bava Bathra 128b.

judge the defendant like someone returning a lost object;[25] those matters over which an oath is not taken by the Torah's law;[26] if produce reaches to the shoulders,[27] whether it is considered as land in regard to taking an oath; if someone says to his fellow, "There is a document [of debt or obligation, of mine] in your possession, and I have some rights in it," whether the other is compelled to give it over;[28] the law for one who comes to pay a debt in the absence of the lender;[29] the law of a loan given for a pawned object whereupon the object was lost, and the two argue over the amount of money lent;[30] the law for a person who lends money in a settled community, and the other wishes to repay him in the wilderness;[31] the law if the borrower says, "I paid half," and witnesses testify that he paid all [the loan];[32] the law if a borrower admits about a document of debt (*sh'tar*) that he had it written, but argues that he paid it, if the lender need prove it genuine;[33] and the law about a *sh'tar* by which a person borrowed money, and then he paid it.[34]

[Further, there is] the law about a person who sends a *maneh* (an amount of money) by messenger to someone to whom he owes it, and then he comes to change his mind;[35] the law about a plea of "paid" regarding a document of debt in the hands of a trustee [who holds the document];[36] the law about a *sh'tar* in which the place or the time [of its writing] is missing, whether it is valid;[37] the law that the omission of the pledge of property in all documents is the scribe's error (oversight) except in deeds of gift;[38] the law of a person who pledges his movable property [as surety for a loan];[39] [the law] when someone mortgages his field or his servant, generally or explicitly;[40] the law about seizing the value of the improvement of land or produce [for his recompense], whether the plaintiff was robbed or he lent money;[41] the law if someone's document of debt was lost or erased;[42] the law on who should pay the fee for writing the *sh'tar*;[43] the law regarding property appraised [by the *beth din* and given to a creditor, *et al.*]—that it can always return [to the original owner] unless he sold it, bequeathed it, or gave it as a gift.[44]

Then there is the law about those matters which do not involve an oath but a general imposition of conditional excommunication;[45] that no oath is taken over the claim of a deaf-mute, a witless fool, or a child;[46] and laws which arise for their cases [of deaf-mutes, *et al.*] with adults.[46]

[There is, moreover, the law] that testimony is to be taken only in the presence of [each] person in the case;[47] that even when a child is present, it is [legally] as if he were not;[47] that a blind man is as a normal

§58: THE COURT TO JUDGE CASES OF PLAINTIFF AND DEFENDANT

חוּץ מֵעֵדוּת, וְדִין חֶנְוָנִי עַל פִּנְקָסוֹ, וּמַעֲמָד שֶׁלָּשְׁתָּן קוֹנֶה וְהִיא הִלְכְתָא בְּלֹא טַעֲמָא, וְכָל הַתָּלוּי בָּזֶה הָעִנְיָן.

וְדִינֵי מְרָשָׁה עִם מִי שֶׁהָרְשָׁה עָלָיו וְעִם מִי שֶׁהִרְשֵׁהוּ, וּלְשׁוֹן הַהַרְשָׁאָה שֶׁהוּא "דּוּן וּזְכֵה וְאַפִּיק לְנַפְשָׁךְ", וְדִין הָאוֹמֵר כְּאוֹמֵר "לָוִיתִי לֹא פָּרַעְתִּי, וְדִינֵי מִי שֶׁהֶחְזִיק כָּפְרָן, וְדִין מִי שֶׁאוֹמֵר לוֹ בֵּית דִּין "צֵא תֵּן לוֹ", וְאָמַר "פָּרַעְתִּי", אוֹ "חַיָּב אַתָּה לִתֵּן לוֹ".

וְדִין הָאוֹמֵר "אַל תִּפְרָעֵנִי אֶלָּא בְּעֵדִים" אוֹ "בִּפְנֵי פְּלוֹנִי וּפְלוֹנִי", וְאִם הָלְכוּ לִמְדִינַת הַיָּם מַה יִּהְיֶה עָלָיו, וְדִין הַמַּאֲמִין הַמַּלְוֶה בִּשְׁטָר כִּשְׁנֵי עֵדִים אִם יוֹעִילוּ לוֹ עֵדֵי פֵּרָעוֹן, וְדִין בְּאֵי זֶה עִנְיָן יָכוֹל אָדָם לוֹמַר "מְשַׁטֶּה הָיִיתִי בָךְ", אוֹ אֵין אָדָם יָכוֹל לוֹמַר.

וְדִין הַמּוֹצִיא מֵחֲבֵרוֹ, וְהַדְּבָרִים שֶׁיֵּשׁ לָהֶן חֲזָקָה שֶׁנִּקְרָא הַתּוֹבְעָן מוֹצִיא, וְדִינֵי חֲזָקוֹת, וְדִינֵי גְּבִיּוֹת בְּאֵי זֶה עִנְיָן יוֹרְדִין לִנְכָסָיו, וְדִינֵי עֲרֵבוּת, וְדִינֵי מְחָאוֹת, וְדִין הָאֲנָשִׁים שֶׁאֵין מַחֲזִיקִין עֲלֵיהֶן וְלֹא הֵם עַל אַחֵר, וְכָל דִּינֵי מְצָרָנוּת.

וְיֶתֶר רְבֵּי פְּרָטֶיהָ, מְבֹאָרִים בְּבָקְמָא, וְעִקָּר בְּפֶרֶק ג' מִמֶּנּוּ, וּבִמְצִיעָא, וְעִקָּר בְּפֶרֶק רִאשׁוֹן, וּשְׁמִינִי דְּבָתְרָא, וּבִשְׁבוּעוֹת פֶּרֶק חֲמִישִׁי שִׁשִּׁי וּשְׁבִיעִי וּבְהַרְבֵּה מְקוֹמוֹת בַּתַּלְמוּד בְּפִזּוּר קְצָת מִן הַדִּינִין.

וְנוֹהֶגֶת מִצְוָה זוֹ, שֶׁאָנוּ חַיָּבִין לָדוּן, בִּזְכָרִים אֲבָל לֹא בִּנְקֵבוֹת שֶׁאֵינָן דָּנוֹת,

---

33. TB K'thuboth 19a, etc. See Rambam MT *hilchoth malveh* xiv 5.

34. I.e. if he reborrowed the money, whether his landed property is again bound by the document as collateral for the loan; TB K'thuboth 85a.

35. I.e. before the messenger has delivered it; TB Gittin 14a.

36. TB Sanhedrin 31a.

37. See TB K'thuboth 110b, Sanhedrin 32a, from which it is evident that such an omission would not disqualify it.

38. TB Bava M'tzi'a 15b; about deeds of gift see *ibid.* 108b and Rashi.

39. TB Bava Bathra 44a.   40. TB Gittin 41a.

41. *Ibid.* 48b (and see Rashi there); Bava M'tzi'a 14–15 (Rambam MT *hilchoth malveh* xxi 1–2).

42. TB Bava Bathra 168a–b.   43. *Ibid.* 167b.   44. TB Bava M'tzi'a 35a.

45. Rambam MT *hilchoth to'én v'nit'an* i 11.

46. Mishnah, Sh'vu'oth vi 4 (TB 38b; Rambam *ibid.* v 10).

47. TB Bava Kamma 112a.

48. *Ibid.* 86b (R. 'Asher to Bava Kamma, chapter 8 §7); Bava Bathra 128a.

49. Mishnah, Sh'vu'oth vii 1 (TB 44b).

50. I.e. if A tells B, "What you are due to give me"—be it a loan or an object left with him for safekeeping—"give it to C"; if all three are there at the time, it takes effect, and none of them can retract; TB Gittin 13b.

51. *Ibid.* 14a.   52. TB Bava Kamma 70a.

53. I.e. if witnesses then testify that he did receive a loan, he must pay; he cannot say, "I meant that I did not remain a borrower—I paid him"; TB Sh'vu'oth 41a, etc.

SIDRAH MISHPATIM

(sighted) man in all respects [legally] except for serving as a witness;[48] the law about a shopkeeper in regard to his account book;[49] [that the transferral of a debt] in the presence of all three takes effect,[50] which is a ruling without a reason,[51] and all that is connected with this subject.

[Then we have] the laws of an authorized person in regard to the one over whom he was given authorization (power of attorney), and in regard to the one who authorized him;[52] the proper phrasing of the authorization, which is, "Impose the law and gain possession, and take [it] for yourself";[52] the law that if someone says, "I did not borrow," it is the same as saying, "I did not pay";[53] the laws about one who becomes known as a liar;[54] the law about a person whom the *beth din* tells, "Go out and pay him," and he says, "I paid," or [alternatively, if the *beth din* tells him] "You are obligated to pay him."[55]

[In addition, we have] the law about a person who said, "Pay me only with witnesses [present]," or "in the presence of these-and-these people," and they went overseas, what should be done about it;[56] the law for one who [promised] in the document of debt (the *sh'tar*) to believe the lender as though there were two witnesses [to his word]—if witnesses to the repayment can avail him;[57] and the law about the situation in which a man can say "I was jesting with you," and where a man cannot say this.[58]

[We have, further] the law about one who would extract [payment or an object] from his fellow;[59] things which have an established status [regarding their possession], so that the man who claims them is called the one who would extract them;[60] the laws on [what establishes] status of possession;[61] the laws of collection [of what rightfully belongs to one]: under which circumstances one goes down to the other's property [to take his due];[62] the laws of guaranty, surety;[63] the laws of protest [against illegal possession];[64] the law about those people for whom no status of possession is established, either for others' property which they hold or for their property which others hold;[65] and all the laws of the rights of neighbors.[66]

[All these] and the rest of its many details are clarified in the Talmud tractate *Bava Kamma*, mainly in its third chapter; in *Bava M'tzi'a*, mainly in the first chapter; in chapter 8 of *Bava Bathra*; in chapters 5, 6 and 7 of *Sh'vu'oth*; and in many [other] places in the Talmud, where some of the laws are scattered.

This precept, that we are required to hold court, applies to men, but not to women, who do not act as judges.[67] They are, however,

§58–59: ABOUT PLAINTIFF & DEFENDANT, PAID CUSTODIAN & HIRER

אֲבָל מִכָּל מָקוֹם בְּתוֹרַת דִּינִין הֵן לְתַשְׁלוּמִין וּלְכָל דָּבָר, אֶלָּא שֶׁיֵּשׁ חִלּוּק קְצָת בְּטַעֲנוֹת הַנְּשׂוּאוֹת בְּעִנְיָנִים יְדוּעִים, כְּמוֹ שֶׁמְּפֹרָשׁ בַּמְּקוֹמוֹת שֶׁנִּזְכָּרְנוּ. וְגַם כֵּן נוֹהֶגֶת בְּכָל מָקוֹם וּבְכָל זְמַן. וּבֵית דִּין הָעוֹבֵר עָלֶיהָ וְלֹא עָשָׂה דִּין אִם יֵשׁ פֹּח בְּיָדוֹ בִּטֵּל עָשָׂה, וְעָנְשׁוֹ גָּדוֹל מְאֹד, שֶׁגּוֹרֵם חֻרְבָּן לָאָרֶץ, שֶׁאֵין הָאָרֶץ מִתְיַשֶּׁבֶת אֶלָּא בְּדִין, וּכְמוֹ שֶׁאָמְרוּ זִכְרוֹנָם לִבְרָכָה: עַל שְׁלֹשָׁה דְּבָרִים הָעוֹלָם עוֹמֵד, וְאַחַת מֵהֶן הוּא הַדִּין.

וְזֹאת אַחַת מִן הַמִּצְווֹת שֶׁנִּצְטַוּוּ עָלֶיהָ כָּל בְּנֵי הָעוֹלָם בִּכְלָלָם, לְפִי שֶׁאִי אֶפְשָׁר לְיִשּׁוּב הָעוֹלָם זוּלָתָהּ.

[מִצְוַת בֵּית דִּין לָדוּן בְּדִין נוֹשֵׂא שָׂכָר וְשׁוֹכֵר]

נט לָדוּן בְּדִין נוֹשֵׂא שָׂכָר וְהַשּׂוֹכֵר. פֵּרוּשׁ נוֹשֵׂא שָׂכָר, שׁוֹמֵר פִּקָּדוֹן בְּשָׂכָר שֶׁנּוֹתְנִין לוֹ עַל הַשְּׁמִירָה, וְשׂוֹכֵר הוּא כְּמַשְׁמָעוֹ, שֶׁשָּׂכַר בְּהֵמָה מֵחֲבֵרוֹ לִרְכֹּב אוֹ לַעֲשׂוֹת בָּהּ מְלָאכָה, אוֹ שֶׁשָּׂכַר מִמֶּנּוּ מִטַּלְטְלִין, וְנָפַל מַחְלֹקֶת בֵּין הַשּׂוֹכֵר וְהַמַּשְׂכִּיר, אוֹ בֵּין בַּעַל הַפִּקָּדוֹן וְהַשּׁוֹמֵר בְּשָׂכָר, שֶׁמִּצְוָה עָלֵינוּ לָדוּן בֵּינֵיהֶם, כְּמוֹ שֶׁכָּתוּב בְּפָרָשָׁה זוֹ: כִּי יִתֵּן אִישׁ אֶל רֵעֵהוּ חֲמוֹר אוֹ שׁוֹר אוֹ שֶׂה וְכָל בְּהֵמָה לִשְׁמֹר וְגוֹמֵר.

שֹׁרֶשׁ הַדִּינִין יָדוּעַ.

דִּינֶיהָ, כְּגוֹן מַה שֶּׁאָמְרוּ זִכְרוֹנָם לִבְרָכָה שֶׁנִּשְׁבָּעִין עַל הָאֳנָסִין הַגְּדוֹלִים, וּמְשַׁלְּמִין הַגְּנֵבָה וְהָאֲבֵדָה לְפִי שֶׁיֵּשׁ בָּזֶה קְצָת פְּשִׁיעָה וּקְצָת אֹנֶס, וּמִפְּנֵי הַשָּׂכָר שֶׁנּוֹטְלִין עַל זֶה חַיָּבִין לְשַׁלֵּם, מַה שֶּׁאֵין כֵּן בְּשׁוֹמֵר חִנָּם שֶׁפָּטוּר עַל הַכֹּל חוּץ מִפְּשִׁיעָה.

וְדִינֵי שְׂכִירוּת פּוֹעֲלִים וּשְׂכִירוּת בְּהֵמוֹת וּבָתִּים, וְדִין הָאֳמָן שֶׁקִּלְקֵל, וּמַרְאֶה

---

54. TB Bava M'tzi'a 17a.   55. Ibid. (MT *hilchoth to'én v'nit'an* vii 6).
56. TB Sh'vu'oth 41b (Rambam MT *hilchoth malveh* xv 1).   57. Ibid. 42a.
58. TB Sanhedrin 29a (see Rambam MT *hilchoth to'én v'nit'an* vi 8, and R. 'Asher to Sanhedrin chapter 3 §25).
59. It is for him to bring evidence that it is due him; TB Bava Kamma 46a, etc.
60. See Rambam *ibid*. viii 1, and *Maggid Mishneh* there.
61. TB Bava Bathra 28a (Rambam *ibid*. xii 1, and viii *et seq*.).
62. Ibid. 169a, 174a (Rambam MT *hilchoth malveh* xxii).
63. Ibid. 173a, 176b.   64. Ibid. 38b.
65. I.e. in these cases, apparent possession of an object or property for any certain length of time does not establish it as the property of the one who has it; e.g. craftsmen (repairmen) and tenants; *ibid*. 37a, 42a, 47a.
66. E.g. that a neighbor has first option on land offered for sale; TB Bava M'tzi'a 108a (Rambam MT *hilchoth sh'chénim* xii–xiv).
67. TJ Sanhedrin iii 9.   68. Mishnah, Avoth i 18.
69. So Ramban on Genesis 34:13.

⟨238⟩

within the scope of the laws in regard to payment and all matters—except that there is a slight difference concerning pleas (arguments) by married women in certain known instances, as it is explained in the places we have mentioned. It applies, too, in every place and every time. If a *beth din* has transgressed it and not effected justice, if it had the power to do so, it has disobeyed a positive precept—and its punishment will be very great, for it causes ruin for the land, since a country cannot be settled (civilized) except by law. As our Sages of blessed memory said,[68] "On three things the world stands," and one of them is law.

This is one of the precepts which all mankind generally was commanded to observe,[69] because the settlement of the world (civilization) cannot do without it.

[THE COURT'S OBLIGATION TO JUDGE CASES INVOLVING A PAID CUSTODIAN OR A HIRER]

59 to judge the case of one who receives payment, and of a *sochér* (one who rents or leases something). "One who receives payment" means a custodian, a keeper of something left with him for safekeeping, for a fee, which he is given for his watchful care. The term *sochér* denotes what the word means, that he leased a domestic animal from his fellow to ride it or do work with it; or, that he leased movable goods from him. Then a controversy arose between the lessee [user] and the leaser [owner], or between the depositor [owner] of the object and the one who guarded it for a fee. It is a *mitzvah*, a religious duty for us to judge between them, as it is written in this *sidrah*: *If a man gives his neighbor a donkey or an ox or a sheep or any beast to safeguard*, etc. (Exodus 22:9).[1]

The root purpose of the [civil] laws is known (§49).

Its laws are, for instance, what our Sages of blessed memory said,[2] that they take an oath over utter accidents,[3] but pay in cases of theft and loss: for there is in this [kind of instance] some element of negligence and some element of accident, and on account of the fee that [the custodians] take, they are obligated to pay compensation—which is not the case with an unpaid custodian, who is free of obligation for everything but outright negligence.

[Then there are] the laws about hiring workers[4] and leasing domestic animals and houses;[5] the law of an artisan who spoiled [an object given him to repair];[6] if someone shows a *dinar* to a trader

§59–60: ABOUT A PAID CUSTODIAN, HIRER, & BORROWER OF OBJECT

דִינָר לַחֶנְוָנִי וְנִמְצָא רַע, וְדִין שׂוֹכֵר בִּבְעָלִים שֶׁפָּטוּר, וְדִין תְּחִלָּתוֹ בִּפְשִׁיעָה וְסוֹפוֹ בְּאֹנֶס.

וְדִינֵי שׁוֹמֵר שֶׁמָּסַר לְשׁוֹמֵר וְהוֹסִיף הַשֵּׁנִי אוֹ גָרַע בַּשְּׁמִירָה, וְעִנְיָן כָּל הַמַּפְקִיד שֶׁעַל דַּעַת אִשְׁתּוֹ וּבָנָיו הַגְּדוֹלִים הוּא מַפְקִיד, וּמָה שֶׁאָמְרוּ זִכְרוֹנָם לִבְרָכָה שֶׁאֵין הַשׂוֹכֵר רַשַּׁאי לְהַשְׂכִּיר.

וְכָתַב הָרַמְבַּ"ם זִכְרוֹנוֹ לִבְרָכָה שֶׁלֹּא אָמְרוּ זֶה אֶלָּא בְּמִטַּלְטְלִין לְפִי שֶׁאֵין רְצוֹנוֹ שֶׁיְּהֵא פִּקְדוֹנוֹ בְּיַד אַחֵר, אֲבָל בְּשׂוֹכֵר בַּיִת וְרָצָה לְהַשְׂכִּירוֹ לְאַחֵר רַשַּׁאי, וּבִלְבַד שֶׁיִּהְיוּ הָאַחֲרוֹנִים כְּמִנְיַן הָרִאשׁוֹנִים, וְכֵן בִּסְפִינָה. וְיֵשׁ חוֹלְקִין עָלָיו.

וְיֶתֶר פְּרָטֶיהָ, מְבֹאָרִים בְּפֶרֶק שִׁשִּׁי וּשְׁבִיעִי מִן קַמָּא, וּשְׁלִישִׁי וְשִׁשִּׁי מִמְּצִיעָא, וּבַשְּׁמִינִי מִשְּׁבוּעוֹת.

וְנוֹהֶגֶת בִּזְכָרִים בְּכָל מָקוֹם וּבְכָל זְמַן. וְאִם עוֹבֵר עָלֶיהָ וְלֹא דָן אִם רָאוּי לְכָךְ בִּטֵּל עֲשֵׂה. וְאַף עַל פִּי שֶׁנִּצְטַוֵּינוּ דֶּרֶךְ כְּלָל לָדוּן בְּדִין טוֹעֵן וְנִטְעָן, רִבְּתָה הַתּוֹרָה צִוּוּי בַּשּׁוֹמְרִים בִּפְרָט לְפִי שֶׁהֵן עִנְיָנִים רְגִילִין בְּיִשּׁוּבֵי בְּנֵי אָדָם.

[מִצְוַת בֵּית דִּין לָדוּן בְּדִין הַשּׁוֹאֵל]

ס לָדוּן בְּדִין הַשּׁוֹאֵל, כְּלוֹמַר אָדָם שֶׁשָּׁאַל מֵחֲבֵרוֹ שׁוּם חֵפֶץ אוֹ בְּהֵמָה, וְהַשְּׁאֵלָה הִיא בְּלֹא שָׂכָר כְּלָל אֶלָּא שֶׁנִּתְחַסֵּד עִמּוֹ לַעֲשׂוֹת לוֹ טוֹבָה זוֹ, וְאַחַר כָּךְ נָפַל מַחֲלֹקֶת בֵּינֵיהֶם עַל הַדָּבָר, שֶׁנָּדוּן בֵּינֵיהֶם הַדִּין שֶׁנֶּאֱמַר עַל זֶה כְּמוֹ שֶׁכָּתוּב בְּפָרָשָׁה זוֹ: וְכִי יִשְׁאַל אִישׁ מֵעִם רֵעֵהוּ, וְגוֹמֵר.

§59   1. That this verse applies to a paid custodian, and the same laws apply to a *sochér*, who rents or leases something, is made quite clear in MdRSbY p. 107; TB Bava M'tzi'a 94b; and Midrash haGadol on the verse.

   2. TB Bava M'tzi'a 93a.

   3. That an accident occurred and no negligence or fraud was involved.

   4. *Ibid.* 75b, 77a.

   5. *Ibid.* 78a, 101b.

   6. TB Bava Kamma 98b.

   7. I.e., he shows it to ask if it is good, with or without payment for the opinion, and he is misled; *ibid.* 99b.

   8. TB Bava M'tzi'a 94a, 95a; see §60.

   9. *Ibid.* 42a (see *tosafoth* s.v. *hilch'tha*; Rambam MT *hilchoth s'chiruth* iii 10).

   10. I.e. if the first was paid and the second unpaid, or vice versa; *ibid.* 36b.

   11. But he wants no outsiders meddling; *ibid.*

   12. TB Gittin 29a, Bava M'tzi'a 29b.

   13. MT *hilchoth s'chiruth* v 5.

   14. Rabad *ad loc.* ("there are those in our generation who say that there are some people who ruin a house by living in it").

   15. See §49, note 15.

⟨240⟩

(money-changer), and it is found to be bad;[7] the law if someone hires the owner [of an animal, etc. along with the animal]—that he is free of obligation;[8] the law if the beginning [of the process by which the rented animal, etc. was lost] was by negligence and its end was an accident.[9]

[We have, further,] the laws about a custodian who gave [the object left him for safekeeping] to another keeper, and the second added to (improved) the watchful care or decreased (worsened) it;[10] the rule that whoever leaves something with another for safekeeping, does so with the understanding that the other's wife and grown children [will attend to it];[11] and the rule that our Sages of blessed memory stated, that the person who hires or rents something may not hire or rent it out to another in turn.[12]

Now, Rambam of blessed memory wrote[13] that this [last rule] was said only about movable property (goods), because it is not a person's wish that what he entrusts for safekeeping should be in another's [an outsider's] hands. But if someone rents or leases a house and he wishes to rent or lease it to another, he may, as long as the later tenants are the same in number as the first (original) tenants. So too about a ship. But there are those who differ.[14]

[These] and the rest of its details are explained in chapters 6 and 7 of the Talmud tractate *Bava Kamma*, chapters 3 and 6 of *Bava M'tzi'a*, and chapter 8 of *Sh'vu'oth*. It applies to men,[15] in every time and every place. If a person transgresses it and does not act as judge, if he is fit to do so, he disobeys a positive precept. And although we were commanded generally to try [every] case of plaintiff and defendant (§54), the Torah added a commandment about custodians specifically, because these [cases] are common occurrences in the settled communities of human beings.

[THE COURT'S OBLIGATION TO JUDGE CASES INVOLVING A MAN WHO BORROWS AN OBJECT FOR USE]

60 to judge the case of a borrower, i.e. a man who borrowed from his fellow some object or domestic animal, the loan being without any payment at all, but merely because the other wished to act kindly toward him by doing him this favor. Afterward, if a quarrel occurs between them over the matter, we are to judge the case between them. For it is stated about this, as written in this *sidrah*, *And if a man borrows anything from his neighbor*, etc. (Exodus 22:13).

§60: REGARDING ONE WHO BORROWS AN OBJECT FOR USE

וּבְדִין הַשּׁוֹאֵל חִיְּבָה הַתּוֹרָה אֲפִלּוּ הָאֲנָסִין לְפִי שֶׁבְּאַחֲרָיוּתוֹ הִיא אַחַר שֶׁשְּׁאָלָהּ וְלֹא הוֹצִיא עָלֶיהָ דָּבָר מִשֶּׁלּוֹ, וַהֲרֵי זֶה כְּעֵין לֹוֶה מָעוֹת שֶׁאִם נֶאֶנְסוּ מִמֶּנּוּ לֹא יִפָּטֵר מִן הַמַּלְוֶה בְּטַעֲנַת אֹנֶס.

וְעַל עִנְיַן שְׁאֵלָה בִּבְעָלִים שֶׁפָּטוּר, נוּכַל לוֹמַר לְפִי הַפְּשָׁט שֶׁהַתּוֹרָה לֹא חִיְּבָה הַשּׁוֹאֵל אַחַר שֶׁבַּעַל הַכְּלִי אוֹ הַבְּהֵמָה עִמּוֹ, דִּמְכֵּיוָן שֶׁהוּא לְשָׁם יִשְׁמֹר הוּא אֶת שֶׁלּוֹ. וְאַף־עַל־פִּי שֶׁהַשּׁוֹאֵל פָּטוּר אַף לְאַחַר שֶׁהָלְכוּ הַבְּעָלִים, מִכֵּיוָן שֶׁהָיוּ שָׁם בִּשְׁעַת שְׁאֵלָה, אֶפְשָׁר לְתָרֵץ בָּזֶה שֶׁלֹּא רָצְתָה הַתּוֹרָה לָתֵת הַדְּבָרִים לְשִׁעוּרִין וְלוֹמַר אִם יֵשְׁבוּ לְשָׁם הַבְּעָלִים הַרְבֵּה יְהֵא פָּטוּר הַשּׁוֹאֵל וְאִם מְעַט יְהֵא חַיָּב, וְצִוְּתָה הַתּוֹרָה דֶּרֶךְ כְּלָל דְּכָל שֶׁהַבְּעָלִים לְשָׁם בִּשְׁעַת שְׁאֵלָה יְהֵא פָּטוּר.

וְזֶהוּ הַטַּעַם שֶׁאָמְרוּ זִכְרוֹנָם לִבְרָכָה שֶׁאִם בִּשְׁעַת שְׁאֵלָה הָיָה עִמּוֹ אַף עַל פִּי שֶׁלֹּא הָיָה עִמּוֹ בִּשְׁעַת שְׁבִירָה וּמִיתָה פָּטוּר, אֲבָל הָיָה עִמּוֹ בִּשְׁעַת שְׁבִירָה וּמִיתָה וְלֹא הָיָה עִמּוֹ בִּשְׁעַת שְׁאֵלָה חַיָּב, כִּי בִּתְחִלַּת הַמַּעֲשֶׂה הָעִנְיָן תָּלוּי. וְזֶה הַטַּעַם בְּעַצְמוֹ מַסְפִּיק לָנוּ בִּשְׂכִירוּת הַבְּעָלִים גַּם כֵּן שֶׁפָּטוּר.

דִּינֵי הַמִּצְוָה, מַה שֶּׁאָמְרוּ זִכְרוֹנָם לִבְרָכָה שֶׁאִם מֵתָה הַבְּהֵמָה מֵחֲמַת מְלָאכָה וְכֵן אִם נִשְׁבַּר הַכְּלִי מֵחֲמַת הַמְּלָאכָה שֶׁפָּטוּר. וְאִם שִׁנָּה מִן הַדֶּרֶךְ שֶׁצִּוּוּהוּ הַבְּעָלִים אֲפִלּוּ מֵתָה מֵחֲמַת מְלָאכָה שֶׁחַיָּב. וְאִם הוֹלִיכָהּ בְּמָקוֹם שֶׁהָרוֹאִים מְצוּיִים חַיָּב לְהָבִיא רְאָיָה עַל טַעֲנָתוֹ שֶׁטָּעַן שֶׁמֵּחֲמַת מְלָאכָה מֵתָה.

וּכְשֶׁמְּשַׁלֵּם מִי שֶׁחַיָּב לְשַׁלֵּם לוֹ שָׁמִין לוֹ תַּשְׁלוּמִין כְּמוֹ בִּנְזָקִין. וְשֶׁחַיָּב הַשּׁוֹאֵל בִּמְזוֹנוֹתֶיהָ מִשְּׁעַת מְשִׁיכָה עַד סוֹף הַשְּׁאֵלָה. וְדִין הִנִּיחַ לָהֶם אֲבִיהֶם פָּרָה שְׁאוּלָה

§60 1. Similarly Rambam, *Guide* III 42. Cf. Rashi to Exodus 22:14, s.v. *'im sachir*.
2. Similarly Ibn Ezra to Exodus 22:14: for he himself saw how it broke or died.
3. TB Bava M'tzi'a 95b.
4. For he can say, "I did not borrow it to keep it in a canopied bed"; *ibid.* 96b.
5. *Ibid.*
6. And he is not believed with a mere oath; *ibid.* 83a.
7. *Ibid.* 97a.

⟨242⟩

In the law of the borrower, the Torah obligated [him] to pay even for accidents, because it is under his responsibility, since he borrowed it and spent nothing of his own for it.[1] Hence he is like a person who borrows money, where, if it is taken from him by force, he cannot be quit of the loan by the plea of accident.

Now, about borrowing something together with its owner (Exodus 22:14), in which case he [the borrower] is free of obligation, we can say, according to the plain meaning [of the matter], that the Torah did not obligate the borrower inasmuch as the owner of the object or the animal is with him: For since he is there, let him watch his own property.[2] It is true, though, that the borrower is free of obligation even after the owner leaves, since he was there at the time it was borrowed. However, it can be said in explanation of this that the Torah did not wish to set limits in these matters and say: If the owner was there at length, the borrower is free of obligation; and if but a short time, he bears the obligation. Hence the Torah ordained generally that as long as the owner was there at the time of the borrowing, he is free of obligation.

This is the reason why our Sages of blessed memory said[3] that if [the owner] was with him at the time of the borrowing, even if he was not with him when breakage [of the object] or death [of the animal] occurred, he remains free of any obligation. However, if [the owner] was with him at the time of breakage or death, but had not been with him at the time of the borrowing, he bears the obligation. For the matter depends on the beginning of the transaction. And this very reason will suffice us in regard to the hiring of the owner also, [to explain] why he is free of obligation.

Now, as to the laws of the precept, what our Sages of blessed memory said: that if the domestic animal died in the course of work, and so too if the object broke in the course of work, he need not pay;[4] but if he varied from the way that the owner ordered him [to work with it], then even if it died in the course of working, he is required to pay.[5] If he took it to a place where observers are generally found, he is required to bring proof for the argument he pleads, that it died in the course of working.[6]

[Further, there are these laws:] When someone obligated to pay makes compensation, the compensation is set for him to pay as for physical damage;[7] that the borrower is required [to provide the animal] with its food from the time he draws it [to him] till the end of the

§60-61: ABOUT THE BORROWER OF AN OBJECT / ABOUT A SEDUCER

וּמָתַי, וְדִין הָאוֹמֵר לַחֲבֵרוֹ "הַשְׁאִילֵנִי דָּבָר פְּלוֹנִי בְּטוֹבָתְךָ" שֶׁמִּשְׁתַּמֵּשׁ בּוֹ לְעוֹלָם וּמַחֲזִיר לוֹ שְׁבָרָיו, וְהַשּׁוֹאֵל סְתָם לְכַמָּה זְמַן מַשְׁמַע, וְהַחִלּוּק שֶׁיֵּשׁ בִּדְבָרִים רַבִּים בְּעִנְיָן זֶה, וְאִי זֶה רַב נִשְׁאַל לְתַלְמִידָיו, וְאֵי זֶהוּ שֶׁהֵם שְׁאוּלִים לוֹ, וְדִין הָאוֹמֵר לִשְׁלוּחוֹ צֵא וְהִשָּׁאֵל עִם פָּרָתִי, וְהַשּׁוֹאֵל מִן הָאִשָּׁה וְנִשְׁאַל לְבַעְלָהּ, אוֹ הַשּׁוֹאֵל מֵאִשְׁתּוֹ, וְשֻׁתָּפִין שֶׁיִּשְׁאֲלוּ זֶה מִזֶּה אוֹ מֵאַחֵר וְנִשְׁאַל לְאֶחָד מֵהֶם, וְדִינֵי הַשּׁוֹאֵל פָּרָה וּשְׁלָחָהּ הַמַּשְׁאִיל בִּמְצֻוַת הַשּׁוֹאֵל אוֹ שֶׁלֹּא בִּמְצֻוָתוֹ, וּמַה שֶּׁאָמְרוּ שֶׁאֵין הַשּׁוֹאֵל רַשַּׁאי לְהַשְׁאִיל; וְיֶתֶר פְּרָטֶיהָ, מְבֹאָרִים בִּמְצִיעָא פֶּרֶק ח', וּבִשְׁבוּעוֹת גַּם כֵּן פֶּרֶק ח'.

וְנוֹהֶגֶת בִּזְכָרִים שֶׁעֲלֵיהֶם לַעֲשׂוֹת דִּין. וּבֵית דִּין הָעוֹבֵר עָלֶיהָ וְלֹא דָן בָּטֵל עֲשֵׂה.

[מִצְוַת בֵּית דִּין לָדוּן בְּדִין מְפַתֶּה]

סא לָדוּן בְּדִין מְפַתֶּה, כְּלוֹמַר מִי שֶׁפִּתָּה בְּתוּלָה שֶׁנְּדִינִין אוֹתוֹ כְּמִשְׁפָּטוֹ הַכָּתוּב עָלָיו בַּפָּרָשָׁה, שֶׁנֶּאֱמַר "וְכִי יְפַתֶּה אִישׁ בְּתוּלָה" וְגוֹמֵר. וְעִנְיַן הַפִּתּוּי הוּא שֶׁאוֹמֵר לָהּ דְּבָרִים שֶׁל שֶׁקֶר אוֹ שֶׁל אֱמֶת עַד שֶׁמִּתְרַצָּה אֵלָיו.

שֹׁרֶשׁ הַדִּין יָדוּעַ. וְאַל תִּתְמַהּ כָּאן בִּהְיוֹת כָּל כְּבוּדָּה בַּת מֶלֶךְ פְּנִימָה נִמְכֶּרֶת לַבּוֹעֵל בַּחֲמִשִּׁים כֶּסֶף בֵּין בַּעֲשִׂירָה בֵּין בַּעֲנִיָּה, שֶׁאֵין הַקְּנָס רַק דְּמֵי הֲנָאַת הַשְּׁכִיבָה בִּלְבָד, אֲבָל מִצַּד אַחֵר חַיָּב הַשּׁוֹכֵב אוֹתָהּ לָתֵת בֹּשֶׁת וּפְגָם לְפִי יִחוּסָהּ וַחֲשִׁיבוּתָהּ, וְכָל מִצְוַת הַשֵּׁם אֱמוּנָה.

דִּינֵי הַמִּצְוָה, כָּתַב הָרַמְבַּ"ם זִכְרוֹנוֹ לִבְרָכָה שֶׁכָּל בָּעִיר בְּחֶזְקַת פִּתּוּי עַד

---

8. TB K'thuboth 34b.
9. I.e. if they must pay if the death was natural or accidental; *ibid*.
10. TB Bava M'tzi'a 103a (MT *hilchoth sh'élah* i 8).
11. TB Makkoth 3b.
12. E.g. if one asks another, "Lend me the tool to hoe this orchard," he may hoe only the one orchard with it; if he said, "to hoe an orchard," he may use it for any one he wishes, or even several; TB Bava M'tzi'a 103a.
13. *Ibid*. 97a; as above, where the owner "lends" himself out together with the object, the borrower is free from payment.
14. I.e. whether this is considered borrowing something along with the owner, so that there is no responsibility in case of accident; *ibid*. 96a.
15. I.e. the man borrows *nichsé m'lug*, property which is itself owned by the woman but whose revenue or benefit belongs to her husband. The question is whether the husband's presence is like an owner's presence (see Exodus 22:14); *ibid*.
16. I.e. if this is called borrowing something along with its owner, since she is always available to do his work; *ibid*. 96b.
17. *Ibid*. 96a (Rambam MT *hilchoth sh'élah* ii 7).
18. *Ibid*.   19. And it died on the way; *ibid*. 98b.
20. TB Gittin 20a, Bava M'tzi'a 29b.   21. See §49, note 15.

borrowing;[8] the law if their father leaves them [his sons] a borrowed cow and it dies;[9] the law if someone says to his fellow, "Lend me that object in your kindness," that he might use it for a time without limit, that [if it breaks] he returns its broken pieces;[10] [the law] if someone simply borrows something [with no time limit specified], what the intended period is;[11] the difference that there is in many instances in this matter;[12] which type of teacher is considered "lent" to his pupils, and when the pupils are considered "lent" to him;[13] the law if someone says to his deputy, "Go and be borrowed (on loan) with my cow;[14] if someone borrows a woman's property, and her husband is lent him [with it];[15] or if one borrows his wife's property;[16] or if partners borrow [an object] from one another;[17] or [if they borrow something] from another person, and he lends himself to one of them;[18] the laws for someone who borrows a cow, whereupon the lender sends it at the borrower's order, or not at his order;[19] and the teaching of the Sages[20] that a borrower has no right to lend [what he has borrowed]. [These] and further details are explained in chapter 8 of *Bava M'tzi'a*, and in the tractate *Sh'vu'oth*, likewise in chapter 8.

It applies to men, for on them lies the obligation to carry out justice.[21] If a *beth din* transgresses it and does not hold court, it has disobeyed a positive precept.

[THE DUTY OF THE COURT TO PASS JUDGMENT ON A SEDUCER]

61 to judge the case of a seducer, which means one who has enticed a virgin—that we should judge him according to his ordinance, written about him in the *sidrah*—as it is stated, *And if a man entices a virgin*, etc. (Exodus 22:15). In substance, seduction means that he tells her matters of falsehood or truth,[1] until she yields to him.

The root reason for the precept is known (evident). Now, do not wonder here why, since *all glorious is the princess within* (Psalms 45:14),[2] she is sold to the man for fifty pieces of silver, whether she is rich or poor. This fine is merely compensation for the enjoyment of the intimacy alone. Apart from this, though, the one who was intimate with her is obligated to pay for shame and impairment [of status] according to her pedigree and her rank.[3] So the *mitzvoth* of the Eternal Lord are trustworthy.

As to the laws of the precept, Rambam of blessed memory wrote[4] that any instance occurring in a city is held to have been seduction,

§61–62: TO JUDGE A SEDUCER / NOT LET A SORCERER LIVE

שֶׁיָּעִידוּ עֵדִים שֶׁהוּא אֹנֶס, וְכָל שֶׁבַּשָּׂדֶה בְּחֶזְקַת אֹנֶס. וְאָמְרוּ זִכְרוֹנָם לִבְרָכָה שֶׁנִּשּׂוּאֵי מְפֻתָּה תְּלוּיִים בִּרְצוֹן הָאָב וְהַמְפֻתָּה, וְאִם כְּנָסָהּ אֵין שָׁם קְנָס.

וְדִין כֹּהֵן גָּדוֹל שֶׁפִּתָּה אוֹ אָנַס, וְדִין קְנָס בִּנְבְעָלָה כְּדַרְכָּהּ, וּזְמַן הַקְּנָס אֵינוֹ אֶלָּא מִשְּׁלֹשָׁה שָׁנִים עַד שֶׁתִּבְגַּר. וּמַה שֶּׁכָּתַב "לְאָבִיהָ" דַּוְקָא לְאָבִיהָ, אֲבָל אֵין לָהּ אָב אֵין דִּין קְנָס עָלֶיהָ, דְּפִתּוּיֵי מִדַּעְתָּהּ הוּא, מַה שֶּׁאֵין כֵּן בְּאָנֵס, וּכְמוֹ שֶׁנִּכְתַּב בִּמְקוֹמוֹ בְּעֶזְרַת הַשֵּׁם. וְהַנָּשִׁים שֶׁאֵין לָהֶן קְנָס, וַעֲשָׂרָה הֵן; וְיֶתֶר פְּרָטֶיהָ, מְבֹאָרִים בְּפֶרֶק שְׁלִישִׁי וּרְבִיעִי מִכְּתֻבּוֹת.

וְנוֹהֶגֶת בְּכָל מָקוֹם שֶׁיֵּשׁ בֵּית דִּין סְמוּכִין, שֶׁאֵין דָּנִין דִּינֵי קְנָסוֹת אֶלָּא בִּסְמוּכִין. וְעוֹבֵר עָלֶיהָ וְלֹא עָשָׂה דִּין בָּזֶה בִּטֵּל עֲשֵׂה.

[שֶׁלֹּא לְהַחֲיוֹת מְכַשֵּׁף]

סב שֶׁלֹּא נְחַיֶּה מְכַשֵּׁפָה אֶלָּא נְמִיתָהּ שֶׁנֶּאֱמַר "מְכַשֵּׁפָה לֹא תְחַיֶּה", וְלָאו דַּוְקָא מְכַשֵּׁפָה אֶלָּא כָּל מִי שֶׁעוֹשֶׂה כִשּׁוּף, אֶלָּא שֶׁיְּדַבֵּר בְּרָגִיל, שֶׁהַנָּשִׁים כַּשְׁפָנִיּוֹת יוֹתֵר מִן הָאֲנָשִׁים.

מִשָּׁרְשֵׁי הַמִּצְוָה שֶׁיָּדוּעַ כִּי עִנְיַן הַכִּשּׁוּף דָּבָר רַע עַד מְאֹד וְגוֹרֵם תַּקָּלוֹת כַּמָּה לִבְנֵי אָדָם, אֵינִי צָרִיךְ לְהַאֲרִיךְ בּוֹ שֶׁיְּדוּעִים הַדְּבָרִים. וְעַל כֵּן נִצְטַוִּינוּ לְסַלֵּק מִן הָעוֹלָם הַמִּשְׁתַּדֵּל בָּזֶה, לְפִי שֶׁהוּא בָּא כְּנֶגֶד חֵפֶץ הַשֵּׁם שֶׁהוּא חָפֵץ בִּישׁוּבוֹ וְשֶׁיִּתְנַהֵג הַכֹּל בְּדֶרֶךְ הַטֶּבַע שֶׁהֻטְבַּע בִּתְחִלַּת הַבְּרִיאָה, וְזֶה בָּא לְשַׁנּוֹת הַכֹּל. וְעִנְיַן הַכִּשּׁוּף הוּא לְפִי דַעְתִּי כֵן, שֶׁהַשֵּׁם בָּרוּךְ הוּא שָׂם בִּתְחִלַּת הַבְּרִיאָה לְכָל

---

§61 1. Rashi on the verse follows Onkelos, that the verb denotes persuasion, while Ramban takes it to indicate diverging from proper behavior.

2. I.e. this is how every Jewish daughter is to be held in esteem, *within*, protected in her parental home. Then why is she given so readily in marriage to the seducer? (The three oldest manuscripts read *bath yisra'él*, a Jewish daughter, instead of *bath melech*, a princess.)

3. So TB K'thuboth 39a, 40a–b.
4. MT *hilchoth na'arah b'thulah* i 2.
5. TB K'thuboth 39a–40a.
6. The chief or head of all the *kohanim*, who ministered at the Holy Temple (often translated "high priest").
7. Whether he may marry the girl (see Leviticus 21:13); TB Y'vamoth 59b.
8. See MT *hilchoth na'arah b'thulah* i 8.
9. I.e. at the age of twelve and a half; TB K'thuboth 29a, etc.
10. So that she has forgiven him the fine.
11. TB K'thuboth 40a (and Rashi).
12. See Rambam *ibid.* 9–10, and the sources noted in *Kessef Mishneh*.

§62 1. So TB Sanhedrin 67a.

⟨246⟩

until (unless) witnesses testify that it was rape; and any instance that occurs in the field is held to have been rape. The Sages of blessed memory said[5] that marriage to an enticed girl depends on the wishes of the father, the daughter, and the seducer; and if he marries her, there is no fine.

[Then we have] the law of a *kohen gadol*[6] who committed seduction or rape[7]; the law that the fine applies [only] when conjugal intimacy occurs by natural connection;[8] that the time the fine applies is when the girl is between the age of three and when she reaches maturity;[9] that when Scripture writes [that the man who was intimate with a girl should give fifty shekels of silver] to her father (Deuteronomy 22:29), it means strictly to her father; but if she has no father, there is no penalty in her case: for seduction is by her consent,[10] which is not the case with rape[11]—as we will write in its proper place (§557) with the help of the Eternal Lord; and those women for whom there is no fine, who are ten in number.[12] [These] and the rest of its details are explained in the third and fourth chapters of the Talmud tractate *K'thuboth*.

It applies in every place where there is an ordained, authorized *beth din*; for cases of fines can be tried only by those ordained. If it is transgressed and this law is not put into effect, a positive precept has been disobeyed.

62 [NOT TO ALLOW A SORCERER TO LIVE]

that we should not let a sorceress live, but should put her to death—as it is stated, *You shall not permit a sorceress to live* (Exodus 22:17). This does not mean a sorceress particularly, but rather anyone who practices sorcery or witchcraft; it is only that Scripture speaks of what is usual, and women are sorcerers to a greater extent than men.[1]

At the root of the precept lies the reason that it is known that the matter of witchcraft is something very bad, and causes people many misfortunes. I need not go on at length about it, for these things are known. Therefore were we commanded to remove from the world anyone who works at this, because he goes against the wishes of the Eternal Lord, who desires that it should be settled (civilized) all in the natural way that was set for it at the beginning of Creation—and this one comes to change everything.

Now, the substance of sorcery, to my mind, is this: At the beginning of Creation, the Eternal Lord (blessed is He) set for every

§62: NOT TO ALLOW A SORCERER TO LIVE

דָּבָר וְדָבָר מִדִּבְרֵי הָעוֹלָם טֶבַע לִפְעֹל פְּעֻלָּתוֹ טוֹבָה לְיֹשֶׁר וִישָׁרָה לְטוֹבַת בְּנֵי הָעוֹלָם אֲשֶׁר בָּרָא, וְצִוָּה כָּל אֶחָד לִפְעֹל פָּעֳלוֹ לְמִינֵהוּ, כְּמוֹ שֶׁכָּתוּב בְּפָרָשַׁת בְּרֵאשִׁית "לְמִינֵהוּ" עַל הַנִּבְרָאִים. וְגַם עַל כָּל כֹּחַ הַמָּשִׁיל כֹּחַ מִלְמַעְלָה לְהַכְרִיחוֹ עַל מַעֲשֵׂהוּ, כְּמוֹ שֶׁאָמְרוּ זִכְרוֹנָם לִבְרָכָה: אֵין לְךָ עֵשֶׂב מִלְּמַטָּה שֶׁאֵין לוֹ מַזָּל מִלְּמַעְלָה שֶׁאוֹמֵר לוֹ: גְּדַל.

וּמִלְּבַד פְּעֻלָּתָן שֶׁעוֹשָׂה כָּל אֶחָד וְאֶחָד בְּטִבְעוֹ יֵשׁ לָהֶם פְּעֻלָּה אַחֶרֶת בְּהִתְעָרְבָם מִין מֵהֶן עִם מִין אַחֵר, וּבִמְלֶאכֶת הַתַּעֲרֹבֶת יֵשׁ בָּהּ צְדָדִין שֶׁלֹּא הֻרְשׁוּ בְּנֵי אָדָם לְהִשְׁתַּמֵּשׁ בָּהֶן, כִּי יוֹדֵעַ אֱלֹהִים שֶׁסּוֹף הַמַּעֲשֶׂה הַיּוֹצֵא לִבְנֵי אָדָם בְּאוֹתָן צְדָדִין רַע לָהֶן וּמִפְּנֵי זֶה מְנָעָם מֵהֶם.

וְזֶהוּ אָמְרָם זִכְרוֹנָם לִבְרָכָה דֶּרֶךְ כְּלָל, כָּל שֶׁיֵּשׁ בּוֹ מִשּׁוּם רְפוּאָה אֵין בּוֹ מִשּׁוּם דַּרְכֵי הָאֱמוֹרִי, כְּלוֹמַר אֵין לְאָסְרוֹ מִפְּנֵי צַד כִּשּׁוּף אַחֵר שֶׁיֵּשׁ תּוֹעֶלֶת בּוֹ מָצוּי בְּנִסָּיוֹן בֶּאֱמֶת אֵין זֶה מִן הַצְּדָדִין הָאֲסוּרִין, כִּי לֹא נֶאֶסְרוּ רַק מִצַּד הַנֶּזֶק שֶׁבָּהֶן.

וְעוֹד יֵשׁ בְּאוֹתָן צִדֵּי הַתַּעֲרֻבוֹת וְהַתַּחְבּוּלוֹת הָאֲסוּרוֹת לַעֲשׂוֹת עִנְיָן אַחֵר שֶׁנֶּאֶסְרוּ בַּעֲבוּרוֹ, לְפִי שֶׁכֹּחַ אוֹתוֹ הַתַּעֲרֹבֶת עוֹלֶה עַל כָּךְ שֶׁמְּבַטֵּל מִפְּעֻלָּתוֹ לְפִי שָׁעָה כֹּחַ הַמַּזָּל הַמְמֻנֶּה עַל שְׁנֵי הַמִּינִין. וְהַמָּשָׁל עַל זֶה, כְּמוֹ שֶׁאַתָּה רוֹאֶה שֶׁהַמַּרְכִּיב מִין בְּשֶׁאֵינוֹ מִינוֹ יְחַדְּשׁוּ לִבְרֹא מִין שְׁלִישִׁי, נִמְצָא שֶׁבְּטֵלָה הַהַרְכָּבָה כֹּחַ שְׁנֵיהֶם, וְעַל כֵּן נִמְנַעְנוּ מִלְּהַעֲלוֹת עַל רוּחֵנוּ אַף כִּי נַעֲשֶׂה בְּיָדֵינוּ דָּבָר שֶׁמַּרְאֶה בָּנוּ רָצוֹן לְהַחֲלִיף דָּבָר בְּמַעֲשֵׂי הָאֵל הַשְּׁלֵמוֹת. וְאֶפְשָׁר שֶׁיַּעֲלֶה בְּיָדֵינוּ.

---

2. B'réshith Rabbah 10, 7; in this paragraph our author follows Ramban on Leviticus 19:19 and Deuteronomy 18:9.

3. I.e. it is permitted to create or prepare medicines even if in some way the process resembles heathen sorcery; TB Shabbath 67b. On the explanation that follows cf. Rashba, *Responsa* I 413.

single thing among the entities of the world a certain nature, to fulfill its good and proper function for the good of the humankind that He created. And He ordered each entity to fulfill its function according to its species, as it is written in the *sidrah b'réshith*, "after its kind" (Genesis 1:12, etc.) in regard to the created organisms. Furthermore, over each and every one He set a ruling force above, to impel it to its task; as the Sages of blessed memory said,[2] "you will find not a blade of grass below [on earth] which does not have a celestial being above that bids it, *Grow!*"

But apart from their [regular] function which each and every organism does by its nature, they have another way of functioning, when one species among them is mingled with another species. In the process of this mingling there are certain aspects, ways which human beings were not permitted to utilize, since God knows that the end of the matter which will result for humanity through those aspects or ways will be harmful for them; and for this reason He withheld them from them.

In this vein our Sages of blessed memory said as a general rule: Whatever contains a purpose of healing, is not considered of "the ways of the Amorites"; in other words, it is not to be forbidden because of an aspect of sorcery [in it];[3] since there is a useful benefit in it, truly found by experience, this is not one of the forbidden ways [of mingling species]. For they were forbidden only on account of the harm in them.

Moreover, in those forbidden ways of mingling and devising [with two species] there is the power to form something new, and on that account they were forbidden: because the power of that mingling (merger) rises up so strongly that it temporarily nullifies the force of the celestial being appointed over the two species. An analogy for this would be, as you see, that when someone grafts one species onto a different one, they create a third species which is new. Then the result is that the grafting has nullified the power of both [angels of the original species].

Therefore we were prohibited from [even] bringing to mind, much less doing with our hands, anything that will show any wish of ours to change anything in the whole, perfect works of God. Perhaps there will come to hand [we will succeed in deriving] from this a hint of the root purpose [of the negative precepts] about mingling species of seeds (§245) and species of animals (§246) and the wearing

§62: NOT TO ALLOW A SORCERER TO LIVE

מִזֶּה רֶמֶז מִשָּׁרְשֵׁי כִּלְאֵי זְרָעִים וּבְהֵמָה וְשַׁעַטְנֵז, וּבִמְקוֹמָם נַאֲרִיךְ בָּם בְּעֶזְרַת הַשֵּׁם.

וְזֵהוּ שֶׁאָמְרוּ זִכְרוֹנָם לִבְרָכָה: לָמָּה נִקְרָא שְׁמָם כְּשָׁפִים, שֶׁמַּכְחִישִׁין פַּמַּלְיָא שֶׁל מַעְלָה וְשֶׁל מַטָּה, כְּלוֹמַר שֶׁכֹּחָן עוֹלֶה לְפִי שָׁעָה יוֹתֵר מִכֹּחַ הַמְמֻנִּים עֲלֵיהֶם. וּרְאֵה כִּוּוּן דִּבְרֵיהֶם זִכְרוֹנָם לִבְרָכָה שֶׁאָמְרוּ פַּמַּלְיָא שֶׁל מַעְלָה וְלֹא אָמְרוּ גְּזֵרַת מַעְלָה, לְפִי שֶׁהַשֵּׁם בָּרוּךְ הוּא גָזְרוֹ וְרָצָה מִתְּחִלַּת הַבְּרִיאָה לִהְיוֹת הַפְּעֻלָּה הַזֹּאת יוֹצֵאת מִבֵּין שְׁנֵיהֶם בְּהִתְעָרְבָם, וּבוֹ תּוֹכַחַת מְגֻלָּה אֶל הַמְמֻנִּים עֲלֵיהֶם, אֲבָל אָמְרוּ שֶׁכֹּחַ הַפַּמַּלְיָא מֻכְחָשׁ מִכֹּל מָקוֹם.

וּמִי שֶׁקְּרֹבַת שְׂכָלוֹ בָּאוֹר פְּנֵי מֶלֶךְ וְכֹחַ זְכוּתוֹ יַעֲלֶה עַל כֹּחַ הַמְמֻנִּים לֹא יִירָא הַמַּעֲשֶׂה הַזֶּה וְהַכְחָשׁוֹתָיו, כְּמוֹ שֶׁמָּצִינוּ בַּגְּמָרָא בְּמַסֶּכֶת שַׁבָּת שֶׁאָמַר הֶחָכָם אֶל הַמְכַשֵּׁפָה.

וִידִיעַת חִלּוּק עִנְיָנִים אֵלֶּה, אֵי זֶה תַעֲרֹבֶת הֶתֵּר לָנוּ וְאֵין בּוֹ צַד כְּשׁוּף וְאֵי זֶהוּ שֶׁיֵּשׁ בּוֹ צַד כְּשׁוּף וְאָסוּר בְּחָכְמַת הַכְּשׁוּף, יָדוּעַ. וְאַל תַּחְשֹׁב כִּי מְלֶאכֶת הַכְּשׁוּף וְהַשֵּׁדִים בְּפֵרוּשׁ שֶׁהֲרֵי אָמְרוּ זִכְרוֹנָם לִבְרָכָה: בְּלָטֵיהֶם, מַעֲשֵׂה שֵׁדִים, בְּלַהֲטֵיהֶם, מַעֲשֵׂה כְשָׁפִים. מַשְׁמַע מִזֶּה שֶׁעִנְיַן הַכְּשׁוּף אֶפְשָׁר לְהֵעָשׂוֹת בִּלְתִּי מַעֲשֵׂה שֵׁדִים, וְאָמְנָם גַּם עִם הַשֵּׁדִים יַעֲשׂוּ לִפְעָמִים אוֹתָן. וְאוֹתָן הַשֵּׁדִים שֶׁמִּשְׁתַּמְּשִׁין בָּהֶן לִמְלֶאכֶת הַכְּשׁוּף נִקְרָאִים מַלְאֲכֵי חַבָּלָה; כֵּן פֵּרְשׁוּ זִכְרוֹנָם לִבְרָכָה, לְפִי שֶׁעִנְיַן הַכְּשׁוּף לְעוֹלָם אֵינוֹ נַעֲשֶׂה רַק לְחַבֵּל.

וּבִפְרָטֵי דִינֵי הַכְּשׁוּף בְּלָאוּ דִמְכַשֵּׁף נַאֲרִיךְ בּוֹ יוֹתֵר בְּעֶזְרַת הַשֵּׁם, כִּי שָׁם מְקוֹמוֹ, שֶׁאֵין כָּאן אֶלָּא אַזְהָרַת הַדִּין, כְּלוֹמַר שֶׁלֹּא נִמְחֹל לָהֶם אֲבָל נְמִיתֵם.

וְנוֹהֶגֶת מִצְוָה זוֹ לַעֲשׂוֹת דִּין בִּמְכַשְּׁפִים בַּזְּכָרִים כִּי לָהֶם יָאוּת וְנִתָּן לַעֲשׂוֹת

4. TB Sanhedrin 67b.

5. The word *k'shafim* (sorceries) is taken as an abbreviation for *kahash* (denied, contradicted) *pamalia shel ma'alah* (the celestial angelic retinue); so Rashi, *ibid*. (The words "and below" are not found in our editions of the Talmud. Our author's point here is that from the beginning of creation, an angel was assigned to supervise the growth of every plant organism, etc. When two species or kinds are combined to form a new variety, the angels assigned to the original species or kinds have no dominion over this new breed. Their function has been nullified here.

6. Expression from Proverbs 16:15.

7. TB 81b end: R. Ḥisda and Rabbah b. R. Huna were once traveling on a boat, when a certain heathen lady asked them, "May I sit near you?"—and they did not permit her. At that she uttered something, casting a spell to still the boat. Then they uttered something [by a Divine name of purity] and released it. Said she to them, "What can I do with you . . ." (bracketed additions from Rashi).

However, our author speaks of "the wise scholar," not two, and of what *he* said to the sorceress. This would indicate that perhaps *Shabbath* is a scribal error and he rather had in mind a passage in TB Sanhedrin 67b: A certain woman kept trying to put earth under R. Ḥanina's feet [to be able to work her sorcery upon him]. Said

of *sha'atnez*, a mixture of wool and linen (§551). In their proper places we will write at greater length, with the help of the Eternal Lord.

Now, this is why our Sages of blessed memory said:[4] Why are they named sorceries?—because they contradict the angelic retinue above and below.[5] In other words, their force rises up for a while stronger than the power of those [angels] appointed over them. Note the precision of their words (be their memory for a blessing): for they said "the angelic retinue above" and not "the edict [decreed] above." For the Eternal Lord, blessed is He, ordained this, desiring from the beginning of Creation that this reaction should result from the two of them when they [the two species] are mingled. And this is clear, open proof about those appointed over them [that they are only angels, not divinities]. But [the Sages] well said that the power of the angelic retinue is in any case contradicted.

However, any person whose intelligence is in close proximity to the light of the King's countenance,[6] the strength of whose virtue is above the power of the appointed [angels], will not fear this activity and its powers of contradiction—as we find in the Talmud tractate *Shabbath*[7] in what the wise scholar said to the sorceress.

Now, the recognition of the division among these subjects—which mingling [of species] was permitted us, having no element of sorcery in it, and which has in it an element of witchcraft and is forbidden [to effect] with the wisdom of sorcery—this is known.[8] And do not think that the work of sorcery and demons are the same thing; for our Sages of blessed memory said distinctly:[9] *b'latéhem* (Exodus 7:22) denotes the work of demons; *b'lahatéhem* (ibid. 11) denotes the work of sorceries. We can infer from this that the business of sorcery can be done without the work of demons, although in truth those [acts of witchcraft] can be effected at times also with demons. The demons which are employed in the work of sorcery are called destroying angels; so our Sages of blessed memory explained,[10] because the business of sorcery is never done except to destroy.

As to the details of the laws of witchcraft, in the negative precept about a sorcerer (§511) we will write about it at greater length, with the Eternal Lord's help, as there is its proper place. For here we have only an injunction to the judge, to convey that we are not to forgive them but rather put them to death.

This precept, to impose justice on sorcerers, applies to men—as

מִשְׁפָּט, אֲבָל לֹא לְנְקֵבוֹת. וְדַוְקָא בְּאֶרֶץ יִשְׂרָאֵל וּבִסְמוּכִין וּבְבֵית דִּין שֶׁל כ"ג. וּבֵית דִּין הָעוֹבֵר עָלֶיהָ אִם יֵשׁ בּוֹ כֹּחַ לַעֲשׂוֹת מִשְׁפָּט עָבַר עַל לָאו זֶה, מִלְּבַד שֶׁבִּטֵּל מִצְוַת עֲשֵׂה שֶׁהוּא לַעֲשׂוֹת דִּין בַּמְחֻיָּבִין דֶּרֶךְ כְּלָל, וְאֵין בָּזֶה מַלְקוּת לְפִי שֶׁאֵין בּוֹ מַעֲשֶׂה, וְכָל לָאו שֶׁאֵין בּוֹ מַעֲשֶׂה אֵין לוֹקִין עָלָיו חוּץ מִנִּשְׁבָּע וּמֵמִיר וּמְקַלֵּל חֲבֵרוֹ בַּשֵּׁם.

[שֶׁלֹּא לְהוֹנוֹת הַגֵּר בִּדְבָרִים]

סג שֶׁנִּמְנַעְנוּ מִלְּהוֹנוֹת הַגֵּר אֲפִלּוּ בִּדְבָרִים, וְהוּא אֶחָד מִן הָאֻמּוֹת שֶׁנִּתְגַיֵּר וְנִכְנַס בְּדָתֵנוּ, שֶׁאָסוּר לָנוּ לְבַזּוֹתוֹ אֲפִלּוּ בִּדְבָרִים, שֶׁנֶּאֱמַר "וְגֵר לֹא תוֹנֶה". וְאַף־עַל־פִּי שֶׁאָנוּ מֻזְהָרִים בָּזֶה בְּיִשְׂרָאֵל, זֶה כֵּיוָן שֶׁנִּכְנַס בְּדָתֵנוּ הֲרֵי הוּא כְּיִשְׂרָאֵל, הוֹסִיף הַכָּתוּב לָנוּ אַזְהָרָה בּוֹ, וְגַם נִכְפְּלָה הָאַזְהָרָה עָלָיו דִּכְתִיב "לֹא תוֹנֵנּוּ" פַּעַם אַחֶרֶת, לְפִי שֶׁעִנְיַן הַהוֹנָאָה אֵלָיו קְרוֹבָה יוֹתֵר מִבְּיִשְׂרָאֵל, כִּי הַיִּשְׂרְאֵלִי יֵשׁ לוֹ גּוֹאֲלִים שֶׁתּוֹבְעִין עֶלְבּוֹנוֹ.

וְעוֹד טַעַם אַחֵר בּוֹ, שֶׁיֵּשׁ חֲשָׁשׁ בּוֹ שֶׁלֹּא יַחְזֹר לְסוּרוֹ מֵעַקַּשׁ הַבִּזְיוֹנוֹת. וְאָמְרוּ בְּסִפְרָא שֶׁלֹּא תֹּאמַר לוֹ "אֶמֶשׁ הָיִיתָ עוֹבֵד עֲבוֹדָה זָרָה וְעַכְשָׁו נִכְנַסְתָּ תַּחַת כַּנְפֵי הַשְּׁכִינָה".

מִשָּׁרְשֵׁי הַמִּצְוָה, מִלְּבַד מַה שֶּׁכָּתַבְנוּ, כְּדֵי לָכֹף אֶת יִצְרֵנוּ לְעוֹלָם לְבַל נַעֲשֶׂה כָּל אֲשֶׁר נִמְצָא בְּכֹחֵנוּ לַעֲשׂוֹת לְרָעָה. עַל כֵּן הִזְהִירַתְנוּ בָּזֶה הָאִישׁ שֶׁהוּא בֵּינֵינוּ בְּלִי עוֹזֵר וְסוֹמֵךְ וְיֵשׁ כֹּחַ בְּיַד כָּל אֶחָד וְאֶחָד מִמֶּנּוּ עִם אוֹהֲבָיו עָלָיו לְבַל נַעֲבִיר

---

he to her, "If you are able to, go ahead and work it. It is written, *there is none else besides Him*" (Deuteronomy 4:35).

8. See TB Sanhedrin 67b.
9. Ibid.
10. Sh'moth Rabbah 9, 11. The standard Hebrew text has "Rashi" instead of "our Sages"; but apparently, as MY writes, the original read *pirshu* (they—the Sages—explained), and mistaking the *vav* at the end for a *yod*, an early scribe thought it an abbreviation for *pirésh Rashi* (Rashi explained). MY's perspicacity can be confirmed: A manuscript from 1345 actually reads *pirshu*; another (MS Parma, de Rossi 741), from 1351, has the word abbreviated as *pi* (פי׳), evidently with the same meaning. Perhaps, though, this was explained in Rashi to TB Sanhedrin 67b, in a different version from our printed text: cf. Rashba, *Responsa ascribed to Ramban*, §283, and I 413.
11. See §49, at note 15.
12. See §47, note 7, which applies here.

§63 1. ShM positive precept §207 gives Leviticus 19:18 as the general precept about an Israelite, which includes the convert: *you shall love your neighbor as yourself*. The source for our author's precept §338 is Leviticus 25:17.
2. So TB Kiddushin 17b, Bava M'tzi'a 59b.

it is appropriate and given [entrusted] to them to carry out justice—but not to women.[11] [It is in effect] specifically in the land of Israel, [to be done] by ordained persons,[12] in a *beth din* of twenty-three [judges]. Should a *beth din* violate this, if it has the power to carry out the law, it has transgressed this negative precept, apart from disobeying a positive precept, i.e. to carry out justice for the guilty generally. No whiplashes are given for this, however, as it involves no physical action [in transgressing it]; and for violating any negative precept which involves no physical action, a person does not receive whiplashes—except one who swears [in vain] (§30), one who exchanges [an animal consecrated for an offering] (§351), and one who curses his fellow by the Divine name (§231).

63 [NOT TO VERBALLY OPPRESS A CONVERT TO JUDAISM]

that we have been restricted from oppressing a proselyte even with words; if he is a member of the heathen nations who converted and entered our faith, it is forbidden for us to shame him, even with words—as it is stated, *And a ger (stranger, proselyte) you shall not oppress* (Exodus 22:20). Even though we were adjured about this in regard to an Israelite (§338),[1] and he, having entered our faith, is now as an Israelite, Scripture added this caution about him for us, and the warning is even repeated, as on another occasion it is written, *you shall not oppress him* (Leviticus 19:33). For the matter of oppression is closer to him [more likely to happen to him] than to an Israelite, since an Israelite has redeemers (defenders) who would demand satisfaction for his disgrace.

Another reason for this is that there is a fear about him that he may revert to his bad ways[2] out of anger at the disgraces and insults. Thus it was stated in the Midrash *Sifra* (Leviticus 19:33): You should not say to him, "Yesterday you were worshipping idols, and now you have entered under the wings of the *shechinah* (the Divine Presence)!"

At the root of the precept, apart from what we have written, lies the aim that we should forever subdue our inclination and not do all the evil that it lies in our power to do. Therefore [the Torah] adjured us about this man who is among us with none to help or uphold him, and in the hands of each and every one of us lies the power over him [to do him evil] despite [the precept about] being his friends, i.e.

§63–64: NOT TO WRONG A CONVERT BY WORDS OR ABOUT PROPERTY

עָלָיו אֶת הַדֶּרֶךְ כְּלָל אֲפִלּוּ בִּדְבָרִים כְּאִלּוּ הוּא כְּאֶחָד מִמֶּנּוּ, וּמִתּוֹךְ גְּדָרִים כָּאֵלּוּ יִקְנֶה נֶפֶשׁ יְקָרָה וּמְסֻלְסֶלֶת וּמְעֻטֶּרֶת הַמִּדּוֹת הָרְאוּיָה לְקַבָּלַת הַטּוֹב, וְיַשְׁלִם בָּנוּ חֵפֶץ הַשֵּׁם שֶׁחָפֵץ לְהֵיטִיב.

דִּינֵי הַמִּצְוָה, כְּגוֹן רֹב הָאַזְהָרוֹת שֶׁהִזְהִירוּנוּ זִכְרוֹנָם לִבְרָכָה עָלָיו, וְהוֹדִיעוּנוּ לְהַזְהִירֵנוּ עוֹד בַּדָּבָר שֶׁבְּעֶשְׂרִים וְאַרְבַּע מְקוֹמוֹת הִזְהִירָה הַתּוֹרָה עָלָיו, וְכָתְבוּ גַם כֵּן לְחִזּוּק הַמִּצְוָה שֶׁבָּאוּתוֹ לָשׁוֹן שֶׁנִּצְטַוֵּינוּ בְּאַהֲבַת הַמָּקוֹם נִצְטַוֵּינוּ בְּאַהֲבַת הַגֵּר, שֶׁבְּאַהֲבַת הַמָּקוֹם כְּתִיב "וְאָהַבְתָּ אֶת יי", וּבְגֵר כְּתִיב "וַאֲהַבְתֶּם אֶת הַגֵּר". וְהַרְבֵּה דְּבָרִים כָּאֵלּוּ, בַּמִּדְרָשִׁים וּבִקְצָת מְקוֹמוֹת בַּתַּלְמוּד.

וְנוֹהֶגֶת בְּכָל מָקוֹם וּבְכָל זְמַן בִּזְכָרִים וּבִנְקֵבוֹת. וְעוֹבֵר עָלֶיהָ וּבִזָּהוּ עָבַר עַל לָאו, וְאֵין לוֹקִין עָלָיו לְפִי שֶׁאֵין בּוֹ מַעֲשֶׂה.

[שֶׁלֹּא לְהוֹנוֹת הַגֵּר בְּמָמוֹן]

סד שֶׁנִּמְנַעְנוּ שֶׁלֹּא לְהוֹנוֹת הַגֵּר בְּמָמוֹן, שֶׁאִם יִהְיֶה לָנוּ עִמּוֹ מַשָּׂא וּמַתָּן שֶׁלֹּא לְהוֹנוֹת אוֹתוֹ, שֶׁנֶּאֱמַר "וְלֹא תִלְחָצֶנּוּ", וְאָמְרוּ בַּמְּכִילְתָּא: וְלֹא תִלְחָצֶנּוּ, בְּמָמוֹן. וְזֶה הַלָּאו נוֹסָף עַל הַלָּאו שֶׁיִּכְלְלֵהוּ עִם יִשְׂרָאֵל כֻּלָּם, שֶׁהֵם בְּלָאו דְּאוֹנָאַת מָמוֹן, וְנִזְהַרְנוּ עָלָיו בִּדְבָרִים וּבְמָמוֹן מִן הַטַּעַם שֶׁכָּתַבְנוּ. כָּל מִשְׁפְּטֵי הַמִּצְוָה הַקּוֹדֶמֶת לָזוֹ. בְּלָאו דְּאוֹנָאַת מָמוֹן בְּיִשְׂרָאֵל נִכְתֹּב קְצָת פְּרָטֵי הַהוֹנָאָה בְּעֶזְרַת הַשֵּׁם.

---

3. The Hebrew means literally, "that we should not make the road pass over (or, bypass) him"—evidently an idiom indicating cheating, exploiting, or making a fool of him. (See last page.)

4. TB Bava M'tzi'a 59b—but our editions read, "thirty-six places, and some say forty-six"; however, *tosafoth* to Kiddushin 70b, s.v. *kashim*, similarly mentions twenty-four.

5. So ShM positive precept §207, and MT *hilchoth de'oth* vi 4.

§64   1. On the verse; the passage begins: "you shall not wrong" him—with words. (See §63.)

that we should not do anything at all to wrong or hurt him,[3] even with words—just as though he were one of us. As a result of restraints like these, we will gain a precious spiritual nature, adorned with noble qualities, fit to receive good favor; and the desire of the Eternal Lord—his wish to do good—will be realized through us.

As to the laws of the precept, [there are] for example, the many warnings that our Sages of blessed memory gave us about it; and to caution us further, they informed us that in twenty-four instances Scripture adjures us about it;[4] moreover, to emphasize the precept, they wrote that with the very expression that we were commanded about love for the omnipresent God, we were commanded about affection for the convert: in regard to love for the omnipresent God it is written, *And you shall love the Lord* (Deuteronomy 6:5), while about the convert it is written, *Therefore love the* ger (ibid. 10:19).[5] There are many similar thoughts in the Midrashim and in a few places in the Talmud.

It is in effect in every place and every time, for both man and woman. Whoever transgresses it and disgraces him has violated a negative precept; but no whiplashes are given, because there is no physical action [necessarily] involved in it.

64 [NOT TO WRONG A CONVERT IN MATTERS OF PROPERTY]

that we were prohibited from wronging a proselyte in matters of monetary value—that if we have business dealings with him, we should not wrong or exploit him. For it is stated, *nor shall you oppress him* (Exodus 22:20); and it was explained in the Midrash *Mechilta*:[1] "you shall not oppress him"—in matters of monetary value. This prohibition is in addition to the negative precept (§337) for which he is included with all Jewry, to whom the ban on wronging or exploitation in matters of monetary value applies. So we were cautioned about him in regard to both words (§63) and monetary matters, for the reason that we have written (§63). All that concerns it [is to be found] in the precept before this. In [connection with] the ban on the exploitation of an Israelite about monetary matters (§337) we will yet write some of the details of such wronging, with the help of the Eternal Lord.

§65: NOT TO AFFLICT ANY ORPHAN OR WIDOW

[שֶׁלֹּא לְעַנּוֹת יָתוֹם וְאַלְמָנָה]

סה שֶׁנִּמְנַעְנוּ מֵהַכְבִּיד בְּמַעֲשֶׂה אוֹ אֲפִלּוּ בְדִבּוּר עַל הַיְתוֹמִים וְהָאַלְמָנוֹת, שֶׁנֶּאֱמַר "כָּל אַלְמָנָה וְיָתוֹם לֹא תְעַנּוּן", אֲבָל כָּל מַשָּׂאוֹ וּמַתָּנוֹ שֶׁל אָדָם עִמָּהֶם יִהְיֶה בְנַחַת וּבְחֶסֶד וּבְחֶמְלָה.

מִשָּׁרְשֵׁי הַמִּצְוָה מַה שֶׁכָּתַבְתִּי בְּסָמוּךְ בְּעִנְיַן הַגֵּר, לְפִי שֶׁאֵלּוּ הֵן תְּשׁוּשֵׁי כֹחַ שֶׁאֵין לָהֶם מִי שֶׁיִּטְעֹן טַעֲנוֹתָם בְּכָל נֶפֶשׁ כְּמוֹ שֶׁהָיָה אִישׁ הָאַלְמָנָה וַאֲבִיהֶן שֶׁל יְתוֹמִים אִם הָיָה קַיָּם, וְעַל כֵּן הִזְהִירַתְנוּ תּוֹרָתֵנוּ הַשְּׁלֵמָה לִקְנוֹת מִדַּת חֶסֶד וְרַחֲמִים בְּנַפְשֵׁנוּ וְנִהְיֶה יְשָׁרִים בְּכָל מַעֲשֵׂינוּ כְּאִלּוּ יֵשׁ כְּנֶגְדֵּנוּ טוֹעֵן בְּכֹחַ הַטַּעֲנָה בְּהֶפְכֵּנוּ, וְנָחוּס וְנַחְמֹל עֲלֵיהֶם וְנִרְאֶה זְכוּתָם בְּכָל דָּבָר יוֹתֵר מִשֶּׁהָיִינוּ עוֹשִׂים אִם הָיָה הָאָב קַיָּם.

מִדִּינֵי הַמִּצְוָה, מַה שֶׁאָמְרוּ שֶׁאֲפִלּוּ אַלְמָנָתוֹ שֶׁל מֶלֶךְ וִיתוֹמָיו בְּאַזְהָרָה זוֹ, וְהֵיאַךְ נוֹהֲגִין עִמָּהֶם, שֶׁלֹּא נְדַבֵּר אֲלֵיהֶם אֶלָּא רַכּוֹת וְלֹא יִנְהַג אָדָם בָּהֶם אֶלָּא מִנְהַג כָּבוֹד, וְלֹא יַכְאִיב גּוּפָן בַּעֲבוֹדָה וְלֹא יַלְבִּינֵם בִּדְבָרִים, וְיָחוּס עַל מָמוֹנָם יוֹתֵר מִמָּמוֹן עַצְמוֹ. וּמִפְּנֵי כֵן אָמְרוּ זִכְרוֹנָם לִבְרָכָה שֶׁהַבָּא לִפָּרַע מִמָּמוֹנָם, אַף־עַל־פִּי שֶׁיֵּשׁ בְּיָדוֹ שְׁטָר מְקֻיָּם לֹא יִפָּרַע אֶלָּא בִּשְׁבוּעָה, מַה שֶּׁאֵין כֵּן בְּאַחֵר. וְעוֹד אָמְרוּ זִכְרוֹנָם לִבְרָכָה שֶׁאִם יֵשׁ לָהֶם רִיב עִם שׁוּם אָדָם, שֶׁבֵּית דִּין חַיָּבִין לִטְעֹן בִּשְׁבִילָם כְּנֶגֶד הַתּוֹבֵעַ אוֹתָם, וְטוֹעֲנִין לְתוֹעַלְתָּם כָּל מַה שֶּׁיַּחְשְׁבוּ שֶׁהָיָה יָכוֹל אֲבִיהֶם לִטְעֹן.

וְאִם יֵשׁ לָהֶם מָעוֹת שֶׁמַּכְרִיחִין בֵּית דִּין כָּל מִי שֶׁיִּמְצְאוּ שֶׁהוּא עָשִׁיר מְנֻכָּסִים שֶׁיֵּשׁ לָהֶם אַחְרָיוּת וְיִהְיֶה אִישׁ נֶאֱמָן וְאוֹהֵב שָׁלוֹם וְכָשֵׁר, וּמַפְקִידִין לוֹ מְעוֹת הַיְתוֹמִים לְהִתְעַסֵּק בָּהֶן בְּעִנְיָן שֶׁיִּהְיֶה קָרוֹב לְשָׂכָר אֶל הַיְתוֹמִים וְרָחוֹק לְהֶפְסֵד, מַה שֶּׁלֹּא הִתִּירוּ בְאָדָם אַחֵר מִשּׁוּם אִסּוּר רִבִּית דְּרַבָּנָן. וּמַכְרִיחִים גַּם כֵּן כָּל אָדָם

---

65   1. I.e. weak, defenseless. Cf. Rashi on Exodus 22:21 (based on Mechilta): The same law applies to every person [not to oppress him], but Scripture spoke of what is usual—because they are powerless, and it is a common thing for them to be oppressed.

2. So MT *hilchoth de'oth* vi 10.

3. I.e. he must swear first that his claim is true; TB Sh'vu'oth 45a, etc. For the reason see Rashi to Gittin 50a, s.v. *lish'vu'ah*.

4. TB Bava Bathra 23a.

5. So that if he mismanages the orphans' money (see below), the *beth din* can collect the loss out of this property.

6. TB Bava M'tzi'a 70a.

7. Cf. MT *hilchoth malveh* iv 14: He [the trustee of the orphans' money] is told: "Deal and trade with it; if there will be a profit, give them their share of the profit; but if there is a loss, you will bear the loss alone." For this is "the dust of usury" [a shade or echo of it], which is forbidden only by the word of the Sages; and in the case of orphans' property they did not apply the ruling.

⟨256⟩

SIDRAH MISHPATIM

65 [NOT TO AFFLICT ANY ORPHAN OR WIDOW] that we were prohibited from oppressing by deed or even by word, orphans and widows—as it is stated, *You shall not afflict any widow or orphan* (Exodus 22:21). Rather, all the dealings that a person has with them should be [conducted] gently, pleasantly, with kindness and compassion.

At the root of the precept lies the reason that I wrote a bit earlier, about a proselyte (§63)—because these [persons] are powerless,[1] since they have no one who will champion them wholeheartedly as the widow's husband or the orphan's father would have done if he were alive. Therefore our complete, perfect Torah adjured us to attain the quality of kindness and mercy in our spirit, and to be honest in all our actions, as though someone opposed us, arguing with force [every possible] argument against us. Let us take pity on them in compassion, and see their right in everything, even more than we would if the father [or the husband] were alive.

As for the laws of the precept, [there is] what the Sages said,[2] that even the widow of a king and his orphans are included in this prohibition; how they should be dealt with—that we should speak nothing but soft (gentle) words to them; that a man should treat them only with respect, and should not make them suffer bodily through [hard] work, or mortally shame them with words; and he should have more concern for their property than for his own.[2] For this reason our Sages of blessed memory said that if someone comes to collect his due out of their possessions, even if he holds a confirmed, validated document [establishing his right] he should collect only with an oath,[3] which is not the case with anyone else. Our Sages of blessed memory said further[4] that if they have a controversy with any man, the *beth din* is required to plead in their behalf against their plaintiff, and they [the justices of the court] argue for their benefit all that they reckon their father could have argued.

Moreover, if they [orphans] have money, the *beth din* imposes a duty on a person rich in landed property from which debts can be collected,[5] who is trustworthy, peace-loving and worthy, and they entrust the orphans' money to him so that he should do business with it in such a way that it is likely to earn profit for the orphans and not likely to incur any loss.[6] This [the Sages] would not permit for anyone else, on account of the prohibition against usury by the law of the Sages.[7] In addition, they compel any man who is beneficial for them to

§65: NOT TO AFFLICT ANY ORPHAN OR WIDOW

שֶׁהוּא טוֹב לָהֶם שֶׁיְּפַקַּח עַל נִכְסֵיהֶם, אִם לֹא הִנִּיחַ לָהֶם אֲבִיהֶם אַפּוֹטְרוֹפָּא.

וְעוֹד אָמְרוּ בָּהֶם שֶׁכָּל מַשָּׂא וּמַתָּן שֶׁיִּהְיֶה לָהֶם עִם כָּל אָדָם יְהֵא יָדָם עַל הָעֶלְיוֹנָה כְּמוֹ הַהֶקְדֵּשׁ וְיוֹתֵר מֵהַהֶקְדֵּשׁ בְּאַחַת.

כֵּיצַד, יְתוֹמִים שֶׁמָּכְרוּ פֵּרוֹת וּמְשָׁכָן מֵהֶם הַלּוֹקֵחַ וְלֹא נָתַן לָהֶם הַדָּמִים עֲדַיִן וְהוּקְרוּ בֵּינְתַיִם חוֹזְרִין בָּהֶן, שֶׁאֵין נִכְסֵיהֶן נִקְנִין אֶלָּא בְּכֶסֶף, כְּהֶקְדֵּשׁ שֶׁכָּתוּב בּוֹ "וְנָתַן הַכֶּסֶף וְקָם לוֹ". הוּזְלוּ הַפֵּרוֹת אֵין יְכוֹלִין הַלּוֹקְחִים לַחֲזֹר בָּהֶם, שֶׁלֹּא יְהֵא כֹּחַ הֶדְיוֹט חָמוּר מִכֹּחָם.

וְכֵן אִם לָקְחוּ הֵם פֵּרוֹת וּמָשְׁכוּ אוֹתָם וְלֹא נָתְנוּ הַדָּמִים וְהוּקְרוּ, אֵין הַמּוֹכֵר יָכוֹל לַחֲזֹר, שֶׁלֹּא יְהֵא כֹּחַ הֶדְיוֹט יָהֵא בִּמְשִׁיכָה גָּדוֹל מִכֹּחָם, וְאִם הוּזְלוּ הָיוּ יְכוֹלִין לַחֲזֹר, אֶלָּא מִפְּנֵי תַקָּנָתָם אָמְרוּ שֶׁלֹּא יְהוּ יְכוֹלִין לַחֲזֹר כְּדֵי שֶׁיִּמָּצְאוּ מִי שֶׁיִּמְכֹּר לָהֶם פֵּרוֹת בְּהַקָּפָה. נָתְנוּ הֵם דָּמִים לַמּוֹכֵר בִּשְׁבִיל פֵּרוֹת וְלֹא מָשְׁכוּ הַפֵּרוֹת וְהוּזְלוּ הַפֵּרוֹת, חוֹזְרִין בָּהֶם. וְזוֹ הִיא הָאַחַת שֶׁאָמַרְנוּ שֶׁיְּתֵרִים הֵם עַל הַהֶקְדֵּשׁ, כִּי הַהֶקְדֵּשׁ אֵינוֹ חוֹזֵר בּוֹ בָּזוֹ: מִכֵּיוָן שֶׁיֵּשׁ בְּכַיּוֹצֵא בָּזֶה מִי שֶׁפָּרַע לַהֶדְיוֹט לֹא רָצוּ חֲכָמִים לְהַטִּיל פְּחִיתוּת מִדָּה בִּשְׁבִיל מְעַט רֶוַח לְגַבֵּי הַהֶקְדֵּשׁ, אֲבָל לְגַבֵּי יְתוֹמִים דַּי לָהֶם לִהְיוֹת כִּשְׁאָר הָעָם, וְכֵיוָן שֶׁשְּׁאָר הָעָם יְכוֹלִים לַחֲזֹר בָּהֶם מִן הַדִּין בָּזוֹ, אֶלָּא שֶׁיֵּשׁ עֲלֵיהֶם מִי שֶׁפָּרַע, יְתוֹמִים שֶׁאֵין לָהֶם דִּין מִי שֶׁפָּרַע, בְּדִין הוּא שֶׁיַּחְזְרוּ בָּהֶם.

נָתְנוּ הַיְתוֹמִים הַדָּמִים וְלֹא מָשְׁכוּ פֵּרוֹת וְהוּקְרוּ, אִם רָצוּ הַמּוֹכָרִים לַחֲזֹר

---

8. I.e. he appointed no one; see Mishnah, Gittin v 4.

9. TB Gittin 52a; this is the source for this and the next two paragraphs.

10. Ownership is generally effected when the buyer lifts or draws the object toward himself.

11. Only when a buyer pays for the goods of orphans do they become his, but not by virtue of his taking them.

12. For had the buyers bought the produce from an ordinary person and drawn it to themselves or into their domain, they could no longer retract; hence these buyers should certainly have no right to do so (Rashi, Gittin 52a, second s.v. *lo y'hé*).

13. MT *hilchoth m'chirah* ix 5.

14. In an ordinary case, not involving orphans or consecrated property, a buyer who merely paid for the wares but did not take them, could retract. But then the *beth din* pronounces this imprecation over him: "He who exacted punishment from the people of the generation of the flood [Genesis 6–7], the people of the generation of the dispersion [*ibid.* 11], the people of Sodom and Gomorrah [*ibid.* 18–19], and from the Egyptians who drowned in the sea—let Him exact punishment from one who will not stand by his word."

⟨258⟩

SIDRAH **MISHPATIM**

keep a watchful eye on their property, if their father did not leave them any guardian.[8]

The Sages said further[9] about them that whatever dealings they may have with any man, [legally] they should have the upper hand, as [in a case involving] consecrated property—and more than [in a case of] consecrated property, in one respect.

How so? Suppose that orphans sold produce, and the buyer drew it from them [toward him][10] but did not yet give them the money for it—and meanwhile its market value rose. Then they can change their mind [and cancel the sale], for their property can be bought only through money,[11] like consecrated property, of which it is written that one gives the money, *and it shall remain his* (Leviticus 27:19). If, however, the produce became worth less, the buyers cannot change their mind and retract—for the rights of an ordinary person [in an ordinary case] should not be stronger than theirs [the orphans'].[12]

So too, if they [orphans] bought produce and drew it [to them] but did not give the money [for it] and its market value rose, the seller cannot change his mind and retract—so that the effectiveness of an ordinary person, who acquires [his purchase] by drawing [it to him], should not be greater than theirs [the orphans']. If [the produce] became worth less, though, they should be able to retract from the sale; however, for their own benefit the Sages ruled that they should not be able to retract, so that they should find someone who will sell them produce on credit.[13] [On the other hand,] if they [orphans] gave the seller money for the produce but did not draw the produce [to them], and the market value of the produce fell, they can change their mind and retract. This is the one respect in which we said that they are superior [in legal power] to consecrated property; for [the custodians of] consecrated property cannot retract in such a case. Since in a similar case, the imprecation of "He who exacted punishment" would be pronounced over an ordinary person,[14] the Sages did not wish to impose a lessening of the measure [of legal effectiveness] in regard to consecrated property, [merely] for the sake of a little profit. As regards orphans, however, it is enough for them to be like the rest of the people; and since the rest of the people can retract by law in such a case, except that they incur the imprecation of "He who exacted punishment," it remains the legal right of orphans—who are not subject to the imprecation—to retract.

Now, if the orphans gave money but did not draw the produce

§65: NOT TO AFFLICT ANY ORPHAN OR WIDOW

בָּהֶם חוֹזְרִים וּמְקַבְּלִים מִי שֶׁפָּרַע, וְזוֹ תַּקָּנָה הוּא לָהֶם, שֶׁאִם יִהְיֶה דִינָם שֶׁיִּקְנוּ בִּנְתִינַת הַמָּעוֹת וְיִהְיוּ שֶׁלָּהֶם לְגַמְרֵי, שֶׁלֹּא יְהֵא הַמּוֹכֵר יָכוֹל לַחֲזוֹר בּוֹ, יֹאמַר לָהֶם הַמּוֹכֵר "נִשְׂרְפוּ" אוֹ "אָבְדוּ בְּאֹנֶס".

וְאִם שֶׁמָּא תֹּאמַר יִהְיוּ בִּרְשׁוּתָם לְכָל תּוֹעַלְתָּם, שֶׁאִם יִרְצוּ יִקְחוּ אוֹתָם עַל־כָּל־פָּנִים, וְאִם לֹא יִרְצוּ לֹא יִקְחוּ אוֹתָם כְּדֵי שֶׁלֹּא יִטְעַן הַמּוֹכֵר דָּבָר זֶה, תְּשׁוּבָתְךָ, כִּי כָּל זֶה אִי אֶפְשָׁר לַעֲשׂוֹת לָהֶם, שֶׁאֵינוֹ בַדִּין שֶׁנִּתֵּן לָהֶם נִכְסֵי בְּנֵי אָדָם, דַּי לָהֶם כִּי אֲנַחְנוּ מַעֲמִידִים אוֹתָם זִמְנִין אַדִּינָא דְאוֹרַיְתָא זִמְנִין אַדִּינָא דְרַבָּנָן לְתוֹעַלְתָּם, אֲבָל לִפְנֵי מִכָּל זֶה אֵינוֹ בַדִּין לָתֵת לָהֶם מָמוֹן הָעוֹלָם. וּכְעֵין מַה שֶּׁאָמוּר עֲלֵיהֶם בַּגְּמָרָא, יַתְמֵי דְאָכְלִי דְּלָאו דִּידְהוּ לֵיזְלוּ בָּתַר שְׁבָקַיְהוּ.

לָקְחוּ הַיְתוֹמִים דָּמִים עַל פֵּרוֹתֵיהֶם וְלֹא מְשָׁכָם מֵהֶם הַלּוֹקֵחַ וְהוּזְלוּ, יְכוֹלִים הַלּוֹקְחִים לַחֲזוֹר בָּהֶם מִן הַדִּין וּמְקַבְּלִים מִי שֶׁפָּרַע, שֶׁאִם אַתָּה אוֹמֵר נַעֲמִידָם עַל דִּין תּוֹרָה, וּמִכֵּיוָן שֶׁנָּתְנוּ הַלּוֹקְחִים הַמָּעוֹת זָכוּ בַּפֵּרוֹת וְלֹא יוּכְלוּ לַחֲזוֹר הַלּוֹקְחִים, יִהְיֶה זֶה רָעָה לַיְתוֹמִים, שֶׁלֹּא יִמְצְאוּ לְעוֹלָם מִי שֶׁיַּקְדִּים לָהֶם מָעוֹת עַל פֵּרוֹתֵיהֶם, וְאוּלַי יִצְטָרְכוּ לְמָעוֹת לְפִי שָׁעָה וְנִמְצָא לָהֶם בְּתַקָּנָה זוֹ הֶפְסֵד גָּדוֹל לִפְעָמִים, וְעַל כֵּן עֵינֵנוּ בְּכָל צִדְדֵי תּוֹעַלְתָּם שֶׁהָיָה אֶפְשָׁר וְתִקְּנוּ לָהֶם.

וּלְעוֹלָם אֵין הַיְתוֹמִים מְקַבְּלִים מִי שֶׁפָּרַע בְּכָל שֶׁיַּעֲשֶׂה הָאַפּוֹטְרוֹפָּא וְלֹא הָאַפּוֹטְרוֹפָּא גַם כֵּן לְפִי שֶׁמִּכֹּחָם הוּא חוֹזֵר בּוֹ. וְכֵן הַדִּין בְּעָלְמָא לְעִנְיַן שָׁלִיחַ הַנּוֹשֵׂא וְנוֹתֵן לָדַעַת מְשַׁלְּחוֹ שֶׁשְּׁנֵיהֶם אֵין מְקַבְּלִין מִי שֶׁפָּרַע.

וּמִכָּל מָקוֹם אָמְרוּ בָּהֶם שֶׁמֻּתָּר לְעַנּוֹתָם קְצָת לְתוֹעַלְתָּם, כְּגוֹן הָרַב לְתַלְמִידוֹ

---

15. And the loss is entirely yours; Rambam *ibid.* 6.
16. That a person gains possession of goods and wares by paying for them.
17. That one takes possession of something purchased by lifting it, or, if it is not to be lifted, by drawing it to him.
18. TB Bava M'tzi'a 70a (bracketed addition: Rashi).
19. TB Gittin 52a; MT *hilchoth m'chirah* ix 4.
20. The deputy, because he does not act in his own behalf; the one who delegated him, because he can say, "I deputized you only to act constructively, not to spoil matters"; TB Bava M'tzi'a 74b; MT *hilchoth malveh* ix 5.

⟨260⟩

SIDRAH MISHPATIM

[into their domain to gain ownership] and its market value rose, should the sellers wish to change their mind and retract, they may do so, receiving the imprecation of "He who exacted punishment." This is a regulation for their [the orphans'] benefit: for were their law that they take possession by giving money and [what they purchase] should be theirs completely, so that the seller should not be able to retract from it, then the seller could say to them: it was burnt, or lost by accident.[15]

You might say, though: Let it be at their disposal for every advantage to them—that if they wish, they can make it theirs in any case, and if they do not wish, they will not make it theirs—so that the seller should not contend this [that it was burnt, etc. by accident]. Your answer is that it is impossible to do all this for them; for it is not justice that we should give them the property of others. It is enough for them that we place them at times under the Torah's law,[16] and at times under the law of the Sages,[17] to their advantage. But beyond this, it would not be fair justice to give them goods generally. This is in keeping with what was said about them in the Talmud:[18] Orphans who eat (consume) what is not theirs will follow the one who left them behind [their father—to the grave].

Now, if orphans have taken money for produce, but the buyer has not drawn it [to him], and its market value fell, the buyer can retract by law, receiving the imprecation of "He who exacted punishment." For if you say, "Let us place them [strictly] under Torah law, and since the buyer gave the money he has acquired the produce, and the buyer cannot retract"—this will be harmful to the orphans: They will never find anyone who will advance them money for their produce; and perhaps they will need money immediately, and the result of this [special] regulation will be a great loss for them at times.[19] Hence the Sages examined all the aspects of benefit and advantage that were possible for them, and enacted this for them.

Orphans never receive the imprecation of "He who exacted punishment" for anything that the guardian does; and neither does the guardian—since it is in their behalf that he makes a retraction. Such is the law, too, generally in regard to a deputy who trades and negotiates in behalf of the person who deputized him—neither receives the imprecation of "He who exacted punishment."[20]

In any case, the Sages said about them [orphans] that it is permissible to make them suffer a bit for their own benefit—for example,

שֶׁל תּוֹרָה אוֹ שֶׁל אוּמָּנוּת, אֲבָל אֲפִלּוּ לְתוֹעַלְתָּם מִצְוָה לְהָקֵל בָּהֶם יוֹתֵר מִשְּׁאָר כָּל אָדָם.

וְאָמְרוּ גַם כֵּן שֶׁבְּרִית כְּרוּתָה לָהֶם שֶׁנַּעֲנִין מִצַּעֲקָתָם, שֶׁנֶּאֱמַר: שָׁמֹעַ אֶשְׁמַע צַעֲקָתוֹ. וְשֶׁהֵם נִקְרָאִים יְתוֹמִים לְעִנְיָן מִצְוָה זוֹ עַד שֶׁלֹּא יְהוּ צְרִיכִין בְּעִסְקֵיהֶם לְאָדָם גָּדוֹל אֶלָּא עוֹשִׂין כָּל צָרְכֵי עַצְמָן כִּשְׁאָר כָּל הַגְּדוֹלִים. וְיֶתֶר פְּרָטֶיהָ מְבֹאָרִים בִּמְקוֹמוֹת מְפֻזָּרִים בַּתַּלְמוּד וּבַמִּדְרָשׁוֹת.

וְנוֹהֶגֶת מִצְוָה זוֹ בְּכָל מָקוֹם וּבְכָל זְמַן בִּזְכָרִים וּנְקֵבוֹת, שֶׁחַיָּבִין בְּנֵי אָדָם לִנְהֹג עִמָּהֶם דֶּרֶךְ נַחַת וְכָבוֹד. וְעוֹבֵר עָלֶיהָ וְהִכְעִיסָן אוֹ הִקְנִיטָן אוֹ רָדָה בָּהֶם אוֹ אִבֵּד מָמוֹנָם, וְכָל שֶׁכֵּן אִם הִכָּה אוֹתָן, הֲרֵי זֶה עוֹבֵר בְּלֹא תַעֲשֶׂה. וְאַף־עַל־פִּי שֶׁאֵין לוֹקִין עַל לָאו זֶה, לְפִי שֶׁאֵין הָעִנּוּי דָּבָר מְסֻיָּם כְּדֵי לְהַלְקוֹת עָלָיו, כִּי לְעוֹלָם יוּכַל הַמְעַנֶּה רָשָׁע לִטְעֹן בְּשֶׁקֶר כִּי מִן הַדִּין עִמּוֹ אוֹ לְטוֹבָתָם, הַשֵּׁם (יִתְבָּרַךְ) שֶׁהוּא בּוֹחֵן לְבָבוֹת תּוֹבֵעַ צַעֲרָן.

וַהֲרֵי עָנְשׁוֹ מְפֹרָשׁ בַּתּוֹרָה, שֶׁנֶּאֱמַר "וְהָרַגְתִּי אֶתְכֶם בֶּחָרֶב", כְּלוֹמַר מִדָּה כְּנֶגֶד מִדָּה שֶׁתִּהְיֶינָה נְשֵׁי הַמְעַנִּים אַלְמָנוֹת וּבְנֵיהֶם יְתוֹמִים וְלֹא יִמְצְאוּ מְרַחֵם, שֶׁבַּמִּדָּה שֶׁאָדָם מוֹדֵד בָּהּ מוֹדְדִין לוֹ. וְאִם נְקֵבָה הִיא הַמְעַנָּה תָּמוּת וְאִישָׁהּ יִשָּׂא אַחֶרֶת שֶׁתְּעַנֶּה בָנֶיהָ. וְדָרְשׁוּ זִכְרוֹנָם לִבְרָכָה: כִּי אִם צָעֹק יִצְעַק אֵלַי, בֵּן קוֹבֵל לְאָבִיו, אִשָּׁה לְבַעְלָהּ, אַלְמָנָה וְיָתוֹם אֵלַי, וְשָׁמַעְתִּי כִּי חַנּוּן אָנִי.

וְהָרַמְבַּ"ן זִכְרוֹנוֹ לִבְרָכָה יִמְנֶה אַזְהָרַת יָתוֹם וְאַלְמָנָה בִּשְׁנֵי לָאוִין מִן הַטַּעַם שֶׁכָּתַבְנוּ לְמַעְלָה.

---

21. Derived from MT *hilchoth de'oth* vi 10.

22. By a scribal oversight the first Hebrew edition (like the old manuscripts) cites a similar passage in Exodus 22:26.

23. A Talmudic dictum, meaning that punishment always fits the sin; TB Sotah 8b.

24. This verse refers to an impoverished borrower in regard to the garment he has pawned; but see note 1.

25. In his commentary (*hassagoth*) to ShM, negative precept §256.

SIDRAH MISHPATIM

an instructor in regard to his pupil in Torah or in [learning] a craft. But even [when it is] for their benefit, it is a religious duty to go easier, more lightly with them than with any other persons.[21]

The Sages said further that a convenant was made for them [orphans] that they would be answered [by Heaven] in their outcry: for it is stated, *I will surely hear their cry* (Exodus 22:22).[22] [They said] too that they are called orphans in regard to this precept until they no longer need an adult in their affairs but rather can attend to all their needs themselves, like all other adults.[21] [These] and the rest of its details are clarified in various, scattered places in the Talmud and Midrashim.

This precept is in effect in every place and every time, for both man and woman—as people [generally] are duty-bound to treat them gently and honorably. If someone transgresses it and angers them, vexes them, treats them tyrannically or loses their property [through mismanagement], and all the more certainly if he beats them, he violates a negative precept. And even though whiplashes are not given over this prohibition, because oppression is not something fixed and certain, so that one can be whipped for it—for the wicked oppressor can always argue falsely that he oppressed them justly, according to the law, or for their good—the Eternal Lord, be He blessed, who examines and reads hearts, exacts satisfaction for their suffering.[21]

His punishment, though, is given explicitly in the Torah: for it is stated, *and I will kill you with the sword* (Exodus 22:23). This is to say [it will be] measure for measure—that the wives of the oppressors should become widows, and their children orphans, and they should find no one to take pity [on them]: for by the yardstick that a man measures, by that he is measured.[23] And if the oppressor is a woman, she will die, and her husband will marry another woman, who will make her children suffer. Moreover, our Sages of blessed memory taught: *if they cry out at all to Me* (ibid. 22)—a child complains to his father, a woman to her husband, a widow and orphan to Me; *I will hear, for I am compassionate* (ibid. 26).[24]

Ramban of blessed memory reckons the injunction about the widow and the orphan as two negative precepts,[25] for the reason we have written above (§7).

§66: THE MITZVAH OF LENDING TO THE POOR

[מִצְוַת הַלְוָאָה לְעָנִי]

סו לְהַלְווֹת לְעָנִי כְּדֵי שַׂגַּת הַיָּד כְּפִי מַה שֶׁצָּרִיךְ לוֹ לְמַעַן הַרְחִיב לוֹ וּלְהָקֵל מֵעָלָיו אַנְחָתוֹ. וְזֹאת הַמִּצְוָה שֶׁל הַלְוָאָה הִיא יוֹתֵר חֲזָקָה וּמְחַיֶּבֶת מִמִּצְוַת נְתִינַת הַצְּדָקָה, שֶׁמִּי שֶׁנִּתְגַּלָּה וְנוֹדַע דָּחֳקוֹ בֵּין בְּנֵי אָדָם וְגִלָּה פָּנָיו לִשְׁאֹל מֵהֶן אֵין דָּחֳקוֹ וְאֲפֵלָתוֹ כְּמִי שֶׁעֲדַיִן לֹא בָא לְאוֹתָהּ בּוּשָׁה וְיִרְאָה מֵהִכָּנֵס בָּהּ, וְאִם יִהְיֶה לוֹ מְעַט סַעַד שֶׁל הַלְוָאָה, בְּמַה שֶׁיָּרוּחַ מְעַט אוּלַי לֹא יִצְטָרֵךְ לִשְׁאֵלָה לְעוֹלָם, וּכְשֶׁיְּרַחֲמֶנּוּ הָאֵל בְּרֶוַח יְשַׁלֵּם נִשְׁיוֹ וְיִחְיֶה בַּנּוֹתָר.

וְעַל כֵּן הִזְהִירַתְנוּ תּוֹרָתֵנוּ הַשְּׁלֵמָה עַל זֶה לִסְעֹד הַדַּךְ בְּהַלְוָאָה טֶרֶם יִצְטָרֵךְ לָבוֹא אֶל הַשְּׁאֵלָה, שֶׁנֶּאֱמַר "אִם כֶּסֶף תַּלְוֶה אֶת עַמִּי", וְאָמְרוּ זִכְרוֹנָם לִבְרָכָה בַּמְּכִילְתָּא כָּל אִם וְאִם שֶׁבַּתּוֹרָה רְשׁוּת חוּץ מִשְּׁלֹשָׁה שֶׁהֵם חוֹבָה, וְזֶה אֶחָד מֵהֶם. וְיַכְרִיחוּ הַדָּבָר מִדִּכְתִיב בְּמָקוֹם אַחֵר בַּתּוֹרָה דֶרֶךְ צַוָּאָה "וְהַעֲבֵט תַּעֲבִיטֶנּוּ".

שֹׁרֶשׁ הַמִּצְוָה, שֶׁרָצָה הָאֵל לִהְיוֹת בְּרוּאָיו מְלֻמָּדִים וּמֻרְגָּלִים בְּמִדַּת הַחֶסֶד וְהָרַחֲמִים כִּי הִיא מִדָּה מְשֻׁבַּחַת, וּמִתּוֹךְ הֶכְשֵׁר גּוּפָם בַּמִּדּוֹת הַטּוֹבוֹת יִהְיוּ רְאוּיִים לְקַבָּלַת הַטּוֹבָה, כְּמוֹ שֶׁאָמַרְנוּ שֶׁחָלוֹת הַטּוֹב וְהַבְּרָכָה לְעוֹלָם עַל הַטּוֹב לֹא בְהִפּוּכוֹ, וּבְהֵיטִיב הַשֵּׁם (יִתְבָּרַךְ) לַטּוֹבִים יַשְׁלִים חֶפְצוֹ שֶׁחָפֵץ לְהֵיטִיב לְעוֹלָם.

וְאִם לֹא מִצַּד שֹׁרֶשׁ זֶה הֲלֹא הוּא בָּרוּךְ הוּא יַסְפִּיק לֶעָנִי דֵי מַחְסוֹרוֹ זוּלָתֵנוּ, אֶלָּא שֶׁהָיָה מֵחַסְדּוֹ בָּרוּךְ הוּא שֶׁנַּעֲשֵׂינוּ שְׁלוּחִים לוֹ לִזְכוּתֵנוּ. וְעוֹד טַעַם אַחֵר בַּדָּבָר, שֶׁרָצָה הָאֵל בָּרוּךְ הוּא לְפַרְנֵס הֶעָנִי עַל יְדֵי בְּנֵי אָדָם מִגֹּדֶל חֶטְאוֹ, כְּדֵי שֶׁיִּתְיַסֵּר בְּמַכְאוֹב בִּשְׁנֵי פָּנִים, בְּקַבָּלַת הַבֹּשֶׁת מֵאֲשֶׁר כְּגִילוֹ וּבְצִמְצוּם מְזוֹנוֹ. וּכְעִנְיָן זֶה שֶׁאָמַרְנוּ כְּדֵי לְזַכּוֹתֵנוּ הֵשִׁיב חָכָם מֵחֲכָמֵינוּ לְמִין אֶחָד שֶׁשְּׁאָלוֹ: אִם

---

1. Literally, as the grasp (or reach) of the hand.
2. Literally, he has revealed his face.
3. So ShM positive precept §197.
4. More literally, from someone about his own age. I.e. even though they started out in life at the same time, now he must receive help from the other.

SIDRAH MISHPATIM

66 [THE MITZVAH OF LENDING TO THE POOR] to lend to a poor man as one can afford,[1] according to what he needs in order to bring him relief and ease (lift) his anguish from him. This religious duty of giving loans is a stronger and greater obligation than the *mitzvah* of giving charity: For if someone's penury has become revealed and known among people, and he has come out into the open[2] to ask [help, charity] of them, his distress and suffering is not as great as that of a person who has not yet been reduced to this ignominy and who fears to enter this state;[3] and if he will have the small help of a loan, so that he can find a little relief, perhaps he will never need to come asking [for charity]; then, when God will mercifully grant him financial ease, he will pay his creditors and live from the rest.

Therefore our complete, perfect Torah adjured us about this, to support a destitute person with a loan before he will be reduced to begging [charity]. For it is stated, *'im (If) you lend money to My people* (Exodus 22:24), and our Sages of blessed memory said in the Midrash Mechilta: Every word *'im* ("if") in the Torah denotes something voluntary, except in three cases, where they denote something obligatory—and this is one of them. And they prove the matter because it is written elsewhere, in an expression of commandment, *and you shall surely lend him enough* (Deuteronomy 15:8).

The root reason for the precept is that God wished for His created humans to be educated and accustomed in the quality of loving-kindness and compassion, since it is a noble quality. Then, out of their physical, bodily training in the good qualities, they will become fit, worthy to receive goodness. As we have stated, the bestowal of goodness and blessing is ever upon the good [person], not on his opposite. And when the Eternal Lord, be He blessed, bestows goodness upon good people, His desire—to do good to the world—is fulfilled.

Now, if not for this root reason, He (blessed is He) could supply a poor man enough for his needs without us. It is only that by His kindness (be He blessed) we have become His agents, to achieve our merit. Another reason for this is that God (blessed is He) wished to sustain a poor man through [the help] of human beings on account of the enormity of his guilt, so that he should be chastised by pain in two respects: by suffering shame from his contemporary,[4] and by the limitation of his sustenance. In the same way that we said it is in order to earn us merit, one of our Sages answered a certain heretic

§66–67: TO LEND TO THE POOR / NOT TO DUN THEM TO REPAY

אֱלֹהִים אוֹהֵב עֲנִיִּים, שֶׁהֲרֵי צִוָּה עֲלֵיהֶם, לָמָּה אֵינוֹ מְפַרְנְסָן, וְכוּלֵּיהּ, כְּמוֹ שֶׁבָּא בְּמַסֶּכֶת עֲבוֹדָה זָרָה.

דִּינֵי הַמִּצְוָה, כְּגוֹן אֵי זֶה עָנִי קוֹדֵם בְּמִצְוָה זוֹ, וְהָאַזְהָרוֹת הַרְבֵּה שֶׁהִזְהִירוּנוּ זִכְרוֹנָם לִבְרָכָה עָלֶיהָ, שֶׁאָמְרוּ שֶׁהָאָדָם מְרֻחָק וְנִמְאָס וְנִתְעָב וְנֶאֱלָח וּמְשֻׁקָּץ עַד שֶׁקָּרוֹב לִהְיוֹת מֵאוּסוֹ כִּמְאוּס עֲבוֹדָה זָרָה, אִם יֵשׁ לוֹ וּמוֹשֵׁךְ יָדוֹ מִמִּצְוָה זוֹ. וְכַמָּה נֶחְמָד וְנֶאֱהָב וּמְרֻחָם וּמִתְבָּרֵךְ בְּכַמָּה בִּרְכוֹת הַמַּחֲזִיק בָּהּ, הַכֹּל מְבֹאָר בִּמְקוֹמוֹת מְכֻתָּבוֹת וּבְבָתְרָא וּבִמְקוֹמוֹת רַבִּים מִן הַתַּלְמוּד.

[שֶׁלֹּא נִתְבַּע חוֹב מֵעָנִי שֶׁאֵין לוֹ בַּמֶּה לִפְרֹעַ]

סז שֶׁנִּמְנַעְנוּ מִלִּתְבֹּעַ הַחוֹב מִן הַלֹּוֶה בְּעֵת שֶׁנֵּדַע לִפְרֹעַ חוֹבוֹ לְפִי שֶׁאֵין לוֹ, שֶׁנֶּאֱמַר: לֹא תִהְיֶה לוֹ כְּנֹשֶׁה. וְדַע כִּי זֹאת הַמְּנִיעָה תִּכְלֹל גַּם כֵּן שֶׁלֹּא לְהַלְווֹת בְּרִבִּית לְיִשְׂרָאֵל.

מִשָּׁרְשֵׁי הַמִּצְוָה לִקְבֹּעַ לָנוּ מִדַּת הַחֶסֶד וְהַחֶמְלָה, וּכְשֶׁיִּהְיוּ קְבוּעוֹת בָּנוּ אָז נִהְיֶה רְאוּיִין לְקַבָּלַת הַטּוֹבָה וִישַׁלֵּם חֵפֶץ הַשֵּׁם בָּנוּ שֶׁחָפֵץ הַשֵּׁם לְהֵטִיב בָּעוֹלָם הַזֶּה וּבַבָּא.

מִדִּינֵי הַמִּצְוָה, מַה שֶּׁאָמְרוּ זִכְרוֹנָם לִבְרָכָה: מִנַּיִן לַנּוֹשֶׁה בַּחֲבֵרוֹ מָנֶה וְיוֹדֵעַ שֶׁאֵין לוֹ שֶׁאָסוּר לַעֲבֹר כְּנֶגֶד בֵּיתוֹ, שֶׁנֶּאֱמַר "לֹא תִהְיֶה לוֹ כְּנֹשֶׁה". וּמַה שֶּׁאָמְרוּ גַּם כֵּן בַּמְּכִילְתָּא, "לֹא תִהְיֶה לוֹ כְּנֹשֶׁה" שֶׁלֹּא יֵרָאֶה לוֹ בְּכָל זְמַן, וּדְבָרִים אֲחֵרִים הַנֶּאֱמָרִים בָּעִנְיָן הַזֶּה בִּמְצִיעָא וּבִמְקוֹמוֹת בַּתַּלְמוּד.

וְנוֹהֶגֶת בִּזְכָרִים וּנְקֵבוֹת בְּכָל מָקוֹם וּבְכָל זְמָן. וְהָעוֹבֵר עָלֶיהָ וְתָבַע הַלְוָאָתוֹ

---

5. The Sage was R. Akiva, and his reply was, "In order that we may be saved through them from the punishment of Géhinnom (purgatory)."

6. TB Bava Bathra 10a: If one turns a blind eye to matters of charity, it is as though he worshipped idols, etc.

7. *Ibid.* 9b: Whoever gives a *p'rutah* (small coin) to a poor man is blessed with six blessings. *Ibid.* 10a: If a man gives a *p'rutah* to a poor person, he will merit to see the visage of the *shechinah* (Divine Presence).

67   1. Apart from the specific prohibitions written elsewhere in the Pentateuch; TB Bava M'tzi'a 75b. The paragraph is based on ShM negative precept §234.

2. TB Bava M'tzi'a 45b.

3. A coin weighing and worth 480 grams of silver.

4. Because this embarrasses or shames the man, and the effect is the same as it he were dunned.

who asked him: If God loves the poor, since He commanded about them [that they should be supported], why does He not sustain them? etc.—as it is recorded in the Talmud tractate *'Avodah Zarah* [*Bava Bathra* 10a].[5]

The laws of the precept are, for example: which poor man takes precedence under this precept; the many admonitions that our Sages of blessed memory gave us about it, saying that a man is repulsive, despicable, abominable, rotten and abhorrent, so much so that his loathsomeness is almost as great as that of an idol-worshipper—if he has the means yet withdraws his hand (holds back) from this religious obligation.[6] [On the other hand,] how delightful, beloved, worthy of compassion, and blessed with many blessings is a person who strongly upholds (fulfills) it.[7] It is all explained in various places in the Talmud tractates *K'thuboth* and *Bava Bathra*, and in many [other] places in the Talmud.

67

[NOT TO DUN A POOR MAN UNABLE TO PAY HIS DEBT]

that we were prohibited from demanding payment of a debt by a borrower at a time when we know that he cannot pay the debt because he does not have the means—for it is stated, *you shall not be to him as a creditor* (Exodus 22:24). And know that this prohibition also includes [an injunction] not to lend money at interest to a Jew.[1]

At the root of the precept lies the purpose to firmly inculcate the qualities of kindness and compassion in us. When they will be firmly set within us, we will be ready, worthy to receive good reward, and what the Eternal Lord desires for us will be fulfilled—for it is the Lord's wish to do good [for us] in this world and the world-to-come.

Among the laws of the precept there is what our Sages of blessed memory said:[2] How do we know that if someone seeks to collect a *maneh*[3] from his fellow and he knows the other does not have the means [to pay it], he is forbidden to pass by opposite the other's house?—for it is stated, *you shall not be to him as a creditor*. Then there is what they said, further, in the Midrash *Mechilta:* "you shall not be to him as a creditor"—[this means] that he should not appear in his sight all the time.[4] Other points are stated about this subject in the tractate *Bava M'tzi'a* and other places in the Talmud.

It applies to both man and woman, in every place and in every time. If a person transgresses it and demands payment of his loan from

§67–68: NOT TO DUN A POOR DEBTOR / ON INTEREST-BEARING LOANS

לַחֲבֵרוֹ וְיוֹדֵעַ שֶׁאֵין לוֹ וְתוֹבְעוֹ כְּדֵי לְצַעֲרוֹ עוֹבֵר עַל לָאו זֶה, וְהוּא כְעוֹבֵר עַל מִצְוַת מֶלֶךְ.

[שֶׁלֹּא נָשִׁית יָד בֵּין לֹוֶה לְמַלְוֶה בְּרִבִּית]

סח שֶׁלֹּא נִתְעַסֵּק בְּמִלְווֹת רִבִּית בֵּין הַלֹּוֶה וְהַמַּלְוֶה, כְּלוֹמַר שֶׁלֹּא נֵעָשֶׂה לָהֶם עֲרֵבוּת וְלֹא נָעִיד אֲלֵיהֶם וְלֹא נִכְתֹּב בֵּינֵיהֶם שְׁטָר שֶׁיֵּשׁ בּוֹ הַזְכָּרַת רִבִּית, שֶׁנֶּאֱמַר: לֹא תְשִׂימוּן עָלָיו נֶשֶׁךְ. וּבָא הַפֵּרוּשׁ בַּמְּצִיעָא שֶׁהַלָּאו הַזֶּה נֶאֱמַר עַל הַמִּתְעַסְּקִים בָּעִנְיָן כְּגוֹן עָרֵב וְעֵדִים וְסוֹפֵר. וְשָׁם נֶאֱמַר גַּם כֵּן שֶׁהַמַּלְוֶה נִכְלָל עִמָּהֶם בְּלָאו זֶה מִלְּבַד הַלָּאוִין הָאֲחֵרִים שֶׁמְּיֻחָדִים בּוֹ. וּכְלַל הָעִנְיָן שֶׁאָמַר אַבַּיֵּי שָׁם שֶׁהַמַּלְוֶה עוֹבֵר עַל ו' לָאוִין בִּשְׁנַיִם וְהַמִּתְעַסְּקִין בְּאֶחָד.

מִשָּׁרְשֵׁי הַמִּצְוָה כִּי הָאֵל הַטּוֹב חָפֵץ בְּיִשּׁוּבוֹ שֶׁל עַמּוֹ אֲשֶׁר בָּחַר, וְעַל כֵּן צִוָּה לְהָסִיר מִכְשׁוֹל מִדַּרְכָּם לְבַל יִבְלַע הָאֶחָד חֵיל חֲבֵרוֹ מִבְּלִי שֶׁיַּרְגִּישׁ בְּעַצְמוֹ עַד שֶׁיִּמָּצֵא בֵיתוֹ רֵיקָן מִכָּל טוּב, כִּי כֵן דַּרְכּוֹ שֶׁל רִבִּית, וְיָדוּעַ הַדָּבָר, וּמִפְּנֵי זֶה נִקְרָא נֶשֶׁךְ. וּבְהִמָּנַע מִן הַמַּעֲשֶׂה הַזֶּה עָרֵב וְסוֹפֵר וְעֵדִים יִמָּנְעוּ בְּנֵי אָדָם מִמֶּנּוּ.

וְיֶתֶר פְּרָטֶיהָ מְבֹאָרִים בִּמְצִיעָא. וְנוֹהֶגֶת בְּכָל מָקוֹם וּבְכָל זְמַן בִּזְכָרִים וּנְקֵבוֹת. וְהָעוֹבֵר עַל זֶה וְנַעֲשָׂה סוֹפֵר אוֹ עָרֵב אוֹ עֵד בְּמִלְוֶה עָבַר עַל לָאו זֶה, אֲבָל אֵין לוֹקִין עָלָיו, שֶׁאֲפִלּוּ הַמַּלְוֶה אֵינוֹ בְּמַלְקוֹת שֶׁהֲרֵי נִתַּן לְהִשָּׁבוֹן, וְאֵינוֹ בְּדִין דְּהַאי דְּאָתוּ מֵחֲמָתֵיהּ יִתְחַיְּבוּ בְּמַלְקוֹת.

---

5. By this our author indicates that whiplashes are not given (since the wickedness of his deed depends on his intent, which he alone knows; he can always contend that he did not know the other was destitute); hence Heaven will call him to account.

68 1. The paragraph is based on ShM negative precept §237; and see MT hilchoth malveh ii, 2, and TB Bava M'tzi'a 60b.

2. Cf. Rashi on Exodus 22:24 (based on Sh'moth Rabbah 31, 6): neshech means interest, because it is like the bite of a snake; a snake makes a small wound in someone's foot, and he does not feel it; but suddenly it bursts forth and swells, until [it infects] his head. So is interest not felt or perceived, until the interest rises and deprives the person of a great amount.

his fellow knowing that he has not the means [to pay it], and yet he duns him in order to make him suffer, he violates this negative precept; and he is as a person who violates the commandment of a king.[5]

[NOT TO HELP A BORROWER OR A LENDER TRANSACT A LOAN AT INTEREST]

68 that we should have no business with a loan at interest made between a borrower and a lender; in other words, we should not provide them with any surety or guarantee, we should not bear witness for them, or write a document [of debt, a *sh'tar*] containing the mention of interest. For it is stated, *nor shall you set interest upon him* (Exodus 22:24); and the explanation was given in the Talmud tractate *Bava M'tzi'a* (75b) that this prohibition was stated for those who have business with such matters: for example, a guarantor, witnesses, and a scribe. There it was taught further that the lender is also included under this prohibition, in addition to all the other injunctions that apply specifically to him. The sum of the matter, as Abbaye states there, is that the lender violates six negative precepts; the borrower, two; and a person who has business with them, one.[1]

At the root of the precept lies the reason that the good, benevolent God desires the settled communal existence of His people that He chose. For this reason He commanded to remove a stumbling-block (source of trouble) from their path, so that one should not swallow up the life-force of another without [the other's] realizing it, until he finds his house empty, bereft of every good. For this is the way of interest; it is a known matter; and for this reason it is called *neshech* ["interest," but literally "biting"].[2] But now, when guarantor, witnesses and scribe will all keep away from this thing, people [generally] will also refrain from it.

The rest of its details are explained in the tractate *Bava M'tzi'a*. It is in effect in every place and every time, for both man and woman. If a person transgresses it and serves as a scribe, guarantor or witness for [such] a loan, he has violated this negative precept. One is not whipped with lashes for it, however, as even the lender is not given lashes, since the matter is given to [rectification by] returning [the money]; it would not be justice, then, that those who incur guilt because of him should receive lashes.

§69: TO UTTER NO CURSE AGAINST A JUDGE

[שֶׁלֹּא לְקַלֵּל הַדַּיָּן]

סט שֶׁלֹּא לְקַלֵּל הַדַּיָּנִים, שֶׁנֶּאֱמַר "אֱלֹהִים לֹא תְקַלֵּל", וּפֵרְשׁוּ דַּיָּנִין כְּמוֹ "אֲשֶׁר יַרְשִׁיעֻן אֱלֹהִים", וְהוֹצִיאָן הַכָּתוּב בִּלְשׁוֹן אֱלֹהִים כְּדֵי שֶׁיְּהֵא נִכְלָל עִם הַלָּאו הַזֶּה לָאו אַחֵר, וְהוּא דְּבִרְכַּת הַשֵּׁם, כְּמוֹ שֶׁאָמְרוּ זִכְרוֹנָם לִבְרָכָה בַּמְּכִילְתָּא וּבְסִפְרֵי: אַזְהָרָה לְבִרְכַּת הַשֵּׁם מִדִּכְתִיב "אֱלֹהִים לֹא תְקַלֵּל" וּמַה שֶּׁכָּתוּב בְּמָקוֹם אַחֵר "וְנֹקֵב שֵׁם יי מוֹת יוּמָת", זֶהוּ הָעֹנֶשׁ, אֲבָל הָאַזְהָרָה הִיא מִכָּאן, כִּי לֹא יַסְפִּיק לָנוּ אַזְהָרַת הָעֹנֶשׁ בְּמִצְוָה מִבְּלִי אַזְהָרָה. וְזֶהוּ שֶׁיֹּאמְרוּ רַבּוֹתֵינוּ (וְזִכְרוֹנָם לִבְרָכָה) תָּמִיד: עֹנֶשׁ שָׁמַעְנוּ אַזְהָרָה מִנַּיִן.

וְהָעִנְיָן הוּא מִפְּנֵי כֵן שֶׁאִם לֹא תָּבוֹא לָנוּ בַּדָּבָר מְנִיעַת הָאֵל אֶלָּא שֶׁיֹּאמַר עוֹשֶׂה דָּבָר פְּלוֹנִי יֵעָנֵשׁ בְּכָךְ, הָיָה בְּמַשְׁמָע שֶׁיִּהְיֶה בְּיַד כָּל הָרוֹצֶה לְקַבֵּל הָעֹנֶשׁ וְלֹא יָחוּשׁ לְצַעֲרוֹ לַעֲבֹר עַל הַמִּצְוָה וְלֹא יָבוֹא בָּזֶה כְּנֶגֶד חֵפֶץ הַשֵּׁם וּמִצְוָתוֹ, וְיַחֲזֹר דְּבַר הַמִּצְוָה כְּעִנְיַן מִקָּח וּמִמְכָּר, כְּלוֹמַר הָרוֹצֶה לַעֲשׂוֹת דָּבָר פְּלוֹנִי יִתֵּן כָּךְ וְכָךְ וְיַעֲשֵׂהוּ אוֹ יִתֵּן שֶׁכְּמוֹ לִסְבֹּל כָּךְ וְיַעֲשֵׂהוּ.

וְאֵין הַכַּוָּנָה עַל הַמִּצְוֹת בְּכָךְ אֶלָּא שֶׁהָאֵל לְטוֹבָתֵנוּ מְנָעָנוּ בִּדְבָרִים וְהוֹדִיעָנוּ בְּמִקְצָתָן הָעֹנֶשׁ הַמַּגִּיעַ לָנוּ מִיָּד מִלְּבַד הַעֲבָרַת רְצוֹנוֹ שֶׁהִיא קָשָׁה מִן הַכֹּל. וְזֶהוּ אָמְרָם זִכְרוֹנָם לִבְרָכָה בְּכָל מָקוֹם: לֹא עָנַשׁ אֶלָּא אִם כֵּן הִזְהִיר, כְּלוֹמַר לֹא יוֹדִיעַ הָאֵל הָעֹנֶשׁ הַבָּא עָלֵינוּ עַל הַעֲבָרַת הַמִּצְוָה אֶלָּא אִם כֵּן הוֹדִיעָנוּ תְּחִלָּה שֶׁרְצוֹנוֹ הוּא שֶׁלֹּא נַעֲשֶׂה אוֹתוֹ הַדָּבָר שֶׁהָעֹנֶשׁ בָּא עָלָיו.

מִשָּׁרְשֵׁי הַמִּצְוָה לְהָסִיר מֵעַל הַדַּיָּנִים יִרְאַת הַנִּדּוֹן וְקִלְלָתוֹ כְּדֵי שֶׁיּוֹצִיאוּ הַדִּין לַאֲמִתּוֹ. וְעוֹד הִזְהִיר עַל זֶה גַּם כֵּן בְּמָקוֹם אַחֵר בַּתּוֹרָה. וְעוֹד נִמְצָא תּוֹעֶלֶת אַחֵר

---

1. The Hebrew has "the blessing," a standard euphemism.
2. Mechilta, *kaspa* 19 (on Exodus 22:27); it is not in our editions of Sifre.
3. E.g. in TB Sanhedrin 54a, 66a.
4. E.g. in TB Yoma 81a.

69 [TO UTTER NO CURSE AGAINST A JUDGE]

not to curse judges: for it is stated, *You shall not curse* Elohim (Exodus 22:27)—which means judges, as in the verse, *he whom* Elohim *shall condemn* (ibid. 8). Scripture, however, used the expression of *Elohim* [which can also mean "God"] so that another prohibition would be included under this negative precept: i.e. the ban on blasphemy[1] of the Divine name, as our Sages of blessed memory stated in the Midrashim *Mechilta* and *Sifre:*[2] [We have] a solemn warning against blasphemy[1] of the Divine name—since it is written, *You shall not curse God.* That which is written elsewhere, *he who blasphemes the name of the Lord shall surely be put to death* (Leviticus 24:16), indicates the punishment; but the warning derives from here. For the warning implicit in the punishment [stated] for a specific precept is not sufficient for us without an [explicit] admonition. This is why our Sages of blessed memory always ask,[3] "We have heard the punishment; from where do we learn the warning?"

The reason for it is that if no deterring caution by God were given us about something, but He merely told us, "Anyone who does this-and-this will be punished thus-and-so," it would imply that anyone who so wishes has the right to take the punishment, not caring about his pain, in order to violate the precept, and by this he will not go against the wishes of the Eternal Lord and His commandment. Hence the subject matter of the precept will turn into something like a trading matter: i.e., if someone wants to do that particular thing, he can pay so much and do it; or he can set his shoulder to bear this-and-this, and do it.

Such was not, however, the [Divine] intention about the precepts. Rather, for our good, God forbade us in [explicit] words [to violate them], and for some He informed us of the punishment that we immediately incur—this apart from the disobedience of His will, which is worst of all. That is why our Sages of blessed memory would say everywhere,[4] "He did not give a punishment unless He stated a prohibition." In other words, God would not let us know the penalty we receive for violating a precept unless He first informed us that it is His will that we should not do this thing for which the penalty is given.

At the root of the precept lies the aim to remove from judges the fear of a person on trial and his curse, so that they can reach a true verdict. Scripture gives another admonition about this, as well,

ספר החינוך §69–70: NOT TO CURSE A JUDGE / OR THE DIVINE NAME

בְּמִצְוָה כִּי בְקִלְלַת הַדַּיָּן תַּקָּלוֹת רַבּוֹת, כִּי הֲמוֹן הָעָם בְּסִכְלוּתָם שׂוֹנְאִים אוֹתוֹ, וְאִם לֹא יִזָּהֲרוּ עַל קִלְלָתוֹ אוּלַי יְקַלְּלוּהוּ וְיִתְעוֹרְרוּ מִתּוֹךְ כָּךְ לָקוּם עָלָיו, כְּמוֹ שֶׁאָמַר הֶחָכָם לַמֶּלֶךְ עַל הֲמוֹן הָעָם: הִזָּהֵר שֶׁלֹּא יֹאמְרוּ, שֶׁאִם יֹאמְרוּ יַעֲשׂוּ, וְיִהְיֶה בָזֶה רָעָה רַבָּה, כִּי הוּא בְמִשְׁפָּט יַעֲמִיד אָרֶץ.

מִדִּינֵי הַמִּצְוָה בַּדַּיָּנִין מַה שֶּׁאָמְרוּ שֶׁאֵין חִיּוּב הַלָּאו אֶלָּא הַמְקַלֵּל הַדַּיָּן בְּשֵׁם מִשְּׁמוֹת הַשֵּׁם, כְּגוֹן יָהּ אוֹ שַׁדַּי וֵאלֹהִים וְכַיּוֹצֵא בָהֶן, אוֹ בְכִנּוּי, כְּגוֹן חַנּוּן קַנּוֹא וְכַיּוֹצֵא בָהֶן, אֲבָל בְּלֹא שֵׁם וְכִנּוּיִים כְּגוֹן אָרוּר פְּלוֹנִי אוֹ אַל יְהִי בָרוּךְ אֵין בּוֹ חִיּוּב לָאו, אֲבָל אָסוּר הוּא; וּמַה שֶּׁפֵּרְשׁוּ זִכְרוֹנָם לִבְרָכָה גַּם כֵּן בְּעִנְיָן זֶה שֶׁהַמְחֻיָּב אֵינוֹ בִּמְקַלְּלוֹ בִּלְשׁוֹן הַקֹּדֶשׁ דַּוְקָא אֶלָּא אֲפִלּוּ בְּכָל לָשׁוֹן, וְכִי צָרִיךְ עֵדִים וְהַתְרָאָה בָזֶה בְּכָל חַיָּבֵי לָאוִין; וְיֶתֶר פְּרָטֶיהָ, מְבֹאָרִין בְּסַנְהֶדְרִין.

וְנוֹהֶגֶת בְּכָל מָקוֹם וּבְכָל זְמַן בִּזְכָרִים וּנְקֵבוֹת. וְעוֹבֵר עָלֶיהָ וְקִלֵּל הַדַּיָּן בְּשֵׁם אוֹ בְכִנּוּי לוֹקֶה שְׁתֵּי מַלְקִיּוֹת, אֶחָד לְפִי שֶׁהוּא בְּכָל אֶחָד מִיִּשְׂרָאֵל הַכְּשֵׁרִים שֶׁהֵם בִּכְלָל אִסּוּר זֶה, כְּמוֹ שֶׁנִּכְתַּב בְּסֵדֶר קְדוֹשִׁים תִּהְיוּ, וְאֶחָד מִפְּנֵי שֶׁהוּא דַּיָּן.

[לָאו דְּבִרְכַּת הַשֵּׁם]

ע וּמִשָּׁרְשֵׁי הַמִּצְוָה בְּבִרְכַּת הַשֵּׁם לְפִי שֶׁמִּתְרוֹקֵן הָאָדָם בְּמַאֲמָר הָרַע הַהוּא מִכָּל טוֹבָה, וְכָל הוֹד נַפְשׁוֹ נֶהְפָּךְ לְמַשְׁחִית, וְהִנֵּה הוּא נֶחְשָׁב כַּבְּהֵמוֹת, כִּי בְאוֹתוֹ דָבָר מַמָּשׁ שֶׁהִבְדִּילוֹ הַשֵּׁם (יִתְבָּרַךְ) לְטוֹבָה וּבוֹ נַעֲשָׂה אָדָם, וְהוּא הַדִּבּוּר שֶׁנִּבְדַּל

---

5. *You shall not be afraid of any man* (Deuteronomy 1:17).
6. Based on Ramban to Leviticus 19:14.
7. Based on MT *hilchoth sanhedrin* xxvi 3–4; cf. TB Sh'vu'oth 35a, 36a.
8. So Rambam *ibid.* 3.
9. *Ibid.* 4 (see *Kessef Mishneh*).

§70   1. In §69 our author wrote that the Scriptural text for it, *You shall not curse God*, contains two negative precepts: one about justices, and one about the Almighty. Having dealt with the first in §69, he now takes up the second. (As usual, the Hebrew has the euphemism, "blessing the Divine name"; see §69, note 1.)

2. Expression based on Daniel 10:8, *my radiance was turned to destruction in me*.

elsewhere in the Torah.[5] And moreover, there is a further benefit from this precept: From the cursing of the judge many misfortunes can ensue. For the general mass of people hate him, and if they were not cautioned against cursing him, perhaps they would revile him, and by that they would be stirred up to rise against him. As the wise man said to the king about the general mass of people, "Beware that they should not speak; for if they speak they will act, and there will be great harm in that." For He *establishes the land by justice* (Proverbs 29:4).[6]

Among the laws of the precept in regard to justices, there is what our Sages said, that guilt over this prohibition is incurred only if a person curses a judge by one of the names of the Eternal Lord: for example, *yah* or *sha-dai*, *elo-him*, and so forth; or by a substitute name [for the Divinity], such as "Gracious," "Impassioned," and so on. But if it is without any Divine name or substitute title, for instance, "Cursed be so-and-so," or "Let him not be blessed," no guilt is incurred for violating a negative precept, although it is forbidden.[7] There is, further, what our Sages of blessed memory explained about this matter, that a person is guilty not only if he curses him in the holy tongue (Hebrew) particularly, but even if he does so in any language;[8] and witnesses and a [prior] warning are necessary in this [for the violator to be punished], as for all who incur guilt over a negative precept.[9] [These] and further details are clarified in the Talmud tractate *Sanhedrin*.

It applies in every place and every time, for both man and woman. If someone disobeys it and curses a judge by a Divine name or a substitute Divine appellation, he receives whiplashes twice: once because he [the judge] is like all worthy Jews, who are included under this [kind of] ban, as we will write in *sidrah k'doshim* (§231); and once because he is a judge.

[THE PROHIBITION AGAINST CURSING THE NAME OF THE ETERNAL LORD]

70 At the root of the precept in regard to blaspheming the Divine name[1] lies the reason that by this evil utterance a man becomes emptied, bereft of every goodness; all the radiance of his spirit turns to destruction,[2] and then he can be reckoned like the animals. For with that very thing by which the Eternal Lord (be He blessed) set him apart for good, beneficently, and by which he became man—i.e. speech,

§70: THE PROHIBITION AGAINST CURSING THE DIVINE NAME

בּוֹ מִמִּינֵי הַבְּהֵמוֹת, מַבְדִּיל הוּא אֶת עַצְמוֹ לְרָעָה וּמוֹצִיא עַצְמוֹ לְגַמְרֵי מִכָּל גֶּדֶר הַדַּעַת וְנַעֲשָׂה כְּשֶׁרֶץ נִמְאָס וְנֶאֱלָח וּלְמַטָּה מִמֶּנּוּ, וְעַל כֵּן הִזְהִירַתְנוּ הַתּוֹרָה עַל זֶה, כִּי הָאֵל הַטּוֹב יַחְפֹּץ בְּטוֹבָתֵנוּ. וְכָל דִּבּוּר וְדִבּוּר הַגּוֹרֵם מְנִיעַת הַטּוֹבָה מִמֶּנּוּ יָבוֹא כְּנֶגֶד חֶפְצוֹ בָּרוּךְ הוּא.

דִּינֵי הַמִּצְוָה, כְּגוֹן מַה שֶּׁפֵּרְשׁוּ שֶׁאֵין הַחִיּוּב עַד שֶׁיְּפָרֵשׁ אֶת הַשֵּׁם הַמְּיֻחָד שֶׁהוּא יוֹ״ד הֵ״א וָי״ו הֵ״א, אוֹ שֶׁל אָלֶ״ף דָּלֶ״ת נוּ״ן יוֹ״ד כְּדַעַת קְצָת מְפָרְשִׁים. וּמַה שֶּׁאָמְרוּ שֶׁבְּכָל יוֹם וָיוֹם שׁוֹאֲלִין אֶת הָעֵדִים בְּכִנּוּי, יַכֶּה יוֹסֵי אֶת יוֹסֵי; נִגְמַר הַדִּין מוֹצִיאִין כָּל הָאָדָם לַחוּץ וְשׁוֹאֲלִין אֶת הַגָּדוֹל שֶׁבָּעֵדִים וְאוֹמְרִים לוֹ ״אֱמֹר מַה שֶּׁשָּׁמַעְתָּ בְּפֵרוּשׁ״, וְהוּא אוֹמֵר, וְהַדַּיָּנִין עוֹמְדִין עַל רַגְלֵיהֶן וְקוֹרְעִין וְלֹא מְאַחִין, וְהָעֵד הַשֵּׁנִי אוֹמֵר ״אַף אֲנִי כָּמוֹהוּ שָׁמַעְתִּי״. וְאִם הָיוּ עֵדִים רַבִּים כֻּלָּם אוֹמְרִים כֵּן.

וּמַה שֶּׁאָמְרוּ זִכְרוֹנָם לִבְרָכָה שֶׁמְּגַדֵּף אַף עַל פִּי שֶׁחָזַר תּוֹךְ כְּדֵי דִּבּוּר נִסְקָל, וּמִי שֶׁגִּדֵּף הַשֵּׁם בְּשֵׁם מֵעֲבוֹדָה זָרָה קַנָּאִין פּוֹגְעִין בּוֹ, וְאִם לֹא פָגְעוּ בוֹ וּבָא לְבֵית דִּין אֵינוֹ נִסְקָל עַד שֶׁיְּבָרֵךְ בְּשֵׁם מִן הַשֵּׁמוֹת הַמְּיֻחָדִין. וְהַטַּעַם שֶׁאֵינוֹ נִסְקָל לְפִי שֶׁהוּא בְּעַצְמוֹ מַכִּיר אֲפִלּוּ בְּעֵת הַכַּעַס שֶׁאֵין דְּבָרָיו אֶלָּא שְׁטוּת גָּמוּר; וּמִכָּל מָקוֹם פּוֹגְעִין בּוֹ קַנָּאִין אַחַר שֶׁהִשְׁחִית וְהִתְעִיב וְהֵעֵז פָּנָיו לְדַבֵּר דְּבָרִים רָעִים כָּאֵלֶּה. וּמַה שֶּׁאָמְרוּ שֶׁכָּל הַשּׁוֹמֵעַ בִּרְכַּת הַשֵּׁם מִפִּי יִשְׂרָאֵל חַיָּב לִקְרֹעַ, אֲבָל הַשּׁוֹמֵעַ מִן הַגּוֹי אֵינוֹ חַיָּב לִקְרֹעַ, וְלֹא קָרְעוּ אֶלְיָקִים וְשֶׁבְנָא אֶלָּא מִפְּנֵי שֶׁרַבְשָׁקֵה מְשֻׁמָּד הָיָה.

וְכָל הָעֵדִים וְהַדַּיָּנִין סוֹמְכִין יְדֵיהֶם אֶחָד אֶחָד עַל רֹאשׁ הַמְּגַדֵּף וְאוֹמְרִים לוֹ

---

3. TB Sanhedrin 56a, Sh'vu'oth 36a.

4. So MT *hilchoth 'avodath kochavim* ii 7 (because both names refer uniquely, specifically to Him).

5. I.e. in taking testimony and examining the witnesses, there was a need to quote the crucial expression of blasphemy which the person on trial uttered. Hence this form was used, with "Yosé" substituted for the Tetragrammaton, since it also starts with a *yod*, and also has four letters; TB Sanhedrin 56a, and Rashi.

6. As a sign of mourning at hearing something so dreadful.

7. TB Sanhedrin 56a.

8. TB N'darim 87a.

9. See §26, note 14.

10. In their jealous wrath at this insult to the Almighty; TB Sanhedrin 81a; MT *hilchoth 'avodath kochavim* ii 9.

11. MT *ibid*.

12. TB Sanhedrin 60a.

13. An Israelite who had left the Hebrew faith and gone over to the Assyrians; hence he spoke fluent Hebrew (II Kings 18:28).

by which he is differentiated from the species of beasts—with that he sets himself apart for evil; he removes himself completely from every boundary of sense, and he becomes as a loathsome, degenerate crawling creature, and even worse. Therefore the Torah adjured us about this: because the good, benevolent God desires our good; and every single utterance that brings a deprivation of that goodness, goes against His wish (be He blessed).

As for the laws of the precept there is, for instance, what our Sages explained:[3] that there is no guilt until a person pronounces His very own name, i.e. the Tetragrammaton, or the name spelled *alef da-led nun yod* ("Lord") in the view of some authorities.[4] There is, further, what our Sages said, that every day [during the examination at the trial] they would question the witnesses with a substitute form [for the blasphemy]: "May Yosé smite Yosé."[5] Once the trial [examination] was ended, everyone was ordered out [of the courtroom], and the older of the witnesses was questioned. They said to him, "Speak what you heard, with your mouth"; and he would utter it. The judges then stood on their feet and made a rent [in their clothing],[6] which was never to be sewn up. Then the second witness would say, "I too heard as he did"; and if there were many witnesses, all would say this [in turn].[7]

There is, moreover, the teaching of our Sages[8] that even if a blasphemer retracted at once, while still occupied with speaking,[9] he is stoned to death; if someone blasphemes the Divine name by the name of an idol, zealots may strike him down;[10] if they did not strike him down, and he comes to the *beth din* [to stand trial], he is not stoned to death—not until he blasphemes by one of the unique names of the Divinity.[11] The reason why he is not stoned is that he himself [obviously] realizes even during his anger that his words are nothing more than utter nonsense. Nevertheless, zealots may strike him down, since he has been destructive and abominable, brazenly daring to speak such evil words.

In addition, there is the teaching of our Sages[12] that whoever hears blasphemy of the Divine name from the mouth of a Jew is duty-bound to rend his clothing,[6] while one who hears it from a heathen is not required to do so; and Eliakim and Shebna rent their clothing (II Kings 18:37) only because Rab-shakeh was an apostate.[13]

All the witnesses and judges rest their hands, one after the other, on the head of the blasphemer, and they say to him, "Your blood be

§70–71 : NOT TO CURSE THE DIVINE NAME / OR A SOVEREIGN RULER

"דָּמְךָ בְרֹאשְׁךָ שֶׁאַתָּה גָרַמְתָּ לָּךְ". וְאֵין בְּכָל הַרוּגֵי בֵית דִּין מִי שֶׁסּוֹמְכִין עָלָיו אֶלָּא מְגַדֵּף בִּלְבַד, שֶׁנֶּאֱמַר: וְסָמְכוּ כָּל הַשֹּׁמְעִים אֶת יְדֵיהֶם עַל רֹאשׁוֹ; וְיֶתֶר פְּרָטֶיהָ, מְבֹאָרִים בְּסַנְהֶדְרִין פֶּרֶק ז'.

וְנוֹהֵג אִסּוּר זֶה בְּכָל מָקוֹם וּבְכָל זְמַן. וְהָעוֹבֵר עַל זֶה וּבֵרֵךְ הַשֵּׁם בָּעִנְיָן שֶׁאָמַרְנוּ נִסְקָל בָּאָרֶץ עַל פִּי סְמוּכִין. וְעַכְשָׁיו בְּחוּצָה לָאָרֶץ שֶׁאֵין לָנוּ סְמוּכִין מַרְחִיקִין כָּל יִשְׂרָאֵל מִמֶּנּוּ וּמַחֲרִימִים אוֹתוֹ.

[שֶׁלֹּא לְקַלֵּל הַנָּשִׂיא]

עא שֶׁלֹּא לְקַלֵּל אֶת הַנָּשִׂיא, שֶׁנֶּאֱמַר "וְנָשִׂיא בְעַמְּךָ לֹא תָאֹר", וּבָא הַפֵּרוּשׁ שֶׁהַנָּשִׂיא זֶה הוּא הַמֶּלֶךְ. וְאָמְנָם זֶה הַלָּאו כּוֹלֵל גַּם כֵּן הַנָּשִׂיא שֶׁבְּיִשְׂרָאֵל, וְהוּא רֹאשׁ סַנְהֶדְרֵי גְדוֹלָה שֶׁנִּקְרָא נָשִׂיא גַּם כֵּן, לְפִי שֶׁכַּוָּנַת הַכָּתוּב לְהַזְהִירֵנוּ עַל כָּל מִי שֶׁהוּא רֹאשׁ שְׂרָרָה עַל יִשְׂרָאֵל בֵּין מֶמְשֶׁלֶת מַלְכוּת אוֹ מֶמְשֶׁלֶת תּוֹרָה.

מִשָּׁרְשֵׁי הַמִּצְוָה לְפִי שֶׁאִי אֶפְשָׁר לְיִשּׁוּב בְּנֵי אָדָם מִבְּלִי שֶׁיַּעֲשׂוּ אֶחָד מִבֵּינֵיהֶם רֹאשׁ עַל הָאֲחֵרִים לַעֲשׂוֹת מִצְוָתוֹ וּלְקַיֵּם גְּזֵרוֹתָיו, מִפְּנֵי שֶׁדֵּעוֹת בְּנֵי אָדָם חֲלוּקִין זֶה מִזֶּה וְלֹא יַסְכִּימוּ כֻּלָּם לְעוֹלָם לַעֲשׂוֹת דָּבָר מִכָּל הַדְּבָרִים, וּמִתּוֹךְ כָּךְ יֵצֵא מִבֵּינֵיהֶם הַבִּטּוּל וְהָאֲסִיפָה בִּפְעֻלּוֹת, וְעַל כֵּן צְרִיכִין לְקַבֵּל דַּעַת אֶחָד מֵהֶם אִם טוֹב וְאִם רַע, לְמַעַן יִצְלְחוּ וְיַעַסְקוּ בְעִסְקֵי שֶׁל עוֹלָם, פַּעַם יִמְצָא בַעֲצָתוֹ וְחֶפְצוֹ תּוֹעֶלֶת רָב וּפְעָמִים הַהֶפֶךְ, וְכָל זֶה טוֹב מִן הַמַּחֲלֹקֶת שֶׁגּוֹרְמָם בִּטּוּל גָּמוּר.

וּמֵאַחַר שֶׁהִסְכַּמְנוּ לְרֹאשׁ סִבָּה אֶל הַתּוֹעֶלֶת שֶׁאָמַרְנוּ, הֵן שֶׁהוּא גָדוֹל לְהַדְרִיכֵנוּ בְּדַרְכֵי הַדָּת אוֹ גָדוֹל לַמַּלְכוּת לִשְׁמֹר אִישׁ מֵרֵעֵהוּ שֶׁיַּתְקִיף מִמֶּנּוּ, רָאוּי הַדָּבָר וְכָשֵׁר שֶׁלֹּא נָקֵל בִּכְבוֹדוֹ, וְגַם שֶׁלֹּא לְקַלְלוֹ אֲפִלּוּ שֶׁלֹּא בְּפָנָיו, וְכָל שֶׁכֵּן

14. So Midrash Sifra, 'emor 19, beginning.
15. So Rabad (R. Abraham b. David of Posquières), commentary on Sifra, ibid.
16. So R. Jacob b. Asher, *Tur Ḥoshen Mishpat*, §425, beginning, in the name of R. Natronai Ga'on.

§71 1. This seems implicit in Mechilta as cited in *Torah Shelemah*, Exodus 22 §643; cf. also R. M'yuḥas on the verse (ibid. note).
2. So ShM negative precept §316, and MT *hilchoth sanhedrin* xxvi 1 (cf. TB Horayoth 10a).

⟨276⟩

on your own head, for you brought this on yourself."[14] Among all that the *beth din* is to put to death, there is none on whom all rest their hands except the blasphemer alone:[15] for it is stated, *and let all who heard him rest their hands on his head* (Leviticus 24:14). [These] and the rest of its details are explained in the Talmud tractate *Sanhedrin*, chapter 7.

This prohibition remains in effect in every place and every time. If someone transgressed it and blasphemed the Divine name in the way that we have stated, he would be stoned to death in the land [of Israel] by the sentence of ordained justices. Now, outside the land, when we have no ordained judges, all Jews withdraw from him, and he is excommunicated.[16]

71 [TO UTTER NO CURSE AGAINST A SOVEREIGN LEADER]

not to curse a *nassi*, a sovereign ruler: for it is stated, *and you shall not curse a ruler of your people* (Exodus 22:27); and the explanation was given [in the Oral Tradition] that this ruler means a king.[1] However, this prohibition includes also the *nassi* of Israel, i.e. the head of the great *sanhedrin* (supreme court), who is also called a sovereign leader.[2] For the intention of Scripture is to caution us about anyone who is a ruling head or chief over the Israelites, whether in the dominion of royal government or in the dominion of Torah.

At the root of the precept lies the reason that it is impossible for a settled community of human beings [to exist and function] without making one among them the head over the others, to obey his order and carry out his decrees. For in their views people are divided from one another, and all will never agree on any one view in order to do any one particular thing. The result will be an idle standstill and the death of all activities. For this reason it is necessary to accept the view of one among them, be it good or bad, that they may successfully engage in the business of the world. Sometimes great benefit will result from his counsel, and sometimes the reverse; but all this is better than quarreling, which causes a complete idle standstill.

Now, since the one appointed as head is the cause of the benefit we have mentioned, whether he is the chief to guide us in the ways of faith or the chief in royal government, to safeguard a man from his neighbor who is stronger than he—it is a fitting and worthy thing that we should not treat his honor lightly, nor curse him, even

§71–72: TO CURSE NO SOVEREIGN RULER / ON DUES FROM PRODUCE

בִּפְנֵי עֵדִים, כְּדֵי שֶׁלֹּא נָבוֹא בְּתוֹךְ כָּךְ לַחֲלֹק עִמּוֹ, לְפִי שֶׁהַהֶרְגֵּל הָרָע שֶׁאָדָם מַרְגִּיל עַצְמוֹ בֵּינוֹ לְבֵין עַצְמוֹ הוּא סוֹף מַעֲשֵׂהוּ, וְהַמַּחְלֹקֶת עָלָיו כְּבָר אָמַרְנוּ הַהֶפְסֵד הַנִּמְצָא בִּשְׁבִילוֹ.

מִדִּינֵי הַמִּצְוָה מַה שֶּׁאָמְרוּ זִכְרוֹנָם לִבְרָכָה שֶׁאֵין חַיָּב עָלָיו אֶלָּא הַמְקַלְּלוֹ בְּשֵׁם אוֹ בְּכִנּוּי, וְשֶׁהַמְקַלְּלוֹ לוֹקֶה שָׁלֹשׁ מַלְקִיּוֹת, מִשּׁוּם אֱלֹהִים לֹא תְקַלֵּל, וּמִשּׁוּם וְנָשִׂיא . . . לֹא תָאֹר, וּמִשּׁוּם לֹא תְקַלֵּל חֵרֵשׁ, שֶׁהוּא לָאו כּוֹלֵל כָּל יִשְׂרָאֵל; וְיֶתֶר פְּרָטֶיהָ, מְבֹאָרִין בְּסַנְהֶדְרִין.

וְנוֹהֶגֶת בִּזְכָרִים וּנְקֵבוֹת, בָּאָרֶץ וּבְכָל מָקוֹם שֶׁיִּהְיֶה עִם מַלְכֵּנוּ אוֹ עִם רֹאשׁ סַנְהֶדְרֵי גְדוֹלָה. וְעוֹבֵר עָלֶיהָ וְקִלְּלוֹ בְּשֵׁם אוֹ בְּכִנּוּי לוֹקֶה שָׁלֹשׁ מַלְקִיּוֹת. וְאִם בֶּן הַנָּשִׂיא קִלְּלוֹ לוֹקֶה אַרְבַּע, שָׁלֹשׁ שֶׁאָמַרְנוּ וְאֶחָד מִשּׁוּם מְקַלֵּל אָבִיו.

[שֶׁלֹּא לְהַקְדִּים חֻקֵּי הַתְּבוּאוֹת]

עב שֶׁלֹּא נַקְדִּים חֻקֵּי הַתְּבוּאָה קְצָתָם עַל קְצָתָם אֶלָּא שֶׁנּוֹצִיאֵם בְּסֵדֶר. וּבֵאוּר עִנְיָן זֶה הוּא שֶׁהַחִטָּה כְּשֶׁתִּתְחַדֵּשׁ וְתִנָּקֶה הִיא טֶבֶל, וּפֵרוּשׁ טֶבֶל הִיא תְבוּאָה שֶׁלֹּא הִתְרְמָה, וְהַחִיּוּב עָלֵינוּ בָּהּ לְהוֹצִיא מִמֶּנָּה תְּחִלָּה תְּרוּמָה גְדוֹלָה, וּמִן הַתּוֹרָה אֲפִלּוּ חִטָּה אַחַת פּוֹטֶרֶת הַכְּרִי, אֲבָל חֲכָמִים אָמְרוּ שֶׁהוּא חֵלֶק אֶחָד מֵחֲמִשִּׁים, וְאַחַר כָּךְ מִמַּה שֶּׁנִּשְׁאַר הַחִיּוּב עָלֵינוּ לְהוֹצִיא מִמֶּנָּה מַעֲשֵׂר וְהוּא נִקְרָא מַעֲשֵׂר רִאשׁוֹן. וְאַחַר כָּךְ מִמַּה שֶּׁנִּשְׁאַר יֵשׁ לָנוּ לְהוֹצִיא מַעֲשֵׂר אַחֵר וְהוּא מַעֲשֵׂר שֵׁנִי, וְתִנָּתֵן תְּרוּמָה לַכֹּהֵן, וּמַעֲשֵׂר רִאשׁוֹן לַלֵּוִי, וּמַעֲשֵׂר שֵׁנִי שֶׁיֹּאכְלוּהוּ בְעָלָיו בִּירוּשָׁלַיִם.

וְעַל זֶה הַסֵּדֶר אָנוּ חַיָּבִים שֶׁנַּפְרִישׁ מִן הַתְּבוּאָה חֲלָקִים אֵלֶּה, וּבָאָה לָנוּ

---

3. TB Sh'vu'oth 35b.
4. The *nassi* in later times was the chief justice of the *sanhedrin*. Cf. Mechilta and MhG on the verse, and MT *hilchoth sanhedrin* xxvi 2.
5. So Mechilta, *kaspa* 19.

§72 1. So TB Kiddushin 59b, etc.
2. I.e. for an average, upright person; a generous man should give one part in forty; and someone ungenerous, at least one part in sixty; Mishnah, T'rumoth iv 3.

when not in his presence, and all the more certainly not before witnesses—so that we should not come, as a result, to quarrel or differ with him. For a bad habit to which a man accustoms himself privately leads ultimately to action; and as regards quarreling or differing with him, we have already written of the great loss that would ensue in its wake.

Among the laws of the precept there is what our Sages of blessed memory said: that guilt is incurred only by a person who curses him by the Divine name or a substitute appellation;[3] that one who curses him is given whiplashes three times: on account of the injunction, *You shall not curse a judge* (Exodus 22:27),[4] on account of the warning, *and a ruler... you shall not curse (ibid.)*, and because of the verse, *You shall not curse the deaf* (Leviticus 19:14; §231), which is a general ban about all Jews. Its other details are explained in the Talmud tractate *Sanhedrin*.

It applies to both man and woman, in the land [of Israel] and wherever we might be with our king or with the head of the great *sanhedrin* (supreme court). Any person who disobeys it and curses him by the Divine name or a substitute Divine title is given whiplashes three times. If the son of a ruler or religious head curses him, he is whipped four times: three times as we have stated, and once on account of cursing his father (§260).[5]

72 [NOT TO SEPARATE THE DUES FROM PRODUCE IN IMPROPER ORDER]

that we should not carry out the laws of dues from grain out of order, but should obey them in proper order. The explanation of this matter is that when wheat is threshed and cleaned, it is *tevel*, which means wheat from which *t'rumah* [the *kohen*'s share, and the tithes] were not separated. Then our obligation over it is to take out from it first the great *t'rumah*. By Torah law, even one kernel of wheat acquits us of the obligation for a whole pile.[1] The Sages said, however, that it should be one part in fifty.[2] Then, out of what remains, we have the obligation to separate *ma'asér*, a tithe [one tenth], which is called "the First Tithe." After that, from that which is left we are to take out another tithe (*ma'asér*), which is "the Second Tithe." The *t'rumah* is to be given to a *kohen*, and the First Tithe to a Levite, while the Second Tithe is for its owner to eat in Jerusalem.

In this order we are required to separate these shares from the

§72: NOT TO TAKE DUES FROM PRODUCE IN IMPROPER ORDER

הַמְּנִיעָה בָּזֶה שֶׁלֹּא נַקְדִּים מִזֶּה מַה שֶּׁרָאוּי לְאַחֵר וְלֹא לְאַחֵר מַה שֶּׁרָאוּי לְהַקְדִּים, שֶׁנֶּאֱמַר "מְלֵאָתְךָ וְדִמְעֲךָ לֹא תְאַחֵר", וְהוּא כְּאִלּוּ אָמַר לֹא תְאַחֵר מִמְּלֵאָתְךָ וְדִמְעֲךָ מַה שֶּׁרָאוּי לְהַקְדִּימוֹ.

מִשָּׁרְשֵׁי הַמִּצְוָה כִּי בְּהֱיוֹת הַדְּבָרוֹת עַל סִדְרָן לֹא יָבוֹא בָּהֶם הָעִרְבּוּב וְהַטָּעוּת, וּכְשֶׁאֵינָן נַעֲשִׂים כֵּן יִהְיֶה הַטָּעוּת נִמְצָא בָּהֶן תָּמִיד. וּבִהְיוֹת הַתְּרוּמוֹת וְהַמַּעַשְׂרוֹת דָּבָר גָּדוֹל בְּקִיּוּם הַדָּת, כְּמוֹ שֶׁנִּפְרָשׁ בְּעֶזְרַת הַשֵּׁם בְּסֵדֶר רָאָה וְשׁוֹפְטִים, צִוָּנוּ הַשֵּׁם (יִתְבָּרַךְ) לְהִזָּהֵר בָּהֶם הַרְבֵּה שֶׁלֹּא לָבוֹא בְּחֶשְׁבּוֹנָן לִידֵי טָעוּת לְעוֹלָם. וּבְשָׁמְעֵנוּ טוֹב מִזֶּה מִן הַמְּקֻבָּלִים נְקַבֵּל.

מִדִּינֵי הַמִּצְוָה מַה שֶּׁאָמְרוּ זִכְרוֹנָם לִבְרָכָה שֶׁאִם עָבַר וְהִקְדִּים בְּעִנְיָן זֶה מַה שֶּׁאֵינוֹ רָאוּי לְהַקְדִּים, מַה שֶּׁעָשָׂה עָשׂוּי, וְלֹא נְחַיְּבֶנּוּ לַחֲזֹר וּלְעָרֵב הַכֹּל וְיַפְרִישֵׁם פַּעַם שְׁנִיָּה. וְכֵן מַה שֶּׁדָּרְשׁוּ בְּמַסֶּכֶת תְּרוּמָה וּבַמִּכִילְתָּא, "מְלֵאָתְךָ" אֵלּוּ הַבִּכּוּרִים הַנִּטָּלִין מִן הַמָּלֵא, כְּלוֹמַר קֹדֶם שֶׁנִּטַּל מִן הַדָּבָר כְּלוּם, וְזֶהוּ לְשׁוֹן מָלֵא כְּלוֹמַר שֶׁהוּא כְּדָבָר שָׁלֵם לְגַמְרֵי. "וְדִמְעֲךָ", זוֹ תְרוּמָה. "לֹא תְאַחֵר", שֶׁלֹּא תַקְדִּים תְּרוּמָה לְבִכּוּרִים, וְכוּלֵּיהּ; וְיֶתֶר פְּרָטֶיהָ, בְּמַסֶּכֶת תְּרוּמָה.

וְנוֹהֶגֶת בִּזְכָרִים וּנְקֵבוֹת, בְּאֶרֶץ יִשְׂרָאֵל, וּבִזְמַן שֶׁיִּשְׂרָאֵל שָׁם, כְּדַעַת הָרַמְבַּ״ם זִכְרוֹנוֹ לִבְרָכָה, שֶׁכָּתַב שֶׁמִּצְוַת תְּרוּמָה וּמַעַשְׂרוֹת מִן הַתּוֹרָה אֵינָהּ אֶלָּא בִּזְמַן שֶׁאֶרֶץ יִשְׂרָאֵל בְּיִשּׁוּבָהּ. וְהָעוֹבֵר עָלֶיהָ וְהִקְדִּים דְּבָרִים אֵלּוּ דִּינוֹ כְּעוֹבֵר עַל מִצְוַת מֶלֶךְ, אֲבָל אֵין לוֹקִין עָלָיו, שֶׁכַּךְ נִתְבָּאֵר שָׁם בִּתְרוּמָה שֶׁאֵין בָּזֶה הַלָּאו מַלְקוֹת.

---

3. Mishnah *ibid.* iii 6; Mechilta; MdRSbY. From the beginning to here is based on ShM negative precept §154.

4. Hebrew, *ha-m'kubbalim* ("the recipients"; very literally, "the received"). Being, however, from the same root as *kabbalah*, it denotes mystics who have received the tradition of Jewish mystic teachings. It thus indicates that our author was aware of reasons in *kabbalah* for the precept.

5. Mishnah *ibid.*

6. This is found in Mechilta on the verse, but not in Mishnah, T'rumah (MY).

7. At the root of the word is the adjective *ma-lé*, "full."

8. The first phrase is taken to denote first-fruits, because they are separated only from dry, solid produce; the second phrase is taken to denote *t'rumah* because it must be separated also from liquid products, such as wine and oil (*tosafoth* to TB T'murah 4a).

9. MT *hilchoth t'rumoth* i 26.

10. This can be inferred from Mishnah, T'rumoth iii 6 (*Kessef Mishneh* to MT *hilchoth t'rumoth* iii 23); it is stated explicitly in TB T'murah 4a–b.

wheat. The injunction was given us about it that we should not do first what should properly be left for later, and not to postpone what should properly be done first. For it is stated, *You shall not delay to offer from the fullness of your harvest and the outflow of your presses* (Exodus 22:28)—which is as though Scripture said, "Do not delay or postpone [separating] from the fullness of your harvest and the outflow of your presses what should properly be taken first."[3]

At the root of the precept lies the principle that when things are done in order, there can be no mix-up or mistake in them; and when they are not done so, error will always occur in them. And since *t'rumah* and the tithes are of great significance in the observance of the faith, as we will explain with the Eternal Lord's help in the *sidroth r'éh* and *shof'tim*, the Eternal Lord (be He blessed) commanded us to be very careful indeed about them, so that we should never come to make any error in their reckoning. And should we hear good [explanations] about this from the mystics,[4] let us accept them.

Among the laws of the precept there is what our Sages of blessed memory said:[5] that if a person acted wrongly and did something first in this kind of situation which should properly not be done earlier, what he did is done [it remains valid]. We are not to require him to turn about and mix everything together again, and then separate out the various parts a second time. There is also what our Sages taught in the Mishnah tractate *T'rumah* and the Midrash *Mechilta:*[6] "the fullness of your harvest" betokens the *bikkurim* (first-fruits) which are taken from the *m'lai*, the stock—in other words, before anything was taken from the mass; this is the connotation of *m'lai*,[7] i.e. that it is like something entirely whole; "and the outflow of your presses" betokens *t'rumah;*[8] "you shall not delay": do not attend to *t'rumah* before *bikkurim*—and so on. The rest of its details are in the Mishnah tractate *T'rumah* [*T'rumoth* iii].

It is in force for both man and woman, in the land of Israel, at the time when the Israelites are there—according to the view of Rambam of blessed memory, who wrote that the precept of *t'rumah* and *ma'asér* (tithes), by Torah law, is in force only at the time when the land of Israel is in its settled, inhabited condition.[9] If a person transgresses it and does these things out of order, his penalty is as for one who violates a king's commandment; but he is not whipped for it. For so is it explained there, in the tractate *T'rumah*, that with this prohibition no whiplashes are involved as punishment.[10]

§73: TO EAT NO MEET FROM AN ANIMAL TORN BY BEASTS (T'RÉFAH)

[שֶׁלֹּא לֶאֱכֹל טְרֵפָה]

עג שֶׁלֹּא לֶאֱכֹל מִן הַטְּרֵפָה, שֶׁנֶּאֱמַר "וּבָשָׂר בַּשָּׂדֶה טְרֵפָה לֹא תֹאכֵלוּ", וּמַשְׁמָעוּת הַנִּגְלָה בַּכָּתוּב זֶה הוּא לְהַזְהִירֵנוּ עַל בְּהֵמָה שֶׁטְּרָפָהּ זְאֵב אוֹ אֲרִי בַּשָּׂדֶה, וְשֶׁטְּרֵפָה בְּעִנְיָן שֶׁהִיא נְטוּיָה לָמוּת בַּטֶּרֶף הַהוּא, דְּוַדַּאי אֵין בְּמַשְׁמַע שֶׁאִם נָגַע בְּרֹאשׁ אָזְנָהּ אוֹ תָלַשׁ מִצַּמְרָהּ שֶׁתִּקָּרֵא טְרֵפָה בְּכָךְ, אֶלָּא וַדַּאי הַמַּשְׁמָעוּת הַנָּכוֹן, וְהַקַּבָּלָה מְסַיַּעַת בְּכָךְ, הוּא שֶׁנִּטְרְפָה בִּכְדֵי שֶׁתָּמוּת לְשָׁעָה אוֹ לִזְמָן קָרוֹב בִּשְׁבִיל הַטֶּרֶף הַהוּא. וְאָמְרוּ זִכְרוֹנָם לִבְרָכָה שֶׁזְּמַן זֶה הוּא שָׁנָה אַחַת. וְעוֹד יֵשׁ לְהָבִין לְכָל מֵבִין כִּי לֹא תַקְפִּיד הַתּוֹרָה כְּשֶׁהִגִּיעַ לָהּ טְרֵפוּת זֶה עַל־יְדֵי זְאֵב אוֹ אֲרִי אוֹ דֹב, אֶלָּא שֶׁתֶּאֱסֹר כָּל בְּהֵמָה מַכָּה הַמְּבִיאָה אוֹתָהּ לִידֵי מָוֶת עַל כָּל פָּנִים, וְהֵם מֵהַמַּכּוֹת שֶׁמָּנוּ אוֹתָן חֲכָמִים שֶׁהֵם מְמִיתוֹת, וּכְמוֹ שֶׁבָּא בַּמִּשְׁנָה: זֶה הַכְּלָל כֹּל שֶׁאֵין כָּמוֹהָ חַיָּה כְּמוֹהָ טְרֵפָה. וְזֶה שֶׁאָמַר הַכָּתוּב בַּשָּׂדֶה לָאו דַּוְקָא אֶלָּא שֶׁדֶּרֶךְ הַכָּתוּב לְדַבֵּר לְעוֹלָם בַּהֹוֶה, וּבַשָּׂדוֹת דֶּרֶךְ בְּהֵמוֹת לִטָּרֵף. וְכֵן הוּא בִּמְכִילְתָּא: דִּבֵּר הַכָּתוּב בַּהֹוֶה.

וְגַם כֵּן נִצְרַךְ לִכְתֹּב "בַּשָּׂדֶה" כְּדֵי לְלַמֵּד בּוֹ עוֹד דְּבָרִים אֲחֵרִים רַבִּים, כִּי דִּבְרֵי הַתּוֹרָה וְדִרְשָׁהּ לְכַמָּה פָנִים, יִתְלַבְּשׁוּ מִבַּחוּץ לְבוּשׁ מַלְכוּת שֵׁשׁ וָמֶשִׁי וְרִקְמָה טְהוֹרִים, וּמִבִּפְנִים יֵשׁ זָהָב וְרֹב פְּנִינִים. וּלְבוּשׁ זֶה הַפָּסוּק הַנִּגְלָה וְהַנִּרְאֶה בּוֹ יוֹתֵר בִּתְחִלַּת הָעִיּוּן הוּא לְלַמֵּד עַל הַטְּרֵפָה לְבַד, כְּמוֹ שֶׁפָּתַחְנוּ, וְעַל בָּשָׂר מִן הַחַי שֶׁבִּכְלָל טְרֵפָה הוּא. וּמַה שֶׁבִּפְנִים בּוֹ הוּא, שֶׁמְּלַמֵּד עַל כָּל בָּשָׂר שֶׁיָּצָא חוּץ מִמְּחִצָּתוֹ שֶׁאָסוּר וְנַעֲשָׂה כִּטְרֵפָה, כְּגוֹן בְּשַׂר קָדָשִׁים שֶׁיָּצָא חוּץ לָעֲזָרָה, וּבְשַׂר

---

§73 1. See e.g. Mishnah, Ḥullin iii 1–2.

2. TB Ḥullin 57b.

3. Mishnah, Hullin iii 1 (TB 42a). The point of the rule which follows is that if the wound ordinarily dooms an animal to die within a year, this animal is considered *tréfah*. Even if it lives longer, it is thus an exceptional case, and we do not change the law of the majority for a minority.

4. For "what difference is there whether a wild beast clawed it or it was [fatally] cut with a knife?"—TB Ḥullin 102b; MT *hilchoth ma'achaloth 'asuroth* iv 10.

⟨282⟩

SIDRAH MISHPATIM

[NOT TO EAT THE FLESH OF AN ANIMAL TORN BY BEASTS, ETC.]

73 not to eat of an animal that is *t'réfah*: for it is stated, *and any flesh that is* t'réfah *(torn of beasts) in the field, you shall not eat* (Exodus 22:30). The overt (plain) meaning of the verse is to caution us about a domestic animal which a wolf or lion tore [clawed as prey] in the field, clawing it in such a way that it is quite sure to die from that tearing attack. For it certainly does not mean that if it [the attacking animal] touched the tip of its ear or pulled out some of its wool, it should be called *t'réfah* (torn of beasts) for that. Rather, the correct meaning, which the Oral Tradition confirms,[1] is that it is so torn (clawed) that it will die in an hour or a short while on account of that clawing. Our Sages of blessed memory stated[2] that this period of time is up to one year.

Moreover, every intelligent person should understand that the Torah is not particularly concerned whether it became *t'réfah*, acquired its fatal condition, through a wolf, a lion, or a bear. Rather, it forbids any animal that was given a wound or blow which dooms it to death, no matter how. This means those wounds which the Sages listed as being fatal. As we read in the Mishnah,[3] this is the rule: Any creature whose like [another animal with the same wound] could not live, is *t'réfah*. Thus, when Scripture says "in the field," it is not meant particularly; it is merely Scripture's way to speak always of what is usual; and in fields domestic animals can ordinarily be torn [by beasts of prey]. So is it also [written] in the Midrash *Mechilta* (Exodus 22:30): Scripture spoke of a usual situation.

Moreover, Scripture needed to write "in the field" in order to teach many other things by it. For the Torah's words can be interpreted in many directions. On the outside they clothe themselves in a royal garment of pure *fine linen, silk and embroidered cloth* (Ezekiel 16:13), while within they contain gold and a great many gems. The "clothing" of this verse, the meaning that is most apparent and visible in it at first consideration, is to teach only about the *t'réfah*, torn by beasts, as we have written, and about [eating] flesh [cut] from a living creature—which must be included in the category of *t'réfah*.[4] But the meaning that lies within is this: It teaches [us] about any meat that went out of its proper boundary, that it is forbidden, having become like [meat of an animal that is] *t'réfah*—for example, flesh of holy offerings that went [was taken] out of the Temple forecourt; flesh of offerings of

§73: TO EAT NO MEAT FROM AN ANIMAL TORN BY BEASTS (T'RÉFAH)

קָדָשִׁים קַלִּים שֶׁיָּצְאוּ חוּץ לַחוֹמָה, וּבְשַׂר הַפֶּסַח שֶׁיָּצָא חוּץ לַחֲבוּרָה, וְכֵן הָעֻבָּר שֶׁיָּצָא חוּץ לִמְעֵי אִמּוֹ.

וּמַשְׁמָעוּתוֹ שֶׁל מִקְרָא יָבוֹא כֵן, כְּאִלּוּ אָמַר וּבָשָׂר בַּשָּׂדֶה טְרֵפָה הוּא, כְּלוֹמַר בָּשָׂר שֶׁיָּצָא חוּץ לִמְחִצָּתוֹ, שֶׁזֶּהוּ לְשׁוֹן שָׂדֶה שֶׁאֵין לוֹ מְחִצּוֹת, טְרֵפָה הוּא. וְכָל אֵלֶּה שֶׁזָּכַרְנוּ יָצְאוּ חוּץ לִמְחִצָּתָן וְדִינָן כִּטְרֵפָה, וּמִי שֶׁאָכַל מֵהֶן כְּזַיִת לוֹקֶה.

מִשָּׁרְשֵׁי מִצְוָה זוֹ, לְפִי שֶׁהַגּוּף כְּלִי לַנֶּפֶשׁ וּבוֹ תַּעֲשֶׂה פְּעֻלָּתָהּ, וְזוּלָתוֹ לֹא תַּשְׁלִים מְלַאכְתָּהּ לְעוֹלָם, וְעַל כֵּן בָּאָה בִּצְלוֹ וְלֹא לְרָעָתָהּ (בֶּאֱמֶת) [בָּאָה], כִּי הָאֵל לֹא יָרֵעַ אֲבָל יֵיטִיב לַכֹּל, נִמְצָא כִּי הַגּוּף בֵּין יָדָיו כְּמוֹ הַצְּבָת בְּיַד הַנַּפָּח אֲשֶׁר עִמּוֹ יוֹצִיא כְּלִי לְמַעֲשֵׂהוּ.

וּבֶאֱמֶת כִּי בִּהְיוֹת הַצְּבָת חָזָק וּמְכֻוָּן לְאֶחָד בּוֹ הַכֵּלִים יַעֲשֶׂה הָאוּמָן טוֹבִים, וְאִם לֹא יִהְיֶה הַצְּבָת טוֹב לֹא יָבוֹאוּ לְעוֹלָם הַכֵּלִים מְכֻוָּנִים וְנָאִים. וּכְמוֹ כֵן בִּהְיוֹת בַּגּוּף שׁוּם הֶפְסֵד מֵאֵי זֶה עִנְיָן שֶׁיִּהְיֶה תִּתְבַּטֵּל פְּעֻלַּת הַשֵּׂכֶל כְּפִי אוֹתוֹ הַהֶפְסֵד, וְעַל כֵּן הִרְחִיקַתְנוּ תּוֹרָתֵנוּ הַשְּׁלֵמָה מִכָּל דָּבָר הַגּוֹרֵם בּוֹ הֶפְסֵד.

וְעַל הַדֶּרֶךְ הַזֶּה לְפִי הַפְּשָׁט נֹאמַר שֶׁבָּא לָנוּ הָאִסּוּר בַּתּוֹרָה בְּכָל מַאֲכָלוֹת הָאֲסוּרִים, וְאִם יֵשׁ מֵהֶם שֶׁאֵין נוֹדָע לָנוּ וְלֹא לְחַכְמֵי הָרְפוּאָה נִזְקָן, אַל תִּתְמַהּ עֲלֵיהֶן, כִּי הָרוֹפֵא הַנֶּאֱמָן שֶׁהִזְהִירָנוּ בָּהֶן חָכָם יוֹתֵר מִמְּךָ וּמֵהֶם, וְכַמָּה נִסְכָּל וְנִבְהָל מִי שֶׁחוֹשֵׁב שֶׁאֵין לַדְּבָרִים נֶזֶק אוֹ תּוֹעֶלֶת אֶלָּא בְּמַה שֶׁהִשִּׂיג הוּא.

וְיֵשׁ לְךָ לָדַעַת כִּי לְתוֹעַלְתֵּנוּ לֹא נִתְגַּלָּה סִבָּתָן וְנִזְקָן, פֶּן יָקוּמוּ אֲנָשִׁים מַחֲזִיקִים עַצְמָן בַּחֲכָמִים גְּדוֹלִים וְיִתְחַכְּמוּ לוֹמַר "נֶזֶק פְּלוֹנִי שֶׁאָמְרָה הַתּוֹרָה שֶׁיֵּשׁ בְּדָבָר פְּלוֹנִי אֵינֶנּוּ כִּי אִם בִּמְקוֹם פְּלוֹנִי שֶׁטִּבְעוֹ כֵן אוֹ בְּאִישׁ שֶׁטִּבְעוֹ כֵן

5. When a pregnant animal is ritually slain, its unborn young also becomes permitted to be eaten, as it is considered part of the mother; if, however, the unborn creature previously put a limb outside the womb, that limb does not become permitted to be eaten by the ritual slaying of the mother. If the unborn creature sticks out its head previously, it remains entirely forbidden, unless it is taken out alive after the mother's death and is ritually slain separately; TB Ḥullin 68a-b, Rashi to 68a, s.v. *u-vasar*. (Here our author has followed ShM negative precept §181.)

6. The spirit gains in merit and standing by resisting the body's temptations and by observing *mitzvoth* with it. Cf. Genesis 19:8, *therefore have they come under the shadow (shelter) of my roof.*

7. Literally, the body between its hands.

8. The Almighty, thus called in the eighth of the nineteen benedictions in *sh'moneh esréh*, the central part of the daily prayers, said silently, standing. (Cf. *Guide* III 48; Ramban to Exodus 22:30.)

lesser holiness that went [was taken] out beyond the wall [of Jerusalem]; meat of a Passover offering that went out of the group [registered for it]; and so too an unborn creature that went out of its mother's innards.[5]

The meaning of the verse thus becomes as though it read, "and flesh in the field is *t'réfah*." In other words, flesh which went out of its boundaries—for this is what "field" signifies, having no boundaries—is *t'réfah*. All these that we mentioned went out of their proper boundaries; then they have the same law as the *t'réfah*; and whoever ate of them the amount of an olive would be given whiplashes.

At the root of this precept lies the reason that the body is an instrument of the spirit: with it, it carries out its activity; without it, it can never complete its work. Therefore did it [the spirit] come into its shadow [for the spirit's benefit][6] and not for its harm; for God never does harm, but only does good to benefit all. Thus we find that the body at its command[7] is like a pair of tongs in the hand of a blacksmith [i.e. any toolmaker]: With it he can produce a tool fit for its purpose.

Now in truth, if the tongs are strong and properly shaped to grasp tools in them, the craftsman can make them well. If the tongs are not good, the tools will never come out properly shaped and fit. In the same way, if there is any loss or damage in the body, of any kind, some function of the intelligence will be nullified, corresponding to that defect. For this reason our whole and perfect Torah removed us far from anything that causes such defect.

In this vein, according to the plain meaning we would say we were given a ban by the Torah against all forbidden foods. And if there are some among them whose harm is known [understood] neither by us nor by the wise men of medicine, do not wonder about them: The faithful, trustworthy Physician[8] who adjured us about them is wiser than both you and them. How foolish and hasty would anyone be who thought that nothing is harmful or useful except as he understands it.

For you should know that for our own good their reason and their harm [i.e. of the forbidden foods] were not revealed—for fear that people would rise up who considered themselves very wise, and becoming overwise they would say, "This harm which the Torah said exists in that thing is so only in that place, since such is its nature; or only for a man whose nature is thus-and-so." Then some fool may

§73: TO EAT NO MEAT FROM AN ANIMAL TORN BY BEASTS (T'RÉFAH)

וְכֵן״, וְיִתְפַּתֶּה לְדִבְרֵיהֶם אֶחָד מִן הַפְּתָאִים, עַל כֵּן לֹא נִתְגַּלָּה טַעְמָן לְהוֹעִיל לָנוּ מִן הַמִּכְשׁוֹל הַזֶּה.

וְיָדוּעַ הַדָּבָר מִדַּרְכֵי הָרְפוּאָה שֶׁבִּבְשַׂר כָּל הַטְּרֵפוֹת הָאֲסוּרוֹת לָנוּ מוֹלִיד הֶפְסֵד אֶל גּוּף אוֹכְלוֹ, מֵחֲמַת שֶׁהַטְּרֵפוּת מוֹרָה חֹלִי בַּבְּהֵמָה. וְאַל תַּקְשֶׁה עָלַי וְתֹאמַר מַה הֶפְסֵד אֶפְשָׁר לִהְיוֹת בִּבְהֵמָה שֶׁנִּטְרְפָה מִיָּד וְנִשְׁחֲטָה, כִּי לֹא מֵחָכְמָה תַּקְשֶׁה עַל זֶה, הֲלֹא יָדַעְתָּ כִּי לְכָל דָּבָר הַתְחָלָה, וְאִם תּוֹדֶה אֵלַי כִּי בְּאֹרֶךְ הַזְּמַן יִמָּצֵא הַהֶפְסֵד בָּהּ מֵחֲמַת הַטְּרֵפוּת תִּתְחַיֵּב לְהוֹדוֹת כִּי בְּרֶגַע הָרִאשׁוֹן הִתְחַל הַהֶפְסֵד אֶלָּא שֶׁהוּא מוּעָט בְּהַתְחָלָה, וְאֵין סָפֵק כִּי מִן הַנֶּזֶק רַע אֲפִלּוּ מְעוּטוֹ. וְעוֹד שֶׁכָּל דִּינֵי הַתּוֹרָה וְכָל דָּבָר שֶׁיֵּשׁ לוֹ קְיָמָה, בְּגֶדֶר כָּזֶה יִתְחַיֵּב לִהְיוֹת, שֶׁאִם תִּתֵּן דְּבָרֶיךָ לְשִׁעוּרִין לֹא יִתְקַיֵּם דָּבָר בְּיָדְךָ לְעוֹלָם.

דִּינֵי הַמִּצְוָה, כְּגוֹן הַטְּרֵפִיּוֹת שֶׁנִּמְסְרוּ לוֹ לְמֹשֶׁה בְּסִינַי, וְהֵן שְׁמוֹנָה אָבוֹת: דְּרוּסָה נְקוּבָה חֲסֵרָה נְטוּלָה פְּסוּקָה קְרוּעָה נְפוּלָה שְׁבוּרָה. וְהַדְּרוּסָה הִיא הַטְּרֵפוּת הֶחָמוּר בְּכֻלָּן, לְפִי שֶׁהוּא מְפֹרָשׁ בַּתּוֹרָה, וּלְפִיכָךְ אָמְרוּ זִכְרוֹנָם לִבְרָכָה שֶׁכָּל סָפֵק הַבָּא לָנוּ עָלָיו אָסוּר, וּבִשְׁאָר הַטְּרֵפוּת יֵשׁ בָּהֶן סְפֵקִין מֻתָּרִין.

וְכָל אֶחָד וְאֶחָד מֵאֵלּוּ הָאָבוֹת יֵשׁ לוֹ כַּמָּה וְכַמָּה תוֹלָדוֹת כְּמוֹ שֶׁבָּא פְּרָטָן בַּגְּמָרָא. וְחֶשְׁבּוֹן בְּכָל הַטְּרֵפִיּוֹת שֶׁאֶפְשָׁר שֶׁיִּמָּצְאוּ בִּבְהֵמָה וְחַיָּה וְעוֹף הָעוֹלֶה בְּיָדֵינוּ בִּפְרָטָן לְפִי הַדּוֹמֶה מִדִּבְרֵי הַגְּמָרָא הֵם ע״ב עִם טְרֵפוּת אֶחָד שֶׁיֵּשׁ בְּעוֹף יָתֵר עַל הַבְּהֵמָה. וַעֲלֵיהֶן אֵין לְהוֹסִיף וּמֵהֶן אֵין לִגְרֹעַ, לְפִי שֶׁכָּל מַכָּה שֶׁתֶּאֱרַע לִבְהֵמָה אוֹ לְחַיָּה אוֹ לְעוֹף חוּץ מֵאֵלּוּ שֶׁמָּנוּ חֲכָמִים בַּדּוֹרוֹת הָרִאשׁוֹנוֹת וְהִסְכִּימוּ

---

9. A similar thought is to be found in ShM end.
10. Expression based on Ecclesiastes 7:10.
11. I.e. by an attacking wild beast.
12. A puncture was made in a vital organ, which will prove fatal.
13. A foot or the lobe of a lung; MT *hilchoth shehittah* viii 1.
14. So Rashi to TB Ḥullin 43a; Rambam *ibid.* 16 includes two other parts of the animal whose removal makes it *t'réfah*.
15. Following TB Ḥullin 43a, the Hebrew reads literally: trampled, perforated, lacking, removed, sundered, torn, fallen, broken. The eight terms have been rendered here according to their explanations in MT *hilchoth shehittah* v–x.
16. Because this is the meaning of *t'réfah*, the term used in the verse.
17. Rambam *ibid.* v 3; and see *Turé Zahav* to Shulḥan 'Aruch Yoreh Dé'ah §29, 1.
18. So Rabad to Rambam *ibid.* x 11; and cf. TB Ḥullin 56a.

⟨286⟩

be foolishly persuaded by their words. Because of this their reason was not revealed, to help us avoid this stumbling-block.[9]

Now, this matter is known from the field of healing: that the meat of all *t'réfah* animals forbidden us will engender damage in the one who eats it, because the fact that it is *t'réfah* indicates illness in the animal. And do not find this difficult and ask, "What loss or damage can there be in an animal which became *t'réfah* instantly and was ritually slaughtered [at once]?" For not out of wisdom would you enquire about this.[10] Certainly you know that everything has a beginning. And if you admit to me that in the course of time spoilage and damage will be found in it on account of its fatal condition, then you will have to admit that the damage began at the first instant, except that it is very little at the beginning. But there is no doubt that harm will come from the damage, even if it is little. Moreover, all the laws of the Torah, and anything which is to endure, must be established within such a "fence": For if you limit your words [of Torah to be observed only] in parts, nothing will ever endure with you permanently.

The laws of the precept are, for example, the kinds of *t'réfah* creatures that were taught to Moses at Sinai, which are the eight "fathers" [main types]: an animal that was lethally clawed,[11] or fatally perforated,[12] or is lacking an organ or limb;[13] if the liver was removed,[14] the spine broken, or the flesh covering most of the abdomen torn away; if it fell from a height smashing a limb, or if it broke most of its ribs.[15]

A torn, clawed animal is the most serious type of *t'réfah* creature, since it is mentioned expressly in the Torah.[16] Therefore our Sages of blessed memory said that any doubtful instance of it that comes to us is forbidden, while of the other kinds of *t'réfah* animals there can be doubtful cases which are permitted.[17]

For each one of these "fathers" [main types] there are any number of "children" [derivative kinds], as they are described in detail in the Talmud. The sum total of all the *t'réfah* kinds which can possibly be found among domestic and wild beasts and birds, by our reckoning, as is apparent from the words of the Talmud, are seventy-two— including one *t'réfah* condition that a bird can have beyond those which a beast can.[18] To these none may be added, and from them none may be taken away. For if any wound should happen to a domestic or wild animal or bird apart from those which the Sages listed in the

§73: TO EAT NO MEAT FROM AN ANIMAL TORN BY BEASTS (T'RÉFAH)

עֲלֵיהֶם בָּתֵּי דִינֵי יִשְׂרָאֵל אֶפְשָׁר שֶׁתִּהְיֶה, וַאֲפִלּוּ נוֹדַע לָנוּ מִדֶּרֶךְ הָרְפוּאָה שֶׁאֵין סוֹפָהּ לִחְיוֹת. וְכָל אֵלּוּ הַמַּכּוֹת שֶׁמָּנוּ וְאָמְרוּ שֶׁהֵן טוֹרְפוֹת, אַף עַל פִּי שֶׁנִּרְאֶה בְּדַרְכֵי הָרְפוּאָה שֶׁבְּיָדֵינוּ שֶׁמִּקְצָתָן אֵין מְמִיתִין וְאֶפְשָׁר שֶׁתִּהְיֶה מֵהֶן, אֵין לְךָ אֶלָּא מָה שֶׁמָּנוּ חֲכָמִים, שֶׁנֶּאֱמַר "עַל פִּי הַתּוֹרָה". וְכָל אֶחָד מִן הָעָ"ב טְרֵפִיּוֹת שֶׁאָמַרְנוּ מְפֹרָשׁ בָּאֲרֻכָּה עִם כָּל תְּנָאָיו בְּמַסֶּכֶת חֻלִּין.

וְכָל טְרֵפִיּוֹת אֵלּוּ שֶׁמָּנוּ חֲכָמִים בִּבְהֵמָה וּבְעוֹף אֵין אָדָם צָרִיךְ לַחֲזֹר אַחֲרֵיהֶן וְלִבְדֹּק אוֹתָם טֶרֶם שֶׁיֹּאכַל בְּשַׂר הַבְּהֵמָה וְהָעוֹף מִפְּנֵי שֶׁחֶזְקָתָן שֶׁכְּשֵׁרִים הֵם, כִּי רֹב בַּעֲלֵי חַיִּים בְּחֶזְקַת חַיִּים בְּרִיאִים אָנוּ מַחֲזִיקִין אוֹתָן, זוּלָתִי בְּאַחַת מֵהֶן שֶׁהִצְרִיכוּ חֲכָמִים לִבְדֹּק טֶרֶם שֶׁנֹּאכַל הַבָּשָׂר מִפְּנֵי שֶׁזֶּה הַטְּרֵפוּת מָצוּי הַרְבֵּה, וְהוּא טְרֵפוּת הָרֵאָה שֶׁמְּצוּיִין בָּהּ רִירִין הַנִּקְרָאִין סִרְכוֹת, וְיֵשׁ לָחוּשׁ בָּהֶן שֶׁלֹּא יִמְשְׁכוּ קְרוּם הָרֵאָה וִינַקְּבוּהוּ.

לְפִיכָךְ צָרִיךְ אָדָם לִרְאוֹת לְעוֹלָם בְּאֵי זֶה צַד יִהְיוּ אוֹתָן רִירִין בָּרֵאָה טֶרֶם שֶׁיֹּאכַל מִן הַבְּהֵמָה, וְאִם יִמְצָא אוֹתָן בְּעִנְיָן שֶׁאֶפְשָׁר כִּי בִּתְנוּעָתָם יִנְקְבוּ הָרֵאָה, טְרֵפָה, שֶׁאָנוּ אוֹמְרִין כָּל הָעוֹמֵד לִנָּקֵב עַל כָּל פָּנִים כְּנָקוּב חֲשָׁבִינָן לֵיהּ וּכְאִלּוּ מֵתָה הִיא, אַחַר שֶׁאִי אֶפְשָׁר לָהּ לְהִנָּצֵל מִן הַמָּוֶת, וְיָדוּעַ הוּא כִּי אוֹתוֹ הַחֲלִי הַגּוֹמֵל אוֹתָן רִירִין בַּמְּקוֹמוֹת הָעֲתִידִין לִנָּקֵב הַתְחָלַת חֳלִי הַמֵּבִיא לִידֵי מָוֶת הוּא אַחַר שֶׁבְּאוֹתָן מְקוֹמוֹת נַעֲשׂוּ הָרִירִין.

וְאֵלּוּ הֵן הַמְּקוֹמוֹת שֶׁהָרִירִין טוֹרְפִין לְפִי הַכְּלָל הָעוֹלֶה בְּיָדֵינוּ מִדִּבְרֵי הַגְּמָרָא עִם הַפֵּרוּשִׁים הַטּוֹבִים: כָּל מָקוֹם בָּעוֹלָם שֶׁהָאֻמָּה סְרוּכָה טְרֵיפָה וְאֵינָהּ נִתֶּרֶת בִּבְדִיקָה, זוּלָתִי בְּעִנְיָן אֶחָד אִם סְרוּכָה לְדֹפֶן וְיֵשׁ מַכָּה בַּדֹּפֶן וְהַסִּירְכָא כֻּלָּהּ

---

19. So Rambam ibid. 12–13.
20. So Rambam ibid. xi 3 (see *Kessef Mishneh*), and Rashi to Ḥullin 12a, top.
21. So *tosafoth* to Ḥullin 47a, s.v. *hainu*.

early generations and which every *beth din* in Israel (Jewry) agreed upon, it can perhaps survive—even if we have learned from the field of healing that ultimately it cannot remain alive. And again, about those wounds which they listed stating that they are fatal, making the creature *t'réfah*—even if it would seem from the knowledge of medicine that we possess that some are not fatal, and the creature could possibly remain alive from them—you have nothing more [to rely on and follow] than what the Sages listed, which was stated according to the Torah.[19] Every one of the seventy-two *t'réfah* types that we have mentioned is explained at length, with all its conditions, in the Talmud tractate *Hullin*.

However, as regards all these conditions of *t'réfah* which the Sages listed for beasts and birds, there is no need for a person to seek after them and ascertain about them before he eats the meat of a beast or a bird: because they have the presumption of being kosher, fit to eat.[20] Since most creatures are held to be healthy, we so regard and consider them—except for one [fatal condition] among them, for which the Sages required us to examine before we eat the meat, because this *t'réfah* state is found very often: This is a *t'réfah* condition of the lungs, when extrusions called adhesions are found in it, and it is to be feared about them that they might have stretched the membrane of the lung and made a hole in it.[21]

Therefore a man always needs to see in what way those extrusions are [formed] on the lung before he eats of the animal; and if he finds them to be in such a manner that by their motion they could perforate the lung, it is *t'réfah*. For we say that if anything is ready (likely) to be perforated in any event, we regard it as though it already had a hole; [so the animal] is as though [already] dead, since it cannot possibly save itself from death. And it is known that the sickness which produces those extrusions in places where they are destined to make holes, is the beginning of an illness leading to death—since it produces the extrusions in those places.

Now, these are the places where the extrusions make an animal *t'réfah*, according to the rule that we gather from the words of the Talmud along with the good commentaries: If a main bronchial tube (bronchus) has an adhesion anywhere at all, it is *t'réfah*, and it cannot become permitted by an examination [to determine that there is no perforation]—except in one instance: If it is adhered to the wall [of the lung] and there is a wound in the wall, and the adhesion goes

§73: TO EAT NO MEAT FROM AN ANIMAL TORN BY BEASTS (T'RÉFAH)

יוֹצֵאת מִמְּקוֹם הַמַּכָּה, שֶׁבְּזוֹ נֹאמַר תִּבָּדֵק. וְיֵשׁ מַתִּירִין בְּלֹא בְדִיקָה. וְיֵשׁ מוֹצִיאִין מִכְּלָל זֶה אִם סְרוּכָה לְאֻנָּה שֶׁבְּצִדָּהּ מֵחִתּוּךְ לְחִתּוּךְ, וְכֵן מִנְהָגֵנוּ הַיּוֹם לְהֶתֵּר.

כָּל מָקוֹם שֶׁבָּעוֹלָם שֶׁהָעֵינוּנִיתָא דְוַרְדָּא שֶׁהִיא מִצַּד יָמִין סְרוּכָה טְרֵיפָה. וְאֻנּוֹת הָרֵאָה הֵם חָמֵשׁ מִלְּבַד הָעֵינוּנִיתָא, וְיֵשׁ מֵהֶן שְׁלֹשָׁה מִצַּד יָמִין הַבּוֹדֵק בְּשָׁעָה שֶׁהַבְּהֵמָה תְּלוּיָה בְרַגְלֶיהָ הָאַחֲרוֹנִים כְּדֶרֶךְ שֶׁתּוֹלִין אוֹתָהּ הַטַּבָּחִים, וּשְׁתַּיִם מִצַּד שְׂמֹאל. אִם סְרוּכוֹת אוֹ סְמוּכוֹת זוֹ אֵצֶל זוֹ וְהַסִּרְכָּא יוֹצֵאת מֵחִתּוּךְ לְחִתּוּךְ, וְכֵן אִם סְרוּכוֹת אֶל צַלְעוֹת הַבְּהֵמָה שֶׁהֵן רְבוּצוֹת בְּתוֹכָן, וְהַסִּרְכָּא יוֹצֵאת מִגַּב הָאֻנּוֹת אֶל הַצְּלָעוֹת וְתוֹפֶשֶׂת בַּצְּלָעוֹת וּבַבָּשָׂר שֶׁבֵּין הַצְּלָעוֹת, וְכָל שֶׁכֵּן בַּבָּשָׂר לְבַד, כָּל זֶה דָנִין אוֹתוֹ לְהֶתֵּר.

אֲבָל אִם הַסִּרְכָא יוֹצֵאת בֵּינֵיהֶן מֵחִתּוּךְ הָאֻנָּה לְגַב חֲבֶרְתָּהּ אוֹ מִגַּב לְגַב, וְכֵן אִם יוֹצֵאת מִן הָאֻנּוֹת אֶל הַצְּלָעוֹת וְאֵינָהּ תּוֹפֶשֶׂת כִּי אִם בַּעֲצָמוֹת לְבַד, וְכֵן כָּל מָקוֹם אַחֵר בָּעוֹלָם שֶׁבַּבְּהֵמָה שֶׁתִּהְיֶינָה הָאֻנּוֹת סְרוּכוֹת שָׁם אוֹ סְמוּכוֹת דָּנִין אוֹתוֹ לְאִסּוּר. וְהָרַמְבַּ״ם זִכְרוֹנוֹ לִבְרָכָה הוֹצִיא מִכְּלָל זֶה כָּל זְמַן שֶׁסְּרוּכוֹת לֶחָזֶה וּלְשַׁמְנוּנִית דֶּחָזֶה וְדָן לְהֶתֵּר, וְלֹא כֵן אָנוּ נוֹהֲגִין.

סִרְכָא הַתְּלוּיָה בְּכָל מָקוֹם בֵּין בָּאֻנּוֹת בֵּין בָּאֻמָּה כְּשֵׁרָה, וְיֵשׁ שֶׁטּוֹרְפָהּ, וְאָנוּ נוֹהֲגִין בָּהּ הֶתֵּר.

נִמְצְאוּ הָאֻנּוֹת שֶׁלֹּא כַּסֵּדֶר הַזֶּה אוֹ חֲסֵרוֹת מֶחְשָׁבוֹן זֶה, טְרֵפָה. וְהָעֵינוּנִיתָא דְוַרְדָּא מַשְׁלֶמֶת חֶסְרוֹן אֶחָד. וְאִם נִמְצְאוּ יְתֵרוֹת מֶחְשָׁבוֹן זֶה הַרְבֵּה אֵין בְּכָךְ כְּלוּם, וּבִלְבַד שֶׁלֹּא יִמָּצֵא הַיִּתְרוֹן מִצַּד גַּבָּן, דְּאִלּוּ מִצַּד גַּבָּן אֲפִלּוּ אַחַת קְטַנָּה

---

22. Rabad to MT *hilchoth shehittah* vii 5.
23. R. Nissim to Rif (R. Isaac Alfasi), Hullin iii (268a), s.v. *ud'amrinan*; Séfer Kolbo, *'issur v'hetter* §101; and see *Béth Yoséf* to Tur Yoreh Dé'ah §39, s.v. *v'ha-rif*, end.
24. Rashi to Hullin 46b, s.v. *hainu*; see also *tosafoth* s.v. *hainu*.
25. So Rashi *ibid*.
26. TB Hullin 47a.
27. *Ibid*. 46b, 48a.
28. MT *hilchoth shehittah* xi 7.
28a. So Rashba, *Torath haBa-yith* ii 3.
29. *Ibid*. 15.
30. R. Aaron haLévi, *Bedek haBa-yith* ii 3.
30a. Cf. Rashba, *Torath haBa-yith* ii 3.
31. TB Hullin 47a.
32. I.e. on the right side, where the small pink lobe is located; Rambam *ibid*. viii 2 (and see *Kessef Mishneh*).
33. See Ramban to TB Hullin 47b, and R. Nissim to Rif, 267a, s.v. *v'hanni milli*.

out entirely from the place of the wound—about this condition it was said to examine,[22] while some permit [the animal to be eaten] without examination.[23] Some make an exception to this rule if it is adhered to a lobe on the side, from one place of articulation [where the lungs begin to divide] to another;[24] and so is it our practice today to permit [the animal to be eaten].

If the small pink lobe, which is [at the bottom of the lung] at the right side, is adhered anywhere at all, the animal is *t'réfah*.[25] There are five lobes of the lung besides this small one; three of them are at the right of the examiner, when the animal is suspended by its hind legs in the way that the butchers suspend it; and two are at the left side.[26] If they are adhered or adjoined one close to another, and the adhesion goes from one point of articulation to another; so also if they are adhered to the ribs of the animal within which they nestle, and the adhesion goes out from the outside of the lobes to the ribs and becomes attached to the ribs and the flesh between the ribs—and all the more certainly if to the flesh alone—in all such cases we rule [the animal] to be permissible.[27]

However, if the adhesion goes out between them, from the articulation (separation) point of a lobe to the exterior of the next one, or from the outside of one to the outside of another; so too if it goes out from the lobes to the ribs but becomes attached to the ribs alone; and so also any other spot whatever within the animal to which the lobes become adhered or adjoined—then the animal is ruled forbidden [to eat].[27] Rambam of blessed memory makes an exception to this rule for any animal as long as [the lobes] are adhered to the breast or the fat of the breast, and considers it permitted.[28] But we do not follow this rule.[28a]

If an adhesion remains suspended anywhere, whether on the lobes or a bronchus [not becoming attached to anything else], the animal is kosher;[29] there is one who rules it *t'réfah*,[30] but in our practice it is permissible.[30a]

If the lobes were found to be not in proper order, or lacking some of this proper number, the animal is *t'réfah*;[31] but the small pink lobe may be considered as a replacement for one that is lacking.[32] If many more than this number were found, it is of no consequence— but only if the extra ones were not found at [the lungs'] back side: For at their back side, even if there is one as tiny as a myrtle leaf, or yet smaller, it makes the animal forbidden.[33] There are those, however,

כַּעֲלֵה הֲדַס אוֹ יוֹתֵר קְטַנָּה אוֹסֶרֶת, וְיֵשׁ מַתִּירִין כְּשֶׁהִיא קְטַנָּה יוֹתֵר מֵעֲלֵי הֲדַס.

וְיֶתֶר רַבֵּי פְּרָטֵי מִצְוָה זוֹ מְבֹאָרִים בְּפֶרֶק ג׳ מֵחוּלִין. וּבְפֶרֶק זֶה בְּעַצְמוֹ כְּמוֹ כֵן, וּבְפֶרֶק אַחֲרוֹן מִמַּכּוֹת וְרִאשׁוֹן מִבְּכוֹרוֹת יִתְבָּאֲרוּ דִּינֵי שְׁאָר הָאֲסוּרִין שֶׁפָּתַבְנוּ לְמַעְלָה שֶׁנִּשְׁמָעִין בִּלְשׁוֹן הַכָּתוּב בַּפָּנִים שֶׁלּוֹ.

וְנִכְפְּלָה אַזְהָרָה זוֹ בַּנְּבִיאִים בְּסֵפֶר יְחֶזְקֵאל בַּכֹּהֲנִים לְבַד, שֶׁכָּתוּב עֲלֵיהֶם: כָּל נְבֵלָה וּטְרֵפָה . . . לֹא יֹאכְלוּ הַכֹּהֲנִים. וְהוֹדִיעוּנוּ חֲכָמִים שֶׁמִּפְּנֵי זֶה נִכְפְּלָה בָּהֶן, לְפִי שֶׁהַכָּתוּב צִנָּם לֶאֱכֹל חַטֹּאת הָעוֹף בִּמְלִיקָה, וְאַף עַל פִּי שֶׁאֲסוּרָה לְיִשְׂרָאֵל בִּנְבֵלָה, וְאוּלַי נַחֲשֹׁב מִתּוֹךְ כֵּן שֶׁיִּתֵּר לָהֶם בַּחֲלָלִין בְּמְלִיקָה אוֹ שְׁחִיטָה נִפְסֶדֶת שֶׁלֹּא מַקְפִּיד תּוֹרָה בָּהֶן, דְּמִכֵּיוָן שֶׁיָּצְאוּ מִן הַגֶּדֶר בְּדָבָר אֶחָד יָצְאוּ לְגַמְרֵי בְּכָל עִנְיַן הַשְּׁחִיטָה, וּלְפִיכָךְ הִזְהִיר הַנָּבִיא בָּהֶם בְּפֵרוּשׁ לְהוֹדִיעֵנוּ שֶׁלֹּא הִתִּירוּ רַק בִּמְלִיקָה לְבַד בְּקָרְבָּן, אֲבָל בַּחֲלָלִין נִשְׁאָרִים הֵם בְּאִסּוּרִין כְּמוֹ יִשְׂרְאֵלִים.

וְנוֹהֶגֶת מִצְוָה זוֹ בְּכָל מָקוֹם וּבְכָל זְמַן בִּזְכָרִים וּנְקֵבוֹת. וְהָעוֹבֵר עָלֶיהָ וְאָכַל כְּזַיִת מִן הַטְּרֵפָה, וּמִכָּל אֵלּוּ שֶׁנִּשְׁמָעִים בְּפֵרוּשׁ הַכָּתוּב שֶׁיָּצְאוּ חוּץ לִמְחִיצָתָן, לוֹקֶה.

וְאַל יַקְשֶׁה עָלֶיךָ: וְאֵיךְ לוֹקֶה, וְהָא קַיְמָא לָן אֵין לוֹקִין עַל לָאו שֶׁבִּכְלָלוֹת, וַהֲרֵי זֶה שֶׁכָּלַל בְּכַמָּה דְּבָרִים, כְּמוֹ שֶׁאָמַרְנוּ. כִּי פֵרוּשׁ עִנְיָן זֶה כְּבָר בֵּאֲרוּהוּ בְּסֵפֶר הַמִּצְוֹת בְּעִקָּר הַתְּשִׁיעִי שְׁנֵי גְּדוֹלֵי הַדּוֹר, וְהֵם הָרַמְבַּ״ם זִכְרוֹנוֹ לִבְרָכָה וְהָרַמְבַּ״ן זִכְרוֹנוֹ לִבְרָכָה, וְהִרְחִיבוּ שָׁם פֵּרוּשֵׁיהֶם וּרְאָיוֹתֵיהֶם בָּזֶה לְבָרֵר הַדָּבָר יָפֶה,

---

34. Rambam *ibid.* VIII 4.
35. TB M'naḥoth 45a.
36. See Rashi to Leviticus 1:15.
37. This paragraph is based on ShM negative precept §181.

who consider it permissible if it [the extra lobe] is smaller than a myrtle leaf.[34]

[These] and the rest of the many details of this precept are explained in chapter 3 of the Talmud tractate *Hullin*. In this chapter, too, and the last chapter of *Makkoth* and the first of *B'choroth*, the laws are explained about the other kinds of prohibition of which we wrote above, that are implied by the language of the verse, by its inner meaning.

Now, this prohibition was repeated in the Prophets, in the *Book of Ezekiel*, but for the *kohanim* alone: for it is written about them, *Anything that has died of itself, or is* t'réfah *(torn) . . . the* kohanim *shall not eat* (Ezekiel 44:31). The Sages informed us[35] that this is the reason why it was repeated for them: Scripture commanded them to eat a fowl brought as a sin-offering whose head was almost severed with a fingernail[36]—although it would be forbidden to an ordinary Israelite as *n'vélah* ("an animal that died of itself"). As a result, you might think that ordinary, non-holy meat was equally permitted them if the animal was almost decapitated with the fingernail or ritually slaughtered in a damaging, spoiling way—that the Torah did not mind about them, for once they were excluded from the regular rule in regard to one thing, they were excluded completely, for everything involving ritual slaughter. Therefore the prophet adjured them explicitly, to let us know that they were given special permission regarding partial decapitation with the fingernail only for a sacrifice; but for ordinary non-holy meat, they are under the same prohibitions as the Israelites.[37]

This precept applies in every place, at every time, for both man and woman. If someone violates it and eats the amount of an olive from a *t'réfah* animal, or from any of all those implied by the meaning of the verse, that went [were taken] out of their proper boundaries, he is given whiplashes.

Now, let this not be a difficulty for you: "But how is he given a whipping? We have an established rule: No lashes are given over an omnibus negative precept [that comprises various implied prohibitions]"—and this includes several [different] matters, as we have stated. The two great luminaries of their time, Rambam and Ramban of blessed memory, made the explanation of this matter quite clear in the past, in the *Séfer haMitzvoth* (Book of Precepts), in the ninth principle. They developed their expositions and proofs amply, to

§73–74: ON T'RÉFAH MEAT / NOT TO HEAR ONE LITIGANT ALONE

וְאַרִיךְ הָעִנְיָן, עַל כֵּן הִנַּחְתִּיו כְּפִי מִנְהָגִי בַּסֵּפֶר. וּמִכָּל מָקוֹם יֵשׁ לְךָ לָדַעַת כִּי הָעוֹלֶה מִדִּבְרֵי שְׁנֵיהֶם, שֶׁאֵין זֶה מִכְּלָל לָאו שֶׁבִּכְלָלוֹת.

[שֶׁלֹּא לִשְׁמֹעַ טַעֲנַת בַּעַל דִּין שֶׁלֹּא בִּפְנֵי בַּעַל־דִּינוֹ]

עד שֶׁלֹּא יִשְׁמַע הַדַּיָּן טַעֲנַת הָאֶחָד שֶׁלֹּא בִּפְנֵי בַּעַל דִּינוֹ, שֶׁנֶּאֱמַר "לֹא תִשָּׂא שֵׁמַע שָׁוְא", וְהַטַּעַם לְפִי שֶׁבְּנֵי אָדָם יְדַבְּרוּ דִּבְרֵי שָׁוְא שֶׁלֹּא בִּפְנֵי בַּעַל דִּינָם, וְצִוָּה הַדַּיָּן עַל זֶה כְּדֵי שֶׁלֹּא יַכְנִיס בְּנַפְשׁוֹ כִּזְבֵי שֶׁל אֶחָד מֵהֶם. וְכֵן בָּא בִּמְכִילְתָּא שֶׁאַזְהָרָה זוֹ שֶׁל "לֹא תִשָּׂא" וְכוֹלֵי עַל זֶה נֶאֶמְרָה. וְעוֹד אָמְרוּ שָׁם שֶׁהִיא אַזְהָרָה גַּם לְבַעַל הַדִּין שֶׁלֹּא יִטְעַן גַּם הוּא טַעֲנוֹתָיו לַדַּיָּן שֶׁלֹּא בִּפְנֵי בַּעַל דִּינוֹ, וַאֲפִלּוּ יִרְצֶה לִשְׁמֹעַ אוֹתָן הַדַּיָּן, וְעַל זֶה נֶאֱמַר גַּם כֵּן "מִדְּבַר שֶׁקֶר תִּרְחָק". וְעוֹד אָמְרוּ זִכְרוֹנָם לִבְרָכָה שֶׁזֶּה הַלָּאו כּוֹלֵל מְסַפֵּר לָשׁוֹן הָרַע וּמְקַבְּלוֹ וּמֵעִיד עֵדוּת שֶׁקֶר.

שֹׁרֶשׁ הַמִּצְוָה יָדוּעַ, כִּי הַשֶּׁקֶר נִתְעָב וְנִגְאָל בְּעֵינֵי הַכֹּל, אֵין דָּבָר מָאוּס מִמֶּנּוּ, וְהַמְאֵרָה וְהַקְּלָלָה בְּבֵית כָּל אוֹהֲבָיו, מִפְּנֵי שֶׁהַשֵּׁם אֵל אֱמֶת וְכָל אֲשֶׁר אִתּוֹ אֱמֶת, וְאֵין הַבְּרָכָה מְצוּיָה וְחָלָה אֶלָּא בַּמִּתְדַּמִּים אֵלָיו בְּמַעֲשֵׂיהֶם, לִהְיוֹתָם אֲמִתִּיִּים כְּמוֹ שֶׁהוּא אֵל אֱמֶת, וְלִהְיוֹת מְרַחֲמִים כְּמוֹ שֶׁיָּדוּעַ שֶׁהוּא רַחוּם, וְלִהְיוֹתָם גּוֹמְלֵי חֲסָדִים כְּמוֹ שֶׁהוּא רַב הַחֶסֶד. אֲבָל כָּל מִי שֶׁמַּעֲשָׂיו בְּהֶפֶךְ מִדּוֹתָיו הַטּוֹבוֹת וְהֵם בַּעֲלֵי הַשֶּׁקֶר, שֶׁהֵם בְּהֶפֶךְ מִדּוֹתָיו מַמָּשׁ, כְּמוֹ כֵן תָּנוּחַ עֲלֵיהֶם לְעוֹלָם מַה שֶּׁהוּא הֶפֶךְ מִדּוֹתָיו, וְהֶפֶךְ מִדַּת הַבְּרָכָה שֶׁהִיא בּוֹ הִיא הַמְּאֵרָה וְהַקְּלָלָה, וְהֶפֶךְ הַשִּׂמְחָה וְהַשָּׁלוֹם וְהַתַּעֲנוּג שֶׁהֵם אִתּוֹ הוּא הַדְּאָגָה וְהַקְּטָטָה וְהַצַּעַר, כָּל אֵלֶּה חֵלֶק אָדָם רָשָׁע מֵאֱלֹהִים.

וְעַל כֵּן הִזְהִירָתְנוּ הַתּוֹרָה לְהַרְחִיק מִן הַשֶּׁקֶר הַרְבֵּה, כְּמוֹ שֶׁכָּתוּב "מִדְּבַר

---

38. Essentially because the one term *basar ba-sadeh t'réfah* ("flesh that is torn of beasts in the field") applies to all the types and conditions which it prohibits.

§74 1. For in the absence of his opponent to refute him, a man will feel no embarrassment in telling lies as easily as truth, or in embellishing and embroidering his argument with falsehood (Rashi, TB Sanhedrin 7b s.v. *shamo'a*; Sh'vu'oth 31a s.v. *shéma shav*).

1a. TB Makkoth 23a. In this paragraph, ShM negative precept §281 is followed.

2. In all these instances, a person "bears a vain or false report" with his mouth or ears. This derives from Mechilta and MdRSbY (in MhG).

clarify the subject well. But the matter is quite lengthy, and I have therefore omitted it, in accordance with my custom in this work. But in any case you should know that what emerges from the words of the two is that this is not to be included among omnibus negative precepts [that include different implied prohibitions].[38]

[NOT TO HEAR A LITIGANT IN COURT IN HIS OPPONENT'S ABSENCE]

74 that the judge should not hear the argument of one party [in a lawsuit] in the absence of his opponent—for it is stated, *You shall not bear (take up) a vain, worthless report* (Exodus 23:1). The reason is that people will speak vain (false) words when their opponent [in a lawsuit] is not present. And so the judge was enjoined about this in order that he should not absorb the lies of one of them. So, too, we read in the Midrash *Mechilta* that this admonition, *You shall not bear*, etc. was given about this. It was stated further there that this is also an admonition to the party in a lawsuit likewise not to present his arguments before the judge when his opponent is not there, even if the judge is willing to listen to them. About this it was also stated, *From a false matter, keep far* (ibid. 7).[1] In addition, our Sages of blessed memory said[1a] that this prohibition applies also to one who tells evil gossip, one who receives (hears) it, and a person who gives false testimony.[2]

The root reason for the precept is known: falsehood is abominable and corrupt in the eyes of all; there is nothing more abhorrent than it; and there is malediction and curse in the house of everyone who loves it. For *the Eternal Lord is a God of truth* (Psalms 31:6), and everything about Him is truth; and blessing abounds and takes effect only for those who liken themselves to Him in their deeds, thus to be truthful even as He is a God of truth; to have compassion even as it is known that He is compassionate; to be doing acts of kindness, even as He abounds in loving-kindness. But if anyone's deeds are the opposite of His good qualities, they are possessed of lies, which are in actual direct opposition to His qualities. Then likewise, the opposite of His qualities will always rest upon them. The opposite of the quality of blessing, which is inherently His, is malediction and curse. The opposite of joy, peace and pleasure, which exist with Him, is worry, quarreling, and suffering. All these are *the lot of a wicked man from God* (Job 20:29).

For this reason the Torah warned us to get far away from falsehood—as it is written, *From a false matter, keep far* (Exodus 23:7).

§74-75: TO HEAR NO LITIGANT ALONE / NO SINNER TO TESTIFY

שֶׁקֶר תִּרְחָק". וְהִנֵּה הַזְכִּירָהּ בּוֹ לָשׁוֹן רִחוּק לָרֹב מְאוּסוֹ מַה שֶּׁלֹּא הִזְכִּירָהּ כֵּן בְּכָל שְׁאָר הָאַזְהָרוֹת. וּמִצַּד הָרִחוּק הַזְהִירָתָנוּ שֶׁלֹּא נַטֶּה אָזְנֵנוּ כְּלָל לְשׁוּם דָּבָר שֶׁנַּחֲשֹׁב שֶׁהוּא שֶׁקֶר, וְאַף עַל פִּי שֶׁאֵין אָנוּ יוֹדְעִין בְּבֵרִיא שֶׁיְּהֵא אוֹתוֹ הַדָּבָר שֶׁקֶר, וּכְעִין מַה שֶּׁאָמְרוּ זִכְרוֹנָם לִבְרָכָה: הַרְחֵק מִן הַכִּעוּר וּמִן הַדּוֹמֶה לוֹ.

וּבְאָמְרִי מִדּוֹת בְּהַקָּדוֹשׁ בָּרוּךְ הוּא, יִתְבָּרַךְ, אֲנִי נִמְשָׁךְ בַּדָּבָר אַחַר דִּבְרֵי רַבּוֹתֵינוּ זִכְרוֹנָם לִבְרָכָה שֶׁיִּחֲסוּ אֵלָיו בָּרוּךְ הוּא שֵׁם מִדּוֹת עַל צַד הַמְּקַבְּלִים, אֲבָל הוּא בָּרוּךְ הוּא לְגָדְלוֹ וְיִחוּדוֹ מִצַּד עַצְמוֹ אֵין לְיַחֵס אֵלָיו מִדּוֹת, כִּי הוּא וְחָכְמָתוֹ וְחֶפְצוֹ וִיכָלְתּוֹ וּמִדּוֹתָיו אֶחָד בְּלִי שׁוּם שִׁתּוּף וּפֵרוּד בָּעוֹלָם.

מִדִּינֵי הַמִּצְוָה מַה שֶּׁאָמְרוּ זִכְרוֹנָם לִבְרָכָה שֶׁכָּל דַּיָּן שֶׁיּוֹדֵעַ בַּדִּין שֶׁהוּא מְרֻמָּה שֶׁחַיָּב לְהִסְתַּלֵּק מִמֶּנּוּ, וְלֹא יֹאמַר אֶחְתְּכֶנּוּ וִיהֵא קוֹלָר תָּלוּי בְּצַוְּארֵי הָעֵדִים. וְהַשְּׁבָחִים הַגְּדוֹלִים שֶׁמְּשַׁבְּחִין חֲכָמִים בְּבַקָּשַׁת הָאֱמֶת וְהַרְחָקַת הַשֶּׁקֶר בַּדִּין, וְיֶתֶר רַבֵּי הַפְּרָטִים, מְבֹאָרִים בְּסַנְהֶדְרִין וּבְמִדְרָשִׁים כְּמוֹ כֵן.

וְנוֹהֶגֶת בְּכָל מָקוֹם וּבְכָל זְמַן בִּזְכָרִים אֲבָל לֹא בִּנְקֵבוֹת, לְפִי שֶׁאֵינָן דַּנּוֹת, וְלָכֵן אֵינָן בִּכְלַל אַזְהָרָה זוֹ שֶׁלֹּא לְקַבֵּל טַעֲנַת בַּעַל דִּין אֶחָד שֶׁלֹּא בִּפְנֵי חֲבֵרוֹ אֲבָל מִכָּל מָקוֹם בִּכְלַל לָאו זֶה הֵן שֶׁלֹּא יַטְעִימוּ טַעֲנוֹתָן לַדַּיָּן שֶׁלֹּא בִּפְנֵי בַּעַל הַדִּין, וְכֵן מֻזְהָרוֹת לְהַרְחִיק מִכָּל שֶׁקֶר כְּמוֹ הָאֲנָשִׁים. וְעוֹבֵר עָלֶיהָ הֲרֵי הוּא כְּעוֹבֵר עַל מִצְוַת מֶלֶךְ, אֲבָל אֵין לוֹקִין עַל לָאו זֶה לְפִי שֶׁאֵין בּוֹ מַעֲשֶׂה.

[שֶׁלֹּא יָעִיד בַּעַל עֲבֵרָה]

עה שֶׁלֹּא נְקַבֵּל עֵדוּת אִישׁ חוֹטֵא וְלֹא נַעֲשֶׂה בִּשְׁבִיל עֵדוּתוֹ שׁוּם דָּבָר,

---

3. TB Ḥullin 44b.

4. Here our author echoes this well-known teaching of Rambam (*Guide*, MT *hilchoth y'sodé torah*) that man ascribes attributes to God subjectively, as a result of his confrontation and interaction with Divinity; it is *as if* He were kind, merciful, etc. But in His essential nature, He is infinitely constant and unchangeable, infinitely beyond human ken.

5. I.e. he discerns from the words of the witnesses that their testimony is not true; TB Sh'vu'oth 30b, and Rashi.

6. Cf. MT *hilchoth sanhedrin* xxv.

7. So TJ Sanhedrin iii 9.

Here, you see, Scripture used for it an expression of keeping a distance, on account of its great loathsomeness—[an expression] which it does not use in any other admonition. And for the sake of keeping far away, it warned us not to incline our ear at all to [hear] anything we believe to be false, even if we do not know for certain that this particular matter is a lie—in keeping with what our Sages of blessed memory said:[3] Keep far away from ugliness and from whatever resembles it.

Now, when I speak of qualities in regard to the Holy One, blessed is He, in this matter I follow in the wake of the words of our Sages of blessed memory, who ascribed to Him (be He blessed) the names of qualities (attributes) from the point of view of those who apperceive [His immanence]. Considering Him alone, however (be He blessed), in His greatness and uniqueness as the Divinity—qualities cannot be attributed to Him. For He, His wisdom, His desire, His prowess, and His attributes are all one, without any cooperation or separation whatever [between them].[4]

Among the laws of the precept there is what the Sages of blessed memory said, that if any judge knows about a case that he is being deceived [by false testimony],[5] he is duty-bound to withdraw from it; he is not to say, "I will decide it, and let the collar [of guilt] lie hung about the neck of the witnesses." Then there are the great praises with which the Sages laud the search for truth and the removal of falsehood in a court case. [These] and the rest of its many details are made clear in the Talmud tractate *Sanhedrin*, and in the Midrashim as well.[6]

It applies in every place and every time, for men but not for women, since they do not judge cases;[7] for this reason they are not included in this injunction not to hear the argument of one party to a lawsuit in the absence of his opponent. However, they are included in this prohibition [in this respect:] that they should not convey their arguments to a judge when [their] opponent is not there. They are likewise adjured to keep well away from every falsehood, in the same way as men. One who transgresses it is like a person who disobeys the command of a king; but no whiplashes are given over this negative precept, since its violation involves no [physical] action.

75 [THAT A SINNER SHOULD NOT GIVE TESTIMONY]

that we should not accept the testimony of a sinful man, nor should we do anything at all on account of his testimony. For it is

§75: THAT A SINNER SHOULD NOT GIVE TESTIMONY

שֶׁנֶּאֱמַר: אַל תָּשֶׁת יָדְךָ עִם רָשָׁע לִהְיוֹת עֵד חָמָס. וּבָא הַפֵּרוּשׁ: אַל תָּשֶׁת רָשָׁע עֵד, אַל תָּשֶׁת חָמָס עֵד, כְּלוֹמַר בַּעַל חָמָס, לְהוֹצִיא הַחַמְסָנִין וְאֶת הַגַּזְלָנִין שֶׁהֵם פְּסוּלִין לְעֵדוּת, שֶׁנֶּאֱמַר: כִּי יָקוּם עֵד חָמָס בְּאִישׁ.

שֹׁרֶשׁ מִצְוָה זוֹ נִגְלֶה, שֶׁכָּל מִי שֶׁעַל עַצְמוֹ לֹא חָס וְלֹא יָחוּס עַל מַעֲשָׂיו הָרָעִים לֹא יָחוּס עַל אֲחֵרִים, וְעַל כֵּן אֵין רָאוּי לְהַאֲמִינוֹ בַּדָּבָר.

מִדִּינֵי הַמִּצְוָה מַה שֶּׁאָמְרוּ זִכְרוֹנָם לִבְרָכָה שֶׁעֲשָׂרָה הֵן הַפְּסוּלִין לְעֵדוּת מִן הַתּוֹרָה, וְאֵלּוּ הֵן: נָשִׁים וַעֲבָדִים וּקְטַנִּים חֵרְשִׁים שׁוֹטִים סוּמִים רְשָׁעִים וַאֲנָשִׁים הַבְּזוּיִין בְּיוֹתֵר וּקְרוֹבִים וְנוֹגְעִים בָּעֵדוּת; הֲרֵי אֵלּוּ עֲשָׂרָה. וְטוּמְטוּם וְאַנְדְּרוֹגִינוּס בִּכְלַל נָשִׁים. וּמִי שֶׁחֶצְיוֹ עֶבֶד בִּכְלַל עֲבָדִים. הַנִּכְפֶּה בְּעֵת כְּפִיָּתוֹ בִּכְלַל שׁוֹטֶה, וְגַם שֶׁלֹּא בְּעֵת כְּפִיָּתוֹ צָרִיךְ הַדַּיָּן לְהִתְיַשֵּׁב בַּדָּבָר אִם דַּעְתּוֹ מְבֻלְבֶּלֶת מִצַּד הַחֳלִי. וְכֵן הַפְּתָאִים בְּיוֹתֵר שֶׁאֵינָם מְבִינִים דְּבָרִים הַסּוֹתְרִין זֶה אֶת זֶה, וְכֵן אֲנָשִׁים מְבֹהָלִים וְנֶחְפָּזִים בְּדַעְתָּן וּמִשְׁתַּגְּעִין בְּיוֹתֵר — כָּל אֵלּוּ בִּכְלַל שׁוֹטִים.

וְכֵן מַה שֶּׁאָמְרוּ זִכְרוֹנָם לִבְרָכָה אֵי זֶהוּ הַנִּקְרָא רָשָׁע שֶׁפָּסוּל מִן הַתּוֹרָה, וְאֵי זֶהוּ רָשָׁע שֶׁפָּסוּל מִדִּבְרֵיהֶם: כְּגוֹן הָעוֹבֵר עַל גֵּזֶל שֶׁל דִּבְרֵיהֶם, שֶׁהוּא פָּסוּל מִדִּבְרֵיהֶם, וּמִכְּלָלָם הוּא מְשַׂחֵק בְּקֻבִּיָּא שֶׁאֵין לוֹ אֻמָּנוּת אֶלָּא הוּא, וּמַפְרִיחֵי יוֹנִים בְּיִשּׁוּב, וּמְגַדְּלֵי בְּהֵמָה דַּקָּה.

וְהַחִלּוּק שֶׁהוּא בֵּין פָּסוּל מִדְּאוֹרַיְיתָא לְפָסוּל מִדִּבְרֵיהֶם, שֶׁבַּפָּסוּל מִן הַתּוֹרָה אָמְרוּ זִכְרוֹנָם לִבְרָכָה בָּטְלָה עֵדוּתוֹ אֲפִלּוּ קֹדֶם שֶׁהִכְרִיזוּ עָלָיו, וְהַפָּסוּל דְּרַבָּנָן עֵדוּתוֹ קַיֶּמֶת עַד שֶׁיַּכְרִיזוּ עָלָיו.

---

75 1. TB Sanhedrin 27a.
2. This term is generally understood to denote forcing a person to sell something against his will, e.g. by seizing it and leaving money for it.
3. Who commit *ḥamas*, as explained in note 2. (In this paragraph our author follows ShM negative precept §286.)
4. I.e. a person who is either deaf or mute; MT *hilchoth 'éduth* ix 11.
5. One who committed a sin punishable by whiplashes, and all the more certainly if he did something deserving a death sentence (*ibid.* x 2).
6. E.g. one who eats his food walking in the square, in the sight of everyone (*ibid.* xi 5).
7. I.e. they stand to gain by it. This listing is given by Rambam in MT *hilchoth 'éduth* ix 1, derived from TB Sh'vu'oth 30a, Bava Kamma 88a, Bava Bathra 43b, 155b, 'Arachin 18a, Sanhedrin 27a-b, Kiddushin 40b; see also *Lehem Mishneh* to Rambam *ibid.* 9.
8. Rambam *ibid.* 3.
9. I.e. if he was owned by two partners and one set him free; see *ibid.* 5.
10. *Ibid.* 9-10.
11. TB Sanhedrin 24b.
12. Those who raise pigeons, because even if raised in the privacy of their own

stated, *you shall not set your hand with a wicked man to be 'éd ḥamas, a malicious [false] witness* (Exodus 23:1); and this was explained[1] to mean, "Do not set a wicked man as a witness; do not set a malicious, lawless man as a witness," i.e. one possessed of *ḥamas*[2]—thus excluding those who seize property illegally[3] and robbers, that they are to be disqualified to bear witness—as it is stated, *If 'éd ḥamas, an illegally grasping witness rises up against any man* (Deuteronomy 19:16).

The root reason for this precept is obvious: Any person who has no concern for himself and will not care about his evil deeds, will have no care or concern for others. Therefore it is not proper to believe him about anything.

Among the laws of the precept there is what our Sages of blessed memory said, that there are ten who are disqualified as witnesses by the law of the Torah; these are: women, servants, children, the deaf and the mute,[4] the witless, the blind, the wicked,[5] very degraded people,[6] close kin, and those personally affected by the testimony;[7] here you have ten. A *tumtum* (one of uncertain gender) and a hermaphrodite are included under the category of women.[8] One who is half slave [and half free][9] is included under the category of servants. An epileptic at the time of a seizure is included under the category of the witless; even when he is not undergoing a seizure, the judge needs to consider the matter [to decide] if his mind is confused because of his illness. So also those who are extremely foolish, not understanding when things contradict one another, as well as people who are hasty and rash in their minds, and the deranged—these fall under the category of the witless.[10]

There is also what our Sages of blessed memory said[11]—who is the sort called wicked, that is disqualified [as a witness] by the Torah's law, and who is a wicked person disqualified by the ruling of the Sages: for example, if a person commits an act that is robbery by the edict of the Sages, he is disqualified by their ruling. Included in this category is a person who plays dice, having no other profession but that [gambling], those who raise pigeons within an inhabited area, and those who raise small domestic animals [e.g. sheep—in the land of Israel].[12]

There is, further, the difference between disqualification by Torah law and disqualification by edict of the Sages: If a person is disqualified by Torah law, the Sages of blessed memory taught[13] that if he gave testimony, his testimony is null and void even before it has been proclaimed about him [that he is unfit to bear witness]; but if he is

§75–76: NO SINNER TO TESTIFY / ON JUDGING A CAPITAL CASE

וְאֵי זוֹ תְשׁוּבָה מַחֲזִירוֹ לְכַשְׁרוּתוֹ, וְהוּא כְּמוֹ שֶׁאָמַר רַב אִידִי בַּר אָבִין בְּפֶרֶק זֶה בּוֹרֵר, דְּאָמַר רַב אִידִי בַּר אָבִין: הֶחָשׁוּד עַל הַטְּרֵפוֹת אֵינוֹ יוֹצֵא מֵחֶזְקָתוֹ עַד שֶׁיֵּלֵךְ לְמָקוֹם שֶׁאֵין מַכִּירִין אוֹתוֹ וְיַחֲזִיר בְּדָבָר אֲבֵדָה חָשׁוּב אוֹ יוֹצִיא טְרֵפָה מִתַּחַת יָדוֹ בְּדָבָר חָשׁוּב וּמִשֶּׁלּוֹ. וּכְמוֹ כֵן נֹאמַר בְּחָשׁוּד עַל עֲבֵרָה אַחֶרֶת לְפִי הַדּוֹמֶה. וְיֶתֶר פְּרָטֶיהָ מְבֹאָרִים שָׁם בְּסַנְהֶדְרִין.

וְנוֹהֶגֶת מִצְוָה זוֹ בְּכָל מָקוֹם וּבְכָל זְמַן בִּזְכָרִים אֲבָל לֹא בְנָשִׁים, שֶׁאֵינָן דָּנוֹת שֶׁיִּצְטָרְכוּ לְקַבֵּל עֵדוּת. וְעוֹבֵר עָלֶיהָ וְקִבֵּל עֵדוּת אִישׁ רָשָׁע וְעָשָׂה דָבָר בִּשְׁבִיל עֵדוּתוֹ עָבַר עַל לָאו, וְאֵין לוֹקִין עַל לָאו זֶה לְפִי שֶׁאֵין בּוֹ מַעֲשֶׂה. וַאֲפִלּוּ עָשָׂה בּוֹ מַעֲשֶׂה, בְּכָל דָּבָר שֶׁבְּמָמוֹן לְפִי שֶׁנִּתָּן לְהִשָּׁבוֹן אֵין לוֹקִין עָלָיו.

[שֶׁלֹּא לִנְטוֹת אַחֲרֵי רַבִּים בְּדִינֵי נְפָשׁוֹת בִּשְׁבִיל אֶחָד]

עו שֶׁלֹּא יֵלֵךְ הַדַּיָּן אַחַר דַּעַת הָרֹב בְּדִינֵי נְפָשׁוֹת כְּשֶׁיִּהְיֶה הַתּוֹסֶפֶת אִישׁ אֶחָד לְבָד. וּבֵאוּר זֶה כִּי כְּשֶׁתִּהְיֶה מַחֲלֹקֶת בֵּין הַדַּיָּנִין בְּדִין אָדָם אֶחָד וְאָמְרוּ קְצָתָם שֶׁהוּא חַיָּב מִיתָה וּקְצָתָם שֶׁאֵינוֹ חַיָּב, וְהָיוּ הַמְחַיְּבִין יוֹתֵר עַל הַמְזַכִּין אֶחָד, שֶׁלֹּא יַעֲשֶׂה הַדַּיָּן בַּחוֹטֵא כְּדִבְרֵי הַמְחַיְּבִין, שֶׁנֶּאֱמַר "לֹא תִהְיֶה אַחֲרֵי רַבִּים לְרָעֹת", כְּלוֹמַר לֹא תֵלֵךְ אַחַר הָרֹב שֶׁיְּזַדְּמֵן לַחְתֹּךְ מִשְׁפַּט מָוֶת, וְזֶהוּ לְשׁוֹן הַכָּתוּב שֶׁאָמַר לְרָעֹת, כְּלוֹמַר לְחִיּוּב מִיתָה, וְזֶהוּ כְּשֶׁיִּהְיֶה רֹב מְצַמְצָם, כְּלוֹמַר שֶׁהַהֶכְרֵעַ אֵינוֹ

---

property, their birds will get about and draw other pigeons to their dovecotes—which is an indirect form of theft (MT *hilchoth 'éduth* x 4; and see *Kessef Mishneh*). Those who raise small animals, because they generally graze in others' fields (TB *ibid.* 25b, Ta'anith 25a).

13. TB Sanhedrin 26b.
14. Literally, go out from.
15. So that his repentance there will not be deceitful, to fool anyone (*ibid.* Rashi).
16. Thus showing that he is no longer bound by a craving for wealth, etc. (the motivation for eating meat of *t'réfah* animals; *ibid.* Rashi).
17. Literally, will bring forth a *t'réfah* animal from under his hand.
18. E.g. if a creditor who lends at interest tears up the promissory notes that he holds (TB Sanhedrin 25b).
19. TJ Sanhedrin iii 9.
20. So that any wrong done can be made right.

disqualified [only] by the ruling of the Sages, then his testimony remains valid until he is proclaimed [to be disqualified].

[Then there is the law about] which kind of repentance returns him to his upright, respectable state. This is as R. 'Idi said in the tractate *Sanhedrin* (25a): For R. 'Idi b. 'Avin said: If someone is suspected about [eating meat of] *t'réfah* animals, he does not lose[14] his reputation and status [as a false, unacceptable witness] until he will go to a place where he is not known[15] and will return something of considerable value that was lost,[16] or will give up from his premises a *t'réfah* animal[17] of considerable value that belongs to him. It was likewise taught about a person suspected of some other transgression [that the requirement for him to be reaccepted would be] according to what parallels [this].[18] [These] and the rest of its details are explained there in the tractate *Sanhedrin*.

This precept is in effect in every place, at every time, for men but not for women, since they do not judge court cases,[19] that they should have to hear witnesses. If someone transgresses this and accepts the testimony of a wicked man, and acts [in the case] on the strength of his testimony, he has violated a negative precept. However, no whiplashes are given over this prohibition, since its violation involves no personal action. And even if he took some action in its regard, over anything to do with goods or possessions, since they are returnable[20] no whipping is given.

[NOT TO FOLLOW A MAJORITY OF ONE AMONG JUDGES IN A CAPITAL CASE]

76 that a [presiding] justice should not follow a majority in a capital case [where a person is on trial for his life] when it is a majority of one man alone. This means that if there is a division of opinion among the judges about the verdict for one man, some saying he deserves death and some saying he does not, if those who condemn are more than those who exonerate by one, the [presiding] judge should not deal with the sinner according to the words of those who condemn. For it is stated, *You shall not follow a majority to do evil* (Exodus 23:2)— i.e. do not follow a majority that will happen to occur, in order to decide on a verdict of death; for this is the sense of Scripture's phrase, "to do evil"—for a sentence of death. This means, though, when it is a minimal majority: i.e. when the dominance [of one side over the other] is due to only one man. However, when the dominance is by

§76–77: ON JUDGING & ARGUING IN CAPITAL CASES

אֶלָּא מֵחֲמַת אִישׁ אֶחָד, אֲבָל כְּשֶׁיִּהְיֶה הֶכְרֵעַ הָרָעָה בִּשְׁנַיִם אֲפִלּוּ לְרָעוֹת מַטִּין עַל פִּיהֶם. וּבִמְכִילְתָּא: הַטָּיָתְךָ לְטוֹבָה עַל פִּי עֵד אֶחָד, וּלְרָעָה עַל פִּי שְׁנָיִם.

מִשָּׁרְשֵׁי מִצְוָה זוֹ לְפִי שֶׁנִּצְטַוֵּינוּ לְהִדַּמּוֹת בְּמַעֲשֵׂינוּ לְמִדּוֹת הַשֵּׁם בָּרוּךְ הוּא, וּמִמִּדּוֹתָיו שֶׁהוּא רַב חֶסֶד כְּלוֹמַר שֶׁעוֹשֶׂה עִם בְּנֵי אָדָם לִפְנִים מִשּׁוּרַת הַדִּין, וְגַם אֲנַחְנוּ נִצְטַוֵּינוּ בְּכָךְ שֶׁיִּהְיֶה הַזְּכוּת בְּדִינֵי נְפָשׁוֹת יָתֵר עַל הַחִיּוּב, לְפִי שֶׁהוּא דָּבָר שֶׁאֵין לוֹ תַּשְׁלוּמִין.

וּמִשְּׁפָּטֵי הַמִּצְוָה בְּפֶרֶק ד׳ מִסַּנְהֶדְרִין, כְּמוֹ שֶׁכָּתַבְתִּי לְמַעְלָה בְּמִצְוַת עֲשֵׂה שֶׁל אַחֲרֵי רַבִּים לְהַטּוֹת. וְהָעוֹבֵר עָלֶיהָ וְחִיֵּב בְּרֹב הַמַּכְרִיעַ בְּאֶחָד עָבַר עַל מִצְוַת מֶלֶךְ, וְעָנְשׁוֹ גָּדוֹל מְאֹד, שֶׁגּוֹרֵם לְאַבֵּד נֶפֶשׁ שֶׁלֹּא כַדִּין.

[שֶׁלֹּא יְלַמֵּד חוֹבָה מִי שֶׁלִּמֵּד זְכוּת תְּחִלָּה בְּדִינֵי נְפָשׁוֹת]

עז שֶׁלֹּא יֵלֵךְ אֶחָד מִן הַדַּיָּנִין אַחַר דַּעַת דַּיָּן אֶחָד גָּדוֹל אוֹ אֲפִלּוּ אַחַר דַּעַת הָרַב עַל צַד שֶׁיַּאֲמִינֵהוּ לְחִיּוּב אוֹ לִזְכוּי מִבְּלִי שֶׁיִּהְיֶה הַדָּבָר מוּבָן אֶצְלוֹ בְּשִׂכְלוֹ, וְאִם הוּא דִּין הַתָּלוּי בִּגְזֵרַת הַכָּתוּב אוֹ מִצַּד גְּזֵרָה שָׁוָה אוֹ הֶקֵּשׁ שֶׁיְּהֵא יוֹדֵעַ אוֹתוֹ הוּא, וְלֹא יִסְמֹךְ וְיִבְטַח עַל אֶחָד מִן הַדַּיָּנִין, וְלֹא עַל הָרַב, שֶׁנֶּאֱמַר: וְלֹא תַעֲנֶה עַל רִב לִנְטֹת, לֹא תֹאמַר עַל הָרִיב דָּבָר לִנְטוֹת, כְּלוֹמַר מִצַּד הַנְּטִיָּה לְבַד, אַחַר דִּבְרֵי דַיָּן אֶחָד גָּדוֹל אוֹ אַחַר הָרַב וְלֹא מִצַּד הֲבָנָתְךָ אוֹ שֶׁתִּרְצֶה לְהַחֲרִישׁ מִמַּה שֶּׁבְּלִבְּךָ עַל הַדִּין וּלְהַטּוֹת אַחַר דִּבְרֵיהֶם, לֹא תַעֲשֶׂה כֵן.

וּלְשׁוֹן מְכִילְתָּא: לֹא תַעֲנֶה עַל רִב לִנְטוֹת, שֶׁלֹּא תֹאמַר דַּי לִי שֶׁאֶהְיֶה כְּר׳

---

76   1. Literally, your inclining or turning. (In this paragraph our author follows ShM negative precept §282.)

2. While this is implicit in Mechilta on the verse, the expression is found in Mishnah, Sanhedrin i 1 (TB 2a), and evidently in MdRSbY (MhG).

3. I.e. to free a man from the death penalty if the judges voting to condemn him are a majority by one vote.

4. In the original work, as found in manuscripts and the first edition (Venice 1523), in each *sidrah* the positive precepts are given first, and then all the negative precepts; hence the original reads "above." In later editions (and so here) all the precepts in each *sidrah* were rearranged strictly in order of the verses; hence this occurs below.

77   1. I.e. MdRSbY (cited in Midrash haGadol), which Rambam similarly quotes in ShM negative precept §283 (which our author follows here in the first four paragraphs).

2. The word *riv* (controversy) is understood as though it were *rav* (rabbi), since it is written in Scripture without a *yod*; see below.

⟨302⟩

two, then even "to do evil" we incline to act on their word. In the Midrash *Mechilta* [it is expressed so]: your decision[1] for good [may be] on the basis of one witness; to do evil, on the basis of two.[2]

At the root of this precept lies the reason that we were commanded to emulate in our actions the qualities of the Eternal Lord, blessed is He. [One] of His attributes is that He abounds in loving-kindness—i.e. He deals with human beings beyond the strict line [letter] of the law. So we were commanded [in turn] about this: that innocence should outweigh guilt in capital cases,[3] because it [an enacted verdict of guilty] is something for which there is no rectification [no way to make it right].

The rules and norms of the precept are in chapter 4 of the tractate *Sanhedrin*, as I have written below, about the positive precept|to|follow a majority (§78).[4] If someone disobeys this and renders a verdict of guilty on account of a majority of one, he has violated a commandment of the King. His punishment will be very great, as he causes a living person to perish unjustly.

77 [A JUDGE WHO ARGUES FOR INNOCENCE IN A CAPITAL CASE SHOULD NOT ARGUE FOR GUILT AFTERWARD]

that one of the judges should not follow the view of a greater [more learned] justice, or even the view of the majority, so as to believe him or it [blindly] to decide for the guilt or the innocence [of the person on trial] without having the matter understood by him, in his mind. Even if it is a matter of law [involved in the case] which depends on a decree of Scripture, or it is learned through a *g'zérah shavah* (an inference made because two verses contain the same root word) or a *hekkesh* (an analogy between two matters which Scripture indicates as having similar laws), he must himself know it, and not rely on and trust to one of the judges, or the majority. For it is stated, *neither shall you respond over a controversy to incline to follow* (Exodus 23 : 2), which means, "Do not say anything about a controversy inclining to follow," i.e. merely by turning to follow the words of one elder, eminent judge or a majority, but not through your own understanding. Should you want to be silent about what is in your heart regarding the trial and turn to follow their words—do not do so.

The Midrash *Mechilta*[1] expresses it so: *neither shall you respond over a controversy to incline to follow:* You should not say, "It is enough for me that I should be like Rabbi[2] So-and-so," but rather declare

§77: ABOUT A JUDGE ARGUING FOR ACQUITTAL IN A CAPITAL CASE

פְּלוֹנִי אֶלָּא אָמַר מַה שֶׁלְּפָנֶיךָ. יָכוֹל אַף דִּינֵי מָמוֹנוֹת כֵּן, תַּלְמוּד לוֹמַר אַחֲרֵי רַבִּים לְהַטּוֹת.

וּבְזֶה הַלָּאו בְּעַצְמוֹ נִכְלָל שֶׁהַמְלַמֵּד זְכוּת בְּדִינֵי נְפָשׁוֹת לֹא יַחֲזֹר וִילַמֵּד חוֹבָה, בְּמָה שֶׁאָמַר "לֹא תַעֲנֶה עַל רִב לִנְטֹת", כְּלוֹמַר לֹא יִהְיֶה פֶּתַח דַּרְכְּךָ לְהַטּוֹת אוֹתוֹ לְחוֹבָה.

וּכְמוֹ כֵן נִכְלָל בּוֹ אֵין פּוֹתְחִין בְּדִינֵי נְפָשׁוֹת לְחוֹבָה, וְיָבֹא הַפֵּרוּשׁ כֵּן: לֹא תַעֲנֶה עַל רִב לִנְטֹת, כְּלוֹמַר לֹא יִהְיֶה פֶּתַח דְּבָרֶיךָ לְהַטּוֹת אוֹתוֹ לְחוֹבָה, כִּי עַל כָּרְחֵנוּ בִּתְחִלַּת הַדִּין יֵשׁ לָנוּ לְפָרֵשׁ אוֹתוֹ, שֶׁאִי אֶפְשָׁר לוֹמַר שֶׁבְּכָל הַדִּין יַזְהִיר שֶׁלֹּא תַעֲנֶה בּוֹ לְחוֹבָה, שֶׁאִם כֵּן לֹא יִהְיֶה שׁוּם אָדָם נִדּוֹן לְעוֹלָם.

וּכְמוֹ כֵן שָׁמַעְנוּ מִזֶּה הַלָּאו שֶׁאֵין מַתְחִילִין בְּדִינֵי נְפָשׁוֹת מִן הַגָּדוֹל אֶלָּא שֶׁלְּמַטָּה הֵימֶנּוּ יַגִּיד תְּחִלָּה דַּעְתּוֹ, וְזֶה "וְלֹא תַעֲנֶה עַל רִב" כְּמוֹ עַל רַב, כִּי בְּלֹא יוּ"ד הוּא נִכְתָּב, כְּלוֹמַר לֹא תַעֲנֶה עַל גָּדוֹל אֶלָּא הוּא יַעֲנֶה אֵלֶיךָ, שֶׁאַתָּה תְדַבֵּר תְּחִלָּה. וְהָעִנְיָן הוּא כְּדֵי שֶׁלֹּא יִסָּמְכוּ עַל דִּבְרֵי הַגָּדוֹל.

כָּל אֵלֶּה הַדְּבָרִים לָמַדְנוּ מִ"לֹא תַעֲנֶה עַל רִב לִנְטֹת", וְעִנְיָן זֶה מִכֹּחַ חָכְמַת הַתּוֹרָה שֶׁיֵּשׁ לְהָבִין מִדָּבָר אֶחָד מִמֶּנָּה כַּמָּה דְּבָרִים; זֶהוּ שֶׁאָמְרוּ זִכְרוֹנָם לִבְרָכָה: שִׁבְעִים פָּנִים יֵשׁ לַתּוֹרָה. וּלְפִי שֶׁיּוֹדֵעַ אֱלֹהִים כִּי הָעָם מְקַבְּלֵי הַתּוֹרָה בְּהִתְנַהֲגָם עַל הַדֶּרֶךְ שֶׁנִּצְטַוּוּ בָּהּ יִהְיוּ נְכוֹנִים אֶל הַחָכְמָה וְאֶל הַתְּבוּנָה וְיָבִינוּ בָהּ כָּל הַצָּרִיךְ לָהֶם אֶל הַנְהָגַת הָעוֹלָם, סָתַם לָהֶם הַדְּבָרִים בִּמְקוֹמוֹת וּמָסַר לָהֶם הַפֵּרוּשׁ עַל יַד הַסַּרְסוּר הַגָּדוֹל אֲשֶׁר בֵּינֵיהֶם וּבֵינוֹ וְלֹא נְתָנָהּ בְּמִלּוֹת רְחָבוֹת יוֹתֵר, לְפִי שֶׁכָּל

2a. MH notes that in civil cases too a judge is not to reach his decision in this way, but if he does so, he does not violate any negative precept.

3. I.e. do not veer away from your original view of acquittal. So ShM *ibid.* and MT *hilchoth sanhedrin* x 2, and Midrash haGadol, evidently from the lost MdRSbY, which Rambam had.

4. This too occurs in the sources given in note 3.

5. The beginning of the trial. Rather, the opening words, addressed to the accused person, are, "If you did not commit the crime, do not be afraid" (see §78, note 11).

6. Since no judge might ever speak to demonstrate his guilt.

7. And Scripture is written without vowel marks; TB Sanhedrin 36b; TJ iv 7.

8. So MT *hilchoth sanhedrin* x 6.

9. In 'Othioth d'R. 'Akiva.

10. I.e. Moses, so designated in TJ M'gillah iv 1.

what there is before you [to say]. I might think that this is so also in civil cases? Hence Scripture states, *after a majority to incline to follow* (Exodus 23:2).[2a]

In this negative precept itself is included [the rule] that if someone argues to show the innocence [of the person on trial] he is not to turn about and argue to show his guilt—inasmuch as Scripture states, *neither shall you respond over a controversy to incline to follow*. In other words: do not open your mouth to incline him to guilt.[3]

So too, included in this [is the rule:] One does not begin in a capital case by [speaking about the accused person's] guilt.[4] This would be the interpretation: *neither shall you respond over a controversy to incline*—i.e. the opening of your words[5] should not be to incline (point) him to a verdict of guilt. For whether we want to or not, we have to interpret this in regard to the beginning of the trial. It is impossible to say that throughout a trial Scripture gives an injunction that "you shall not respond" about him regarding his [possible] guilt—for if that were the case, no man in the world will ever be condemned [in a capital case].[6]

We likewise learn from this negative precept that we do not begin in a capital case with a greater judge but rather one below him (in learning, rank, etc.) should speak his mind first. Here the verse, *neither shall you respond over riv, a controversy*, is [understood] as though [it read] "over *rav*, a master scholar," since the word is written without a *yod*.[7] In other words: do not respond to someone greater, but rather let him respond to you—you are to speak first. The reason is that they [the younger ones] should not rely on the words of the elder, greater judge.[8]

All these matters we have learned from the verse, *neither shall you respond over a controversy, to incline*. This sort of thing derives from the power of the wisdom of the Torah: for out of one point in it many points are to be understood. In this sense our Sages of blessed memory said:[9] There are seventy facets to the Torah. Now, God knows that the people who received the Torah, as they behave in the way they were commanded in it, will be given to wisdom and understanding, and will comprehend in it everything they need about the conduct of the world. Therefore He left the words "closed up" for them (terse, elliptic) in certain places, and transmitted the interpretation through the great mediator[10] who stood between them and Him, and He did not give it [the Torah] in more ample, expanded

§77: ABOUT A JUDGE ARGUING FOR ACQUITTAL IN A CAPITAL CASE

מְלוּתֶיהָ גְּזוּרוֹת וּמְחֻיָּבוֹת בְּחֶשְׁבּוֹנָן וּבְצוּרָתָן לִהְיוֹת כָּכָה, כִּי מִלְּבַד מַשְׁמָעוֹת מִצְווֹתֶיהָ הַיְקָרוֹת שֶׁאָנוּ מְבִינִין בָּהּ נִכְלְלוּ בָהּ חָכְמוֹת גְּדוֹלוֹת וּמְפֹאָרוֹת, עַד שֶׁהֶעֱלוּ רַבּוֹתֵינוּ זִכְרוֹנָם לִבְרָכָה גֹּדֶל הַחָכְמָה שֶׁהִנִּיחַ הָאֵל בָּרוּךְ הוּא בְּתוֹכָהּ, שֶׁאָמְרוּ עָלֶיהָ שֶׁהִבִּיט הַקָּדוֹשׁ בָּרוּךְ הוּא בָּהּ וּבָרָא אֶת הָעוֹלָם.

מִשָּׁרְשֵׁי מִצְוָה זוֹ כְּמוֹ שֶׁאָמַרְנוּ תְּחִלָּה שֶׁלֹּא יֵלֵךְ אֶחָד מִן הַדַּיָּנִין אַחַר חֲבֵרָיו אֶלָּא יָבִין הַדְּבָרִים מֵעַצְמוֹ. הַטַּעַם מִפְּנֵי שֶׁאֶפְשָׁר שֶׁמִּתּוֹךְ כָּךְ יָבֹא הַדִּין כֻּלּוֹ לִפְעָמִים עַל דַּעַת אֶחָד מֵהֶם, הָבֵן הַדָּבָר כִּי כֵן הוּא, וְלֹא רָצָה הַשֵּׁם לִמְסֹר דִּין נֶפֶשׁ לְדַעַת אֶחָד. אֲבָל בְּדִין מָמוֹן שֶׁנִּתַּן לְהֶשְׁבּוֹן אֵין חוֹשְׁשִׁין לְכָל זֶה, וַאֲפִלּוּ לִשְׁלֹשָׁה מוֹסְרִין אוֹתוֹ לְכַתְּחִלָּה עַל סָמַךְ דְּאִי אֶפְשָׁר דְּלֵיכָּא בְהוּ חַד דְּגָמִיר. וּשְׁאָר הַדְּבָרִים שֶׁנִּלְמְדוּ מִמֶּנּוּ, כְּגוֹן מְלַמֵּד זְכוּת מְלַמֵּד חוֹבָה, וְשֶׁאֵין פּוֹתְחִין לְחוֹבָה, וְאֵין מַתְחִילִין מִן הַגָּדוֹל, כָּל זֶה לְחֶמְלַת הַשֵּׁם עַל בְּרִיּוֹתָיו כְּאָדָם הַחוֹמֵל עַל בָּנָיו, דֶּרֶךְ מָשָׁל, כְּמוֹ שֶׁכָּתוּב: בָּנִים אַתֶּם לַיְיָ אֱלֹהֵיכֶם, וְגוֹמֵר.

וְהַגַּע עַצְמְךָ עַל דֶּרֶךְ מָשָׁל: אִם יוֹלִיד אִישׁ מֵאָה וּבָנָה לָהֶם עִיר וְהוֹשִׁיבָם שָׁם וְרָאָה שֶׁלֹּא יִתְקַיְּמוּ בַּיִּשּׁוּב אֶלָּא אִם כֵּן יִגְזֹר עֲלֵיהֶם שֶׁכָּל הַמַּכֶּה רֵעֵהוּ יֵעָנֵשׁ בְּמָמוֹנוֹ, וְאִם יְמִיתֵהוּ יוּמָת, וְקָם הָאֶחָד וְעָבַר עַל גְּזֵרָתוֹ, אִם יִמְחַל לוֹ הֲרֵי הַיִּשּׁוּב בָּטֵל, שֶׁלֹּא תִּשָּׁאֵר מוֹרָא עַל הַנִּשְׁאָרִים, מַה יֵּשׁ לוֹ לַעֲשׂוֹת וְאַל יִרְאֶה בְּמוֹת בְּנוֹ הַשֵּׁנִי, יַחֲזֹר עַל כָּל פָּנִים בְּכָל צַד שֶׁיּוּכַל לְפָטְרוֹ מִן הַדִּין, אִם יוּכַל מוּטָב, וְאִם אִי אֶפְשָׁר בְּשׁוּם צַד יְצַוֶּה לַהֲמִיתוֹ כְּדֵי לְקַיֵּם יִשּׁוּב הָאֲחֵרִים; וְכֵן הַדָּבָר הַזֶּה, וַהֲבִינֵיהוּ.

---

11. In B'réshith Rabbah 1, 1.
12. I.e. if each follows either him or another judge who followed him, etc.
13. By Torah law one learned judge is sufficient; the Sages permitted using any three as judges because it is assumed that one of them will be learned enough to rule; TB Sanhedrin 3b.
14. Expression derived from Ecclesiastes 6:3.
15. By murdering one of the 100 sons.

SIDRAH MISHPATIM

words. For all its words are decreed and required, in their sum and their form, to be such—since apart from the meaning of its precious *mitzvoth* which we understand in it, great and resplendent wisdoms were included in it, so much so that our Sages of blessed memory exalted the greatness of the wisdom that God, blessed is He, set down within it by saying about it[11] that the Holy One, blessed is He, looked in it and [thus] created the world.

At the root of this precept, as we stated at the beginning, lies the purpose that no one of the judges should follow his colleagues, but each should understand matters for himself. The reason is that [otherwise] it is possible, as a result, that the verdict reached will be entirely according to the thinking of one of them.[12] Understand the matter, that it is so. And the Eternal Lord (be He blessed) did not want to give over the verdict on a man's life to one person's view. In a civil case, though, where the verdict is given to rectification [one can make amends for it], there is no fear of all this; and it can be given over at the start even to [a *beth din* of] three, on the basis of the fact that it is impossible that not even one of them will be learned.[13]

As to the other rules that were derived from it [from the verse], for instance, that one who speaks for exoneration [of the accused] should not speak to demonstrate his guilt; the trial is not begun [by speaking] of his guilt; and one does not begin [with] the view of a greater scholar—all this is on account of the compassion the Eternal Lord has for His creatures, by way of analogy like a man who has compassion for his children—as it is written, *You are children to the Lord your God*, etc. (Deuteronomy 14:1).

Now, imagine this by way of a parable: A man fathered 100 [sons],[14] and he built a city for them and settled them there. Then he saw that they would not endure in the settlement unless he decreed for them that whoever wounded his neighbor would be punished through his wealth, and if he killed him he would be put to death. Then one rose up and disobeyed the decree.[15] If he should forgive him, the settlement will be reduced to nothing, for no [restraining] fear will remain upon them. What is there for him to do, then, that he should not see his second son die? Let him, in every possible way, go over every possible aspect by which he can set him free by law. If he is able to, good. If it is not possible from any angle, he will order him put to death, in order to uphold the settled communal existence of the others. So is this matter. Understand it.

§77: ABOUT A JUDGE ARGUING FOR ACQUITTAL IN A CAPITAL CASE

מִדִּינֵי הַמִּצְוָה מַה שֶּׁאָמְרוּ זִכְרוֹנָם לִבְרָכָה שֶׁאִם פָּתְחוּ כֻלָּם לְחוֹבָה שֶׁפָּטוּר, וְאִם הַמְחַיְּבִים וְהַמְזַכִּים שָׁוִים שֶׁמּוֹסִיפִין עֲלֵיהֶם, וְעַד כַּמָּה מוֹסִיפִין, וְאִם אוֹמַר אֶחָד אֵינִי יוֹדֵעַ מַה יְּהֵא בְּכָךְ, וּמַה שֶּׁאָמְרוּ שֶׁהַמְלַמֵּד זְכוּת אֵינוֹ חוֹזֵר וּמְלַמֵּד חוֹבָה, דַּוְקָא בִּשְׁעַת מַשָּׂא וּמַתָּן נֶאֱמַר, אֲבָל בִּגְמַר דִּין חוֹזֵר לְהִמָּנוֹת עִם הַמְחַיְּבִין. וְאִם פָּתַח וְאָמַר אֶחָד "יֵשׁ לִי לְלַמֵּד זְכוּת" וְנִשְׁתַּתֵּק אוֹ מֵת, שֶׁהוּא כְּמִי שֶׁאֵינוֹ, וְהַמְזַכֶּה נָמַק מַשְׁקִין אוֹתוֹ בִּגְמַר דִּין כְּאִלּוּ הוּא בִּמְקוֹמוֹ. וְתַלְמִיד הַבָּא לְלַמֵּד חוֹבָה מְשַׁתְּקִין אוֹתוֹ, וְאִם אָמַר לְלַמֵּד זְכוּת מַעֲלִין אוֹתוֹ עִם סַנְהֶדְרִין, וְאִם יֵשׁ מַמָּשׁ בִּדְבָרָיו שׁוֹמְעִין לוֹ וְאֵינוֹ יוֹרֵד מִשָּׁם לְעוֹלָם, וְאִם אֵין מַמָּשׁ בִּדְבָרָיו אֵינוֹ יוֹרֵד מִשָּׁם כָּל אוֹתוֹ הַיּוֹם דֶּרֶךְ מוּסָר, וְהַנִּדּוֹן בְּעַצְמוֹ שֶׁאָמַר "יֵשׁ לִי לְלַמֵּד עַל עַצְמִי זְכוּת" שׁוֹמְעִין לוֹ וְהוּא שֶׁיֵּשׁ מַמָּשׁ בִּדְבָרָיו, וְיֶתֶר פְּרָטֶיהָ, מְבֹאָרִים. בְּפֶרֶק ז' מִסַּנְהֶדְרִין.

וְנוֹהֶגֶת מִצְוָה זוֹ בִּזְכָרִים אֲבָל לֹא בְּנָשִׁים, שֶׁאֵינָן דָּנוֹת, כְּמוֹ שֶׁאָמַרְנוּ לְמַעְלָה בְּהַרְבֵּה מְקוֹמוֹת. וְאַל יִקְשֶׁה עָלֶיךָ מַה שֶּׁכָּתוּב בִּדְבוֹרָה הַנְּבִיאָה: הִיא שֹׁפְטָה אֶת יִשְׂרָאֵל. שֶׁאֶפְשָׁר לָנוּ לְתָרֵץ שֶׁלֹּא לְתָרֵץ הַדִּין נֶחְתָּךְ עַל פִּיהָ אֲבָל הָיְתָה אִשָּׁה חֲכָמָה וּנְבִיאָה וְהָיוּ נוֹשְׂאִים וְנוֹתְנִים עִמָּהּ בִּדְבָרִים שֶׁל אִסּוּר וְהֶתֵּר וְדִינִין גַּם כֵּן, וְלָכֵן כָּתוּב עָלֶיהָ "הִיא שֹׁפְטָה אֶת יִשְׂרָאֵל". אוֹ נֹאמַר שֶׁקִּבְּלוּהָ לָדוּן עֲלֵיהֶם רָאשֵׁי יִשְׂרָאֵל וְאַחֲרֵיהֶן כָּל אָדָם דָּן עַל פִּיהָ, דִּבְקַבָּלָה וַדַּאי הַכֹּל כְּשֵׁרִים, דְּכָל תְּנַאי שֶׁבְּמָמוֹן קַיָּם.

וּמִכָּל מָקוֹם כָּל זֶה שֶׁאָמַרְנוּ שֶׁאֵינָן דָּנוֹת הוּא כְּדַעַת קְצָת הַמְפָרְשִׁים וּכְדַעַת

---

16. TB Sanhedrin 17a; MT *hilchoth sanhedrin* ix 1.

17. Since a *beth din* would never have an even number of judges, this necessarily means that at least one judge said, "I do not know" (see note 19) or after rising to speak in the accused person's favor, he was struck dumb or died (see below, at note 21).

18. TB Sanhedrin 41a.

19. He is considered as though not there, and he may not speak thereafter for a verdict to condemn; *ibid*. (MT *ibid*. 2).

20. TB Sanhedrin 34a.

21. Because he never made his point or gave his reason. *Ibid*. 43a; MT *ibid*. x 4.

22. I.e. voting for acquittal—because he gave his reason; *ibid*. 34a.

23. *Ibid*. 42a.

24. So as not to embarrass him; *ibid*.

25. I.e. she would not act as judge but merely instruct them in the law (*tosafoth* to TB Niddah 50a, s.v. *kol*); but the male judges would give the verdicts.

26. So TB K'thuboth 56a, etc. In other words, all agreed to abide by Deborah's rulings in civil cases; but she did not judge capital cases.

⟨308⟩

SIDRAH **MISHPATIM**

Among the laws of the precept there is what our Sages of blessed memory said, that if all [the judges] began by speaking of [the accused person's] guilt, he goes free;[16] if those who would condemn him and those who would acquit him are equal in number,[17] more [judges] are added—and up to what number may be added;[18] and if one [judge] says, "I do not know" [how to decide the case], what should be [done] about it.[19] Then there is what the Sages said, that [the rule that] one who speaks for the exoneration [of the accused] may not turn about and speak for his condemnation, holds only during the discussion; but at the conclusion of the trial, he can turn about to be counted with those who consider him guilty.[20] If one opened his statement saying, "I have something to say to show his innocence," and he was struck dumb or he died, then he is [considered] as one who is [simply] not [there at all].[21] If someone spoke for acquittal and he died, he is regarded at the end of the trial as if he were in his place.[22] If a disciple comes to demonstrate the guilt [of the accused] he is silenced.[23] But if he proposed to speak in his favor, he is brought up [to take a place] with the *sanhedrin* (high court); and if there is substance in his words, he is heeded, and he does not go down [is not demoted] from there ever.[23] If there is nothing of substance in his words, he does not go down from there the entire day, for ethical reasons.[24] If the person on trial himself said, "I have something to say to show something in my favor," he is listened to—that is, if there is substance in his words.[23] These and the rest of its details are explained in chapter 7 of the Talmud tractate *Sanhedrin*.

This precept applies to men, but not to women, since they do not judge [court cases], as we have stated above in many places. Now, let it not be a difficulty for you that it is written about Deborah the prophetess, *she was judging Israel* (Judges 4:4). We can answer that the verdict [in a case] was not decided by her word, but rather, she was a wise woman and a prophetess, and they would discuss and consider with her even questions of what is permitted and forbidden, and so too cases of law;[25] and therefore it is written of her, *she was judging Israel*. Or, we can say that the leaders of Israel accepted her [granted her the authority] to judge for them, and following them everyone would decide cases by her word. For upon acceptance [as judges] all are properly fit [to sit in judgment], since any condition [accepted] in matters of goods and possessions remains in force.[26]

⟨309⟩ In any case, though, all this that we have said, that women do not

הַיְרוּשַׁלְמִי, שֶׁכֵּן נִמְצָא שָׁם מְפֹרָשׁ. אֲבָל לָדַעַת קְצָת מִן הַמְּפָרְשִׁים כְּשֵׁרוֹת הֵן לָדוּן, וְאָמְרוּ כִּי מִקְרָא מָלֵא הוּא, שֶׁנֶּאֱמַר "הִיא שֹׁפְטָה". וּמַה שֶּׁאָמְרוּ בְּסַנְהֶדְרִין, דְּכָל שֶׁאֵינוֹ כָּשֵׁר לְהָעִיד אֵינוֹ כָּשֵׁר לָדוּן, וְנָשִׁים וַדַּאי אֵינָן כְּשֵׁרוֹת לְהָעִיד כִּדְמוּכָח שָׁם, אֶפְשָׁר שֶׁיֹּאמְרוּ לְפִי דַעְתָּם זֶה לְפִי שֶׁאֵין לְמֵדִין מִן הַכְּלָלוֹת. וְהַנִּרְאֶה מִן הַדְּבָרִים וּמִן הַסְּבָרָא שֶׁאֵינָן בְּתוֹרַת דִּין, כִּדְאִיתָא בִּירוּשַׁלְמִי וְכִדְמַשְׁמַע לְפִי גְמָרִין דֶּרֶךְ פְּשִׁיטוּת.

וְנוֹהֶגֶת מִצְוָה זוֹ בְּאֶרֶץ יִשְׂרָאֵל בִּלְבָד, שֶׁאֵין דִּינֵי דִינֵי נְפָשׁוֹת אֶלָּא שָׁם. וְהָעוֹבֵר עַל זֶה וְלֹא רָצָה לִלְמֹד בַּדִּין מַה שֶּׁרוֹאֶה בְּדַעְתּוֹ וְסוֹמֵךְ עַל חֲבֵרָיו, אוֹ שֶׁפָּתַח לְחוֹבָה, אוֹ שֶׁחָזַר וְלִמֵּד חוֹבָה אַחַר הַזְּכוּת, אוֹ גָדוֹל שֶׁפָּתַח תְּחִלָּה, עָבְרוּ עַל לָאו; וְאֵין לוֹקִין עָלָיו לְפִי שֶׁאֵין בּוֹ מַעֲשֶׂה.

[מִצְוַת הַטָּיָה אַחֲרֵי רַבִּים]

עח לִנְטוֹת אַחֲרֵי רַבִּים, וְהוּא כְּשֶׁיִּפֹּל מַחֲלֹקֶת בֵּין הַחֲכָמִים בְּדִין מִדִּינֵי הַתּוֹרָה כֻּלָּהּ, וּכְמוֹ כֵן בְּדִין פְּרָטִי, כְּלוֹמַר שֶׁיִּהְיֶה בֵּין רְאוּבֵן וְשִׁמְעוֹן, עַל דֶּרֶךְ מָשָׁל, כְּשֶׁתִּהְיֶה הַמַּחֲלֹקֶת בֵּין דַּיָּנֵי עִירָם שֶׁקְּצָתָם דָּנִין לְחִיּוּב וּקְצָתָם לִפְטוֹר, לִנְטוֹת אַחַר הָרֹב לְעוֹלָם, שֶׁנֶּאֱמַר: אַחֲרֵי רַבִּים לְהַטֹּת. וּבְבֵאוּר אָמְרוּ זִכְרוֹנָם לִבְרָכָה: רַבָּה דְּאוֹרַיְתָא.

וּבְחִירַת רֹב זֶה לְפִי הַדּוֹמֶה הוּא כְּשֶׁשְּׁנֵי הַכִּתּוֹת הַחוֹלְקוֹת יְדוּעוֹת בְּחָכְמַת הַתּוֹרָה בְּשָׁוֶה, שֶׁאֵין לוֹמַר שֶׁכַּת חֲכָמִים מוּעֶטֶת לֹא תַכְרִיעַ כַּת בּוּרִים מְרֻבָּה

---

27. TJ Sanhedrin iii 9, Sh'vu'oth iv 1 (quoted in *tosafoth, ibid.*).

28. Wherever we learn a general rule [in the Talmud] we do not say there are no exceptions, since there can be a general rule under which certain matters are not covered (Rashi, TB 'Eruvin 27a).

29. See §47, note 7, which applies equally here.

§78   1. TB Ḥullin 11a. The paragraph is based on ShM positive precept §175. (The verse is rendered here literally, in keeping with the context. It is generally translated quite differently.)

2. It is evident from TB Yevamoth 14a.

judge [cases of law], is according to the view of some authorities, and by the ruling of the Jerusalem Talmud, for so is it to be found there explicitly.[27] In the view of certain other authorities, however, they are properly fit to act as judges; and they asserted that this is a direct, full [ruling by] a verse, since it is stated, "she was judging." As to what our Sages said in the tractate *Sanhedrin* (34b) that whoever is not qualified to bear witness is not qualified to act as judge, and women are certainly not qualified to act as witnesses, as is proven there—perhaps they would say, following their view, that this is because we do not draw specific inferences from general rules.[28] It would seem right, though, from the subject matter and by logical reasoning, that they do not belong in the judgment of court cases, as we read in the Jerusalem Talmud, and as is apparent from the [relevant] Talmudic passages in their plain meaning.

This precept would be in force in the land of Israel alone: for capital cases may be judged nowhere else but there.[29] If someone transgresses this and does not wish to present at a trial what he sees in his mind, but relies on his colleagues; or if he opens [the trial] by referring to the accused person's guilt; or if he retracts and speaks for condemnation after [speaking for the accused person's] exoneration; or if a great (very learned) judge opened his discourse first—they have violated a negative precept. No whipping is given for it, though, since it involves no [physical] action.

[THE PRECEPT OF FOLLOWING THE MAJORITY IN LEGAL DECISIONS]

78 to follow a majority: i.e. when a controversy occurs among the Sages about some law among the laws of the entire Torah; and so too about a particular [matter of] law—in other words, a court case between Reuben and Simeon, to give an example. If the controversy is among the justices of their city, some judging [a man] guilty (liable) and some innocent—the majority is always to be followed. For it is stated, *after a majority, to follow* (Exodus 23:2). In clarifying it, our Sages of blessed memory said that [the rule of] the majority is a law of the Torah.[1]

The choice of this majority is evidently when the two contending groups know the wisdom of the Torah equally.[2] For it cannot be said that a small group of Torah scholars should not outweigh a large group of ignoramuses, even if it is as immense [in number] as those

§78: TO FOLLOW THE MAJORITY IN LEGAL DECISIONS

וַאֲפִלּוּ כְיוֹצְאֵי מִצְרַיִם, אֲבָל בְּהַשָּׂגַת הַחָכְמָה אוֹ בְּקֵרוּב הוֹדִיעָתְנוּ הַתּוֹרָה שֶׁרִבּוּי הַדֵּעוֹת יַסְכִּימוּ לְעוֹלָם אֶל הָאֱמֶת יוֹתֵר מִן הַמְּעוּט. וּבֵין שֶׁיַּסְכִּימוּ לָאֱמֶת אוֹ לֹא יַסְכִּימוּ לְפִי דַּעַת הַשּׁוֹמֵעַ, הַדִּין נוֹתֵן שֶׁלֹּא נָסוּר מִדֶּרֶךְ הָרֹב.

וּמַה שֶּׁאֲנִי אוֹמֵר כִּי בְּחִירַת הָרֹב לְעוֹלָם הוּא בְּשֶׁשְּׁנֵי הַחוֹלְקִים שָׁוִוּת בְּחָכְמַת הָאֱמֶת, כִּי כֵן נֶאֱמַר בְּכָל מָקוֹם חוּץ מִן הַסַּנְהֶדְרִין, שֶׁבָּהֶם לֹא נְדַקְדֵּק בְּהִיוֹתָם חוֹלְקִין אֵי זוֹ כַת יוֹדַעַת יוֹתֵר אֶלָּא לְעוֹלָם נַעֲשֶׂה כְּדִבְרֵי הָרֹב מֵהֶם. וְהַטַּעַם לְפִי שֶׁהֵם הָיוּ בְּחֶשְׁבּוֹן מְחֻיָּב מִן הַתּוֹרָה, וְהוּא כְּאִלּוּ צִוְּתָה הַתּוֹרָה בְּפֵרוּשׁ אַחַר רֹב שֶׁל אֵלּוּ תַּעֲשׂוּ כָּל עִנְיְנֵיכֶם, וְעוֹד שֶׁהֵם כֻּלָּם הָיוּ חֲכָמִים גְּדוֹלִים.

וּמִשָּׁרְשֵׁי מִצְוָה זוֹ שֶׁנִּצְטַוֵּינוּ בָּזֶה לְחִזּוּק קִיּוּם דָּתֵנוּ, שֶׁאִלּוּ נִצְטַוֵּינוּ קִיְּמוּ הַתּוֹרָה כַּאֲשֶׁר תּוּכְלוּ לְהַשִּׂיג כַּוָּנַת אֲמִתָּתָהּ, כָּל אֶחָד וְאֶחָד מִיִּשְׂרָאֵל יֹאמַר דַּעְתִּי נוֹתֶנֶת שֶׁאֲמִתַּת עִנְיַן פְּלוֹנִי כֵּן הוּא, וַאֲפִלּוּ כָּל הָעוֹלָם בְּהֶפְכּוֹ לֹא יִהְיֶה לוֹ רְשׁוּת לַעֲשׂוֹת הָעִנְיָן בְּהֶפֶךְ הָאֱמֶת לְפִי דַּעְתּוֹ, וְיֵצֵא מִזֶּה חֻרְבָּן שֶׁתֵּעָשֶׂה הַתּוֹרָה כְּכַמָּה תוֹרוֹת, כִּי כָל אֶחָד יָדִין כְּפִי עֲנִיּוּת דַּעְתּוֹ. אֲבָל עַכְשָׁיו שֶׁבְּפֵרוּשׁ נִצְטַוֵּינוּ לְקַבֵּל בָּהּ דַּעַת רֹב הַחֲכָמִים יֵשׁ תּוֹרָה אַחַת לְכֻלָּנוּ וְהוּא קִיּוּמֵנוּ גָּדוֹל בָּהּ וְאֵין לָנוּ לָזוּז מִדַּעְתָּם וִיהִי מָה.

וּבְכֵן בַּעֲשׂוֹתֵנוּ מִצְוָתָם אָנוּ מַשְׁלִימִין מִצְוַת הָאֵל, וַאֲפִלּוּ אִם לֹא יְכַוְּנוּ לִפְעָמִים הַחֲכָמִים אֶל הָאֱמֶת חָלִילָה, עֲלֵיהֶם יִהְיֶה הַחֲטָאת וְלֹא עָלֵינוּ. וְזֶהוּ הָעִנְיָן שֶׁאָמְרוּ שֶׁאָמְרוּ זִכְרוֹנָם לִבְרָכָה בְּהוֹרָיוֹת שֶׁבֵּית דִּין שֶׁשָּׁעוּ דִּין בְּהוֹרָאָה וְעָשָׂה הַיָּחִיד עַל פִּיהֶם שֶׁהֵם בְּחִיּוּב הַקָּרְבָּן לֹא הַיָּחִיד כְּלָל, זוּלָתִי בִּצְדָדִים מְפֹרָשִׁים שָׁם.

דִּינֵי הַמִּצְוָה, כְּגוֹן הַחִלּוּקִים שֶׁיֵּשׁ בָּרֹב זֶה בֵּין דִּינֵי מָמוֹנוֹת לְדִינֵי נְפָשׁוֹת,

---

3. I.e. the chief court of a city, with twenty-three judges, and the supreme court in Jerusalem, with seventy-one.
4. So TB Sanhedrin 2a.
5. Only such men were appointed as justices; TB Sanhedrin 17a.
6. TB Horayoth 4b, etc.

⟨312⟩

who left Egypt. But when the wisdom [of the two groups] is equal or close, the Torah has instructed us that the greater number of minds will always agree more closely with the truth than the smaller number. But whether they are in accord with the truth or not in the view of the listener, the law requires that we should not deviate from the way of the majority.

Now, what I am stating, that the majority is preferred always when the two contending groups are equal in the wisdom of truth—this we say everywhere (in all cases) except in regard to the *sanhedrin*.[3] For with them [its justices] we do not pay careful attention, when they are divided, to which group knows more; rather, we always act according to the ruling of the majority among them. The reason is that they are of a number made mandatory by the Torah;[4] hence it is as though the Torah had ordained explicitly, "According to the majority of them shall you conduct all your affairs." Moreover, they were all great Torah scholars.[5]

At the root of the precept lies the reason that we were thus commanded to strengthen the observance and fulfillment of our faith. For were we commanded, "Observe the Torah as you are able to grasp the intention of its truth," every single Jew would say, "I am inclined to think the truth of this particular matter is thus and so"; and then, even if all the world should hold the opposite, he would have no right to carry out (observe) that particular matter in opposition to the truth as he understands it. The result would be a disaster: the Torah would become as if many Torahs, since everyone would judge and rule according to the limitation of his mind. But now that we were commanded explicitly to accept the view of the majority of Sages about it, there is one Torah for us all. This is our great way of survival with it; and we are not to budge from their ruling, no matter what.

So, by obeying their commandments, we complete and perfect our observance of God's commandments. And even if the Sages should fail sometimes to arrive at the truth (perish the thought), the sin would be upon them and not on us. This is the reason why our Sages of blessed memory taught in the Talmud tractate *Horayoth* (2a) that if a *beth din* made a mistake in a ruling and an individual acted on their word, the duty to bring an offering [in atonement] lies on them, and not on the individual at all—except in certain special cases, as explained there.[6]

As for the laws of the precept, [there are] for example, the differen-

שֶׁבְּדִינֵי נְפָשׁוֹת צָרִיךְ שֶׁיְּהֵא הָרֹב יוֹתֵר נִכָּר, וְכַמָּה אֲנָשִׁים צְרִיכִים לְדִינֵי נְפָשׁוֹת מֵחֲמַת שֶׁאָנוּ מְצַוִּין לַעֲשׂוֹת כְּדִבְרֵי הָרֹב, וְאֵין רָאוּי לְהָמִית אִישׁ אֶחָד בִּשְׁנֵי דַיָּנִין שֶׁהֵם רֹב כְּנֶגֶד אֶחָד. וְכֵן מַה שֶׁאָמְרוּ לְבִרְכָה זִכְרוֹנָם שֶׁצְּרִיכִין גַּם־כֵּן אֵלוּ הָעוֹשִׂים רֹב בְּדִינֵי נְפָשׁוֹת לִהְיוֹת סְמוּכִין, וְהַסְּמִיכָה עֵדוּת לָהֶם שֶׁהֵם חֲכָמִים וּנְבוֹנִים וּשְׁלֵמִים שֶׁרְאוּיִים לַעֲשׂוֹת כָּל דָּבָר עַל יָדָם, וְלֹא נָמִית אֲנָשִׁים עַל פִּי אֲנָשִׁים חַסְרֵי חָכְמָה פֶּן יִטְעוּ בַּדִּין, וּלְמִיתָה אֵין תַּשְׁלוּמִין.

וְשֶׁבְּדִינֵי נְפָשׁוֹת הַמְלַמְּדִים זְכוּת אֵין חוֹזְרִין וּמְלַמְּדִין חוֹבָה, וּבְדִינֵי מָמוֹנוֹת אֵינוֹ כֵן, וְשֶׁפּוֹתְחִין בִּזְכוּת בְּדִינֵי נְפָשׁוֹת, וְהִנֵּה נִסְתַּלֵּק הַפּוֹתֵחַ בְּכָךְ מִכַּת הַמְּחַיֶּבֶת, וְשֶׁהַכֹּל מְלַמְּדִין זְכוּת, בֵּין רַב בֵּין תַּלְמִיד, וְיֶתֶר פְּרָטֶיהָ, מְבֹאָרִין בְּסוֹף סַנְהֶדְרִין.

וְנוֹהֶגֶת בְּכָל מָקוֹם וּבְכָל זְמַן בִּזְכָרִים וּנְקֵבוֹת. וְעוֹבֵר עָלֶיהָ וְלֹא נָטָה אַחֲרֵיהֶם בִּטֵּל עֲשֵׂה וְעָנְשׁוֹ גָּדוֹל מְאֹד, שֶׁהוּא הָעַמּוּד שֶׁהַתּוֹרָה נִסְמֶכֶת בּוֹ.

[שֶׁלֹּא לְרַחֵם עַל עָנִי בַּדִּין]

עט שֶׁלֹּא יַחְמֹל הַדַּיָּן עַל הֶחָלָשׁ וְהַדַּל בִּשְׁעַת הַדִּין אֶלָּא שֶׁיָּדִין דִּינוֹ לַאֲמִתּוֹ, לֹא עַל צַד הַחֶמְלָה עָלָיו, אֲבָל יַשְׁוֶה בֵּין הֶעָשִׁיר וְהַדַּל לְהַכְרִיחוֹ לִפְרֹעַ מַה שֶׁהוּא חַיָּב, שֶׁנֶּאֱמַר: וְדָל לֹא תֶהְדַּר בְּרִיבוֹ. וְנִכְפַּל זֶה הָעִנְיָן בְּמָקוֹם אַחֵר, שֶׁנֶּאֱמַר: לֹא תִשָּׂא פְנֵי דָל. וּלְשׁוֹן סִפְרָא: שֶׁלֹּא תֹאמַר עָנִי הוּא זֶה, וַאֲנִי וְהֶעָשִׁיר חַיָּבִים

---

7. TB Sanhedrin 2a; see also above, §76.
8. TB *ibid.*
9. TB Sanhedrin 37a.
10. *Ibid.* 32a.
11. I.e. the person on trial is told by a member of the *beth din*, "If you did not commit murder (or do what the witnesses say), do not be afraid"; *ibid.* a-b (MT *hilchoth sanhedrin* x 7).
12. By the rule given at the beginning of the paragraph. It does not refer, however, to the one who opens the trial, since he merely speaks a standard formula (note 11).
13. But if a disciple would speak for the guilt of the accused, he is silenced; TB Sanhedrin 32a, 33b.

ces regarding this majority between a civil and a capital case [where a person is on trial for his life]: that in a capital case the majority must be larger, more pronounced;[7] how many people [justices] are needed for a capital case, because we were commanded to follow the majority;[8] and that it is not proper to put a person to death by the verdict of two justices when they are a majority against one.[8] There is also the teaching of our Sages[9] that in addition, those who form the majority in a capital case must be ordained scholars; their ordination attests that they are wise, understanding and perfect [in integrity], men by whose word it is proper to carry out every matter. So let us not put any persons to death by the verdict of people lacking in wisdom, for fear that they may make a mistake—and for death there can be no rectification [to make it right].

[There is, further, the law] that in capital cases those who speak in favor [of the accused] may not turn around and speak to demonstrate [his] guilt, although this rule does not apply in civil cases;[10] that in a capital case, one opens [the trial] by speaking of the innocence [of the accused].[11] Thus, one who begins [his views by speaking for acquittal] is ruled out of the group that may argue for his guilt;[12] and all may speak to show his innocence, whether a master scholar or a disciple.[13] These and the rest of its details are explained toward the end of the Talmud tractate *Sanhedrin*.

It applies in every place and every time, for both man and woman. If someone transgresses it and does not follow them [the majority of Sages, to obey them], he has disobeyed a positive precept, and his punishment will be very great—for this is the pillar by which the Torah is upheld.

79

[NOT TO TAKE PITY ON A POOR MAN IN JUDGMENT] that the judge should not take pity on a powerless or destitute person during a court trial, but should decide his case in its truth, not by way of pity for him. Rather, he should judge equally, whether it is a rich or poor man [on trial], to force him to pay what he owes— for it is stated, *nor shall you favor a poor man in his contention* (Exodus 23:3). This theme was repeated in another place in Scripture: as it is stated, *you shall not show favor to the poor* (Leviticus 19:15). The expression in the Midrash *Sifra* [about this second verse] is this: For you should not say, "This is a poor man, and I and the rich man [his opponent

לְפַרְנְסוֹ, אָזְכֶּנּוּ וְנִמְצָא מִתְפַּרְנֵס בִּנְקִיּוּת, תַּלְמוּד לוֹמַר "לֹא תִשָּׂא פְנֵי דָל".
וְשֹׁרֶשׁ הַמִּצְוָה יָדוּעַ, שֶׁהַשֵּׂכֶל מֵעִיד בְּהַשְׁוָיַת הַדִּין שֶׁדָּבָר רָאוּי וְכָשֵׁר הוּא.
וְנוֹהֶגֶת בְּכָל מָקוֹם וּבְכָל זְמַן בַּזְּכָרִים. וְעוֹבֵר עָלֶיהָ וְהִטָּה הַדִּין לְחֶמְלָתוֹ עַל
הַדַּל עָבַר עַל מִצְוַת מֶלֶךְ; וְאֵין בָּהּ מַלְקוֹת, שֶׁאֵין בָּהּ מַעֲשֶׂה.

[מִצְוַת פְּרִיק מַשָּׂא]

פ לְהָסִיר הַמַּשָּׂא מֵעַל הַבְּהֵמָה שֶׁיָּגְעָה בְמַשָּׂאָהּ בַּדֶּרֶךְ, שֶׁנֶּאֱמַר "כִּי תִרְאֶה
חֲמוֹר שֹׂנַאֲךָ" וְגוֹמֵר. וְהַשּׂוֹנֵא זֶה פֵּרוּשׁוֹ יִשְׂרָאֵל, וְאַף עַל פִּי שֶׁכָּתוּב "לֹא תִשְׂנָא
אֶת אָחִיךָ", דְּהַיְנוּ יִשְׂרָאֵל, אָמְרוּ חֲכָמִים שֶׁעִנְיָן זֶה הוּא כְּגוֹן שֶׁרָאָהוּ עוֹבֵר
עֲבֵרָה בְּיִחוּד וְהִתְרָה בוֹ וְלֹא חָזַר שֶׁזֶּה מֻתָּר לִשְׂנֹאתוֹ. וּמַה שֶּׁאָמַר חֲמוֹר לָאו
דַּוְקָא חֲמוֹר אֶלָּא כָּל בְּהֵמָה, אֶלָּא שֶׁדִּבֵּר הַכָּתוּב בַּהֹוֶה, שֶׁהַחֲמוֹרִים לְמַשָּׂא.
וּכְתִיב "עָזֹב תַּעֲזֹב עִמּוֹ", כְּלוֹמַר עָזְרֵהוּ, מִלְּשׁוֹן וַיַּעַזְבוּ יְרוּשָׁלַיִם, שֶׁהוּא לְשׁוֹן
חֹזֶק.

מִשָּׁרְשֵׁי הַמִּצְוָה לְלַמֵּד נַפְשֵׁנוּ בְּמִדַּת הַחֶמְלָה שֶׁהִיא מִדָּה מְשֻׁבַּחַת, וְאֵין צָרִיךְ
לוֹמַר שֶׁחוֹבָה עָלֵינוּ לַחְמֹל עַל הָאִישׁ הַמִּצְטַעֵר בְּגוּפוֹ, אֶלָּא אֲפִלּוּ הַמִּצְטַעֵר
בַּאֲבֵדַת מָמוֹנוֹ מִצְוָה עָלֵינוּ לַחְמֹל עָלָיו וּלְהַצִּילוֹ.

דִּינֵי הַמִּצְוָה, כְּגוֹן אִם הַבְּהֵמָה שֶׁל גּוֹי וּמַשָּׂאוֹ שֶׁל יִשְׂרָאֵל אוֹ בְהֶפֶךְ, וְדִין
הַפּוֹגֵשׁ בְּאוֹהֲבוֹ יִשְׂרָאֵל וּבְשׂוֹנְאוֹ שֶׁמִּצְוָה בְשׂוֹנֵא לְכַךְ הַיֵּצֶר, וַאֲפִלּוּ אוֹהֵב לִפְרֹק

§79 1. In this paragraph our author follows ShM negative precept §277.

2. But not women, as they are not permitted to judge cases, as our author wrote in §77.

3. See MT *hilchoth sanhedrin* xviii 2 that in this sort of instance, even if the judge did some physical action to implement his wrong verdict, he would receive no whipping, since anything wrongly given to the poor man can be returned or repaid.

§80 1. I.e. when the observer was alone, so that he cannot testify against him afterward, since at least two witnesses are needed to convict a person.

2. So TB P'saḥim 113b.

3. So TB Bava Kamma 54b.

4. In §540 our author states explicitly that the religious duty to help unload a burden applies also to a man laden.

5. TB Bava M'tzi'a 32b.

6. So that his animal is suffering pain; *ibid*.

⟨316⟩

in the lawsuit] are duty-bound to provide him his needs. I will have him win [the lawsuit] and in consequence he will support himself in sober dignity." Therefore Scripture states, *you shall not show favor to the poor.*[1]

The root reason for the precept is known: For human intelligence avows about judging a case equally [impartially, no matter who are the people in it], that it is a proper and nobly worthy matter.

It applies in every place and every time, for men.[2] If someone violates it and perverts justice out of his pity for a poor man, he has disobeyed a commandment of the King; but whiplashes are not given for it, since it involves no [physical] action.[3]

[THE MITZVAH OF UNLOADING ANOTHER PERSON'S BURDEN]

80 to remove a load from an animal which has wearied under its burden on the road—for it is stated, *If you see the donkey of one that you hate*, etc. (Exodus 23:5). Now, this "one that you hate" denotes an Israelite; and although it is stated, *You shall not hate your brother* (Leviticus 19:17), which means an Israelite (Jew), the Sages said that the situation here is, for example, that he saw him committing a transgression when he was alone;[1] he cautioned him, and the other did not desist. This one, it is permitted to hate.[2] As to Scripture's saying "a donkey," it does not mean a donkey particularly, but any beast.[3] It is only that Scripture spoke of what is usual, as donkeys are for carrying burdens. And it is written, "'*azov ta'azov* with him" (Exodus 23:5)—i.e. help him, in the sense of *va-ya'azvu y'rushalayim* (Nehemiah 3:8), where the word denotes strengthening.

At the root of the precept lies the purpose to teach our spirit the quality of compassion, which is a noble trait of character. There is no need to say that a duty lies on us to take pity on a man who is suffering bodily pain;[4] but even if he suffers only at the loss of his goods and possessions, it is a *mitzvah*, a religious obligation for us to take pity on him and rescue him.

The laws of the precept are, for example: if the animal belongs to a heathen and the load to a Jew, or vice versa;[5] the law if one encounters both his Jewish friend and one whom he hates—that it is a religious duty [rather to help] the hated one, in order to subdue the evil inclination—and this even if the friend [needs his animal] to be unloaded,[6] and the hated one, to be loaded. This "hated one" is

§80–81: HELP UNLOAD A BURDEN / NOT TO DENY A SINNER JUSTICE

וְשׂוֹנֵא לִטְעֹן. וְשׂוֹנֵא זֶה אֵינוֹ כַּשּׂוֹנֵא שֶׁזְּכַרְנוּ מֵחֲמַת עֲבֵרָה אֶלָּא שֶׁאֵין לִבּוֹ שָׁלֵם עִמּוֹ.

וּפֵרוּשׁ "כִּי תִרְאֶה" מֵאֵימָתַי הוּא הַחִיּוּב, וְשִׁעֲרוּ חֲכָמִים אֶחָד מִשִּׁבְעָה וּמֶחֱצָה בְּמִיל וְזֶהוּ רִיס, אֲבָל רָחוֹק מִזֶּה הַשִּׁעוּר אֵין חַיָּב לְהַטּוֹת הַדֶּרֶךְ אֵלָיו, וְהָעוֹשֶׂה לִפְנִים מִן הַשּׁוּרָה תָּבוֹא עָלָיו בְּרָכָה, וְדִין זָקֵן אוֹ נִכְבָּד וְאֵינָהּ לְפִי כְּבוֹדוֹ הַכֹּל נִדּוֹן לְפִי מַה שֶּׁיִּהְיֶה עוֹשֶׂה בְּשֶׁלּוֹ, וְדִין פְּרִיקָה בְּחִנָּם וּטְעִינָה בְּשָׂכָר, וְשֶׁמְּדַדֶּה עִמּוֹ עַד פַּרְסָה, וְנוֹטֵל שָׂכָר עַל הַלְוָיָה, כְּמוֹ שֶׁמְּבֹאָר הַכֹּל בְּפֶרֶק שְׁנֵי מִמְצִיעָא.

וְנוֹהֶגֶת בְּכָל מָקוֹם וּבְכָל זְמַן בִּזְכָרִים וּנְקֵבוֹת. וְעוֹבֵר עָלֶיהָ בָּטֵל עֲשֵׂה וּמַרְאֶה בְּעַצְמוֹ מִדַּת הָאַכְזָרִיּוּת שֶׁהִיא מִדָּה מְכֹעֶרֶת, וְכָל שֶׁאֵינוֹ מְרַחֵם אֵין מְרַחֲמִין עָלָיו מִן הַשָּׁמַיִם, שֶׁאֵין רָאוּי גּוּפוֹ לְקַבֵּל הָרַחֲמָנוּת.

[שֶׁלֹּא לְהַטּוֹת מִשְׁפַּט חוֹטֵא מִפְּנֵי רִשְׁעוֹ]

פא שֶׁלֹּא לְהַטּוֹת הַדִּין עַל אֶחָד מִבַּעֲלֵי הַדִּין כְּשֶׁיֵּדַע הַדַּיָּן שֶׁהוּא רָשָׁע בַּעַל עֲבֵרוֹת, שֶׁנֶּאֱמַר "לֹא תַטֶּה מִשְׁפַּט אֶבְיוֹנְךָ בְּרִיבוֹ". וּפֵרוּשׁוֹ שֶׁהוּא אֶבְיוֹן בְּמִצְוֹת, שֶׁאֵין בְּמַשְׁמַע שֶׁיְּהֵא אֶבְיוֹן בְּמָמוֹן צָרִיךְ שֶׁאֵין לוֹמַר שֶׁלֹּא יַטּוּ עָלָיו הַדִּין לִגְזֹל מִמֶּנּוּ בְּעָנְיוֹ, אֶלָּא נִצְטַוֵּינוּ שֶׁאַף עַל פִּי שֶׁהוּא רָשָׁע לֹא יֹאמַר הַדַּיָּן "הוֹאִיל וְרָשָׁע הוּא אַטֶּה עָלָיו אֶת הַדִּין". כִּי הַמִּשְׁפָּט בָּרְשָׁעִים לֵאלֹהִים הוּא וְלֹא לוֹ. וְכֵן הוּא בִּמְכִילְתָּא: רָשָׁע וְכָשֵׁר עוֹמְדִין לְפָנֶיךָ בַּדִּין, שֶׁמָּא תֹּאמַר, וְכוּלֵי.

שֹׁרֶשׁ הַשְׁוָיַת הַדִּין בְּכָל אָדָם דָּבָר מֻשְׂכָּל הוּא. וְנוֹהֶגֶת בְּכָל מָקוֹם וּבְכָל זְמַן בִּזְכָרִים אֲבָל לֹא בִּנְקֵבוֹת, שֶׁאֵינָן דָּנוֹת. וְעוֹבֵר עָלֶיהָ וְהִטָּה הַדִּין עַל הָרָשָׁע עָבַר עַל מִצְוַת מֶלֶךְ.

7. Hence the need and duty to subdue his inclination, since such hatred is forbidden.
8. *Ibid.* In one view, a *mil* is three fifths of mile (960 meters), and a *ris* 140 yards (128 meters). Another view is that a *mil* is 0.72 miles (1152 meters), and a *ris* is 172.4 yards (153.6 meters).
9. Evidently derived from the instance of R. Ishmael b. R. Yosé in TB Bava M'tzi'a 30b (MY).
10. This much he is required to do for another; *ibid.*
11. *Ibid.* 32a.
12. Literally, he jogs or trips along with him; a parasang (*parsah*) is four *mils* (see note 8). The purpose of it is that if the animal falls again (or even a hundred times) he must help him unload and reload; *ibid.* 33a.
13. So TB Shabbath 151b.

81 1. This paragraph is based on ShM negative precept §278.
2. As our author wrote in §77.
3. But, as our author adds in similar instances, no whiplashes are given since no physical action is involved in the violation.

⟨318⟩

not as the disliked man whom we have mentioned, [hated] on account of sin, but merely one with whom his heart is not at peace, in harmony.[7]

Then there is the meaning of "If you see": from which distance does the obligation apply? The Sages established the measure as two fifteenths of a *mil*, which is a *ris*.[8] At a distance greater than this measure, there is no obligation to turn from one's way toward him. But if a person acts beyond the letter of the law, let blessing come upon him.[9]

[There is, further,] the law about an elder or distinguished man, with whose honor it is not in accord [to help load or unload a beast of burden]: all is judged according to what he would do with [an animal of]'his own;[10] the law that unloading is to be done without charge, but loading for a fee;[11] that he helps him continue for a parasang,[12] but takes payment for the escort—as it is all explained in the second chapter of the tractate *Bava M'tzi'a*.

It is in effect in every place, at every time, for both man and woman. If someone violates it, he has disobeyed a positive precept; and he displays a quality of cruelty, which is an ugly character trait. For him who has no compassion, there will be no compassion from Heaven,[13] for his physical, corporeal self is not fit to receive compassion.

[NOT TO PERVERT JUSTICE FOR A SINNER ON ACCOUNT OF HIS WICKEDNESS]

81 not to pervert justice for one party in a lawsuit when [the judge] knows that he is a wicked sinner. For it is stated, *You shall not pervert the justice due your poor in his contention* (Exodus 23:6); and this denotes that he is poor in *mitzvoth* [in observance of the precepts]. It cannot mean that he is poor in wordly goods, for then there is no need to state that justice should not be perverted for him to rob him in his poverty. We were rather commanded that even though he is sinful, the judge should not say, "Because he is wicked, I will pervert justice for him." For taking the wicked to account is for God [to do], not for him. And so is it [taught] in the Midrash *Mechilta*: If a wicked and a worthy man stand before you in a lawsuit, perhaps you would say, etc.[1]

The root reason for giving equal justice to every man is something logical, understandable. It applies in every place, in every time, for men but not for women, since they do not judge lawsuits.[2] If someone violates it and perverts justice for a wicked man, he has disobeyed a [Divine] royal commandment.[3]

§82: NOT TO DECIDE A CAPITAL CASE ON PROBABILITY

[שֶׁלֹּא לַחְתּוֹךְ הַדִּין בְּאֹמֶד הַדַּעַת]

פב שֶׁלֹּא יַהַרְגוּ בֵּית דִּין הַנִּדּוֹן כִּי אִם בְּעֵדִים מְעִידִין עַל אוֹתוֹ עִנְיָן שֶׁהוּא נֶהֱרָג עָלָיו שֶׁרְאוּהוּ אוֹתוֹ שֶׁעָשָׂה בְּעֵינֵיהֶם מַמָּשׁ, לֹא שֶׁיָּעִידוּ עָלָיו מִצַּד אוֹתוֹת חֲזָקוֹת; וְעַל זֶה נֶאֱמַר "וְנָקִי וְצַדִּיק אַל תַּהֲרֹג", כְּלוֹמַר הִזָּהֵר עַד מְאֹד לְבַל תַּהֲרֹג אָדָם שֶׁיְּהֵא בְּאֶפְשָׁרוּת שֶׁלֹּא עָשָׂה מַה שֶּׁאָמְרוּ עָלָיו שֶׁעָשָׂה.

וְכֵן הוּא מְפֹרָשׁ בִּמְכִילְתָּא, שֶׁאָמְרוּ שָׁם: רָאוּהוּ רוֹדֵף אַחַר חֲבֵרוֹ לְהָרְגוֹ וְהִתְרוּ בוֹ "יִשְׂרָאֵל הוּא, בֶּן בְּרִית הוּא, אִם הֲרַגְתָּ אוֹתוֹ תֵּהָרֵג", וְהֶעֱלִימוּ עֵינֵיהֶם שֶׁלֹּא רָאוּ בְּהַכּוֹתוֹ אוֹתוֹ וּמְצָאוּהוּ מִיַּד הָרוּג וּמְפַרְפֵּר וְהַסַּיִף מְנַטֵּף דָּם מִיַּד הַהוֹרֵג, שׁוֹמֵעַ אֲנִי יְהֵא חַיָּב, תַּלְמוּד לוֹמַר: וְנָקִי וְצַדִּיק אַל תַּהֲרֹג.

הֲרֵי שֶׁמִּפְּנֵי שֶׁהֶעֱלִימוּ עֵינֵיהֶם בְּעֵת הַהַכָּאָה נִפְטַר זֶה. וְכָשֵׁר הַדָּבָר וְרָאוּי לִהְיוֹת כֵּן, שֶׁאִלּוּ הִתִּירָה הַתּוֹרָה לָקִים לְהָקִים גְּבוּלֵי הָעֹנֶשׁ בְּאֶפְשָׁרוּת הַקָּרוֹב יֵצֵא מִן הָעִנְיָן לִפְעָמִים לְהָקִים גְּבוּלֵי הָעֹנֶשׁ בְּאֶפְשָׁרוּת רָחוֹק עַד שֶׁנְּמִית בְּנֵי אָדָם לִפְעָמִים עַל מַה שֶּׁלֹּא עָשׂוּ, כִּי יֵשׁ לָאֶפְשָׁרוּת רֹחַב גָּדוֹל.

וְדַע זֶה וַהֲבִינֵהוּ כִּי דָּבָר בָּרוּר הוּא. וּלְפִיכָךְ סָגַר יִתְבָּרַךְ זֶה הַשַּׁעַר וְצִוָּה אוֹתָנוּ עַל זֶה, וְכָל פִּקּוּדֵי הַשֵּׁם יִתְבָּרַךְ יְשָׁרִים.

וְעוֹד נִכְלָל בִּכְלָל זֶה מִי שֶׁהֵעִידוּ עָלָיו שְׁנֵי עֵדִים שֶׁרְאוּהוּ שֶׁעָבַר עֲבֵרָה אַחַת כְּגוֹן שֶׁהָאֶחָד מֵעִיד עָלָיו שֶׁעָשָׂה מְלָאכָה בְּשַׁבָּת וְהָאֶחָד שֶׁעָבַד עֲבוֹדָה זָרָה, שֶׁזֶּה אֵינוֹ נִדּוֹן בְּעֵדוּתָם, שֶׁנֶּאֱמַר: וְנָקִי וְצַדִּיק אַל תַּהֲרֹג. וְכֵן אָמְרוּ זִכְרוֹנָם לִבְרָכָה: הָיָה אֶחָד מְעִידוֹ שֶׁרָאָהוּ עוֹבֵד לַחַמָּה וְאֶחָד לַלְּבָנָה, שׁוֹמֵעַ אֲנִי יִצְטָרְפוּ, תַּלְמוּד לוֹמַר "וְנָקִי וְצַדִּיק אַל תַּהֲרֹג".

שֹׁרֶשׁ הַמִּצְוָה נִגְלֶה הוּא כְּמוֹ שֶׁאָמַרְנוּ.

---

§82   1. Since we find in Scripture, *and he is a witness, whether he has seen* (Leviticus 5:1), the witnesses must actually see the deed. As they did not, the killer emerges "righteous," free of penalty (Ramban on ShM negative precept §290). In these paragraphs our author follows Rambam *ibid*.

  2. In Mechilta on the verse.

  3. And he should be convicted because two witnesses testify that he deserves death.

82 [NOT TO DECIDE A CAPITAL CASE ON PROBABILITY]

that a *beth din* should not send a person on trial [in a capital case] to his death except where witnesses testify about the matter for which he is to suffer death, that they actually saw him do it, with their own eyes, and not where they testify about him on account of strong signs and indications [that he did it]. About this it is stated, *and the innocent and righteous, do not slay* (Exodus 23:7): in other words, be extremely careful not to put a person to death when it is possible that he did not do what they asserted that he did.

And so was it explained in the Midrash *Mechilta;* for it was stated there: If they saw him pursuing his fellow to kill him, and they warned him, "He is an Israelite; he is a member of the covenant; if you kill him, you will be put to death"—and they shut their eyes, so that they did not see when he struck him, but then they found him murdered and in his death throes, the sword dripping blood in the hand of the killer—I might infer that he has incurred a death sentence. Hence Scripture states, *and the innocent and righteous, do not slay.*[1]

Thus you see, because they shut their eyes at the time of the [murderous] attack, this one is set free. And the matter is quite right, and should properly be so. For if the Torah allowed us to establish the boundaries of punishment around strong likelihood [to include what is very probable] the consequence of this would be at times to establish the boundaries of punishment to include remote possibility, until we would put people to death sometimes for what they did not do. For possibility [and probability] cover a wide range. Know this and understand it, as it is a clear matter.

Therefore He (be He exalted) shut this gate and commanded us about it. All *the precepts of the Eternal Lord are right* (Psalms 19:9).

Also included in this negative precept is a person about whom two witnesses testified that they saw him commit a certain sin, for example thus: One attests about him that he did work on the Sabbath, and one, that he was guilty of idol-worship. This person is not sentenced to death on the strength of their testimony, because it is stated, *and the innocent and the righteous, do not slay.* And so our Sages of blessed memory taught:[2] If one testified about him that he saw him worship the sun, and one [that he saw him worship] the moon, I might understand that [the two testimonies] should be joined and merged into one.[3] Hence Scripture states, *and the innocent and righteous, do not slay.*

The root reason for the precept is obvious, as we said.

דִּינֶיהָ, כְּגוֹן מַה שֶּׁאָמְרוּ זִכְרוֹנָם לִבְרָכָה לְבָרְכָה שֶׁאֵין עֵדוּתָן מִצְטָרֶפֶת אֲפִלּוּ מְעִידִים בַּעֲבֵרָה אַחַת עַד שֶׁיִּרְאוּ שְׁנֵיהֶם כְּאֶחָד. וְעוֹד שֶׁיִּהְיוּ רוֹאִין זֶה אֶת זֶה בִּשְׁעַת הַמַּעֲשֶׂה, לְהוֹצִיא אִם הָאֶחָד רָאָהוּ מֵחַלּוֹן זֶה וְהָאֶחָד מֵחַלּוֹן אַחֵר וְאֵין יְכוֹלִין לִרְאוֹת זֶה אֶת זֶה, וְשֶׁהַמַּתְרֶה מְצָרְפָן אִם רָאָה שְׁנֵיהֶם, וְיֶתֶר פְּרָטֶיהָ, בְּסַנְהֶדְרִין.

וְנוֹהֶגֶת בְּאֶרֶץ יִשְׂרָאֵל בִּזְכָרִים כְּמוֹ שֶׁאָמַרְנוּ, לְפִי שֶׁבָּהֶם הַמִּשְׁפָּט, כְּמוֹ שֶׁאָמַרְנוּ כַּמָּה פְּעָמִים, אֲבָל לֹא בִּנְקֵבוֹת לְפִי שֶׁאֵינָן דָּנוֹת. וְהָעוֹבֵר עָלֶיהָ דָּן עַל פִּי עֵדוּת שֶׁאֵינָהּ מְכֻוֶּנֶת כְּמוֹ שֶׁאָמַרְנוּ עָבַר עַל מִצְוַת מֶלֶךְ, וְעָנְשׁוֹ גָּדוֹל מְאֹד שֶׁגּוֹרֵם לַהֲרֹג נְפָשׁוֹת שֶׁלֹּא כַּדִּין.

וְהָרַמְבַּ״ן זִכְרוֹנוֹ לִבְרָכָה חָשַׁב זֶה הַמִּקְרָא בִּשְׁנֵי לָאוִין וּלְעִנְיָן אַחֵר, וְהוּא שֶׁנִּפְטָר בְּדִינֵי נְפָשׁוֹת בְּצִדְדִין שֶׁנִּתְחַיֵּב בְּדִינֵי מָמוֹנוֹת. וְסָמַךְ עַל מַה שֶּׁאָמְרוּ בִּגְמָרַת סַנְהֶדְרִין: תָּנוּ רַבָּנָן מִנַּיִן לְיוֹצֵא מִבֵּית דִּין חַיָּב וְאָמַר אֶחָד ״יֵשׁ לִי לְלַמֵּד עָלָיו זְכוּת״ שֶׁמַּחֲזִירִין אוֹתוֹ, שֶׁנֶּאֱמַר וְנָקִי וְצַדִּיק אַל תַּהֲרֹג, כְּלוֹמַר וְזֶה נָקִי הוּא דְּשֶׁמָּא זֶה יְלַמֵּד שֶׁהוּא נָקִי. וּמִנַּיִן לְיוֹצֵא מִבֵּית דִּין זַכַּאי וְאָמַר אֶחָד ״יֵשׁ לִי לְלַמֵּד עָלָיו חוֹבָה״ שֶׁאֵין מַחֲזִירִין אוֹתוֹ, תַּלְמוּד לוֹמַר וְצַדִּיק אַל תַּהֲרֹג, וְזֶה צַדִּיק הוּא שֶׁכְּבָר יָצָא צַדִּיק. הִנֵּה דִקְדְּקוּ הַמִּקְרָא לִשְׁנֵי לָאוִין.

וְכָל עִנְיָנִים אֵלֶּה מִן הַשֹּׁרֶשׁ שֶׁכָּתַבְתִּי, שֶׁרָצָה הָאֵל שֶׁנְּהַפֵּךְ בְּכָל זְכוּת הַנִּדּוֹן, שֶׁמָּא עָשָׂה תְּשׁוּבָה וְנִחַם עַל רָעָתוֹ שֶׁעָשָׂה, וְיִהְיֶה עֲדַיִן מִמְּיַשְּׁבֵי עוֹלָם, וְהוּא בָּרוּךְ הוּא חָפֵץ בְּיִשּׁוּבוֹ.

---

4. TB Makkoth 6b.
5. In his commentary (*hassagoth*) to ShM negative precept §290.
6. I.e. live as productive members of a community.

⟨322⟩

Its laws are, for example, what our Sages of blessed memory said,[4] that their testimony is not linked together [to be considered as one] even if they bear witness about one transgression, unless they both saw it together, as one person; and, moreover, unless they could see each other at the time of the event—which excludes a case where one saw him through one window, and the other through another window, and they could not see one another. But the one who warned [the sinner] can "weld" them [to be considered as giving one testimony] if he saw both. [These] and further details are in the tractate *Sanhedrin*.

It would be in force in the land of Israel, for men, as we have stated, since judging at trials is their province, as we said many times; but not for women, because they do not act as judges. If someone transgresses it and renders a verdict on the basis of testimony that is not harmonized [merged into one] as we have conveyed, he has disobeyed a [Divine] royal commandment. His punishment will be very great, because he brings death to human beings in violation of the law.

Ramban of blessed memory[5] reckons this verse to contain two prohibitions, about another matter: i.e. that we should set a person free of penalty in a capital case in certain circumstances where we would declare him guilty in a civil case involving property. He bases himself on what was stated in the tractate *Sanhedrin* (33b): Our Sages learned: How do we know that if a person leaves the *beth din* condemned, and one says, "I have something to say in his favor," he is brought back?—for it is stated, *and the innocent and righteous, do not slay*. In other words, this one is [in the category of] the innocent, as that man may perhaps demonstrate that he is innocent. And how do we know that if a person leaves the *beth din* [having been declared] free of penalty, and one [judge] says, "I have something to say to demonstrate his guilt," he is not brought back?—because Scripture states, *and the righteous, do not slay*, and this man is righteous, since he already emerged [from his trial declared] righteous. Thus the verse is analyzed to yield two negative precepts.

Yet all these matters stem from the root reason I have written: God wished that we should cast about and consider every possible point and argument in favor of the person on trial. Perhaps he became penitent and had remorse for the evil that he did, and he will yet be among those who settle the world;[6] and He (blessed is He) desires its settlement and habitation.

§83: A JUDGE IS NOT TO TAKE ANY BRIBE / ספר החינוך

[שֶׁלֹּא לָקַח שֹׁחַד]

פג שֶׁלֹּא יִקַּח הַדַּיָּן שֹׁחַד מִבַּעֲלֵי הַדִּין אֲפִלּוּ לָדוּן דִּין אֱמֶת, שֶׁנֶּאֱמַר: וְשֹׁחַד לֹא תִקָּח; וְנִכְפַּל הַלָּאו בַּתּוֹרָה בְּזֶה הָעִנְיָן בְּמָקוֹם אַחֵר. וְכֵן אָמְרוּ בְסִפְרֵי: לֹא תִקַּח שֹׁחַד, אֲפִלּוּ לְזַכּוֹת זַכַּאי וּלְחַיֵּב חַיָּב.

מִשָּׁרְשֵׁי הַמִּצְוָה שֶׁנֶּאֱסַר עָלֵינוּ לָקַחַת הַשֹּׁחַד אֲפִלּוּ לָדוּן אֶת הַדִּין לַאֲמִתּוֹ, כְּדֵי לְהָסִיר מִבֵּינֵינוּ הַהֶרְגֵּל הָרָע פֶּן נָבֹא מִתּוֹךְ כָּךְ לָדוּן בְּשֹׁחַד דִּינֵי שֶׁקֶר, וְדָבָר בָּרוּר הוּא, אֵין צָרִיךְ מוֹפֵת.

מִדִּינֵי הַמִּצְוָה מַה שֶּׁאָמְרוּ זִכְרוֹנָם לִבְרָכָה שֶׁהַנּוֹתֵן וְהַמְקַבֵּל עוֹבְרִין בְּלָאו, הַנּוֹתֵן מִשּׁוּם "וְלִפְנֵי עִוֵּר לֹא תִתֵּן מִכְשֹׁל", וְהַמְקַבְּלוֹ שֶׁהוּא בִּכְלָל אָרוּר, וְחַיָּב לְהַחֲזִירָם, וְשֶׁאָסוּר לַדַּיָּן לְהַגְדִּיל מַעֲלָתוֹ לְבַנָּיו כְּדֵי לְהַרְבּוֹת שָׂכָר לְסוֹפְרָיו וְשֶׁאֲפִלּוּ שֹׁחַד דְּבָרִים אָסוּר אֶלָּא יִרְאֶה עַצְמוֹ כְּאִלּוּ אֵינוֹ מֵשִׂים לִבּוֹ בְּכָל אֵל הַדְּבָרִים אִם אוּלַי יְכַבְּדוּהוּ בַּעֲלֵי הַדִּין בִּדְבָרִים. בְּלָלוֹ שֶׁל דָּבָר, אָסוּר לַדַּיָּן לְקַבֵּל הֲנָאָה מִבַּעֲלֵי הַדִּין כְּלָל בִּשְׁבִיל דִּינָיו, אֲבָל אִם הַדַּיָּן הוּא בַּעַל מְלָאכָה הִתִּירוּ לוֹ חֲכָמִים לִשְׁאֹל מִבַּעֲלֵי הַדִּין שָׂכָר בַּטָּלָתוֹ מִמְּלַאכְתּוֹ בְּעוֹד שֶׁיַּעֲסֹק בְּדִינָם, וְהוּא שֶׁיִּהְיֶה הַדָּבָר נִכָּר שֶׁהוּא שְׂכַר הַבַּטָּלָה בִּלְבָד וְלֹא יוֹתֵר, וְיִטֹּל מִשְּׁנֵיהֶם בְּשָׁוֶה, וְיֶתֶר פְּרָטֶיהָ, בְּסַנְהֶדְרִין.

וְנוֹהֶגֶת בְּכָל מָקוֹם וּבְכָל זְמַן בִּזְכָרִים, שֶׁהֵם דַּיָּנִים. וְהָעוֹבֵר עָלֶיהָ וְקִבֵּל שֹׁחַד עָבַר עַל מִצְוַת מֶלֶךְ, וְאֵינוֹ לוֹקֶה לְפִי שֶׁנִּתָּן לְהִשָּׁבוֹן.

---

§83 1. In the verse now to be cited.

2. On the verse which follows; Deuteronomy §144. Here our author follows ShM negative precept §274.

3. So MT *hilchoth sanhedrin* xxiii 1–2.

4. Which the litigants must pay; derived from TB Shabbath 56b.

5. Cf. TB K'thuboth 105b: A judge was entering a small fishing boat to cross a river, and a man held out his hand to help him. When the judge learned that the man was a litigant in a case that he was to try, he disqualified himself.

6. *Ibid.* 105a.

SIDRAH MISHPATIM

83 [A JUDGE IS NOT TO TAKE ANY BRIBE] that the judge should not take a bribe from parties to a lawsuit, even to render true judgment. For it is stated, *And you shall take no bribe* (Exodus 23:8); and the prohibition about this matter was repeated in the Torah in another place.[1] So was it stated, too, in the Midrash *Sifre:*[2] *neither shall you take a bribe* (Deuteronomy 16:19)— even to declare the guiltless innocent and to impose punishment on the guilty.

At the root of the precept, that it is forbidden for us to take a bribe even to judge a case truly, lies the purpose to remove this evil habit from our midst, for fear that in consequence, with a bribe we will come to render false judgments. This is a clear, certain matter, requiring no proof.

Among the laws of the precept, there is what our Sages of blessed memory said, that both the one who gives and the one who accepts [the bribe] violate a negative precept: the one who gives it, on account of the injunction, *before the blind, you shall not put a stumbling-block* (Leviticus 19:14); and the one who receives it, who is [also] subject to the imprecation, *Cursed [be he who takes a bribe]* (Deuteronomy 27:25); moreover, he is under obligation to return it.[3]

Then [there is the law] that a judge is forbidden to raise his rank deliberately in order to increase the fees of his scribes;[4] even a bribe of words [flattery] he is forbidden to accept, but he must rather regard himself as though paying no attention at all to such matters if the parties to a lawsuit should perhaps honor him with words. In short, it is forbidden for a judge to receive any benefit at all from the litigants on account of his cases.[5] However, if the judge is a skilled worker, the Sages permitted him to ask a fee from the litigants for being idled [kept] from his work while he is occupied with their case; but this [on condition] that it should be evident that it is only a fee for being idled, and nothing more; and he should take equally from both.[6] [These] and the rest of its details are in the Talmud tractate *Sanhedrin*.

It is in effect in every place and every time, for men, since they judge cases. If someone violated it and accepted a bribe, he would disobey a [Divine] royal command. He is not given whiplashes, however, because it is given to rectification [the bribe can be returned].

⟨325⟩

§84: SH'MITTAH—TO LEAVE THE LAND FALLOW IN THE 7TH YEAR

[מִצְוַת שְׁמִטַּת קַרְקָעוֹת]

פד לְהַפְקִיר כָּל מַה שֶּׁתּוֹצִיא הָאָרֶץ בַּשָּׁנָה הַשְּׁבִיעִית שֶׁהִיא נִקְרֵאת מִפְּנֵי הַמַּעֲשֶׂה הַזֶּה שֶׁנִּתְחַיַּבְנוּ בָּהּ שְׁנַת הַשְּׁמִטָּה, וְיִזְכֶּה בְּפֵרוֹתֶיהָ כָּל הָרוֹצֶה לִזְכּוֹת, שֶׁנֶּאֱמַר: וְהַשְּׁבִיעִית תִּשְׁמְטֶנָּה וּנְטַשְׁתָּהּ וְאָכְלוּ אֶבְיֹנֵי עַמֶּךָ וְיִתְרָם תֹּאכַל חַיַּת הַשָּׂדֶה כֵּן תַּעֲשֶׂה לְכַרְמְךָ לְזֵיתֶךָ.

וּלְשׁוֹן מְכִילְתָּא: וַהֲלֹא הַכֶּרֶם וְהַזַּיִת בִּכְלָל הָיָה, כְּלוֹמַר שֶׁרֹאשׁ הַפָּסוּק שֶׁאָמַר "תִּשְׁמְטֶנָּה וּנְטַשְׁתָּהּ" יִכְלֹל כָּל מַה שֶּׁיִּצְמַח בָּאָרֶץ, בֵּין פֵּרוֹת אִילָן אוֹ פֵּרוֹת אֲדָמָה, וְלָמָּה פֵּרְטָן הַכָּתוּב שְׁנֵי אֵלֶּה, לְהַקִּישׁ לַכֶּרֶם שְׁאָר מִינֵי אִילָן, לְלַמֵּד שֶׁכְּמוֹ שֶׁיֵּשׁ בַּכֶּרֶם עֲשֵׂה וְלֹא תַעֲשֶׂה, שֶׁהֲרֵי בְּפֵרוּשׁ נִכְתַּב עָלָיו "וְאֶת עִנְּבֵי נְזִירֶךָ לֹא תִבְצֹר", כְּמוֹ כֵן כָּל שְׁאָר הָאִילָן יֵשׁ בָּהֶן עֲשֵׂה וְלֹא תַעֲשֶׂה.

וּלְפִיכָךְ פֶּרֶט כֶּרֶם וָזַיִת לְלַמֵּד עַל עִנְיָן זֶה, כִּי כַּוָּנַת הַכָּתוּב דְּלָאו דַּוְקָא כֶּרֶם וָזַיִת לְבַד אֶלָּא הוּא הַדִּין לְכָל שְׁאָר פֵּרוֹת הָאִילָן, אֶלָּא שֶׁהִזְכִּיר אֶחָד מֵהֶם וְהוּא מְלַמֵּד לְכֻלָּן, שֶׁזֶּה מִן הַמִּדּוֹת שֶׁהַתּוֹרָה נִדְרֶשֶׁת בָּהֶן. וּמִצְוָה זוֹ לְהַפְקִיר שֶׁתְּהֵא כָּל פֵּרוֹתֶיהָ, וְהַמִּצְוָה הָאַחֶרֶת שֶׁצִּוָּנוּ הָאֵל לִשְׁבֹּת בָּהּ, כְּמוֹ שֶׁכָּתוּב בְּכִי תִשָּׂא, "בֶּחָרִישׁ וּבַקָּצִיר תִּשְׁבֹּת", קֶשֶׁר אֶחָד לָהֶן.

וּמִשָּׁרְשֵׁי הַמִּצְוָה לִקְבֹּעַ בְּלִבֵּנוּ וּלְצַיֵּר צִיּוּר חָזָק בְּמַחְשַׁבְתֵּנוּ עִנְיַן חִדּוּשׁ הָעוֹלָם "כִּי שֵׁשֶׁת יָמִים עָשָׂה יְיָ אֶת הַשָּׁמַיִם וְאֶת הָאָרֶץ", וּבַיּוֹם הַשְּׁבִיעִי שֶׁלֹּא בָרָא דָבָר הִכְתִּיב מְנוּחָה עַל עַצְמוֹ. וּלְמַעַן הָסִיר וְלַעֲקֹר וְלִשְׁרֹשׁ מֵרַעְיוֹנֵינוּ דְּבַר הַקַּדְמוּת אֲשֶׁר יַאֲמִינוּ הַכּוֹפְרִים בַּתּוֹרָה וּבוֹ יֶהֶרְסוּ כָּל פִּנּוֹתֶיהָ וְיִפְרְצוּ חוֹמוֹתֶיהָ,

---

1. I.e. MdRSbY, as cited in Midrash haGadol and in ShM positive precept §134, which our author here follows in the first four paragraphs.
2. There is a positive precept to leave all seventh-year produce free for all to take, and a negative precept (§329) not to harvest it as private property.
3. I.e. one or two.
4. The eighth of the thirteen rules listed by R. Ishmael in the introduction to Midrash Sifra (recited at the end of the preliminary, private part of the morning prayers).
5. This expression is found in Rashi to Exodus 31:17.

SIDRAH **MISHPATIM**

[THE PRECEPT OF SH'MITTAH, TO LEAVE THE LAND FALLOW IN THE SEVENTH YEAR]

84 to leave ownerless all that the land will grow in the seventh year, which, on account of this procedure that we were commanded about it, is called the year of *sh'mittah* ("relinquishing, abandoning"); and anyone who wishes to obtain its produce may obtain it—for it is stated, *but the seventh year you shall let it rest and lie fallow, that the poor of your people may eat; and what they leave, the beast of the field may eat. You shall deal likewise with your vineyard and your olive orchard* (Exodus 23:11).

Now, this is the exposition of the Midrash *Mechilta:*[1] But were the vineyard and the olive orchard not included in the general rule? In other words, when the beginning of the verse states, "you shall let it rest and lie fallow," it includes all that the land will grow, whether fruit of the tree or produce of the earth. Then why did Scripture mention these two specifically?—It is to liken to the vineyard all other kinds of trees, to teach that just as in regard to a vineyard there are both a positive and a negative precept—for it is explicitly written about it, *and the grapes of your uncultivated vine you shall not gather* (Leviticus 25:5)—so are there for every other tree both a positive and a negative precept.[2]

For this reason Scripture mentioned the vineyard and olive orchard specifically, to teach about this subject [generally]; for Scripture's purpose is not strictly about the vineyard and olive orchard, but that the same law should apply to all other fruits of the tree. In truth, then, it mentioned one[3] of them, and this teaches [us] about all. For this is one of the rules by which the Torah is interpreted.[4]

Now this precept, to leave all its produce ownerless, and the other precept which God commanded us, to rest [from working the land]—as written in *sidrah ki thissa, in plowing time and in harvest you shall rest* (Exodus 34:21)—are linked together.

At the root of the precept lies the purpose to establish in our heart and set in our thought a firm conception of the doctrine that the world was brought into being as a new entity, out of nothing—*for in six days the Lord made heaven and earth* (Exodus 20:11), and on the seventh day, when He created nothing, He had Himself described [in Scripture] as "resting."[5] Then in order to remove, uproot and extirpate from our thinking any concept of the world's timeless pre-existence, in which those who deny the Torah believe, thereby demolishing its every

⟨327⟩

§84: SH'MITTAH—TO LEAVE THE LAND FALLOW IN THE 7TH YEAR

בָּאָה חוֹבָה עָלֵינוּ לְהוֹצִיא כָּל זְמַנֵּנוּ יוֹם וָיוֹם וְשָׁנָה וְשָׁנָה עַל דָּבָר זֶה לִמְנוֹת שֵׁשׁ שָׁנִים וְלִשְׁבֹּת בַּשְּׁבִיעִית, וּבְכֵן לֹא תִפָּרֵד הָעִנְיָן לְעוֹלָם מִבֵּין עֵינֵינוּ תָּמִיד, וְהוּא כְּעִנְיָן שֶׁאָנוּ מוֹצִיאִין יְמֵי הַשָּׁבוּעַ בְּשֵׁשֶׁת יְמֵי עֲבוֹדָה וְיוֹם מְנוּחָה.

וְלָכֵן צִוָּה בָּרוּךְ הוּא לְהַפְקִיר כָּל מַה שֶׁתּוֹצִיא הָאָרֶץ בְּשָׁנָה זוֹ מִלְּבַד הַשְּׁבִיתָה בָּהּ, כְּדֵי שֶׁיִּזְכֹּר הָאָדָם כִּי הָאָרֶץ שֶׁמּוֹצִיאָה אֵלָיו הַפֵּרוֹת בְּכָל שָׁנָה וְשָׁנָה לֹא בְכֹחָהּ וּסְגֻלָּתָהּ תּוֹצִיא אוֹתָם, כִּי יֵשׁ אָדוֹן עָלֶיהָ וְעַל אֲדוֹנֶיהָ, וּכְשֶׁהוּא חָפֵץ הוּא מְצַוֶּה אֵלָיו לְהַפְקִירָם. וְעוֹד יֵשׁ תּוֹעֶלֶת נִמְצָא בַּדָּבָר לִקְנוֹת בָּזֶה מִדַּת הַוַּתְרָנוּת, כִּי אֵין נָדִיב כַּנּוֹתֵן מִבְּלִי תִקְוָה אֶל הַגְּמוּל.

וְעוֹד יֵשׁ תּוֹעֶלֶת אַחֵר נִמְצָא בָּזֶה שֶׁיּוֹסִיף הָאָדָם בִּטָּחוֹן בַּשֵּׁם בָּרוּךְ הוּא, כִּי כָּל הַמּוֹצֵא עִם לְבָבוֹ לָתֵת וּלְהַפְקִיר לְעוֹלָם כָּל גִּדּוּלֵי קַרְקְעוֹתָיו וְנַחֲלַת אֲבוֹתָיו הַגְּדֵלִים בְּכָל שָׁנָה אַחַת וּמְלַמֵּד בְּכָךְ הוּא וְכָל הַמִּשְׁפָּחָה כָּל יָמָיו, לֹא תֶחֱזַק בּוֹ לְעוֹלָם מִדַּת הַכִּילוּת הַרְבֵּה וְלֹא מְעוּט הַבִּטָּחוֹן.

מִדִּינֵי הַמִּצְוָה, מַה הֵן הַדְּבָרִים מֵעֲבוֹדוֹת הָאָרֶץ שֶׁהֵן לָנוּ בְחִיּוּב שְׁבִיתָה זוֹ מִן הַתּוֹרָה, כְּגוֹן זְרִיעָה זְמִירָה קְצִירָה בְצִירָה, וַאֲשֶׁר הֵן אֲסוּרוֹת מִדְּרַבָּנָן, כְּגוֹן מְזַבֵּל וְחוֹפֵר, וַעֲבוֹדוֹת שֶׁבָּאִילָן כְּגוֹן חוֹתֵךְ מִמֶּנּוּ יַבֶּלֶת, פּוֹרֵק מִמֶּנּוּ עָלִין אוֹ בַדִּין יְבֵשִׁין, מְאַבֵּק בְּאָבָק אוֹ מְעַשֵּׁן תַּחְתָּיו לְהָמִית הַתּוֹלַעַת, סָךְ הַנְּטִיעוֹת, קוֹטֵם אוֹ מְפַסֵּג הָאִילָנוֹת, וּמַה שֶׁהִתִּירוּ לַעֲשׂוֹת כְּגוֹן סוֹקְרִין בְּסִיקְרָא, וְעוֹדֵר תַּחַת הַגְּפָנִים, וְדִין עֲבוֹדַת בֵּית הַשְּׁלָחִין, וְשֶׁלֹּא יַעֲשֶׂה אַשְׁפָּה בְּתוֹךְ שָׂדֵהוּ עַד שֶׁיַּעֲבֹר זְמַן הַזִּבּוּל וְאַחַר כָּךְ שֶׁתְּהֵא גְדוֹלָה וְלֹא יְהֵא נִרְאֶה כִמְזַבֵּל, וְשִׁעוּרָהּ מִמֵּאָה וַחֲמִשִּׁים סְאָה זֶבֶל וּלְמָעְלָה.

וּמַה שֶׁאָמְרוּ שֶׁהֶחְיֵיב לִמְנֹעַ מֵעֲבוֹדַת הָאָרֶץ שְׁלֹשִׁים יוֹם קֹדֶם שָׁנָה

---

6. Leviticus 25:4–5.
7. "Coating saplings": with an odious ointment or oil to keep off birds that would otherwise injure them in their search for food; "thinning" trees: Hebrew, *m'faség*, which generally denotes splitting, cutting or breaking off (see '*Aruch* s.v. *pasag*), hence "thinning" here. Rashi, however, explains it as tying tender trees to supports. TB Mo'ed Katan 3a; MT *hilchoth sh'mittah* i.
8. I.e. a tree which sheds its fruit, for the purpose that people should pray for it.
9. *Ibid.* 2a.
10. So that the owner should not be thought a sinner who is fertilizing the field.
11. Mishnah, Sh'vi'ith iii 1 (Rambam *ibid.* ii 1). A *se'ah*, in one view, is 0.3 cubic feet (8294 cubic centimeters); and 0.5 cubic feet (14,333 cubic centimeters) by another view.

basis and breaking its every wall, the obligation was imposed on us to spend our entire time, day by day, year by year, in reference to this—[hence] to count six years and rest on the seventh. And thus the matter will never ever depart from between our eyes [from our mind], as it is akin to our practice of spending the days of the week as six working days and a day of rest.

For this reason He (blessed is He) commanded [us] to leave free, ownerless, all that the land will produce in this year, apart from resting in it—so that a man will remember that the land which grows produce for him every single year does not grow it by its own power and aptitude: There is a Lord and Master over it and its owner, and when He so desires, He commands him to leave it all ownerless.

There is another useful benefit to be gained from it: to attain through it the quality of yielding and relinquishing. There is no one so generous as a person who gives with no hope of receiving anything in return.

Yet another useful benefit to be found in this is that a man increases [thereby his] trust in the Eternal Lord, blessed is He. For any man who finds it in his heart to give and leave free, ownerless for all the world, all the produce grown by his lands and the inheritance of his fathers for one whole year, and he and his family become trained in this all his life—neither the quality of miserliness nor a lessening of Divine trust will ever seize hold of him.

[These are some] of the laws of the precept: what are the kinds of labor on the land from which we are obligated to rest by the law of the Torah—for instance, sowing, pruning and trimming, reaping and vintage (grape-gathering);[6] and which are forbidden by the law of the Sages—such as fertilizing and digging, and forms of work on a tree, such as cutting away from it any thickening on the bark, removing dried leaves or twigs, covering [exposed roots] with dust or making smoke under it to kill worms, coating saplings, breaking off [the tops of twigs] or thinning trees.[7] Then we have what they permitted doing: for instance, marking [a tree] with red,[8] or hoeing under grapevines;[7] the law of work in an irrigated field;[9] that a compost pile (dunghill) should not be made within the field until the time of fertilization has passed,[10] and after that it should be large, and he should not appear to be fertilizing [the field]; and its volume should be from 150 *se'ah* and up.[11]

Then there is the teaching of the Sages that the duty to refrain from

§84: SH'MITTAH—TO LEAVE THE LAND FALLOW IN THE 7TH YEAR

שְׁבִיעִית, וְהִיא הֲלָכָה לְמֹשֶׁה מִסִּינַי. וְדִין שְׂדֵה אִילָן, כַּמָּה זְמַן אָסוּר בַּעֲבוֹדָה מִשָּׁנָה שִׁשִּׁית, וּמַהוּ נִקְרָא שְׂדֵה אִילָן, וְאִסּוּר הַבְרָכָה וְהַרְכָּבָה, וְאִם עָבַר וְעָשָׂה מַה יְּהֵא בִּנְטִיעוֹתָיו, וּפֵרוֹת שְׁבִיעִית מַה דִּינָן, דְּכָל שֶׁהוּא מְיֻחָד לְמַאֲכַל אָדָם כְּגוֹן חִטִּים וּשְׂעוֹרִים וּפֵרוֹת אֵין עוֹשִׂין מֵהֶן מְלוּגְמָא אוֹ רְטִיָּה, שֶׁנֶּאֱמַר בָּהֶן "לְאָכְלָה", וְשֶׁאֵינוֹ מְיֻחָד לְמַאֲכַל אָדָם כְּגוֹן קוֹצִים וְדַרְדָּרִים עוֹשִׂין מֵהֶן מְלוּגְמָא לְאָדָם וְלֹא לִבְהֵמָה, וְשֶׁאֵינוֹ מְיֻחָד לְאָדָם וְלִבְהֵמָה כְּגוֹן פּוּאָה וְאֵזוֹב וְקוֹרָנִית הֲרֵי הוּא תָּלוּי בְּמַחְשֶׁבֶת הָאָדָם, חֲשָׁבָן לַאֲכִילָה דִּינָן כְּמַאֲכָל, חֲשָׁבָן לְעֵצִים דִּינָן כְּעֵצִים; וְיֶתֶר רַבֵּי פְרָטֶיהָ כֻּלָּן, מְבֹאָרִים בְּמַסֶּכְתָּא הַבְּנוּיָה עַל זֶה וְהִיא מַסֶּכֶת שְׁבִיעִית.

וְנוֹהֶגֶת בִּזְכָרִים וּנְקֵבוֹת בְּאֶרֶץ יִשְׂרָאֵל בִּלְבַד, וּבִזְמַן שֶׁיִּשְׂרָאֵל שָׁם, שֶׁנֶּאֱמַר עָלֶיהָ "כִּי תָבוֹאוּ אֶל הָאָרֶץ", וּמִדִּרְבָּנָן נוֹהֶגֶת אֲפִלּוּ בַּזְּמַן הַזֶּה בָּאָרֶץ דַּוְקָא, וְכָל מָקוֹם שֶׁהֶחֱזִיקוּ בּוֹ עוֹלֵי בָבֶל עַד כְּזִיב וְלֹא כְזִיב בִּכְלָל אָסוּר בַּעֲבוֹדָה, וְכָל הַסְּפִיחִין הַצּוֹמְחִין שָׁם אֲסוּרִין בַּאֲכִילָה, כִּי הֵם קִדְּשׁוּ הַמְּקוֹמוֹת שֶׁהֶחֱזִיקוּ בָּהֶן לְעוֹלָם, וְהַמְּקוֹמוֹת שֶׁהֶחֱזִיקוּ בָּהֶן כְּבָר עוֹלֵי מִצְרַיִם וְלֹא עוֹלֵי בָבֶל שֶׁהֵן מִכְּזִיב וְעַד הַנָּהָר וְעַד אֲמָנָה, אַף עַל פִּי שֶׁהֵן אֲסוּרִין הַיּוֹם מִדִּרְבָּנָן בַּעֲבוֹדָה בַּשְּׁבִיעִית שֶׁהֶחְמִירוּ בָּהֶן, הַסְּפִיחִין שֶׁצּוֹמְחִין שָׁם מֻתָּרִין בַּאֲכִילָה אַחַר שֶׁלֹּא נִתְקַדֵּשׁ בְּעוֹלֵי בָבֶל. וּמִן הַנָּהָר וַאֲמָנָה וָהָלְאָה מֻתָּר בַּעֲבוֹדָה.

סוּרְיָא, וְהוּא מִן הַמְּקוֹמוֹת שֶׁכָּבַשׁ דָּוִד קֹדֶם שֶׁנִּכְבְּשָׁה אֶרֶץ יִשְׂרָאֵל כֻּלָּהּ, וְזֶהוּ נִקְרָא לְרַבּוֹתֵינוּ זִכְרוֹנָם לִבְרָכָה כִּבּוּשׁ יָחִיד, וְהָאָרֶץ הַזֹּאת הִיא כְּנֶגֶד אֲרַם

---

12. TB Mo'éd Katan 3b.
13. Mishnah, Sh'vi'ith i 1.
14. Ibid. 2.
15. Ibid. 6, TB Yevamoth 83b.
16. Mishnah, Sh'vi'ith viii 1 (MT hilchoth sh'mittah v 11).
17. I.e. 'Achziv (Joshua 19:29), north of 'Acco.
18. I.e. hor ha-har (Numbers 34:7), at the northernmost tip of the land of Israel.
19. Mishnah, Sh'vi'ith vi 1 (Rambam ibid. iv 26).
20. TB Gittin 8b, etc.

working the land thirty days before the seventh year is a normative law given to Moses at Sinai;[12] the law of an orchard: how much time out of the sixth year is work on it forbidden;[13] what is called a cultivated field of trees;[14] the prohibition against implanting growing vine shoots and against grafting;[15] and if someone transgressed and did [one of these forbidden labors] what should be done with the saplings;[15] what the law is for produce of the seventh year—that whatever is specifically for humans to eat, such as wheat, barley, and fruit, no poultice or compress should be made of them, since it is stated about them, *for food* (Leviticus 25:6); and out of what is not specifically food for humans, such as thorns and thistles, a poultice may be made for a man but not for an animal; as for what is not specifically food for humans and animals, such as madder (*Rubia Tinctorum*), hyssop and thyme, it depends on the thought of the man: if he intended them for food, they have the same law as food; if he intended them for wood (fuel), they have the same law as wood.[16] [These] and the rest of its many details are all explained in the tractate composed about this subject: *Sh'vi'ith*.

It applies to both man and woman, in the land of Israel alone, at the time that the Israelites are there: for it is stated about it, *When you come into the land* (Leviticus 25:2). By the law of the Sages, though, it is in effect at this time too, but solely in the land [of Israel]. Every area of which those who came up from Babylonia [returning from exile with Ezra and Neḥemiah] took possession, until K'ziv but not including K'ziv,[17] comes under the ban of labor [on the land], and all produce that grows of itself there is forbidden to be eaten; for they hallowed forever the places where they took possession. As for those areas of which those who came up from Egypt took possession long before, but those who came up from Babylonia did not—from K'ziv to the river [Shiḥor] and on to 'Amanah[18]—even though they are forbidden nowadays to be worked in the seventh year, by the law of the Sages, because they were stringent about them—produce which grows there of itself is allowed to be eaten, since [that territory] was not hallowed by those who came up from Babylonia. And from the river and 'Amanah and further out, [the land] is allowed to be worked.[19]

Syria is among the regions that David took in battle before the entire land of Israel was conquered. This is what was called by our Sages of blessed memory "the conquest of an individual."[20] That land corresponds to 'Aram-naharayim (Mesopotamia) and 'Aram-ẓoba,

§84–86: SH'MITTAH / SABBATH REST / NOT TO SWEAR BY AN IDOL

נְהָרִים וַאֲרַם צוֹבָא כָּל יַד פְּרָת עַד בָּבֶל, כְּגוֹן דַּמֶּשֶׂק וְאַחְלָב וְחָרָן וּמְקוֹמוֹת אֲחֵרִים סְמוּכִין לָאֵלּוּ, אַף־עַל־פִּי שֶׁאֵין שְׁבִיעִית נוֹהֶגֶת בָּהֶן מִן הַתּוֹרָה, גָּזְרוּ עֲלֵיהֶן שֶׁיִּהְיוּ אוֹתָן מְקוֹמוֹת אֲסוּרִין בַּעֲבוֹדָה כְּאֶרֶץ יִשְׂרָאֵל. אֲבָל עַמּוֹן וּמוֹאָב וּמִצְרַיִם וְשִׁנְעָר אַף־עַל־פִּי שֶׁהֵן חַיָּבִין בְּמַעֲשֵׂר אֵין שְׁבִיעִית נוֹהֶגֶת בָּהֶן, וְכָל שֶׁכֵּן שֶׁאֵין נוֹהֶגֶת בִּשְׁאָר חוּצָה לָאָרֶץ.

וְעוֹבֵר עָלֶיהָ וְנָעַל כַּרְמוֹ אוֹ שֶׁדֵּהוּ בַּשְּׁבִיעִית אוֹ אָסַף כָּל פֵּרוֹתָיו לְבֵיתוֹ בִּזְמַן שֶׁיִּשְׂרָאֵל עַל אַדְמָתָן בִּטֵּל עֲשֵׂה. וּמִכָּל מָקוֹם מֻתָּר לֶאֱסֹף מֵהֶן מְעַט מְעַט לַבַּיִת לֶאֱכֹל, וּבִלְבַד שֶׁתְּהֵא יַד הַכֹּל שָׁוָה בָּהֶן כְּאִלּוּ אֵין לַקַּרְקַע בְּעָלִים יְדוּעִים.

[מִצְוַת שְׁבִיתָה בְּשַׁבָּת]

פה לִשְׁבֹּת מִמְּלָאכָה בְּיוֹם הַשַּׁבָּת, שֶׁנֶּאֱמַר "וּבַיּוֹם הַשְּׁבִיעִי תִּשְׁבֹּת". כָּל עִנְיָנָהּ כָּתוּב לְמַעְלָה, בַּלָּאו הַבָּא עַל זֶה. וְנִכְפְּלָה מִצְוַת שַׁבָּת עַד י"ב פְּעָמִים.

[שֶׁלֹּא לִשָּׁבַע בַּעֲבוֹדָה זָרָה]

פו שֶׁלֹּא נִשָּׁבַע בְּשֵׁם עֲבוֹדָה זָרָה אֲפִלּוּ לְעוֹבְדֶיהָ, וְלֹא נַשְׁבִּיעַ לְגוֹי בָּהּ, שֶׁנֶּאֱמַר "וְשֵׁם אֱלֹהִים אֲחֵרִים לֹא תַזְכִּירוּ". וּבִכְלָל הַהַזְכָּרָה שֶׁמַּשְׁמָעֵנוּ בֵּין נִשְׁבַּע בֵּין מַשְׁבִּיעַ. וְיֵשׁ מְפָרְשִׁים שֶׁעִקַּר לָאו זֶה אֵינוֹ בָּא אֶלָּא בְּעוֹסֵק עִם הַגּוֹי בְּיוֹם אֵידוֹ וּמַרְוִיחוֹ דְּאָזִיל וּמוֹדֶה, וְקָא עָבַר עַל "לֹא תַזְכִּירוּ", כְּלוֹמַר שֶׁלֹּא יִזְכְּרוּם אֲחֵרִים עַל יָדְךָ הַזְכָּרָה הָאֲסוּרָה לָהֶם, דְּהַיְנוּ עַל דַּעַת לְעָבְדָם שֶׁהוּא אָסוּר אַף לָהֶם מִן הַתּוֹרָה, שֶׁבְּנֵי נֹחַ מֻזְהָרִים עַל עֲבוֹדָה זָרָה. וְעוֹד הוֹסִיפוּ זִכְרוֹנָם לִבְרָכָה הַרְחָקָה וְאָמְרוּ בְּסַנְהֶדְרִין שֶׁלֹּא יֹאמַר אָדָם לַחֲבֵרוֹ "שְׁמֹר לִי בְּצַד עֲבוֹדָה זָרָה פְּלוֹנִית".

---

21. So that people should not leave the land of Israel and settle there (Rambam ibid.); Mishnah ibid. 2; see also MT hilchoth t'rumoth i 3, 9.

22. Mishnah, Yadayim iv 3 (MT hilchoth sh'mittah iv 27).

23. See Leviticus 25:6.

§85 1. So ShM root principle 9.

§86 1. So Mechilta, first edition.

2. So ShM negative precept §14, evidently from his version of Mechilta; see *Torah Shelemah*, Exodus 23, §183 and note.

3. So Rashi, TB 'Avodah Zarah 6a, s.v. *m'shum*.

4. See §26, note 32.

the entire bank of the Euphrates up to Babylonia—for instance, Damascus, Aḥlav, Ḥaran, and other places close to these. Even though the precept of the seventh year does not apply to them by the law of the Torah, the Sages decreed about them that work [in the fields] should be forbidden in those regions as in the land of Israel.[21] However, in Ammon, Moab, Egypt and Shin'ar, even though they are under the obligation of *ma'asér* (tithes), the law of the seventh year does not apply;[22] and it is all the more certainly not in force elsewhere outside the land [of Israel].

If a person violates it and locks up his vineyard or field in the seventh year, or if he gathers all his produce into his house—this in a period when the Israelites are on their homeland—he has disobeyed a positive precept. It is, however, permitted to gather from it a little at a time into the house, to eat, as long as everybody has equal rights and access to it, as though the land (field) had no known owner.[23]

85 [THE MITZVAH OF RESTING ON THE SABBATH]

to rest from work on the Sabbath day: for it is stated, *but on the seventh day you shall rest* (Exodus 23:12). Its whole content was written above, in the negative precept that applies to this (§32). The *mitzvah* of the Sabbath was repeated [in Scripture] as much as twelve times.[1]

86 [NOT TO SWEAR BY ANY IDOL]

that we should not swear by the name of an idol, even to its worshippers,[1] nor should we have a non-Jew swear by it—as it is stated, *make no mention of the name of other gods* (Exodus 23:13). [In the Oral Tradition] we learned that "mention" includes both taking and imposing an oath.[2] Some explain that principally this prohibition applies to none but a person who has dealings with a heathen on his holyday, and he brings him profit, so that [the heathen] goes and gives thanks [to his idol][3]—and thus [the Jew] has violated the injunction, "make no mention"—i.e. that others should not mention them on account of you in a way that is forbidden to them, which means with the intention of worshipping them. For this is forbidden to them as well by the Torah's law, as the descendants of Noah are adjured about idolatry.[4] In addition, our Sages added a measure of distance [from it] and ruled in the tractate *Sanhedrin* (63b) that a man should not say to his fellow, "Wait for me at the side of that certain idol."

§86–87: TO SWEAR BY NO IDOL / TO LEAD NO JEW INTO IDOLATRY

מִשָּׁרְשֵׁי הַמִּצְוָה לְהַרְחִיק כָּל עִנְיְנֵי עֲבוֹדָה זָרָה בֵּין בְּמַעֲשֶׂה בֵּין בְּדִבּוּר עַד שֶׁלֹּא יַעֲלֶה זִכְרָהּ בִּלְבָבֵנוּ לְעוֹלָם. וְהִשְׂגִּיחוּ רַבּוֹתֵינוּ זִכְרוֹנָם לִבְרָכָה וְאָמְרוּ שֶׁבְּמָ"ד מְקוֹמוֹת הִזְהִירָתְנוּ הַתּוֹרָה עָלֶיהָ לְרֹב מְאוּסָהּ, צֵא וַחֲשֹׁב.

מִדִּינֵי הַמִּצְוָה, מַה שֶּׁאָמְרוּ שֶׁאָפִלּוּ לְהַזְכִּיר שֵׁם עֲבוֹדָה זָרָה בְּדֶרֶךְ שְׁבוּעָה אָסוּר, וְשֶׁכָּל עֲבוֹדָה זָרָה הַכְּתוּבָה בַּסְּפָרִים הַקֹּדֶשׁ מֻתָּר לְהַזְכִּיר שְׁמָהּ, כְּגוֹן פְּעוֹר וּבֵל וּנְבוֹ וְכַיּוֹצֵא בָּהֶן; וְשֶׁאָסוּר לִגְרֹם לַאֲחֵרִים שֶׁיִּדְּרוּ וְשֶׁיְּקַיְּמוּ בְּשֵׁם עֲבוֹדָה זָרָה, אֲבָל אֵינוֹ לוֹקֶה אֶלָּא הַנּוֹדֵר וְהַמְּקַיֵּם בִּשְׁמָהּ, דְּהַיְנוּ הַנִּשְׁבָּע בְּעַצְמוֹ וְלֹא הַמַּשְׁבִּיעַ, וְאַף־עַל־פִּי שֶׁהַמַּשְׁבִּיעַ כְּמוֹ כֵן בַּכְּלָל הַלָּאו הוּא לְפִי דַּעַת הָרַמְבָּ"ם זִכְרוֹנוֹ לִבְרָכָה; וְיֶתֶר פְּרָטֶיהָ, מְבֹאָרִים בְּפֶרֶק ז' מִסַּנְהֶדְרִין.

וְנוֹהֶגֶת בְּכָל מָקוֹם וּבְכָל זְמַן בִּזְכָרִים וּנְקֵבוֹת. וְהָעוֹבֵר עָלֶיהָ וְנִשְׁבַּע בְּדָבָר מִכָּל הַנִּבְרָאִים שֶׁיַּאֲמִינוּ בָּם הַכּוֹפְרִים הַסְּכָלִים עַל צַד הַגְּדֻלָּה, חַיָּב מַלְקוֹת; כֵּן כָּתַב הָרַב זִכְרוֹנוֹ לִבְרָכָה, וְאַף־עַל־פִּי שֶׁאֵין בּוֹ מַעֲשֶׂה, מֵרֹב חֹמֶר עֲבוֹדָה זָרָה הוּא.

[שֶׁלֹּא לְהַדִּיחַ בְּנֵי יִשְׂרָאֵל אַחַר עֲבוֹדָה זָרָה]

פז שֶׁלֹּא יִקְרָא אָדָם בְּנֵי־אָדָם לַעֲבוֹדָה זָרָה וִיזָרֵז אוֹתָם עַל כָּךְ, וְאַף־עַל־פִּי שֶׁזֶּה הַקּוֹרֵא לֹא יַעֲבְדֶנָּה וְלֹא יַעֲשֶׂה לָהּ פְּעֻלָּה מִן הַפְּעֻלּוֹת רַק הַקְּרִיאָה לְבַד, וְזֶהוּ נִקְרָא מַדִּיחַ. וְכֵן אָמְרוּ בְּסַנְהֶדְרִין "לֹא יִשָּׁמַע עַל פִּיךָ", אַזְהָרָה לַמַּדִּיחַ. וְכֵן אָמְרוּ בִּמְכִלְתָּא.

שֹׁרֶשׁ הַמִּצְוָה יָדוּעַ.

דִּינֶיהָ בְּפֶרֶק עֲשִׂירִי מִסַּנְהֶדְרִין. וּמִי שֶׁלֹּא הִדִּיחַ בְּעִנְיָן זֶה אֶלָּא אָדָם אֶחָד אֵינוֹ נִקְרָא מַדִּיחַ אֶלָּא מֵסִית, וּבַסֵּדֶר רְאֵה אָנֹכִי נִכְתֹּב אַזְהָרַת מֵסִית בְּעֶזְרַת הַשֵּׁם

---

5. Tanḥuma, *va-yikra* 2 (ed. Buber, 3) mentions forty-eight places.
6. TB Sanhedrin 63b.
7. MT *hilchoth ʿavodath kochavim* v 11.
8. ShM negative precept §14.
9. For which the standard rule is that no whiplashes are given (TB P'saḥim 63b, etc.)

§87 1. Evidently the lost MdRSbY, as cited in Midrash haGadol and ShM negative precept §15.
2. So Rambam *ibid*.

At the root of the precept lies the purpose to move the entire matter of idolatry far away, both in action and in speech, until any remembrance of it will not ever arise in our heart. Our Sages of blessed memory took note and said that in forty-four instances [in Scripture] the Torah adjured us about it,[5] on account of its great abhorrence. Go forth and count.

Among the laws of the precept there is what our Sages said,[6] that even to mention the name of an idol not by way of taking an oath, is forbidden; but if any idol is found written in the sacred Scriptures, one is allowed to mention its name—for instance, Pe'or (Numbers 23:28), Bel and Nebo (Isaiah 46:1), and so on. It is forbidden to cause others to take a vow or swear in the name of an idol;[6] but no one other than the person who takes the vow or the oath in its name is given whiplashes—i.e. the one who himself swears, but not the one who imposes the oath—even though the one who imposes the oath falls equally within the scope of the negative precept; this is the view of Rambam of blessed memory.[7] The rest of its details are clarified in chapter 7 of the Talmud tractate *Sanhedrin*.

It is in effect in every place, at every time, for both man and woman. If someone transgresses it and swears by any one of the created entities in which foolish heretics believe, on account of [its supposed] greatness, he is given whiplashes. So wrote the master scholar [Rambam] of blessed memory.[8] And even though it involves no physical action,[9] this is so [he is flogged] on account of the immense seriousness of idolatry.

87 [NOT TO LEAD ISRAELITES ASTRAY INTO IDOLATRY] that a man should not call people to idol-worship and urge them on to it, even if this summoner will himself not worship it or do any action on its behalf other than the calling alone. He is what is called *madi-aḥ*, "one who leads astray." And so our Sages said in the tractate *Sanhedrin* (63b): *nor let this be heard out of your mouth* (Exodus 23:13)—this is an admonition to one who would lead others astray. The same was taught in the Midrash *Mechilta*.[1]

The root reason for the precept is known (evident).

Its laws are [to be found] in chapter 10 of the tractate *Sanhedrin*. If someone seeks to mislead no more than one person in this way, he is not called *madi-aḥ*, "one who leads astray," but rather *mésith*, "an inciter."[2] In *sidrah r'éh* I will write of the admonition about an inciter,

§87: NOT TO LEAD ISRAELITES ASTRAY INTO IDOL-WORSHIP

בְּלָאו כ"א. אֲבָל כְּשֶׁמַּדִּיחַ שְׁנֵי אֲנָשִׁים אוֹ יוֹתֵר נִקְרָא מַדִּיחַ.

וְזֶה שֶׁאַתָּה מוֹצֵא כָּל הַרְחָקוֹת אֵלּוּ בַּעֲבוֹדָה זָרָה וְגֹדֶל הָעֹנֶשׁ בָּהּ עַד שֶׁנִּכְפְּלָה בְּמ"ד מְקוֹמוֹת בַּתּוֹרָה, וְשֶׁתִּמְצָא הַתּוֹרָה לַשֵּׁם בָּרוּךְ הוּא קַנָּא עַל עוֹבְדֶיהָ, אַל יַעֲלֶה בְלִבְּךָ שֶׁקִּנְאַת הָאֵל וְהַהַרְחָקוֹת אֵלּוּ נִכְתְּבוּ זוּלָתִי מִצַּד הָעוֹבְדִים, כִּי הַשֵּׁם בָּרוּךְ הוּא וּבָרוּךְ שְׁמוֹ בֵּין שֶׁיַּעֲבְדוּ אוֹתוֹ בְּנֵי אָדָם אוֹ יַעַבְדוּ מַלְאָךְ אוֹ גַלְגַּל אוֹ כּוֹכָב אוֹ אֶחָד מִכָּל בְּרוּאָיו אֵין שׁוּם צַד תּוֹסֶפֶת וְגֵרוּעַ נוֹפֵל בָּזֶה בִּכְבוֹדוֹ בָּרוּךְ הוּא, כִּי תַּכְלִית הַכָּבוֹד וְהַהוֹד לֹא נוֹסַף וְלֹא נִגְרַע בִּשְׁבִיל דָּבָר, אַף כִּי בְּמַעֲשָׂיו אֲנַחְנוּ פְּעֻלּוֹתָיו אַנְשֵׁי הַגּוּפוֹת.

אַךְ תֵּדַע בֶּאֱמֶת כִּי כָּל עִנְיָנִים אֵלֶּה נֶאֱמָרִים עַל צַד הַמְּקַבְּלִים, יֹאמַר כִּי בְּעֵת שֶׁהָאָדָם מוֹצִיא עַצְמוֹ לְגַמְרֵי וּמִתְפַּשֵּׁט מֵאֱמוּנַת הַשֵּׁם בָּרוּךְ הוּא וּמוֹלִיךְ גּוּפוֹ וּמַתְפִּיס מַחְשְׁבוֹתָיו אַחֲרֵי הַהֶבֶל, לֹא יִהְיֶה בּוֹ כְּלָל רָאוּי לְהָנִיחַ בּוֹ שׁוּם בְּרָכָה וְשׁוּם טוֹבָה, אֲבָל יִהְיֶה רָאוּי לְהָנִיחַ עָלָיו כָּל מַה שֶּׁהוּא הֵפֶךְ הַבְּרָכָה, וְהוּא הַקְּלָלָה וְהַמְּאֵרָה וְהֶחֳלָאִים וְכָל רָעוֹת, כִּי הוּא נִתְרַחֵק תַּכְלִית הָרִחוּק מִכָּל גְּבוּלֵי הַטּוֹב, וְעַל-כֵּן לֹא תַשִּׂיגֵהוּ כִּי אִם רַע מִכָּל צְדָדָיו. וְעַל דֶּרֶךְ הַמָּשָׁל יֵאָמֵר עָלָיו כְּאִלּוּ הַשֵּׁם (יִתְבָּרַךְ) שֶׁהוּא אֲדוֹן הַטּוֹבָה נַעֲשָׂה לוֹ לְאוֹיֵב וְעוֹצֵר מִמֶּנּוּ כָּל הַטּוֹבוֹת, וּכְאִלּוּ הוּא מְקַנֵּא בּוֹ בְּהַנִּיחוֹ עֲבוֹדָתוֹ וְעוֹבֵד אֶת אֲחֵרִים.

וְאוּלָם הָאֵל בָּרוּךְ הוּא לֹא אוֹיֵב לִבְרִיָּה וְלֹא יְקַנֵּא בְּבֶן-אָדָם, כִּי בְיָדוֹ לְהַחֲזִירָם כֻּלָּם עִם כָּל שְׁאָר הָעוֹלָם כֻּלּוֹ לְתֹהוּ וָבֹהוּ בְּהַנַּחַת חֶפְצוֹ בְּבִטּוּל, כַּאֲשֶׁר בְּרָאָם בְּהַנַּחַת חֶפְצוֹ בַּבְּרִיאָה, אֲבָל יְכֻנּוּ שְׁמוֹ בָּרוּךְ הוּא בְּקַנָּא עַל דֶּרֶךְ מַעֲשֵׂה בְּנֵי הָאָדָם לְפִי שֶׁאֵין בֵּינֵיהֶם שִׂנְאָה גְּדוֹלָה כְּמִי שֶׁמְּקַנֵּא בְּאִישׁ עַל שׁוּם

---

3. See §86, note 5.

4. E.g. in Exodus 20:5. Cf. Rambam, *Guide* I 36: Know that when you will look through the Torah and all the Books of the Prophets, you will not find the expression of fury or anger or vengeful jealousy [ascribed to the Almighty] except in connection with idolatry; nor will you find anyone called an enemy of the Lord ... except someone who worships idols.

with the help of the Eternal Lord, in the twenty-first negative precept (§462). But when he urges two people or more to idolatry, he is called "one who leads astray."

Now, it is a fact that you find all these measures about idolatry to keep it far away, and the immensity of the punishment for it, to the extent that it was repeated in forty-four instances in the Torah;[3] and the Torah describes the Eternal Lord as vengefully jealous toward its worshippers.[4] Yet let the thought not arise in your heart that the vengeful jealousy of God and these measures for keeping far away from it were written in any other sense but from the point of view of the worshippers. For as regards the Eternal Lord (blessed be He and blessed His name), whether human beings worship Him or an angel, a constellation or a star, or any one of His creations, no element whatever of increase or diminution occurs thereby in His glory (blessed is He). The ultimate perfection of glory and majesty is not to be augmented or decreased by anything, even if among His handiwork we are His [personal] creations, as physical human beings.

Know, then, in truth, that all these matters were said from the point of view of those who receive [these matters]. It means that when a man removes himself completely and divests himself of faith in the Eternal Lord (blessed is He), and he directs his body and attaches his thoughts to vapid nonsense, he will not be worthy at all for any blessing or any good to be bestowed upon him. Rather, he will be fit to have whatever is the opposite of blessing bestowed upon him, which means curse and malediction, afflictions and every evil. For he has moved utterly far away from all the boundaries of goodness. Therefore nothing but evil can reach him, from all sides. By way of metaphor it would be said of him that it is as if the Eternal Lord (be He blessed), who is the Master of goodness, became an enemy to him and withheld every goodness from him; and it is as if He is vengefully jealous about him, as he abandoned His worship and now worships others.

God, however (blessed is He), is not hostile to any human being and is not vengeful toward any person. For it lies in His power to return them all, with the entire rest of the world, to a state of chaos and void, by setting His desire on the nullification [of existence]—just as He created them by setting His desire on the Creation. But the attributive name "vengefully jealous" is ascribed to Him out of the terms of human activity: for there is no greater hatred among them

§87–88: LEAD NO JEW INTO IDOLATRY / CELEBRATING FESTIVALS

דָּבָר אוֹ מְקַנֵּא בְּאִשְׁתּוֹ בִּזְנוֹתָהּ עִם אֲחֵרִים. וְעַל כֵּן נִכְתְּבוּ בַּתּוֹרָה דִּמְיוֹנוֹת אֵלּוּ אֶצְלוֹ בָּרוּךְ הוּא כְּדֵי שֶׁיְּבִינֵם אֹזֶן הַשּׁוֹמֵעַ.

וְנוֹהֵג אִסּוּר זֶה בְּכָל מָקוֹם וּבְכָל זְמַן בִּזְכָרִים וּנְקֵבוֹת. אֲבָל דִּין הָעוֹבֵר עָלֶיהָ בֵּין אִישׁ וְאִשָּׁה, שֶׁהֵן בִּסְקִילָה, אֵינוֹ אֶלָּא בַּמָּקוֹם הָרָאוּי לַמִּשְׁפָּט שֶׁהוּא הָאָרֶץ הַנִּבְחֶרֶת.

[מִצְוַת חֲגִיגָה בָּרְגָלִים]

פח לָחֹג בָּרְגָלִים, וְהוּא שֶׁנִּצְטַוֵּינוּ לַעֲלוֹת לָרֶגֶל לַמִּקְדָּשׁ שָׁלֹשׁ פְּעָמִים בַּשָּׁנָה, וְהֵן סָמוּךְ לְפֶסַח וְשָׁבוּעוֹת וְסֻכּוֹת, כְּדֵי שֶׁנָּחֹג שָׁם, שֶׁנֶּאֱמַר "שָׁלֹשׁ רְגָלִים תָּחֹג לִי בַּשָּׁנָה". וּמֵעִנְיַן הַחֲגִיגָה הוּא שֶׁנַּעֲלֶה שָׁם קָרְבָּן וְנַקְרִיבֵהוּ שְׁלָמִים לִכְבוֹד הֶחָג. וְנִכְפְּלָה מִצְוָה זוּ פַּעֲמַיִם בַּתּוֹרָה, וְאָמְרוּ זִכְרוֹנָם לִבְרָכָה בְּמַסֶּכֶת חֲגִיגָה: שָׁלֹשׁ מִצְוֹת נִצְטַוּוּ יִשְׂרָאֵל בָּרֶגֶל, חֲגִיגָה רְאִיָּה שִׂמְחָה.

מִשָּׁרְשֵׁי מִצְוָה זוּ לְפִי שֶׁאֵינוֹ בַּדִּין לָבוֹא בְּיָדַיִם רֵיקָנִיּוֹת לְפָנָיו בָּרוּךְ הוּא, וְאַף־עַל־פִּי שֶׁהָאֱמֶת כִּי אֵינוֹ צָרִיךְ דָּבָר מִיָּדֵינוּ, כְּמוֹ שֶׁכָּתוּב, "אִם אֶרְעַב לֹא אֹמַר לָךְ", אַף־עַל־פִּי־כֵן בְּדִמְיוֹן מַחֲשַׁבְתֵּנוּ אֲנַחְנוּ רוֹאִין כְּאִלּוּ נַעֲמֹד לְפָנָיו. וְהָאֱמֶת שֶׁהַנְּפָשׁוֹת קְרוֹבוֹת אֶל הַטּוֹב בַּמָּקוֹם הַהוּא יוֹתֵר מִשְּׁאָר מְקוֹמוֹת וְאוֹר פְּנֵי מֶלֶךְ נֹגַהּ עֲלֵיהֶם שָׁם. וְעַל כֵּן רָאוּי לָנוּ לַעֲשׂוֹת מַעֲשֵׂה הַקָּרְבָּן בָּעֵת הַהִיא, כִּי בִּפְעֻלַּת הַקָּרְבָּן נִתְכַּן לְקַבָּלַת הַטּוֹבָה וְתִתְעַלֶּה נַפְשׁוֹתֵינוּ מַעֲלָה מַעֲלָה, כְּמוֹ שֶׁכָּתוּב בְּעֶזְרַת הַשֵּׁם.

מִדִּינֵי הַמִּצְוָה, מַה שֶּׁאָמְרוּ זִכְרוֹנָם לִבְרָכָה שֶׁקָּרְבָּנוֹת אֵלּוּ אֵין לָהֶן שִׁעוּר,

---

5. See, however, §47, note 7.

§88 1. Exodus 34:23–24, Deuteronomy 16:16.
2. Paragraph based on ShM positive precept §52.
3. One may bring any acceptable animals, in any amount; Mishnah, Pe'ah i 1.

than that of one who is jealous of a man over something, or one who is jealous over his wife when she acts immorally with others. For this reason these terms of similitude were written in the Torah in regard to Him (blessed is He), so that the ear of the listener should be able to understand them.

This prohibition is in force in every place, at every time, for both man and woman. But the punishment of one who violates it, whether man or woman, who is to be stoned to death, is given only in the place that is proper for a [capital] trial, which is the chosen land.[5]

[THE PRECEPT OF CELEBRATION ON THE PILGRIMAGE FESTIVALS]

88 to celebrate on the pilgrimage festivals, as we were commanded to go up on pilgrimage to the Sanctuary three times a year, i.e. shortly before Passover, *Shavu'oth* and *Sukkoth*, so that we should celebrate [the festivals] there. For it is stated, *Three pilgrimage festivals shall you celebrate to Me in the year* (Exodus 23:14). The substance of the celebration is that we should ascend there with an animal offering and sacrifice it as *sh'lamim*, a peace-offering, in honor of the festival. This precept is repeated twice in the Torah.[1] And our Sages of blessed memory taught in the tractate *Ḥagigah* (6b): The Israelites were commanded [to observe] three *mitzvoth* on a pilgrimage festival: celebration [with the festival peace-offering], appearance (§489), and rejoicing (§488).[2]

At the root of this precept lies the reason that it is not right to come empty-handed before Him (blessed is He). Even though the truth is that He needs nothing from our hands—as it is written, *If I were hungry, I would not tell you* (Psalms 50:12)—nevertheless, in the image of our thoughts we see it as though we are to stand in His presence. And in truth, people are closer to goodness at that place, more than in any other place; *the light of the King's countenance* (Proverbs 16:15) is a radiance upon them there. Therefore it is fitting for us to perform the deed of bringing the offering at that time. For through the act of bringing the offering we would become prepared to receive the reward of goodness, and our spirits would be exalted to an ever higher degree, as we will write (§95), with the help of the Eternal Lord.

Among the laws of the precept there is what our Sages of blessed memory said, that these offerings have no fixed limit,[3] although

§88–89: ON PILGRIMAGE FESTIVALS / ON THE PASSOVER OFFERING

אֶלָּא אֲפִלּוּ אֶחָד יַסְפִּיק, בֵּין בְּהֵמָה בֵּין עוֹף תּוֹר אוֹ גוֹזָל, וְשֶׁחַיָּב לַעֲלוֹת לִירוּשָׁלַיִם עַל כָּל פָּנִים בְּקָרְבָּן אוֹ בְכֶסֶף שֶׁיִּקְנֶה בּוֹ קָרְבָּן בִּירוּשָׁלַיִם, אֲבָל בְּשָׁוֶה כֶסֶף אֵינוֹ פָטוּר. וְאִם לֹא הִקְרִיב קָרְבָּנוֹ בְּיוֹם רִאשׁוֹן יֵשׁ לוֹ תַשְׁלוּמִין כָּל שִׁבְעָה, וּבִלְבַד שֶׁיִּהְיֶה הוּא שָׁם בְּיוֹם רִאשׁוֹן; וְיֶתֶר פְּרָטֶיהָ, מְבֹאָרִים בְּמַסֶּכֶת חֲגִיגָה.

וְנוֹהֶגֶת בִּזְמַן הַבַּיִת בִּזְכָרִים אֲבָל לֹא בִנְקֵבוֹת, וְלֹא כָל הַזְּכָרִים, שֶׁחֵגֵּר וְסוּמָא אֲפִלּוּ בְּאַחַת מֵעֵינָיו וְחוֹלֶה וְזָקֵן וְעִנֵּג הַרְבֵּה שֶׁאֵינוֹ יָכוֹל לַעֲלוֹת בְּרַגְלָיו כֻּלָּן פְּטוּרִין, וְכֵן טֻמְטוּם וְאַנְדְּרוֹגִינוּס וַעֲבָדִים. אֲבָל כָּל שְׁאָר הַזְּכָרִים חַיָּבִין, וַאֲפִלּוּ יֵשׁ לָהֶן אוּמָנוּת מְכֹעָר כְּגוֹן מְקַמֵּץ וּמְצָרֵף וְעַבְדָן מְטַהֲרִין גּוּפָן וּמַלְבּוּשָׁן וְעוֹלִין לִפְנֵי הַשֵּׁם (יִתְבָּרֵךְ). וְהֵם מְקֻבָּלִין לְפָנָיו כִּשְׁאָר יִשְׂרָאֵל, שֶׁטִּנּוּף הַנֶּפֶשׁ הוּא הַמְמָאֵס בְּנֵי אָדָם לִפְנֵי הַמָּקוֹם וְלֹא הָאוּמָנוּת כָּל זְמַן שֶׁעוֹשִׂין אוֹתוֹ בֶּאֱמוּנוּת.

וְעוֹבֵר עָלֶיהָ וְנִרְאָה בָּעֲזָרָה בְּיוֹם רִאשׁוֹן שֶׁל חַג וְלֹא הֵבִיא קָרְבָּן בִּטֵּל עֲשֵׂה, וְגַם עָבַר עַל לַאו שֶׁנֶּאֱמַר עַל זֶה: וְלֹא יֵרָאוּ פָנַי רֵיקָם.

[שֶׁלֹּא נִשְׁחַט שֶׂה הַפֶּסַח בְּאַרְבָּעָה עָשָׂר בְּנִיסָן בְּעוֹד שֶׁהֶחָמֵץ בִּרְשׁוּתֵנוּ]

פט שֶׁלֹּא נִשְׁחַט שֶׂה הַפֶּסַח בְּאַרְבָּעָה עָשָׂר בְּנִיסָן בְּעוֹד שֶׁיִּהְיֶה בִּרְשׁוּתֵנוּ עַד שֶׁנּוֹצִיאֶנּוּ; וּזְמַן בְּעוּרוֹ עַד חֲצִי הַיּוֹם, כְּמוֹ שֶׁדְּרָשׁוּ זִכְרוֹנָם לִבְרָכָה אַף, חָלָק; שֶׁנֶּאֱמַר "לֹא תִזְבַּח עַל חָמֵץ דַּם זִבְחִי", וּבָא הַפֵּרוּשׁ בּוֹ: לֹא תִשָּׁחֵט שֶׂה הַפֶּסַח

---

4. I.e. for an 'olah (burnt-offering), called *korban r'iyah* or *r'a-yon*, in addition to the *korban hagigah*, which, being a *sh'lamim* (peace-offering) as mentioned above, had to be a domestic animal, not a fowl; MT *hilchoth hagigah* i 1, based on his version of TB Ḥagigah 6a (*Kessef Mishneh*).

5. TB B'choroth 51a.

6. TB Ḥagigah 9a.

7. Mishnah, Ḥagigah i 1 (TB 2a).

8. Used e.g. in tanning leather.

9. MT *hilchoth hagigah* ii 2 (see *Kessef Mishneh*).

10. He equally disobeys this positive precept, of course, if he fails to appear at all (MH); and the negative precept, as R. Judah Rosanes (author of *Mishneh l'Melech*) notes, refers to the *korban r'iyah* (see note 4), not the *korban hagigah* dealt with in this precept—as our author writes in §490.

§89 1. I.e. *hamétz* is permitted in the first half of the day, forbidden in the second half; TB P'saḥim 5a.

⟨340⟩

even one is enough, whether it is a domestic animal or a fowl—a mature turtle-dove or a fledgling;[4] that a person is duty-bound to go up to Jerusalem, in any event, with an offering in hand or with money to buy an offering with it in Jerusalem—but with something [goods] worth money he does not acquit himself of the obligation;[5] and if he did not offer up his sacrifice on the first day [of the festival] it can be made right all the seven days [by sacrificing it then]—but this only if he is there on the first day.[6] [These] and the rest of its details are clarified in the Talmud tractate *Ḥagigah*.

It is in effect at the time that the Temple is extant, for the men, but not for women; and not for all men, either: a person who is lame, blind—even if only in one of his eyes—sick, old, or very delicate, so that he cannot go up [to Jerusalem] on foot—all such people are free of the obligation.[7] So also a *tumtum* (one of uncertain gender), a hermaphrodite, and servants (slaves);[7] but all other males have the obligation. Even if they have a vile, offensive occupation—for instance, a collector [of dog excrement],[8] a copper miner, and a leather tanner[9]— they cleanse their bodies and their clothing, and go up into the presence of the Eternal Lord (be He blessed), and they are as acceptable before Him as the other Israelites. For the foulness of the spirit is what makes human beings abhorrent before the omnipresent God, and not the occupation, as long as they work at it in honesty.

If someone transgressed it and appeared in the Temple forecourt on the first day of a festival without bringing an offering, he would thus disobey a positive precept. Moreover, he would violate a negative precept: for it is stated about this, *and none shall appear before Me empty-handed* (Exodus 23:15).[10]

[NOT TO RITUALLY SLAY THE PASSOVER OFFERING ON THE EVE OF PASSOVER WHILE THERE IS YET ḤAMÉTZ IN OUR POSSESSION]

89 that we should not sacrifice the lamb of the Passover offering on the fourteenth of Nissan while there is yet *ḥamétz* (leavened food) in our possession—[not] until we remove it. The time to eradicate it is until midday; as our Sages of blessed memory taught: the word *'aḥ*, "but" [in the verse, *but on the first day you shall put away leaven out of your houses* (Exodus 12:15)] divides it in two.[1] For it is stated, *You shall not offer over leavened bread the blood of My sacrifice* (Exodus 23:18); and the explanation was given for it [in the Midrash *Mechilta*]:

וְיִהְיֶה עֲדַיִן חָמֵץ קַיָּם בִּרְשׁוּתְךָ. וְנִכְפְּלָה זֹאת הַמְּנִיעָה בְּלָשׁוֹן אַחֵר בַּתּוֹרָה. וְגַם כֵּן שָׁמַעְנוּ בִּכְלַל הַפֵּרוּשׁ שֶׁלֹּא יִהְיֶה חָמֵץ אֵצֶל הַשּׁוֹחֵט אוֹתוֹ וְלֹא אֵצֶל הַזּוֹרֵק דָּמוֹ וְלֹא אֵצֶל הַמַּקְטִיר חֶלְבּוֹ וְלֹא אֵצֶל אֶחָד מִבְּנֵי חֲבוּרָה הַנִּמְנִין עָלָיו.

מִשָּׁרְשֵׁי הַמִּצְוָה לְפִי שֶׁקְּבִיעוּת זְמַן בְּכָל הָעִנְיָנִים הוּא קִיּוּם עֲשִׂיָּתָן, יָדוּעַ הַדָּבָר אֵצֶל כָּל אָדָם. וְעַל כֵּן בִּדְבַר הַפֶּסַח שֶׁהוּא דָּבָר גָּדוֹל אֶצְלֵנוּ בְּקִיּוּם הַדָּת, כְּמוֹ שֶׁכָּתַבְנוּ לְמַעְלָה, צִוָּה הָאֵל בָּרוּךְ הוּא שֶׁנַּעֲשֵׂהוּ עִנְיָנוֹ בְּסֵדֶר וּבִקְבִיעוּת זְמַן לְכָל דָּבָר וְדָבָר מִדְּבָרָיו, וְלֹא תָבוֹא מִצְוָה מִמִּצְווֹת עִנְיְנֵי הַמּוֹעֵד הַזֶּה בִּגְבוּל חֲבֶרְתָּהּ. וְעַל כֵּן נִזְהַרְנוּ לְהַשְׁבִּית הֶחָמֵץ הַנִּמְאָס בְּעֵינֵינוּ לְשַׁעְתּוֹ תְּחִלָּה, וְאַחַר כָּךְ לְהַתְחִיל בְּקָרְבַּן הַפֶּסַח שֶׁהוּא הַתְחָלַת שִׂמְחַת הַמּוֹעֵד הַטּוֹב. וְעַד שֶׁשָּׁמַעְנוּ טוּב מִזֶּה נַחֲזִיק בּוֹ.

מִדִּינֵי הַמִּצְוָה, מַה שֶּׁאָמְרוּ שֶׁזִּמַּן שְׁחִיטָתוֹ אַחַר חֲצוֹת, וְאִם שְׁחָטוֹ קֹדֶם חֲצוֹת שֶׁפָּסוּל, וְאַף־עַל־פִּי שֶׁאַחַר חֲצוֹת הוּא זְמַנּוֹ אֵינוֹ נִשְׁחָט לְכַתְּחִלָּה אֶלָּא אַחַר תָּמִיד שֶׁל בֵּין הָעַרְבַּיִם, אַחַר שֶׁמַּקְטִירִים קְטֹרֶת שֶׁל בֵּין הָעַרְבַּיִם, גַּם לְאַחַר שֶׁמֵּיטִיב אֶת הַנֵּרוֹת, וְיֶתֶר פְּרָטֶיהָ, בִּפְסָחִים.

וְנוֹהֶגֶת בִּזְמַן הַבַּיִת בִּזְכָרִים וּבִנְקֵבוֹת. וְהָעוֹבֵר עָלֶיהָ וְהִנִּיחַ מִדַּעְתּוֹ בַּיִת חָמֵץ בִּרְשׁוּתוֹ בִּשְׁעַת הַקְרָבָתוֹ, אֶחָד שׁוֹחֵט אוֹ זוֹרֵק אוֹ מַקְטִיר הָאֵמוּרִין אוֹ אֲפִלּוּ אֶחָד מִבְּנֵי הַחֲבוּרָה הַנִּמְנִין בַּאֲכִילָתוֹ לוֹקֶה, וְהַפֶּסַח כָּשֵׁר מִכָּל מָקוֹם.

[שֶׁלֹּא נַנִּיחַ אֵמוּרֵי הַפֶּסַח לְפָסֵל בְּלִינָה]

צ שֶׁלֹּא לְהָנִיחַ אֵמוּרִין שֶׁל פֶּסַח עַד הַבֹּקֶר, שֶׁלֹּא יַקְרִיבוּ אוֹתָן וְהֵן נִפְסָלִין

---

2. Exodus 34:25.
3. TB P'saḥim 63b. (The paragraph is based on ShM negative precept §115.)
4. Ibid. 61a.
5. Ibid. 59a (MT *hilchoth korban pesaḥ* i 4).
6. So *tosafoth*, TB T'murah 4b, s.v. *rava*, citing TJ P'saḥim v 4.

do not sacrifice the paschal lamb while there is yet *hamétz* extant in your possession. This restriction was repeated, expressed differently, in the Torah.[2] We learned further, in the range of the interpretation,[3] that there should be no *hamétz* in the possession of the one who ritually slaughters it, the one who sprinkles its blood, the one who burns its fat, or any one of the group that was registered for it.

At the root of the precept lies the reason that to set a proper time in all matters is to assure their observance; this is something known (evident) to everyone. Therefore, in the matter of Passover, which is an important theme for us in viably upholding our religion, as we wrote above (§21), God (blessed is He) commanded that we should observe its content in order and with a fixed time for every one of its elements, and no precept among the *mitzvoth* connected with this festival should infringe on the boundary of any other. Therefore we were commanded first to clear away the *hamétz*, which is repulsive to our eyes at that time, and afterward to commence with the Passover offering, which marks the beginning of the rejoicing at the good [festive] period. And until we hear some better [reason] than this, let us hold fast to it.

Among the laws of the precept, there is what our Sages said: that the time to sacrifice it is after midday, and if one sacrificed it before midday, it is not valid;[4] and even though its proper time [starts] after midday, originally, at first it is not to be sacrificed until after the daily burnt-offering of the afternoon, after the afternoon incense has been burnt, and the lamps [of the *menorah*] kindled.[5] [These] and the rest of its details are in the Talmud tractate *P'sahim*.

It is in force at the time when the Temple is extant, for both man and woman. If someone violates it and knowingly leaves *hamétz* in the amount of an olive in his possession during his sacrifice, whether while it is ritually slain, while its blood is sprinkled or certain parts of it are burnt on the altar, or even [if *hamétz* was then in the possession of] any one of all the members of the group that were registered for eating it, he is given whiplashes. But the Passover sacrifice remains kosher, fit to eat, in any event.[6]

[NOT TO LET THE 'ÉMURIM OF THE PASSOVER OFFERING REMAIN OVERNIGHT AND THUS BECOME IMPERMISSIBLE]

90 not to leave until morning the *'émurim*, the parts of the Passover sacrifice to be burnt on the altar, without offering them up, as they

§90–91: ABOUT THE PASSOVER OFFERING / BRINGING FIRST-FRUITS

בִּשְׁהָיָה זוֹ וְנִקְרָאִין נוֹתָר, שֶׁנֶּאֱמַר "וְלֹא יָלִין חֵלֶב חַגִּי עַד בֹּקֶר", וְהוּא הַדִּין לִשְׁאָר אֵמוּרִין וְלִשְׁאָר קָרְבָּנוֹת. וּלְשׁוֹן מְכִילְתָּא: "לֹא יָלִין חֵלֶב", בָּא הַכָּתוּב לְלַמֵּד עַל הַחֲלָבִים שֶׁנִּפְסָלִין בְּלִינָה. וּכְבָר נִכְפְּלָה זֹאת הַמְּנִיעָה בְּמָקוֹם אַחֵר, שֶׁנֶּאֱמַר: וְלֹא יָלִין לַבֹּקֶר זֶבַח חַג הַפָּסַח.

מִשָּׁרְשֵׁי הַמִּצְוָה כִּי כְבוֹד הַקָּרְבָּן לְהַקְרִיבוֹ בִּזְמַנּוֹ הַקָּבוּעַ אֵלָיו, וְהַמַּעֲבִיר הַמּוֹעֵד נִרְאֶה כְּמִתְיָאֵשׁ וּמַשְׁלִיךְ הַדָּבָר אַחֲרֵי גֵוּוֹ וְאֵינֶנּוּ מִתְעוֹרֵר וּמִתְפַּיֵּס כַּנָּוֹתָיו אֶל הָעֲבוֹדָה יָפֶה, וּמִפְּנֵי כֵן נִפְסָלִין בְּכָךְ.

מִדִּינֵי הַמִּצְוָה, מַה שֶּׁאָמְרוּ שֶׁמִּצְוָה לְהַקְטִיר אֵמוּרֵי כָל זֶבַח וָזֶבַח בִּפְנֵי עַצְמוֹ; וּמַה שֶּׁאָמְרוּ שֶׁמִּצְוַת הַקְטָרָתָן אַחַר שְׁחִיטָה סָמוּךְ, וְאִם לֹא הִקְטִיר כֵּן מַקְטִירָן כָּל הַלַּיְלָה עַד שֶׁיַּעֲלֶה עַמּוּד הַשַּׁחַר. וְדַוְקָא בְּשָׁחַל אַרְבָּעָה־עָשָׂר בְּנִיסָן לִהְיוֹת בְּשַׁבָּת, שֶׁחֶלְבֵי שַׁבָּת קְרֵבִין בְּיוֹם טוֹב, אֲבָל אִם אַרְבָּעָה עָשָׂר חֹל אֵין מַקְטִירִין בַּלַּיְלָה, שֶׁאֵין מַקְטִירִין חֶלְבֵי חֹל בְּיוֹם טוֹב, דְּיוֹם טוֹב עֲשֵׂה וְלֹא תַעֲשֶׂה, וְדוֹחֶה לָאו דְּלֹא יָלִין; וְיֶתֶר פְּרָטֶיהָ, בִּפְסָחִים.

וְנוֹהֶגֶת בִּזְמַן הַבַּיִת בִּזְכָרִים כֹּהֲנִים. וְהָעוֹבֵר וְלֹא הִקְרִיבָן אֵינוֹ לוֹקֶה, לְפִי שֶׁאֵין בּוֹ מַעֲשֶׂה.

[מִצְוַת הֲבָאַת בִּכּוּרִים]

צא לְהָבִיא בִכּוּרִים לַמִּקְדָּשׁ, וְהוּא הַפְּרִי הָרִאשׁוֹן שֶׁמִּתְבַּשֵּׁל בָּאִילָן שֶׁחַיָּבִין אָנוּ לַהֲבִיאוֹ שָׁם וְלִתְּנוֹ לַכֹּהֵן; וְלֹא כָל הָאִילָנוֹת בַּמִּצְוָה זוֹ מִן הַתּוֹרָה, אֶלָּא שִׁבְעַת

---

§90 1. Paragraph based on ShM negative precept §116.

2. I.e. not to mix the parts of fat of any two offerings when those parts are burned on the altar; TB P'saḥim 64b.

3. TB P'saḥim 65b, M'naḥoth 72a.

4. MT hilchoth korban pesaḥ i 8 (TB P'saḥim 59b, 83a).

⟨344⟩

become disqualified, unacceptable, through this delay, and they are then called *nothar*, "remainder." For it is stated, *and the fat of My festival shall not remain until the morning* (Exodus 23:18). The same law applies to other *'émurim*, of other offerings. The Midrash *Mechilta* expresses it so: "the fat shall not remain"—the Writ comes to teach [us] about the parts of fat, that they become disqualified, unacceptable by being left overnight. This prohibition was repeated elsewhere, for it is stated, *neither shall the sacrifice of the Passover festival remain till morning* (Exodus 34:25).[1]

At the root of the precept lies the reason that to honor the sacrifice means to offer it up in its time, that was set for it. If someone goes past the proper time, he seems like a person who gives up hope and throws the [whole] matter behind him, not bestirring himself and fixing his intentions well on the [Divine] service. For this reason they thus become disqualified.

Among the laws of the precept there is what the Sages said, that it is a religious duty to offer up the *'émurim* of every single sacrifice separately.[2] Then there is the teaching of the Sages that the duty of burning them comes close, directly after the ritual slaying; but if they were not burnt thus, they may be burnt the entire night, until dawn rises.[3] But this is only when the fourteenth of Nissan fell on a Sabbath, when the parts of fat of the Sabbath sacrifices were offered up on the festival. However, if the fourteenth occurred on a weekday, [the *'émurim*] were not to be burnt at night, since the fat parts of a weekday sacrifice might not be burnt during a festival; for on the festival, a positive and a negative precept apply [against burning these *'émurim*], and it thus thrusts aside the negative precept, [*the fat of My festival*] *shall not remain*.[4] [These] and the rest of its details are in the tractate *P'saḥim*.

It is in force when the Temple exists, for male *kohanim*. However, if someone transgressed it and did not offer them up [on the altar for burning] he would not be given whiplashes, since no physical action was involved.

[THE PRECEPT OF BRINGING FIRST-FRUITS TO THE HOLY TEMPLE]

91 to bring *bikkurim* (first-fruits) to the Sanctuary, i.e. the first fruit that ripens on a tree: we are duty-bound to bring it there and give it to a *kohen*. Not all trees, though, are included under this precept by the law of the Torah, but only the seven kinds for which the land [of Israel]

§91: ABOUT BRINGING FIRST-FRUITS TO THE HOLY TEMPLE

הַמִּינִין לְבַד שֶׁנִּשְׁתַּבְּחָה הָאָרֶץ בָּהֶן, וְהֵם חִטָּה וּשְׂעוֹרָה גֶּפֶן וּתְאֵנָה וְרִמּוֹן זֵיתִים וּתְמָרִים, שֶׁנֶּאֱמַר: רֵאשִׁית בִּכּוּרֵי אַדְמָתְךָ תָּבִיא בֵּית יי אֱלֹהֶיךָ, וּבָא הַפֵּרוּשׁ שֶׁלֹּא נֶאֱמַר אֶלָּא עַל ז' פֵּרוֹת אֵלוּ.

וּלְפִי הַדּוֹמֶה כִּי בְדֶרֶךְ זוֹ לָמְדוּ זִכְרוֹנָם לִבְרָכָה לוֹמַר כֵּן, כִּי אַחַר שֶׁלֹּא הֻזְכְּרוּ פֵּרוֹת אֲחֵרִים חוּץ מֵאֵלּוּ בַּתּוֹרָה בְּשׁוּם מָקוֹם, וְצִוָּנוּ בָּרוּךְ הוּא לְהָבִיא מֵאַרְצֵנוּ בִּכּוּרֵי פֵּרוֹת סְתָם, בֶּאֱמֶת יֵשׁ לָדוּן כִּי עַל הַפֵּרוֹת שֶׁהוֹדִיעָנוּ בַּתּוֹרָה שֶׁהֵן בְּאֶרֶץ יִשְׂרָאֵל וְשֶׁשִּׁבְּחָהּ בָּהֶן עַל אוֹתָן צִוָּנוּ. וְאֶפְשָׁר כִּי יֵשׁ לְרַבּוֹתֵינוּ זִכְרוֹנָם לִבְרָכָה עוֹד הֶכְרֵחַ הַכָּתוּב בָּעִנְיָן, אוֹ שֶׁמָּא דִבְרֵי קַבָּלָה הֵם.

וְכֵן הָיָה דַרְכָּם לְהָבִיא אוֹתָן: הַסְּמוּכִין לִירוּשָׁלַיִם מְבִיאִין אוֹתָן רַכִּים וְהָרְחוֹקִים מְיַבְּשִׁין אוֹתָן.

מִשָּׁרְשֵׁי הַמִּצְוָה כְּדֵי לְהַעֲלוֹת דְּבַר הַשֵּׁם יִתְבָּרַךְ עַל רֹאשׁ שִׂמְחָתֵנוּ, וְנִזְכֹּר וְנֵדַע כִּי מֵאִתּוֹ בָּרוּךְ הוּא יַגִּיעוּ לָנוּ כָּל הַבְּרָכוֹת בָּעוֹלָם. עַל כֵּן נִצְטַוֵּינוּ לְהָבִיא לִמְשָׁרְתֵי בֵּיתוֹ רֵאשִׁית הַפְּרִי הַמִּתְבַּשֵּׁל בְּאִילָנוֹתֵינוּ, וּמִתּוֹךְ הַזְּכִירָה וְקַבָּלַת מַלְכוּתוֹ וְהוֹדָאָתֵנוּ לְפָנָיו כִּי מֵאִתּוֹ בָּאוּ, נִהְיֶה רְאוּיִין לְבְרָכָה וְיִתְבָּרְכוּ פֵּרוֹתֵינוּ.

מִדִּינֵי הַמִּצְוָה, מַה שֶּׁאָמְרוּ זִכְרוֹנָם לִבְרָכָה שֶׁהֵן אֲסוּרִין לְזָר כִּתְרוּמָה מִשֶּׁנִּכְנְסוּ לִירוּשָׁלַיִם, וּמֵאֵי זֶה פֵּרוֹת מְבִיאִין מֵהֶם בִּכּוּרִים מִדְּרַבָּנָן, וְשֶׁנּוֹתְנִין הַבִּכּוּרִים לְאַנְשֵׁי מִשְׁמָר, וְשֶׁטּוֹעֲנִין כְּלִי וְהוּא לַכֹּהֵן אִם הוּא שֶׁל עֵץ, וְשֶׁלֹּא יְבִיאֵם בְּעַרְבּוּב אֶלָּא דֶּרֶךְ נוֹי, כְּגוֹן שֶׁמְּשִׂימִים הַחֻצִּין אוֹ עָלִין בַּסַּל בֵּין כָּל מִין וָמִין, וּמַקִּיף אֶשְׁכּוֹלוֹת עֲנָבִים לַסַּל שֶׁל תְּאֵנִים עַל שְׂפָתוֹ, וּמְבִיאִין בִּידֵיהֶן תּוֹרִים וּבְנֵי יוֹנָה לִכְבוֹד הַבִּכּוּרִים וְנוֹתְנִין אוֹתָן לַכֹּהֲנִים, וְכֵיצַד הָיוּ מַעֲלִין אוֹתָם,

---

§91   1. Sifre, Deuteronomy §297; TB M'naḥoth 84b; TJ Bikkurim i 3.

2. I.e. as significant among the crops of the Holy Land. Actually, Genesis 43:11 mentions *botnim* (pistachio nuts) and almonds as "choice fruits of the land," and Leviticus 23:40 has "the beautiful fruit of trees," i.e. the citron. Only Deuteronomy 8:8, however, describes the country as "a land of wheat and barley," etc.—indicating that *these* are the regular, staple crops which distinguish the land, and no other. The other three, from all we can infer from Scripture, might have been grown only at certain times (Genesis) or in small quantity as luxury items. (The answer given in ed. Chavel p.810 is rather forced, as the plain meaning of *kol* in the context is not "all" but "any"—i.e. none.)

3. Mishnah, Bikkurim iii 3.
4. Literally, a stranger; TB Makkoth 19a.
5. MT *hilchoth bikkurim* ii 1 (Mishnah, Bikkurim i 10).
6. The *kohanim* were divided by family groups into *mishmaroth* ("watches"), i.e. groups which took turns to minister at the Sanctuary, each serving a week; Mishnah, Bikkurim iii 12.
7. Tosefta, Bikkurim ii (MT *hilchoth bikkurim* iii 7).
8. Mishnah, Bikkurim iii 8.

⟨346⟩

SIDRAH MISHPATIM

was praised. These are: wheat, barley, grapes, figs, pomegranates, olives, and dates (Deuteronomy 8:8). For it is stated, *The earliest of the first-fruits of your soil you shall bring into the house of the Lord your God* (Exodus 23:19); and the explanation was given [in the Oral Tradition][1] that this was stated about none but these seven fruits.

It would seem that in this way our Sages of blessed memory learned to teach this: Since no other produce except these is mentioned anywhere in the Torah,[2] and He (blessed is He) commanded us to bring from our land simply "first-fruits," it can be inferred in truth that it was about those fruits—which, He informed us, are in the land of Israel and it is to be praised for them—that He commanded us. It is possible, though, that our Sages of blessed memory had some other proof written [in Scripture] about the matter; or perhaps this is a teaching [purely] of the Oral Tradition.

This was their way of bringing them: Those close to Jerusalem would bring them soft (fresh), and those who were distant would dry them.[3]

At the root of the precept lies the purpose to set the thought of the Eternal Lord (be He blessed) above our rejoicing and happiness, that we should remember and know that from Him (blessed is He) all the blessings in the world reach us. For this reason we were commanded to bring to the ministering servants of His house [the Temple] the first of the fruit that ripens on the trees. Out of this remembrance, this acceptance of His kingship, and our avowal in thanks before Him that the fruits and every other goodness come from Him, we will become worthy of blessing, and our produce will be blessed.

Among the laws of the precept there is what our Sages of blessed memory taught, that they are as forbidden to a non-*kohen*[4] as *t'rumah*, once they have entered Jerusalem; from which produce *bikkurim* are brought by the ruling of the Sages;[5] that the *bikkurim* are given to the members of the watch [the *kohanim* on duty that week];[6] that they require a vessel [to hold them],[7] which becomes the *kohen*'s if it is of wood;[8] that a man should not bring them mixed up (in disarray) but in a beautiful way: for instance, he puts palm foliage or leaves in the basket around every single species, and sets clusters of grapes about a basket of figs, at the edge;[7] and they would bring turtle-doves and pigeons in their hands in honor of the first-fruits, and give them to the *kohanim*.[9] [Then there is the law on] how they would bring them up; the rejoicing that there would be by those who brought them and by

§91–92: BRINGING FIRST-FRUITS / NOT TO COOK MEAT IN MILK

וְהַשִּׂמְחָה שֶׁהָיוּ עוֹשִׂין הַמְּבִיאִין אוֹתָן וְהַיּוֹצְאִים לִקְרָאתָם, וְהַמִּזְמוֹרִים שֶׁהָיוּ קוֹרִין סָמוּךְ לָעִיר, וְיֶתֶר פְּרָטֶיהָ, מְבֹאָרִים בְּמַסֶּכֶת בִּכּוּרִים.[10]

וְנוֹהֶגֶת בִּזְמַן הַבַּיִת בִּזְכָרִים וּבִפָרוֹת אֶרֶץ יִשְׂרָאֵל וְסוּרְיָא וְעֵבֶר הַיַּרְדֵּן, אֲבָל לֹא בְּפֵרוֹת חוּצָה לָאָרֶץ. וְעוֹבֵר עָלֶיהָ בִּטֵּל עֲשֵׂה.[11]

[שֶׁלֹּא לְבַשֵּׁל בָּשָׂר בְּחָלָב]

צב שֶׁלֹּא נְבַשֵּׁל בָּשָׂר בְּהֵמָה בְּחָלָב, שֶׁנֶּאֱמַר "לֹא תְבַשֵּׁל גְּדִי בַּחֲלֵב אִמּוֹ",[1] וּבָא הַפֵּרוּשׁ דְּלָאו דַּוְקָא גְּדִי אֶלָּא אֲפִלּוּ כָּל בְּשַׂר בְּהֵמָה בְּמַשְׁמָע, שֶׁאֵין לְשׁוֹן גְּדִי אֶלָּא לְשׁוֹן בָּשָׂר בְּהֵמָה, וְהוֹצִיאוּ בִּלְשׁוֹן גְּדִי לְפִי שֶׁהַבָּשָׂר דָּבָר רַךְ כִּגְדִי. וְאֵיךְ אַתָּה לָמֵד כֵּן, מִמַּה שֶּׁאַתָּה מוֹצֵא בְכַמָּה מְקוֹמוֹת בַּתּוֹרָה שֶׁכָּתוּב גְּדִי וְהֻצְרַךְ לְפָרֵשׁ גְּדִי עִזִּים,[2] הָא לָמַדְתָּ שֶׁבִּמְקוֹם שֶׁנֶּאֱמַר גְּדִי סְתָם לָאו דַּוְקָא גְּדִי עִזִּים אֶלָּא אַף כָּל בְּשַׂר בְּהֵמָה כַּיּוֹצֵא בּוֹ בְּמַשְׁמָע.

מִשָּׁרְשֵׁי מִצְוָה זוֹ לְפִי הַדּוֹמֶה שֶׁהוּא כְעִנְיָן מַה שֶּׁכָּתַבְנוּ בְּמִצְוַת כִּלְאַיִם,[2a] כִּי יֵשׁ בָּעוֹלָם דְּבָרִים שֶׁנֶּאֱסַר לָנוּ תַּעֲרֻבְתָּן בְּסִבַּת הָעִנְיָן שֶׁאָמַרְנוּ שָׁם. וְאֶפְשָׁר שֶׁתַּעֲרֹבֶת הַבָּשָׂר עִם הֶחָלָב בְּמַעֲשֵׂה הַבִּשּׁוּל יִהְיֶה סִבַּת אִסּוּרוֹ מִן הַיְסוֹד הַהוּא.

וּקְצָת רְאָיָה לָזֶה לְפִי שֶׁבָּא הָאִסּוּר לָנוּ בְּמַעֲשֶׂה הַתַּעֲרֹבֶת אַף־עַל־פִּי שֶׁלֹּא נֹאכְלֶנּוּ, שֶׁנִּרְאֶה בָּזֶה שֶׁאֵין אִסּוּרוֹ מֵחֲמַת נֶזֶק אֲכִילָתוֹ כְּלָל, רַק שֶׁלֹּא נַעֲשֶׂה פְּעֻלַּת אוֹתוֹ הַתַּעֲרֹבֶת וּלְהַרְחִיק אוֹתוֹ עִנְיָן שֶׁאָמַרְנוּ. וְהִזְהִירָנוּ גַם־כֵּן בְּמָקוֹם אַחֵר שֶׁאִם אוּלַי נַעֲשָׂה הַתַּעֲרֹבֶת לְבַל נֹאכְלֵהוּ וְלֹא נֶהֱנֶה בּוֹ, לְהַרְחִיק הָעִנְיָן.[3] וַאֲפִלּוּ אֲכָלוֹ מִבְּלִי שֶׁיֵּהָנֶה מִמֶּנּוּ כְּלָל לוֹקֶה, מַה שֶּׁאֵין כֵּן בִּשְׁאָר כָּל אִסּוּרֵי

---

9. Ibid. 5.
10. Ibid. 2–4 (MT hilchoth bikkurim iii 16–17).
11. Cf. §84, next to last paragraph.

§92 1. TB Ḥullin 113a–b.
2. E.g. Genesis 27:9, 38:17, 20; so Rashi to Exodus 23:19, based on TB *ibid*.
2a. When two ingredients are blended to form a new, hybrid substance, the original substances no longer exist here in their original proper state, and thus the power of the angels appointed over their growth and existence is refuted.
3. E.g. if something bitter was added, spoiling the taste; TB P'sahim 25a.

⟨348⟩

those who went out to greet them, and the psalms they would recite close to the city.[10] [These] and the rest of its details are made clear in the Mishnah tractate *Bikkurim*.

It is in force when the Temple is extant, for men, and in regard to the produce of the land of Israel, Syria[11] and Transjordan, but not in regard to produce outside the land. One who violates it disobeys a positive precept.

92 [NOT TO COOK MEAT IN MILK]

that we should not cook the meat of an animal in milk: for it is stated, *You shall not boil a kid in its mother's milk* (Exodus 23:19); and the explanation was given [in the Oral Tradition][1] that this does not mean a kid particularly; it rather denotes any animal meat, since the term "kid" is no more than an expression for animal flesh; Scripture merely used this particular term because meat is something as soft as a kid. How can you learn [that it is] so?—from what you find in several instances in the Torah: that "a kid" is written, and it has to be explained as "a kid of the goats";[2] hence you learn that where "kid" alone is stated, it does not mean a kid of the goats particularly, but rather any animal meat is equally denoted.

At the root of the precept there would seem to be the same kind of reason that we wrote about the precept of the sorceress (§62)—that there are certain things in the world which it was forbidden to us to mix, on account of the reason we stated there. Perhaps, then, the reason for the ban on mixing meat with milk during the process of boiling would derive from the same basis.[2a]

Some proof for this lies in the fact that there is a prohibition for us about making the mixture even though we will not eat it. It would appear from this that its prohibition is not at all because of harm [that will result from] eating it, but only in order that we should not do the act of making that mixture, and to keep that matter which we stated [creating hybrid substances] well away from us.

Moreover, Scripture adjured us in another instance (§113) that if we should perhaps make the mixture, we should not eat it or have any benefit from it—in order to keep the matter [of such mixing] distant [from us]. And even if someone eats it without enjoying or benefiting from it at all, he receives a whipping[3]—which is not the case with any other bans on foods. All this indicates that the fundamental reason for it

הַמַּאֲכָלוֹת; וְכָל זֶה מוֹרֶה שֶׁיְּסוֹד טַעֲמוֹ הוּא מֵחֲמַת הַתַּעֲרֹבֶת וּכְעִנְיָן שֶׁאָמַרְנוּ בְּכִשּׁוּף.

זֶה נֹאמַר מִתּוֹךְ הַדֹּחַק, וַעֲדַיִן צְרִיכִים אָנוּ לְמוֹדִעַי הַמְקֻבָּל. וְהָרַמְבַּ״ם זִכְרוֹנוֹ לִבְרָכָה כָּתַב בְּעִנְיָן טַעַם אַחֵר: אָמַר כִּי יֵשׁ עוֹבְדֵי עֲבוֹדָה זָרָה יַעַבְדוּהָ בְּמַעֲשֵׂה תַּעֲרֹבֶת בָּשָׂר עִם חָלָב, וְלָכֵן הִרְחִיקָה הַתּוֹרָה אוֹתוֹ הַתַּעֲרֹבֶת; וְכָל זֶה אֵינֶנּוּ שָׁוֶה לִי.

דִּינֵי הַמִּצְוָה נִכְתָּב בְּעֶזְרַת הַשֵּׁם בְּקִצּוּר כְּמִנְהָגֵנוּ בְּמַצְוֹת אִסּוּר הָאֲכִילָה וְהַהֲנָאָה בְּסֵדֶר כִּי תִשָּׂא.

וְנוֹהֶגֶת בְּכָל מָקוֹם וּבְכָל זְמַן בִּזְכָרִים וּנְקֵבוֹת. וְעוֹבֵר עָלֶיהָ וּבִשֵּׁל בָּשָׂר בְּחָלָב, וְאַף עַל פִּי שֶׁלֹּא אֲכָלָן, לוֹקֶה.

[שֶׁלֹּא לִכְרֹת בְּרִית לְשִׁבְעָה עֲמָמִים וְכֵן לְכָל עוֹבֵד עֲבוֹדָה זָרָה]

צג שֶׁלֹּא נִכְרֹת בְּרִית, כְּלוֹמַר שֶׁלֹּא נַבְטִיחַ בְּאַהֲבָתֵנוּ אֶל הָעָם הָרַע הַכּוֹפְרִים שֶׁהֵם שִׁבְעָה עֲמָמִים שֶׁבַּתּוֹרָה שֶׁהָיוּ מַחֲזִיקִים בְּאַרְצֵנוּ טֶרֶם בּוֹאֵנוּ שָׁם, וְהֵן הַחִתִּי וְהָאֱמוֹרִי וְכוּלֵּי, שֶׁנֶּאֱמַר "לֹא תִכְרֹת לָהֶם וְלֵאלֹהֵיהֶם בְּרִית", כְּלוֹמַר שֶׁלֹּא נַעֲשֶׂה עִמָּהֶם שָׁלוֹם וְנַנִּיחַ אוֹתָם לַעֲבֹד הָעֲבוֹדָה זָרָה.

מִשָּׁרְשֵׁי מִצְוָה זוֹ לְאַבֵּד עֲבוֹדָה זָרָה וְכָל מְשַׁמְּשֶׁיהָ מִן הָעוֹלָם, וְאִלּוּ הַשִּׁבְעָה עֲמָמִים הָיוּ עִקַּר עֲבוֹדָה זָרָה וִיסוֹדָהּ הָרִאשׁוֹן, וְעַל כֵּן נֶעֶקְרוּ מֵאַרְצָם, וְנִצְטַוֵּינוּ לְשָׁרֵשׁ אַחֲרֵיהֶם וּלְאַבֵּד זִכְרָם לְעוֹלָם, וּכְמוֹ שֶׁכָּתוּב עֲלֵיהֶם בַּתּוֹרָה, "הַחֲרֵם תַּחֲרִים אוֹתָם", וְהִיא מִצְוַת עֲשֵׂה בְּסֵדֶר וָאֶתְחַנָּן. וְשָׁם אַאֲרִיךְ בַּמִּצְוָה בְּעֶזְרַת הַשֵּׁם, וְנַגִּיד סִבַּת הֱיוֹת בָּעוֹלָם הָאֻמּוֹת הָרָעוֹת לָמָּה, וְכִי מִצְוָה זוֹ בִּכְלַל הַמִּצְוֹת הַנּוֹהֲגוֹת.

וּמִן הָאַזְהָרָה בָּהֶם נִשְׁמַע אַזְהָרָה שֶׁלֹּא לִכְרֹת בְּרִית לְכָל עוֹבֵד עֲבוֹדָה זָרָה, אֲבָל יֵשׁ חִלּוּק בֵּין שִׁבְעָה עֲמָמִים לִשְׁאָר הָאֻמּוֹת עוֹבְדֵי עֲבוֹדָה זָרָה, כִּי שְׁאָר הָאֻמּוֹת אִם אֵין נִלְחָמִים עִמָּנוּ אֵין מִצְוָה עָלֵינוּ לְהָרְגָם אֶלָּא שֶׁלֹּא יֵשְׁבוּ בְּאַרְצֵנוּ

---

4. Rambam, *Guide* III 48.

§93   1. I.e. Girgashites, Canaanites, Perizzites, Hivvites, Jebusites.
2. So ShM positive precept §187.
3. I.e. for all time, even though the seven nations disappeared long ago.

[the ban on either eating or benefiting from it] is on account of the mixing; and it thus suggests what we said about sorcery.

This, however, has been said out of compulsion [to find a plausible reason]; but we are still in need of the knowledge of a master of mystic tradition. Rambam of blessed memory wrote a different reason for the matter:[4] He said that there are idolaters who worship it [their idol] by the act of mixing meat with milk, and therefore the Torah outlawed that mixture. *Yet all this is without sufficient worth for me* (Esther 5:13).

The laws of the precept we will write with the Eternal Lord's help, briefly, as is our custom, in the precept (§113) of the ban on eating or benefiting [from it], in the *sidrah ki thissa*.

It is in force in every place, at every time, for both man and woman. If someone violates it and boils meat with milk, even if he does not eat them, he is given whiplashes.

[TO MAKE NO TREATY WITH THE SEVEN NATIONS TO BE EXTIRPATED, OR WITH ANY IDOL-WORSHIPPER]

93 that we should not make a covenant with—i.e. that we should not set our trust in our love for—the wicked heretical people, these being the seven nations [listed] in the Torah who possessed our land before we came there. These are the Hittites, Amorites, and so on.[1] For it is stated, *You shall make no covenant with them or with their gods* (Exodus 23:32); in other words, we should not make peace with them and leave them to worship idols.

At the root of this precept lies the purpose of eradicating from the world idolatry and all who serve it. These seven nations were a main center of idol-worship and its first base.[2] Therefore they were extirpated from their land, and we were commanded to seek out and destroy their roots, and to eradicate their memory forever—as it is written about them in the Torah, *you shall utterly destroy them* (Deuteronomy 7:2), which is a positive precept (§425) in the *sidrah va'eth-ḥanan*. There I will write at length about the precept, with God's help, and we will convey the reason why these evil nations were [given existence] in the world, and how this precept is among the *mitzvoth* that remain in force.[3]

From the admonition about them we understand a solemn warning not to make a covenant with any idol-worshippers. But there is a difference between the seven nations and other idol-worshipping peoples: In regard to other nations, if they do not wage war with us,

§93–94: BANS ON 7 NATIONS & IDOL-WORSHIPPER IN ERETZ ISRAEL

עַד שֶׁיַּעַזְבוּ עֲבוֹדַת עֲבוֹדָה זָרָה, וְאִלּוּ שִׁבְעָה עֲמָמִים נִצְטַוִּינוּ לְהָרְגָם בְּכָל מָקוֹם שֶׁנּוּכַל לָהֶם אֶלָּא אִם כֵּן יַנִּיחוּ עֲבוֹדָה זָרָה. וְהָעִנְיָן לְפִי שֶׁהֵם הָיוּ עִקַּר עֲבוֹדָה זָרָה וִיסוֹדָהּ הָרִאשׁוֹן, כְּמוֹ שֶׁכָּתַבְתִּי. וְכָל מִי שֶׁבָּא לְיָדוֹ אֶחָד מֵהֶם וְיָכוֹל לְהָרְגוֹ בְּלֹא סַכָּנָה וְלֹא הֲרָגוֹ, עוֹבֵר בְּלָאו.

וְזֶה שֶׁאָמַרְנוּ שֶׁעוֹבְדֵי עֲבוֹדָה זָרָה בִּשְׁאֵין נִלְחָמִים עִמָּנוּ שֶׁלֹּא נַהַרְגֵם, דַּוְקָא עוֹבְדֵי עֲבוֹדָה זָרָה מִן הָאֻמּוֹת, אֲבָל יִשְׂרָאֵל עוֹבֵד עֲבוֹדָה זָרָה, כְּגוֹן הַמִּינִין וְהָאֶפִּיקוֹרוּסִין וְהַמְשֻׁמָּדִין, מִצְוָה עָלֵינוּ לְהָרְגָם, לְפִי שֶׁהֵם מְצֵרִים לְיִשְׂרָאֵל, וּמוּטָב יֹאבְדוּ אֶלֶף כַּיּוֹצֵא בָם וְלֹא יִשְׂרָאֵל אֶחָד כָּשֵׁר.

מִדִּינֵי הַמִּצְוָה, מַה שֶּׁאָמְרוּ שֶׁמְּקַבְּלִין אוֹתָן אִם רָצוּ לַחֲזֹר בִּתְשׁוּבָה, וְיֶתֶר פְּרָטֶיהָ, מְבֹאָרִין בְּסַנְהֶדְרִין.

[שֶׁלֹּא לְהוֹשִׁיב עוֹבֵד עֲבוֹדָה זָרָה בְּאַרְצֵנוּ]

צד שֶׁלֹּא לְשַׁכֵּן עוֹבְדֵי עֲבוֹדָה זָרָה בְּאַרְצֵנוּ, שֶׁנֶּאֱמַר: לֹא יֵשְׁבוּ בְּאַרְצְךָ פֶּן יַחֲטִיאוּ אֹתְךָ לִי.

מִשָּׁרְשֵׁי הַמִּצְוָה מַה שֶּׁנִּגְלֶה בַּכָּתוּב, בִּשְׁבִיל שֶׁלֹּא נִלְמַד מִכְּפִירָתָם.

מִדִּינֵי הַמִּצְוָה מַה שֶּׁאָמְרוּ זִכְרוֹנָם לִבְרָכָה שֶׁאִלּוּ רָצוּ לְהַנִּיחַ עֲבוֹדָה זָרָה, אַף־עַל־פִּי שֶׁעֲבוֹדָתוֹ מִתְחַלֶּפֶת, שֶׁמֻּתָּרִין לִשְׁכֹּן בְּאַרְצֵנוּ, וְזֶהוּ הַנִּקְרָא גֵּר תּוֹשָׁב, כְּלוֹמַר שֶׁהוּא גֵּר לְעִנְיָן שֶׁהֻתַּר לֵישֵׁב בְּאַרְצֵנוּ, כְּמוֹ שֶׁאָמְרוּ זִכְרוֹנָם לִבְרָכָה: אֵי זֶהוּ גֵּר תּוֹשָׁב, זֶה שֶׁקִּבֵּל שֶׁלֹּא לַעֲבֹד עֲבוֹדָה זָרָה. וְאִם לֹא הִנִּיחַ עֲבוֹדָה זָרָה אֵין צָרִיךְ לוֹמַר שֶׁאֵין מוֹכְרִין לוֹ קַרְקַע שֶׁיֵּשֵׁב בְּאַרְצֵנוּ אֶלָּא אֲפִלּוּ לְשַׂכֵּר לוֹ אָסוּר כָּל זְמַן שֶׁיִּשְׂכֹּר לְדִירָה, לְפִי שֶׁמַּכְנִיסִים שָׁם עֲבוֹדָה זָרָה, אֲבָל לִסְחוֹרָתוֹ מֻתָּר וּבִלְבַד

---

4. So TB Gittin 45a.
5. TB 'Avodah Zarah 26a (MT *hilchoth 'avodath kochavim* x 1).
6. So Sifre Deuteronomy §202; TB Sotah 35b (Tosefta viii 7).

§94 1. TB 'Avodah Zarah 64b.
2. *Ibid.* and Gittin 45a.
3. TB 'Avodah Zarah 21a.

we have no religious duty to kill them out, but merely [a duty to ensure] that they should not dwell in our land until they have forsaken idolatry.[4] As for these seven nations, however, we were commanded to kill them out wherever we could prevail against them, except in the event that they had forsaken idolatry.[5] The reason is that they were a main center of idol-worship and its first base, as I have written. Hence, if one of them fell into a person's power and he could kill him without peril, and he did not slay him, he would violate a negative precept.

Now, what we said, that when idol-worshippers do not wage war with us, we are not to kill them—this means specifically idol-worshippers among the nations. But if Israelites worship idols—for instance, infidel sectarians, apostates and heretics—a religious duty lies upon us to kill them, because they make oppressive trouble for the Israelites.[5] It were better that a thousand like them die, and not one worthy Israelite.

Among the laws of the precept there is what the Sages said,[6] that they are accepted if they wish to return in repentance. The rest of its details are explained in the Talmud tractate *Sanhedrin*.

94 [NOT TO SETTLE ANY IDOL-WORSHIPPER IN OUR LAND] not to have idol-worshippers dwell in our land: for it is stated, *They shall not dwell in your land, lest they make you sin against Me* (Exodus 23:33).

At the root of the precept lies the reason revealed in the Writ: it is in order that we shall not learn from their heresy.

Among the laws of the precept there are what the Sages of blessed memory said,[1] that if they wanted to forsake the worship of [their] idol, even though they did worship it from their very beginning, they are permitted to live in our land—and this kind is what is called *gér toshav*, "a resident proselyte": i.e. he is a proselyte to an extent that gains him permission to live in our land. As our Sages of blessed memory said:[2] Who is a *gér toshav?*—one who accepted and resolved not to worship idols. If he did not forsake idolatry, there is no need to say that he is not to be sold any ground so that he can dwell in our land; but even to rent to him is forbidden, as long as he wishes to rent [property] for a residence, since he will bring an idol into it;[3] however, if it is [for a warehouse] for his merchandise, it is permissible—on

§94–95: ON AN IDOL-WORSHIPPER / BUILDING THE HOLY TEMPLE

שֶׁלֹּא יִשְׂכֹּר לִשְׁלֹשָׁה בְּנֵי אָדָם, לְפִי שֶׁשְּׁלֹשָׁה דְּבַר קְבִיעוּת הוּא וְאֵין רָאוּי לְקָבְעָם.

וְחִלּוּק הַדִּינִין שֶׁאָמְרוּ זִכְרוֹנָם לִבְרָכָה שֶׁיֵּשׁ בְּעִנְיָן זֶה בֵּין בָּתִּים לְשָׂדוֹת וּכְרָמִים וּבֵין סוּרְיָא לְאֶרֶץ יִשְׂרָאֵל, וְיֶתֶר פְּרָטֶיהָ, מְבֹאָרִין בְּסַנְהֶדְרִין וַעֲבוֹדָה זָרָה.

וְנוֹהֶגֶת בִּזְכָרִים וּנְקֵבוֹת בָּאָרֶץ. וְעוֹבֵר עָלֶיהָ וּמָכַר לָהֶם קַרְקַע אוֹ שְׂכָרוֹ לָהֶם בְּמָקוֹם שֶׁאֵינוֹ רַשַּׁאי, עָבַר עַל מִצְוַת מֶלֶךְ; וְאֵינוֹ לוֹקֶה, לְפִי שֶׁאֶפְשָׁר לִמְכֹּר לָהֶם קַרְקַע אוֹ לְהַשְׂכִּיר בְּלֹא עֲשִׂיַּת מַעֲשֶׂה.

✡ וְיִקְחוּ לִי תְּרוּמָה

יֵשׁ בָּהּ שְׁתֵּי מִצְוֹת עֲשֵׂה וְאַחַת מִצְוַת לֹא תַעֲשֶׂה.

[מִצְוַת בִּנְיַן בֵּית הַבְּחִירָה]

צה לִבְנוֹת בַּיִת לְשֵׁם יְיָ, כְּלוֹמַר שֶׁנִּהְיֶה מַקְרִיבִים שָׁם קָרְבְּנוֹתֵינוּ אֵלָיו, וְשָׁם תִּהְיֶה הָעֲלִיָּה לָרֶגֶל וְקִבּוּץ כָּל יִשְׂרָאֵל בְּכָל שָׁנָה, שֶׁנֶּאֱמַר "וְעָשׂוּ לִי מִקְדָּשׁ". וְזֹאת הַמִּצְוָה כּוֹלֶלֶת עִמָּהּ הַכֵּלִים הַצְּרִיכִים לַבַּיִת אֶל הָעֲבוֹדָה, כְּגוֹן הַמְּנוֹרָה וְהַשֻּׁלְחָן וְהַמִּזְבֵּחַ וְכָל שְׁאָר הַכֵּלִים כֻּלָּם.

מִשָּׁרְשֵׁי מִצְוָה זוֹ מַה שֶּׁתִּתְרָאֶה בְּסוֹף דְּבָרַי. וְאָכֵן מִיִּרְאָתִי לְהִתְקָרֵב אֶל מִשְׁכַּן יְיָ, כִּי יָדַעְתִּי כָּל הַקָּרֵב הַקָּרֵב אִם לֹא הִתְקַדֵּשׁ לְמַדַּי לֹא יִרְאֶה הַבַּיִת וָחָי, גַּם הַכֹּהֲנִים הַנִּגָּשִׁים לַעֲבוֹדָה יִתְקַדְּשׁוּ בְּבוֹאָם אֶל הַקֹּדֶשׁ לְפָנַי, וְהַלְוִיִּם אַחַי הַשְׁתַּחֲווּ בְנֵי אַהֲרֹן אוֹתָם תְּנוּפָה טֶרֶם יִתְּנוּ קוֹלָם בְּהֵיכַל יְיָ, אָמַרְתִּי גַּם אֲנִי אַגִּיד עֲצָתִי וְאֶעֱרֹךְ הִתְנַצְּלוּתִי נֶגֶד זִקְנֵי וְאֶרְחַץ בְּנִקָּיוֹן כַּפַּי טֶרֶם אֶעֱלֶה בֵית יְיָ. יָדוּעַ הַדָּבָר וּמְפֻרְסָם בֵּינֵינוּ הָעָם מְקַבְּלֵי הַמִּצְוֹת כִּי שִׁבְעִים פָּנִים לַתּוֹרָה,

---

4. *Ibid.* 20b–21a (MT *hilchoth 'avodath kochavim* x 3).

5. See §13, note 6.

§95 1. Paragraph based on ShM positive precept §20.

2. Here our author echoes Exodus 33:20, *for man shall not see Me and live.* With literary license, he writes of his intention to write on the Sanctuary as though he were intending to go up to it.

3. Here, as in his introduction, our anonymous author indicates that he was a Levite (of the tribe of Levi). This is the reading of the three oldest manuscripts and the first edition; the fourth manuscript and other editions read *'ahar hitaharu*, so that it would mean, "and the Levites, after they purified themselves, Aaron then raised them up," etc.

condition that one should not rent it to three people: for three [indicate that it is] a permanent matter, and it is not proper to make them permanent tenants.[3]

Then there is the difference in the laws which, our Sages of blessed memory said,[4] apply in this regard between houses and fields and vineyards, and between Syria and the land of Israel. [These] and its further details are explained in the tractates *Sanhedrin* and *'Avodah Zarah*.

It applies to both man and woman in the land [of Israel]. If a person violates it and sells them land or rents to them in an instance where it is forbidden, he has disobeyed a [Divine] royal command; but he is not given whiplashes since it is possible to sell them land or to rent to them without doing any physical action.[5]

sidrah t'rumah
(Exodus 25–27:19)

There are two positive precepts and one negative in it.

95 [THE PRECEPT OF BUILDING THE HOLY TEMPLE] to build a House for the sake of the Lord, which means that we will offer up our sacrifices there to Him, and there will be [the focus of] the ascent for the pilgrimage festivals and the gathering of all Israelites every year. For it is stated, *And let them make Me a sanctuary* (Exodus 25:8). This precept includes, too, the vessels and objects needed in the House for the [Divine] service, such as the *menorah* (lamp), the table and the altar, and all the other objects.[1]

What lies at the root of this precept, you will see [below] after these words of mine. But indeed I have a reverent fear of drawing close to the dwelling of the Lord: for I know that *every one who comes near, who comes near* (Numbers 17:28), if he has not adequately hallowed himself, will not see the House and live.[2] *And also the* kohanim *who would come near* for [His] service *would sanctify themselves* (Exodus 19:22) as they came into the holiness within; and my brethren *the Levites*[3] *purified themselves, ... and Aaron raised them up in offering* (Numbers 8:21) before they would raise their voices [in praise-song] in the Temple of the Lord. Yet said I: Let me also speak my thought and present my apology before my elders; and I will wash my hands in innocence (Psalms 73:13) before I go up to the House of the Lord.

It is a known and widely recognized tenet among us, the people

§95: THE MITZVAH OF BUILDING THE HOLY TEMPLE

וּבְכָל אַחַת מֵהֶן שָׁרָשִׁים גְּדוֹלִים וְרַבִּים, וּלְכָל שֹׁרֶשׁ וְשֹׁרֶשׁ עֲנָפִים, כָּל אֶחָד יִשָּׂא אֶשְׁכּוֹל גָּדוֹל שֶׁל פֵּרוֹת נֶחְמָדִים לְהַשְׂכִּיל לְבוֹת, יוֹם יוֹם יוֹצִיאוּ פֶּרַח לַשְּׁקֵדִים עֲלֵיהֶם, פִּרְחֵי חָכְמָה וְשֵׂכֶל טוֹב, כָּל עֵינַיִם מְאִירוֹת וְרָחָבָה וְעֲמֻקָּה עֹמֶק חָכְמָתָהּ עַד שֶׁאֵין כֹּחַ בָּאָדָם לְהַשִּׂיג תַּכְלִיתָהּ, כְּמוֹ שֶׁהֵעִיד הֶחָכָם הַמֶּלֶךְ "אָמַרְתִּי אֶחְכָּמָה וְהִיא רְחוֹקָה מִמֶּנִּי", וְעִם כָּל זֶה אֵין לְהַרְפּוֹת יְדֵי הָעוֹסֵק בָּהּ, כִּי אִם מְעַט וְאִם הַרְבֵּה מִמֶּנָּה יֹאכַל כֻּלָּהּ מְתוּקָה, וְאִם יֵשׁ כַּמָּה מִפֵּרוֹת אֲשֶׁר הַגַּן לֹא תַשִּׂיג יָדָם לָקַחַת יִקְחוּ לָהֶם עָלֵהוּ לִתְרוּפָה. וְאָנֹכִי עִם דַּעְתִּי גֹּדֶל עֶרְכָּהּ וְרֹב עָמְקָהּ, וְכִי פְלִיאָה מִמֶּנִּי נִשְׂגָּבָה, פָּעַרְתִּי פִי לְדַבֵּר בָּהּ וְאֶסְמֹךְ בַּמֶּה שֶׁלִּמְדוּנִי רַבּוֹתַי, לִגְרֹס אִינִישׁ וְאַף־עַל־גַּב דְּלָא יָדַע מַאי קָאָמַר, שֶׁנֶּאֱמַר: גָּרְסָה נַפְשִׁי לְתַאֲבָה.

דַּע בְּנִי, כִּי כָל אֲשֶׁר יַגִּיעַ אֵצֶל הַשֵּׁם בַּעֲשׂוֹת בְּנֵי־אָדָם כָּל מִצְווֹתָיו אֵינֶנּוּ רַק שֶׁחָפֵץ הַשֵּׁם לְהֵיטִיב לָנוּ, וּבִהְיוֹת הָאָדָם מֻכְשָׁר וּמוּכָן בַּעֲשִׂיַּת אוֹתָם מִצְווֹת לְקַבֵּל הַטּוֹבָה אָז יֵיטִיב אֵלָיו הַשֵּׁם, וְעַל כֵּן הוֹדִיעָם דֶּרֶךְ טוֹב לִהְיוֹתָם טוֹבִים, וְהִיא דֶּרֶךְ הַתּוֹרָה כִּי בָהּ יִהְיֶה הָאָדָם טוֹב; נִמְצָא שֶׁכָּל הַמְקַיֵּם מִצְווֹתָיו הַשְּׁלֵמִים חֲפָצוֹ בַּאֲשֶׁר הוּא רָאוּי אָז לְקַבֵּל טוּבָתוֹ; וְכָל שֶׁאֵינוֹ מֵכִין עַצְמוֹ לְכָךְ רָעָתוֹ רַבָּה, שֶׁיּוֹדֵעַ חֵפֶץ הַשֵּׁם בַּמֶּה וְהוּא יַעֲשֶׂה מַעֲשָׂיו כְּנֶגֶד חֶפְצוֹ.

וּפָרָשָׁה אַחַת נִכְתְּבָה בַּתּוֹרָה לְהוֹדִיעֵנוּ עִקָּר זֶה לְבָד, וְהִיא מַה שֶּׁכָּתוּב בְּסֵדֶר וְהָיָה עֵקֶב, "וְעַתָּה יִשְׂרָאֵל מָה יְיָ אֱלֹהֶיךָ שׁוֹאֵל מֵעִמָּךְ" וְגוֹמֵר עַד "לְטוֹב לָךְ", כְּלוֹמַר אֵינֶנּוּ שׁוֹאֵל מֵעִמְּךָ דָּבָר בַּעֲשׂוֹתְךָ מִצְווֹתָיו רַק שֶׁיִּרְצֶה בְּטוּבוֹ הַגָּדוֹל

---

4. So Ba-midbar Rabbah 13, 15 and 'Othioth d'R. Akiva. On this paragraph cf. Rashba, *Responsa* I 94.

5. The original is a verb meaning both to pound or crunch, and to study; TB 'Avodah Zarah 19a. Thus the verse which follows is taken to mean: In my great longing for the Torah (to know it), I would "crunch" it or "pound" it as best I could, although I could not "grind it fine" to penetrate its depths of meaning (Rashi *ibid.*).

who accept the *mitzvoth*, that there are seventy facets to the Torah;[4] for each one of them there are great and manifold roots, and every root has branches, each of which bears a great cluster of desirable fruit, to make hearts wise. Every day they produce blossoms for those who attend them diligently—blossoms of wisdom and good intelligence, bringing light to all eyes. The depth of its wisdom widens and winds about until a man has not the power to grasp its ultimate sense. As the wise king [Solomon] avowed, *I said, "I will get wisdom"; but it was far from me* (Ecclesiastes 7:23).

With all that, however, the hands of anyone who occupies himself with it should not be slackened. For if he eats a little or much of it, it is all sweet. And if there are many whose hand will not attain to take *of the fruit of the trees of the garden* (Genesis 3:2), let them take themselves *its leaf for healing* (Ezekiel 47:12). So I, although I know its great worth and immense depth, and that it is *too wondrous for me, too exalted* (Psalms 139:6), *I have opened wide my mouth* (Psalms 119:131) to speak of it, relying on what my master teachers taught me: Let a man pound away at his study[5] even if he does not know what he is saying—as it is stated, *My soul pounds on with longing* (Psalms 119:20).

Know, my son, that all that is attained in regard to the Eternal Lord when people observe all his *mitzvoth*, is only this: It is the desire of the Eternal Lord to do us good, and as a man becomes capable and ready, by observing those precepts, to receive the good, then the Eternal Lord grants him beneficence. He therefore made them know the good way, so that they may be good—this being the way of the Torah; for by it a man becomes good. Consequently, anyone who fulfills His precepts fulfills His desire, by being worthy then to receive His beneficence. On the other hand, if any person does not prepare himself for this, his evil is great: For he knows wherein the desire of the Eternal Lord lies, yet he carries out his deeds in opposition to His desire.

One portion was written in the Torah to inform us of this principle alone. This is what was set down in the *sidrah 'ékev: And now, Israel, what does the Lord your God require of you, but to fear the Lord your God, to walk in all His ways and to love Him, and to serve the Lord your God with all your heart and with all your soul; to keep the commandments of the Lord and His statutes, which I command you this day, for your good* (Deuteronomy 10:12–13). In other words, He asks nothing of you when you observe the *mitzvoth*, but this: It is His desire, in His great benevolence, to do you good—as it is written afterward: *Behold, to the Lord your God*

§95: THE MITZVAH OF BUILDING THE HOLY TEMPLE

לְהֵיטִיב לָךְ, וּכְמוֹ שֶׁכָּתוּב אַחֲרָיו: הֵן לַיי אֱלֹהֶיךָ הַשָּׁמַיִם וּשְׁמֵי הַשָּׁמַיִם הָאָרֶץ וְכָל אֲשֶׁר בָּהּ, כְּלוֹמַר וְאֵינוֹ צָרִיךְ לְמִצְוֹתֶיךָ, רַק מֵאַהֲבָתוֹ אוֹתְךָ לְזַכּוֹתְךָ.

וְיֵשׁ בְּעוֹשֵׂי הַמִּצְוֹת יָשִׂימוּ מְגַמַּת פְּנֵיהֶם אֶל הַטּוֹבָה הַמְעֻתֶּדֶת אֲלֵיהֶם בַּעֲשִׂיָּתָן לְבַד, כִּי יֵדְעוּ שֶׁבִּסְבָתָן תָּנוּחַ עֲלֵיהֶם הַבְּרָכָה וְהַטּוֹב, וְאֶל הַכַּוָּנָה הַהִיא יִתְעַסְּקוּ בָּהֶן לְעוֹלָם; וְאֵלֶּה חֶלְקָם בַּחַיִּים וְזוֹכִין לְעֵדֶן גַּן אֱלֹהִים, וְאוּלָם לֹא הִגִּיעוּ אֶל תַּכְלִית הַכַּוָּנָה הַטּוֹבָה.

אֲבָל יֵשׁ אֲשֶׁר זָכוּ וְנָתַן לָהֶם הַשֵּׁם לֵב לָדַעַת וּלְהַכִּיר בְּמִדּוֹתָיו הַמַּעֲלוֹת, וּמִתּוֹךְ הַכָּרָתָם יִתְקַשְּׁרוּ מוֹרָשֵׁי לְבָבָם בְּאַהֲבָתוֹ קֶשֶׁר חָזָק וְאַמִּיץ עַד שֶׁיָּשִׂימוּ כָּל כַּוָּנַת הֲכָנַת גּוּפָם כְּדֵי לְהַשְׁלִים חֵפֶץ הַשֵּׁם לָרֹב חֶשְׁקָם אוֹתוֹ, וְאֶל הַתּוֹעֶלֶת הַמְעֻתָּד לָהֶם בָּעֵסֶק הַהוּא לֹא יָשִׁיתוּ לֵב, וְהִיא הַמַּעֲלָה הַגְּדוֹלָה שֶׁעָלוּ אֵלֶיהָ הָאָבוֹת הַקְּדוֹשִׁים הַשְּׁלֹשָׁה, וְהִרְבָּה מִבְּנֵיהֶם אַחֲרֵיהֶם, זֵכֶר כֻּלָּם לִבְרָכָה; וְזֹאת הִיא הַמַּדְרֵגָה הָעֶלְיוֹנָה שֶׁאֶפְשָׁר לְבֶן-אָדָם לַעֲלוֹת.

וּמֵעַתָּה בִּהְיוֹת הַנַּחַת דַּעְתֵּנוּ עַל זֶה בְּעִנְיְנֵי מִצְוֹתָיו בָּרוּךְ הוּא, תְּחַיֵּב אוֹתָנוּ לֵאמֹר כִּי בִּנְיַן בֵּית לַשֵּׁם וַעֲשׂוֹתֵנוּ בָּהּ תְּפִלּוֹת וְקָרְבָּנוֹת אֵלָיו הַכֹּל לְהָכִין הַלְּבָבוֹת לַעֲבוֹדָתוֹ יִתְעַלֶּה, לֹא מֵהִיוֹתוֹ צָרִיךְ לָשֶׁבֶת בֵּית אֲנָשִׁים וְלָבוֹא בְּצֵל קוֹרָתָם, וְאִם אַרְזֵי לְבָנוֹן יִבְנוּהוּ אוֹ בְרוֹתִים, כִּי הַשָּׁמַיִם וּשְׁמֵי הַשָּׁמַיִם לֹא יְכַלְכְּלוּהוּ, וּבְרוּחוֹ יַעֲמֹדוּ, אַף כִּי הַבַּיִת אֲשֶׁר בָּנוּ בְנֵי הָאָדָם צָרִיךְ כְּבוֹדוֹ חָלִילָה, הֲלֹא יְדוּעִים הַדְּבָרִים וּבְרוּרִים שֶׁהַכֹּל לְהַכְשֵׁר גּוּפוֹתֵינוּ, כִּי הַגּוּפוֹת יְכָשְׁרוּ עַל יְדֵי הַפְּעֻלּוֹת, וּבְרַבּוֹת הַפְּעֻלּוֹת הַטּוֹבוֹת וְרֹב הִתְמָדָתָן מַחְשְׁבוֹת הַלֵּב מִשְׁתַּהֲרוֹת מִתְלַבְּנוֹת מִזְדַּקְּקוֹת.

וְהַשֵּׁם חָפֵץ בְּטוֹבָתָן שֶׁל בְּרִיּוֹת כְּמוֹ שֶׁאָמַרְנוּ. וְעַל כֵּן צִוָּנוּ לִקְבֹּעַ מָקוֹם שֶׁיִּהְיֶה טָהוֹר וְנָקִי בְּתַכְלִית הַנְּקִיּוּת לְטַהֵר שָׁם מַחְשְׁבוֹת בְּנֵי אִישׁ וּלְתַקֵּן לְבָבָם

---

6. Based on Ramban to Deuteronomy 10:12.

7. Cf. TB P'saḥim 8a: If someone says, "This coin is for charity in order that my son may live," or "that I may deserve life in the world-to-come," he is a complete *tzaddik*, an utterly righteous person.

8. Expression based on Genesis 19:8.

9. Expression based on I Kings 8:27.

⟨358⟩

belong the heaven and the heaven of heavens, the earth with all that is in it (*ibid.* 14)—as much as to say: and he does not need your *mitzvoth*, except, out of His love for you, in order to make you worthy.[6]

Among people who observe the *mitzvoth*, there are those who set their sights solely on the good that is destined for them, knowing that because of them [the *mitzvoth*] blessing and good will be bestowed upon them; and with that intention they occupy themselves with them [the *mitzvoth*] perpetually. They have their portion in [eternal] life, and merit to attain to Eden, the paradise of God.[7] Yet they did not attain to the ultimate level of the good [Divine] intention.

There are those who have merited, however, that the Eternal Lord should give them the heart to know and recognize His noble, exalted qualities; and as a result of their understanding, the thoughts of their heart become attached to His love with a strong and mighty bond, until they set the entire intent of their physical ability on the purpose of completing the desire of the Eternal Lord, out of their great yearning for Him. To the benefit which is destined for them on account of this preoccupation, they pay no attention. This is the great level to which the three Patriarchs ascended, and many of their descendants after them (may the memory of all be for a blessing). And this is the highest level to which a man can possibly ascend.

Now, with this settled clearly in our mind in regard to the precepts, it compels us to say that building a Temple for the Eternal Lord, there to offer up our prayers and our sacrifices to Him, would be entirely in order to prepare our hearts for His worship (be He exalted)—not because He needs to dwell in a house of human beings and come under the shelter of their roof,[8] even if it should be built of the cedars of Lebanon or of cypress wood. For heaven and the heaven of heavens cannot contain Him,[9] as by His spirit they endure. All the more certainly would His glory have no need of a house built by human beings, perish the thought. This is surely a known and clear matter, that it was all [meant] for making our physical selves worthy. For the physical self becomes qualified through [its] actions. As good actions are multiplied and as they are continued with great perseverance, the thoughts of the heart become purified, cleansed and refined.

Now, the Eternal Lord desires good for human beings, as we have stated. Therefore He commanded us to establish a site that should be pure and clean to the ultimate degree of cleanness, there to purify the thoughts of people and to rectify and perfect their heart toward Him.

אֵלָיו בּוֹ, וְהוּא בָּרוּךְ הוּא בָּחַר אוֹתוֹ הַמָּקוֹם וַהֲכִינוֹ אֶל הַטּוֹבָה לִבְנֵי־אָדָם אוּלַי מֵהָיוֹתוֹ אֶמְצָעוּת הָעוֹלָם בְּכִוּוּן, וְהָאֶמְצָעוּת נִבְחָר מִן הַקְּצָווֹת, אוֹ מִן הַטַּעַם שֶׁיִּהְיֶה הוּא הַיּוֹדֵעַ. וּמִתּוֹךְ הֶכְשֵׁר הַמַּעֲשֶׂה וְטָהֳרַת הַמַּחֲשָׁבָה שֶׁיִּהְיֶה לָנוּ שָׁם יַעֲלֶה שִׂכְלֵנוּ אֶל הַדְּבֵקוּת עִם שֵׂכֶל הָעֶלְיוֹנִי.

וְעַל דֶּרֶךְ הַפְּשָׁט עַל הַצַּד הַזֶּה נֶאֱמַר שְׁרִיַּת הַשְּׁכִינָה בַּמָּקוֹם הַהוּא, וְאַף־עַל־פִּי שֶׁהָאֱמֶת כִּי אָמְרוּ זִכְרוֹנָם לִבְרָכָה קְדֻשָּׁתָן עֲלֵיהֶם אֲפִלּוּ כְּשֶׁהֵן שׁוֹמְמִין, שֶׁמַּשְׁמַע בָּזֶה שֶׁאֵין כָּל סִבַּת שְׁרִיַּת הַשְּׁכִינָה שָׁם מִצַּד הָעוֹבְדִים, אֶפְשָׁר לוֹמַר כִּי אוֹתוֹ הַמָּקוֹם בְּחָרוֹ הָאֵל לִבְרֹךְ בְּנֵי־אָדָם אֲשֶׁר בָּרָא מִתּוֹכוֹ, כְּמוֹ שֶׁאָמַרְנוּ, וּכְמוֹ שֶׁהָיָה חָפֵץ לִשְׁלֹחַ לִבְנֵי־אָדָם נָבִיא לְהוֹרוֹתָם דֶּרֶךְ יֵלְכוּ בָהּ וְיִזְכּוּ לְקִיּוּם נַפְשׁוֹתָם, כְּמוֹ־כֵן חָפֵץ בַּחֲסָדָיו הַגְּדוֹלִים לִקְבֹּעַ לָהֶם מָקוֹם בָּאָרֶץ שֶׁיִּהְיֶה נָכוֹן אֶל טוֹבַת הַבְּרִיּוֹת וּזְכוּתָם, וְכָל זֶה מֵחֲסָדָיו עַל בְּרִיּוֹתָיו.

וּמִכָּל מָקוֹם לְעוֹלָם תִּתְרַבֶּה שָׁם הַבְּרָכָה וְהַקְּדֻשָּׁה לְפִי הַפְּעֻלּוֹת הַטּוֹבוֹת שֶׁיַּעֲשׂוּ שָׁם בְּנֵי־אָדָם, וְאָז עִם הַפְּעֻלּוֹת הַטּוֹבוֹת יִפָּתְחוּ מַעְיְנוֹת הַטּוֹב כְּנֶגְדּוֹ, כִּי בֶאֱמֶת אֵינוֹ דוֹמֶה קְדֻשַּׁת הַמָּקוֹם בְּחֻרְבָּנוֹ לִקְדֻשָּׁתוֹ בְּיִשּׁוּבוֹ.

וְהַנָּחַת הַטַּעַם הַזֶּה בְּעִנְיָן הַבַּיִת תְּחַיֵּב אוֹתָנוּ גַּם כֵּן לִסְמֹךְ אֶל הַטַּעַם הַזֶּה בְּעַצְמוֹ לְפִי הַפְּשָׁט עִנְיַן הַקָּרְבָּנוֹת וְשֵׁבֶט עוֹבֵד וְכֵלִים יְקָרִים יְדוּעִים. הֲלֹא אָמַרְנוּ כִּי עִקְּרֵי הַלְּבָבוֹת תְּלוּיִין אַחַר הַפְּעֻלּוֹת, וְעַל־כֵּן כִּי יֶחֱטָא אִישׁ לֹא יִטָּהֵר לְבּוֹ יָפֶה בְּדָבָר שְׂפָתַיִם לְבַד, שֶׁיֹּאמַר בֵּינוֹ וְלַכֹּתֶל "חָטָאתִי לֹא אוֹסִיף עוֹד", אֲבָל בַּעֲשׂוֹתוֹ מַעֲשֶׂה גָדוֹל עַל דְּבַר חֶטְאוֹ, לָקַחַת מִמִּכְלְאוֹתָיו עַתּוּדִים וְלִטְרֹחַ לַהֲבִיאָם אֶל הַבַּיִת אֶל הַכֹּהֵן, וְכָל הַמַּעֲשֶׂה הַכָּתוּב בְּקָרְבְּנֵי הַחוֹטְאִים, מִתּוֹךְ כָּל הַמַּעֲשֶׂה הַגָּדוֹל הַהוּא יִקְבַּע בְּנַפְשׁוֹ רֹעַ הַחֵטְא, וְיִמָּנַע מִמֶּנּוּ פַּעַם אַחֶרֶת.

---

10. The tradition that the Temple site marks the center or starting-point of the formation of the earth's surface can be found most explicitly in Zohar II 222a-b; cf. also TB Yoma 54b.

11. Cf. Rambam, *Sh'monah P'rakim* ("Eight Chapters"), §4.

12. TB M'gillah 28a.

13. Expression based on Psalms 50:9.

He (blessed is He) chose that site and prepared it for the good of human beings—perhaps because it is the directional center of the world,[10] and the center was chosen in preference to the extremities;[11] or for some [other] reason that He (blessed is He) knows. Then by the worthiness of deed and the purification of thought that we would attain there, our intelligence would ascend to [find] adherence with the supernal [Divine] intelligence.

Thus, in plain, direct interpretation, with this approach, we can explain the dwelling of the *shechinah*, the Divine Presence, at that site—although the truth is that our Sages of blessed memory said that their sanctity remains in force over them [the sites of the Sanctuaries] even when they are desolate;[12] and this would imply that on account of the worshippers there was no cause whatever for the immanence of the *shechinah* there. It can be said, though, that God chose that place in order to bless from its center the human beings whom He created, as we stated. Just as it was His wish to send mankind a prophet to show them the way in which they should walk, and so they should merit the endurance (survival) of their souls, so did He wish, in His great kindness, to set a place for them in the land [of Israel] that should be prepared for the good of people and for their merit—all this out of His loving-kindness for His humans.

In any case, though, in truth, blessing and holiness would increase there according to the good actions that people would do there; and with the good actions, the wellsprings of good would open in response. For indeed, the holiness of the place in its state of ruin is not to be compared to its holiness in its inhabited condition.

Having set down this reason concerning the Temple, we are impelled, moreover, to apply this same reason, according to the plain meaning, to the matter of offerings, the tribe [of Lévi] that served [at the Sanctuary], and the known precious objects. Now, we said that the main ways of the heart depend on [a person's] actions. Therefore, should a man sin, he will not cleanse his heart well by word of the lips alone, i.e. that he should say, between himself and the wall, "I have sinned; I will not do so any more." But when he does some important deed on account of his sin, taking "he-goats out of his fold"[13] and toiling to bring them to the Temple, to the *kohen*—and so all the activity written about the offerings of sinners—out of that entire immense act, the evil of the sin will be impressed on his spirit, and he will refrain from it another time.

וּכְעֵין טַעַם זֶה מָצָאתִי לָרַמְבַּ"ן זִכְרוֹנוֹ לִבְרָכָה עַל צַד הַפְּשָׁט, שֶׁכָּתַב בְּשֵׁם אֲחֵרִים, וְזֶה לְשׁוֹנוֹ: כִּי בַּעֲבוּר שֶׁמַּעֲשֵׂה בְּנֵי־אָדָם נִגְמָרִים בְּמַחֲשָׁבָה וּבְדִבּוּר וּבְמַעֲשֶׂה, צִוָּה הַשֵּׁם (יִתְבָּרֵךְ) כִּי כַּאֲשֶׁר יֶחֱטָא יָבִיא קָרְבָּן וְיִסְמֹךְ עָלָיו יָדָיו כְּנֶגֶד הַמַּעֲשֶׂה, וְיִתְוַדֶּה בְּפִיו כְּנֶגֶד הַדִּבּוּר, וְיִשְׂרֹף בָּאֵשׁ הַקֶּרֶב וְהַכְּלָיוֹת שֶׁהֵם כְּלֵי הַמַּחֲשָׁבָה וְהַתַּאֲוָה, וּכְרָעַיִם כְּנֶגֶד יָדָיו וְרַגְלָיו שֶׁל אָדָם הָעוֹשִׂים כָּל מְלַאכְתּוֹ, וְיִזְרֹק הַדָּם עַל הַמִּזְבֵּחַ כְּנֶגֶד דָּמוֹ בְּנַפְשׁוֹ כְּדֵי שֶׁיַּחֲשֹׁב אָדָם בַּעֲשׂוֹתוֹ כָּל אֵלֶּה כִּי חָטָא לֵאלֹהִים בְּגוּפוֹ וְנַפְשׁוֹ, וְרָאוּי לוֹ שֶׁיִּשָּׁפֵךְ דָּמוֹ וְיִשָּׂרֵף גּוּפוֹ, לוּלֵי חֶסֶד הַבּוֹרֵא שֶׁלָּקַח מִמֶּנּוּ תְּמוּרָה וְכֹפֶר הַקָּרְבָּן שֶׁיִּהְיֶה דָּמוֹ תַּחַת דָּמוֹ, נֶפֶשׁ תַּחַת נֶפֶשׁ, וְרָאשֵׁי אִבְרֵי הַקָּרְבָּן כְּנֶגֶד רָאשֵׁי אֵבָרָיו, וְהַמָּנוֹת לְהַחֲיוֹת בָּהֶן מוֹרֵי הַתּוֹרָה שֶׁיִּתְפַּלְּלוּ עָלָיו. וְקָרְבָּן הַתָּמִיד בַּעֲבוּר שֶׁלֹּא יִנָּצְלוּ הָרַבִּים מֵחֲטֹא תָמִיד. וְאֵלֶּה דְּבָרִים מִתְקַבְּלִים מוֹשְׁכִין הַלֵּב כְּדִבְרֵי הַגָּדָה; עַד כָּאן.

וְהֶאֱרִיךְ הוּא עוֹד בָּעִנְיָן, וְכָתַב: וְעַל דֶּרֶךְ הָאֱמֶת יֵשׁ בַּקָּרְבָּנוֹת סוֹד נֶעֱלָם וְכוּלֵי, כְּמוֹ שֶׁכָּתוּב בְּפֵרוּשָׁיו בְּפָרָשַׁת וַיִּקְרָא. וְעוֹד נוֹסִיף דְּבָרִים עַל צַד הַפְּשָׁט, וְנֹאמַר כִּי מִזֶּה הַשֹּׁרֶשׁ צִוָּנוּ הָאֵל לְהַקְרִיב לְעוֹלָם מֵהַדְּבָרִים שֶׁלֵּב בְּנֵי אָדָם הוֹמֶה בָּהֶן כְּמוֹ הַבָּשָׂר וְהַיַּיִן וְהַפַּת, כְּדֵי שֶׁיִּתְעוֹרֵר הַלֵּב יוֹתֵר עִם הָעֵסֶק בָּהֶם, וְלֶעָנִי חַיָּב לְהָבִיא מְעַט קֶמַח מֵחֲמַת אֲשֶׁר עֵינָיו וְלִבּוֹ עָלָיו כָּל הַיּוֹם.

וְעוֹד יֵשׁ הִתְעוֹרְרוּת אַחֵר לַלֵּב בַּקָּרְבָּן מִצַּד הַדִּמְיוֹן שֶׁגּוּף הָאָדָם וְהַבְּהֵמָה יְדַמּוּ בְּכָל עִנְיְנֵיהֶם, לֹא יִתְחַלְּקוּ רַק שֶׁבָּזֶה נִתַּן הַשֵּׂכֶל וְלֹא בָזֶה, וּבִהְיוֹת גּוּף הָאָדָם יוֹצֵא מִגֶּדֶר הַשֵּׂכֶל בְּעֵת הַחֵטְא יֵשׁ לוֹ לָדַעַת שֶׁנִּכְנַס בְּעֵת הַהִיא בְּגֶדֶר הַבְּהֵמוֹת אַחַר שֶׁלֹּא יְחַלְּקֵם רַק הוּא לְבַדּוֹ. וְעַל־כֵּן נִצְטַוָּה לָקַחַת גּוּף בָּשָׂר כְּגוּפוֹ

---

14. Ramban to Leviticus 1:9.

15. Based on TB Sotah 3a: A man does not commit a sin unless a spirit of lunacy has possessed him.

SIDRAH T'RUMAH

I found something similar to this reason [written] by Ramban of blessed memory, in the way of simple, direct explanation, which he wrote in the name of others. These are his words:[14] Because human deeds are carried to completion by thought, speech, and action, the Eternal Lord (be He blessed) ordained that when a person sins he is to bring an offering and rest his hands upon it—which constitutes action; he is to confess [his sin] with his mouth—which constitutes speech; and he is to burn in the [altar] fire the entrails and the kidneys, which are the vessels of thought and desire, and the legs, which correspond to a man's hands and feet, that do all his work. The blood is to be sprinkled on the altar, corresponding to his blood, which gives him life—so that a man will consider, as he does all these [acts], that he sinned toward God with his body and his spirit, and he deserves that his blood should be spilled and his body burned—if not for the kindness of the Creator, that He has taken from him the offering as exchange and ransom, that its blood should be instead of his blood, one life in lieu of another. The main limbs and organs of the offering correspond to his main limbs and organs, and the portions [are eaten by the *kohanim*] in order to sustain the instructors of the Torah, that they should pray for him. Moreover, the daily offering is sacrificed because people generally cannot avoid sinning continually. These words are plausible, drawing the heart like words of homiletic teaching. Thus far [the exposition of Ramban].

He went on at length about the subject, writing: "On the level of truth, though, there is a hidden mystic meaning, etc."—as written in his commentary, in *sidrah va-yikra*.[14] Well, we can continue by way of plain explanation and say that for this root reason, God commanded us always to bring offerings of those things for which the heart longs, such as meat, wine, and bread: so that the heart should be the more aroused as one has recourse to them; and the poor man is obligated to bring a bit of his flour, over which his eyes and heart are concerned the entire day.

There is yet another way in which the heart is bestirred by an animal offering: through the similarity—since the bodies of man and animal resemble one another in all their features, being differentiated only by the fact that intelligence was given the one and not the other. Now, since the physical man leaves the boundary of intelligence at the time of the sin,[15] he ought to know that then he enters the boundary of the animals, as this alone sets them apart. For this reason he

§95: THE MITZVAH OF BUILDING THE HOLY TEMPLE

וְלַהֲבִיאוֹ אֶל הַמָּקוֹם הַנִּבְחָר לְעִלּוּי הַשֵּׂכֶל וְלִשְׂרְפוֹ שָׁם, וּלְהַשְׁכִּיחַ זִכְרוֹ, כָּלִיל יִהְיֶה, לֹא יִנָּכֵר וְלֹא יִפָּקֵד, תַּחַת גּוּפוֹ, כְּדֵי לְצַיֵּר בְּלִבָּבוֹ צִיּוּר חָזָק שֶׁעִנְיָנֵנוּ שֶׁל גּוּף בְּלִי שֵׂכֶל אָבֵד וּבָטֵל לְגַמְרֵי.

וְיִשְׂמַח בְּחֶלְקוֹ בַּנֶּפֶשׁ הַמַּשְׂכֶּלֶת שֶׁחֲנָנֲנוּ הָאֵל שֶׁהִיא קַיֶּמֶת לְעוֹלָם, וְגַם לַגּוּף הַשָּׁתָּף עִמָּהּ יֵשׁ קִיּוּם בִּתְחִיָּה בִּסְבָתָהּ בְּלֶכְתּוֹ בַּעֲצָתָהּ, כְּלוֹמַר שֶׁיִּשָּׁמֵר מִן הַחֵטְא. וּבְקָבְעוֹ צִיּוּר זֶה בְּנַפְשׁוֹ יִזָּהֵר מִן הַחֵטְא הַרְבֵּה, וְהַבְטִיחָהּ הַתּוֹרָה שֶׁבַּמַּעֲשֶׂה הַגָּדוֹל הַזֶּה וּבְהִסְתַּכְּמַת עוֹשֵׂיהוּ שֶׁיִּתְנַחֵם עַל חֶטְאוֹ מִלֵּב וּמִנֶּפֶשׁ, תְּכֻפַּר אֵלָיו שִׁגְגָתוֹ. אֲבָל הַזְּדוֹנוֹת לֹא יַסְפִּיק לְכַפְּרָם דִּמְיוֹן זֶה, כִּי הַזֵּד לֹא יִנָּכַח בְּדִמְיוֹנוֹת וּדְבָרִים; שֵׁבֶט לְגֵו כְּסִילִים.

וְאַל יַקְשֶׁה עָלֶיךָ בַּהֲנָחַת טַעַם זֶה אֵיךְ נָבִיא קָרְבָּן נְדָבָה לְעוֹלָם, כִּי טַעֲמֵנוּ זֶה יְסֻבַּל גַּם הַנְּדָבוֹת: שֶׁאַחַר שֶׁאָמַרְנוּ שֶׁהַקָּרְבָּן דִּמְיוֹן לְהַשְׁפָּלַת הַגּוּפוֹת וּלְעִלּוּי הַנְּפָשׁוֹת, אַף בְּלֹא חֵטְא יָדוּעַ יִמָּצֵא בּוֹ הַמַּקְרִיב תּוֹעֶלֶת לָקַחַת הַמּוּסָר.

וּבְקָרְבַּן עֲזָאזֵל שֶׁנִּשְׁתַּלַּח חַי אֶל מְקוֹם הַחֻרְבָּן וְהַכִּלָּיוֹן נֹאמַר בִּפְשַׁט הָעִנְיָן לְבַל יְדַמֶּה הַחוֹטֵא הַגָּמוּר שֶׁאַחַר שֶׁתְּקַבֵּל נַפְשׁוֹ עֹנֶשׁ עַל חַטָּאָיו, תָּשׁוּב לַעֲמֹד בִּמְקוֹם הַטּוֹבִים אוֹ תִּהְיֶה לָהּ הַשָּׁאֲרוּת וְטוֹבָה קְצָת וַאֲפִלּוּ יִהְיֶה כְּיָרָבְעָם בֶּן נְבָט וַחֲבֵרָיו, כְּמוֹ שֶׁהוּא רוֹאֶה כָּל הַשָּׁנָה כֻּלָּהּ שֶׁיֵּשׁ לַגּוּף הַבְּהֵמָה שֶׁהוּא לְדִמְיוֹן גּוּף הַחוֹטֵא הַשָּׁאֲרוּת קְצָת בֵּית הַשֵּׁם בָּאֵפֶר שֶׁנִּשְׁאַר שָׁם בְּעֵת הַשְּׂרֵפָה, לֹא יוֹצִיאוּהוּ מִן הַבַּיִת עַד אַחַר זְמַן הַרְבֵּה.

was commanded to take a body of flesh like himself and bring it to the site chosen for the ennobling exaltation of the intelligence; and there he is to burn it—to eradicate its memory it is burnt completely; *it shall not come to mind or be remembered* (Jeremiah 3:16)—in place of his body; this, in order to form a strong conception in his heart that the entire business of a body without intelligence must perish and become completely void.

Thus let him be happy with his lot, with the intelligent spirit with which God endowed him, that endures forever. Even for the body that was joined with it there is eternal life [ultimately] through resurrection on its account, if he will follow its counsel, i.e. to guard against sin. Hence, by fixing this conception firmly in his spirit, he will beware of sin greatly; and the Torah gave assurance that through this great deed and the compliance of the one who performs it—that he regrets his iniquity heart and soul—his inadvertent sin will be forgiven him. For deliberate sins, however, this similarity [between the human and the animal body] is not enough to bring forgiveness. The willful transgressor is not chastised by similarities and words; *a rod for the back of fools* (Proverbs 26:3).

Now, let it not be a difficulty for you to understand, if we accept this reason as a basis, how we could ever bring a voluntary animal offering. For this explanation of ours can also account for voluntary (gift) offerings: Since we have said that an animal offering [points by its] resemblance to the degrading lowliness of the physical body and the superiority of the spirit, then [even] without any known sin, the person bringing an offering will find useful benefit in it, to learn an ethical lesson.

About the offering [taken on *Yom Kippur* to] Azazel, though, which was sent alive into a place of desolation and destruction, let us say this out of the simple meaning of the matter: The total utter sinner should not imagine that after his spirit will receive punishment for its sins, it will return to stand in the place of the virtuous, or it will have some survival and good [portion in the afterlife], even if he should be [as wicked] as Jeroboam the son of Nebat and his colleagues—as he sees through the entire year that for the animal's body, which is [offered up] as a semblance of the sinner's body, there is some slight survival in the House of the Eternal Lord, through [its] ash, which remains there at the time of the burning: it is not removed from the Temple until after a considerable period.

§95: THE MITZVAH OF BUILDING THE HOLY TEMPLE

עַל־כֵּן בַּשָּׂעִיר הַחַי הַנּוֹשֵׂא כָּל הָעֲווֹנוֹת יִרְאוּ רֶמֶז כִּי הַחוֹטְאִים שֶׁעֲווֹנוֹתָיו מְרֻבִּין כְּמוֹ הָאֶפִּיקוֹרוֹסִין וְשֶׁכָּפְרוּ בַּתּוֹרָה וּבִתְחִיַּת הַמֵּתִים וְכָל הַמֵּצֵרִים לְיִשְׂרָאֵל בִּכְלָל, לֹא יִרְאוּ בְּטוֹבָה לְעוֹלָם וְתוֹלַעְתָּם לֹא תָמוּת וְאִשָּׁם לֹא תִכְבֶּה, כְּמַעֲשֵׂה הַשָּׂעִיר בְּנָשְׂאוֹ רֻבֵּי עֲווֹנוֹת כָּל יִשְׂרָאֵל יְשַׁלַּח לִגְמָרֵי אֶל אֶרֶץ גְּזֵרָה, לֹא יִמָּצֵא בֵית יְיָ לֹא לִשְׁחִיטָה וְלֹא לִזְרִיקָה, זִכְרוֹ יֹאבַד מִנִּי אָרֶץ. וְזֶהוּ שֶׁאָמְרוּ זִכְרוֹנָם לִבְרָכָה כִּי בְשָׁעָה שֶׁיִּשְׂרָאֵל מְרַצִּין לֹא הִגִּיעַ לַחֲצִי הָהָר עַד שֶׁנַּעֲשֶׂה אֲבָרִים אֲבָרִים, לְהוֹדִיעָן דִּמְיוֹן הַחוֹטֵא הַגָּמוּר כִּי כֵן יֹאבַד מְהֵרָה וְיִהְיֶה כָּלֶה כָּלָיוֹן גָּמוּר, לְמַעַן יִלְמְדוּ וְיִקְחוּ מוּסָר וְיֵיטִיבוּ דַרְכֵיהֶם, וְזֶהוּ הַסִּימָן הַטּוֹב לָהֶם, שֶׁאֵין מְלַמֵּד מוּסָר אֶלָּא הָאוֹהֵב, כְּמוֹ שֶׁכָּתוּב: וְאוֹהֲבוֹ שִׁחֲרוֹ מוּסָר.

וּבְעִנְיַן חִלּוּק הַקָּרְבָּנוֹת בִּשְׁחִיטָתָן וּבְמַתְּנוֹת הַדָּם וּבְחֵלֶק הַכֹּהֲנִים וְיֶתֶר פְּרָטֶיהָ רַבִּים, אִם נֹאמַר לְפִי הַפְּשָׁט שֶׁהָיָה כֵן לִהְיוֹת מַחֲשֶׁבֶת הָעוֹבֵד מְכֻוֶּנֶת אֶל הָעֲבוֹדָה הַרְבֵּה, כִּי הַחִלּוּקִין יַכְרִיחוּ כִּוּוּן הַמַּחֲשָׁבָה בַּדָּבָר, לֹא נַעֲלֶה בְיָדֵינוּ רַק דִּבְרֵי נַעֲרוּת. וּכְלָל הַדְּבָרִים כִּי גַם בַּפְּשָׁטִים לֹא נִמְצָא יָדֵינוּ וְרַגְלֵינוּ בִּלְתִּי סַעַד הַמְקֻבָּלִים, וַאֲלֵיהֶם נִכְרַע אַפַּיִם וְיִפְתְּחוּ לָנוּ בְכָל אֵלֶּה הָעֵינָיִם.

וְאוּלָם אֵין לִקְרוֹתֵנוּ מִכַּת הַכְּסִילִים בְּהוֹצִיאֵנוּ כָּל רוּחֵנוּ בִדְבָרִים, כִּי בְפָסֹלֶת רַב מְעַט אֹכֶל נִמְצָא לְעִתִּים; גַּם כִּי רָאִינוּ לְרַבּוֹתֵינוּ זִכְרוֹנָם לִבְרָכָה כַּיּוֹצֵא בִדְבָרֵינוּ אוֹמְרִים, שֶׁאָמְרוּ בְּקָרְבַּן סוֹטָה: הִיא עָשְׂתָה מַעֲשֵׂה בְהֵמָה, לְפִיכָךְ תַּקְרִיב שְׂעוֹרִים; וּבְקָרְבָּן מְצֹרָע: הוּא עָשָׂה מַעֲשֵׂה פָטִיט, יַקְרִיב צִפֳּרִים; וּבְדוֹמֶה לָזֶה אָמְרוּ זִכְרוֹנָם לִבְרָכָה בְּעִנְיַן הַנִּדָּה: מִפְּנֵי מָה אָמְרָה תוֹרָה לֵישֵׁב שִׁבְעָה

---

16. Listed thus in MT *hilchoth t'shuvah* iii 6.

17. TB Yoma 67a; cf. TJ vi 3: All the days that Simeon the *tzaddik* lived, it did not reach halfway down the mountain before it was torn limb from limb; from the time Simeon the *tzaddik* died, it would flee into the wilderness.

18. Literally, we will not find our hands and our feet.

19. Cf. Proverbs 29:11, *A fool expends all his spirit*.

20. I.e. the food of animals; TB Sotah 14a.

21. The Sages teach that *tzara'ath*, the skin ailment of a *m'tzora*, is a punishment for *lashon ha-ra*, idle, evil gossip—i.e. "chattering"; hence the offering should be of birds (fowl), which also chatter; TB 'Arachin 16b.

⟨366⟩

Therefore, in the goat [sacrificed] alive, which carries all the sins, let them see a hint that sinners whose iniquities are enormous—such as heretics and those who have denied the Torah and the resurrection of the dead;[16] and those who make oppressive trouble for the people Israel are included too—will never see any good; *for their worm shall not die, and their fire shall not be quenched* (Isaiah 66:24). [Theirs will be a fate] like the course of the goat: carrying as it does the multitude of sins of all the Israelites, it is hurled altogether *into a stark land* (Leviticus 16:22). It is not found at all in the House of the Lord, neither for ritual slaughter nor for sprinkling of the blood; its *remembrance perishes from the earth* (Job 18:17). And this is why our Sages of blessed memory said that when the Israelites were acceptable [beloved to the Almighty], it did not reach halfway down the mountain [precipice] before it was completely torn limb from limb[17]—to give them an analogy for the utter, total sinner, that even so will he perish swiftly and be utterly, totally destroyed—that they might learn and take heed of this, and improve their ways. This was a good augury for them, for none but a good friend teaches moral lessons, as it is written, *but he who loves him chastens him with morality* (Proverbs 13:24).

As to the differences between the [various] offerings in their ritual slaughter, the utilization of the blood, the portion for the *kohanim*, and the rest of their many details—if we were to say, according to the plain meaning, that all was so [arranged] in order that the thought of the [Divine] servant should be attuned in its intention to the great, manifold service, for the differences would compel attuning, focusing one's thought in the matter—we would succeed in producing nothing more than child's talk. The sum of the matter is that even in the plain meanings we cannot move hand or foot[18] without help from the masters of the mystic tradition. To them we must bow face down, and they will open our eyes [with insight] on all these [points].

However, we should not be called [a member] of the group of fools as we expend all our spirit in words:[19] for [even] in much waste matter a little food is found at times. Moreover, we have seen our Sages of blessed memory say things similar to our words: for they taught about the offering of a *sotah* (a woman suspected, with reason, of adultery): She acted like an animal; therefore let her bring barley;[20] and about the offering of a [cured] *m'tzora*: He did a deed of chattering; let him offer up birds.[21] Similarly, our Sages of blessed memory said by way of homily: Why did the Torah say (for a woman) to wait seven clean

§95: THE MITZVAH OF BUILDING THE HOLY TEMPLE

נְקִיִּים, שֶׁתְּהֵא חֲבִיבָה עָלָיו בְּיוֹתֵר. וּבֶאֱמֶת שֶׁאֵין כָּל זֶה לְדַעְתָּם תַּכְלִית הַכַּוָּנָה בַּדְּבָרִים, רַק לְהוֹדִיעַ כִּי עִנְיַן הַמִּצְוָה יִסְבֹּל הַרְבֵּה רְמָזִים מִלְּבַד עִקָּרֶיהָ גְּדוֹלִים וַחֲזָקִים.

מִדִּינֵי הַמִּצְוָה, מַה שֶּׁאָמְרוּ זִכְרוֹנָם לִבְרָכָה שֶׁקֹּדֶם שֶׁנִּבְנָה הַבַּיִת בִּירוּשָׁלַיִם הָיוּ מַקְרִיבִין קָרְבָּנוֹת בִּשְׁאָר מְקוֹמוֹתָם, אֲבָל מִשֶּׁנִּבְנָה הַבַּיִת נֶאֶסְרוּ כָּל הַמְּקוֹמוֹת לִבְנוֹת בָּם בַּיִת לַשֵּׁם וּלְהַקְרִיב שָׁם, שֶׁנֶּאֱמַר: זֹאת מְנוּחָתִי עֲדֵי עַד. וְאֵלּוּ הֵם הַדְּבָרִים שֶׁהֵם עִקָּר בְּבִנְיַן הַבַּיִת: עוֹשִׂין בּוֹ קֹדֶשׁ וְקֹדֶשׁ קָדָשִׁים, וְיִהְיֶה לִפְנֵי הַקֹּדֶשׁ מָקוֹם אֶחָד וְהוּא הַנִּקְרָא אוּלָם, וְשָׁלָשְׁתָּן נִקְרָאִין הֵיכָל. וְעוֹשִׂין מְחִצָּה אַחַת סָבִיב לַהֵיכָל רְחוֹקָה מִמֶּנּוּ כְּעֵין קַלְעֵי הֶחָצֵר שֶׁהָיוּ בַּמִּדְבָּר, וְכָל הַמֻּקָּף בִּמְחִצָּה זוֹ שֶׁהוּא כְּעֵין חֲצַר אֹהֶל מוֹעֵד הוּא הַנִּקְרָא עֲזָרָה, וְהַכֹּל נִקְרָא מִקְדָּשׁ.

וְעוֹשִׂין בַּמִּקְדָּשׁ הַכֵּלִים הַכְּתוּבִים בַּתּוֹרָה שֶׁצְּרִיכִים שָׁם. וּמַה שֶּׁאָמְרוּ שֶׁכָּל כְּלֵי הַקֹּדֶשׁ שֶׁנִּקְּבוּ אוֹ נִסְדְּקוּ שֶׁמְּתַקְּנִין אוֹתָן וְעוֹשִׂין אוֹתָן חֲדָשִׁים, וְסַכִּין שֶׁנִּשְׁמַט מְקָתוֹ אוֹ נִפְגַּם אֵין מְתַקְּנִין אוֹתוֹ אֶלָּא גּוֹנְזִין אוֹתוֹ מִיָּד, שֶׁאֵין עֲנִיּוּת בִּמְקוֹם עֲשִׁירוּת. וְעוֹשִׂין בְּתוֹךְ הָעֲזָרָה גְּבוּלִין, עַד כָּאן לְיִשְׂרָאֵל, עַד כָּאן לַכֹּהֲנִים, וּבוֹנִין סָמוּךְ לָהּ בָּתִּים לְהִשְׁתַּמֵּשׁ בָּהֶן כָּל צָרְכֵי הַמִּקְדָּשׁ, וְכָל אַחַת נִקְרֵאת לִשְׁכָּה.

וְיֶתֶר פְּרָטֶיהָ, כְּגוֹן בִּנְיַן הַבַּיִת כֵּיצַד, וְתַבְנִיתוֹ וְכָל מִדּוֹתָיו, וּבִנְיַן הַמִּזְבֵּחַ וּמִשְׁפָּטָיו, מְבֹאָרִים בְּמַסֶּכֶת מִדּוֹת. וְכֵן תַּבְנִית הַמְּנוֹרָה וְהַשֻּׁלְחָן וּמִזְבַּח הַזָּהָב וּמְקוֹמָם בַּהֵיכָל, בִּגְמָרָא מְנָחוֹת וְיוֹמָא.

וְנוֹהֶגֶת מִצְוָה זוֹ בִּזְמַן שֶׁרֹב יִשְׂרָאֵל עַל אַדְמָתָן, וְזוֹ מִן הַמִּצְוֹת שֶׁאֵינָן

---

22. TB Niddah 31b.
23. TB Z'vaḥim 112b.
24. *Ibid.* 119a.
25. Mishnah, Middoth iv 6.
26. MT *hilchoth béth ha-b'ḥirah* i 5 (based on Mishnah, Kélim i 8—MY).
27. But the damaged one is not repaired, as that would seem an act of penury; see below; TB Z'vaḥim 88a.
28. *Ibid.*
29. Mishnah, Middoth ii 6.

⟨368⟩

days [after the menses]?—so that she should be very beloved to him [her husband].[22] The truth is that in their view these are not the final, ultimate purposes of those matters. It is only to inform us that the subject-matter of a precept can bear many implications, apart from its main and mighty principles.

Among the laws of the *mitzvah* there is what our Sages of blessed memory said,[23] that before we would build the Temple in Jerusalem, they could offer up sacrifices in their other places; but from the time the Temple was built, all [other] places became banned to build a temple and offer up sacrifices there; for it is stated, *This is My resting-place forever* (Psalms 132:14).[24] These are the matters of main importance in the construction of the Temple: A holy chamber and a holy of holies are to be made in it; before the holy chamber there should be a certain place, called *'ulam* (the entrance hall); and all three [together] are called *héchal* (the Temple "palace").[25] One partition is erected around the *héchal*, but distant from it, similar to the hangings of the court that were in the wilderness (Exodus 27:9); all that is surrounded by this partition, corresponding to the court of the *'ohel mo'éd* (Tent of Meeting), is called the *'azarah* (the Temple court); and all [these together] are called *mikdash*, the Sanctuary.[26]

Then the objects and utensils written in the Torah, that are needed there, would be made [for use] in the Sanctuary. And [there is the law] that our Sages taught, that every sacred utensil that developed a hole or became cracked is to be melted down at once, and it is to be made anew;[27] if a knife-blade slipped out of its handle or became nicked, it is not to be repaired but rather hidden at once—for there is no poverty in a place of wealth.[28] Within the *'azarah* (Temple forecourt), boundaries are set: till here for Israelites; till here for *kohanim*. Near it, houses (rooms) are built, to be used for all the needs of the Sanctuary; and each one is called *lishkah* (compartment).[29]

The rest of its details, such as how the construction of the Temple is carried out; its plan and all its dimensions; the construction of the altar and its laws—are explained in the Mishnah tractate *Middoth*. So too, the plan of the *menorah* (lamp), the table and the altar of gold, and their proper places in the *héchal* [are explained] in the Talmud tractates *M'nahoth* and *Yoma*.

This *mitzvah* is in force when the majority of Israelites (Jewry) are settled in their homeland. It is one of the precepts that are not imposed on any individual, but rather on the entire community. When the

§96: NOT TO REMOVE ITS STAVES FROM THE HOLY ARK

מוּטָּלוֹת עַל יָחִיד כִּי אִם עַל הַצִּבּוּר כֻּלָּן, כְּשֶׁיִּבָּנֶה הַבַּיִת בִּמְהֵרָה בְיָמֵינוּ יִתְקַיֵּם מִצְוַת עֲשֵׂה.

[שֶׁלֹּא לְהוֹצִיא בַּדֵּי הָאָרוֹן מִמֶּנּוּ]

צו שֶׁלֹּא לְהוֹצִיא בַּדֵּי הָאָרוֹן מִתּוֹךְ הַטַּבָּעוֹת, שֶׁנֶּאֱמַר: בְּטַבְּעֹת הָאָרֹן יִהְיוּ הַבַּדִּים לֹא יָסֻרוּ מִמֶּנּוּ. וּמְבֹאָר הוּא שֶׁמִּצְוָה זוֹ בִּכְלַל מִצְוֹת הַנּוֹהֲגוֹת לְדוֹרוֹת הִיא, שֶׁאֵין פֵּרוּשׁ נוֹהֲגוֹת לְדוֹרוֹת שֶׁלֹּא יִפְסֹק מִיִּשְׂרָאֵל מַעֲשֵׂה אוֹתָהּ מִצְוָה לְעוֹלָם בְּשׁוּם זְמַן, אֶלָּא כֵן הוּא הָעִנְיָן: כָּל מִצְוָה שֶׁלֹּא נִצְטַוֵּינוּ עָלֶיהָ לַעֲשׂוֹתָהּ רַק בִּזְמַן יָדוּעַ וְלֹא יוֹתֵר, כְּגוֹן מַה שֶּׁכָּתוּב "הֱיוּ נְכֹנִים לִשְׁלֹשֶׁת יָמִים", וּכְמוֹ־כֵן אַזְהָרָה דְסִינַי, "גַּם הַצֹּאן וְהַבָּקָר אַל יִרְעוּ אֶל מוּל הָהָר הַהוּא", וְכָל כַּיּוֹצֵא בָזֶה, שֶׁלֹּא הָיְתָה הַצִּוָּאָה אֶלָּא לְשָׁעָה בִּלְבַד; אֵלּוּ יִקָּרְאוּ מִצְוֹת שֶׁאֵינָן נוֹהֲגוֹת לְדוֹרוֹת.

אֲבָל כָּל מִצְוָה שֶׁלֹּא נִצְטַוֵּינוּ עָלֶיהָ לִזְמַן יָדוּעַ, אַף־עַל־פִּי שֶׁיֵּשׁ לָהּ הֶפְסֵק בִּזְמַן מִן הַזְּמַנִּים מִצַּד גָּלוּתֵנוּ אוֹ בְּסִבַּת דָּבָר אַחֵר, כְּגוֹן עַכְשָׁיו בַּעֲווֹנוֹתֵינוּ שֶׁאֵין לָנוּ אָרוֹן, מִצְוָה הַנּוֹהֶגֶת לְדוֹרוֹת נִקְרֵאת, לְפִי שֶׁכָּל זְמַן שֶׁיִּהְיֶה לָנוּ אָרוֹן חַיָּבִין אָנוּ לְבַל נָסִיר בַּדָּיו מִמֶּנּוּ כְּדֵי שֶׁיּוֹצִיאוּהוּ בָּהֶם הַלְוִיִּם אִם נִצְטָרֵךְ לַהֲבִיאוֹ מִמָּקוֹם לְמָקוֹם בְּסִבַּת מִלְחָמָה אוֹ מֵאַי זֶה סִבָּה שֶׁתָּבֹא.

מִשָּׁרְשֵׁי הַמִּצְוָה לְפִי שֶׁהָאָרוֹן מִשְׁכַּן הַתּוֹרָה, וְהִיא כָּל עִקָּרֵנוּ וּכְבוֹדֵנוּ, וְנִתְחַיַּבְנוּ לִנְהֹג בּוֹ כָּל כָּבוֹד וְכָל הָדָר בְּכָל יְכָלְתֵּנוּ, עַל כֵּן נִצְטַוֵּינוּ לְבַל נָסִיר בַּדֵּי הָאָרוֹן מִמֶּנּוּ פֶּן נִהְיֶה צְרִיכִים לָצֵאת עִם הָאָרוֹן לְשׁוּם מָקוֹם בִּמְהִירוּת, וְאוּלַי מִתּוֹךְ הַטִּרְדָּה וְהַחִפָּזוֹן לֹא נִבְדֹּק יָפֶה לִהְיוֹת בַּדָּיו חֲזָקִים כָּל הַצֹּרֶךְ, וְשֶׁמָּא חַס־וְשָׁלוֹם יִפֹּל מִיָּדָם וְאֵין זֶה כְּבוֹדוֹ. אֲבָל בִּהְיוֹתָם בּוֹ מוּכָנִים לְעוֹלָם וְלֹא יָסוּרוּ מִמֶּנּוּ נַעֲשֶׂה אוֹתָן חֲזָקוֹת הַרְבֵּה וְלֹא יֶאֱרַע תַּקָּלָה בָּהֶן.

וְעוֹד טַעַם אַחֵר, שֶׁכָּל כְּלֵי הַמִּקְדָּשׁ צוּרָתָן מְחֻיֶּבֶת לִרְמֹז עִנְיָנִים עֶלְיוֹנִים כְּדֵי

---

§96 1. Otherwise it could not be included among the 613 precepts (see "The Order of the *Mitzvoth*," note 1); ShM root principle 3.

2. So ShM *ibid*.

3. Cf. ShM positive precept §187.

Temple will be rebuilt—soon, in our days—a positive precept will be fulfilled.

96 [NOT TO REMOVE THE STAVES OF THE ARK FROM IT] not to remove the poles of the ark from within the rings: for it is stated, *In the rings of the ark shall the poles be; they shall not be taken from it* (Exodus 25:15); and it is clear that this precept is included among the *mitzvoth* that remain in effect for all generations.[1] For "remain in effect for all generations" does not mean that the observance of that particular precept will never stop among the Israelites, at any time whatever; but it rather means this: Any *mitzvah* that we were commanded to observe only at a certain time and no more, such as the injunction written in Scripture, *Be ready by the third day* (Exodus 19:15), the warning about Sinai, *neither let the flocks or herds feed before that mountain*, and anything similar, where the command was only for a brief time—these are called precepts which do not apply for all generations.[2]

However, any precept that we were not commanded to observe [only] for a certain known time, even if it has a period of interruption for some amount of time, on account of our exile or because of something else—for example, now, for our sins, [in regard to this precept,] when we have no ark—this is called a *mitzvah* that remains in effect for all generations.[3] For as long as we will have an ark, we will have the obligation not to remove the poles from it, so that the Levites can take it out by using them if it will be necessary to bring it from one place to another on account of war, or for any reason that may occur.

At the root of the precept lies the reason that the ark is the "dwelling-place" of the Torah, and it is our entire mainstay and glory. So we became obligated to treat it with every honor and majesty that lies in our power. Therefore we were commanded not to remove the poles of the ark from it, for fear that we might need to go with the ark out to some place swiftly, and perhaps, amid the anxiety and haste, we will not check well if its poles are as strong as necessary, and then, Heaven forfend, it may fall from their hands—and this is not an honor for it. But as they will be with it, forever ready, and will not be removed from it, we will make them extremely strong, and no disaster will occur with them.

Another reason is that the form of every object in the Sanctuary must imply and connote sublime supernal themes, so that a man will be

שֶׁיִּהְיֶה הָאָדָם נִפְעָל לְטוֹבָה מִתּוֹךְ מַחְשַׁבְתּוֹ בָּהֶן, וְרָצָה הָאֵל לְטוֹבָתֵנוּ שֶׁלֹּא תֻּפְסַד אוֹתָהּ הַצּוּרָה אֲפִלּוּ לְפִי שָׁעָה.

[מִצְוַת סִדּוּר לֶחֶם הַפָּנִים וּלְבוֹנָה]

צז לָשִׂים בְּבֵית הַמִּקְדָּשׁ לִפְנֵי יְיָ לֶחֶם תָּמִיד, שֶׁנֶּאֱמַר: וְנָתַתָּ עַל הַשֻּׁלְחָן לֶחֶם פָּנִים לְפָנַי תָּמִיד.

מִשָּׁרְשֵׁי הַמִּצְוָה שֶׁצִּוָּנוּ הָאֵל בָּרוּךְ הוּא מִצְוָה תְּמִידִית בַּלֶּחֶם לְפִי שֶׁבּוֹ יִחְיֶה הָאָדָם, וְעַל־כֵּן צָרִיךְ אֵלָיו לִהְיוֹת הַבְּרָכָה מְצוּיָה בּוֹ תָּמִיד, וּמִתּוֹךְ עָסְקֵנוּ בּוֹ לְקַיֵּם עָלָיו מִצְוַת הַשֵּׁם יִהְיֶה הָרָצוֹן וְהַבְּרָכָה חָלִים עָלֵינוּ וְיִתְבָּרֵךְ בִּמְעֵינוּ, כִּי בְּכָל שֶׁיַּעֲשֶׂה בּוֹ הָאָדָם רְצוֹן הַשֵּׁם בּוֹ הוּא מִתְבָּרֵךְ, וּלְפִי כָּל עִנְיָן וְעִנְיָן שֶׁיָּשִׂים מְגַמַּת פָּנָיו וּמַחְשְׁבוֹתָיו וַעֲסָקָיו בְּדָבָר מִצְוָה לְפִיהֶן מַעֲיַן הַבְּרָכָה נוֹבֵעַ עָלָיו. וְכֵן מָצָאתִי לְהָרַמְבַּ״ן זִכְרוֹנוֹ לִבְרָכָה, וּבְעֵצֶם מַה שֶּׁאָמְרוּ זִכְרוֹנָם לִבְרָכָה: הָבִיאוּ לְפָנַי עֹמֶר בַּפֶּסַח כְּדֵי שֶׁיִּתְבָּרְכוּ לָכֶם תְּבוּאָה שֶׁבַּשָּׂדוֹת; נַסְּכוּ לְפָנַי מַיִם בֶּחָג כְּדֵי שֶׁיִּתְבָּרְכוּ לָכֶם גִּשְׁמֵי שָׁנָה; תִּקְעוּ לְפָנַי שׁוֹפָר שֶׁל אַיִל כְּדֵי לִזְכֹּר עֲקֵדַת יִצְחָק.

וְעַל הַלֶּחֶם הַזֶּה בְּעַצְמוֹ אָמְרוּ כִּי מִפְּנֵי שֶׁהוּא תַּשְׁמִישׁ הַמִּצְוָה וּבוֹ נַעֲשָׂה רְצוֹן הָאֵל, הָיְתָה הַבְּרָכָה דְּבֵקָה בּוֹ בְּיוֹתֵר, וְכָל אֶחָד מִן הַכֹּהֲנִים שֶׁהִגִּיעַ לוֹ מִמֶּנּוּ כְּפוֹל הָיָה שָׂבֵעַ.

וְאֵלֶּה הַדְּבָרִים כְּגוֹן שֻׁלְחָן וּמְנוֹרָה וְלֶחֶם הַפָּנִים וְהַקָּרְבָּנוֹת בְּכֻלָּן נִצְטַוִּינוּ מִצַּד הַמְּקֻבָּלִים, וּכְעִנְיָנִים שֶׁכָּתַבְתִּי, אֵין סָפֵק וּפִקְפּוּק לְכָל מֵבִין עִם תַּלְמִיד, שֶׁאֵין חֲסַר־תְּבוּנוֹת בָּעוֹלָם יַחֲשֹׁב שֶׁבְּסִדּוּר לֶחֶם בַּבַּיִת עַל שֻׁלְחָן שֶׁנַּנִּיחֵהוּ שָׁלֵם וְנִקָּחֵנוּ שָׁלֵם וּמְבֹרָךְ תְּקַבֵּל שׁוּם הֲנָאָה לְמַעֲלָה חָלִילָה, לֹא בְּמַרְאֶה וְלֹא בְּרֵיחַ וְלֹא בְּשׁוּם

---

§97 1. Commentary, Exodus 25:24.
2. TB Rosh haShanah 16a.
3. TB Yoma 39a.

influenced toward the good through his contemplation of them. And God wished, for our good, that it should not lose that form even for a moment.

[THE PRECEPT OF ARRANGING THE SHOWBREAD AND THE FRANKINCENSE]

97 to place bread continually in the Sanctuary, before the Lord: for it is stated, *And you shall set on the table the showbread, before Me, always* (Exodus 25:30).

At the root of the precept lies the point that God (blessed is He) gave us the obligation of a continual precept about bread because by this a man lives. Therefore he requires that a blessing should be found in it always. Then as a result of our being occupied with it [bread] to fulfill with it the precept of the Eternal Lord, the [Divine] will and benison will take effect upon us, and we will be blessed in our diet. For whatever a man uses to do the will of the Eternal Lord, in that he is blessed. In whatever way one sets the direction of his face, his thoughts and his activities in a matter of *mitzvah* (religious duty), the wellspring of blessing flows to him accordingly. And so I found [in the writings] by Ramban of blessed memory.[1]

This is akin to what our Sages of blessed memory taught:[2] Bring the *'omer* (sheaf) offering before Me on Passover, so that the grain in the fields will be blessed for you; pour libations of water before Me on the [*Sukkoth*] festival, so that the rains of the year will come for you in beneficence; sound before Me the *shofar* (horn) of a ram, to bring the binding of Isaac to mind.

About this bread itself the Sages said, too,[3] that because it was used for a *mitzvah*, and with it the wish of God was done, blessing would greatly adhere to it; and every *kohen* who received of it the amount of a bean, was satiated.

Now, about all these matters, such as the table, *menorah* (lamp), showbread, and offerings, we were commanded for the benefit of the "receivers" [the people who receive the precepts and their reward]. As I have written (§88), no understanding person or student who is not lacking in worldly comprehension can have any doubt or uncertainty, that he should think that by the arrangement of bread in the Temple on a table, when we set it down whole and remove it whole and blessed, any benefit can be received above, in the Divine realm (perish the thought)—either through its appearance or fragrance, or in any way

§97: ON ARRANGING THE SHOWBREAD AND FRANKINCENSE

צַד, רַק שֶׁצִּוָּנוּ בְּכָךְ לַחֲפְצוֹ בָּרוּךְ הוּא שֶׁנִּתְבָּרֵךְ מִמֶּנּוּ מֵרֹב מִדַּת טוּבוֹ.

גַּם הַלְּבוֹנָה הַבָּאָה עִם הַלֶּחֶם שֶׁנִּכְתַּב בָּהּ אִשֶּׁה לַיְיָ, וְאָמְרוּ הַמְפָרְשִׁים שֶׁאֵין מִן הַלֶּחֶם לַגָּבוֹהַּ כְּלוּם אֶלָּא הַלְּבוֹנָה שֶׁנִּקְטֶרֶת בְּכָל שַׁבָּת כְּשֶׁמְּסַלְּקִין הַלֶּחֶם, אֵין בְּוַנָּתָם חָלִילָה לִהְיוֹת חִלּוּק כְּלָל בֵּין הַלְּבוֹנָה וְהַלֶּחֶם לְמַעְלָה, וְקִיּוּם מִצְוַת הָאֵל בַּלֶּחֶם וּבַלְּבוֹנָה אֶחָד הוּא, כִּי כְּמוֹ שֶׁצִּוָּה הָאֵל בָּרוּךְ הוּא לְהַסְדִּיר הַלֶּחֶם לְפָנָיו וְנַעֲשָׂה רְצוֹנוֹ וְסִדְּרוּהוּ, כֵּן נַעֲשָׂה רְצוֹנוֹ בַּלְּבוֹנָה שֶׁצִּוָּה לְהַקְטִיר וְהִקְטִירוּהָ, קֶצֶב אֶחָד לַכֹּל.

אֲבָל כָּל אֵלֶּה הָעִנְיָנִים יִכָּתְבוּ עַל צַד הָעוֹסְקִים, כִּי הַלֶּחֶם שֶׁנֶּאֱכַל לַכֹּהֲנִים אֵין לִכְתֹּב עָלָיו שֶׁכֻּלּוֹ לַשֵּׁם כִּי הֵם יֹאכְלוּהוּ, נִמְצָא שֶׁאֵין כֻּלּוֹ לַשֵּׁם כִּי אֲחֵרִים יַחְלְקוּ בוֹ, אֲבָל בְּכָל מַה שֶּׁלֹּא יֵהָנֶה בּוֹ הָאָדָם כְּלָל אֶלָּא שֶׁעוֹשֶׂה מִמֶּנּוּ מִצְוַת בּוֹרְאוֹ וְכָלָה לְגַמְרֵי בַּמִּצְוָה, בָּזֶה נוּכַל לוֹמַר עָלָיו כִּי כֻלּוֹ לַיְיָ, כְּלוֹמַר שֶׁנִּכְנַס כֻּלּוֹ בְּמִצְוָתוֹ, לֹא אָכַל מִמֶּנּוּ אָדָם וְלֹא נֶהֱנָה בּוֹ הֲנָאָה גוּפָנִית כְּלָל. וְעַל שֶׁהָרֵיחַ אֵינֶנּוּ מִן הַהֲנָאוֹת שֶׁל גּוּף רַק מֵהֲנָאַת הַנֶּפֶשׁ, כִּי הַגּוּף לֹא יְקַבֵּל רַק הֲנָאַת הַמִּשּׁוּשׁ, יְכַנּוּ לְעוֹלָם עִנְיַן הָרֵיחַ אֶל הַשֵּׁם בָּרוּךְ הוּא, אַף־עַל־פִּי שֶׁהוּא בָּרוּךְ הוּא וּבָרוּךְ שְׁמוֹ אֵינֶנּוּ לְרֹב מַעֲלָתוֹ וְגֻדְלוֹ בְּגֶדֶר עִנְיָנִים אֵלֶּה כְּלָל לְפִי שֶׁאֵינוֹ גוּף וְלֹא כֹחַ בְּגוּף, יָדוּעַ הוּא אֵצֶל כָּל מֵבִין. וּכְבָר פֵּרְשׁוּ זִכְרוֹנָם לִבְרָכָה: בְּכָל מָקוֹם שֶׁנֶּאֱמַר רֵיחַ נִיחוֹחַ לַיְיָ, שֶׁאָמַרְתִּי וְנַעֲשָׂה רְצוֹנִי, וְכֵן "וַיָּרַח יְיָ אֶת רֵיחַ הַנִּיחֹחַ" בַּדֶּרֶךְ הַזֶּה. זֶהוּ שֶׁנִּרְאֶה לָנוּ בְּעִנְיַן סִדּוּר הַלֶּחֶם בְּבֵית הַשֵּׁם. וְהָרַמְבַּ"ם זִכְרוֹנוֹ לִבְרָכָה

---

4. I.e. Rashi on the verse.
5. Cf. TB B'rachoth 43b: What is it that the soul benefits from it and the body does not?—it can well be said: scent.
6. Expression of Rambam, commentary to Mishnah, Sanhedrin x, the third fundamental principle.
7. Midrash Sifra on the verse which follows.

whatever. He commanded us about it only out of His desire (blessed is He) that we should receive blessing from Him, by His abounding quality of goodness.

Similarly the frankincense that comes with the bread, of which it is written, *an offering by fire to the Lord* (Leviticus 24:7)—and the commentaries [4] noted that Heaven has nothing from the bread but the frankincense, which is burnt every Sabbath when the bread is removed: Their meaning is not (perish the thought) that there is any difference at all between the bread and the frankincense for the supernal realm [of the Divinity]; fulfilling the precept of God, whether with bread or with frankincense, is all one and the same. Just as God (blessed is He) ordained to have the bread arrayed before Him, and His will was done and it was set out, so was His will done with the frankincense, which He ordered burnt, and it was burned—one measure for all.

All these matters, however, are written from the point of view of those who are occupied [with them]. Since the bread is eaten by the *kohanim*, one cannot write about it that it is entirely for the Eternal Lord, as they will eat it; consequently, it is not entirely for the Eternal Lord, since others share in it. But anything from which man does not benefit at all, but he rather fulfills the commandment of his Creator with it and it is entirely consumed (used up) for the commandment— in such a case we can say about it that it is wholly for the Lord; i.e. it entered (was used) completely in its *mitzvah*; no man ate of it or enjoyed any physical benefit from it at all. And if someone smelled [its odor], this is not one of the physical enjoyments but rather a spiritual benefit: [5] for the body receives only the gratification of touch; the matter of odor or fragrance is always attributed metaphorically to the Eternal Lord, blessed is He, even though He (blessed be He and blessed His name) is not, in His most exalted state and His grandeur, within the range of these matters at all, since He has no physical body or bodily faculty, [6] the which is known to every understanding person. Long ago, our Sages of blessed memory explained: [7] Wherever it is stated [in Scripture], *a pleasing scent to the Lord* (Leviticus 1:9), [it means] that "I asserted [My wish] and My will was done." Similarly, *the Lord smelled the pleasing scent* (Genesis 8:21) [is to be understood] in the same way.

This is [the meaning] that seems to us [to lie] in the matter of the array of bread in the House of the Eternal Lord. However, Rambam of blessed memory wrote, in these words, "But as for the table, and the

כָּתַב וְזֶה לְשׁוֹנוֹ: אֲבָל הַשֻּׁלְחָן וִהְיוֹת הַלֶּחֶם עָלָיו תָּמִיד לֹא אֵדַע לוֹ סִבָּה, וְאֵינִי יוֹדֵעַ לְאֵי זֶה דָבָר אֲיַחֵס אוֹתוֹ עַד הַיּוֹם.

מִדִּינֵי הַמִּצְוָה מַה שֶּׁאָמְרוּ זִכְרוֹנָם לִבְרָכָה שֶׁבְּכָל אַחַת מִן הַמַּעֲרָכוֹת הָיוּ נוֹתְנִין כְּלִי שֶׁיֵּשׁ בּוֹ קֹמֶץ לְבוֹנָה, שֶׁנֶּאֱמַר "וְנָתַתָּ עַל הַמַּעֲרֶכֶת", כְּלוֹמַר עַל כָּל אַחַת מֵהֶן, לְבוֹנָה זַכָּה, וּכְלִי זֶה נִקְרָא בָזָךְ. וְאָמְרוּ זִכְרוֹנָם לִבְרָכָה שֶׁשְּׁנֵי הַסְּדָרִין מְעַכְּבִין זֶה אֶת זֶה, וּשְׁנֵי הַבָּזִיכִין מְעַכְּבִין זֶה אֶת זֶה, וּמִיּוֹם שַׁבָּת לְיוֹם שַׁבָּת מוֹצִיאִין אֶת הַלֶּחֶם וּמְסַדְּרִין לֶחֶם אַחֵר מִיָּד. וְזֶה שֶׁמּוֹצִיאִין הוּא שֶׁחוֹלְקִין שְׁתֵּי הַמִּשְׁמָרוֹת הַנִּכְנָסוֹת וְהַיּוֹצְאוֹת עִם כֹּהֵן גָּדוֹל וְאוֹכְלִין אוֹתוֹ.

וְכֵיצַד מְסַדְּרִין אוֹתוֹ, שֶׁאַרְבָּעָה נִכְנָסִין בַּלֶּחֶם וּבַבָּזִיכִין וְאַרְבָּעָה מַקְדִּימִין לִפְנֵיהֶם לִטֹּל הַלֶּחֶם מֵעַל הַשֻּׁלְחָן. וְאָמְרוּ זִכְרוֹנָם לִבְרָכָה שֶׁהָיוּ מְכַוְּנִין בְּהַנָּחָתוֹ לִהְיוֹת טִפְחוֹ שֶׁל זֶה בְּצַד טִפְחוֹ שֶׁל זֶה, לְקַיֵּם מַה שֶּׁנֶּאֱמַר "לְפָנַי תָּמִיד". וְצוּרַת הַלֶּחֶם וְעִנְיַן הַנָּחָתוֹ כֵּיצַד הָיָה כְּדֵי שֶׁיְּהֵא הָאֲוִיר שׁוֹלֵט בּוֹ, וְיֶתֶר פְּרָטֶיהָ, מְבֹאָרִים בְּפֶרֶק י"א מִמְּנָחוֹת.

וְנוֹהֶגֶת בִּזְמַן הַבַּיִת בַּזְּכָרִים הַכֹּהֲנִים, כִּי לָהֶם הָעֲבוֹדָה, לֹא לַנָּשִׁים. שְׁלֹשֶׁת מִצְוֹת סֵדֶר זֶה אֵינָן נוֹהֲגוֹת הַיּוֹם.

🕎 וְאַתָּה תְּצַוֶּה

יֵשׁ בָּהּ אַרְבַּע מִצְווֹת עֲשֵׂה וְשָׁלֹשׁ לֹא־תַעֲשֶׂה

[מִצְוַת עֲרִיכַת נֵרוֹת הַמִּקְדָּשׁ]

צח לְהֵיטִיב נֵרוֹת תָּמִיד לִפְנֵי הַשֵּׁם, שֶׁנֶּאֱמַר: יַעֲרֹךְ אוֹתוֹ אַהֲרֹן וּבָנָיו, כְּלוֹמַר יַעֲרֹךְ הַנֵּר לִפְנֵי הַשֵּׁם, וְזֶהוּ מִצְוַת הֲטָבַת נֵרוֹת הַנִּזְכֶּרֶת בַּגְּמָרָא.

---

8. Rambam, *Guide* III 45.

9. Sifra on Leviticus 24:7. There were twelve loaves, arranged in two rows of six, one above the other.

10. I.e. if something disqualifies one row of loaves or one censer of frankincense, the other is not acceptable either before Heaven; TB M'naḥoth 27a.

11. Literally, from Sabbath day to Sabbath day; *ibid.* 99b.

12. See §91, note 6.

13. TB Yoma 17b.

14. TB M'naḥoth 99b.

15. I.e. as one *kohen* moved an old loaf a handbreadth away from its original position, another *kohen* moved a new loaf a handbreadth in to take its place. Thus the table was never left without bread for even an instant, in keeping with the verse that follows.

16. TB M'naḥoth 96a.

17. As remarked in §76, note 4, our author's original arrangement in each *sidrah* was to give the positive precepts first and then the negative (following, in this respect,

bread being on it always, I do not know a reason for it, and I do not know, to this day, to what theme I can attribute it."[8]

Among the laws of the precept there is what our Sages of blessed memory said,[9] that in each of the rows they would set a vessel containing a handful of frankincense: for it is stated, *And you shall put with the row*—i.e. with each of them—*pure frankincense* (Leviticus 24:7); and this vessel is called *bazach*, a censer. Our Sages said further that the two rows can hinder one another [from being valid, acceptable]; and the two censers [of frankincense likewise] can hinder each other.[10] Every Sabbath[11] the bread is taken out, and other bread is arrayed at once. That which is taken out is what the two "watches" [of *kohanim*],[12] those coming in and those going out, share with the *kohen gadol*; they eat it.[13]

[Then there is the law on] the way in which it is arranged: that four enter with the bread and the censers [of frankincense], and four go before them to take the [old] bread from the table.[14] And the Sages of blessed memory said[14] that they would be intent, when putting it down, to have the handbreadth of one next to the handbreadth of the other,[15] to fulfill what Scripture states, *before Me always* (Exodus 25:30). There are, too, the form of the bread and the way it was set down, how it was done so that the air should have access to it [to prevent it from turning moldy].[16] These and the rest of its details are clarified in chapter 11 of the Talmud tractate *M'nahoth*.

It is in effect when the Temple is extant, for male *kohanim*, for the service [at the Temple] is for them [to carry out], not for women.

The three precepts of this *sidrah* are not in force today.[17]

sidrah tetzavveh
(Exodus 27:20–30:10)

There are four positive and three negative precepts in it.

[THE PRECEPT OF KINDLING THE MENORAH IN THE SANCTUARY]

98 to kindle the perpetual lights before the Eternal Lord, as it is stated, *Aaron and his sons shall tend it* (Exodus 27:21)—i.e. he should tend the lamp before the Eternal Lord; and this is the *mitzvah* of kindling the lights which is mentioned in the Talmud.[1]

§98: THE PRECEPT OF KINDLING THE MENORAH IN THE SANCTUARY

מִשָּׁרְשֵׁי הַמִּצְוָה שֶׁצִּוָּנוּ הַשֵּׁם יִתְבָּרַךְ לִהְיוֹת נֵר דּוֹלֵק בַּבַּיִת הַקָּדוֹשׁ לְהַגְדִּיל הַבַּיִת לְכָבוֹד וּלְתִפְאֶרֶת בְּעֵינֵי הָרוֹאִים, כִּי כֵן דֶּרֶךְ בְּנֵי אִישׁ לְהִתְכַּבֵּד בְּבָתֵּיהֶם בְּנֵרוֹת דּוֹלְקִין. וְכָל עִנְיַן הַהַגְדָּלָה בּוֹ כְּדֵי שֶׁיִּכְנְסוּ הָאָדָם בְּלִבּוֹ כְּשֶׁיִּרְאֵהוּ מוֹרָא וַעֲנָוָה, וּכְבָר אָמַרְנוּ כִּי בַּמַּעֲשֶׂה הַטּוֹב הֻכְשַׁר הַנֶּפֶשׁ. וְכָל זֶה סוֹבֵב עַל הַיְסוֹד הַבָּנוּי לָנוּ כִּי הַכֹּל נִגְזַר מִצַּד הַמְּקַבְּלִים, עִם הֱיוֹתִי מַאֲמִין בֶּאֱמֶת כִּי יֵשׁ לַמְקֻבָּלִים בְּעִנְיָנִים אֵלֶּה חָכְמוֹת נִכְבָּדוֹת וִיסוֹדוֹת נִפְלָאִים. וְאוּלָם גַּם אֲנַחְנוּ נִכְתֹּב הַנִּרְאָה כְּפַשְׁטוּטָן שֶׁל דְּבָרִים, וְהַכֹּל לְשֵׁם שָׁמָיִם.

דִּינֵי הַמִּצְוָה, כְּגוֹן מַה שֶּׁאָמְרוּ הַדְלָקַת הַנֵּרוֹת דּוֹחָה שַׁבָּת כְּקָרְבָּנוֹת, שֶׁקָּבוּעַ לָהֶם זְמַן, שֶׁנֶּאֱמַר בּוֹ תָּמִיד, וְשֶׁנּוֹתֵן לְכָל נֵר וָנֵר חֲצִי לוֹג שֶׁמֶן, שֶׁנֶּאֱמַר "מֵעֶרֶב עַד בֹּקֶר", וְשֶׁעָרְווּ חֲכָמִים שֶׁזֶּה הַשִּׁעוּר יַסְפִּיק בְּלֵילֵי טֵבֵת, וְכֵן נוֹתְנִין בְּכָל הַלֵּילוֹת, וְאִם יּוֹתֵר אֵין בְּכָךְ כְּלוּם.

וּמֵעִנְיַן מִצְוַת הַהֲטָבָה הוּא הַדִּשּׁוּן, וְדִשּׁוּן הַמְּנוֹרָה וַהֲטָבָתָהּ מִצְוַת עֲשֵׂה בַּבֹּקֶר וּבֵין הָעַרְבַּיִם; וְהַדִּשּׁוּן הוּא שֶׁכָּל נֵר שֶׁכָּבָה מֵסִיר הַפְּתִילָה וְכָל שֶׁמֶן שֶׁבַּנֵּר וּמְקַנְּחוֹ וְנוֹתֵן בּוֹ פְּתִילָה אַחֶרֶת וְשֶׁמֶן אַחֵר, וְנֵר שֶׁלֹּא כָבָה מְתַקְּנוֹ; וְנֵר אֶמְצָעִי אִם כָּבָה מַדְלִיקוּ מֵאֵשׁ שֶׁעַל מִזְבֵּחַ הַחִיצוֹן, וְהָאֲחֵרִים מַדְלִיקָן זֶה מִזֶּה, שֶׁמּוֹשֵׁךְ הַפְּתִילָה וּמַטֶּה אוֹתָהּ עַד שֶׁהָאוֹר נִתְפֶּשֶׂת בָּהּ, לְפִי שֶׁאֵין כְּבוֹד הַמִּצְוָה לְהַדְלִיקָן מִנֵּר אַחֵר; וְיֶתֶר פְּרָטֶיהָ, מְבֹאָרִים בְּפֶרֶק שְׁמִינִי מִמְּנָחוֹת וּמְקוֹמוֹת מִתָּמִיד.

זֶהוּ דַּעַת הָרַמְבַּ"ם זִכְרוֹנוֹ לִבְרָכָה בְּמִצְוָה זוֹ שֶׁהֲהֲטָבָה הִיא הַדְלָקָתָן כְּמוֹ שֶׁפֵּרַשְׁנוּ, אֲבָל דַּעַת מְפָרְשִׁים רַבִּים שֶׁהַהֲטָבָה הִיא הַדִּשּׁוּן וְהַקִּנּוּחַ וְתִקּוּן

ShM). Hence our §96 was originally §97, the last precept in *sidrah t'rumah*, and this sentence came at its end. Since the present translation follows the order of the later editions, which rearranged the precepts in each *sidrah* in accordance with their order in the Written Torah, this last sentence has been moved to here, so that it should remain (as intended) the conclusion to the *mitzvoth* of *sidrah t'rumah*.

§98 1. E.g. TB Yoma 14a. The Hebrew for "kindle" is *l'hétiv*; as noted toward the end of this section, this is how Rambam understands it, while for Ramban it means trimming the lamps of the *menorah*.

2. Cf. *T'shuvoth haRashba* (Responsa of R. Sh'lomoh ibn 'Adreth, whose disciple our author evidently was), I 94: "And know that for all these [precepts] the masters of the mystic meanings of the Torah have most distinguished reasons."

3. Hence the *menorah* was to be lit on the Sabbath too, as this was the Almighty's will; Sifra, *'emor, parashah* 13, 11.

4. TB M'nahoth 89a (here our author followed Rashi to Exodus 27:21).

5. So MT *hilchoth t'midin* iii 10.

6. TB M'nahoth 88b.

7. I.e. he fixes the wick; Rambam *ibid.* 12.

8. Rambam *ibid.* 13; the first Hebrew edition reads, "If the western light," etc. But as Rambam explains it, "the western light" means the middle one of the *menorah*'s seven lamps, as it was placed with the wick toward the west; the other six,

SIDRAH TETZAVVEH

At the root of the precept lies the fact that the Eternal Lord (be He blessed) commanded us that a lamp should burn in the Sanctuary, to magnify the glory and splendor of the Temple in the eyes of those who behold it. For such is the way of people, to attain distinction in their houses with burning lights. And the entire reason for the magnification [of splendor] in it is that a man's heart should become infused, when he sees it, with reverent awe and humility. We have said previously (§16) that through the good deed the spirit is made worthy.

Now, this entire theme revolves about the basic point established for us, that all is postulated from the point of view of those who receive [and respond to it]; although I do believe, in truth, that the masters of the mystic tradition possess in these matters distinguished wisdoms and wondrous hidden truths.[2] Nevertheless, we as well shall write what appears to us the plain meanings of the matters, all [our intention being] for the sake of Heaven.

The laws of the precept are, for example, what the Sages said: the kindling of the lights thrusts aside [the forbiddance of] the Sabbath, like animal offerings for which a specific time was set, since the word *tamid*, "continually," is stated about it (Exodus 27:20);[3] that half a *log* of oil was poured into each light: for it is stated, *from evening to morning* (*ibid.* 21), and the Sages gauged that this measure would be enough for the [long winter] nights of Téveth; so this amount would be given every night, and if some remained, it did not matter.[4]

Part of the religious duty of kindling [the lights] is the removal of ash. Cleaning out the ash from the *menorah* and lighting it is a positive precept in the morning and in the afternoon.[5] "Removing the ash" means that from every light which went out one removes the wick and any oil that [remains] in the light; then he wipes it clean and puts in other oil.[6] If a light did not go out, he fixes it.[7] If the middle light went out, he kindles it from the fire on the outer altar.[8] As for the rest, he lights one from another: he draws the wick over and bends it until the flame catches in it[9]—for it is not a way of reverence for the *mitzvah* to kindle them from any other light. The rest of its details are explained in the eighth chapter of the Talmud tractate *M'nahoth* and in certain places in *Tamid*.

This is the view of Rambam of blessed memory about this precept[10]—that *hatavath ha-néroth* means kindling the lights, as we have explained. The view of many other authorities, however,[11] is that *hatavah* means removing the ash, wiping the lamp clean, and fixing

§98–99: KINDLING THE MENORAH / ON THE KOHANIM'S GARMENTS

הַפְּתִילוֹת, וְזוֹ הִיא מִצְוָה בִּפְנֵי עַצְמָהּ, וְכֵן נִרְאָה בַּפֶּרֶק הַתְּכֵלֶת בְּמַסֶּכֶת מְנָחוֹת. וְנוֹהֶגֶת בִּזְמַן הַבַּיִת בַּכֹּהֲנִים. וְכֹהֵן הָעוֹבֵר עָלֶיהָ וְלֹא עָרַךְ הַנֵּרוֹת כַּמִּצְוָה, בִּטֵּל עֲשֵׂה.

[מִצְוַת לְבִישַׁת בִּגְדֵי הַכֹּהֲנִים]

צט שֶׁנִּצְטַוּוּ הַכֹּהֲנִים לִלְבּשׁ בְּגָדִים מְיֻחָדִים לִגְדֻלָּה וְכָבוֹד וְאָז יַעַבְדוּ בַּמִּקְדָּשׁ, שֶׁנֶּאֱמַר: וְעָשׂוּ בִגְדֵי קֹדֶשׁ לְאַהֲרֹן . . . וּלְבָנָיו.

מִשָּׁרְשֵׁי הַמִּצְוָה הַיְסוֹד הַקָּבוּעַ לָנוּ כִּי הָאָדָם נִפְעָל לְפִי פְעֻלּוֹתָיו וְאַחֲרֵיהֶם מַחְשְׁבוֹתָיו וְכַוָּנוֹתָיו, וְהַשָּׁלִיחַ הַמְכַפֵּר צָרִיךְ לְהִתְפִּיס כָּל מַחְשַׁבְתּוֹ וְכַוָּנָתוֹ אֶל הָעֲבוֹדָה, עַל־כֵּן רָאוּי לְהִתְלַבֵּשׁ בִּבְגָדִים מְיֻחָדִים אֵלֶיהָ שֶׁכְּשֶׁיִּסְתַּכֵּל בְּכָל מָקוֹם שֶׁבְּגוּפוֹ מִיָּד יִהְיֶה נִזְכָּר וּמִתְעוֹרֵר בְּלִבּוֹ לִפְנֵי מִי הוּא עוֹבֵד, וְזֶה כְּעֵין תְּפִלִּין שֶׁנִּצְטַוּוּ הַכֹּל לְהָנִיחַ בִּקְצָת הַגּוּף שֶׁיִּהְיֶה לְזִכָּרוֹן מַחֲשֶׁבֶת הַכָּשֵׁר. וְאַף־עַל־פִּי שֶׁגַּם הַכֹּהֵן הָיָה מֵנִיחַ תְּפִלִּין, לְגֹדֶל עִנְיָנֵנוּ הָיָה צָרִיךְ גַּם זֶה.

וּמִן הַטַּעַם הַזֶּה נֹאמַר שֶׁנִּתְחַיְּבוּ לִהְיוֹת אֹרֶךְ הַכֻּתֹּנֶת עַל כָּל גּוּפוֹ עַד לְמַעְלָה מִן הֶעָקֵב מְעַט, וְאֹרֶךְ בֵּית יַד שֶׁלָּהּ עַד פַּס יָדוֹ, וְהַמִּצְנֶפֶת אָרְכָּהּ שֵׁשׁ עֶשְׂרֵה אַמָּה וּמַקִּיפָהּ בְּרֹאשׁוֹ כְּדֵי שֶׁיֵּרָאֶה אוֹתָהּ בְּכָל עֵת שֶׁיִּשָּׂא עֵינָיו, וְהָאַבְנֵט שֶׁחֲגוֹר בְּמָתְנָיו אָרְכּוּ שְׁתַּיִם וּשְׁלֹשִׁים אַמָּה וּמַקִּיפוֹ וּמַחֲזִירוֹ עַל גּוּפוֹ כֶּרֶךְ עַל כֶּרֶךְ, וְנִמְצָא שֶׁמַּרְגִּישׁ בּוֹ בְּכָל־עֵת בִּזְרוֹעוֹתָיו, שֶׁמְּתוּךְ גָּבְהוֹ בְּרֹב הַהֶקֵּפִין הַזְּרוֹעוֹת נוֹגְעוֹת בּוֹ עַל כָּל פָּנִים.

וְכָל זֶה רְאָיָה לְמַה שֶּׁאָמַרְתִּי לְמוֹדֶה עַל הָאֱמֶת, מִלְּבַד שֶׁיֵּשׁ בָּעִנְיָן כָּבוֹד לַבַּיִת וְלָעֲבוֹדָה בִּהְיוֹת הָעוֹבֵד מְלֻבָּשׁ בִּלְבוּשׁ מְיֻחָד לָעֲבוֹדָה. וּכְבָר כָּתַבְנוּ כִּי בְהַגְדָּלַת

---

three on either side of it, were placed with the wicks toward this middle one (Rambam, Commentary to Mishnah, ed. Kafiḥ, Tamid iii 9).

9. MT *hilchoth t'midin* iii 13–14.

10. *Ibid.* 12.

11. Rashi to Exodus 27:20 and TB Ḥagigah 26b s.v. *menorah*; Rabad to MT *hilchoth 'avodath yom ha-kippurim* ii 2; Ramban to Exodus 27:20; Rashba, per *Kessef Mishneh* to MT *hilchoth t'midin* iii 12 (cf. Rashba, *Responsa* I 309).

12. TB M'naḥoth 50a; see *Leḥem Mishneh* to MT *ibid*.

§99 1. I.e. the *kohen*, who acts as the agent of the person who brings the offering, to achieve atonement for him.

2. See TB Z'vaḥim 19a that while he served in the Sanctuary he might not wear the *t'fillin* of the hand, since it would come between his body and his sacred garments; and he had no duty to put on the *t'fillin* of the head (while busy with one *mitzvah*, a person is free of the obligation to observe any others). At other times, however, he had the obligation like anyone else.

3. TB P'saḥim 65b.

4. TB Yoma 72b.

⟨380⟩

the wicks, while this [kindling] is a separate precept in its own right; and so it would seem in chapter 4 of the tractate *M'nahoth*.[12]

It is in force when the Temple is extant, for *kohanim*. If a *kohen* violated it and did not prepare the lights in accordance with the commandment, he would disobey a positive precept.

[THE PRECEPT THAT THE KOHANIM SHOULD WEAR THEIR SPECIAL GARMENTS]

99 that the *kohanim* were commanded to put on special clothing, for grandeur and honor, and then they are to serve in the Sanctuary: for it is stated, *and they shall make holy clothing for Aaron . . . and his sons* (Exodus 28:4).

At the root of the precept lies the basic tenet, firmly established for us, that a man is influenced and acted upon according to his activities, and his thoughts and intentions follow them. So the agent who brings atonement[1] must attach (concentrate) his entire thought and intention on the [Divine] service. It is therefore fitting for him to put on these garments that are especially intended for it: When he will gaze at any place on his body, he will be reminded at once, bestirred in his heart, [of the One] in whose presence he serves. It is thus akin to *t'fillin* (phylacteries), which all were commanded to place on part of the body, that it might serve as a reminder of the thought [to bear in mind] of becoming worthy. And even though the *kohen* would also put on *t'fillin*,[2] for the greatness of his calling he needed this too.

For this reason, we may say, the length of the tunic was required to cover his entire body, until slightly above the heel,[3] and the length of its sleeve to reach to his wrist.[4] The *mitznefeth* [turban, of the *kohen gadol*] had a length of sixteen cubits,[5] and it enveloped his head so that he would see it whenever he raised his eyes (looked up). The sash, which he girded about his hips, had a length of thirty-two cubits;[6] he put it around him and wound it about his body, wrapping it over itself. As a result, he would feel it all the time with his arms: On account of its thickness, because of the many windings, the arms would touch it under all circumstances.

All this is evidence in support of what I have said, for one who would admit to the truth—apart from the honor to the Temple and the service which lies in the matter, when the [Divine] servant is dressed in the garb made especially for the service. And we have written earlier (§98) that as the glory and awe of the Temple are magnified,

§99: THAT THE KOHANIM SHOULD WEAR THEIR SPECIAL GARMENTS

הַבַּיִת וּבְמוֹרָאוֹ יִתְרַכְּכוּ שָׁם לִבּוֹת הַחוֹטְאִים וְיָשׁוּבוּ אֶל יְיָ.

דִּינֵי הַמִּצְוָה, כְּגוֹן בֵּאוּר הַמַּלְבּוּשִׁים שֶׁהֵן שְׁלֹשֶׁת מִינִין: בְּבִגְדֵי כֹהֵן הֶדְיוֹט מִין אֶחָד, וּבְבִגְדֵי כֹהֵן גָּדוֹל שְׁנֵי מִינִין, בְּבִגְדֵי זָהָב וּבְבִגְדֵי לָבָן: וְשֶׁל כֹּהֵן הֶדְיוֹט הֵם אַרְבָּעָה כֵלִים וּשְׁמָם כֵּן: כֻּתֹּנֶת וּמִכְנָסַיִם וּמִגְבַּעַת וְאַבְנֵט. הַכֻּתֹּנֶת הִיא כְּעֵין חָלוּק רָחָב שֶׁל יִשְׁמְעֵאלִים, וְהַמִּכְנָסַיִם צוּרָתָן יְדוּעָה בְּכָל מָקוֹם וְהָיוּ שֶׁלָּהֶם גְּדוֹלִים מִמָּתְנַיִם וְעַד הַיְרֵכַיִם, כְּלוֹמַר עַד הַיְרֵכַיִם שֶׁהוּא הַנִּקְרָא גִּינוּי.

(אָמְנָם) הַמִּגְבַּעַת הוּא כְלִי שֶׁמַּנִּיחִין עַל הָרֹאשׁ עָשׂוּי כְּכוֹבַע. הָאַבְנֵט הוּא כְּמִין אֵזוֹר שֶׁחוֹגְרִין בּוֹ אֶלָּא שֶׁהֵם הָיוּ מַקִּיפִין בּוֹ הַרְבֵּה הֶקֵּפִין מַה שֶּׁאֵין אָנוּ עוֹשִׂין כֵּן בְּאֵזוֹר.

וְאַרְבַּעַת כֵּלִים אֵלֶּה שֶׁל פִּשְׁתָּן הָיוּ, לְבָנִים וְחוּטָן כָּפוּל שִׁשָּׁה, וְהָאַבְנֵט לְבַדּוֹ רָקוּם בְּצֶמֶר, וּבְאֵלּוּ הָיָה עוֹבֵד לְעוֹלָם כֹּהֵן הֶדְיוֹט, וּמֻתָּר לְלָבְשָׁן בַּיּוֹם בֵּין בִּשְׁעַת עֲבוֹדָה אוֹ שֶׁלֹּא בִּשְׁעָתָהּ, דְּמֻתָּר לֵהָנוֹת בָּהֶן, חוּץ מִן הָאַבְנֵט לְפִי שֶׁהוּא שַׁעַטְנֵז וּלְפִיכָךְ אָסוּר שֶׁלֹּא בִּשְׁעַת עֲבוֹדָה.

וְשֶׁל כֹּהֵן גָּדוֹל הֵם שְׁמוֹנָה וּשְׁמָם כֵּן: כֻּתֹּנֶת וּמִכְנָסַיִם וְאַבְנֵט, כְּשֵׁם הַשְּׁלֹשָׁה שֶׁל כֹּהֵן הֶדְיוֹט, וּמִצְנֶפֶת לְכֹהֵן גָּדוֹל בִּמְקוֹם מִגְבַּעַת שֶׁל כֹּהֵן הֶדְיוֹט, שֶׁזֶּה וְזֶה עַל הָרֹאשׁ נָתוּן אֶלָּא שֶׁהַמִּצְנֶפֶת הוּא עָשׂוּי כְּמוֹ בֶגֶד אָרוּךְ שֶׁצּוֹנְפִין בּוֹ הַנָּשִׁים רֹאשָׁן, וְכֹהֵן גָּדוֹל צוֹנֵף בָּהּ, וְהַמִּגְבַּעַת עָשׂוּי כְּמִין כּוֹבַע; הֲרֵי אַרְבָּעָה שֶׁל כֹּהֵן גָּדוֹל, שֶׁהָיוּ אַרְבַּעְתָּן שֶׁל פִּשְׁתָּן לְבַדּוֹ לְבָנִים וְחוּטָן כָּפוּל שִׁשָּׁה; וּמַעֲשֵׂה רוֹקֵם הָיוּ עֲשׂוּיִין אֲבָל לֹא הָיָה דוֹמֶה רְקִימָתָן לִרְקִימַת הָאַבְנֵט שֶׁל כֹּהֵן הֶדְיוֹט.

וְעוֹד הָיוּ לוֹ אַרְבָּעָה אֲחֵרִים שֶׁל זָהָב, וּשְׁמָם חֹשֶׁן אֵפוֹד מְעִיל צִיץ. וּבְכָל הַשְּׁמֹנָה הָיָה עוֹבֵד עֲבוֹדַת חוּץ, אֲבָל בִּפְנִים שֶׁהוּא לִפְנִים מִן הַפָּרֹכֶת לֹא הָיָה

---

5. So MT *hilchoth k'lé ha-mikdash* viii 19; and *Kesseʃ Mishneh* there notes that Ramban also states this, in the name of the Talmudic Sages.

6. TJ Yoma vii, toward the end (MT *ibid.*)

7. TB Yoma 71b.

8. *Ibid.* 12b.

9. *Ibid.* 69a.

10. This apparently follows a view of Rambam that in the sash of the *kohen gadol* an embroidered figure appeared on one surface, while the sash of an ordinary *kohen* was of plain, unfigured embroidery (see *Mishneh l'Melech* to MT *hilchoth k'lé ha-mikdash* viii 2; and cf. MT *ibid.* 15—which cites verbatim R. Nehemiah's statement in *Baraitha diM'lecheth haMishkan*, iv).

11. I.e. on the Day of Atonement.

the hearts of sinners will be softened there and they will return to the Lord.

The laws of the precept are, for example, the explanation about the garments, that they are of three kinds: the clothes of the ordinary *kohen* are one kind; and the clothes of the *kohen gadol* are of two kinds—garments [with threads] of gold, and garments of white. Those of the ordinary *kohen* are four articles, named tunic, breeches, *migba'ath* (hat), and sash. The tunic is like the broad robe of the Ishmaelites (Arabs). As for the breeches, their shape is known everywhere; theirs [of *kohanim*] were large, [reaching] *from the hips to the thighs* (Exodus 28:42), i.e. to [the end of] the thigh, which is called *genojo* [in Spanish, = the kneecap].

On the other hand, the *migba'ath* (hat) is an article of clothing placed on the head, made like a *kova* (cap). The sash is like a kind of belt which is girded on, except that they would wrap it many times about, which we do not do with a belt.

These four articles of clothing, [made] of linen, were white, their thread being woven of six strands;[7] and the sash alone was embroidered with wool.[8] In these an ordinary *kohen* would always serve. It was permitted to wear them by day, both during and outside the hours of the service—for it was permissible to derive personal benefit from them[9]—except the sash, because it was *sha'atnéz* (made of linen and wool) and hence forbidden outside the time of [Divine] service.[9]

Those of the *kohen gadol* were eight, named so: tunic, breeches, sash—named like the three of the ordinary *kohen*. Then there was a *mitznefeth* (turban) for the *kohen gadol* in place of the *migba'ath* (hat) of the ordinary *kohen*: both were placed on the head, but the *mitznefeth* was made like a long garment (cloth) which women wrap or coil about their heads, and the *kohen gadol* would envelop [his head] with it; but the *migba'ath* was made like a kind of cap. Here, then, are four [garments] of the *kohen gadol*. All four were of linen only, white, their thread being woven of six strands. They were embroidered work, but their embroidery was unlike that of the sash of the ordinary *kohen*.[10]

He had, in addition, four other [articles of clothing], of cloth with gold thread. Their names are: breastplate, éphod, robe, plate. In all eight articles he would attend to the service outside [the holy of holies], but within, meaning inside the curtain [that separated the holy chamber from the holy of holies] he would never serve in any but the garments of linen;[11] and after he served in them on one Day of Atone-

§99–100: ON THE KOHANIM'S GARMENTS / ABOUT THE BREASTPLATE

עוֹבֵד לְעוֹלָם כִּי אִם בְּבִגְדֵי הַבַּד. וְאַחַר שֶׁעָבַד בָּהֶן בְּיוֹם הַכִּפּוּרִים אֶחָד אֵינוֹ חוֹזֵר וְעוֹבֵד בָּהֶן לְעוֹלָם, שֶׁנֶּאֱמַר וְהִנִּיחָם שָׁם.

וְכָל זְמַן שֶׁיַּעֲבֹד הַכֹּהֵן בֵּין הֶדְיוֹט בֵּין גָּדוֹל בְּפָחוֹת מִבְּגָדָיו הַמְיֻחָדִין לָעֲבוֹדָה הַהִיא אוֹ בְּיוֹתֵר מֵהֶן עֲבוֹדָתוֹ פְּסוּלָה, וְגַם יִתְחַיֵּב מִיתָה בִּידֵי שָׁמַיִם, כְּמוֹ שֶׁלָּמְדוּ הַדָּבָר וְכָרְנָם לִבְרָכָה מִ"וְחָגַרְתָּ אוֹתָם אַבְנֵט ... וְהָיְתָה לָהֶם כְּהֻנָּה" בִּזְמַן שֶׁבִּגְדֵיהֶם עֲלֵיהֶם כְּהֻנָּתָם עֲלֵיהֶם, אֵין בִּגְדֵיהֶם עֲלֵיהֶם אֵין כְּהֻנָּתָם עֲלֵיהֶם, וְיֵחָשְׁבוּ כְּזָר הָעוֹבֵד שֶׁהוּא בְּמִיתָה.

וְיֶתֶר פְּרָטֶיהָ מְבֹאָרִים בְּפֶרֶק שְׁנֵי מִזְבְּחִים וּבִמְקוֹמוֹת מְפֻזָּרִים וְסָבָּה. וְנוֹהֶגֶת מִצְוָה זוֹ בִּזְמַן הַבַּיִת בְּזִכְרֵי כְהֻנָּה. וְעוֹבֵר עָלֶיהָ וְעָבַד מְחֻסָּר בְּגָדִים אוֹ יוֹתֵר חַיָּב מִיתָה בִּידֵי שָׁמַיִם כְּמוֹ שֶׁכָּתַבְנוּ.

[שֶׁלֹּא יִזַּח הַחֹשֶׁן מֵעַל הָאֵפוֹד]

ק שֶׁלֹּא נָסִיר הַחֹשֶׁן מֵעַל הָאֵפוֹד. וְעִנְיַן חֹשֶׁן וְאֵפוֹד כְּבָר זְכַרְנוּם לְמַעְלָה שֶׁהֵם שְׁנַיִם מִשְּׁמוֹנָה בִּגְדֵי כֹהֵן גָּדוֹל, וְהַחֹשֶׁן הָיָה נָתוּן כְּנֶגֶד לִבּוֹ שֶׁל כֹּהֵן לְפָנָיו, וְהָאֵפוֹד מֵאֲחוֹרָיו מְכֻוָּן כְּנֶגֶד הַחֹשֶׁן שֶׁלְּפָנָיו, וְהָיָה בָּאֵפוֹד מִמַּעֲשֵׂה הָאֵפוֹד בְּעַצְמוֹ כְּמִין שְׁתֵּי יָדוֹת יוֹצְאוֹת מִמֶּנּוּ, שֶׁחוֹגֵר עַצְמוֹ הַכֹּהֵן בָּהֶן, וְהוּא נִקְרָא חֵשֶׁב הָאֵפוֹד. וְאוֹתוֹ חֵשֶׁב הָאֵפוֹד, אַחַר שֶׁחָגַר עַצְמוֹ בּוֹ וְנָתַן הַחֹשֶׁן עַל לִבּוֹ, הָיָה עוֹמֵד תַּחַת הַחֹשֶׁן.

וְצִוָּה הַכָּתוּב לִקְשׁוֹר טַבָּעוֹת שֶׁהָיוּ קְבוּעִים בַּחֹשֶׁן עִם טַבָּעוֹת שֶׁהָיוּ קְבוּעִין בָּאֵפוֹד בִּפְתִיל תְּכֵלֶת כְּדֵי שֶׁיִּהְיֶה נָתוּן הַחֹשֶׁן עַל הַחֵשֶׁב דֶּרֶךְ קְבִיעוּת וְהָדָר, שֶׁאִם לֹא יִקְשֹׁר אוֹתָם בְּאוֹתָם טַבָּעוֹת יִהְיֶה הַחֹשֶׁן נָד וְנִבְדָּל מֵחֵשֶׁב הָאֵפוֹד וְנוֹקֵשׁ עַל

---

12. Implying that they should remain hidden thereafter; TB P'sahim 26a, Yoma 24a.

13. TB Sanhedrin 83b, Z'vahim 17b, 18a.

14. In TB Z'vahim 17b.

§100   1. Literally, the table of his heart.

ment, he would not serve in them ever again—for it is stated, *and he shall leave them there* (Leviticus 16:23).[12]

Now, as long as any *kohen*, an ordinary one or the *kohen gadol*, serves in less than [the proper number] of his garments that were expressly for that service, or in more than them, his service is disqualified;[13] and moreover, he incurs death at the hands of Heaven—as our Sages of blessed memory derived the ruling[14] from the verse, *And you shall gird them with sashes . . . and* k'hunah [*the position of* kohen] *shall be theirs* (Exodus 29:9): At the time their garments are upon them, their status of *kohen* lies upon them; if their garments are not upon them, their status of *kohen* is not bestowed upon them—and they are regarded as a non-*kohen* who serves [at the Sanctuary], who deserves death [at Heaven's hands].

The rest of its details are explained in chapter 2 of the Talmud tractate *Z'vaḥim*, and in various places in *Yoma* and *Sukkah*. This precept is in effect when the Temple is extant, for male *kohanim*. If someone violated it and served [at the Sanctuary] with a lack or an excess of [his] garments, he incurs death at the hands of Heaven, as we have written.

100 [THE BREASTPLATE SHOULD NOT COME LOOSE FROM THE ÉPHOD WORN BY THE KOHEN GADOL]

that we should not move the breastplate away from the éphod. Now, as regards the breastplate and éphod, we noted about them previously, above (§99), that they are two of the eight articles of clothing of the *kohen gadol*. The breastplate was placed against the heart of the *kohen*, in front; and the éphod was behind him, corresponding [in its position] to the breastplate before him. With the éphod, made with its own material and workmanship, there was something akin to two straps coming out from it, with which the *kohen* [*gadol*] girded himself; this was called the band of the éphod. After he girded himself with it and placed the breastplate over his heart, this band of the éphod would remain in position under the breastplate.

Now, Scripture ordained to tie rings which were set in the breastplate to rings that were set in the éphod, with a blue thread, so that the breastplate should remain placed on the band in permanence and majesty. For if he would not tie them by those rings, the breastplate would drift and separate from the band of the éphod, and keep striking against the chest[1] of the *kohen*. But about this, Scripture states, *and the*

לוּחַ לִבּוֹ שֶׁל כֹּהֵן, וְעַל זֶה נֶאֱמַר: וְלֹא יִזַּח הַחֹשֶׁן מֵעַל הָאֵפוֹד, כְּלוֹמַר מֵעַל חֵשֶׁב הָאֵפוֹד, וְתַרְגּוּמוֹ לֹא יִתְפָּרֵק. וְהַמְפָרֵק חִבּוּרָן בִּשְׁעַת עֲבוֹדָה לוֹקֶה מִלָּאו זֶה.

מִשָּׁרְשֵׁי הַמִּצְוָה, שֶׁרָצָה הַשֵּׁם לְטוֹבָתֵנוּ לְזַכּוֹתֵנוּ בְּהַגְדָּלַת אוֹתוֹ הַבַּיִת הַגָּדוֹל וְהַקָּדוֹשׁ וְלִהְיוֹת כָּל אֲשֶׁר בּוֹ מְכֻוָּן וְקָבוּעַ עַל מְכוֹנוֹ, בֵּין עִנְיָן כֵּלָיו שֶׁיִּהְיוּ בְּתַכְלִית הַשְּׁלֵמוּת בֵּין עִנְיַן כְּלֵי הַמְשָׁרְתִים כְּגוֹן מַלְבּוּשִׁים אֵלֶּה שֶׁהֵם מְלֻבָּשִׁים בָּהֶן בִּשְׁעַת הָעֲבוֹדָה, שֶׁהַכֹּל יִהְיֶה נָכוֹן וְשָׁלֵם בְּתַכְלִית הַשְּׁלֵמוּת, לֹא יֶחְסַר שׁוּם נוֹי בְּכָל הַדְּבָרִים. וּבֶאֱמֶת כִּי מִנּוּי הָעִנְיָן הוּא שֶׁלֹּא יִהְיֶה הַחֹשֶׁן נָע וְנָד עַל לוּחַ לִבּוֹ אֶלָּא יַעֲמֹד שָׁם קָבוּעַ כְּמִין חֹמֶר. וְעַד שֶׁשְּׁמָעְנוּ טוֹב מִזֶּה נַחֲזִיק בָּזֶה.

דִּינֵי הַמִּצְוָה, כְּגוֹן מַעֲשֵׂה הַחֹשֶׁן וְהָאֵפוֹד וְסֵדֶר לְבִישָׁתָן, וְיֶתֶר פְּרָטֶיהָ, מְבֹאָרִים בְּמִדּוֹת. וְנוֹהֶגֶת מִצְוָה זוֹ, שֶׁלֹּא נָסִיר הַחֹשֶׁן מֵעַל הָאֵפוֹד, בִּזְמַן הַבַּיִת, בִּזְכָרִים וּנְקֵבוֹת, כְּלוֹמַר שֶׁאֶחָד אִישׁ אוֹ אִשָּׁה שֶׁפֵּרַק חִבּוּרָם לוֹקֶה.

[שֶׁלֹּא לִקְרֹעַ הַמְּעִיל שֶׁל כֹּהֲנִים]

קא שֶׁלֹּא לְהַכְרִית פִּי הַמְּעִיל שֶׁל כֹּהֵן גָּדוֹל, שֶׁנֶּאֱמַר: לֹא יִקָּרֵעַ.

מִשָּׁרְשֵׁי הַמִּצְוָה, לְפִי שֶׁהַקְּרִיעָה דָּבָר שֶׁל גְּנַאי אֶצְלֵנוּ וְעִנְיַן הַשְׁחָתָה. וְאַף כִּי בְּפִי הַבֶּגֶד, נִתְרַחֲקָנוּ מִן הַדָּבָר וְהֻזְהַרְנוּ עָלָיו בְּלָאו כְּדֵי שֶׁיִּלְבָּשֵׁהוּ הַלּוֹבְשׁוֹ בְּאֵימָה בְּיִרְאָה וּבְנַחַת דֶּרֶךְ כָּבוֹד, שֶׁיִּירָא מִלְּקָרְעוֹ וּמִלְּהַשְׁחִית בּוֹ דָּבָר.

וְנוֹהֶגֶת בִּזְמַן הַבַּיִת בִּזְכָרִים וּבִנְקֵבוֹת, כְּלוֹמַר שֶׁכָּל מִי שֶׁקְּרָעוֹ בֵּין אִישׁ בֵּין אִשָּׁה, אוֹ אֲפִלּוּ הִכְרִיתוֹ בְּמִסְפָּרַיִם בְּמֵזִיד, לוֹקֶה.

---

2. On this basic concept cf. *Guide* III 45.

breastplate shall not come loose from the éphod (Exodus 28:28)—i.e. from over the band of the éphod. Onkelos translates it, "it shall not go apart." If someone takes their fastening apart at the time of service [in the Sanctuary] he is given whiplashes on the strength of this negative precept.

At the root of the precept lies the principle that for our good, the Lord desired to make us meritorious by magnifying the grandeur of that great, holy Temple; hence everything in it should be set right and fixed in its proper place—both as regards its objects and utensils, that they should be utterly complete and perfect, and as regards the articles of the servitors who minister, such as these garments in which they are clothed during the service—that all should be right and perfect to the utmost degree of perfection. No esthetic excellence should be lacking in any of the objects.[2] And truly, it is for the esthetic aspect of the matter that the breastplate should not drift and wander about on his chest[1] but should stay there, admirably set. And until we hear any better [reason or explanation] than this, let us hold fast to this.

The laws of the precept—for example, the workmanship of the breastplate and the éphod, and the order of putting them on—and the rest of its details, are clarified in the Mishnah tractate *Middoth*.

This precept, that we should not move the breastplate away from the éphod, is in force when the Temple is in existence, for both man and woman. In other words, whether a man or a woman loosened their fastening, there is a punishment of whiplashes.

101 [NOT TO TEAR THE ME'IL OF THE KOHANIM]

not to slit the opening (neck) of the robe (*me'il*) of the *kohen gadol*: for it is stated, *it is not to be torn* (Exodus 28:32).

At the root of the precept lies the reason that tearing is a matter of disgrace for us, and a matter of destruction, this even if the tear is only at the opening (neck). Hence we were bidden to keep well away from the matter, and were adjured about it by a negative precept, so that the one who is to wear it [the *kohen gadol*] will put it on in awe and fear, gently, reverently, fearing to tear it or damage anything in it.

It applies when the Temple is extant, for both man and woman. In other words, whoever tears it, man or woman, or even if one cuts it with scissors—if it is done deliberately, whiplashes are given.

§102: ON EATING THE FLESH OF THE ḤAṬṬATH & 'ASHAM OFFERINGS

[מִצְוַת אֲכִילַת בְּשַׂר חַטָּאת וְאָשָׁם]

קב שֶׁנִּצְטַוּוּ הַכֹּהֲנִים לֶאֱכֹל מִן בְּשַׂר קְצָת מִן הַקָּרְבָּנוֹת כְּגוֹן הַחַטָּאת וְהָאָשָׁם, שֶׁנֶּאֱמַר עֲלֵיהֶם: וְאָכְלוּ אוֹתָם אֲשֶׁר כֻּפַּר בָּהֶם, וְאָמְרוּ זִכְרוֹנָם לִבְרָכָה: כֹּהֲנִים אוֹכְלִים וּבְעָלִים מִתְכַּפְּרִים. וְעִנְיַן מַעֲשֵׂה הַחַטָּאת וְהָאָשָׁם אֵיךְ הָיוּ עוֹשִׂין אוֹתָן וּמְקוֹם וּזְמַן אֲכִילָתָן בְּסֵדֶר שֶׁלּוֹ נִכְתְּבֶנּוּ בְּעֶזְרַת הַשֵּׁם. וּכְלָל הַדָּבָר שֶׁכָּל בְּשַׂר קָרְבַּן הַחַטָּאת וְהָאָשָׁם הָיָה לְזִכְרֵי כְהֻנָּה נֶאֱכָל בָּעֲזָרָה חוּץ מִן הָאֲמוּרִין שֶׁבָּהֶן, וְאֵין לַבְּעָלִים בָּהֶן כְּלוּם, וְשָׁם יִתְפָּרֵשׁ גַּם־כֵּן מַה הֵן הָאֲמוּרִין.

וּבִכְלַל מִצְוָה־עֲשֵׂה זֶה גַּם־כֵּן שֶׁיֹּאכְלוּ חֶלְקָם הַמַּגִּיעַ אֲלֵיהֶם מִכָּל הַקָּרְבָּנוֹת שֶׁנִּקְרָאִין קָדָשִׁים קַלִּים, וְכֵן אֲכִילַת הַתְּרוּמָה בִּכְלַל הַמִּצְוָה. וְאוּלָם אֵין אֲכִילַת קָדָשִׁים קַלִּים וּתְרוּמָה כְּמוֹ אֲכִילַת בְּשַׂר חַטָּאת וְאָשָׁם, שֶׁבַּאֲכִילַת חַטָּאת וְאָשָׁם תֻּשְׁלַם כַּפָּרַת הַמִּתְכַּפֵּר, כְּמוֹ שֶׁאָמְרוּ זִכְרוֹנָם לִבְרָכָה: כֹּהֲנִים אוֹכְלִין וּבְעָלִים מִתְכַּפְּרִין, וַאֲכִילַת קָדָשִׁים קַלִּים וּתְרוּמָה לֹא יוֹסִיף וְלֹא יִגְרַע בְּמִצְוַת הַמַּקְרִיב וְהַנּוֹתֵן.

מִשָּׁרְשֵׁי הַמִּצְוָה, הַיְסוֹד הַקָּבוּעַ אֶצְלֵנוּ כִּי כָּל פְּעֻלּוֹת הַקָּרְבָּנוֹת לְהַכְשִׁיר מַחְשְׁבוֹתֵינוּ וְכַוָּנוֹתֵינוּ לְטוֹב, וּלְהַשְׁפִּיל הַנֶּפֶשׁ הַמִּתְאַוָּה אֲשֶׁר בָּנוּ, וּלְהַגְדִּיל וּלְחַזֵּק נֶפֶשׁ הַשֵּׂכֶל אֶל הַמִּצְווֹת, וְעַל־כֵּן נִצְטַוֵּינוּ לְהִתְנַהֵג בְּכָל עִנְיְנֵי הַבַּיִת וְהַקָּרְבָּנוֹת דֶּרֶךְ מַעֲלָה וּגְדֻלָּה וְכָבוֹד לְמַעַן תָּנוּחַ בְּלִבָּבֵנוּ יִרְאָה וַעֲנָוָה וְשִׁפְלוּת הָרוּחַ בִּהְיוֹתֵנוּ שָׁם, גַּם בְּזָכְרֵנוּ אוֹתוֹ מִמְּקוֹמֵנוּ. וּבֶאֱמֶת כִּי מִן הַהַנְהָגָה הַכָּבוֹד אֶל הַקָּרְבָּן שֶׁהַכַּפָּרָה תְּלוּיָה בּוֹ לִהְיוֹתוֹ נֶאֱכָל אֶל הַמְשָׁרְתִים בְּעַצְמָם וְלֹא שֶׁיִּתְּנוּהוּ

---

§102 1. TB P'saḥim 59b.
   2. So ShM positive precept §89 (on which these first two paragraphs are based).

[THE PRECEPT TO EAT THE FLESH OF THE ḤATTATH AND THE 'ASHAM]

102 that the *kohanim* were commanded to eat the flesh of some offerings, such as the *ḥattath* (sin-offering) and the *'asham* (guilt-offering): for it is stated about them, *they shall eat those things with which atonement was made* (Exodus 29:33); and our Sages of blessed memory said:[1] the *kohanim* eat, and the owners [of the offerings] find atonement. As for the process of the *ḥattath* and *'asham*—how they were treated, and the time and place for eating them—in its proper *sidrah* we will write it (§§138, 140), with the Eternal Lord's help. The crux of the matter is that all the flesh of the *ḥattath* and *'asham* was eaten by the male *kohanim* in the Temple forecourt, except for the *'émurim* in them [the fatty parts burned on the altar]; and the owners receive nothing from them. There (§138) it will also be explained what the *'émurim* are.

Included in this positive precept too is the rule that [the *kohanim*] should eat their due portion from all the sacrifices that are called offerings of lesser holiness. So too, the eating of *t'rumah* [the *kohen*'s portion from all produce] is included under this precept. However, the consumption of offerings of lesser holiness and *t'rumah* is not [of] the same [significance] as the consumption of the flesh of the *ḥattath* and *'asham*: For when the *ḥattath* and *'asham* are eaten, the atonement of the man seeking forgiveness is completed;[2] as the Sages of blessed memory said,[1] the *kohanim* eat, and the owners find atonement. But eating offerings of lesser holiness and *t'rumah* neither adds anything to nor detracts anything from the *mitzvah* of the one who brings or gives them.

At the root of the precept lies the fundamental tenet that is firmly established for us—that all things done with the offerings are in order to prepare our thoughts and intentions for goodness, to humble the desiring, craving spirit within us, and to augment and encourage the spirit of intelligence toward the *mitzvoth*. For this reason we were commanded to behave in all matters of the Temple and the offerings in a manner of nobility, grandeur and honor, so that reverent awe, humility and lowliness of spirit may settle in our heart when we are there, and also when we remember it from our own location. So in truth, it is part of the respectful treatment of an offering on which atonement depends, that it should be eaten by the ministers [servitors, *kohanim*] themselves, and they should not give it to their servants and

§102–103: ON EATING THE ḤATTATH & 'ASHAM / BURNING INCENSE

לְעַבְדֵיהֶם וּלְכַלְבָּם אוֹ יִמְכְּרוּהוּ לְכָל קוֹנֶה, וְכֵן מִן הַכָּבוֹד הוּא שֶׁיֵּאָכֵל בְּמָקוֹם קָדוֹשׁ, וְכֵן שֶׁלֹּא יַשְׂהוּ אֲכִילָתוֹ הַרְבֵּה כְּדֵי שֶׁלֹּא יַסְרִיחַ וְיִהְיֶה הַנֶּפֶשׁ קָצָה בּוֹ, הֲלֹא כָל זֶה מַרְאֶה בָעִנְיָן גְּדֻלָּה וַחֲשִׁיבוּת.

דִּינֵי הַמִּצְוָה בִּמְקוֹמָן נֶאֱרִיךְ בָּהֶן קְצָת כְּמִנְהָגֵנוּ.

וְנוֹהֶגֶת מִצְוָה זוֹ בִּזְמַן הַבַּיִת בְּזִכְרֵי כְהֻנָּה. וְעוֹבֵר עָלֶיהָ וְלֹא אָכַל חֶלְקוֹ הַמַּגִּיעַ מֵהֶן בִּזְמַן הַמְגֻבָּל לוֹ בִּטֵּל עֲשֵׂה וְנֶעֱנַשׁ עוֹד מִצַּד כַּפָּרַת הַבְּעָלִים שֶׁתְּלוּיָה בּוֹ, כְּמוֹ שֶׁאָמַרְנוּ.

וְהָרַמְבְּ"ן זִכְרוֹנוֹ לִבְרָכָה לֹא יִמְנֶה מִצְוָה זוֹ, כִּי אָמַר שֶׁזֶּה חֵלֶק מֵחֶלְקֵי מִצְוַת הַקָּרְבָּנוֹת הוּא, שֶׁצִּוָּה הַשֵּׁם בָּהֶם מִי יֹאכְלֵם וּלְמִי יִהְיוּ; הָאֱמֶת שֶׁהַכַּפָּרָה תְּלוּיָה בָזֶה.

[מִצְוַת הַקְטָרַת קְטֹרֶת]

קג שֶׁנִּצְטַוּוּ הַכֹּהֲנִים לְהַקְטִיר קְטֹרֶת סַמִּים פַּעֲמַיִם בְּכָל יוֹם עַל מִזְבַּח הַזָּהָב, שֶׁנֶּאֱמַר: וְהִקְטִיר עָלָיו אַהֲרֹן קְטֹרֶת סַמִּים בַּבֹּקֶר בַּבֹּקֶר בְּהֵיטִיבוֹ אֶת הַנֵּרֹת יַקְטִירֶנָּה. וּבְכָל שָׁנָה וְשָׁנָה מִצְוָה עֲלֵיהֶם לַעֲשׂוֹת מִמֶּנָּה כְּדֵי לְהַקְטִיר בָּהּ כְּמוֹ שֶׁאָמַרְנוּ. וַעֲשִׂיָּתָהּ וְהַמִּצְוָה שֶׁנַּעֲשֵׂית בָּהּ בְּכָל יוֹם נֶחְשָׁב לְמִצְוָה אַחַת, לְפִי שֶׁסּוֹף מִצְוַת עֲשִׂיָּתָהּ אֵינָהּ אֶלָּא לְהַקְטִיר בָּהּ, וְאַף־עַל־פִּי שֶׁשְּׁנֵי כְתוּבִים כְּתוּבִים שֶׁל צִוָּאָה מָצָאנוּ בֵּין הָעֲשִׂיָּה וְהַהַקְטָרָה, שֶׁנֶּאֱמַר בְּסֵדֶר כִּי תִשָּׂא "קַח לְךָ סַמִּים" וְגוֹמֵר עַל עֲשִׂיָּתָהּ, וְכָאן כָּתוּב "וְהִקְטִיר עָלָיו אַהֲרֹן" וְגוֹמֵר, אַף־עַל־פִּי־כֵן רָאִיתִי לִמְחַשְּׁבֵי הַמִּצְוֹת שֶׁחוֹשְׁבִין הַכֹּל מִצְוָה אַחַת, אֵין בָּזֶה מַחֲלֹקֶת בֵּינֵיהֶם כְּלָל, אֲבָל יַחְלְקוּ בָהּ בְּעִנְיָן אַחֵר, כִּי הָרַמְבְּ"ם זִכְרוֹנוֹ לִבְרָכָה יִמְנֶה קְטֹרֶת שַׁחֲרִית וְשֶׁל עַרְבִית מִצְוָה אַחַת, וְהָרַמְבְּ"ן זִכְרוֹנוֹ לִבְרָכָה כָּתַב שֶׁהֵן נִמְנוֹת שְׁתַּיִם, וּרְאָיוֹתָיו בְּסִפְרוֹ.

מִשָּׁרְשֵׁי מִצְוָה זוֹ גַּם־כֵּן לְהַגְדִּיל כְּבוֹד הַבַּיִת וְלִהְיוֹת מַעֲלָתוֹ וּמוֹרָאוֹ עַל פְּנֵי

---

3. In his commentary on ShM, root principle 12.

4. I.e. when the flesh is eaten, the process of atonement (the purpose of the offering) is completed. Hence, Ramban holds, this is certainly but a detail of the general precept of the offering.

§103   1. Rambam: ShM positive precept §28; Ramban: in his commentary to ShM, in the listing of the precepts at the end, at the completion of the negative precepts, s.v. *v'attah 'im tavin*.

dogs, or sell it to every buyer. Similarly, it is a mode of respect that it should be eaten in a hallowed place; and so also that they should not postpone eating it very long, so that it should not develop a stench, whereupon the spirit would find it repulsive. All this quite certainly endows the matter with distinction and importance.

As to the laws of the precept, we will write somewhat at length about them in their proper place, as our custom is.

This precept is in force when the Temple exists, for male *kohanim*. If someone violated it and did not eat his due share of them in the time limited for it, he would disobey a positive precept; and he would be further punished on account of the atonement of the owner, which depends on it, as we said.

Ramban of blessed memory, however,[3] does not count this precept [in his reckoning of the 613 *mitzvoth*]. For he says it is part of the subdivisions of the precept of offerings, about which the Eternal Lord ordained who should eat them and to whom they will be [credited for atonement]. The truth is that the atonement depends on it.[4]

[THE PRECEPT OF BURNING INCENSE]

103 that the *kohanim* were commanded to burn incense of spices twice every day on the altar of gold: as it is stated, *And Aaron shall burn on it incense of spices; every morning when he kindles the lamps he shall burn it* (Exodus 30:7). Every year, too, a religious duty lies on them to make [enough] of it in order to [be able] to burn it as we have stated. Its manufacture and the religious act done with it every day are [together] considered one precept, since the end purpose of the religious duty to make it is only to use it for burning. Then even though we find two verses of commandment [respectively] concerning the making and the burning—for it is stated in the *sidrah ki thissa*, *Take yourself spices*, etc. (*ibid.* 34) in regard to its manufacture; and here it is written, *Aaron shall burn on it*, etc.—I have nevertheless seen that those who reckon the precepts count it all as one *mitzvah*; there is no division of opinion about it at all. They do differ, though, about another matter: for Rambam of blessed memory counts the morning and afternoon incense [together] as one precept; whereas Ramban of blessed memory wrote that they are counted as two, and his proofs are [given] in his work.[1]

At the root of this precept too lies the purpose to make the glory

§103: THE PRECEPT OF BURNING INCENSE IN THE SANCTUARY

כָּל אָדָם, וְאִי אֶפְשָׁר לְהַגְדִּיל דָּבָר בְּלֵב בְּנֵי־אָדָם וּמַחֲשַׁבְתּוֹ רַק בִּדְבָרִים שֶׁהוּא חוֹשֵׁב אוֹתָם לְגַדְּלָה וְיִמְצָא בָּהֶם תַּעֲנוּג וְשִׂמְחָה, וְיָדוּעַ כִּי עִנְיָן הָרֵיחַ הַטּוֹב הוּא דָּבָר שֶׁנֶּפֶשׁ אָדָם נֶהֱנֵית בּוֹ וּמִתְאַוָּה אֵלָיו וּמוֹשֵׁךְ הַלֵּב הַרְבֵּה, וְרֵיחַ הַקְּטֹרֶת הָיָה הַטּוֹב שֶׁאֶפְשָׁר לַעֲשׂוֹת עַל־יְדֵי אָדָם, עַד שֶׁאָמְרוּ זִכְרוֹנָם לִבְרָכָה בְּפֵרֶק אָמַר לָהֶם הַמְמֻנֶּה כִּי מֵרֵיחוֹ הָיוּ מְרִיחִין בּוֹ בִּשְׁעַת הַקְּטָרָה מִירִיחוֹ עַד יְרוּשָׁלַיִם.

מִדִּינֵי הַמִּצְוָה, מַה שֶּׁאָמְרוּ (בַּבָּרַיְתָא בִּכְרִיתוֹת) שֶׁפִּטּוּם הַקְּטֹרֶת הָיְתָה חֲמִשָּׁה־עָשָׂר סַמָּנִין, אַרְבָּעָה מֵהֶן מְפֹרָשִׁין בַּתּוֹרָה וְאֶחָד־עָשָׂר קַבָּלָה. וּמַה שֶּׁאָמְרוּ שֶׁהַקְּטֹרֶת נַעֲשֵׂית בֵּין עַל־יְדֵי כֹּהֵן גָּדוֹל אוֹ הֶדְיוֹט, וְאָמְרוּ שֶׁאִם לֹא הִקְטִיר בַּבֹּקֶר מַקְטִיר בֵּין הָעַרְבַּיִם כָּל הַשִּׁעוּר שֶׁל יוֹם אֶחָד שֶׁהוּא מִשְׁקַל מֵאָה דִּינָרִין, וּמִשְׁקַל הַדִּינָר יָדוּעַ. וּבְכָל יוֹם הָיָה מַקְטִיר חֶצְיָן בַּבֹּקֶר וְחֶצְיָן בָּעֶרֶב אַחַר תָּמִיד שֶׁל בֵּין הָעַרְבַּיִם, קֹדֶם הֲטָבַת הַנֵּרוֹת כֻּלָּן, אַחַר הֲטָבַת חָמֵשׁ פְּתִילוֹת מֵהֶן, כִּי לֹא הָיָה מַדְלִיקָן רְצוּפִין.

וְכָךְ הָיוּ עוֹשִׂין עִנְיָן זֶה: כֹּהֵן שֶׁזָּכָה לְהַקְטִיר הַקְּטֹרֶת נוֹטֵל כְּלִי מָלֵא קְטֹרֶת גָּדוּשׁ (וְנוּנִי) [וּטְנִי] שְׁמוֹ, וּפוֹרְשִׁין כָּל הָעָם מִן הַהֵיכָל וּמִבֵּין הָאוּלָם וְלַמִּזְבֵּחַ, שֶׁנֶּאֱמַר: וְכָל אָדָם לֹא יִהְיֶה בְּאֹהֶל מוֹעֵד וְגוֹמֵר, וּמַקְטִיר כְּדֶרֶךְ שֶׁמְּפֹרָשׁ שָׁם בַּגְּמָרָא, שֶׁמַּשְׁלִיךְ הַקְּטֹרֶת בְּנַחַת עַל הַגֶּחָלִים (בַּמַּחְתָּה) [בַּמִּזְבֵּחַ] הַזָּהָב וּמִשְׁתַּחֲוֶה וְיוֹצֵא.

וְיֶתֶר פְּרָטֶיהָ וְכֵיצַד הִיא נַעֲשֵׂית, וּמַה שֶּׁהָיוּ אוֹמְרִים בִּשְׁחִיקַת הַסַּמָּנִין: הֵיטֵב הָדֵק הָדֵק הֵיטֵב, לְפִי שֶׁאָמְרוּ רַבּוֹתֵינוּ לִבְרָכָה כִּי הַקּוֹל יָפֶה לַסַּמָּנִין בְּעוֹד שֶׁשּׁוֹחֲקִין אוֹתָם, הַכֹּל בִּכְרִיתוֹת וּבְתָמִיד.

וְנוֹהֶגֶת בִּזְמַן הַבַּיִת בְּזִכְרֵי כְהֻנָּה, וְהַמַּקְטִיר כְּדִינֵנוּ קִיֵּם עֲשֵׂה זֶה.

    2. The part in parentheses is not in the oldest manuscripts, and was apparently added later. The standard Hebrew editions read, "that the compounding... was of eleven ingredients... and seven [known] in the Oral Tradition"; our version is that of the oldest manuscripts. While the *baraitha* in TB K'rithoth 6a states, "There were eleven ingredients in it," after the eleven it lists an additional four, used to improve two of the eleven ingredients and to enhance the incense generally.
    3. TB Yoma 26a; Mishnah, Tamid vii 3.
    4. TB M'naḥoth 49a.
    5. Literally, between the evenings; see §5, note 1.
    6. So TB K'rithoth 6a.
    7. I.e. 4.8 grams.
    8. TB Yoma 14b (MT *hilchoth t'midin* vi 3–4).
    9. Lots were cast for it; Mishnah, Yoma ii 4.
    10. In Mishnah, Tamid vi 3 (and MT *ibid.*) it is called *bazach*, a censer.
    11. Mishnah, Kélim i 9.
    12. The Hebrew editions generally have "censer"; but from Mishnah, Tamid vi 2–3 and MT *hilchoth t'midin* iii 7 it is apparent that this must be a scribal error (MY). In one old manuscript (MS Vatican 163) from the year 1333, it was so corrected in the

of the Temple great, and that its excellence and awe may be impressed upon every man. Now, it is possible to make something great in the heart and thought of a person only through matters which he regards as grand, finding delight and joy in them. And it is known that good scent is something which a man's spirit enjoys and desires; it greatly attracts the heart. The scent of the incense was the best that could possibly be made by human beings, so much so that our Sages of blessed memory said in the Mishnah tractate *Tamid* (iii 8) that at the time it was burned its aroma was sensed from Jericho to Jerusalem.

Among the laws of the precept, there is what the Sages said (in a *baraitha* in the Talmud tractate *K'rithoth*—6a), that the compounding of the incense was of fifteen ingredients, four of them named explicitly in the Written Torah (Exodus 30:34), and eleven [known] in the Oral Tradition.[2] And there is what they taught further,[3] that the incense might be burned by either a *kohen gadol* or an ordinary *kohen*. They said, too,[4] that if it was not burned in the morning, in the evening[5] the entire measure for one day would be burned, which has the weight of 100 dinars,[6] the weight of a dinar being known.[7] Every day [normally] half of it would be burned in the morning and half in the evening,[6] after the daily burnt-offering of the afternoon,[5] before all the lights [of the *menorah*] were kindled after five of the wicks had been lit[8]— for they were not lit [all] in succession.

So the matter was done: The *kohen* who won the right to burn the incense[9] would take a vessel, called *t'ni*,[10] packed full with incense; everyone would then leave the *héchal* and the area between the *'ulam* and the altar—as it is written, *And no man shall be in the Tent of Meeting*, etc. (Leviticus 16:17);[11] and he would burn it in the way explained there in the Talmud: He would spill the incense gently on the burning embers on the altar[12] of gold, bow down to the ground, and leave.

The rest of its details, and how it was made; what they would say during the pounding of the ingredients—"Well do grind it, grind it well"—because our Sages of blessed memory taught that the human voice was good (beneficial) for the ingredients while they were being pounded[13]—all [will be found] in the tractates *K'rithoth* and *Tamid*.

It is in effect when the Temple is in existence, for male *kohanim*. One who burns the incense in accordance with its law, has fulfilled a positive precept.

§104: TO BURN NOTHING [BUT INCENSE] ON THE GOLDEN ALTAR

[שֶׁלֹּא לְהַקְטִיר וּלְהַקְרִיב עַל מִזְבַּח הַזָּהָב]

קד שֶׁלֹּא לְהַקְרִיב בְּמִזְבַּח הַזָּהָב שֶׁבַּהֵיכָל כִּי־אִם קְטֹרֶת שֶׁבְּכָל יוֹם, זוּלָתִי הַזָּאַת הַדָּמִים מִיּוֹם הַכִּפּוּרִים לְיוֹם הַכִּפּוּרִים, שֶׁנֶּאֱמַר: לֹא תַעֲלוּ עָלָיו קְטֹרֶת זָרָה וְעֹלָה וּמִנְחָה וְנֵסֶךְ לֹא תִסְּכוּ עָלָיו.

כְּבָר כָּתַבְנוּ לְמַעְלָה תְּשׁוּבָה לַשּׁוֹאֵל עַל צַד הַפְּשָׁט עַל עִנְיַן מִצְוַת בִּנְיַן הַבַּיִת הַקָּדוֹשׁ לָאֵל בָּרוּךְ הוּא, וְעִנְיַן הֱיוֹת שָׁם כֵּלִים יְקָרִים לַעֲבוֹדָה וְשֻׁלְחָן וּמְנוֹרָה, וְאַחֲרֵי זֹאת אֵין לְיַגֵּעַ מַחְשַׁבְתֵּנוּ בַּמֶּה שֶׁאֵינוֹ צָרִיךְ וּלְחַפֵּשׂ טַעַם לָמָּה יְצַוֶּה הָאֵל לְבַל נַקְטִיר בְּמִזְבַּח הַזָּהָב קְטֹרֶת זָרָה, שֶׁאִם כֵּן יְחַיְּבֵנוּ לַחֲפֹשׂ לָמָּה צִוָּה אוֹתָנוּ לִהְיוֹת נֵרוֹת הַמְּנוֹרָה שִׁבְעָה וְלֹא שְׁמוֹנָה, וְאֶל הַפְּרָטִים אֵין חֵקֶר לָנוּ וְלֹא תַשִּׂיג בָּהֶן הַמַּחֲשָׁבָה לְעוֹלָם.

וְאִם תִּלְחָצֵנִי לְהָשִׁיב בַּפְּרָטִים בְּכָל פָּנִים, אֹמַר, עַל צַד הַפְּשָׁט, אִם לֹא שֶׁהַקַּבָּלָה תַכְרִיחַ לְפִי דִּבְרֵי רַבּוֹתֵינוּ זִכְרוֹנָם לִבְרָכָה הַקְּדוֹשִׁים הַמְקֻבָּלִים שֶׁלֹּא יִהְיֶה בַּפְּרָטִים טַעַם אַחֵר, אֶלָּא נֹאמַר שֶׁאַחַר שֶׁנִּתְחַיַּבְנוּ לִבְנוֹת בַּיִת וְלַעֲשׂוֹת כֵּלִים נְצַטַּוֵּנוּ בָּהֶם עַל צַד אֶחָד מִן הַצְּדָדִין, וּבָא בָּהֶן אֶחָד מִן הַחֶשְׁבּוֹנוֹת שֶׁאִי אֶפְשָׁר לַמַּעֲשֶׂה בִּלְתִּי אֶחָד מֵהֶן, וְאוּלָם אַחַר שֶׁנִּצְטַוֵּינוּ בָּהֶם בָּאָה הַצְוָאָה עֲלֵיהֶם לַעֲשׂוֹתָם בַּמִּצְוָה דֶּרֶךְ קֶבַע לְעוֹלָם, וְלֹא נוֹסִיף וְלֹא נִגְרַע, כִּי הַתּוֹסֶפֶת וְהַגֵּרוּעַ בִּמְכֻוָּן בִּשְׁלֵמוּת קִלְקוּל, וְכָל מִצְווֹתָיו בָּרוּךְ הוּא שְׁלֵמוֹת וּתְמִימוֹת. וְאוּלָם שָׁמַעְתִּי כִּי יֵשׁ לַמְקֻבָּלִים בְּכָל אֶחָד מִן הַפְּרָטִים טְעָמִים נִפְלָאִים וִיסוֹדוֹת עֲמֻקִּים.

וְנוֹהֶגֶת מִצְוָה זוֹ שֶׁלֹּא לְהַקְרִיב בְּמִזְבַּח הַזָּהָב כִּי־אִם קְטֹרֶת בִּזְמַן הַבַּיִת בַּכֹּהֲנִים. וְהָעוֹבֵר עַל זֶה וְהִקְרִיב אוֹ זָרַק בּוֹ, כִּי־אִם דָּבָר הָרָאוּי לְהַקְרִיב בּוֹ כְּמוֹ שֶׁאָמַרְנוּ, חַיָּב מַלְקוֹת.

margin by the scribe. (The incense was burned on glowing coals in a censer only on *Yom Kippur*, in the holy of holies, by the *kohen gadol*.)

13. TB K'rithoth 6b.

§104 1. I.e. in the holy chamber, which was part of the *héchal* (§95).

2. I.e. of the bullock and goat which were offered up (Leviticus 16:18). The Hebrew reads literally "from Day of Atonement to Day of Atonement."

3. Cf. Rambam, *Guide* III 26: "For a precept in its totality necessarily has a reason; He commanded it for some use or benefit. But as for its parts, details that were given about it, they are merely for [the sake of] commandment"—i.e. to obey with precision and clarity.

4. See §98, note 2.

SIDRAH TETZAVVEH

[NOT TO BURN OR OFFER UP ANYTHING ON THE GOLDEN ALTAR]

104 not to offer up anything on the altar of gold in the *héchal*,[1] but only the incense every day—except for the sprinkling of the blood every Day of Atonement:[2] for it is stated, *You shall offer no alien incense on it, nor burnt-offering nor meal-offering; and you shall pour no libation on it* (Exodus 30:9).

We wrote earlier, above (§95), a reply, in terms of the plain meaning, to one who might ask the reason for the commandment to build the holy Temple for God (blessed is He), and the reason why there were precious objects there for the [Divine] service, and a table and a *menorah* (lamp). After that there is no need [for us] to weary our minds unnecessarily, seeking a reason why God would ordain that we should not burn alien [unholy] incense on the altar of gold. For if there were [such a need], it would obligate us to seek [a reason] why He commanded us that the lights of the *menorah* should be seven and not eight. About the details there can be no enquiry for us, and the mind will never grasp [any significance] about them.[3]

However, if you will press me to respond [with an explanation] about details under all circumstances, I would answer by way of simple, direct interpretation—unless the *kabbalah* (mystic tradition), according to the words of our holy sages of blessed memory who are masters of the *kabbalah*, shows that there is another reason for the details. Then let us merely say that having been commanded to build a Temple and make objects and utensils [for it], we were commanded about them in one of the [many possible] ways, and one of the [various possible] calculations was given for them, since the manufacture would be impossible without one of them. However, once we were commanded about them, the order was given for them to produce them as commanded, in the set, fixed way always. We are not to add anything or take anything away, for to impose any addition or diminution on what was planned to perfection, is to spoil it; and all His commandments are perfect and whole. I have heard, though, that about every one of the details, the masters of mysticism possess wondrous reasons and deep secrets.[4]

This precept, to offer up nothing other than incense on the altar of gold, applies when the Temple is extant, for the *kohanim*. If someone violated it and offered or sprinkled on it anything other than what should properly be offered on it, as we have stated, he would incur whiplashes.

⟨395⟩

כִּי תִשָּׂא

יֵשׁ בָּהּ אַרְבַּע מִצְווֹת עֲשֵׂה וְחָמֵשׁ מִצְווֹת לֹא־תַעֲשֶׂה

[מִצְוַת נְתִינַת מַחֲצִית הַשֶּׁקֶל בְּשָׁנָה]

קה שֶׁיִּתֵּן כָּל אֶחָד מִיִּשְׂרָאֵל מִבֶּן עֶשְׂרִים שָׁנָה וָמַעְלָה בֵּין עָנִי בֵּין עָשִׁיר מַחֲצִית הַשֶּׁקֶל, שֶׁהוּא מִשְׁקַל עֲשָׂרָה גֵּרָה כֶּסֶף, בְּכָל שָׁנָה לְיַד הַכֹּהֲנִים, שֶׁנֶּאֱמַר: זֶה יִתְּנוּ כָּל הָעֹבֵר עַל הַפְּקֻדִים. וְהָיוּ מַנִּיחִין הַכֹּל בְּלִשְׁכָּה אַחַת שֶׁבַּמִּקְדָּשׁ וּמִשָּׁם הָיוּ מוֹצִיאִין לִקְנוֹת תְּמִידִין וּמוּסָפִין וְכָל קָרְבָּן הַקָּרֵב עַל הַצִּבּוּר, וְנִסְכֵּיהֶם, וְהַמֶּלַח שֶׁמּוֹלְחִין בּוֹ אֶת הַקָּרְבָּנוֹת, וַעֲצֵי הַמַּעֲרָכָה, וְלֶחֶם הַפָּנִים, וְהָעֹמֶר, וּשְׁתֵּי הַלֶּחֶם, וּפָרָה אֲדֻמָּה, וְשָׂעִיר הַמִּשְׁתַּלֵּחַ, וְלָשׁוֹן שֶׁל זְהוֹרִית.

מִשָּׁרְשֵׁי מִצְוָה זוֹ, שֶׁרָצָה הַקָּדוֹשׁ־בָּרוּךְ־הוּא לְטוֹבַת כָּל יִשְׂרָאֵל וְלִזְכוּתָם שֶׁיִּהְיֶה יַד כֻּלָּם שָׁוָה בַּדָּבָר הַקָּרְבָּנוֹת הַקְּרֵבִים לְפָנָיו כָּל הַשָּׁנָה בְּהִתְמָדָה, וּבְעִנְיָנִים אֵלּוּ הַנִּזְכָּרִים, וְשֶׁיִּהְיוּ הַכֹּל, אֶחָד עָנִי וְאֶחָד עָשִׁיר, שָׁוִים בְּמִצְוָה אַחַת לְפָנָיו לְהַעֲלוֹת זִכָּרוֹן כֻּלָּן עַל־יְדֵי הַמִּצְוָה שֶׁהֵם כְּלוּלִים בָּהּ יַחַד לְטוֹבָה לִפְנֵי, וַעֲלִיַּת הַזִּכָּרוֹן הַכֹּל נֶאֱמַר מִצַּד הַמְקַבֵּל, עַל הַדֶּרֶךְ שֶׁכָּתַבְנוּ לְמַעְלָה.

מִדִּינֵי הַמִּצְוָה (כְּגוֹן) מַה שֶּׁאָמְרוּ זִכְרוֹנָם לִבְרָכָה שֶׁבְּאֶחָד בַּאֲדָר מַשְׁמִיעִים עַל הַשְּׁקָלִים, וְשֶׁאֲפִלּוּ דַּל שֶׁבַּדַּלִּים חַיָּב בּוֹ, וְאִם אֵין לוֹ שׁוֹאֵל מֵאֲחֵרִים אוֹ מוֹכֵר כְּסוּתוֹ שֶׁעָלָיו וְנוֹתְנוֹ, שֶׁנֶּאֱמַר: וְהַדַּל לֹא יַמְעִיט; וְאֵינוֹ נִתָּן בְּפַרְעוֹנוֹת הַרְבֵּה אֶלָּא הַכֹּל בְּפַעַם אַחַת, וְהוּא מִשְׁקַל שְׁמוֹנִים גַּרְעִינֵי שְׂעוֹרָה, שֶׁהַשֶּׁקֶל הַשָּׁלֵם הָיָה בִּימֵי

---

§105 1. I.e. 19.2 grams.
2. Offered on the second day of Passover; Leviticus 23:10–11.
3. Offered on *Shavu'oth*; ibid. 17.
4. Numbers 19.
5. Leviticus 16:10, 20–22.
6. To be tied to the horns of the goat hurled into the wilderness; Mishnah, Yoma iv 2, vi 6; TB 67b. This whole sentence is based on MT *hilchoth sh'kalim* iv 1, which derives in turn from Mishnah, Sh'kalim iv 1 and TB K'thuboth 106a.
7. Messengers were sent by the chief *beth din* to alert people to give their coins; Mishnah, Sh'kalim i 1.
8. MT *hilchoth sh'kalim* i 1; see *Minhath Yitzhak*.
9. Rambam *ibid*.

⟨396⟩

sidrah ki thissa
(Exodus 30:11–34:35)

There are four positive and five negative precepts in it.

105 [THE PRECEPT OF GIVING HALF A SHEKEL EACH YEAR] that every one of the people Israel from the age of twenty and up, whether rich or poor, should give half a shekel, which has the weight of ten *gérah* of silver,[1] every year into the hand (possession) of the *kohanim*: for it is stated: *This they shall give, every one that passes among those who are counted* (Exodus 30:13). They [the *kohanim*] would leave it all in one *lishkah* (compartment) in the Sanctuary, and from there they would take out [funds] to buy the daily burnt-offerings, the additional (*musaf*) offerings, and every sacrifice that was offered up in behalf of the public, and their libations; the salt with which the offerings were salted, the ordered piles of wood [for the altar fire], the showbread, and the wages for the one who made the showbread; the '*omer* (sheaf-offering),[2] the two loaves of bread,[3] the red heifer,[4] the goat despatched [into the wilderness],[5] and the cloth strip of crimson.[6]

At the root of this precept lies the principle that the Holy One, blessed is He, desired for the good of all the Israelites, and to make them meritorious, that all should have an equal hand [share] in regard to the sacrifices that were offered up before Him the entire year, consistently, and in those [other] matters mentioned [above]; and that all, the poor and the rich, should be equal in one *mitzvah* before Him, to make the remembrance of all ascend to His presence through the *mitzvah* in which they are included together, for good reward. But this "ascent of the remembrance" is said entirely from the point of view of the receiver [the human being involved], in the way that we have written above (§30).

Among the laws of the precept there are, for example, what our Sages of blessed memory said,[7] that on the first of Adar, proclamation was made about the *sh'kalim*; that even the poorest of the poor was duty-bound about it; if someone did not have it [the half-shekel], he was to borrow from others or sell the cloak that he wore, and give it—for it is stated, *and the poor shall not give less* (Exodus 30:15).[8] It was not to be given in many payments, but all at once.[9] It should have the weight of eighty kernels of barley, since the full, perfect

§105–106: THE ANNUAL HALF-SHEKEL / KOHEN RINSES HANDS & FEET

מֹשֶׁה מִשְׁקַל מֵאָה וְשִׁשִּׁים שְׂעוֹרָה. וְהַכֹּל חַיָּבִין לִתְּנָם, כֹּהֲנִים לְוִיִּים וְיִשְׂרְאֵלִים, גֵּרִים וַעֲבָדִים מְשֻׁחְרָרִין, אֲבָל לֹא נָשִׁים וַעֲבָדִים וּקְטַנִּים, וְאִם נָתְנוּ מְקַבְּלִין מֵהֶן, אֲבָל לֹא מִן הַגּוֹיִים, חֵלֶק וְנַחֲלָה לֹא יִהְיֶה לָהֶם בְּתוֹכֵנוּ.

וְעוֹד אָמְרוּ זִכְרוֹנָם לִבְרָכָה שֶׁכָּל מִי שֶׁאֵינוֹ נוֹתֵן חֲצִי שֶׁקֶל מַמָּשׁ שֶׁהָיָה מַטְבֵּעַ בְּאוֹתוֹ זְמַן וְנוֹתֵן בַּעֲבוּרוֹ כֶּסֶף בְּמִשְׁקָלוֹ אוֹ פְרוּטוֹת, שֶׁמּוֹסִיף עַל מִשְׁקַל שִׁקְלוֹ זֶה מְעַט, וְאוֹתוֹ הַמְּעַט נִקְרָא קָלְבּוֹן, וְאוֹתוֹ הַמְּעַט הוּא שְׂכַר הַשֻּׁלְחָנִי שֶׁמְּשַׁתֵּר כְּשֶׁהוּא מַחֲלִיף חֲצִי שֶׁקֶל שֶׁהָיָה טָבוּעַ בִּשְׁבִיל פְּרוּטוֹת. וּלְפִיכָךְ שְׁנַיִם שֶׁהֵבִיאוּ שֶׁקֶל שָׁלֵם בֵּין שְׁנֵיהֶם חַיָּבִים בְּקָלְבּוֹן שֶׁאִלּוּ רָצוּ לְהַחֲלִיפוֹ צְרִיכִין הָיוּ לִתֵּן הַקָּלְבּוֹן לַשֻּׁלְחָנִי, וּכְמוֹ־כֵן יִתְּנוּהוּ לַגִּזְבָּר, לְפִי שֶׁבַּחֲצִי שֶׁקֶל חִיְּבוֹ הַכָּתוּב, וְלָכֵן חַיָּבִים בּוֹ אוֹ בְּעֶרְכּוֹ בְּכִוּוּן.

וְכֵן מַה שֶּׁאָמְרוּ (זִכְרוֹנָם לִבְרָכָה) בְּמִי שֶׁאָבַד שִׁקְלוֹ בַּדֶּרֶךְ מַה דִּינוֹ, וְיֶתֶר רַבֵּי פְּרָטֶיהָ, מְבֹאָרִים בַּמַּסֶּכְתָּא הַבְּנוּיָה עַל זֶה וְהִיא מַסֶּכֶת שְׁקָלִים.

וְנוֹהֶגֶת בִּזְמַן הַבַּיִת, שֶׁחַיָּבִין לָתֵת אוֹתָהּ כָּל יִשְׂרָאֵל בֵּין הָעוֹמְדִין בָּאָרֶץ אוֹ חוּצָה לָאָרֶץ; וְשֶׁלֹּא בִזְמַן הַבַּיִת אֵין חַיָּב בָּהּ אָדָם וַאֲפִלּוּ הָעוֹמְדִין בָּאָרֶץ. וְהָעוֹבֵר עָלֶיהָ וְלֹא נָתְנוֹ, בִּטֵּל עֲשֵׂה, וְעָנְשׁוֹ גָדוֹל שֶׁפֵּרֵשׁ עַצְמוֹ מִן הַצִּבּוּר, וְאֵינוֹ בִכְלַל כַּפָּרָתָן.

וַעֲכָשָׁיו בַּעֲוֹנוֹתֵינוּ שֶׁאֵין לָנוּ מִקְדָּשׁ וְלֹא שְׁקָלִים נָהֲגוּ כָל יִשְׂרָאֵל לְזֵכֶר הַדָּבָר לִקְרוֹת בְּבֵית־הַכְּנֶסֶת בְּכָל שָׁנָה וְשָׁנָה פָּרָשָׁה זוּ שֶׁל כִּי תִשָּׂא עַד "וְלָקַחְתָּ אֶת כֶּסֶף הַכִּפֻּרִים" בַּשַּׁבָּת שֶׁהוּא לִפְנֵי רֹאשׁ־חֹדֶשׁ אֲדָר לְעוֹלָם.

[מִצְוַת קִדּוּשׁ יָדַיִם וְרַגְלַיִם בִּשְׁעַת עֲבוֹדָה]

קו לִרְחֹץ הַיָּדַיִם וְהָרַגְלַיִם בְּכָל עֵת הִכָּנֵס לַהֵיכָל, וְהַבָּא לַעֲבֹד עֲבוֹדָה, וְזֹאת

---

10. Rambam *ibid.* 5. (The standard editions have "in the days of Solomon," but the old manuscripts read "Moses.") The editions generally have a note inserted in the text: "This is puzzling, because according to Rambam's words the *me'ah* has the weight of 16 kernels of barley [so MT *hilchoth sh'kalim* i 3]; hence the shekel [equal to 20 *me'ah* or *gérah*; *ibid.*, Exodus 30:13] has the weight of 320 barley kernels, and half the shekel, of 160 barley kernels." In MT *ibid.* 5, Rambam writes, "Regarding this half-shekel, the religious duty is to give half the coin [the standard unit of currency] of the time, even if that coin [unit] is larger than the "holy shekel" [designated in Scripture]. But it may never weigh less than half the shekel that was current in our Master Moses' days, whose weight was 160 barley kernels." Perhaps the figures in our text were originally double their present value, and were "emended" by some early copyist who understood this last number in MT (160) to refer to the *shekel* in Moses' time, and took the weight of 320 (given in MT *ibid.* 2–3) to refer to Talmudic or post-Talmudic times.

11. Mishnah, Sh'kalim i 3–5. 12. *Ibid.* 6. 13. So Rambam *ibid.* iii 1.
14. Mishnah, Sh'kalim ii 1. 15. MT *hilchoth sh'kalim* i 8.

⟨398⟩

shekel, in the days of Moses, weighed as much as 160 kernels of barley.[10] All were obligated to give it: *kohanim*, Levites and ordinary Israelites, converts and freed slaves—but not women, servants and children; however, if they gave it, it was accepted from them—but not from heathens: they were to have no portion or inheritance in our midst.[11]

Furthermore, our Sages of blessed memory taught that if anyone did not give an actual half-shekel, which was a coin [extant] at that time, but gave instead its weight in silver, or pennies, he was to add on a bit to the weight of his [half] shekel, this little bit being called *kolbon* (agio).[12] This small amount is the fee of a money-changer, who would take payment if he exchanged a half-shekel that was cast as a coin, for pennies. For this reason, if two brought a whole shekel between the two of them, they had to pay the *kolbon*: for if they wanted to change it [into two half-shekels] they would have to give the *kolbon* to the money-changer; hence they must similarly give the *kolbon* to the treasurer[13]—because Scripture obligated them to give a half-shekel; therefore they must pay that or its exact value.

There is, also, what our Sages of blessed memory said about one who lost his [half] shekel on the way, what his law is.[14] The rest of its many details are explained in the tractate built about this theme, i.e. the tractate *Sh'kalim*.

It is in effect when the Temple is in existence: then all Israelites are required to give it, whether they live in the land [of Israel] or outside the land. When the Temple does not exist, no one has the duty, not even those who live in the land.[15] If someone violated it and did not give it, he would [thus] disobey a positive precept; his punishment would be very great, for he separated himself from the community, and he would not be included in their atonement.[16]

Now, when for our sins we have neither Temple nor *sh'kalim*, all Jews have the custom, in commemoration of the matter, to read aloud in the synagogue every year this section of *ki thissa* [from Exodus 30:11] until the verse, *And you shall take the atonement money* (ibid. 16)—always on the Sabbath which occurs before the beginning of the month of Adar.[17]

[THE PRECEPT OF RINSING HANDS AND FEET WHEN MINISTERING AT THE SANCTUARY]

106 to wash the hands and feet every time [a *kohen*] enters the *héchal*[1] and when one comes to do [Divine] service. This is the religious

§106: A KOHEN RINSES HANDS & FEET TO SERVE AT THE TEMPLE

הִיא מִצְוַת קִדּוּשׁ יָדַיִם וְרַגְלַיִם, שֶׁנֶּאֱמַר: וְרָחֲצוּ אַהֲרֹן וּבָנָיו מִמֶּנּוּ אֶת יְדֵיהֶם וְאֶת רַגְלֵיהֶם בְּבֹאָם אֶל אֹהֶל מוֹעֵד . . . אוֹ בְגִשְׁתָּם אֶל הַמִּזְבֵּחַ, וְגוֹמֵר.

מִשָּׁרְשֵׁי הַמִּצְוָה, הַיְסוֹד הַקָּבוּעַ שֶׁאָמַרְנוּ, לְהַגְדִּיל כְּבוֹד הַבַּיִת וְכָל הַמְּלָאכוֹת הַנַּעֲשׂוֹת שָׁם, עַל־כֵּן רָאוּי לְנַקּוֹת הַיָּדַיִם, שֶׁהֵן הָעוֹשׂוֹת בִּמְלָאכָה, בְּכָל־עֵת יִגְּעוּ הַכֹּהֲנִים בְּעִנְיְנֵי הַבַּיִת. וּמִזֶּה הַשֹּׁרֶשׁ אָמְרוּ זִכְרוֹנָם לִבְרָכָה שֶׁאֵין הַכֹּהֵן צָרִיךְ לְקַדֵּשׁ יָדָיו בֵּין עֲבוֹדָה לַעֲבוֹדָה אֶלָּא פַּעַם אַחַת בַּבֹּקֶר, וְעוֹבֵד כָּל הַיּוֹם וְכָל הַלַּיְלָה, וְהוּא שֶׁלֹּא יִישַׁן וְלֹא יָטִיל מַיִם וְלֹא יַסִּיחַ דַּעְתּוֹ.

נִרְאֶה מִכָּל זֶה שֶׁאֵין הַכַּוָּנָה בִּרְחִיצָה מִתְּחִלָּה אֶלָּא לְהַגְדִּיל כְּבוֹד הַבַּיִת, שֶׁאֲפִלּוּ הָיָה טָהוֹר וְנָקִי בִּתְחִלַּת בּוֹאוֹ שָׁם צָרִיךְ לִרְחֹץ, וּמִשֶּׁהִתְחִיל בָּעֲבוֹדָה אֵין צָרִיךְ עוֹד לִרְחִיצָה בֵּין עֲבוֹדָה לַעֲבוֹדָה, זוּלָתִי בְּיוֹם הַכִּפּוּרִים לְרֹב חֻמְרוֹ שֶׁל יוֹם, לְפִי שֶׁכָּל עֵסֶק עֲבוֹדַת הַבַּיִת אָנוּ מַחֲזִיקִין וְרוֹאִין בִּלְבָבֵנוּ טָהוֹר וְנָקִי וְקָדוֹשׁ.

מִדִּינֵי הַמִּצְוָה, מַה שֶּׁאָמְרוּ זִכְרוֹנָם לִבְרָכָה שֶׁהַיּוֹצֵא חוּץ לְחוֹמַת הָעֲזָרָה טָעוּן קִדּוּשׁ יָדַיִם, וְאִם קִדֵּשׁ יָדָיו הַיּוֹם צָרִיךְ לַחֲזֹר וּלְקַדֵּשׁ לְמָחָר, אַף־עַל־פִּי שֶׁלֹּא יָשֵׁן כָּל הַלַּיְלָה שֶׁהַיָּדַיִם נִפְסָלוֹת בְּלִינָה, וְשֶׁמִּצְוָה לְכַתְּחִלָּה לִרְחֹץ בְּשַׁחֲרִית פָּנָיו יָדָיו וְרַגְלָיו, וְשֶׁמִּצְוָה לְקַדֵּשׁ בְּמֵי הַכִּיּוֹר, וְאִם קִדֵּשׁ מֵאֶחָד מִכְּלֵי שָׁרֵת כָּשֵׁר דִּיעֲבַד, אֲבָל לֹא מִכְּלֵי חוֹל אֲפִלּוּ דִיעֲבַד.

וְשֶׁאֵין מַכְנִיסִין יְדֵיהֶן לְתוֹכוֹ אֶלָּא שׁוֹפְכִין מִמֶּנּוּ עַל יְדֵיהֶם, וְגַם זֶה דֶּרֶךְ כָּבוֹד; וְאֵין אָנוּ מַצְרִיכִין כֵּן בְּעִנְיָן נְטִילַת יָדַיִם לְחֻלִּין לִטֹּל מִן הַכְּלִי וְלֹא בְתוֹכוֹ, שֶׁאַף־עַל־פִּי שֶׁאָנוּ מַצְרִיכִין כְּלִי לִנְטִילַת חֻלִּין, וִיסוֹד הַדָּבָר הוּא מִפְּנֵי שֶׁמָּצָאנוּ כְּלִי לִנְטִילָה בַּקֹּדֶשׁ, מִכָּל־מָקוֹם בַּקְּדֻשָּׁה הוּא דְּמִיעֵט רַחֲמָנָא מִמֶּנּוּ וְלֹא בְתוֹכוֹ,

---

16. I.e. in the atonement granted for the offerings sacrificed in behalf of all the people, which were bought for this money.

17. So TB M'gillah 29a.

106   1. I.e. even without performing any Temple service; so *tosafoth* to TB Yoma 5b, s.v. *l'havi* (see MY).

2. TB Z'vaḥim 19b (MT *hilchoth bi'ath ha-mikdash* v 3).

3. *Ibid.* 20b; TB Yoma (Rambam *ibid.*).

4. TB Yoma 30a.

5. I.e. upon his return; TB Z'vaḥim 20b.

6. *Ibid.* 19b (Rambam *ibid.* 8).

7. TB Shabbath 50b (a general rule for all, which our author applies also to the *kohen* at the Sanctuary).

8. TB Z'vaḥim 22b (Rambam *ibid.* 10)

9. *Ibid.* 21a.

10. I.e. not to put the hands into a vessel of water to rinse them. This refers to the duty of washing before a meal. Here our author follows the view of *Halachoth G'doloth*, cited in *tosafoth* to TB Ḥullin 106a, s.v. *d'lo*; this view is also upheld by

duty of sanctifying hands and feet—as it is stated, *And Aaron and his sons shall wash their hands and their feet from it, when they go into the Tent of Meeting . . . or when they come near the altar*, etc. (Exodus 30:19–20).

At the root of the precept lies the constant, established fundamental reason that we have stated [before]: to make great the glory of the Temple and of all the labors done there. It is therefore fitting to cleanse the hands which do the labor, every time the *kohanim* touch any matters of the Temple. And for this root reason our Sages of blessed memory said[2] that a *kohen* did not need to hallow (wash) his hands between one labor and another, but merely once in the morning, and then he could serve the entire day and night—but this only if he did not sleep, pass water, or divert his attention.[3]

It is evident from all this that from the start, the purpose of this washing is nothing else but to magnify the glory of the Temple. For even if someone was pure and clean when he originally came there, he would need to wash; and from the time he began the [Divine] work, he would no longer need to wash, [i.e.] between one labor and another, except on the Day of Atonement,[4] on account of the great solemnity of the day. For we hold every activity of Temple service to be—and see it in our heart as—pure, clean and holy.

Among the laws of the precept, there is what the Sages of blessed memory said, that if someone goes outside the wall of the Temple court, he requires sanctification (washing) of the hands;[5] if someone sanctified his hands today, he must sanctify them again tomorrow, even if he did not sleep all night: for the hands become disqualified, unacceptable by the passage of a night.[6] Then [there is the law] that it is a religious duty originally to wash one's face, hands and feet in the morning;[7] and it is a duty to do the sanctification with water from the laver (*ki-yor*); yet if someone did the sanctification from one of the vessels of the Temple service, it remains acceptable after the fact—but not from a profane, non-holy vessel, in which case it is not valid even after the fact.[8]

Then [there is the law] that they are not to put their hands into it, but pour from it onto their hands;[9] this too [because it] is a way of honor. We do not require this in regard to washing the hands for non-holy purposes—to wash from the vessel (cup) but not within it:[10] For even though we require a vessel for ordinary, non-holy hand-washing, and the basis of the ruling is that we find a vessel [used] in hand-washing in holiness, nevertheless, it is only in holiness that

§106: A KOHEN RINSES HANDS & FEET TO SERVE AT THE TEMPLE

אֲבָל בְּחֻלִּין אֵין לָנוּ מָעוּט, וְאַף־עַל־פִּי שֶׁנְּטִילַת הַחֻלִּין מִשּׁוּם סֶרֶךְ הַקָּדָשִׁים הִיא, וּכְמוֹ שֶׁאָמְרוּ זִכְרוֹנָם לִבְרָכָה מִשּׁוּם סֶרֶךְ תְּרוּמָה, מִכָּל־מָקוֹם אֵין לָנוּ לְהַשְׁווֹתָם לְגַמְרֵי בְּכָל דִּינֵיהֶם, וְדַי לָנוּ לַחַיֵּב בִּנְטִילָה וּבִכְלֵי בְחֻלִּין מִשּׁוּם סֶרֶךְ זֶה, וּלְהַנִּיחַ מָעוּטוֹ דְ"מִמֶּנּוּ" שֶׁנֶּאֱמַר בּוֹ בִּמְקוֹמוֹ. וַאֲפִלּוּ בִּתְרוּמָה עַצְמָהּ נְטִילַת יָדַיִם בָּהּ מִדְּרַבָּנָן הוּא, כִּי מִן הַתּוֹרָה לֹא נִמְצָא טָהֳרָה רַק בְּכָל הַגּוּף בְּבַת־אַחַת. וּמַה שֶּׁאָמְרוּ זִכְרוֹנָם לִבְרָכָה שֶׁהַנְּטִילָה מִדִּכְתִיב "וְיָדָיו לֹא שָׁטַף בַּמָּיִם" וְגוֹמֵר, אַסְמַכְתָּא בְעָלְמָא הוּא; כֵּן כָּתוּב בְּסֵפֶר הַמִּצְווֹת שֶׁל הָרַמְבַּ"ן זִכְרוֹנוֹ לִבְרָכָה.

וְכֵן מַה שֶּׁאָמְרוּ זִכְרוֹנָם לִבְרָכָה, כַּמָּה מַיִם צָרִיךְ לִהְיוֹת בַּכִּיּוֹר, אֵין פָּחוֹת מִשִּׁעוּר מַיִם הָרְאוּיִין לִנְטִילַת אַרְבָּעָה אֲנָשִׁים, שֶׁנֶּאֱמַר: וְרָחֲצוּ אַהֲרֹן וּבָנָיו מִמֶּנּוּ אֶת יְדֵיהֶם, וְהָיוּ אַהֲרֹן אֶלְעָזָר וְאִיתָמָר וּפִנְחָס עִמָּהֶם.

וְכָל מַיִם כְּשֵׁרִין לְקִדּוּשׁ, בֵּין מֵי מַעְיָן אוֹ מֵי מִקְוֶה, וְנִפְסָלִין בְּלִינָה. וְכֵיצַד מִצְוַת קִדּוּשׁ, מַנִּיחַ יָדוֹ הַיְמָנִית עַל רַגְלוֹ הַיְמָנִית וְיָדוֹ הַשְּׂמָאלִית עַל רַגְלוֹ הַשְּׂמָאלִית, וְרוֹחֵץ עוֹמֵד וְלֹא יוֹשֵׁב, לְפִי שֶׁמִּכְּלַל הָעֲבוֹדָה הוּא קִדּוּשׁ יָדַיִם וְרַגְלַיִם, וְכָל עֲבוֹדוֹת הַמִּקְדָּשׁ מְעֻמָּד הֵן, שֶׁנֶּאֱמַר: לַעֲמֹד לְשָׁרֵת, וְכָל זֶה לְמַעֲלַת הַבַּיִת; וְיֶתֶר פְּרָטֶיהָ, מְבֹאָרִים בְּפֶרֶק שְׁנֵי מִזְבְּחִים.

וְנוֹהֶגֶת בִּזְמַן הַבַּיִת בְּזִכְרֵי כְהֻנָּה לְבַד. וְעוֹבֵר עָלֶיהָ וְלֹא קִדֵּשׁ יָדָיו וְרַגְלָיו

Rashba (evidently our author's master teacher) in *Torath haBa-yith* vi 4, and in his commentary to Ḥullin 106a.

11. So that those who eat t'rumah [the *kohanim*] should become accustomed to washing their hands, they made it a rule for non-holy food (Rashi); TB Ḥullin 106a.
12. I.e. after uncleanness.
13. *Ibid*.
14. I.e. it is only an allusion or implication in Scripture, but the law is essentially a decree of the Sages.
15. In his commentary to ShM, root principle 1, s.v. *uvit'shuvah*.
16. TB Z'vaḥim 21b.
17. Aaron's two sons.
18. The son of El'azar (see Numbers 25:13).
19. TB Z'vaḥim 22b, Yoma 37a.
20. TB Z'vaḥim 19b (MT *hilchoth bi'ath ha-mikdash* v 16).

the merciful God set the limitation, *from it* (Exodus 30:19), and not within it; but for non-holy purposes we have no such limitation. Even though non-holy hand-washing [was necessitated] for the sake of following the pattern of holiness [to make the practice uniform]—as our Sages of blessed memory said, "for the sake of consistency with *t'rumah*"[11]—nevertheless, we are not to equate them completely, in all their laws; it is enough for us to impose the duty of hand-washing, and that with a vessel, in non-holy circumstances, for the sake of this consistency—but to let its strict limitation, derived from the words *from it*, remain in its place. Even for *t'rumah* itself [the *kohen*'s portion from produce] the duty of washing the hands for it is [only] by a ruling of the Sages; for by Torah law the only type of purification ever required is of the entire body at once.[12]

Now, what the Sages of blessed memory said,[13] that [we learn the duty of] hand-washing from the verse, *and his hands he has not rinsed in water*, etc. (Leviticus 15:11)—this is merely a connotation of support for it.[14] So is it written in the *Book of Precepts* of Ramban of blessed memory.[15]

There is, moreover, the law that the Sages of blessed memory taught:[16] How much water must there be in the laver?—not less than a measure of water fit for the washing of four people. For it is stated, *And Aaron and his sons shall wash their hands... from it* (Exodus 30:19), and there were Aaron, El'azar and Ithamar,[17] and Pinḥas (Phinehas) was with them too.[18]

All water is fit to use for sanctification, whether from a wellspring or a *mikveh* (collected water), but it becomes unfit to use if left overnight.[19] And [there is the law on] how the *mitzvah* of sanctification is performed: He [the *kohen*] puts his right hand on his right leg, and his left hand on his left leg, and he washes standing, not sitting. For sanctification (washing) of hands and feet is considered part of the Temple service, and all sacred labors at the Sanctuary were done standing: for it is stated, *to stand and minister* (Deuteronomy 18:5).[20] And this was all on account of the noble, exalted state of the Temple. The rest of its details are clarified in the second chapter of the Talmud tractate *Z'vaḥim*.

It is in force when the Temple is extant, for the male *kohanim* only. If someone violated it and did not sanctify (wash) his hands and feet in the morning, or if he left the Sanctuary and his mind was distracted, and he returned and served without sanctification, he would

שַׁחֲרִית, אוֹ שֶׁיָּצָא מִן הַמִּקְדָּשׁ וְהֵסִיחַ דַּעְתּוֹ וְחָזַר וְעָבַד בְּלֹא קִדּוּשׁ, חַיָּב מִיתָה בִּידֵי שָׁמַיִם, וַעֲבוֹדָתוֹ פְּסוּלָה, בֵּין כֹּהֵן גָּדוֹל אוֹ הֶדְיוֹט.

[מִצְוַת מְשִׁיחַת כֹּהֲנִים גְּדוֹלִים וּמְלָכִים בְּשֶׁמֶן הַמִּשְׁחָה]

קז לַעֲשׂוֹת שֶׁמֶן הַמִּשְׁחָה עַל הָעִנְיָן שֶׁצִּוְּתָה הַתּוֹרָה לַעֲשׂוֹתוֹ, שֶׁנֶּאֱמַר: וְעָשִׂיתָ אֹתוֹ שֶׁמֶן מִשְׁחַת קֹדֶשׁ, שֶׁיִּהְיֶה מוּכָן לִמְשֹׁחַ בּוֹ כָּל כֹּהֵן גָּדוֹל שֶׁיִּתְמַנֶּה, כְּמוֹ שֶׁכָּתוּב "וְהַכֹּהֵן הַגָּדוֹל וכו' אֲשֶׁר יוּצַק עַל רֹאשׁוֹ שֶׁמֶן הַמִּשְׁחָה", וְכֵן מוֹשְׁחִין בּוֹ קְצָת הַמְּלָכִים, וְכֵן גַּם מָשְׁחוּ בּוֹ הַכֵּלִים שֶׁל בֵּית-הַמִּקְדָּשׁ; וְלֹא יִצְטָרְכוּ לִמְשֹׁחַ לֶעָתִיד אֶלָּא בַּעֲבוֹדָה יִתְקַדְּשׁוּ, וְזֶהוּ שֶׁכָּתוּב "יִהְיֶה זֶה לִי לְדֹרֹתֵיכֶם", כֵּן אָמְרוּ זִכְרוֹנָם לִבְרָכָה בְּסִפְרֵי.

מִשָּׁרְשֵׁי הַמִּצְוָה, שֶׁרָצָה הָאֵל שֶׁנַּעֲשֶׂה פְּעֻלָּה בְּנַפְשׁוֹתֵינוּ בְּיוֹם שֶׁנַּעֲלֶה לְהִתְחַנֵּךְ בִּכְבוֹד עֲבוֹדָתוֹ הַקְּדוֹשָׁה, תּוֹרָה בָּנוּ גְּדֻלָּה וָשֶׁבַח, וְזֶהוּ מְשִׁיחַת הַשֶּׁמֶן, לְפִי שֶׁעִנְיַן הַמְּשִׁיחָה בַּשֶּׁמֶן הַטּוֹב לֹא יַעֲשׂוּהוּ רַק הַמְּלָכִים וְהַשָּׂרִים הַגְּדוֹלִים.

וְגַם מִיְּסוֹד הַמִּצְוָה לִהְיוֹת מוּכָן בַּבַּיִת לְעֵת הַצֹּרֶךְ לְמַעֲלַת הַמָּקוֹם, כִּי יָדוּעַ עַל דֶּרֶךְ מָשָׁל כִּי מַעֲלַת בַּעַל-הַבַּיִת הַנִּכְבָּד לִהְיוֹת מוּכָן בַּבַּיִת כָּל הַצָּרִיךְ בָּהּ וְלֹא תִתְעַכֵּב שָׁם מְלָאכָה עַד הָכֵן הַצָּרִיךְ אֵלֶיהָ.

דִּינֵי הַמִּצְוָה, כְּגוֹן מַעֲשֵׂה הַשֶּׁמֶן כֵּיצַד נַעֲשָׂה, מוֹר קִנָּמוֹן קִדָּה חֲמֵשׁ-מֵאוֹת שֶׁקֶל מִכָּל אֶחָד, אֶלָּא שֶׁהַקִּנָּמוֹן נִשְׁקָל בֵּין שְׁתֵּי פְעָמִים לְהַרְבּוֹת בּוֹ שְׁתֵּי הַכְרָעוֹת, וּקְנֵה-בֹשֶׂם חֲמִשִּׁים וּמָאתַיִם שֶׁקֶל, וְכֻלָּן נִמְצָאִים בְּאִיֵּי הֹדּוּ, וְשֶׁמֶן-זַיִת שְׁעוּר הִין שֶׁהוּא שְׁנֵים-עָשָׂר לֹג; וְאַחַר שֶׁיִּתְבַּשֵּׁל הַכֹּל כְּדֵי צָרְכּוֹ חוֹזֵר הַכֹּל לְמִדַּת הַשֶּׁמֶן

---

107   1. Descendants of David, over whose coronation there was controversy (so our author writes below, §108). In this paragraph our author follows ShM positive precept §35.

2. The Hebrew has "of the Sanctuary," but it is evident from Talmudic sources (and ShM *ibid.*) that this must be a scribal error (MY).

3. I.e. since the precept remains for every future *kohen gadol* and for certain kings.

4. Since it is quite impossible to measure an amount on a scales with absolute precision, a small amount (boot) is added to tip the scales a bit over. For cinnamon we learn from Exodus 30:23 that it is to be weighed as our author describes (TB K'rithoth 5a, and Rashi).

5. See Rambam MT *hilchoth k'lé ha-mikdash* i 3.

6. Exodus 30:23–24.

7. I.e. a miracle occurred in the making of it: far more than a *hin* of oil could have been absorbed by the ingredients and consumed by the fire in the boiling process; yet after the boiling, the original twelve *log* remained (TJ Sotah viii 3, etc.).

8. Hebrew letters also serve as numbers; in the word *zeh*, the *zayin* = 7, *hé* = 5; TB Horayoth 11b.

[THE PRECEPT OF ANOINTING OIL FOR EACH KOHEN GADOL AND KING]

107 to make the anointing oil in the manner that the Torah ordained to make it—for it is stated, *And you shall make it a holy anointing oil* (Exodus 30:25)—so that it should be prepared for every *kohen gadol* who will be appointed, to be anointed with it: as it is written, *And the kohen who is highest among his brethren, upon whose head the anointing oil is poured* (Leviticus 21:10). Similarly, some kings were to be anointed,[1] and so too the objects and utensils of the *mishkan* (Tabernacle)[2] were anointed with it. However, there will be no need to anoint [the objects and utensils] in the future; instead, they will be sanctified by the [Divine] service. This is why it is written, *this shall be to Me throughout your generations* (Exodus 30:31).[3] So our Sages of blessed memory said in the Midrash *Sifre* (Numbers §146).

At the root of the precept lies the reason that God wished that we should perform an activity with our souls on the day we go up to be initiated and consecrated in the glory of His sacred service, which should manifest greatness and excellence in us—and this is anointing with oil. For the matter of anointing with fine oil is something [generally] done by none but kings and great princes.

It is also a fundamental part of the precept that it [the oil] should be ready in the Temple for any time of need, on account of the exalted nature of the [holy] place. For, to give an analogy, we know it is a mark of distinction for a respected householder that in the house there should be ready whatever may be needed in it, and no task should be delayed there until something needed for it is prepared.

The laws of the precept are, for example, the making of the oil, how it is compounded: myrrh, cinammon and cassia—500 shekels' [weight] of each, except that the cinammon was weighed in two batches, to add two minims of overweight;[4] sweet calamus, 250 shekels' [weight]; all are found in the Indian Islands.[5] Then there was olive oil, in the measure of a *hin*, which is twelve *log*.[6] After all was boiled sufficiently, it was returned entirely to the measure of oil, which was twelve *log*.[7] The mnemonic sign for it is [in the verse], *this*, zeh, *shall be* (Exodus 30:31), the word *zeh* (this) having the numerical value of twelve.[8]

שֶׁהוּא י״ב ל״ג, וְסִימָן יִהְיֶה ז״ה בְּגִימַטְרִיָּא י״ב הֲוֵי; וְיֶתֶר פְּרָטֶיהָ, מְבֹאָרִים בְּפֶרֶק רִאשׁוֹן מִכְּרִיתוֹת.

וְנוֹהֶגֶת בִּזְמַן הַבַּיִת, וְהִיא מִמִּצְווֹת הַמֻּטָּלוֹת עַל הַצִּבּוּר כְּמוֹ בִּנְיַן הַבַּיִת וְכֵלָיו.

[שֶׁלֹּא יָסוּךְ זָר בְּשֶׁמֶן הַמִּשְׁחָה]

קח שֶׁלֹּא לִמְשֹׁחַ בְּשֶׁמֶן הַמִּשְׁחָה שֶׁעָשָׂה מֹשֶׁה אֶלָּא כֹּהֲנִים לְבַד, שֶׁנֶּאֱמַר: עַל בְּשַׂר אָדָם לֹא יִיסָךְ, וְנִתְבָּאֵר בַּכָּתוּב שְׁמִי שֶׁמִּשְׁתַּמֵּשׁ בּוֹ בְּמֵזִיד חַיָּב כָּרֵת, שֶׁנֶּאֱמַר: וַאֲשֶׁר יִתֵּן מִמֶּנּוּ עַל זָר וְנִכְרָת, וְאִם נִמְשַׁח בּוֹ בְּשׁוֹגֵג חַיָּב חַטָּאת קְבוּעָה. פֵּרוּשׁ קְבוּעָה, כְּלוֹמַר שֶׁאֵין חִלּוּק בּוֹ בֵּין הַדַּל וְהֶעָשִׁיר אֶלָּא דָּבָר קָבוּעַ הוּא לַכֹּל.

מִשָּׁרְשֵׁי מִצְוָה זוֹ גַם כֵּן לְהַגְדָּלַת הַבַּיִת וְכָל אֲשֶׁר בָּהּ, וְלָכֵן אֵין רָאוּי לַהֶדְיוֹטוֹת לְהִשְׁתַּמֵּשׁ בְּאוֹתוֹ הַשֶּׁמֶן הַנִּכְבָּד רַק הַנִּבְחָרִים בָּעָם לְבַד שֶׁהֵם כֹּהֲנִים וּמְלָכִים, וּבְכֵן בְּהִמָּנַע הֶהָמוֹן מִמֶּנּוּ יִיקַר בְּעֵינֵיהֶם עַד מְאֹד וְיִתְאַוּוּ אֵלָיו, כִּי גֹדֶל עֶרֶךְ הַדְּבָרִים בְּלֵב רֹב בְּנֵי־אָדָם לְפִי מְעוּט הִמָּצְאָם אֶצְלָם.

מִדִּינֵי הַמִּצְוָה (כְּגוֹן) מַה שֶּׁאָמְרוּ זִכְרוֹנָם לִבְרָכָה שֶׁחַיָּב כָּרֵת וְהַקָּרְבָּן אֵינוֹ עַד שֶׁיָּסוּךְ מִמֶּנּוּ שִׁעוּר זַיִת, וְשֶׁלֹּא חִיְּבוּנוּ הַכָּתוּב אֶלָּא עַל אוֹתוֹ שֶׁעָשָׂה מֹשֶׁה וְלֹא עַל אַחֵר שֶׁיַּעֲשֶׂה שׁוּם אָדָם, וְקַבָּלָה בְּיָדֵינוּ שֶׁנֵּס נַעֲשָׂה בּוֹ שֶׁיַּסְפִּיק לְעוֹלָם.

וּמַה שֶּׁאָמְרוּ זִכְרוֹנָם לִבְרָכָה שֶׁאֵין מוֹשְׁחִין בּוֹ לְדוֹרוֹת כָּל הַכֹּהֲנִים הַמִּתְחַנְּכִים לַעֲבוֹדָה אֶלָּא כֹּהֵן גָּדוֹל וּמְשׁוּחַ מִלְחָמָה וּמַלְכֵי בֵית־דָּוִד, וְכָל שְׁאָר מְלָכִים אֵינָם נִמְשָׁחִין בָּזֶה הַשֶּׁמֶן אֶלָּא בְּשֶׁמֶן אֲפַרְסְמוֹן, וְהַחִלּוּק שֶׁיֵּשׁ בְּמַעֲשֵׂה מְשִׁיחַת הַמֶּלֶךְ לְמַעֲשֵׂה מְשִׁיחַת הַכֹּהֵן. וּמַה שֶּׁאָמְרוּ (זִכְרוֹנָם לִבְרָכָה) שֶׁאֵין

---

§108 1. Paragraph based on Rambam ShM negative precept §84.
2. TB K'rithoth 6b.
3. Ibid. 5a.
4. I.e. that which Moses prepared; ibid. 5b; Horayoth 11b.
5. I.e. the kohen chosen to go with the army and proclaim to the soldiers, before battle, the instructions given in Deuteronomy 20:3 ff.
6. TB K'rithoth 5b, Horayoth 11b (Rambam MT hilchoth k'lé ha-mikdash i 7).
7. Ibid. MT ibid. 9.

⟨406⟩

The rest of its details are clarified in the first chapter of the tractate *K'rithoth*. It is in effect when the Temple is extant; and it is one of the precepts whose obligation lies upon the community, like the construction of the Temple, and its objects and utensils.

108 [THAT AN OUTSIDER SHOULD NOT HAVE ANOINTING OIL APPLIED TO HIMSELF]

not to anoint with the anointing oil that Moses made any but but the *kohanim* alone: for it is stated, *On the flesh of an ordinary man it shall not be poured* (Exodus 30:32); and it is made clear in the Writ that if someone used it deliberately for anointing, he would incur *karéth* [Divine severance of existence]: for it is stated, *or whoever puts any of it on an outsider, he shall be cut off* (Exodus 30:33). If someone was anointed with it unintentionally, he is duty-bound to bring a standard unvarying *ḥattath* (sin-offering), the meaning of "standard" being that there is no difference [in law] between the poor and the rich: rather, it is a standard, set matter for all.[1]

At the root of this precept too lies the principle of magnifying the glory of the Temple and everything in it. It is therefore not fitting for ordinary people, commoners, to make use of that distinguished oil in the Temple, but solely the chosen of the people, i.e. *kohanim* and kings. Then as the mass of people abstains from [using] it, it will be most precious in their eyes, and they will find it desirable. For how great a value things have in the heart of most people, depends on how little it is available to them.

Among the laws of the precept there is, for instance, what the Sages of blessed memory said,[2] that one does not incur the penalty of *karéth* or an offering until he pours the measure of an olive's amount of it; that Scripture imposed the penalties on us only in regard to [the oil] that Moses prepared, and not over any other that anyone else might make;[3] and we have an oral tradition that a miracle occurred with it that it should last perpetually.[4]

Then there is what the Sages of blessed memory said, that through the generations, not all the *kohanim* who became initiated and consecrated for the Divine service were to be anointed with it, but only the *kohen gadol*, the *kohen* anointed for war,[5] and the kings of the House (dynasty) of David. All other kings, though, were not to be anointed with this oil, but with balsam oil.[6] There is, further, the difference between the act of anointing a king and the act of anointing a *kohen*.[7]

ספר החינוך §108-110: ON USING OR MAKING ANOINTING OIL / OR INCENSE

מוֹשְׁחִין מֶלֶךְ בֶּן מֶלֶךְ אֶלָּא אִם־כֵּן יֵשׁ עָלָיו מַחֲלֹקֶת, וְעַל־כֵּן נִמְשַׁח שְׁלֹמֹה; וְיֶתֶר פְּרָטֶיהָ, מְבֹאָרִים בְּפֶרֶק שְׁלִישִׁי מִכְּרֵיתוֹת.

וְנוֹהֶגֶת מִצְוָה זוֹ שֶׁל אִסּוּר מְשִׁיחַת הַשֶּׁמֶן בְּכָל מָקוֹם שֶׁיִּמָּצֵא וּבְכָל זְמָן בִּזְכָרִים וּנְקֵבוֹת. וְעוֹבֵר עָלֶיהָ וְסָךְ מִמֶּנּוּ כַּזַּיִת בְּמֵזִיד חַיָּב כָּרֵת, בְּשׁוֹגֵג חַיָּב חַטָּאת קְבוּעָה.

[שֶׁלֹּא לַעֲשׂוֹת בְּמַתְכֹּנֶת שֶׁמֶן הַמִּשְׁחָה]

קט שֶׁלֹּא לַעֲשׂוֹת שֶׁמֶן הַמִּשְׁחָה, שֶׁנֶּאֱמַר: וּבְמַתְכֻּנְתּוֹ לֹא תַעֲשׂוּ.

מִשָּׁרְשֵׁי הַמִּצְוָה, מַה שֶּׁכָּתַבְנוּ בְּאִסּוּר מְשִׁיחָתוֹ. עִנְיַן הַמִּצְוָה שֶׁאָמְרוּ זִכְרוֹנָם לִבְרָכָה, כִּי מֵעוֹלָם לֹא נַעֲשָׂה מִמֶּנּוּ אֶלָּא אוֹתוֹ שֶׁעָשָׂה מֹשֶׁה בַּמִּדְבָּר, וְאָמְרוּ שֶׁנֵּס נַעֲשָׂה בּוֹ שֶׁכֻּלּוֹ קַיָּם לֶעָתִיד לָבוֹא, וּמַה שֶּׁהוֹצִיאוּ מִמֶּנּוּ לִמְשִׁיחַת הַמִּשְׁכָּן וְכֵלָיו, הַבְּרָכָה הִשְׁלִימוֹ.

וְשֶׁאֵין חַיָּבִין עַל עֲשִׂיָּתוֹ אֶלָּא בְּשֶׁעֲשָׂהוּ בְּסַכּוּם סַמְמָנָיו, וְזֶהוּ לְשׁוֹן "בְּמַתְכֻּנְתּוֹ" מִלְּשׁוֹן חֶשְׁבּוֹן, כְּלוֹמַר בְּחֶשְׁבּוֹן סַמְמָנָיו. וְיֶתֶר פְּרָטֶיהָ, מְבֹאָרִים בְּפֶרֶק רִאשׁוֹן מִכְּרֵיתוֹת.

וְנוֹהֶגֶת מִצְוָה זוֹ שֶׁל אִסּוּר עֲשִׂיַּת הַשֶּׁמֶן בְּכָל מָקוֹם וּבְכָל זְמַן בִּזְכָרִים וּנְקֵבוֹת, וְעוֹבֵר עָלֶיהָ וְעָשָׂה מִמֶּנּוּ בְּמֵזִיד כַּזַּיִת חַיָּב כָּרֵת, בְּשׁוֹגֵג חַיָּב חַטָּאת קְבוּעָה.

[שֶׁלֹּא לַעֲשׂוֹת בְּמַתְכֹּנֶת הַקְּטֹרֶת]

קי שֶׁלֹּא לַעֲשׂוֹת קְטֹרֶת כִּדְמוּת קְטֹרֶת, כְּלוֹמַר שֶׁתִּהְיֶה הַרְכָּבָתוֹ עַל עִנְיַן אוֹתָן

---

8. Because Adonijah tried to seize the crown; TB K'rithoth 5b, Horayoth 11b.
9. The term is explained in the first paragraph.

§109 1. TB K'rithoth 5b, Horayoth 11b.
2. TB K'rithoth 5a.
3. See §108, first paragraph, end.

And [we have] what the Sages of blessed memory said, that a king who was the son of a king was not to be anointed unless there was controversy about him; for this reason Solomon was anointed.[8] [These] and the rest of its details are explained in the third chapter of the Talmud tractate *K'rithoth*.

This precept, forbidding anointing with the oil, applies wherever it may be found, at every time, for both man and woman. If someone violates it and pours an olive's amount of it deliberately, he incurs *karéth* [Divine severance of existence]; and if it was done unintentionally, he is obligated to bring a standard, unvarying *hattath* (sin-offering).[9]

[NOT TO MAKE ANOINTING OIL ACCORDING TO THE SCRIPTURAL FORMULA]

109 not to reproduce the anointing oil: for it is stated, *and according to its composition you shall not make any* (Exodus 30:32).

At the root of the precept lies what we have written about the ban on anointing with it (§108). Concerning the precept, our Sages of blessed memory said[1] that never was any of it produced but that which Moses made in the wilderness. And they said[1] that a miracle was wrought with it, so that all of it will exist in the [Messianic] future; whatever was taken out (used) from it for anointing the *mishkan* (Tabernacle) and its objects and utensils, the [Divine] blessing replenished it.

Then [there is the law] that one does not become guilty for producing it unless he makes it with the exact amount of its ingredients:[2] for this is the meaning of "according to its composition" (*ibid.*)—in the sense of a sum or reckoning, i.e. according to the reckoning of its ingredients. The rest of its details are explained in chapter 1 of the tractate *K'rithoth*.

This precept, of the ban on producing the oil, applies in every place and every time, for both man and woman. If someone violated it and made an olive's amount of it deliberately, intentionally, he would deserve *karéth* [Divine severance of existence]; if it was unintentional, he would be obligated to bring a standard unvarying *hattath* (sin-offering).[3]

[THE PROHIBITION AGAINST MAKING INCENSE ACCORDING TO THE TORAH'S FORMULA]

110 not to make incense in the form of [the original] incense, i.e. with its composition according to those weights, and intending to

§110–111: ON MAKING INCENSE / ON FOOD FROM AN IDOL'S OFFERING

הַמִּשְׁקָלִים וְיִתְכַּוֵּן לְהַקְטִיר עַצְמוֹ בָּהּ, שֶׁנֶּאֱמַר: בְּמַתְכֻּנְתָּהּ לֹא תַעֲשׂוּ לָכֶם, וְנֶאֱמַר עָלֶיהָ: אִישׁ אֲשֶׁר יַעֲשֶׂה כָמוֹהָ לְהָרִיחַ בָּהּ, כְּלוֹמַר שֶׁיִּתְכַּוֵּן בַּעֲשִׂיָּתָהּ לְהַקְטִיר עַצְמוֹ.

מִשָּׁרְשֵׁי הַמִּצְוָה, מַה שֶּׁכָּתַבְנוּ בְּאִסּוּר מְשִׁיחַת הַשֶּׁמֶן.

מִדִּינֵי הַמִּצְוָה, מַה שֶּׁאָמְרוּ זִכְרוֹנָם לִבְרָכָה שֶׁהָעוֹשָׂהּ אוֹתָהּ לְהִתְלַמֵּד אוֹ לְמָכְרָהּ לַצִּבּוּר פָּטוּר; וְהָעוֹשָׂה אֲפִלּוּ קְצָת מִמֶּנָּה, כָּל זְמַן שֶׁנַּעֲשָׂה אוֹתוֹ קְצָת לְפִי מִשְׁקֹלֶת הַקְּטֹרֶת שֶׁחַיָּב. וּמַה שֶּׁאָמְרוּ שֶׁהַקְּטֹרֶת הָיְתָה נַעֲשֵׂית בִּזְמַן הַבַּיִת בְּכָל שָׁנָה וְשָׁנָה, וְאִם חָסַר הָעוֹשֶׂה אוֹתָהּ אַחַת מִסַּמְמָנֶיהָ חַיָּב מִיתָה, וְיֶתֶר פְּרָטֶיהָ, מְבֹאָרִים בְּפֶרֶק א׳ מִכְּרִיתוֹת.

וְנוֹהֶגֶת מִצְוָה זוֹ שֶׁל אִסּוּר עֲשִׂיָּתָהּ בְּכָל מָקוֹם וּבְכָל זְמַן בִּזְכָרִים וּנְקֵבוֹת. וְעוֹבֵר עָלֶיהָ וְעָשָׂה מִמֶּנָּה לְפִי מִשְׁקֹלָהּ לְהָרִיחַ בָּהּ בְּמֵזִיד חַיָּב כָּרֵת, בְּשׁוֹגֵג חַיָּב חַטָּאת קְבוּעָה. אֲבָל הַמֵּרִיחַ בָּהּ לְבַד וְלֹא עֲשָׂאָהּ אֵינוֹ חַיָּב כָּרֵת אֶלָּא דִּינוֹ כְּדִין כָּל הַנֶּהֱנֶה מִן הַהֶקְדֵּשׁ.

[שֶׁלֹּא לֶאֱכֹל וְלִשְׁתּוֹת תִּקְרֹבֶת עֲבוֹדָה זָרָה]

קיא שֶׁלֹּא לֶאֱכֹל וְלִשְׁתּוֹת תִּקְרֹבֶת עֲבוֹדָה זָרָה, שֶׁנֶּאֱמַר: הִשָּׁמֶר לְךָ פֶּן תִּכְרֹת בְּרִית לְיוֹשֵׁב הָאָרֶץ וְכוּ׳ וְזָבְחוּ לֵאלֹהֵיהֶם וְקָרָא לְךָ וְאָכַלְתָּ מִזִּבְחוֹ.

מִשָּׁרְשֵׁי הַמִּצְוָה, לְהַרְחִיק, וּלְסַלֵּק כָּל עִנְיַן עֲבוֹדָה זָרָה וְכָל דָּבָר הַמְיֻחָס אֵלֶיהָ מִבֵּין עֵינֵינוּ וּמִמַּחְשַׁבְתֵּנוּ, וּבִיסוֹד רִחוּק הָעֲבוֹדָה זָרָה כָּתַבְנוּ לְמַעְלָה מַה שֶּׁיָּדַעְנוּ בּוֹ.

מִדִּינֵי הַמִּצְוָה, מַה שֶּׁאָמְרוּ זִכְרוֹנָם לִבְרָכָה שֶׁכָּל דָּבָר שֶׁעָשׂוּ מִמֶּנּוּ תִּקְרֹבֶת

---

§110   1. So Rambam ShM negative precept §85, based on TB P'saḥim 26a.

2. TB K'rithoth 5a; MT hilchoth k'lé ha-mikdash ii 10. These have l'mos'rah latzibbur, "to transmit it to the public"; but our reading is in all four manuscripts consulted and in the first edition, and thus may well be our author's paraphrase rather than a scribal error.

3. I.e. if he made it for his own use; TB ibid. MT ibid. 9.

4. TB K'rithoth 6a; MT ibid. 1.

5. TB ibid. MT ibid. 8. TB Yoma 53a indicates that this refers to the kohen who burns the incense in the Sanctuary. A compounder who omitted an ingredient would cause the sin, but would not commit it.

6. I.e. even if he did not actually smell the incense (Rambam MT hilchoth k'lé ha-mikdash ii 9); see Kessef Mishneh there, however, that one incurs the penalty only if he makes at least enough for a day's supply at the Sanctuary, to burn morning and evening; or, according to Rashi, half a day's supply).

7. See §108, first paragraph, end.

8. I.e. of the holy incense made for the Sanctuary.

9. TB K'rithoth 6a; MT ibid. 10.

⟨410⟩

burn it oneself as incense. For it is stated, *according to its composition, you shall not make for yourselves* (Exodus 30:37); and it was stated further about this, *Whoever shall make any like it to inhale its perfume* (*ibid.* 38)—i.e. if he intends in making it to burn it himself.[1]

At the root of the precept lies the thought that we have written about the ban on anointing with the oil (§108).

Among the laws of the precept there is what the Sages of blessed memory said,[2] that if someone makes it in order to train himself or to sell it to the public, he is free of guilt. But if a person made even a bit of it, as long as that bit was made according to the measurements [proportions] of the [holy] incense, he is guilty.[3] There is, further, their teaching[4] that when the Temple was in existence, the incense would be made every single year. And if the person making it left out [even] one of its ingredients, he deserved death [at Heaven's hands].[5] The rest of its details are explained in chapter 1 of the tractate *K'rithoth*.

This precept, of the prohibition against making it, is in force in every place, at every time, for both man and woman. If a person violated it and made some of it according to its composition in order to inhale its scent—if he did it deliberately [knowing it was forbidden] he would incur *karéth* [Divine severance of existence];[6] if he did it inadvertently, he would be duty-bound to bring a standard unvarying *ḥattath* (sin-offering).[7] However, if someone merely inhaled its scent[8] but did not make it, he would not deserve *karéth*; rather, he would incur the penalty of a person who derives benefit from the sacred.[9]

[THE BAN ON EATING OR DRINKING ANYTHING FROM AN OFFERING TO AN IDOL]

111 not to eat or drink of anything offered up to an idol: for it is stated, *Take heed to yourself, lest you make a covenant with the inhabitants of the land ... and they sacrifice to their gods, and they call you, and you will eat of their sacrifice* (Exodus 34:12, 15).

At the root of the precept lies the purpose to remove and eradicate the whole matter of idolatry and everything related to it, from between our eyes and our thoughts. And about the fundamental principle of being rid of idolatry we wrote above (§26) what we knew of it.

Among the laws of the precept there are [for example] what our Sages of blessed memory said,[1] that anything out of which an offering

§111: THE BAN ON FOOD & DRINK FROM AN OFFERING TO AN IDOL

לַעֲבוֹדָה זָרָה אָסוּר וַאֲפִלּוּ מַיִם וָמֶלַח, כְּלוֹמַר שֶׁאַף־עַל־פִּי שֶׁמַּיִם וָמֶלַח הֵם דְּבָרִים קַלִּים וְאֶפְשָׁר לוֹמַר בָּהֶם שֶׁאֵינָם לְתִקְרֹבֶת וְלֹא הִנִּיחוּם לִפְנֵי הָעֲבוֹדָה זָרָה לְכַוָּנַת כָּבוֹד כְּלָל, אַף־עַל־פִּי־כֵן אָסוּר.

וְכֵן אָסְרוּ זִכְרוֹנָם לִבְרָכָה לְרֹב רִחוּק זֶה כָּל יַיִן שֶׁל גּוֹיִם אַף־עַל־פִּי שֶׁלֹּא יָדַעְנוּ בּוֹ שֶׁנִּסְּכוּהוּ לַעֲבוֹדָה זָרָה, וְהוּא נִקְרָא לָהֶם סְתָם יֵינָם, אֶלָּא שֶׁחִלְּקוּ זִכְרוֹנָם לִבְרָכָה בֵּין הַנֶּסֶךְ לִסְתָם יֵינָם, שֶׁהַיָּדוּעַ אָסוּר בְּמַשֶּׁהוּ מִן הַתּוֹרָה וְלוֹקִין עָלָיו, מִדִּכְתִיב: וְלֹא יִדְבַּק בְּיָדְךָ מְאוּמָה מִן הַחֵרֶם, וּבִסְתָם יֵינָם אֵין אִסּוּרָם אֶלָּא מִדִּבְרֵיהֶם אֵין בְּחִיּוּבוֹ שְׁתִיָּתוֹ אֶלָּא מַכַּת מַרְדוּת, וּבִשְׁתִיָּתָה מִמֶּנּוּ רְבִיעִית, אֲבָל בְּפָחוֹת מֵרְבִיעִית אֵין בּוֹ מַכַּת מַרְדוּת, וּמִכָּל מָקוֹם אָסוּר הוּא מִדִּבְרֵיהֶם אֲפִלּוּ בְּמַשֶּׁהוּ בַּהֲנָאָה.

וּבִשְׁאָר דְּבָרִים שֶׁבָּעוֹלָם חוּץ מִיַּיִן לֹא הֶחְמִירוּ זִכְרוֹנָם לִבְרָכָה לֶאֱסֹר כָּל הַנִּמְצָא בְּיַד אָדָם בִּסְתָם מִפְּנֵי חֲשַׁשׁ תִּקְרֹבֶת עֲבוֹדָה זָרָה אוֹ חֲשַׁשׁ עֲבוֹדָה זָרָה עַצְמָהּ זוּלָתִי בִּדְבָרִים שֶׁבָּהֶם נָכְרִי עֲשָׂאָם לְכָךְ, כְּגוֹן מַה שֶּׁאָמְרוּ זִכְרוֹנָם לִבְרָכָה בְּעִנְיַן צְלָמִים, שֶׁסְּתָם הַצְּלָמִים לַעֲבוֹדָה זָרָה יַעֲשׂוּם, וּלְפִיכָךְ אָסְרוּ אוֹתָם; וַאֲפִלּוּ הַמּוֹצֵא אוֹתָם מֻשְׁלָכִים אֵינוֹ רַשַּׁאי לִטְלָם כִּי־אִם בְּתָנָאִים יְדוּעִים, כְּמוֹ שֶׁפֵּרְשׁוּ הֵם זִכְרוֹנָם לִבְרָכָה. וְכֵן נִרְאֶה בְּוַדַּאי בְּכָל דָּבָר שֶׁהַיִּשְׂרָאֵל חוֹשֵׁב שֶׁנַּעֲשָׂה בּוֹ תִּקְרֹבֶת שֶׁאָסוּר לוֹ לְלָקְחוֹ מֵהֶם.

וְעוֹד עָשׂוּ הַרְחָקוֹת רַבּוֹת בְּעִנְיַן הַיַּיִן לְפִי שֶׁהוּא עִקָּר שִׂמְחַת הַזֶּבַח לָהֶם, וְעוֹד שֶׁהַתּוֹרָה הִזְכִּירָה אִסּוּרוֹ בְּפֵרוּשׁ, כְּמוֹ שֶׁכָּתוּב בְּפָרָשַׁת הַאֲזִינוּ: יִשְׁתּוּ יֵין

---

§111 1. TB 'Avodah Zarah 51b.
2. Ibid. 31a.
3. Ibid. 73a; Rambam ShM negative precept §194, MT *hilchoth ma'achaloth 'asuroth* xvii 1–2.
4. I.e. the number of lashes is at the discretion of the *beth din*.
5. Rambam MT *ibid.* 3.
6. TB 'Avodah Zarah 41a; MT *hilchoth 'avodath kochavim* vii 7.
7. I.e. the Torah equates the two: just as the law about "the fat of their sacrifices" is that any benefit from it is banned, so is the law about their wine of libation.

⟨412⟩

to an idol was made, is [thus] forbidden—even water and salt. In other words, even though water and salt are minor, insignificant things, so that it is possible to say of them that they are not [fit] for an offering, and they were not set before the idol with the intention of honoring it at all—they are nevertheless forbidden. Similarly, for the sake of keeping it so very distant, our Sages of blessed memory banned all wine of non-Jews, even if we do not know about it that it was poured as a libation to an idol. This is what is called, in regard to them, *s'tham yénam*, their general, unknown wine.[2] However, our Sages of blessed memory did differentiate between known wine of libation and their general, unknown wine: With known wine of libation, the slightest amount of it is forbidden by the law of the Torah, and whiplashes are to be given on account of it—since it is written, *and let nought of the banned devoted thing cleave to your hand* (Deuteronomy 13:18);[3] but with their general, unknown wine, which is forbidden only by the word of the Sages, for the guilt of drinking it only "whiplashes of disobedience" are given,[4] and that [only] if one drank a *r'vi'ith*, a fourth of a *log*;[5] for less than a *r'vi'ith*, though, no "lashes of disobedience" are given. Nevertheless, by the ruling of the Sages it is forbidden to benefit from even the slightest amount of it.[5]

In regard to anything else in the world, however, other than wine, our Sages of blessed memory were not stringent, to ban anything of a general, unknown nature that may be found in someone's possession, out of suspicion [that it may have been made] an offering to an idol, or an object of idol-worship itself—except for those things which are recognizable as having been made for this purpose: For instance, as the Sages of blessed memory said about sculptured figures, that in general, sculptured figures were probably made for idol-worship; and therefore they banned them. Even if a person finds them thrown away, he is not allowed to take them, except under certain conditions, as the Sages of blessed memory explained.[6] So it would seem quite certain that if there is anything which an Israelite thinks was made an idolatrous offering, it is forbidden for him to acquire it from them [from heathens].

Our Sages imposed many other barriers as well in regard to wine, for it is a main element in their rejoicing at sacrifices. Moreover, the Torah refers to its forbiddance explicitly, as it is written in *sidrah ha'azinu*, [*who ate the fat of their sacrifices*] *and drank the wine of their drink-offering* (Deuteronomy 32:38).[7] Hence they said, to keep the

§111: THE BAN ON FOOD & DRINK FROM AN OFFERING TO AN IDOL

נְסִיכָם, וְעַל־כֵּן הֶחְמִירוּ זִכְרוֹנָם לִבְרָכָה בּוֹ וְאָמְרוּ לְהַרְחָקַת הָעִנְיָן שֶׁאֲפִלּוּ יַיִן שֶׁל יִשְׂרָאֵל מִיָּד שֶׁיִּגַּע בּוֹ גוֹי יְהֵא אָסוּר אֲפִלּוּ בַּהֲנָאָה.

וְאַל יַקְשֶׁה עָלֶיךָ אֵיךְ יוּכַל הַגּוֹי לֶאֱסֹר יַיִן שֶׁל יִשְׂרָאֵל, וְהָא קַיְמָא לָן אֵין אָדָם אוֹסֵר דָּבָר שֶׁאֵינוֹ שֶׁלּוֹ. שֶׁלֹּא נֶאֱמַר זֶה אֶלָּא כְּגוֹן מִשְׁתַּחֲוֶה לְבֶהֱמַת חֲבֵרוֹ שֶׁלֹּא עָשָׂה מַעֲשֶׂה בְּגוּף הַדָּבָר, אֲבָל כָּל זְמַן שֶׁיַּעֲשֶׂה מַעֲשֶׂה בְּגוּף הַדָּבָר וַאֲפִלּוּ מַעֲשֶׂה מוּעָט כִּי הַאי דִּנְגִיעָה, יֵשׁ לוֹ כֹחַ לֶאֱסֹר דָּבָר שֶׁאֵינוֹ שֶׁלּוֹ מִדְּרַבָּנָן, שֶׁהֶחְמִירוּ בַּדָּבָר, אֲבָל לֹא מִדְּאוֹרַיְיתָא עַד שֶׁיַּעֲשֶׂה מַעֲשֶׂה גָדוֹל כְּמוֹ שְׁחִיטַת בְּהֵמָה, שֶׁהוּא מַעֲשֶׂה גָדוֹל. וְכֵן אִם נִסֵּךְ הַיַּיִן לִפְנֵי הָעֲבוֹדָה זָרָה מַמָּשׁ גַּם זֶה הוּא מַעֲשֶׂה גָדוֹל.

אֲבָל נְגִיעָה בְיַיִן שֶׁלֹּא בִּפְנֵי עֲבוֹדָה זָרָה מַעֲשֶׂה מוּעָט הוּא, וּמִכֵּיוָן שֶׁהוּא מוּעָט וְאֵין הָאִסּוּר אֶלָּא מִדְּרַבָּנָן הִתִּירוּ זִכְרוֹנָם לִבְרָכָה לִטֹּל תַּשְׁלוּם מַה שֶּׁאָסַר מִיַּד הָאוֹסֵר, וְאַף־עַל־פִּי הַדָּבָר שֶׁאָסַר שֶׁהֶחְמִירוּ לְאָסְרוֹ בַּהֲנָאָה, בְּתַשְׁלוּמִין לֹא הֶחְמִירוּ לְפִי שֶׁאֵין הַתַּשְׁלוּמִין אֶלָּא כְּעֵין תַּשְׁלוּמֵי נֶזֶק וְאֵינוֹ נֶהֱנֶה מִן הַדָּבָר הָאָסוּר אֶלָּא שֶׁלּוֹקֵחַ תַּשְׁלוּמֵי נִזְקוֹ מִיַּד הָאוֹסֵר.

וְכֵן הֶחְמִירוּ זִכְרוֹנָם לִבְרָכָה הַרְבֵּה בְּרִחוּק יַיִן שֶׁנִּתְנַסֵּךְ מַמָּשׁ לַעֲבוֹדָה זָרָה אוֹ בְּכָל דָּבָר שֶׁהוּא מֵעֲבוֹדָה זָרָה יוֹתֵר מִכָּל אִסּוּרִין שֶׁבַּתּוֹרָה, שֶׁאֵין לְךָ דָּבָר שֶׁאָסוּר בַּהֲנָאָה בְּכָל הַתּוֹרָה שֶׁנִּתְעָרֵב בְּהֶתֵּר וְאֵינֶנּוּ נִכָּר, שֶׁלֹּא יְהֵא לוֹ תַּקָּנָה בַּהֲנָאָתוֹ, וַאֲפִלּוּ לַח בְּלַח, עִם מַה שֶּׁאָמַר רַבָּן שִׁמְעוֹן בֶּן גַּמְלִיאֵל בַּגְּמָרָא שֶׁיִּמָּכֵר כֻּלּוֹ לְגוֹיִים חוּץ מִדְּמֵי הָאִסּוּר שֶׁבּוֹ, וְהוּא שֶׁיְּהֵא מִן הַדְּבָרִים שֶׁאֵינָן נִקָּחִין מִן הַגּוֹיִים כְּדֵי שֶׁלֹּא יִכָּשֵׁל בָּהֶן שׁוּם אָדָם מִיִּשְׂרָאֵל שֶׁיִּקָּחֵנוּ מִן הַגּוֹי, אֲבָל בְּיַיִן נֶסֶךְ גָּמוּר

---

8. TB 'Avodah Zarah 58a.
9. So TB P'saḥim 90a, Y'vamoth 83b.
10. So Rashi, TB Ḥullin 40b, s.v. *'én 'adam*.
11. TB 'Avodah Zarah 59b.
12. *Ibid.* 74a.

matter far removed, that even the wine of a Jew, so soon as a heathen touches it, becomes forbidden even to derive benefit from it.[8]

Now, let this not be a difficulty for you: How can a heathen make an Israelite's wine forbidden? We have an established rule that a man cannot impose a ban on something that is not his![9] We can apply this rule only, for example, when someone prostrates himself [in worship] to the domestic animal of his fellow, in which case he did no direct action with the object itself. But so long as he does any action with the object itself, even a minimal action like the matter of touching, he has the power to make something that is not his forbidden—by the ruling of the Sages, who were stringent in the matter; but not by the law of the Torah, until he does some major action, like the ritual slaying of an animal, which is a major action [indeed]. So too, if he actually poured the wine in libation before an idol: this too is a major action.[10]

Merely touching the wine, though, not in the presence of an idol, is a small, minor action. And since it is minor, and the forbiddance is only by the ruling of the Sages, they (of blessed memory) permitted a person to exact compensation from the man who brought on the ban, for whatever he made forbidden.[11] Even though they were stringent about the object itself that he made forbidden, to prohibit deriving any benefit from it, about compensation they were not stringent, since the compensation is only akin to the payment of damages for injury. He does not benefit from the forbidden object, but rather takes recompense for his damage (loss) from the one who brought on the ban.

So too, our Sages of blessed memory were far more stringent in removing from us wine that was actually used in libation for an idol, or anything to do with idolatry, than about anything else forbidden by Torah law. For in the entire Torah you will find nothing whose benefit is forbidden for which, if it became mixed in with permitted matter so that it cannot be recognized, there should be no rectification to allow benefiting from it, even if it is liquid mixed into liquid—in accordance with the teaching of R. Shim'on b. Gamli'él in the Talmud,[12] that it may be sold entirely to a heathen, except for the price of the forbidden matter in it. This applies, though, only if it is one of the things which are not to be bought from heathens, so that no Israelite whatever will [possibly] come to grief over it by buying it [in turn] from the heathen. However, for pure wine of libation and

⟨415⟩

§111: THE BAN ON FOOD & DRINK FROM AN OFFERING TO AN IDOL

וּבְכָל דִּבְרֵי עֲבוֹדָה זָרָה אֵין לָהֶם תַּקָּנָה בִּמְכָר כֻּלּוֹ לַגּוֹי וְכוּלֵּי, וְכָל שֶׁכֵּן שֶׁאֵין לָהֶן תַּקָּנָה בְּיוֹלִיךְ הֲנָאָה לְיָם הַמֶּלַח.

וּמִיהוּ דַּוְקָא בְּשֶׁנִּתְעָרֵב יֵין נֶסֶךְ מַמָּשׁ, וַאֲפִלּוּ טִפָּה מִמֶּנּוּ, בְּקַנְקָן מַחֲזִיק כַּמָּה סְאִין, הוּא דִּין שֶׁאֵין לוֹ תַּקָּנָה לַהֲנָאָתוֹ לְעוֹלָם, אֲבָל אִם נִתְעָרֵב מִמֶּנּוּ חָבִית אַחַת בְּחָבִיּוֹת אֲחֵרוֹת שֶׁל יַיִן כָּשֵׁר, כֵּיוָן שֶׁלֹּא נִתְעָרֵב גּוּף הָאִסּוּר מַמָּשׁ אֶלָּא כָּל אֶחָד בִּפְנֵי עַצְמוֹ הוּא עוֹמֵד, יֵשׁ לוֹ תַּקָּנָה בְּתַקָּנַת רַבָּן שִׁמְעוֹן בֶּן גַּמְלִיאֵל שֶׁיִּמָּכֵר כֻּלּוֹ לַגּוֹיִים וְכוּלֵּי. וְכֵן בִּסְתַם יֵינָם יֶשׁ לָנוּ תַּקָּנָה בְּתַקָּנַת רַבָּן שִׁמְעוֹן בֶּן גַּמְלִיאֵל, וַאֲפִלּוּ נִתְעָרֵב מַמָּשׁ, כְּדִין שְׁאָר אִסּוּרִין, כֵּיוָן שֶׁאֵינוֹ יֵין נֶסֶךְ גָּמוּר.

וְעוֹד יֶשׁ לָדַעַת שֶׁכָּל אִסּוּרִין שֶׁבַּתּוֹרָה שֶׁאוֹסְרִין תַּעֲרָבְתָן בַּהֲנָאָה אֵין אוֹסְרִין אוֹתָן אֶלָּא-אִם-כֵּן יֵשׁ מִן הָאִסּוּר שֶׁנִּתְעָרֵב בַּהֶתֵּר בִּכְדֵי נְתִינַת טַעַם בַּהֶתֵּר, זוּלָתִי אִם יִהְיֶה אוֹתוֹ אִסּוּר דָּבָר חָשׁוּב, כִּי כָּל דָּבָר חָשׁוּב כְּגוֹן חֲתִיכָה הָרְאוּיָה לְהִתְכַּבֵּד וְכַיּוֹצֵא בָהּ אוֹסְרִין בְּכָל-שֶׁהֵן, אֲבָל כָּל שֶׁאֵינוֹ דָּבָר חָשׁוּב אֵינוֹ אוֹסֵר תַּעֲרָבְתּוֹ בַּהֲנָאָה אֶלָּא-אִם-כֵּן יִהְיֶה בּוֹ בִּכְדֵי נְתִינַת טַעַם, כְּמוֹ שֶׁאָמַרְנוּ, חוּץ מִיֵּין נֶסֶךְ וְכָל עִנְיְנֵי עֲבוֹדָה זָרָה שֶׁאוֹסְרִין בְּמַשֶּׁהוּ בַּהֲנָאָה כָּל שֶׁנִּתְעָרֵב עִמָּהֶם. וְאֵין שׁוּם דָּבָר אַחֵר בָּעוֹלָם יוֹצֵא מִכְּלָל זֶה חוּץ מִכִּלְאֵי הַכֶּרֶם וְחָמֵץ בְּפֶסַח לָדַעַת מִקְצָת מְפָרְשִׁים, שֶׁהֵן בַּהֲנָאָה תַּעֲרָבְתָּן בְּאֶחָד וּמָאתַיִם בֵּין בְּמִינָן בֵּין שֶׁלֹּא בְמִינָן, וּתְרוּמָה בְּאֶחָד וּמֵאָה.

וּלְעִנְיַן הַתַּקָּנָה שֶׁיֵּשׁ לָהֶם כְּבָר אָמַרְנוּ כִּי לְכָל הָאִסּוּרִין יֵשׁ תַּקָּנָה בְּתַקָּנַת רַבָּן

---

13. I.e. any large amount.
14. On the last two paragraphs, see TB 'Avodah Zarah 74a; *tosafoth* to Yevamoth 81b, s.v. *kulan*; Rashi, 'Avodah Zarah 49b, s.v. *'aval ḥavith*; Rambam MT *hilchoth ma'achaloth 'asuroth* xvi 28–29.
15. TB Ḥullin 100a.
16. R. Aaron haLévi, cited by Ritba to TB 'Avodah Zarah 74a.
17. Mishnah, 'Orlah ii 1. (The correct reading of *t'rumah* is found in a manuscript of 1345—MS Casanatense 134. The editions read *'orlah*, or "and it retains its significance.") MH notes that the preceding phrase "or another kind" must be the result of a scribal error and should be expunged, for when mixed with food of another kind, the forbidden ingredients become null and void if there is sixty times as much of the other kind.

⟨416⟩

all things [used] in idolatry there is no way of saving the situation by selling it all to a heathen, etc. And all the more certainly can there be no amends for it by taking the profit [from it to throw] into the Dead Sea.

Yet it is only when wine of libation itself, if only a drop of it, became mixed into a wine-vessel containing several se'ah,[13] that the law holds that there is no way of repairing matters ever to be able to benefit from it. But if a jug of it became mixed up with other jugs, containing kosher [permissible] wine, since the actual forbidden matter itself did not become merged or blended, but rather each [quantity] remained by itself, the matter can be set right by the rectification of R. Shim'on b. Gamli'él—that it should all be sold to heathens, etc. So too, for their general, unknown wine we can make matters right by the rectification of R. Shim'on b. Gamli'él—and this even if it was actually mixed in [with kosher wine], as the law is for other forbidden foods, since it is not absolute wine of libation.[14]

Now, you should also know that when any foods banned by Torah law make other foods forbidden by being mixed into them, they do not thus make them forbidden unless enough of the prohibited element merged into the permissible matter to give the permitted food a taste [affect its flavor]—unless [alternatively] that forbidden element is something significant [by itself]; for all significant things, such as a portion fit to be served with pride,[15] etc., bring forbiddance [to their mixture] in any amount. However, anything that is not itself of significance does not make it forbidden to have any benefit from its mixture unless there was enough of it to give [add] a taste, as we have stated—except for wine of libation and whatever is connected with idolatry: These prohibit deriving benefit from anything into which they become mixed in any amount. There is nothing else in the world which forms an exception to this rule, except mixed produce grown in a vineyard (§ 549) and *hametz* during Passover, in the view of some authorities,[16] who forbid having any benefit from something into which they become mixed in the proportion of one part in 201, whether they were mixed with their own kind or another kind [of food]; and *t'rumah*, [which retains its significance] at one part in 101.[17]

As to what way of saving the situation there is for them, we have stated earlier that for all forbidden foods [in cases of mixture] matters can be amended by the rectification of R. Shim'on b. Gamli'él, except

§111: THE BAN ON FOOD & DRINK FROM AN OFFERING TO AN IDOL

שִׁמְעוֹן בֶּן גַּמְלִיאֵל חוּץ מִכָּל אִסּוּרֵי עֲבוֹדָה זָרָה שֶׁנִּתְעָרֵב גּוּף הָאָסוּר מַמָּשׁ שֶׁאֵין לוֹ שׁוּם תַּקָּנָה לְעוֹלָם, וְזֶהוּ מֵחֹמֶר עֲבוֹדָה זָרָה.

וַהֲפֹךְ וַהֲפֹךְ בַּגְּמָרָא, כִּי כָל זֶה תִּמְצָא בָהּ מְבֹאָר עִם הַפֵּרוּשִׁים הַטּוֹבִים, וּשְׁמֹר הַדְּבָרִים כִּי בְהַרְבֵּה מְקוֹמוֹת בַּתַּלְמוּד תִּצְטָרֵךְ אֲלֵיהֶן, וְעַל־כֵּן הֶאֱרַכְתִּי בָהֶן שֶׁלֹּא כְמִנְהָגִי בְּקוּנְדְּרֵיסִין אֵלּוּ.

וְעוֹד הִרְחִיקוּנוּ זִכְרוֹנָם לִבְרָכָה מֵאִסּוּר יֵין נֶסֶךְ לוֹמַר שֶׁאֲפִלּוּ שֵׁכָר שֶׁל יֵין נֶסֶךְ יְהֵא אָסוּר בַּהֲנָאָה, גַּם הִפְלִיגוּ בְּרִחוּקוֹ לוֹמַר שֶׁאֲפִלּוּ הַנִּשְׁכָּר לִשְׁבֹּר חָבִיּוֹת יֵין נֶסֶךְ שֶׁ[מָּא] שְׂכָרוֹ אָסוּר מִפְּנֵי שֶׁהוּא רוֹצֶה בְקִיּוּמוֹ זְמַן מוּעָט, כְּלוֹמַר שֶׁרוֹצֶה שֶׁיִּהְיֶה קַיָּם הַיַּיִן בֶּחָבִיּוֹת עַד שֶׁיִּשְׁבְּרֵם הוּא כְּדֵי שֶׁיַּרְוִיחַ שְׂכָרוֹ עַל הַשְּׁבִירָה, כִּי הֵם זִכְרוֹנָם לִבְרָכָה רָצוּ לַעֲקֹר מִמַּחֲשַׁבְתֵּנוּ שֶׁלֹּא נִהְיֶה חֲפֵצִים בְּקִיּוּמוֹ אֲפִלּוּ רֶגַע אֶחָד לָרֹב מְאוּסֵנוּ בְּכָל מִינֵי עֲבוֹדָה זָרָה. (וְהָיְתָה הַתְּשׁוּבָה: יִשְׁבֹּר וְתָבֹא עָלָיו בְּרָכָה שֶׁמְּמַעֵט אֶת הַתִּפְלָה.)

וְיֶתֶר פְּרָטֶיהָ הָרַבִּים, כְּגוֹן מִי עוֹשֵׂה יֵין נֶסֶךְ לְאָסְרוֹ בַּהֲנָאָה, וּמִי אוֹסְרוֹ בִּשְׁתִיָּה דַּוְקָא, וּמֵאֵימָתַי נַעֲשֶׂה יֵין נֶסֶךְ, וְדִינֵי מַגָּעוֹ שֶׁל גּוֹי בְּכַוָּנָה וְשֶׁלֹּא בְכַוָּנָה, וְכֹחוֹ וְכֹחַ כֹּחוֹ וְסִיּוּעַ יִשְׂרָאֵל עִמּוֹ, וְאֵי זוֹ שְׁמִירָה תַּסְפִּיק לָנוּ בְּיֵינֵנוּ בְּבֵיתוֹ שֶׁל גּוֹי אוֹ בְבֵיתֵנוּ אִם יֵשׁ שָׁם גּוֹי אוֹ בְקָרוֹן וְהִנִּיחַ שָׁם גּוֹי, כְּגוֹן הַנִּכְנָס וְיוֹצֵא, שֶׁמֻּתָּר הַיַּיִן; וְדִינֵי הָאָסוּר שֶׁיֵּשׁ לָנוּ בִּכְלֵי יֵינָן, וְדִינֵי הֶכְשֵׁרָן, וְרַבֵּי הַפְּרָטִים שֶׁבָּאוּ לָנוּ גַּם־כֵּן בִּכְלֵי בִשּׁוּלֵיהֶן וְהוּא הָעִנְיָן הַנִּקְרָא גִּעוּלֵי גוֹיִים, וְדִינֵי רִחוּקֵנוּ שֶׁלֹּא לְשַׁקֵּץ

---

18. Literally, saying; TB 'Abodah Zarah 63b.
19. And he may keep the wages; MT *ibid.* xiii 17. This part in parentheses is not in the old manuscripts; it is apparently a later addition.
20. TB 'Avodah Zarah 55b; MT *ibid.* xi 5.
21. TB *ibid.*
22. *Ibid.* 60a-b, 58b; MT *ibid.*
23. *Ibid.* 72b.
24. *Ibid.* 61a. (The reading "in a coach or wagon"—*b'karon*—is from the old manuscripts; the editions have *b'fikadon*, "left for safekeeping.")
25. *Ibid.* 74b-75b.
26. *Ibid.* 39b, etc.

⟨418⟩

for items banned on account of idolatry, where the banned substance itself became intermingled, so that there can be no way for them ever of saving the situation—this on account of the seriousness of idol-worship.

Turn and turn about in the Talmud, because all this will you find there, explained, with the good commentaries. And keep these matters [in your memory] as in many places in the Talmud you will have need of them. For this reason I have dwelt at length on them, unlike my usual custom in these pages.

Our Sages of blessed memory removed us yet further from the prohibition on wine of libation by ruling that even from any wages earned on account of wine of libation, it is forbidden to benefit.[18] And they went still further in seeking to keep the matter far away, by asking[18] that even if a person was hired to smash jugs of wine of libation, perhaps the wages should be strictly forbidden, because he desired their existence for a short while: In other words, he wished that the wine should be in the jugs until he would break them, so that he should earn his wages for the breakage. For our Sages of blessed memory wished to extirpate [the entire matter] from our thoughts, that we should not desire its existence for even a moment, on account of our great loathing for all kinds of idolatry. (However, the decision was: "Let him break them, and may blessing come upon him,"[19] because he reduces the folly) [of idolatry in the world].

The rest of its many details are, for example: who can make [dedicate] wine for libation, so that it becomes forbidden even to benefit from it; and who makes it only forbidden to drink;[20] from when it becomes wine of libation;[21] the laws about the touch (contact) of a heathen, deliberately or unintentionally, by his own force or by a force derived from his power,[22] or if [he had] the help of a Jew with him.[23] [Then there is the law of] what guard or protection is enough for our wine in a heathen's house, or in our house if there is a heathen there; or [if there is wine] in a coach or wagon and one left a heathen there, but, as it happens, he [the Jew] goes in and out—that the wine should be permissible.[24] And there are the laws of the prohibition that obtains for us about a vessel used for their wine, and the laws of making them kosher, fit for use.[25]

There are, too, the many details that were also transmitted to us about a vessel used in their cooking—which is a subject called the cleansing of impure vessels of heathens.[26] Further, we have the laws

§111: THE BAN ON FOOD & DRINK FROM AN OFFERING TO AN IDOL

נָפְשֵׁנוּ גַם־כֵּן בְּעִנְיָנִים הַנִּגְרָרִין אַחַר דְּבָרִים אֵלּוּ הַמְּאוּסוֹת, כְּגוֹן מַה שֶּׁאָמְרוּ זִכְרוֹנָם לִבְרָכָה שֶׁלֹּא לֶאֱכֹל וְלִשְׁתּוֹת בְּכֵלִים מְאוּסִים כְּגוֹן כְּלֵי הַשֶּׁתֶן וְהַצּוֹאָה וְקַרְנָא דְאוּמָנָא לְפִי שֶׁיֵּשׁ בַּדָּבָר שִׁקּוּץ הַנֶּפֶשׁ, וְיֶתֶר פְּרָטֶיהָ, מְבֹאָרִים בַּפְּרָקִים הָאַחֲרוֹנִים שֶׁל עֲבוֹדָה זָרָה וּקְצָת מֵהֶן בְּחֻלִּין.

וְנוֹהֶגֶת אַזְהָרָה זוֹ בְּכָל מָקוֹם וּבְכָל זְמַן בִּזְכָרִים וּנְקֵבוֹת. וְעוֹבֵר עָלֶיהָ וְאָכַל כָּל־שֶׁהוּא אוֹ שָׁתָה אֲפִלּוּ טִפַּת יֵין נֶסֶךְ גָּמוּר לוֹקֶה, שֶׁאֵין דִּין דְּבָרִים אֵלּוּ כְּדִין שְׁאָר אִסּוּרֵי מַאֲכָלוֹת, שֶׁהֵן בִּכְזַיִת, וְדִין שְׁתִיָּה בִּרְבִיעִית, לְפִי שֶׁעַל עֲבוֹדָה זָרָה הַזְהִירָה תּוֹרָה וְאָמְרָה: לֹא יִדְבַּק בְּיָדְךָ מְאוּמָה מִן הַחֵרֶם, כְּלוֹמַר וַאֲפִלּוּ כָּל־שֶׁהוּא.

בְּזֹאת הַמַּנִּיעָה שֶׁל יֵין נֶסֶךְ הָרַמְבַּ"ם זִכְרוֹנוֹ לִבְרָכָה וְהָרַמְבַּ"ן זִכְרוֹנוֹ לִבְרָכָה שְׁנֵיהֶם יוֹדוּ שֶׁיֵּשׁ בָּזֶה לָאו וְשֶׁהוּא נִמְנֶה בְּחֶשְׁבּוֹן הַלָּאוִין, אָמְנָם נֶחְלְקוּ בּוֹ בְּעִנְיָן זֶה, כִּי הָרַמְבַּ"ם זִכְרוֹנוֹ לִבְרָכָה יוֹצִיא אִסּוּר יֵין נֶסֶךְ מִן הַמִּקְרָא שֶׁכָּתוּב בְּפָרָשַׁת הַאֲזִינוּ שֶׁנֶּאֱמַר: יִשְׁתּוּ יֵין נְסִיכָם, וְאִסּוּר שְׁאָר תִּקְרֹבֶת עֲבוֹדָה זָרָה מִ"לֹּא יִדְבַּק בְּיָדְךָ מְאוּמָה מִן הַחֵרֶם", וּמִ"לֹּא תָבִיא תוֹעֵבָה", וְהָרַמְבַּ"ן זִכְרוֹנוֹ לִבְרָכָה כָּתַב כִּי מִפָּסוּק זֶה דְ"הִשָּׁמֶר לְךָ וְגוֹמֵר" נִלְמַד אִסּוּר כָּל תִּקְרֹבֶת עֲבוֹדָה זָרָה וְיֵין נֶסֶךְ בִּכְלָל.

וַאֲנִי כָּתַבְתִּי זֶה הַמִּקְרָא כְּדַעְתּוֹ שֶׁלֹּא כְמִנְהָגִי בְּכָל הַסֵּפֶר כִּי כֻלָּם כְּתַבְתִּים כְּדַעַת הָרַמְבַּ"ם זִכְרוֹנוֹ לִבְרָכָה, אֲבָל בְּכָאן רָאִיתִי שֶׁהַפָּסוּק הַזֶּה נָאֶה מְאֹד לִדְרֹשׁ מִמֶּנּוּ הָעִנְיָן, וְעוֹד שֶׁיֵּשׁ בּוֹ אַזְהָרָה, וּכְמוֹ שֶׁאָמְרוּ זִכְרוֹנָם לִבְרָכָה: כָּל מָקוֹם

---

27. TB Makkoth 16b.
28. Rambam MT *hilchoth ma'achaloth 'asuroth* xi 1.
29. Ran[b]am ShM negative precept §194.
30. *Ibid.* See note 7.
31. In his commentary to *ibid.*
32. Which our author quoted at the beginning of the section on this precept.
33. TB 'Eruvin 96a.

about keeping well away, not to make our souls abhorrent, too, in matters which follow in the wake of these vile matters: for instance, the teaching of the Sages of blessed memory not to eat or drink from such loathsome vessels as urinals and chamber pots, and a surgeon's horn [for collecting blood], since the matter involves the abomination of the soul.[27] [These] and its further details are explained in the last chapters of the Talmud tractate *'Avodah Zarah*, and some of them in *Ḥullin*.

This injunction is in effect in every place, at every time, for both man and woman. If a person violates it and eats any amount at all [of food linked with idolatry] or drinks even a drop of absolute wine of libation, he should be given whiplashes.[28] For the law of these matters is unlike the laws of other forbidden foods, where [punishment is due only] for the amount of an olive, and the law of [forbidden] drink, which is punishable in the amount of a *r'vi'ith*—because about idolatry the Torah adjured us and said, *and let none of the banned devoted thing cleave to your hand* (Deuteronomy 13:18), i.e. not even the slightest amount.[29]

About this prohibition on wine of libation, Rambam and Ramban of blessed memory are both in accord that there is a negative precept regarding it, which is counted in the reckoning of the negative precepts. However, they do differ on the subject: for Rambam of blessed memory derives the ban on wine of libation from the verse written in *sidrah ha'azinu*, as it is stated, *and drank the wine of their drink-offering* (Deuteronomy 32:38);[30] the ban on other offerings to idols [he derives] from the verse, *let none of the banned devoted thing cleave to your hand* (ibid. 13:18), and from the verse, *you shall not bring an abomination [into your house, and be accursed like it]* (ibid. 7:26). On the other hand, Ramban of blessed memory wrote[31] that from this verse, *Take heed to yourself*, etc. (Exodus 34:12),[32] we learn the ban on all offerings in idolatry, including wine of libation.

Now, I have written [the precept out of] this verse, in accord with his view, unlike my custom throughout the work; for all of them have I written according to the opinion of Rambam of blessed memory. Here, though, I saw that it is most felicitous to derive and expound the subject from this verse. Moreover, it contains an admonition; and as the Sages of blessed memory said,[33] wherever [in Scripture] it is stated, *take heed*, *lest*, or *do not*, [it is nothing other than a negative precept]. But in the verse, *and drank the wine of their drink-*

שֶׁנֶּאֱמַר בּוֹ הִשָּׁמֶר, פֶּן, וְאַל, וְכוּלֵּי, וּבַפָּסוּק "יִשְׁתּוּ יֵין נְסִיכָם" אֵין שָׁם אַזְהָרָה. גַּם רָאִיתִי גְדוֹלִים מִמְחַשְּׁבֵי הַמִּצְווֹת שֶׁכָּתְבוּ כֵן.

[מִצְוַת שְׁבִיתַת הָאָרֶץ בִּשְׁנַת הַשְּׁמִטָּה]

קיב לְבַטֵּל עֲבוֹדַת הָאָרֶץ בַּשָּׁנָה הַשְּׁבִיעִית, שֶׁנֶּאֱמַר: בֶּחָרִישׁ וּבַקָּצִיר תִּשְׁבֹּת, וּבָא הַפֵּרוּשׁ שֶׁעַל שָׁנָה הַשְּׁבִיעִית נֶאֱמַר, שֶׁנִּצְטַוִּינוּ שֶׁלֹּא לַעֲסֹק בָּהּ כְּלָל בַּעֲבוֹדַת הָאָרֶץ. וְנִכְפְּלָה הַמִּצְוָה בָּזֶה בְּאָמְרוֹ בְּמָקוֹם אַחֵר: שְׁנַת שַׁבָּתוֹן יִהְיֶה לָאָרֶץ, וְכֵן וְשָׁבְתָה הָאָרֶץ שַׁבָּת לַיְיָ. וּכְבָר כָּתַבְתִּי כָּל עִנְיָנָהּ מְשֻׁלָּם לְמַעְלָה בְּסֵדֶר וְאֵלֶּה הַמִּשְׁפָּטִים בְּמִצְוַת "וְהַשְּׁבִיעִית תִּשְׁמְטֶנָּה וּנְטַשְׁתָּהּ", שֶׁבָּאָה לְצַוּוֹת עַל הֶפְקֵר פֵּרוֹת שָׁנָה זוֹ לַכֹּל, וְאַף־עַל־פִּי שֶׁכָּאן הָיָה מְקוֹמוֹ.

[שֶׁלֹּא לֶאֱכֹל בָּשָׂר בְּחָלָב]

קיג שֶׁלֹּא לֶאֱכֹל בָּשָׂר וְחָלָב שֶׁנִּתְבַּשְּׁלוּ בְּיַחַד, שֶׁנֶּאֱמַר: לֹא תְבַשֵּׁל גְּדִי בַּחֲלֵב אִמּוֹ, וְזֶה הַכָּתוּב בָּא לֶאֱסֹר הָאֲכִילָה וְהַהֲנָאָה בְּבָשָׂר בְּחָלָב. וְאַל יִקְשֶׁה עָלֶיךָ אִם־כֵּן לָמָּה לֹא נֶאֱמַר בְּפֵרוּשׁ אִסּוּרוֹ בְּלֹא תֹאכַל וְהוֹצִיאוֹ בִּלְשׁוֹן בִּשּׁוּל, שֶׁהַתְּשׁוּבָה בָּזֶה מִפְּנֵי שֶׁנִּתְחַדְּשָׁה אִסּוּר אֲכִילָתוֹ מֵאִסּוּר שְׁאָר אֲכִילַת אִסּוּרִין, שֶׁשְּׁאָר אִסּוּרִין אֵין חִיּוּבָן אֶלָּא אִם־כֵּן נֶהֱנֶה בַּאֲכִילָתָן, וְכָאן אֲפִלּוּ לֹא נֶהֱנָה בַּאֲכִילָתָן מִכֵּיוָן שֶׁבִּלְעוֹ וַאֲפִלּוּ יְבַלְעֶנּוּ חַם שׂוֹרֵף גְּרוֹנוֹ בּוֹ וְכַיּוֹצֵא בָזֶה שֶׁאֵין לוֹ הֲנָאָה בּוֹ מִכָּל־מָקוֹם לוֹקֶה, כְּמוֹ שֶׁאָמְרוּ זִכְרוֹנָם לִבְרָכָה בְּפֶרֶק שְׁנֵי מְפַסְחִים: לְהָכִי לֹא כָתַב רַחֲמָנָא אֲכִילָה בְּגוּפֵיהּ לְמֵימְרָא שֶׁלּוֹקִין עָלָיו שֶׁלֹּא כְּדֶרֶךְ הֲנָאָתוֹ. וּמִכָּל־מָקוֹם אֵין לוֹקִין עָלָיו אֶלָּא דֶרֶךְ בִּשּׁוּל כַּלָּשׁוֹן שֶׁהוֹצִיא הַכָּתוּב אִסּוּרוֹ.

SIDRAH KI THISSA

offering, there is no admonition. I have seen, too, that great authorities among those who reckon the precepts have written so.³⁴

112 [THE PRECEPT OF LETTING THE LAND LIE FALLOW IN THE YEAR OF SH'MITTAH]
to cease the working of the land in the seventh year—as it is stated, *in plowing time and in harvest you shall rest* (Exodus 34:21); and the explanation was given in the Oral Tradition that this was stated about the seventh year—that we were [thus] commanded not to engage throughout it [the year] in any labor of the land at all.¹ This precept was repeated when Scripture stated elsewhere, *it shall be a year of solemn rest for the land* (Leviticus 25:5); and so too, *then shall the land keep a sabbath to the Lord* (ibid. 2). I have already written its entire substance, completely, in *sidrah mishpatim*, in the precept (§84), *but the seventh year you shall let it rest and lie fallow* (Exodus 23:11), which came to ordain about leaving ownerless, free for all, the produce of this year—although its proper place is here.

113 [THE PROHIBITION ON MEAT WITH MILK]
not to eat meat and milk that were cooked together—for it is stated, *You shall not cook a kid in its mother's milk* (Exodus 34:21); and this verse comes to forbid eating or deriving benefit from meat in milk. Now, do not let this be a difficulty in your eyes: If this is so, why was its prohibition not stated explicitly as "You shall not eat," but Scripture rather expressed it in terms of cooking? For the answer to that is this: it is because the ban on eating it was made a new law, [differing] from the prohibition on other forbidden foods: With other forbidden foods, there is no guilt unless one benefited by eating them; but here, even if one did not benefit by eating it, while swallowing it—even if he should swallow it hot, burning his throat, and so forth, so that he has no enjoyment or benefit from it at all—he is to be given whiplashes. As our Sages of blessed memory said in chapter 2 of the tractate *P'saḥim* (25a): For this reason the merciful God did not write the term "eating" in [the precept] itself, to convey that a person can receive whiplashes over it [for consuming the food in a manner] unlike its usual way of enjoyment or benefit.

In any case, though, whiplashes are not given for it unless [it

וְאַף־עַל־פִּי שֶׁאָמְרוּ זִכְרוֹנָם לִבְרָכָה שֶׁזֶּה שֶׁנִּכְתַּב בַּתּוֹרָה אָסוּר בַּבִּשּׁוּל שָׁלֹשׁ
פְּעָמִים שֶׁהוּא לְלַמֵּד אָסוּר אֲכִילָה וְאָסוּר בִּשּׁוּל וְאָסוּר הֲנָאָה, אֵין רָאוּי לָנוּ
לִמְנוֹת בְּחֶשְׁבּוֹן הַלָּאוִין אֶלָּא הַשְּׁנַיִם, לְפִי שֶׁאָסוּר אֲכִילָה וַהֲנָאָה דָּבָר אֶחָד הוּא,
כְּמוֹ שֶׁאָמְרוּ זִכְרוֹנָם לִבְרָכָה: כָּל מָקוֹם שֶׁנֶּאֱמַר לֹא תֹאכַל, לֹא תֹאכְלוּ, אֶחָד
אָסוּר אֲכִילָה וְאֶחָד אָסוּר הֲנָאָה בְּמַשְׁמָע, כִּי הַתּוֹרָה תּוֹצִיא כָּל הַהֲנָאוֹת דֶּרֶךְ כְּלָל
בִּלְשׁוֹן אֲכִילָה לְפִי שֶׁהִיא הֲנָאָה תְּמִידִית לָאָדָם וְצָרִיךְ אֵלֶיהָ, וּכְעִנְיָן שֶׁכָּתוּב:
וַיֶּחֱזוּ אֶת הָאֱלֹהִים וַיֹּאכְלוּ וַיִּשְׁתּוּ, שֶׁיְּכַנֶּה הַהֲנָאָה לַאֲכִילָה.

וְאִם תִּתְפֹּשׂ עָלַי: אִם־כֵּן לָמָּה נִכְתְּבוּ שְׁלֹשָׁה לָאוִין, דִּשְׁנַיִם יַסְפִּיקוּ לְפִי זֶה
שֶׁאָמַרְתִּי; יֵשׁ לַהֲשִׁיבְךָ דְּוַדַּאי אִם נִכְתַּב בְּמָקוֹם אֶחָד "לֹא תְבַשֵּׁל" שֶׁיְּלַמֵּד עַל
אָסוּר בִּשּׁוּל, וּבְמָקוֹם אַחֵר "לֹא תֹאכַל", שֶׁיִּכְלֹל אָסוּר הֲנָאָה וַאֲכִילָה כְּמוֹ
שֶׁאָמַרְנוּ, הָיָה בְדִין שֶׁלֹּא יִכְתֹּב הַשְּׁלִישִׁי, שֶׁאֵין צֹרֶךְ עוֹד בּוֹ, שֶׁכְּבָר הָיִינוּ לְמֵדִים
אֲכִילָה וַהֲנָאָה בְּ"לֹא תֹאכַל" מִן הַכְּלָל שֶׁבְּיָדֵינוּ דִּבְכִלְלַל אֲכִילָה הֲנָאָה בְּמַשְׁמָע,
אֲבָל עַכְשָׁיו שֶׁלֹּא הֻזְכְּרָה בּוֹ אֲכִילָה בְּשׁוּם מָקוֹם לֹא הָיִינוּ לְמֵדִים הַהֲנָאָה אֶלָּא
עִם הַלָּאו הַשְּׁלִישִׁי.

וְאֵין לְךָ לִשְׁאֹל עוֹד, וְלָמָּה לֹא כָּתַב רַחֲמָנָא "לֹא תֹאכַל" בְּאֶחָד מֵהֶם וְיַסְפִּיק
בִּשְׁנַיִם, שֶׁכְּבָר הוֹדַעְתִּיךָ כִּי לְעִנְיָן נִצְטָרֵךְ שֶׁלֹּא יַזְכִּיר בּוֹ הַכָּתוּב לְשׁוֹן אֲכִילָה
מִפְּנֵי שֶׁהַחִיּוּב בּוֹ אֲפִלּוּ שֶׁלֹּא כְּדֶרֶךְ הֲנָאָתוֹ. לָמַדְנוּ מֵעַתָּה כִּי מַה שֶּׁאָמְרוּ זִכְרוֹנָם
לִבְרָכָה חַד לְאָסוּר אֲכִילָה וְחַד לְאָסוּר הֲנָאָה וְחַד לְאָסוּר בִּשּׁוּל אֵין הַכַּוָּנָה בָּהֶם
שֶׁיִּהְיֶה נֶחְשָׁב הַכָּתוּב הַשְּׁלִישִׁי לְלָאו אַחֵר, אֶלָּא שֶׁנִּצְטָרֵךְ לִלְמֹד מִמֶּנּוּ הֲנָאָה.
וּבָרוּךְ שֶׁבָּחַר בְּדִבְרֵיהֶם.

---

§113   1. So TB Hullin 108a.
2. *Ibid.* 115b.
3. TB P'sahim 21b, etc.
4. The last two paragraphs are based on Rambam ShM negative precept §187.

was prepared] by boiling, in keeping with the term in which Scripture expressed its prohibition.[1]

Now, the Sages of blessed memory said[2] that the reason why the prohibition against boiling is written in the Torah three times is that it is to teach a ban against eating it, a ban against boiling it, and a ban against benefiting from it. Nevertheless, it would not be proper for us to count them as other than two in the reckoning of the negative precepts: because the ban on eating and benefiting is one thing. As our Sages of blessed memory said,[3] wherever it is stated [in Scripture] "you shall not eat," in the singular or plural, both a ban on eating and a ban on deriving benefit are equally meant. For the Torah expresses all derivations of benefit, generally, in terms of eating—since it is a constant form of benefit for a man, that he needs, in keeping with the verse, *they beheld God, and ate and drank* (Exodus 24:11), which thus designates enjoyment and benefit as eating.

Now, you might seize upon me [with the question]: In that case, why were three injunctions written, since two would have been enough, according to what I have stated? The answer can be given you that certainly, if it were written in one instance, "You shall not boil," that would teach about the prohibition against boiling it, and in another instance, "You shall not eat," which would comprise a ban on deriving benefit and eating it, as we said, it would then be right that the third should not be written [in Scripture]: There would be no need for it, as we would already learn about both eating and benefiting from the words "You shall not eat," by the rule we have, that benefiting is included in the meaning of eating. Now, however, that eating is not mentioned about it anywhere [in Scripture], we can learn about deriving benefit only from the third injunction.

Nor should you ask, further: But why did the merciful God not write "You shall not eat" in one of the instances, and then two would have been enough? For I have already told you that it was necessary for a reason that the Writ should not mention the term "eating," as guilt is incurred for this even [if eaten in a manner] unlike its usual way of enjoyment and benefit. Hence we have learned that when the Sages of blessed memory said, "One is for a ban on eating, one for a ban on benefiting, and one for a ban on boiling," their meaning was not that the third verse should denote a third negative precept, but that it was needed [for us] to learn from it about deriving benefit. Blessed is He who chose to accept their words.[4]

§113: THE PROHIBITION ON MEAT WITH MILK

מִשָּׁרְשֵׁי הַמִּצְוָה, כָּתַבְנוּ בְּאִסּוּר הַבִּשּׁוּל בְּפָרָשַׁת וְאֵלֶּה הַמִּשְׁפָּטִים עַל צַד הַפְּשָׁט מַה שֶּׁיָּכֹלְנוּ.

מִדִּינֵי הַמִּצְוָה, מַה שֶּׁאָמְרוּ זִכְרוֹנָם לִבְרָכָה שֶׁאֵין אָסוּר בָּשָׂר בְּחָלָב מִן הַתּוֹרָה אֶלָּא בִּבְשַׂר בְּהֵמָה טְהוֹרָה אֲבָל לֹא בִּבְהֵמָה טְמֵאָה וְלֹא בְחַיָּה אֲפִלּוּ טְהוֹרָה, וְלֹא בְעוֹף בֵּין טָהוֹר בֵּין טָמֵא, וְנִסְמְכוּ בָזֶה בְּמַה שֶׁכָּתוּב שָׁלֹשׁ פְּעָמִים גְּדִי שֶׁהוּא לָשׁוֹן מְחֻדָּשׁ, שֶׁהָיָה לוֹ לִכְתֹּב בָּשָׂר, וּבָא הַפֵּרוּשׁ עַל זֶה: גְּדִי וְלֹא בְהֵמָה טְמֵאָה, גְּדִי וְלֹא חַיָּה, גְּדִי וְלֹא עוֹף. וּלְפִיכָךְ אָמְרוּ זִכְרוֹנָם לִבְרָכָה כִּי שְׁלֹשָׁה אֵלֶּה מֻתָּר לְבַשְּׁלָם בְּחָלָב וּמֻתָּרִים בַּהֲנָאָה, אֲבָל בַּאֲכִילָה אָסְרוּם זִכְרוֹנָם לִבְרָכָה לִגְדֵר בִּבְהֵמָה טְהוֹרָה דְּבַר תּוֹרָה, כְּדֵי שֶׁלֹּא יִתְחַלֵּף לִבְנֵי־אָדָם בָּשָׂר בְּבָשָׂר, וּלְפִיכָךְ, מִפְּנֵי שֶׁהַדָּבָר קָרוֹב שֶׁבָּשָׂר בְּבָשָׂר מִתְחַלֵּף, הֶחֱמִירוּ זֶה כְּמוֹ שֶׁהֶחֱמִירוּ בִּבְשַׂר בְּהֵמָה מַמָּשׁ בִּקְצָת עִנְיָנִים, שֶׁאָסְרוּ בָּהֶם שֶׁלֹּא לְהַעֲלוֹתָם עַל הַשֻּׁלְחָן כְּלָל.

וּלְפִי דַעַת קְצָת מִן הַמְפָרְשִׁים חִיְּבוּ בָּהֶם גַּם־כֵּן שֶׁהָיָה בֵּין אֲכִילָתָם לַאֲכִילַת הַגְּבִינָה, כְּמוֹ בְּעִקַּר הָאִסּוּר, דְּהַיְנוּ בִּבְשַׂר בְּהֵמָה, אֲבָל בִּבְשַׂר דָּגִים וַחֲגָבִים לֹא גָדְרוּ בָהֶם כְּלָל, שֶׁאֵין בְּשָׂרָם דּוֹמֶה כְּלָל לִבְשַׂר בְּהֵמָה וְלֹא יָבוֹאוּ בְנֵי־אָדָם לִטְעוֹת בָּזֶה.

וְעוֹד הֶחֱמִירוּ בְעִנְיָן זֶה שֶׁאָמְרוּ גַּם־כֵּן שֶׁיֵּשׁ אִסּוּר מְחֻדָּשׁ בָּהּ יוֹתֵר מִשְּׁאָר אִסּוּרֵי מַאֲכָלוֹת לְפִי קְצָת מִן הַפֵּרוּשִׁים, שֶׁבְּעִנְיַן בָּשָׂר בְּחָלָב אִם נִתְעָרֵב חָלָב עִם הַבָּשָׂר וְאֵין בַּחֲתִיכַת הַבָּשָׂר שֶׁנִּתְעָרֵב בּוֹ שִׁשִּׁים כְּנֶגֶד הֶחָלָב, אָנוּ רוֹאִים שְׁנֵיהֶם כַּחֲתִיכַת אִסּוּר, וְאִם נָפְלָה אוֹתָהּ חֲתִיכָה בִּקְדֵרַת בָּשָׂר אוֹ בִּקְדֵרַת חָלָב מְשַׁעֲרִין

---

5. TB Ḥullin 113a.
6. I.e. when dairy products are being eaten, even if they are kosher, fit to eat; ibid. 104b.
7. Rambam MT *hilchoth ma'achaloth 'asuroth* ix 28; Rashba, *Torath haBa-yith*.
8. Permissible by Torah law (Leviticus 11:22), and eaten in some parts of the world.
9. If the quantity of one is sixty times the amount of the other, we consider the other to have been rendered null and void.

⟨426⟩

SIDRAH KI THISSA

What lies at the root of the precept, we have written about the prohibition against boiling it, in *sidrah mishpatim* (§92), by way of the plain meaning, as we were able.

Among the laws of the precept, there is what the Sages of blessed memory said,[5] that by the law of the Torah, the prohibition on meat and milk applies only to the flesh of a "pure" [permissible] domestic animal, but not an unclean [forbidden kind of] domestic animal, nor a wild animal, even if it is "pure" [permissible], nor a fowl, whether "pure" or unclean (of a forbidden kind). They based themselves in this on the fact that the word "kid" is written three times in the Torah— an unusual expression, since Scripture should have written "meat"; hence the interpretation was given for it: "a kid" and not an unclean [forbidden] domestic animal; "a kid" and not a wild animal; "a kid" and not fowl.

Therefore our Sages of blessed memory said[5] that these three may be boiled with milk, and it is permissible to have benefit from them. But as for eating them, our Sages of blessed memory forbade them, to [impose] a "fence" [a protective restriction] about animal meat that is forbidden by Torah law, so that among people, one kind of meat should not be confused with another. And for this reason, because it is a likely thing [to happen], that one kind of meat should become confused with another, they were stringent also about this protective restriction, as they were strict about the meat of a domestic animal itself, in certain respects: Thus they banned them, that they may not be brought to the table at all.[6]

In the view of some of the authorities,[7] the Sages also imposed an obligation about them to wait between eating them and eating cheese, as there is about the main forbidden kind, i.e. the meat of a domestic animal. However, as regards the flesh of fish and grasshoppers,[8] they set no "fences" [protective restrictions] at all, since their flesh is not at all like animal meat, and people will not come to make mistakes about it.

They were further stringent about this matter by teaching, in addition,[1] that there is a new prohibition about it, more than on other forbidden foods—according to some of the authorities: In the matter of meat in milk, if milk became mixed into meat, and the piece of meat into which it was mixed does not contain sixty times the amount of the milk,[9] we regard both of them as quantities of forbidden food. And if that piece fell [in turn] into a pot of meat or a pot of milk, we

§113: THE PROHIBITION ON MEAT WITH MILK

בִּכְלָלָה, וְזֶהוּ אָמְרָם זִכְרוֹנָם לִבְרָכָה חֲתִיכָה עַצְמָהּ נַעֲשֵׂית נְבֵלָה, וְהַטַּעַם מִפְּנֵי שֶׁמְּעָרְבְתָּם אוֹסְרָם, וּלְפִיכָךְ אַחַר שֶׁנִּתְעָרְבוּ הֲרֵי הֵן כַּחֲתִיכַת נְבֵלָה. וּבִשְׁאָר אִסּוּרִין אֵינוֹ כֵן, שֶׁאִסּוּר שֶׁנִּתְעָרֵב בַּחֲתִיכַת הֶתֵּר וְאֵין בַּחֲתִיכָה שִׁשִּׁים לְבַטֵּל הָאִסּוּר וְאַחַר־כָּךְ נָפְלָה לִקְדֵרָה אֵין מְשַׁעֲרִין אֶלָּא בְשִׁעוּר הָאִסּוּר שֶׁנָּפַל בָּהּ וְהִיא בְעַצְמָהּ תְּסַיֵּעַ לַעֲלוֹת הָאִסּוּר, לְפִי שֶׁאוּתָהּ חֲתִיכָה לֹא נַעֲשֵׂית נְבֵלָה, וְנִמְצָא הַהֶתֵּר שֶׁבָּהּ כְּמוֹ שְׁאָר הַהֶתֵּר שֶׁבַּקְּדֵרָה וּמְסַיֵּעַ לְהַעֲלוֹת הָאִסּוּר. וְאָמְנָם הַחֲתִיכָה עַצְמָהּ אִם הִיא נִכֶּרֶת אֲסוּרָה לְעוֹלָם כְּדַעַת קְצָת הַמְפָרְשִׁים.

וְאָמְרוּ זִכְרוֹנָם לִבְרָכָה שֶׁאֲפָרוּ שֶׁל בָּשָׂר בְּחָלָב אָסוּר כְּאֵפֶר כָּל אִסּוּר הֲנָאָה, שֶׁטְּעוּנִין קְבוּרָה, וְאָמְרוּ גַּם־כֵּן שֶׁלֹּא אָסְרָה תּוֹרָה בָּשָׂר בְּחָלָב אֶלָּא בְחָלָב שֶׁל בְּהֵמָה חַיָּה אֲבָל בַּחֲלֵב הַמֵּתָה אֵינוֹ נֶאֱסַר, וּלְפִיכָךְ הַכֹּחַל מֻתָּר מִן הַתּוֹרָה בַּחֲלָבוֹ, אֶלָּא שֶׁחֲכָמִים אֲסָרוּהוּ לִגְדֹּר עַד שֶׁיְּמָרֵק חֲלָבוֹ מִמֶּנּוּ, כְּמוֹ שֶׁנִּתְבָּאֵר בִּמְקוֹמוֹ.

וְחָלָב הַנִּמְצָא בְקֵבַת הַבְּהֵמָה יֵשׁ בּוֹ שְׁנֵי הֶתֵּרִין, אֶחָד שֶׁהוּא בִכְלַל חָלָב שֶׁל מֵתָה, וְעוֹד שֶׁאֵינוֹ אֶלָּא כְּפֶרֶשׁ בְּעָלְמָא שֶׁכְּבָר נִתְעַכֵּל שָׁם, וּלְפִיכָךְ מֻתָּר לְכַתְּחִלָּה, וְאֵין צָרִיךְ לוֹמַר שֶׁהַנִּמְצָא שָׁם קָרוּשׁ מֻתָּר, שֶׁהוּא וַדַּאי כְּפֶרֶשׁ, אֶלָּא אֲפִלּוּ הַצָּלוּל הִתִּירוּ הַגְּאוֹנִים.

הַמְבַשֵּׁל שָׁלִיל בְּחָלָב חַיָּב, וְכֵן הָאוֹכְלוֹ, אֲבָל הַמְבַשֵּׁל שִׁלְיָא אוֹ עוֹר וְגִידִין וַעֲצָמוֹת וְעִקְּרֵי קַרְנַיִם וּטְלָפַיִם פָּטוּר. וְיֶתֶר פְּרָטֵי הַמִּצְוָה מְבֹאָרִים בְּפֶרֶק שְׁמִינִי מֵחֻלִּין.

וְנוֹהֶגֶת בְּכָל מָקוֹם וּבְכָל זְמַן בִּזְכָרִים וּנְקֵבוֹת. וְהָעוֹבֵר עָלֶיהָ וְאָכַל כַּזַּיִת מִן הַבָּשָׂר וְהֶחָלָב שֶׁנִּתְבַּשְּׁלוּ יַחַד בְּמֵזִיד לוֹקֶה, אֲבָל נֶהֱנֶה בּוֹ כְּגוֹן שֶׁנְּתָנוֹ אוֹ מְכָרוֹ

---

10. I.e. we calculate if the original contents of the pot are sixty times as much as the combined meat and milk that fell into it.
11. I.e. like the forbidden meat of an animal that died of itself; TB Ḥullin 100a.
12. Although originally, each by itself was perfectly permissible.
13. So Rashba, *Torath haBa-yith* iv 1 (cited in Tur Yoreh Dé'ah, §106).
14. TB T'murah 33b-34a.
15. TB Ḥullin 113b.
16. Ibid. 109b.
17. Ibid. 116b.
18. So indicated by R. Isaac Alfasi (Rif), *ibid*.
19. TB Ḥullin 113b-114a (Rambam MT *hilchoth ma'achaloth 'asuroth* ix 7).

measure according to its entire amount.[10] In this sense our Sages of blessed memory said: The piece itself becomes *n'vélah*, "carrion"[11]— the reason being that their mixture makes them forbidden.[12] Therefore, after they mixed together, they are like a piece of carrion.

With other forbidden foods, though, this is not so. If something prohibited became mixed into a piece of permissible food, and the piece does not contain sixty [times its amount] so as to nullify the forbidden food, and then it fell into a pot [of other food], we measure only according to the amount of forbidden food that fell into it, and [the piece] itself helps to count [prevail] against the forbidden element. For that piece did not become carrion; hence it is permitted food like the rest of the permissible food in the pot, and it helps to count [prevail] against the forbidden element. However, if it is recognizable, the piece itself remains forbidden forever, in the view of some authorities.[13]

Moreover, our Sages of blessed memory taught[14] that the ash of meat in milk [that was burnt] is forbidden, like the ash of anything from which all benefit is forbidden, which thus must be buried. They said, furthermore,[15] that the Torah forbade meat in milk only if it was [mixed] with milk from a living animal; but if it was with milk from a dead animal, it does not become forbidden. Therefore the udder is permissible by Torah law, with its milk. Nevertheless, the Sages forbade it, by a protective restriction, until its milk is washed out of it[16]—as we will explain in its proper place.

As to milk found in the maw (stomach) of an animal, there are two reasons for ruling it permissible: First, it is in the category of milk from a dead animal; moreover, it is only like mere waste matter, since it was already digested there.[17] Hence it is permissible from the start. Needless to say, whatever is found there congealed is permissible, as it certainly is like waste matter; but even liquid, the Ge'onim ruled permissible.[18]

If someone boils a fetus in milk, he is punishable; so too one who eats it. But if a person boils [in milk] the placenta, or skin, tendons, bones, the root parts of horns, or hooves, he bears no guilt.[19] The remaining details of the precept are explained in the eighth chapter of the Talmud tractate *Hullin*.

It remains in force in every place, at every time, for both man and woman. If someone transgresses it and eats the amount of an olive of meat and milk that were cooked together, if it was deliberate,

§113-114: THE BAN ON MEAT & MILK / NO EXECUTION ON SABBATH

אֵינוֹ לוֹקֶה, לְפִי שֶׁאֶפְשָׁר לַהֲנָאָה בְּלִי מַעֲשֶׂה, וְכָל שֶׁאֵין בּוֹ מַעֲשֶׂה אֵין לוֹקִין עָלָיו, וַאֲפִלּוּ סָךְ מִמֶּנּוּ אֶפְשָׁר דְּלָא לָקֵי לְפִי שֶׁהוּא שֶׁלֹּא כְּדֶרֶךְ הֲנָאָתוֹ, שֶׁאֵינוֹ עָשׂוּי לָסוּךְ, וְיֵשׁ לָדוּן בּוֹ גַּם־כֵּן שֶׁיִּלְקֶה.

שׁ וַיַּקְהֵל מֹשֶׁה

[שֶׁלֹּא יַעֲשׂוּ בֵית־דִּין מִשְׁפַּט מָוֶת בְּשַׁבָּת]

קיד יֵשׁ בָּהּ מִצְוַת לֹא־תַעֲשֶׂה אַחַת, וְהִיא שֶׁלֹּא יַעֲשׂוּ הַדַּיָּנִין דִּינִים בְּשַׁבָּת, כְּלוֹמַר שֶׁמִּי שֶׁנִּתְחַיֵּב מִיתָה בְּבֵית־דִּין לֹא יְמִיתוּהוּ בְּשַׁבָּת, שֶׁנֶּאֱמַר: לֹא תְבַעֲרוּ אֵשׁ בְּכֹל מֹשְׁבֹתֵיכֶם בְּיוֹם הַשַּׁבָּת, וּבָא הַפֵּירוּשׁ עָלָיו בָּזֶה שֶׁלֹּא יִשְׂרְפוּ בֵּית־דִּין בְּשַׁבָּת מִי שֶׁנִּתְחַיֵּב שְׂרֵפָה, וְהוּא הַדִּין לִשְׁאָר מִיתוֹת.

וְיֵשׁ לָנוּ לִדְרשׁ מִמֶּנּוּ דָּבָר זֶה, שֶׁהֲרֵי לְגוּפֵיהּ אֵינוֹ צָרִיךְ, שֶׁהֲרֵי כְּבָר כָּתוּב בְּמָקוֹם אַחֵר: לֹא תַעֲשֶׂה בוֹ מְלָאכָה, וְהַבְעָרָה לְצֹרֶךְ מְלָאכָה הִיא, אֶלָּא לְלַמֵּד עִנְיָן בִּפְנֵי עַצְמוֹ נִכְתַּב, וּפֵרְשׁוּ בּוֹ שֶׁבָּא לְלַמֵּד אֶת זֶה שֶׁאָמַרְנוּ. וְכֵן לְשׁוֹן הַמְּכִלְתָּא, לֹא תְבַעֲרוּ אֵשׁ, שְׂרֵפָה בִּכְלָל הָיְתָה וְיָצְאָה לְלַמֵּד: מַה שְׂרֵפָה מְיֻחֶדֶת שֶׁהִיא אַחַת מִמִּיתוֹת בֵּית־דִּין וְאֵינָהּ דּוֹחָה אֶת הַשַּׁבָּת, אַף כָּל שְׁאָר מִיתוֹת בֵּית־דִּין לֹא יִדְחוּ אֶת הַשַּׁבָּת.

וְעִם כָּל זֶה שֶׁלָּמַדְנוּ בְּפָסוּק זֶה יֵשׁ לִדְרשׁ בּוֹ מַה שֶּׁדָּרְשׁוּ בוֹ עוֹד גַּם־כֵּן:

---

20. Since a person is punished for eating it even if he did so in such an unusual way that he derived no benefit or enjoyment from it, as our author wrote above. Hence one may become equally guilty, perhaps, for making absolutely any kind of direct, immediate use of meat boiled with milk (see MY).

114   1. TB Yevamoth 6b.
       2. E.g. in Exodus 20:10, 31:14–15, Leviticus 23:3.   ⟨430⟩

he should be given whiplashes. But if he [merely] benefited from it—for instance, if he gave it [as a gift] or sold it—he receives no whiplashes, since it is possible to derive benefit without any action [on his part]; and whatever [transgression of a negative precept] does not necessitate physical action, no whiplashes are given for it. Even if a person rubbed some of it on himself, it is possible that he is not whipped, since this is a use unlike the usual way of benefiting from it, as it is not usually put on as a salve. However, it could equally be decided that he should receive a whipping for it.[20]

sidrah va-yakhel
(Exodus 35–38:20)

[THAT THE COURT SHOULD NOT CARRY OUT ANY EXECUTION ON THE SABBATH]

114 It contains one negative precept, which is that judges should not carry out judgments on the Sabbath. In other words, if a person has incurred the death penalty in the court, they should not have him put to death on the Sabbath. For it is stated, *You shall kindle no fire throughout your habitations on the sabbath day* (Exodus 35:3), and the interpretation was given for it [in the Oral Tradition][1] in this way—that the court should not execute by burning on the Sabbath someone who has incurred death by burning; and the same law holds for other forms of execution.

We have the right to derive this matter from it [the verse], for you see, it is not needed for its own meaning, since it was already written elsewhere, "do not do any work on it,"[2] and fire is for the purpose of work. Hence it was rather written to teach something separate; and so the Sages explained about it that it comes to teach us what we have stated. So also is it expressed in the Midrash *Mechilta*: "You shall kindle no fire"—burning a fire was included [among the labors forbidden on the Sabbath], and it went out [was singled out] in order to teach [us an additional point of law]: What is specifically characteristic about burning with fire? It is one of the forms of death imposed by the court, and it does not thrust aside [the precept of] the Sabbath [to be able to be carried out on that day]. Then so too all other death sentences by the court are not to thrust the Sabbath aside.

However, with all that we have learned from this verse, it can

§114: NO EXECUTIONS BY THE COURT ON THE SABBATH

הבערה לחלק יצאת, כלומר שהעושה בשבת הרבה אבות מלאכות בבת־אחת בהעלם אחד שיהיה חיב חטאת על כל מלאכה ומלאכה בפני עצמה. ובגמרא דבני מערבא אמרו: בכל מושבתיכם, רבי אילא בשם רבי ינאי מכאן לבתי־דינים שלא יהו דנין בשבת.

משרשי המצוה, שרצה השם לכבד היום הזה שימצאו בו מנוחה הכל גם החוטאים והחיבים, משל למלך גדול שקרא בני המדינה יום אחד לסעודה שאינו מונע הפתח מכל אדם, ואחר יום הסעודה יעשה משפט, כן הדבר הזה שהשם ברוך הוא צונו לקדש ולכבד יום השבת לטובתנו ולזכותנו, כמו שכתבתי למעלה, וזה גם־כן מכבודו של יום הוא.

ונוהגת מצוה זו בזמן הבית בזכרים, שהם בעלי המשפט וחיבים להזהר לבל יעשו דין בשבת. ואם עברו וצוו לשרף או ברי"ה בשבת עברו על לאו זה, ואין לוקין עליו אם לא עשו בו מעשה. ואם עשו בו מעשה, כגון ששרפוהו הם בידיהם, אם יש עדים והתראה נסקלין, בשוגג מביאים חטאת לכפרה.

שׁ פָּרָשַׁת אֵלֶּה פְקוּדֵי
אֵין בָּהּ מִצְוָה.

תָּם סֵפֶר וְאֵלֶּה שְׁמוֹת
בְּעֶזְרַת נוֹתֵן עֹז וְתַעֲצוּמוֹת

---

3. Mechilta, on the verse; TB Shabbath 70a.

4. Because the Hebrew word for "your habitations" occurs also in Numbers 35:29, *And these things shall be for a statute ... in all your habitations;* just as that verse is an instruction to the court, so is this; TJ Sanhedrin iv 6. (These first three paragraphs are based on Rambam ShM negative precept §322).

5. Having forgotten (or being unaware) that this was forbidden on the Sabbath.

* This is the ending in MS Vatican and the first edition. The oldest manuscript ends with the couplet given here in the Hebrew text, which might be rendered thus:

    Completed and done
      is the Book of Exodus,
    by the aid of the One
      who grants His strength to us.

SIDRAH VA-YAKHÉL

be further interpreted as they expounded it in addition:[3] Kindling fire was singled out in order to separate [labors on the Sabbath into individual transgressions]: In other words, if someone does many major kinds of work on the Sabbath in one period of forgetfulness, he becomes duty-bound to bring a *ḥattath* (sin-offering) for every single kind of work separately. And in the Talmud of the westerners [Jerusalem Talmud] it was taught: "throughout your habitations": R.. 'Ila quoted R. Yannai: From here [we learn] about every court that it should not carry out judgment on the Sabbath.[4]

At the root of the precept lies the reason that the Eternal Lord wished to honor this day, that all should find rest in it, even the sinners and the guilty. To give a parable: A great king summoned the people of the country one day to a feast, when he would not withhold entry from any man, and after the day of the feast he would sit in judgment. So is this matter: the Eternal Lord commanded us to hallow and honor the Sabbath day for our good, and to make us meritorious, as I have written above (§ 32). This too is for the honor of the day.

This precept applies when the Temple is extant, for males, as they are in charge of judgment, and they have to beware not to carry out a verdict [of death] on the Sabbath. If they transgressed and ordered some person burnt to death on the Sabbath, they would violate this injunction; but no whiplashes should be given for it if they did no physical action in regard to it. If they did some physical action about it, for instance, if they burnt him with their own hands, then if there were witnesses and a [prior] warning, they would be stoned to death. If they did it inadvertently,[5] they should bring a *ḥattath* (sin-offering) for atonement.

sidrah p'kudé
(Exodus 38:21–40:38)

There is no precept in it.

⟨433⟩   THE BOOK OF EXODUS HAS BEEN COMPLETED.*

Addendum to §18, note 18 (p. 128)

This statement is patently puzzling. As a rule, our author invariably follows Rambam, if he has no reason to do otherwise. Yet in ShM positive precept §89, having cited Midrash Sifre (as our author did here, following him), Rambam declares that the precept of the firstling is in force only in the land of Israel; a firstling born outside the land, he continues, may not be offered up anywhere as an altar sacrifice, but it is in a state of holiness, and only if it becomes blemished or disfigured may it be ritually slain and eaten like any kosher animal. In MT *hilchoth b'choroth* i 5, despite apparent differences from ShM, Rambam's ruling is the same. (In MT we read of a firstling outside the land, *haré hu k'hullin*, it is non-holy; but a note in voweled ed. Mossad R. Kook informs us that in MS Yemen, the first edition — Rome before 5240/1480, and the reading of *Kessef Mishneh*, these three words are absent.) Why, then, does our author write that outside the land, a firstling must be considered and treated as in a state of holiness *only by decree of the Sages?*

Let it be noted, first, that in both ShM and MT a number of *rishonim* (Early Scholars) cite a very different prescript by Rambam, which they decidedly refute: that a firstling born outside the land is to be regarded as completely non-holy, in all respects (see *Kessef Mishneh* on MT *loc. cit.* and ShM ed. Heller, p. 57 note 9, last part). The veteran scholar R. Yosef Kafiḥ concludes from the evidence that *rishonim* had before them not *séfer mut'eh*, an erroneous manuscript copy of MT, as *Kessef Mishneh* posits, but Rambam's ruling in his first versions of ShM and MT, which he corrected afterward (ShM bilingual ed. Kafiḥ, *loc. cit.* note 56; the phrase *haré hu k'hullin*, cited above, may well be a trace of Rambam's original view).

Hence here in our text we evidently have yet a third view that Rambam held, at some time between his original and final rulings — that outside the land of Israel a firstling *is* in a state of holiness, but only by decree of the Sages. This supposition is confirmed by a responsum of R. Yisrael miBruna (R. Israel of Bruenn, mid-15th century: *Responsa*, ed. Stettin, §244; ed. Jerusalem, §245), in which he indeed cites this, from his manuscript copy of MT, as Rambam's ruling.

Addendum to §63, note 3 (p. 254)

It should be added that the idiom is found in TB Sanhedrin 31b: Ukban the Babylonian complained before us, "My brother Jeremiah made the road pass over (or bypass) me..." The commentaries explain it: He did not deal justly, or properly, with me, i.e. in regard to property (Rashi, 2nd part; Yad Ramah; Me'iri); or, he did me a grievous physical injury (R. Ḥannan'él). The phrase occurs again in Midrash Sifre, Deut. §29:... as one might tell another, "So-and-so passed a road over so-and-so" (reading of MhG) which R. Hillel similarly explains: The one did not treat the other properly; it implies that the first person transgressed the way of civilized and moral behavior and dealt with the other person wrongly.